THE OXFORD HISTORY of ISLAM

THE OXFORD
HISTORY
of ISLAM

EDITED BY John L. Esposito

OXFORD
UNIVERSITY PRESS

OXFORD
UNIVERSITY PRESS

Oxford   New York
Athens   Auckland   Bangkok   Bogotá   Buenos Aires   Calcutta
Cape Town   Chennai   Dar es Salaam   Delhi   Florence   Hong Kong   Istanbul
Karachi   Kuala Lumpur   Madrid   Melbourne   Mexico City   Mumbai
Nairobi   Paris   São Paulo   Singapore   Taipei   Tokyo   Toronto   Warsaw

and associated companies in
Berlin   Ibadan

Library of Congress Cataloging-in-Publication Data
The Oxford History of Islam/[edited by] John Esposito.
p.   cm.
Includes bibliographical references and index.
ISBN 0-19-510799-3 (alk. paper)
1. Islam--History.   I. Esposito, John. L.
BP50.095 1999   99-13219
297'.09--dc21   99-13219

Design by POLLEN

7 9 8 6
Printed in Hong Kong on acid-free paper

For Hasib Sabbagh
Builder of bridges
of steel
and of mutual understanding
and
Ismail R. al-Faruqi
scholar and pioneer
in Muslim-Christian dialogue

CONTENTS

Introduction

John L. Esposito

Although Islam is the youngest of the major world religions, with 1.2 billion followers, Islam is the second largest and fastest-growing religion in the world. To speak of the world of Islam today is to refer not only to countries that stretch from North Africa to Southeast Asia but also to Muslim minority communities that exist across the globe. Thus, for example, Islam is the second or third largest religion in Europe and the Americas.

Both the Muslim world and the West have experienced the impact of Islam politically, culturally, and demographically. Events in the contemporary Muslim world have led to an explosion of interest and scholarly work on Islam and the Muslim world. Much of this work in religion, history, and the social sciences has contributed toward the redressing of earlier imbalances of coverage and stereotyping. *The Oxford History of Islam* is part of this process.

The cognitive, ideological, political, and demographic map of the Muslim world changed dramatically in the second half of the twentieth century. Modern nation-states emerged from centuries of European colonization, often as a result of successful independence movements. However, contemporary Muslim history challenged the expectation that modernization would result in the progressive westernization and secularization of societies. Secularization of society has not proved a necessary precondition for social, economic, and political development.

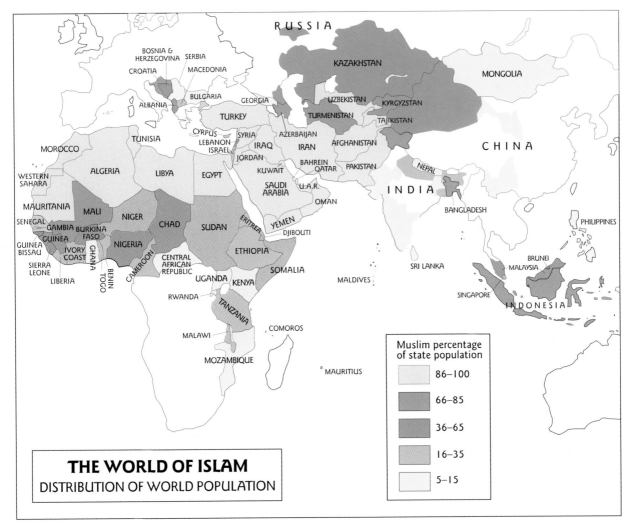

THE WORLD OF ISLAM
DISTRIBUTION OF WORLD POPULATION

Muslim percentage
of state population

- 86–100
- 66–85
- 36–65
- 16–35
- 5–15

Islam today is the dominant symbolic and ideological force in the Muslim world, informing social institutions (education, clinics, hospitals, social welfare services, and banks) and politics. In contrast to the expectations of only a few decades ago, Islam (Islamic symbols, ideology, organizations, and institutions) has reemerged as a significant force in public life. Mainstream Islamic organizations have become major social and political actors in society. The reassertion of Islam produced new Islamic republics in Iran, Sudan, and Afghanistan. At the same time, Islamic movements emerged as the major opposition in Algeria, Egypt, Kuwait, Yemen, Tunisia, Jordan, Pakistan, Palestine/Israel, Kashmir, Central Asia, and elsewhere. Radical Islamic movements have used violence in attempts to destabilize and topple governments and attack Muslim elites as well as Western governments and interests. Of equal importance, Muslims are a significant presence in the West.

In the 1950s and 1960s large numbers of Muslims emigrated to Europe and America as laborers, students, and professionals. Today they are a significant minority, addressing issues of identity (assimilation or integration), values, political and social participation, and pluralism in Western secular societies.

The Oxford History of Islam is designed to provide ready access to the history of Islam. Written for the general reader but also appealing to specialists, our goal is to present the best of scholarship in a readable style, complemented by a rich use of illustrations. Technical terms have been severely limited and diacriticals omitted. The approach to understanding Islam and Muslim history and civilization is interdisciplinary, relying on historians of Islamic religion, history, art, and science as well as social sciences. Contributors represent different disciplinary perspectives and include scholars from diverse national and religious traditions. As with *The Oxford Encyclopedia of the Modern Islamic World*, it has been especially important to include Muslim as well as non-Muslim scholars.

While it is not possible to cover this topic exhaustively in a single volume, *The Oxford History* is comprehensive in its coverage. The first part of the book provides an overview of the origins and development of classical Islam: its faith, community, institutions, sciences, and art. It also surveys the historic encounter of Islam and Christianity, critical to world history and to relations between the Muslim world and the West.

The Mongol invasion and destruction of the Abbasid empire in the thirteenth century appeared to bring to an end Islam's phenomenal expansion as faith and as empire. Instead, as seen in the next chapters, the thirteenth to the seventeenth centuries saw a period of sultanates and empires, extending from Timbuktu to Mindanao. Sultanates from Africa to China and Southeast Asia emerged alongside great empires—the Ottoman and Safavid empires in the Middle East and the Mughal in South Asia. Within each, Islam expressed itself in diverse ways and flourished as both a faith and a civilization. However, by the eighteenth century, across the Muslim world the fortunes of Muslim societies were in decline.

The next group of chapters tracks the domestic and international challenges faced by premodern and modern Muslim societies, in particular movements of Islamic renewal and reform. The seventeenth and eighteenth centuries witnessed the rise of premodern reform movements from Africa to Southeast Asia, including the Wahhabi, Mahdi, and Sanusi, which responded to internal causes of stagnation and decline. By the nineteenth century, much of the Muslim world faced an external threat, the onslaught of European colonialism. The colonial legacy and the history of Muslim responses to the political, economic, and religious challenges of European imperialism in the nineteenth and twentieth centuries have had a profound impact on Muslim societies and upon relations between the Muslim world and the West.

The final chapters of the book provide perspectives on the contemporary landscape. The resurgence of Islam in the late twentieth century has been a testimony to the vitality of Islam. At the dawn of the twenty-first century, Islam is indeed a global presence that blurs old distinctions between the Muslim world and the West. Islam is truly a world religion, necessitating coverage of both Islam *and* the West and Islam *in* the West. Islam is to be found not only in the more than 55 Muslim countries of the world but also in significant Muslim minority communities in Europe and America as well as such diverse countries as China, Australia, Thailand, and the Philippines. As a result, Islam and Muslim history have played and continue to play a dynamic and major role in world history.

I wish to especially acknowledge my colleagues, the contributors to this volume, who have been responsive to my requests for revision and additions. I am indebted to James Piscatori (Oxford University), Tamara Sonn (College of William and Mary), and John O. Voll (Georgetown University) for their invaluable assistance. Natana DeLong-Bas, my senior research assistant, was especially helpful in gathering the chronology. Sheila Blair and Jonathan Bloom were a pleasure to work with, invaluable in identifying the many illustrations to be found in this volume. Jean Esposito, as always, was there with advice and encouragement.

THE OXFORD HISTORY of ISLAM

CHAPTER ONE

Muhammad and the Caliphate

POLITICAL HISTORY OF THE ISLAMIC EMPIRE UP TO THE MONGOL CONQUEST

Fred M. Donner

Islam as a religion and civilization made its entry onto the world stage with the life and career of the Prophet Muhammad ibn Abd Allah (ca. 570–632) in western Arabia. After his death, a series of successors called *caliphs* claimed political authority over the Muslim community. During the period of the caliphate, Islam grew into a religious tradition and civilization of worldwide importance. A properly historical view of Islam's appearance and early development, however, demands that these processes be situated against the cultural background of sixth-century Arabia and, more generally, the Near East.

Historical Setting

The Near East in the sixth century was divided between two great empires, the Byzantine or Later Roman Empire in the west and the Sasanian Empire in the east, with the kingdoms of Himyar in southern Arabia and Axum in the Horn of Africa constituting smaller players in the political arena. This Byzantine-Sasanian rivalry was merely the most recent phase in a long struggle between Rome and Persia that had lasted for more than five hundred years. The two empires not only raised competing claims to world dominion, they also represented different cultural traditions: the Byzantines espoused Hellenistic culture, while the Sasanians looked to ancient Iranian and Semitic cultural traditions and rejected Hellenism as alien.

(Left) Pilgrims to Mecca worshiping around the Kaaba, the cubical stone structure covered with cloth, which stands in the middle of the Masjid al-Haram in Mecca. Muslims revere the Kaaba as the House of God and direct their prayers toward it five times a day.

This cultural antagonism was specifically exacerbated by religious rivalry; in the third and fourth centuries the Byzantine emperors had declared themselves champions of Christianity, which itself had been heavily imbued with Hellenistic culture, whereas the Sasanian Great Kings espoused the Iranian faith known as Zoroastrianism (Magianism) as their official religion. On the eve of Islam, religious identities in the Near East, particularly Greek or Byzantine Christianity and Zoroastrianism, had thus acquired acutely political overtones.

Although both the Byzantine and Sasanian empires espoused official religions, neither empire had a religiously homogeneous population. Large populations of Jews were scattered throughout the Near East; they were especially numerous in such cities as Alexandria, Jerusalem, Antioch, Hamadan, Rayy, Susa, the Byzantine capital at Constantinople, and the Sasanian capital at Ctesiphon. Many more Jews were settled in places like Tiberias in Palestine and in southern Mesopotamia, where Jewish academies continued a long tradition of religious learning and contributed to producing the Palestinian and Babylonian Talmuds (the authoritative bodies of Jewish tradition) during the fourth, fifth, and sixth centuries. Christians were numerous, perhaps the majority of the Near Eastern population in the sixth century, but they were divided into several sects that differed on points of theology. Each sect viewed itself as the true or orthodox ("right-confessing") Christianity and dismissed the others as heterodox. The Byzantine (or Greek Orthodox) faith, the official church of the Byzantine Empire, was widely established in Greece, the Balkans, and among the large Greek-speaking populations of Anatolia (Asia Minor). In Syria-Palestine and Egypt, however, the Byzantine church was mainly limited to the towns. A few Byzantine Christians were even found in the Sasanian Empire, mainly in Mesopotamia, but their position was precarious. Christians following the teachings of Bishop Nestorius (Nestorianism)

The great church of Hagia Sophia in Istanbul was built by the Byzantine emperor Justinian in the sixth century. It was transformed into a mosque after the Ottomans conquered Constantinople in 1453, and the minarets were added then.

had been forced to leave the Byzantine Empire after Nestorius was deposed for heresy by the Council of Ephesus in 431. They had to take refuge in the Sasanian Empire, scattered widely between Mesopotamia, Iran, and the fringes of Central Asia. Another Christian sect, the Monophysites, had been declared a heresy by the Council of Chalcedon in 451, but Monophysitism was nonetheless the creed of most indigenous Christians of Axum, Egypt, Syria-Palestine, Mesopotamia, Armenia, and Iran, particularly in the countryside. Zoroastrians were found mainly in Iran and southern Mesopotamia; few lived outside the Sasanian Empire. Communities of all three religions (Christianity, Judaism, and Zoroastrianism)— which are called the scriptural religions because they shared the idea of a divinely inspired, revealed scripture—were also found in Arabia.

The Byzantines and Sasanians fought many wars between the fourth and sixth centuries in an effort to secure and extend their own territories. They competed with particular intensity for key border zones such as upper Mesopotamia and Armenia. They also tried to seize key towns from one another to gain control over, and therefore to tax, the lucrative "Orient trade." This commerce brought southern Arabian incense, Chinese silk, Indian pepper and cottons, spices, and other goods from the Indian Ocean region to the cities of the Mediterranean basin. The Byzantines and Sasanians also attempted to gain the advantage by establishing alliances with lesser states in the region. The most important of these client states was the Christian kingdom of Axum, with which the Byzantines established an uneasy alliance. Both Byzantines and Sasanians also formed alliances with tribal groups who lived on the Arabian fringes of their territories. Arabia was wedged between the two empires. The Sasanians established a series of protectorates over tribes and small states on the east Arabian coast and in Oman, whereas the Byzantines brought tribes on the fringes of Palestine and Syria into their orbit.

Arabia occupied a strategic position in relation to the Orient trade, a fact that led both empires to intervene decisively in its affairs during the sixth century. In 525 the Byzantines persuaded Axum to invade and occupy the kingdom of Himyar in Yemen and its important trading ports, thus bringing the Red Sea trade to the Indian Ocean securely within the Byzantine orbit. In 575, however, the Sasanians, invited by the Himyarites, sent an expedition to oust the Axumites from Yemen, which for the next several decades was a Sasanian province ruled

The Sasanians, rulers of Iran and adjacent areas in the centuries before Islam, maintained their capital at Ctesiphon, near present-day Baghdad. The main room of their palace was a giant iwan, a barrel-vaulted space, under which the ruler sat.

by a governor appointed by the Great King. Some time later, the Sasanians inaugurated the last and greatest of the Sasanian-Byzantine wars by launching a series of assaults on Byzantine territories farther north. Between 611 and 620 the Sasanians seized most of Anatolia, all of Syria-Palestine, and Egypt from the Byzantines. But in the next decade the Byzantine emperor Heraclius regained these territories, and in 628 he was able to conquer the Sasanians' Mesopotamian heartlands, depose the Great King, and install another, more docile king. These dramatic events formed the political backdrop to the career of Islam's Prophet Muhammad in the western Arabian towns of Mecca and Medina.

Although distant from the main centers of high civilization in the Near East, Arabia was not isolated. The Arabian peoples were aware of and affected by political, economic, and cultural developments in the more highly developed surrounding lands of the Near East. Trends in religion in particular resonated in various parts of Arabia. Many religions had established themselves in Arabia on the eve of Islam. Christianity was well-established in parts of eastern Arabia along the Persian Gulf coast and in Oman as well as in Yemen. The Yemeni city of Najran in particular later became famous because of the martyrdom of Christians there during the sixth century. Christianity had also spread among some of the pastoral nomadic tribes that occupied the northern fringes of the peninsula, where it bordered on Syria and Mesopotamia, and may also have been current among some pastoral groups farther south, in northern and central Arabia itself. Judaism was similarly widespread; important Jewish communities existed in the string of oasis towns stretching southward along the northern Red Sea coast of Arabia, including the towns of Khaybar and Yathrib (later called Medina, the Prophet Muhammad's adoptive home). Jews were also found in eastern Arabia and especially in Yemen. Zoroastrianism was far less widespread in Arabia than either Christianity or Judaism, but a small following existed, particularly in parts of eastern Arabia and Oman, where the Sasanian Empire had established protectorates among the local populations. Arabian communities of all three scriptural religions—Christianity, Judaism, and Zoroastrianism—sometimes maintained contact with their co-religionists in the lands surrounding Arabia, where these religions were much more firmly established. For example, bishops from lower Mesopotamia were sent to Yemen, and Arabian Jews may have had some contact with the great academies of Jewish learning in Mesopotamia.

In addition to the scriptural religions, Arabia also was home to a host of local animist cults, which attributed divine powers to natural objects—the sun, the moon, Venus, certain sacred rocks or trees, and so on. These cults seem to have been late vestiges of the animist religions once widespread among the peoples of the ancient Near East, such as the Babylonians and Canaanites. Although animism still existed in Arabia in the sixth century, it was being supplanted by the scriptural religions in many areas. The remaining strongholds of these animistic cults were in central and western Arabia, especially in towns such as Taif and

Mecca, which contained sanctuaries (*harams*) within whose confines members of the cult were forbidden to fight and had to observe other rules of the cult—a feature that made such harams important centers for markets and for social transactions of all kinds. In Mecca the cultic center was a cube-shaped building called the Kaaba, embedded in which was a meteoric black stone around which cult members performed circumambulations to gain the favor of the cult's dieties.

The religious, cultural, economic, and political environment in Arabia and the Near East was thus a very complex one. Before examining Islam's rise, however, it is important to note a feature of the Near Eastern landscape that profoundly influenced the course of the region's history, including its history during the early Islamic centuries. There are extensive tracts of agriculturally marginal land in the Near East; these marginal lands consist either of arid steppe and desert, as in much of Arabia, or of semiarid mountainous terrain, as in parts of Iran and Anatolia. In these regions settled life, particularly larger towns and cities, tended to be widely scattered and in some cases virtually nonexistent. Some such areas, however, could sustain thinly scattered populations of pastoral nomads or mountaineering peoples living in small settlements and relying on a mixture of subsistence agriculture and herding. These nomadic or mountaineering peoples were often outside the effective control of any state, and they organized themselves politically in kinship-based entities (tribes) or in larger confederations of tribes. In many cases they also had strong martial traditions, apparently rooted in such diverse factors as their skill with riding animals and a culturally based attitude of superiority toward nonpastoralists or lowlanders. The result was that for several millennia the history of the Near East was marked by the repeated intrusion of powerful pastoral nomads or mountain tribespeople into the richer, settled lands and towns belonging to the various states of the region. Sometimes these intrusions were merely raids along a state's borders, usually undertaken when a state was not strong enough to defend a district effectively. During other intrusions, however, nomads or mountain tribes toppled the ruling dynasties of moribund states and supplanted the rulers with members of their own group, who became a new ruling dynasty—usually settling down in the state's heartlands in the process, but keeping a power base in the marginal region from which they had come. This process of periodic intrusion by peoples from the marginal regions into the state-dominated areas of the Near East is one of the main themes in the area's history.

The Prophet Muhammad and the Nascent Community of Believers

The historian, whether Muslim or non-Muslim, who wishes to write about the life of the Prophet Muhammad faces grave problems of both documentation and interpretation. The first rule of the historian is to rely whenever possible on contemporary documents—yet for the life of the Prophet these are virtually nonexistent. Fortunately, many accounts produced within the Muslim community in later times provide us with copious information about the Prophet. When dealing with such accounts, however, the historian must try to identify and set aside those features that reflect not the Prophet's life and times but later attitudes and values of all kinds that have been interpolated into the story of his life by subsequent writers, whether consciously or unconsciously. This is never an easy task, and a significant measure of honest disagreement inevitably emerges among historians engaged in the work of evaluating the reported events and providing a sound interpretation of them. The brief sketch of the Prophet Muhammad's life and career that follows is drawn largely on the basis of the traditional narratives, but the choice of traditional materials selected, and the interpretation of their overall meaning, reflect mainly the author's general concerns as an historian interested in questions of social and political integration and in the evolution of religious movements.

Little is known with certainty about the Prophet Muhammad's early life. He was born Muhammad ibn (son of) Abd Allah in the small western Arabian town of Mecca some time around 570 C.E. (traditional accounts differ on the date). He belonged to the Hashim clan, one of the smaller segments of the tribe of Quraysh that dominated Mecca. At an early age Muhammad was orphaned and came under the guardianship of his paternal uncle, Abu Talib, head of the Hashim clan. Mecca was the site of an important pagan shrine, the Kaaba, during Muhammad's youth. The Quraysh tribe served as guardians and stewards of the cult of Hubal, centered on this shrine. The tribe was also involved in trade; although they probably dealt mainly in humble goods such as hides, their commercial activity gave them contact with much of Arabia and the surrounding lands, and it provided them with a measure of experience in the organization and management of people and materials.

Traditional sources portray Muhammad as having been a promising and respected young man who participated in both Mecca's cultic activities and its commerce. He also seemed to have had an inward, contemplative side, however, which expressed itself in his periodic withdrawal to secluded spots for prolonged periods of meditation and reflection. It was during such a retreat, in about 610, that he began to have religious experiences in the form of visions and sounds that presented themselves as revelations from God. These experiences initially so terrified him that he sought comfort from his first wife, Khadijah, but the visions occurred again and slowly Muhammad came to accept both the message itself and his own role as God's messenger. The revelations, coming to Muhammad as sonorous utterances, were eventually collected to form the Quran (sometimes spelled "Koran" in earlier English writings), which is sacred scripture for Muslims.

To Muhammad and to all who have since followed his message, the Quran is literally the word of God, God's own eternal speech.

The message Muhammad received in these revelations was a warning that only through devotion to the one and only God and through righteous observance of the revealed law could people attain salvation in the afterlife. Some revelations thus emphasized the oneness and omnipotence of God, Creator of the world and of everything in it, including humankind. Others warned that the Last Judgment was near; and then those who had lived righteously would be sent to heaven and those who had lived evil lives would be sent to eternal damnation in hell. Other revelations laid out the general guidelines for a righteous existence. These included worship of the one God and rejection of idols and false gods; regular prayer; almsgiving and charitable treatment of the poor, widows, orphans, and other unfortunates; observance of strict modesty in dealing with the opposite sex, and of humility in all one's affairs; the need to work actively for the good and to stand up against evil when one sees it; and many other injunctions. Still other revelations retold stories of earlier prophets (among them Abraham, Moses, David, and Jesus) who, like Muhammad, had been charged with bringing God's truth to their people, and who provided for Believers inspiring models of righteous conduct: as the Quran put it, "Surely in this there is a sign for you, if you believe."

Many aspects of Muhammad's message were conveyed in concepts and sometimes in words that were already familiar in Arabia. In part, this was what made Muhammad's message comprehensible to his first audience. The ideas of

In the first centuries of Islam, many fine manuscripts of the Quran were copied on parchment in the distinctive angular script known as Kufic and embellished with gold chapter headings.

monotheism, a Last Judgment, heaven and hell, prophecy and revelations, and the emphasis on intense, even militant, piety were widespread in the Near Eastern scripturalist religions in the sixth century. In this sense Muhammad's message can be seen as an affirmation and refinement of certain trends among the scripturalist religions of the late antique era, perhaps as an effort at their reformation. To adherents of the pagan cults of western Arabia, however, including Muhammad's fellow tribespeople of Quraysh, his message came as a blunt repudiation of all they stood for. He proclaimed their polytheism as incorrect and profoundly sinful, an affront to the one God's unity, in itself sufficient to condemn them eternally to hellfire. He made it clear that in their behavior, they failed in many ways to meet God's demands for humility, for modesty, for charity for the less fortunate, and especially for pious dedication to God himself through regular prayer. Muhammad pointed out that the tribe's pagan ancestors, even his own grandfathers, were similarly destined for perdition—an idea certain to generate outrage in a tribal society that highly revered ancestors. The Quraysh were aghast.

Much of Muhammad's prophetic career, from the time he began publicly preaching in about 613 until his death in 632, was consumed with warding off and eventually overcoming the opposition of his own tribe, the Quraysh. His early followers included some close relatives, such as his paternal cousin, Ali ibn Abi Talib (ca. 600–61), as well as a few prominent Meccans of leading clans, such as Uthman ibn Affan (ca. 575–656) of the Umayya clan. He was also joined at first by many people of lower social stature in Mecca—clients, freed slaves, and individuals of lesser clans of Quraysh—perhaps because their weaker family ties made it easier for them to act in accordance with their conscience. As his following grew, however, the opposition and abuse by the remaining Quraysh hardened; conditions became so bad for some that Muhammad arranged for a number of them to take refuge with the ruler of Axum in perhaps about 615. His situation in Mecca became critical with the death, in close succession, of his wife Khadijah and his uncle Abu Talib, in about 619; almost simultaneously, he had lost his main source of emotional support and his main protector, because Abu Talib, although he never embraced the Prophet's message, had nonetheless used the solidarity of the Hashim clan to defend Muhammad.

As Muhammad's situation worsened, he began to look to other towns in western Arabia for supporters. It was around 620 that Muhammad won over a few people from Yathrib, an oasis town about 250 miles (400 km) north of Mecca. For some years the population of Yathrib, which included two predominantly pagan tribes and a number of Jewish tribes, had been riven by intractable internal strife. Over the next two years more people of Yathrib agreed to observe the Prophet's message, until finally a large delegation of people from Yathrib agreed to follow his teachings and invited him to come to Yathrib as arbiter of their disputes and de facto ruler of the town. Muhammad gradually sent his beleaguered followers from Mecca to safety in Yathrib, following them himself and taking up residence in 622. Yathrib henceforth came to be known as Medina (from the Arabic *madinat al-nabi*, "the Prophet's city"). The Prophet's move (the *hijra*, emigration) to Medina marked the beginning of a new chapter in his life and that of his followers. They were no longer a small, oppressed religious group in Mecca; they were now an autonomous religio-political community of Believers that dominated the oasis of Medina. Muhammad's hijra to Medina in 622 was thus the beginning of Islam's long life as a political force, a fact symbolized by the selection of that year to serve as the first year of the Islamic era.

During his roughly ten years in Medina (622–32), Muhammad consolidated his control over the town's disparate population, and he extended Medina's power and influence in Arabia. When Muhammad first arrived, Medina was still full of smouldering rivalries: between the town's two main Arab tribes; between the *muhajirun* ("emigrants," the Believers who had emigrated to Medina from Mecca or elsewhere) and the *ansar* ("helpers," Muhammad's first followers in Medina, who had invited him and his Meccan followers to find refuge with them); and between some of Medina's Jews and the new Believers. While some of Medina's Jews appear to have supported Muhammad, those who challenged Muhammad's claim to prophecy, and in some cases cooperated with his political enemies (or whose leaders did), were handled harshly in a series of confrontations—exiled with loss of

R. J. Burton's nineteenth-century drawing of Medina with the Mosque of the Prophet in the center. The Prophet settled here in 622, and his new house became the first mosque in Islam and later served as his place of burial.

their lands, enslaved, or executed, depending on the case. Beyond Medina the most determined opponents of Muhammad's efforts to extend his influence and his message were his erstwhile fellow citizens, the Quraysh of Mecca.

Mecca and Medina became locked in an intense struggle to win over other towns and groups of nomads, a struggle in which Mecca, with its established commercial and tribal ties, initially appeared to have the advantage. Muhammad, however, launched raids against Meccan caravans, seizing valuable booty and hostages, and, more important, disrupting the commercial lifeblood of Mecca. After a series of raids and battles against the Quraysh that seem to have been indecisive in their results (at Badr in 624; Uhud, 625; and Khandaq, 627), Muhammad negotiated a truce with the Quraysh at Hudaybiya in 628. In exchange for some short-term concessions, the truce gave Muhammad and his followers the right to make the pilgrimage to Mecca's shrine, Kaaba, in the following year. The treaty also gave Muhammad a free hand to subdue one of Mecca's key allies, the oasis of Khaybar north of Medina, whose large Jewish population (some of them refugees from Medina) was hostile to the Prophet. This done, it was relatively easy for Muhammad to turn on Mecca itself, which submitted virtually without bloodshed in 630. Aware of how dangerous the Quraysh could be if their opposition continued, and wishing to win their support, Muhammad was careful to spare their pride. He tied them to his movement by awarding many of their leaders important commands and positions of authority.

While Muhammad was engaged in his struggle against Mecca, he was also slowly working to bring more and more nomadic groups and towns within Medina's orbit, either as loose allies or as full-fledged members of the community of Believers. In doing so, he used the appeal of his religious message, promises of material gain, or, on occasion, outright force to bring recalcitrant groups under Medina's sway. His conquest of Mecca opened the way for victorious campaigns—with the help of the Quraysh—against the other main town of western Arabia, Taif, and against the remaining groups of powerful nomads in the region. By this time Muhammad's position as the most powerful political leader in western Arabia had become apparent to all, and tribal groups that had until then tried to hold Medina at arm's length now sent delegations to tender their submission. By Muhammad's death in 632, his community had expanded—more by religious persuasion and political alliance than by force—to include all of western Arabia, and he had made fruitful contact with some groups in the northern Hijaz, Nejd, eastern Arabia, Oman, and Yemen.

Early Expansion of the Community and State

Upon Muhammad's death in 632, the young community of Believers faced a set of difficult challenges. The first and most basic challenge was to resolve the question: Were the Believers to form a single polity under one leader even after Muhammad's death, or were they to belong to separate communities, each headed by its own political leader? In the end the Believers chose to remain a single community and selected the Prophet's father-in-law and staunch supporter, Abu Bakr, to be his first successor. Abu Bakr and subsequent successors as leaders of the Islamic community are known in Islamic tradition as caliphs (from the Arabic *khalifa*, meaning "successor" or "representative").

Abu Bakr and the Believers in Medina faced a second immediate challenge. Although the towns of Medina, Mecca, and Taif and the nomadic groups between them were for the most part quite steadfast in their support of Abu Bakr, many groups in Arabia that had once tendered their submission to Muhammad tried to sever their political or religious ties with Medina once the Prophet was dead. Some claimed that they would remain Believers but contended that they did not owe the tax that the Prophet had collected, which Abu Bakr continued to demand. Other groups gave no assurances that they would remain Believers. In still other cases religious leaders arose claiming to be prophets themselves.

Against these threats, Abu Bakr acted quickly and decisively in what is usually called the Apostasy (or *Ridda*) wars, during which he sent armed bands of Believers to the main centers of opposition in Arabia: Yemen, Nejd, and Yamama. By making shows of force first among wavering tribes, these campaigns picked up allies as they proceeded, and grew large enough to defeat the more serious opponents, such as the "false prophet" Musaylima of Yamama. These campaigns were followed by incursions into Oman and northward toward the Arabian fringes of Syria and Mesopotamia (what is now Iraq). In 634, at the end of two years of campaigning, Abu Bakr and the Believers of Medina had brought the entire Arabian peninsula under their control, opening the way to further conquests that would, within a few more decades, make the Believers the masters of a vast empire. This was possible partly because the almost ceaseless military activity of the Ridda wars provided the setting in which the loosely organized war parties formed at the beginning of the Ridda wars began to assume the character of a standing army, with a core of devoted supporters (mainly townsmen of Medina, Mecca, and Taif) leading a larger mass of allies drawn from a wide variety of Arabian tribes. It also represented the domination of the pastoral and mountaineer populations of Arabia by the embryonic new state in Medina, which was headed by an elite group composed almost exclusively of settled townsmen.

The Ridda wars brought the Believers to the very doorsteps of the Byzantine and Sasanian empires, but they also did more. The emergence in Arabia of a state where none had been before, one that could harness the military potential of the Arabian population, made it possible for the Believers to organize campaigns of conquest that penetrated the great empires and wrested vast territories from them. The great wave of early conquests was the main work of the second caliph, Umar ibn al-Khattab (r. 634–44), whom Abu Bakr upon his deathbed selected to lead the Believers. The conquests were further continued during the first years of the reign of the third caliph, Uthman ibn Affan (r. 644–56).

The caliphs launched one set of offensives against the Byzantine-controlled territories of Palestine and Syria, home to many Arabic-speaking tribes (part of the primary audience to which the Quran had been addressed). These incursions elicited defensive reactions from the Byzantine authorities in Syria, against whom several battles were fought. Eventually, the Byzantine emperor Heraclius sent a large army from Anatolia to secure Syria against the threatening Believers, but to no avail; his force was decimated at a battle along the Yarmuk valley (east of the Sea of Galilee) in 636. Most of the countryside and towns of Syria and Palestine fell to the Believers shortly thereafter; the only exceptions were some coastal towns such as Ascalon and Tripoli, which held out for years longer because the Byzantines could supply them by sea. From Syria the Believers sent campaigns into northern Mesopotamia, Armenia, and against the Byzantine frontier in southern Anatolia. An expeditionary force from Syria also wrested the rich province of Egypt from the Byzantines, conquering the commercial and cultural hub of Alexandria in 642.

At the same time as the offensives in Syria and Palestine, the Believers were faced with impending clashes with the Sasanian Empire in what is now southern Iraq. The early contacts of the Believers with the Arabic-speaking pastoral nomads of this region, and their increasing boldness in penetrating Iraq's interior, had caused the Sasanians to mobilize their armies to resist them, but they fared no better than the Byzantines. In a great battle in 637 at al-Qadisiyah (modern Kadisiya) in southern Iraq, the Sasanians were decisively broken, opening the rich alluvial lands of Iraq to occupation by the armies of the Believers. From southern Iraq the Believers sent campaigns into Khuzestan and Azerbaijan, and others pursued the fleeing Sasanians into the Iranian highlands. Gradually the main towns of western Iran, and with time areas farther east, fell to the Believers. By the mid-650s the Believers ruling from Medina had loose control over a vast area stretching from Yemen to Armenia and from Egypt to eastern Iran. And from various staging centers in this vast area, the Believers were organizing raids into areas yet further afield: from Egypt into Libya, North Africa, and Sudan; from Syria and northern Mesopotamia into Anatolia; from Armenia into the Caucasus region; from lower Mesopotamia into many unconsolidated districts in Iran and eastward toward Afghanistan and the fringes of Central Asia.

An important feature of the early expansion of the Believers was its quality as a religious movement, but this was colored by the presence of the state. The caliphs and their followers believed, of course, in Muhammad's message of the need to acknowledge God's oneness and to live righteously in preparation for the imminent Last Day. They saw their mission as *jihad*, or militant effort to combat evil and to spread Muhammad's message of monotheism and righteousness far and wide. But their goal seems to have been to bring the populations they encountered into submission to the righteous order they represented, not to make them change their religion—not, at least, if they were already monotheists, such as Christians and Jews. For this reason the early Believers collected tribute from conquered populations but generally let them worship as they always had; only pagans and at times Zoroastrians appear to have been coerced into embracing Islam or had their places of worship sacked.

The astonishing extent and rapidity of this process of expansion and conquest can only be understood if the nature of the expansion it represented is recognized. It was, first and foremost, the expansion of a new state based in Medina. The ruling elite of this state were mostly settled townsmen of Mecca, Medina, and Taif, who commanded growing armies composed mainly of pastoral nomads from northern and central Arabia or mountaineers from Yemen. It was not an expansion of nomadic or mountaineering peoples as such. The state-sponsored quality of the expansion is reflected in a significant measure of centralized direction of the expansion movement by the caliphs and their circle, who appear to have coordinated strategy between various fronts, as well as in certain bureaucratic institutions that were established during the early conquests. The institutions included the creation of a regular payroll (*diwan*) for the soldiers, as well as the gathering of the expeditionary forces in distant areas into tightly clustered garrison settlements that became the nucleus of new cities: Kufa and Basra in southern Mesopotamia, Fustat in Egypt, and somewhat later, Marv in northeastern Iran (651) and Qayrawan in Tunisia (670). These garrisons helped the Believers live apart from the vast conquered populations they ruled, and so to avoid assimilation; later, as cities, these garrisons would be among the most important centers in which early Islamic culture was elaborated.

The consequences of the conquests were momentous. They established a large new empire in the Near East, destroying the Sasanian Empire completely and occupying important parts of the Byzantine Empire. Moreover, the leadership of this new empire was committed to a new religious ideology. New economic structures were created with the demise of the old ruling classes and the rise of a new one, consisting at first largely of people of Arabian origin. Property and wealth—as well as political power—were redistributed on a grand scale. Most important, the newly emergent state provided the political framework within which the religious ideas of the ruling Believers, who were but a small part of the population, could gradually spread among the conquered peoples. The many captives taken during the conquests came to be integrated into the tribes and families of their captors as clients (*mawali*), a fact that facilitated this transformation.

The Early Caliphate and the Question of Legitimacy

It was widely accepted in the early community of Believers that Muhammad could have no successor in his role as Prophet. But the early Believers decided that someone should succeed Muhammad as temporal head of the community. The first documentary references call the leader of the community of Believers not caliph but *amir al-mu minin* ("commander of the Believers"), and this may be the

Interior of the Great Mosque at Qayrawan in Tunisia. Founded in the late seventh century, the mosque owes much of its present aspect to extensive rebuilding by the Aghlabid governors in the ninth century.

original term for the heads of the community, replaced only some time later by the term caliph, which was seen as synonymous but had the advantage of being found in the Quran. Whatever it was called, community leadership was at first informal and personal, much like tribal leadership. Only gradually did the caliphate acquire greater prestige and formality, as the original Islamic state grew into a far-flung empire during the early conquest era.

Although the first two caliphs, Abu Bakr and Umar, appear to have enjoyed widespread support among the Believers, dissension arose under the third caliph, Uthman. The reasons for this discontent probably included practical concerns, such as a tapering off in the ready supply of conquest booty for individual soldiers, or feelings that newly conquered lands outside the garrison towns were not being made available for settlement by the soldiers and were instead being dominated by wealthy families. But they also seem to have involved perceptions that Uthman was not ruling with the fairness and disdain for private gain that most pious Believers expected of their commander. Uthman was accused (whether rightly, it may never be known) of favoring his relatives when making important and sometimes lucrative appointments, of diverting monies from the treasury, and of other transgressions, some fiscal, some moral. This dissension grew into a violent uprising, which culminated in the murder of the caliph in 656. These developments began the complicated series of events known as the First Civil War (656–61), which was a struggle for leadership of the community of Believers waged by the prominent heads of several families within the Prophet's tribe, the Quraysh. This is a chapter of the utmost importance in Islamic history, because this is when the main subgroups or sects that have constituted the Muslim community up to the present day first emerged.

After Uthman's murder the people of Medina, including some of the conspirators, recognized as the next caliph Ali ibn Abi Talib—cousin and son-in-law of the Prophet, therefore a member of his clan, the Hashim. Ali's acclamation as caliph was opposed by significant segments of the community of Believers, however—in particular by Uthman's kinsmen of the Umayyad clan, led by Muawiyah, and by leading members of some other Quraysh families, including the Prophet's favorite wife, Aishah, and two of Muhammad's early supporters, Talha ibn Ubaydallah and al-Zubayr ibn al-Awwam.

The bid for power by Talha, al-Zubayr, and Aishah was thwarted when their forces were decisively defeated at the "battle of the camel" near Basra in southern Iraq by the supporters of Ali (shiat Ali, Arabic for "party of Ali," often referred to simply as the Shia or Shiites). Ali and his backers established their base in the garrison town of Kufa. They eventually felt strong enough to march northward along the Euphrates River, intending to take the war to Muawiyah's base in Syria. Armies of the two sides met at Siffin along the middle Euphrates, near the frontier of Syria and Iraq, but many on both sides were uneasy about launching an attack against men who also considered themselves Believers, and who until recently had been their own comrades-at-arms. Skirmishing gave way, after many days, to a battle that was broken off when Ali and Muawiyah agreed that the matter should be settled by arbitration rather than fighting and withdrew to Kufa and Syria, respectively, to await the arbiters' decision. Eventually neither side was satisfied with the arbitration results, and a period of desultory raiding between Syria and Iraq ensued. During the period of arbitration and thereafter, Ali's situation was weakened by the withdrawal from his camp of some militant pietists, who came to be known as Kharijites (from the Arabic *khawarij*, possibly meaning "seceders"). Some of them may have broken with Ali because they feared that if he reached an accommodation with Muawiyah, they would be called to account for their participation in the mutiny against Uthman. Others may have felt that Ali's agreement to arbitrate revealed an impious lack of trust in God's ability to render a just verdict between the two rivals on the battlefield. As they said in their battle cry, "Only God has the right to decide." Ali was forced to massacre many Kharijites in a battle at Nahrawan in eastern Iraq, an event that shocked many and did little to advance his cause, because many Kharijites were renowned for their piety.

The First Civil War finally came to an end in 661, when a Kharijite assassin killed Ali (another was thwarted before he could assassinate Muawiyah). Shortly thereafter, the majority of Believers agreed to recognize Muawiyah as caliph, perhaps less because they thought him the ideal ruler than because, after five years of turmoil, they yearned for stability and unity among the Believers. Muawiyah's recognition as caliph marks the beginning of the Umayyad caliphate (661–750). During his two decades as caliph, Muawiyah relied on careful diplomacy and strong governors, especially in Iraq and the east, to maintain an uneasy peace in the community. He kept discontented Shiite supporters of Ali's family under control, and either subdued small uprisings of rebellious Kharijites or forced them to take refuge in frontier zones, beyond the effective reach of the caliph's agents. The relative stability of his reign enabled the Muslim armies once again to embark on raids and campaigns of conquest against neighboring areas.

But the issues that were at the heart of the First Civil War—how leaders of the community of Believers were to be selected, and above all what were the criteria for leadership—remained unresolved. It is hardly surprising that a new wave of internal turmoil, the Second Civil War (680–92), broke out upon Muawiyah's death. The Second Civil War was a continuation of the first, because the same groups were involved, at the remove of one generation. The Umayyads, whose hold on the caliphate from their capital in Damascus was being challenged, were represented first by Muawiyah's son Yazid (r. 680–83), and then, after Yazid's early death and a period of confusion within the Umayyad family, by another relative, the caliph Abd al-Malik ibn Marwan (r. 685–705). The Umayyads faced widespread opposition. From Ali's old stronghold in Kufa, the Shiites, who claimed that the caliphate should belong to someone of Ali's family, rallied first around Ali's younger son, al-Husayn. After al-Husayn and his family were massacred in 680 by Umayyad troops at Karbala in Iraq, the Shiites continued to resist Umayyad rule in Kufa under the leadership of a charismatic leader named al-Mukhtar, who claimed to be acting in the name of one of Ali's sons.

Abd Allah ibn al-Zubayr (624–92), son of that al-Zubayr whose bid for the caliphate had been so quickly ended in the First Civil War, established himself in Mecca and was recognized by many in the empire as caliph. His determination and broad support made his resistance to the Umayyads as formidable as his father's had been ephemeral. Meanwhile, several groups of Kharijites took advantage of the political disarray prevailing in the community of Believers to establish themselves in various parts of Arabia, Iraq, and Iran. In the end, after a dozen years of bitter strife, Abd al-Malik and his ruthless lieutenant, al-Hajjaj ibn Yusuf, were able to pacify first Iraq, then Arabia, and to bring the whole empire under Umayyad control.

The road the Umayyads had followed to victory, however, was littered with mangled dreams, memories of which would haunt the dynasty's future and contribute to its downfall. Yazid's generals, in the first unsuccessful efforts to subdue Abd Allah ibn al-Zubayr in Mecca, had ruthlessly crushed an uprising in Medina while en route, and had even laid siege to the sacred precincts in Mecca, in the process starting a fire that destroyed part of the Kaaba. The Shiites had seen their hopes dashed, but the pitiless slaughter of Ali's son al-Husayn and his family at Karbala provided them with an act of martyrdom of mythical proportions.

The golden dome of the shrine at Karbala in Iraq marks the burial site of the Prophet's grandson Husayn and his family, who were murdered by the Umayyads in 680. This act of martyrdom marks the beginning of the separation of Shiites as a political party and distinct subgroup within the Islamic community.

Nurturing the memory of this martydom deepened their hatred of the Umayyads and started a process whereby the Shiites began to feel themselves to be not merely a political party but a distinct subgroup within the Islamic community. In the course of working out the differences within their own house, the Umayyads had even managed to set some Syrian tribes against others in a way that would later undermine their efforts to build a cohesive army on these tribal groups.

The importance of the two civil wars goes far beyond their immediate political impact, however. These civil wars represented the arena in which Believers first openly debated the ways in which authority to lead the Islamic community could be legitimately claimed. Kharijites held that true piety and impeccably righteous behavior were the only qualities that provided true legitimation in an Islamic context. Others, notably the Alids and their Shiite supporters, who contended that only a member of Ali's family or of the Prophet's clan of Hashim should hold power, argued that legitimacy was essentially genealogical. Still others—such as the Umayyads—claimed that the consensus of the community of Believers (jamaa, or coming together) was the most important element in establishing a legitimate claim to head the Islamic community. Later, some (including the Umayyads) would argue that their very ascent to power was an expression of God's will and therefore legitimate in its own right. These claims and counterclaims would be raised repeatedly in the centuries ahead.

It is therefore during the civil wars that the main sectarian subdivisions of the Islamic community first emerged: the Shiites, the Kharijites, and (retrospectively, through an ephemeral group known as the Murjia) the Sunni or orthodox majority sect of Islam, which came to be defined as much as anything by their rejection of the central beliefs of the Shiites and Kharijites. All members of these subgroups within the Islamic community justify their particular identity on the basis of their differing readings of the events of the civil wars, particularly the first war. The civil wars are thus the lens through which radiates the spectrum of groups making up the Muslim community. The ideal of a politically unified community of Believers (ummah) headed by a caliph eventually became unrealizable in practice, as the empire came to span thousands of kilometers and the community to embrace millions of people. Nonetheless, the institution of the caliphate (and indeed, the caliph himself) played an important role because it stood as a symbolic embodiment of Muslim religious unity. For this reason the institution was retained long after it had ceased to have real political meaning.

Apogee of the Caliphal Empire (700–950 c.e.)

The age of the first conquests and the civil wars (roughly 630–700 c.e.) had seen the establishment of the community of Believers as a loosely organized political

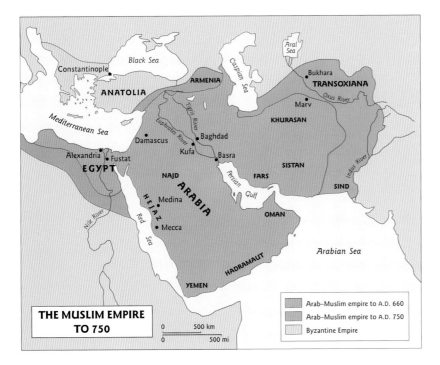

entity headed by the first caliphs. The early community and state had been united (when they were united) not so much by institutional structures, most of which were still embryonic, but mainly by ideology—that is, by the Believers' conviction that they were engaged in a common effort to establish, in God's name, a new and righteous regime on earth. The depth of this conviction underlay the intensity with which the Believers had disagreed over the legitimacy of various rivals for the caliphate during the civil wars; but their commitment to a common cause also enabled the Believers to come together once again as a single political unit after the wars.

By the end of the second war in 692, the Believers had embraced more clearly than before their identity as *Muslims*—that is, as a monotheist confession following the teachings of Muhammad and the Quran, and for this reason distinct from other monotheists such as Jews or Christians. During the two and a half centuries that followed the second war (ca. 700–ca. 950 C.E.), the rudimentary institutional structures of the early community of Believers fully matured, providing the caliphs with the military and administrative machinery needed to contain the divisions that have reverberated down through the subsequent history of the Islamic community since the civil wars. The period of 700 to 950, then, represented the apogee of the caliphal empire—an age of political and communal expansion, great institutional and cultural development, and economic growth. The Umayyad dynasty was overthrown in 750 C.E. by a military uprising organized by the Abbasid family, descendants of the Prophet Muhammad's uncle al-Abbas ibn Abd al-Muttalib (ca. 566–ca. 653), resulting in a shift of the imperial capital eastward from Damascus, in Syria, to Iraq, where the early Abbasids founded a new capital, Baghdad. But several key aspects of the evolution of the caliphate and the empire continued under both the late Umayyad and the early Abbasid caliphs, and for this reason, despite the change of ruling dynasty, it is fair to view the period of 700 to 950 as a single phase in the history of the caliphate and of the Islamic community.

The most basic fact about this period is that the caliphal empire and the Muslim community continued to expand. The early conquests had ground to a halt during the Second Civil War, as the Umayyads and their rivals devoted military resources to fighting each other. After the war, however, the Umayyads inaugurated a second phase of imperial expansion (the first half of the eighth century). Some of the conquests sponsored by the later Umayyads were motivated by a desire to extend Islamic rule. For example, expansion seems to have been the objective of the great (if unsuccessful) campaigns by land and sea against Constantinople, the capital of the Byzantine Empire (669, 674–80, and 716–17), as well as the annual summer raids into Byzantine border territories (a policy continued under the Abbasids until the middle of the ninth century). The caliphs also doubtless hoped to affirm their legitimacy among Muslims by sponsoring such campaigns of jihad against non-Muslim states. The incentive for launching other campaigns, however, seems to have been the desire to benefit from the seizure of booty, particularly captives who could be employed or sold as slaves; this may have been the case with many raids in North Africa organized by the later Umayyads. The throngs of recruits who participated in these campaigns were, of course, responding to a wide range of motivations—from zeal

The mighty land walls of Constantinople, built in the centuries preceding the revelation of Islam, protected the city against repeated invasions, including the unsuccessful Arab campaigns in the seventh and eighth centuries.

to spread the faith or the hope of attaining martyrdom on the battlefield (and hence eternal salvation), to lust for booty or hope of finding new lands to settle, to a simple thirst for adventure. Without the organizing activity of the caliphs and their governors, however, most of these campaigns would not have occurred.

Whatever the motivations, the scope of the second phase of conquests was astonishing. In North Africa the Muslims, who during the civil wars had stayed close to their strong points, such as the garrison town of Qayrawan, finally dislodged the last Byzantine outposts, such as Carthage, and pushed all the way to the Atlantic coast of Morocco. The local Berber population began to embrace Islam, and some were drawn into the expansion process. In 711 general Tariq ibn Ziyad led an army consisting largely of Berbers across the Straits of Gibraltar (named after him) into Spain. Other troops, Berber and Arab, poured in and within a few brief years seized the southern and eastern two-thirds of the Iberian peninsula from the faltering Visigothic kingdom, which vanished, leaving small, impoverished Christian kindgoms only in the northern mountains. From Spain the Muslims sent raids across the Pyrenees into the Languedoc and adjacent regions of France, reaching the high water mark of their expansion in the west somewhere near the Loire region, where in 732 they were defeated by the Frankish ruler Charles Martel. Although the Muslims held several cities in southern France for a few decades, ultimately their conquests there were ephemeral; by the late eighth century they seldom ventured north of the Pyrenees. During the ninth century the Abbasids' governors of Tunisia, the Aghlabids, raided Sicily (starting in 827), southern Italy, and the French and Italian Rivieras, and established over much of Sicily a Muslim political presence that endured until the arrival of the Normans in the mid-eleventh century.

In the east, Umayyad governors launched renewed campaigns from their garrisons in Khurasan (in northeast Iran), particularly Marv and Balkh, into the regions beyond the Oxus River on the fringes of Central Asia. Between 705 and 713, Bukhara in Transoxiana, the region of Fergana and its capital, Shash (modern-day Tashkent), the rich district of Khwarizm (modern-day Khorezm) south of the Aral Sea—all located in what is now known as Uzbekistan—and much of Sogdiana, including its capital at Samarqand, were brought into the Umayyad Empire. Despite numerous rebellions and efforts by local groups to overthrow Muslim rule during the early ninth century, these areas remained forever after part of the Islamic world. Meanwhile, between 711 and 713, the caliphate was establishing its first permanent foothold in Sind (part of the Indus River valley); the teenage commander of Muslim troops, Muhammad ibn al-Qasim, marched through southern Iran to conquer and establish an initial base at Daibul, the main city in the Indus delta. From it he conquered other major cities in the region now known as Pakistan, including the religious center at Multan and the political capital of Sind, Brahmanabad (where the city of Mansura would later be built under the Abbasids). These first Muslim colonies in Sind lived on, but little about them is documented, and they were doubtless almost completely autonomous. Nevertheless, recent archaeological evidence suggests that they maintained ties of trade, at least with other parts of the Islamic world such as Iran and Syria.

During the expansion of the caliphal empire, the Islamic community itself spread beyond the empire. Whereas the spread of the empire was carried out mainly by armies, the spread of the Islamic faith beyond the caliphate's borders was usually the work of merchants and pious preachers. Kharijite merchants from North Africa, for example, appear to have been the first to bring Islam to the populations of sub-Saharan West Africa. The main spreading of the Islamic community, however, took place within the caliphal empire itself. In many parts of the empire, even in those conquered early on, such as Egypt or Iran, the population remained predominantly non-Muslim for centuries. With time, more of these conquered peoples embraced Islam; estimates suggest that in the Near Eastern provinces Muslims became the majority only after about 850 C.E. In other words, during the golden age of the Umayyad and Abbasid caliphates Muslims were still a minority in the lands they ruled. The empire's conquered populations were gradually won over to Islam for various reasons. Forced conversions were rare, but in some cases the imposition of higher taxes on non-Muslims may have created an economic incentive for embracing Islam. For the most part, however, the gradual Islamization of the empire's populations was part of a complex transformation of the whole social environment, involving many factors that impinged simultaneously on the individual and the family: economic and political advantage, social mobility, linguistic and cultural affinities, marriage and kinship requirements, and, above all, the intrinsic appeal of Islam as a belief system.

Another important feature of this period was continuing rivalry for the caliphate itself, that is, for supreme political power in the empire. On the pragmatic side there were grumblings or actual uprisings directed against established caliphs, and various measures (such as transforming the army) were taken by the caliphs themselves to safeguard their power. But the ideological struggle over the meaning of the caliphate and the legitimacy of various contenders' claims to it also continued unabated in this period. Although the Umayyad caliph Abd al-Malik and his successors were able to build a fairly firm support base for themselves after the Second Civil War, they nonetheless faced widespread opposition. The long-standing opposition of the Shiites and Kharijites continued. The Umayyads used garrison troops to control numerous small Kharijite insurrections as well as more serious uprisings such as that mounted by the Alid leader Zayd ibn Ali in Kufa in 740. But the Umayyads were also opposed by many new converts to Islam, most of them mawali, or clients, of Arab tribes, who felt that their conversion should have entitled them to equal treatment with other Muslims, particularly the lower rate of taxes that Arab Muslims enjoyed. A number of pious Muslims backed the new converts in this claim, however, or felt that the Umayyads had discredited themselves in some other way by their earlier actions. Such concerns may have underlain the obscure *qadariyya* movement (on the surface, a debate over the degree to which God's omnipotence limited human independence and responsibility) that plagued the last decades of Umayyad rule. On a more mundane level, the later Umayyads faced a crisis as agricultural lands were abandoned in the two richest provinces of the empire, Egypt and Iraq. The full reasons for this phenomenon are not known—it was probably linked in part to the conversion to Islam of the indigenous peasantry—but whatever the causes, this abandonment disrupted the flow of taxes and in some cases was reversed only through draconian measures that further enhanced the Umayyads' reputation for harsh and unjust rule.

The Umayyads were not blind to their opponents' varied claims, and they made serious efforts to establish themselves as legitimate heads of the Islamic community and rulers of the state. They encouraged scholars to gather and compile reports about the origins of Islam (the Prophet's life and career, the history of the early community, and so on). In this way, the Umayyads played a central role in establishing a Muslim identity, because the origin story affirmed that the Islamic com-

The Dome of the Rock in Jerusalem is the third holiest site in Islam. Built over the remains of Solomon's temple, the structure is thought by many Muslims to mark the spot from which Muhammad began his night journey to heaven.

munity they led was the direct descendant of Muhammad's own, and that it followed his teachings and those of the Quran—propositions to which Muslims still adhere. The Umayyads also asserted their legitimacy by continuing the ancient tradition of royal patronage for sumptuous religious buildings, notably the Dome of Rock in Jerusalem and the Umayyad mosque in Damascus—two of the first outstanding examples of Islamic architecture. The Umayyads' support for campaigns of expansion and conquest also helped bolster their claim to being legitimate rulers of the Islamic community.

Despite these efforts, however, opposition to the Umayyads intensified during the second quarter of the eighth century. At the same time divisions within their Syrian-based army—the product of clashes during the Second Civil War and rivalry over royal patronage—made the army an increasingly unreliable support for the Umayyad regime. Yet it was just at this time that ceaseless campaigning on the Byzantine frontiers and stubborn internal opposition made firm support indispensable. The Alids and their Shiite supporters proved especially troublesome to the Umayyads, fomenting numerous uprisings in the last decades of Umayyad rule. Eventually, it was another branch of Muhammad's family (the Abbasids), however, that finally overthrew the Umayyads and occupied the caliphate in 750. Unlike the Alids and their Shiite partisans, the Abbasids had patiently organized an underground opposition movement and built up a secure power base before rising in open revolt. Moreover, when they organized their rebellion against the Umayyads from the province of Khurasan in northeastern

Courtyard of the Great Mosque in Damascus, founded in the early eighth century. The walls were once entirely covered with glittering mosaics, largely covered with whitewash in this photograph taken in the early twentieth century but now restored.

Iran, the Abbasids carefully kept secret their own identity as claimants to the caliphate, rallying supporters instead in the name of "the family of Muhammad." This vague appeal enabled them both to avoid detection by the Umayyads and to win the backing of many among the Shiites (who naturally assumed that the movement was in favor of an Alid) and of many other disgruntled groups who yearned for more righteous leadership than they thought the Umayyads had provided. Only after decisively defeating Umayyad armies in several battles in Iran and Iraq, and killing the caliph and many Umayyad princes, did the Abbasid leader Abu l-Abbas al-Saffah come out in the open and receive the oath of allegiance as caliph.

For several turbulent years the Abbasid caliphs al-Saffah (r. 750–54) and Abu Jafar al-Mansur (r. 754–75) consolidated their power against rivals within the Abbasid family, disgruntled Alids, and former powerful supporters such as the Abbasids' agent Abu Muslim, who had largely engineered the rebellion in Khurasan. By about 756, however, the Abbasid dynasty's power was securely established, and the Abbasids were to occupy the caliphate for the remainder of its existence (that is, from 750 until 1258), although after about 950 their real power was severely curtailed by a succession of secular powerholders. The first Abbasids claimed to be starting the caliphate anew, purging it of the evils of their Umayyad predecessors. Shortly after coming to power, the second Abbasid caliph, al-Mansur, founded a new imperial capital at Baghdad, on the Tigris River in Iraq, to symbolize this break with the impious Umayyad past. Many Islamic rulers of later periods would follow this precedent by founding new capitals to symbolize the start of what they claimed to be a new era.

Even the Abbasids' overthrow of the Umayyads did not end the struggle over the caliphate, however. The Shiites still believed that only an Alid could legitimately lead the community, so they were usually no more favorably disposed to the Abbasids than they had been to the Umayyads. The complex relationship between these two branches of the Prophet's family, the Abbasids and the Alids, is a central theme of Abbasid history (and of many historical texts written in this and later periods). The reverence that many early Muslims felt for the family of the Prophet Muhammad, indeed for the entire Hashim clan, led some Abbasid caliphs, such as al-Mansur and al-Mahdi (r. 775–85), to favor their Alid contemporaries by including them at court, seeking their advice, and otherwise trying to win their support. Other Abbasids, such as Harun al-Rashid (r. 786–809), were suspicious of the Alids, whom they assumed to be conspiring for the caliphate. For their part, the Alids were also divided in their attitude toward the Abbasids, which naturally varied in some measure with the Abbasids' policies toward them. Some Alids—such as the brothers Ibrahim and Muhammad ibn Abd Allah (d. 762–763) and al-

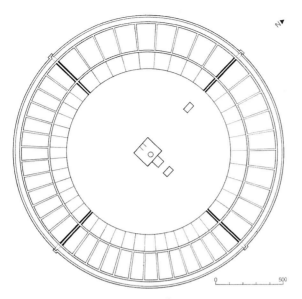

The Abbasid capital at Baghdad, founded in 762 as reconstructed on the basis of medieval descriptions. The caliph's palace and mosque stood in the center of a vast esplanade surrounded by shops and residences.

Husayn ibn Ali (d. 786), and their more radical supporters—could not let go of the idea that they were more entitled to rule than the Abbasid "upstarts," and rose in rebellion, particularly if the reigning Abbasid had taken a hard line toward them. Others, such as Jafar al-Sadiq (702/3–765), were more prudent in dealing with the Abbasids and advanced a special Alid claim to rule in terms of a strictly religious leadership. By the late eighth century, if not earlier, some Shiites had developed a clearly articulated concept of the imamate (the office of the imam, or head of the community), which posited that only an Alid in a certain line of descent from the Prophet's cousin and son-in-law Ali ibn Abi Talib could rightfully claim leadership of the Muslim community. The social upshot of this was a gradually hardening sense among the Alids' Shiite supporters that they formed a distinct, separate group within the Muslim community, identified with the fortunes of the Alid imams.

This sense of Shiite separateness from what was becoming the Sunni majority in the Islamic community begins to be visible by the beginning of the ninth century at the latest; from that time on, Shiites and Sunnis often appear as rival social and political factions in the life of Baghdad and many other places in the Islamic world, independent of the existence in a particular historical moment of an Alid claimant to power. Following the abortive rebellion of al-Husayn ibn Ali in the Hejaz in 786, some Alids and their supporters seem to have decided that the Abbasids were too powerful near the empire's centers of power to be challenged there, and they established small, independent states in inaccessible regions, such as the wild mountain country south of the Caspian Sea, in Yemen, or in the far western reaches of North Africa. From these new bases, and from underground movements secretly organized in the heart of the empire, the Shiites eventually mounted more effective challenges to Abbasid rule.

This struggle for the position of caliph also raged within the ruling dynasty (whether Umayyad or Abbasid), because there was no clear tradition or rule of succession. Many caliphs found themselves confronted by insurrections mounted by, or in the name of, their own brothers, uncles, or other close relatives. Powerful factions in the army, bureaucracy, caliphal court, and caliphal family (the different mothers of two rival half-brothers, for example) lent their support to the claimant whom they thought would best serve their own interests. Some caliphs, remembering their own close call at accession, hoped to spare their offspring the same tribulations and drew up detailed wills laying out the exact order of succession of several sons. Such arrangements seldom worked out as intended, however.

A major example of this was the bitter civil war that broke out following the death of the Abbasid caliph Harun al-Rashid in 809. Despite the fact that al-Rashid had made strenuous efforts to regulate the succession, al-Rashid's son Muhammad al-Amin (r. 809–813) was overthrown by his brother al-Mamun (r. 813–33), who had been governor of Khurasan. Underlying the dispute was a long-lasting tension between Baghdad and Khurasan, with pro-Baghdad and pro-Khurasan factions in the army, the court, and the landed aristocracy backing either al-Amin or al-Mamun. Al-Mamun's attempt to govern the empire from Marv, his capital in Khurasan, aroused great discontent, and in 819 he moved his court to Baghdad. By then, however, the civil war's disruptive events had done much to undermine the Abbasids' legitimacy. These included not only the long siege of Baghdad and its inhabitants and the execution of al-Amin but also al-Mamun's effort to win Shiite support by backing, for a time, an Alid as his heir-apparent—only to drop him from succession later, when the idea proved a political embarrassment. This episode exacerbated tensions between Sunni backers of the Abbasids and the Shiites, both of whom felt victimized in ways that caused people to question Abbasid legitimacy.

Abbasid legitimacy was also undermined by clashes with a religious elite increasingly jealous of its right to interpret nascent Islamic law. By the ninth century religious scholars expert in the Quran and the sayings of the prophet had come to feel that they—not the caliphs—should be the final arbiters in matters of law. The mihna, or inquisition, instituted by the Abbasid caliphs between 833 and 848—which revolved around a theological doctrine known as Mutazilism and focused on the question of whether the Quran text was created or eternal—was in part an effort by the caliphs to enforce their claims to legal absolutism. The main result of this episode, however, was to make heroes out of Ahmad ibn Hanbal (780–855) and other religious scholars in Baghdad who had led the opposition.

Development of the Caliphal Army and Administration

This period (700–950) was also marked by important developments in key institutions of the caliphate and the Muslim empire, particularly the army and the imperial bureaucracy. The later Umayyads tried to build a potent new army based on the Arab tribes of Syria, which they tied to their interests through lavish caliphal patronage. The early Abbasid armies, by contrast, relied especially on soldiers from Khurasan (often settlers of Arabian origin) whom the first Abbasids had ridden to power. Although the Arabian and Syrian tribes that constituted the core of the Umayyad army were not completely swept away, it was the Khurasanians and their descendants—the *abna al-dawla*, or "sons of the revolution," now mostly settled in Iraq—who dominated the Abbasid military establishment for almost a century after the Abbasids' accession in 750. But both the Umayyad and early Abbasid armies were composed mainly of ordinary men with ordinary social ties (that is, to their families, tribes, places of origin, and so on). In many cases, soldiers were only on duty part time or were recruited by the army as auxiliaries as occasion demanded. Despite their loose structure and lack of professional training, such armies enabled the Umayyads and Abbasids to extend the empire's borders, quell dissident movements, and launch the annual summer raids against the Byzantines in Anatolia.

This pattern of loose army organization was gradually replaced during the ninth century by a new model built around smaller, highly trained corps of full-time professional soldiers (*ghulams*), who lived and worked as tight cadres and who often had few permanent ties to the rest of society (many were not even married). The change began when the caliph al-Mutasim (r. 833–42) assembled a bodyguard of mercenaries—many but not all of them slaves (*mamluks*) of Turkish origin, or recently freed slaves. The idea was that such soldiers would be completely loyal to the ruler who had raised them to power, because they had few ties to the families, tribes, or institutions of the capital and central lands of the empire. Because these mercenaries were professionally trained, they were more effective in the field than other recruits, and they came to form an increasingly large segment of the army. They helped secure al-Mutasim against potential rivals and enabled him to impose much tighter control over the provinces of the empire (especially over their taxes). To reduce frictions between the Arabic-speaking population of Baghdad and the soldiery, who often did not even speak Arabic, al-Mutasim constructed an enormous new capital at Samarra, roughly sixty-five miles (one hundred km) north of Baghdad on the east bank of the Tigris. The vast scale of the new capital offers some indication of the size of his army, and of the wealth he was able to collect in taxes to pay for it.

The growth of the professional army continued under al-Mutasim's successors al-Wathiq (r. 842–47) and al-Mutawakkil (r. 847–61). Moreover, governorships of important provinces were increasingly assigned to key commanders in the new army rather than to the caliph's kinsmen or other civilian notables, and more traditional units of the army were sidelined. Eventually, this mighty military machine got out of hand, however, proving itself more effective as an agent of factional politics than as a force of imperial defense. In 861 army commanders conspired to assassinate the caliph al-Mutawakkil, ushering in a decade of chaos during which military factions fought among themselves for supremacy and for dwindling revenues, making and unmaking four caliphs in Samarra in the process. Meanwhile, the empire's affairs outside Iraq were neglected; many provinces were left on their own, and numerous rebellions sprang up, some of which seized entire regions and established virtually independent states, while others threatened to seize Baghdad itself.

Under the late Umayyads and Abbasids the imperial administration also underwent significant changes, aimed at creating a unified bureaucracy under caliphal oversight that could manage the empire—and particularly its taxes—more effectively. Talented administrators such as Abd al-Hamid ibn Yahya (d. 750) and Ibn al-Muqaffa (720–756) oversaw the first efforts to professionalize the bureaucracy, including the development of a new, lucid Arabic prose style. The Abbasids' rise to power brought an increase in the prominence of individuals and families hailing from Iran, especially Khurasan, not only in the army but also in the caliphal court and in governmental institutions generally, including the administration. The viziers or heads of this administration, such as the famed viziers of the Barmakid family, were highly educated, and as heads of a vast bureaucracy, they often held great power in the Abbasid government. At its height around the mid-ninth century the Abbasid administration was composed of a large number of separate departments (*diwans*), staffed by thousands of clerks or secretaries (*kuttab*) who ran this administrative machinery. The administration dealt with assessment and collection of land taxes from the various provinces, with incomes from state lands and confiscated property and with other kinds of income, as well as with disbursements to the army and to administrators and others on government salary. It included a treasury that balanced receipts and expenses, an accounting office, an intelligence service, a chancery office to handle official correspondence, and a department for the caliph's special court of appeal (*mazalim*). Eventually, the costs of running such a vast bureaucracy outstripped revenues, however. Struggles arose between the caliphs and their increasingly petulant army commanders and troops for control of the bureaucracy and the revenues it could provide. In a few cases, powerful army chiefs actually secured appointments as viziers—usually with disastrous results because most military men lacked the extensive scribal training, in everything from tax assessment and accounting to literature and composition, required of an effective vizier.

After the chaos of the 860s, the caliphate enjoyed a temporary resurgence of power because several caliphs had close ties to the army chiefs. With the help of some cooperative viziers, they were able to put down the most threatening rebellions. The caliph al-Mutadid (r. 892–902) was able to regain control over Iraq, northern Mesopotamia, Al-Jazirah, northern Syria, and parts of western Iran.

Other areas of the empire—including much of Armenia, Azerbaijan, Egypt, Iran, North Africa, and Yemen—were effectively autonomous under their "governors" or local dynasties, however, and made little or no real financial or military contribution to the caliphate. But even areas that were under Abbasid control at the beginning of the tenth century now consisted of a mosaic of units headed by powerful governors, tribes, or local families, and they were weakly integrated with the caliphate. A vigorous and skillful caliph such as al-Mutadid could rely on them for support, but when the caliphal grip weakened again these areas also could venture to stand on their own. The caliphal grip weakened decisively after 908, and the next forty years in Baghdad were marked by continual infighting of bureaucratic and army factions for control of the caliphs and whatever revenues could be raised by his bureaucracy, culminating in a military takeover in 932. Thereafter the Abbasid caliphs had no trustworthy units to rely on, and key army factions ensured that the civilian bureaucracy paid them first.

The intensity of the struggle was exacerbated by a general shortage of money, generated by disarray and extravagance in the bureaucracy, loss of revenues from independent provinces and recalcitrant tax farmers, and an unfortunate decline in the agrarian productivity of Iraq itself, formerly the caliphate's financial mainstay. To cope with the revenue shortage, the Abbasids began to rely on an institution called iqta (loosely translated as "fief," although the term had a wide and variable range of meanings). Iqta was a kind of administrative shortcut whereby a general or soldier was given the right to collect tax revenues directly from a certain district. The advantage in the short term was that the troops were paid even if the treasury was empty, and the relevant parts of the bureaucracy could be eliminated. The disadvantages, however, particularly the potential for abuse of the peasantry and loss of administrative oversight, were significant.

As a result of these developments the once powerful Abbasid caliphs were little more than figureheads by the 940s, endowed with symbolic religious authority, but lacking real political or military power or financial resources of their own. That power and access to resources had passed to powerful military figures, especially the one who could occupy the coveted position as the caliph's commander-in-chief (amir al-umara). As the power of the caliphate was choked off, leaders of the regional and local polities that emerged competed against one another for control of Baghdad and the privilege of being the caliph's "protector." The most noteworthy of these protectors were the chiefs of the powerful Buyid family of northwestern Iran (who played this role from 945 to 1055) and the sultans of the Turkish Seljuk dynasty (who dominated Baghdad from 1055 until the mid-twelfth century). From the mid-tenth century until the Mongols ended the caliphate in 1258, the Abbasid caliphs were recognized as overlords in many parts of the Islamic world, but only in a symbolic sense. Only on a few occasions did the Abbasids succeed in regaining, albeit briefly, some of their lost power.

Knowledge of the caliphs' eventual demise, however, must not overshadow the many positive achievements that took place during the age of the imperial caliphate. The expansion of the empire created the political haven in which the new faith of Islam established itself among new populations from Spain to India. Moreover, the imperial caliphate gave birth to a sophisticated and richly varied new civilization in Eurasia, culturally the most advanced of its day. This cultural genesis was linked to a noteworthy process of urbanization that took place during the early Islamic centuries; although urban life in the Mediterranean basin had declined sharply in late antiquity, the early Islamic era saw a revival of urban centers and of the commerce and culture usually associated with them. The early military garrisons of the first conquest days—Kufa, Basra, Marv, Hims, Fustat, Qayrawan—soon grew into bustling towns to which Muslims of divergent cultural backgrounds, especially new converts, were drawn. In the government offices, private salons, and marketplaces of such towns, as well as of the imperial capitals of Damascus and Baghdad, a new Islamic literary culture in Arabic began to crystallize—all the more remarkable because before the rise of Islam, Arabic had no tradition of written literature. Poetry, grammar, Quranic studies, history, biography, law, theology, philosophy, geography, the natural sciences—all were elaborated in Arabic and in a form that was distinctively Islamic.

The social base supporting this new Arabic-Islamic culture was to a certain extent bipartite. The religiously inclined cultivated such fields as Quranic studies, prophetic traditions, religious law, and theology, while topics such as history, philosophy, and statecraft were sponsored particularly by the scribes of the imperial bureaucracy, who were often learned in Sasanian and other traditions of statecraft. Poetry, from the start the soul of the Arabic literary tradition, was cultivated by both groups in religious and secular varieties. The full development of Arabic-Islamic literary culture continued long after 950, of course, but its foundations were laid, its first remarkable monuments completed, and many of its distinctive genres and forms were first established during the age of the imperial caliphate.

The caliphs also presided, wittingly or not, over economic developments that had global repercussions. The vast extent and relative stability of the empire over almost two centuries—as well as the continuous circulation within it of soldiers, administrators, pilgrims heading to or from Mecca, and scholars wishing to study with renowned teachers—helped to keep routes open and made it easier for merchants to travel far and wide. The rise of Arabic as a common written language made it easier for merchants from distant parts of the empire to communicate. Moreover, merchants in the Islamic domains in this era were usually unencumbered by duties or the need for special travel documents. Meanwhile, the rise of large cities created a base of demand for a variety of products, as well as centers of culture. In its heyday in the early ninth century, Baghdad appears to have been a city of about a million inhabitants—a staggeringly large size for preindustrial times—and had to import even its basic food supplies from sources some distance away. Some luxury goods in demand in Baghdad, particularly among the political and commercial elites, were brought from halfway around the globe. Baghdad grew to a size unmatched by other cities, but smaller cities also contributed to the economic boom. The flourishing port city of Siraf, on the eastern coast of the Persian Gulf, symbolizes one dimension of this commercial activity. It was a key transit point for foodstuffs coming from Oman, as well as textiles and other goods entering the caliphal domains from east Africa, India, and beyond.

In the other direction hoards of Abbasid gold coins found around the Baltic Sea are silent reminders of a once-thriving commercial connection that helped revitalize the economy of northern Europe and may have helped stimulate the ninth-century revival of culture and economy commonly called the Carolingian renaissance. The discovery of North African coins in Abbasid-period archaeological sites in Jordan, or Iraqi (or Chinese) ceramics found in Egypt, attest to yet other dimensions of this thriving commerce. It is appropriate to think of much of Eurasia in this period as a single, vast economic body, of which Abbasid Baghdad in particular was the heart, pumping the commercial lifeblood that kept the system alive. Iraq's prosperity in particular, with its rich tax base and thriving commerce, was an important element contributing to the political power and cultural brilliance of the high caliphate. When Iraq's agrarian prosperity began to wane in the tenth century—a result of such varied factors as deterioration of vital irrigation works, salinization of the soil, and sheer administrative mismanagement—the caliphs found themselves increasingly unable to pay the bills of their enormous government operations. This in turn sparked the infighting among military and administrative factions that characterized the long decline of Abbasid power.

Local Autonomy, Decentralization, and Regionalism Through 1100

The capture of Baghdad by the Buyids in 945, and their reduction of the caliphs to little more than figureheads, was merely the climax of a long process of change that saw ever more parts of the Islamic empire gradually slip beyond the caliphs' real control. The emergence on the former empire's terrain of autonomous or independent political units—what some historians call a "commonwealth" of regional Muslim states, united by their participation in an emerging Islamic culture—makes tracing the political history of the Islamic community after about 900 C.E. much more difficult than it is for earlier periods, when there existed a single main center of political power. This section mentions some of the main political units that emerged and gives a general idea of their significance and of larger patterns of political and cultural evolution of which these units were part.

Given the nature of communications and travel in preindustrial times, many provinces of the Islamic empire, particularly those distant from the capital at Damascus or Baghdad, enjoyed a significant measure of autonomy even at the apogee of caliphal power. The caliphs in Damascus or Baghdad simply did not have the means to keep lands as far away as Ifriqiya or Khurasan, not to mention Spain or India, under close supervision. The caliphs therefore had to rely on strong governors to manage distant provinces. It was taken for granted that provincial governors would operate with a good deal of autonomy, and the caliphs were usually well satisfied if governors recognized their overlordship, contributed to the caliphal treasury, and put additional military units at their disposal when they were needed. One important measure of truly centralized control under such conditions, however, is whether governors, despite the great independence of action they wielded within their provinces, could effectively be replaced by the caliphs. In this regard, it is noteworthy that the Umayyad and early Abbasid caliphs engaged in frequent (sometimes almost annual) rotation of their governors. Even provinces in which the governorship was granted for life or made hereditary, however, could remain loyal to the caliphs and offer meaningful support in the form of tax revenues, military backing, and diplomatic support.

The first province to be definitively detached from the caliphate was Spain. After the Abbasids overthrew the Umayyad caliphs and slaughtered many of their kinsmen, one Umayyad prince who escaped made his way to North Africa, and in 756 he invaded Spain. It then became an independent state under Umayyad rulers, who at first called themselves simply *amir* (commander). Eventually, in 929, the greatest of the Spanish Umayyad rulers, Abd al-Rahman III (891–961), assumed the title of *amir al-mu'minin* (caliph), in defiance of the Abbasids and of the Ismaili Fatimids, who were closer and more dangerous rivals. During the ninth to the twelfth centuries a splendid and distinctive Islamic culture developed in Spain, enshrined in major works of Arabic poetry and prose literature, in signal contributions to Islamic philosophy, theology, and law, and in major architectural monuments such as the Great Mosque of Córdoba and Abd al-Rahman's palace complex at Medinat al-Zahra. Many Christians and Jews in Islamic Spain began to adopt their rulers' Arabic language and culture, and in turn made their own contributions to the culture's brilliance. The great Jewish philosopher Maimonides, for example, who composed works in both Arabic and Hebrew, was as much a product of Islamic as of Jewish culture.

The Umayyads in Spain faced significant challenges, however. Tension among Arab settlers, Berber settlers, and local converts (*muwallads*) sometimes resulted in armed clashes. Some Christians steadfastly resisted both acculturation and assimilation, and tensions between Muslims and Christians sometimes ran high. Disaffected elements—whether Christian or Muslim—often did not hesitate to call on the Christian kingdoms of northern Spain or even on the Carolingians beyond the Pyrenees for aid, and this embroiled the Umayyads in persistent raiding and warfare along their northern borders. The powerful strongman Abu Amir al-Mansur (commonly known as Almanzor), who came to power as protector of a young caliph and remained in control of affairs until his death in 1002, campaigned tirelessly in the north, using a new army composed of Berber recruits. After Almanzor's death, however, the caliphate fell under dispute among various claimants, backed by dominant families in the main cities of Islamic Spain. Finally, in 1031, the leading families decided to abolish the Spanish Umayyad caliphate altogether, ushering in the era of the "petty kings" (*muluk al-tawaif* in Arabic, *reyes de taifas* in Spanish), during which Islamic Spain was divided into an unstable aggregation of competing city-states: Seville, Córdoba, Toledo, Badajoz, Saragossa, Valencia, Granada, and others.

Although the competition among these local rulers was partly responsible for the brilliant cultural flowering of Islamic Spain during the eleventh century, the same competition, played out on the political plane, sapped the economic and mil-

The Great Mosque of Córdoba, founded in the late eighth century, was repeatedly enlarged to meet the needs of the expanding Muslim population. The ingenious system of two-tiered supports allowed builders to create a forest of supports using the short stubby columns from Visigothic buildings.

itary strength of each of the petty kings, who often raided one another's territories or agreed to pay tribute to Christian kingdoms of northern Spain when threatened with attack. The era of the petty kingdoms thus helped to make possible the relentless expansion of the Christian kingdoms of northern Spain at the expense of the Islamic south that began with the union of Castile and Léon in the late eleventh century—what is known in later Spanish historiography as the *reconquista*. The first landmark in the reconquista occurred in 1085, when Toledo fell to the astute and dynamic king of Castile and Léon, Alfonso VI. The petty kings, recognizing that they were too weak to avoid suffering Toledo's fate, yet too divided by petty jealousies to agree on any one of them as ruler of them all, invited the powerful ruler of the Almoravids in Morocco, Yusuf ibn Tashfin, to cross the Strait of Gibraltar and lead their defense against Alfonso in 1086. Thus began the period of Almoravid and Almohad domination, which delayed for more than a hundred years the expansion of the Christian kingdoms into Islamic Spain.

Parts of North Africa also became independent of the caliphate, in fact or in principle, at an early date. Unlike Spain, which had a prosperous agrarian base and boasted numerous thriving cities even in early Islamic times, most of North Africa was thinly populated by pastoralists or marginal farming communities, and there were few large towns. Under the Umayyad caliphs (before 750) the Muslim garrison center at Qayrawan—situated in Ifriqiya, the most fertile part of North Africa, modern Tunisia—replaced Byzantine Carthage as the center of government, and it long remained the nucleus both of caliphal authority and of Islamic orthodoxy in North Africa. Even though all of North Africa was theoretically subject to the caliphate, vast areas, especially those more distant from Qayrawan, remained effectively outside the control of the caliphs and their governors. Moreover, during the seventh and eighth centuries, many Berbers were won over to Kharijite Islam by Kharijite merchants, preachers, and refugees fleeing oppression in their earlier centers in Iraq and Oman. Their egalitarian and puritanical variety of Islam, with its emphasis on pious "bearers of religious knowledge," seems to have struck a sympathetic chord among the Berbers, in whose traditional beliefs holy (sometimes miracle-working) men played a

The Ribat at Monastir in Tunisia, founded at the end of the eighth century, is one of a series of fortress/monasteries established to protect the North African coast and extend Muslim power to Sicily.

prominent role. The Kharijites established numerous small states in Libya, Tunisia, and Algeria during the eighth and ninth centuries, such as that of the Rustamids of Tahert.

Because many Kharijites were heavily involved in commerce, they seem to have been the first to carry Islam across the Sahara to the peoples of the western Sudan (modern Chad, Niger, and Mali). Other refugees from Abbasid rule also found shelter in the difficult mountain terrain of North Africa, including the Alid prince Idris ibn Abd Allah, who fled after the abortive Alid rebellion in the Hejaz in 786 and established a small state in Morocco, which his successors ruled from their new capital at Fez. By the late eighth century much of North Africa beyond the outskirts of Qayrawan was a checkerboard of independent tribes and small states that tendered neither recognition nor taxes to the caliphs in Baghdad. In 800 C.E. the Abbasid caliph Harun al-Rashid resorted to recognizing his governor, Ibrahim ibn al-Aghlab, as hereditary governor of Ifriqiya ("Africa," as the province of North Africa was then called) in exchange for an agreed annual tribute. This arrangement had the advantage of bringing at least some revenue to Baghdad and of preserving the appearance of Abbasid rule. During the century of their rule the Aghlabid governors were often criticized by the strictly orthodox population and religious scholars of Qayrawan for their abuses of power. Partly to quell such criticism, they struggled mightily against the Kharijite states around them, built mosques and irrigation works, and sponsored naval campaigns against Sicily, leading to the establishment of Muslim rule on that island. Aghlabid Qayrawan also developed as a major center for theology and law, but much of North Africa nevertheless remained effectively beyond Aghlabid rule. Their rule was brought to an abrupt halt by the rise of the Ismaili Fatimids in Ifriqiya during the first decade of the tenth century.

The Aghlabid basins at Qayrawan were among the many waterworks built in the mid-ninth century by the rulers of present-day Tunisia. Water from aqueducts flowed into the smaller basin where the silt was deposited; the clear water then flowed into the adjoining larger basin from which it was distributed to the city.

From the time of its conquest in 639–42, Egypt was an important part of the Islamic empire. The "province" of Egypt included North Africa and Spain until these were split off to form a separate province in 705. Despite a steady flow of Arabic-speaking settlers to Egypt, the local Copts (Monophysite Christians) remained the majority of the population for at least several centuries, and they long remained important as administrators for their Muslim rulers. The ancient city of Alexandria continued to be a major trade emporium, but the Muslims

developed their new garrisontown of Fustat (Old Cairo), which was from the start the province's administrative center. By the ninth century Fustat was beginning to develop as an important economic and Islamic cultural center. The rich farmland of the Nile valley made Egypt a major source of revenue for the Umayyad and early Abbasid caliphs. Despite its importance, however, Egypt slipped out of the effective grasp of the Abbasid caliphs when they were overwhelmed by military factions in Samarra and Baghdad; for most of a century after 868, Egypt was virtually independent of the caliphate under autonomous military governors (the Tulunids, 868–905, and the Ikhshidids, 935–69) or powerful financial administrators (especially the Madharai family in the early tenth century). During this time Egypt's economy seems to have suffered from mismanagement of the tax system. But also during this period Egypt began to emerge, for the first time since the Roman conquest almost a thousand years earlier, once again as an independent state. Egypt took another giant step in this direction when the Fatimid caliphs, coming from Ifriqiya, conquered it in 969 and made it the seat of their caliphate shortly thereafter.

Much of northern and central Arabia was the preserve of local pastoral nomadic groups, over which the caliphs in Baghdad often had minimal control. The caliphs did, however, endeavor to keep the holy cities of Mecca and Medina, important for symbolic and cultic reasons as the focus of the annual pilgrimage, firmly under their governors' supervision, and to keep open the main pilgrimage roads through tribal territory from Syria and Iraq. Southern Arabia (Yemen, Hadramawt, and parts of Oman) was only loosely held by the caliphate even in

The great Mosque at Sanaa in Yemen was founded in early Islamic times and repeatedly restored and repaired. The Sulayhids, adherents of Ismaili Shiism who ruled Yemen from Sanaa and Dhu Jibla from 1014 to 1138, were one of the many dynasties that established local control as the power of the Abbasid caliphs declined.

the best of times. Under the Umayyads and early Abbasids, governors were regularly dispatched to Yemen, but generally they had little influence beyond the capital at Sanaa. Yemen's rugged terrain was mostly dominated by various tribal chiefs, who often resided in mountaintop castles and controlled local market towns. Kharijism and particularly Shiism of various varieties took hold at an early date among some groups in this natural refuge zone. After the mid-ninth century, as the power of the Abbasid caliphs declined, local dynasties of diverse origins became established in various centers, particularly Sanaa in the mountains and Zabid along the Red Sea coast. Commerce with the Indian Ocean basin was an important element in the economic life of the main coastal towns, such as Sohar, Aden, and Zabid.

The rise of local and regional autonomy on the Iranian plateau occurred in very diverse ways and at different times in different parts of Iran. The first trend toward autonomy (not yet independence) can be seen in the career of the Tahirid family, which rose to prominence in Abbasid service during the civil war of 809–13. During the middle of the ninth century the Tahirids were recognized as hereditary governors of much of eastern Iran, centered on the rich province of Khurasan and including adjacent provinces such as Sistan and much of Transoxiana, which they governed by co-opting important local families. The Tahirids (who also held important posts in Baghdad and elsewhere) remained loyal to the Abbasid caliphs and consistently delivered considerable revenues to the caliphal treasury, in exchange for which the Abbasids allowed the Tahirids virtually free rein in their provinces.

Tahirid domination of eastern Iran was brought to an end abruptly in 873 when their capital Nishapur (in the province of Khurasan) was conquered by the Saffarids of Sistan, whose attitude toward the caliphate was as aggressive and hostile as the Tahirids' had been supportive. The rugged and impoverished province of Sistan, though conquered early by the Muslims, had been only marginally integrated into the caliphal empire. During the Umayyad and early Abbasid periods, Kharijite bands and other local rebellions kept the region turbulent. The freebooting Saffarid leaders, rising in this context, expanded their control first into Khurasan and western Afghanistan, then into the provinces of Kerman (in southeast Iran) and Fars (in southwest Iran). By the 870s they had seized Khuzestan (in southwest Iran) and parts of southern Iraq and came close to overthrowing the Abbasids in 876, when they were finally turned back by the caliph's armies only a few days' march from Baghdad. For many years thereafter, however, the Saffarids remained powerful and essentially independent of the caliphs, who were forced to recognize the Saffarids as "governors" of their home province of Sistan, as well as of Fars and Kerman (until at least 898), and even awarded them key posts in Baghdad. After about 900 the

Saffarids were restricted to Sistan, as they were supplanted in much of eastern Iran by the Samanids, a "loyalist" dynasty of governors who had risen from the wreckage of the former Tahirid domains.

The Samanid family came to prominence as subordinates of the Tahirids, for whom they governed key towns of Transoxiana. When the Saffarids seized Khurasan, the Samanids retained control over Transoxiana. By about 900 the Samanids had reconquered Khurasan in the name of the Abbasids, who recognized them as governors, and extended their control over much of northern Iran, Khwarizm (modern Khorezm), and further east in Transoxiana and Afghanistan as well, paying special attention to warding off depredations into settled districts by the nomadic Turkish tribes of Transoxiana. Like the Tahirids, the Samanids remained loyal to the Abbasids, but they never contributed revenues to the caliphate and were, in effect, an independent state. They prospered especially because of the lucrative trade in slaves, captured among Turkish tribes living on the fringes of their domains. Many of these slaves were trained in martial skills

The tomb of the Samanids at Bukhara is one of the earliest mausolea to survive in the Islamic lands. It covers the graves of several members of the Samanid family, governors of Khurasan and Transoxiana for the Abbasid caliphs in the early tenth century.

and sold as mercenaries or used to staff their own burgeoning army. But the Samanid period also saw the conversion of parts of Transoxiana's Turkish population to Islam by itinerant merchants and missionaries, and the beginnings of the peaceable migration of Turkish converts into Samanid domains to settle.

To manage their domains, the Samanids established an extensive bureaucracy, based on the Abbasid model and staffed by cadres of highly literate scribes. As earlier in Abbasid Baghdad, the highly educated administrators in the Samanid bureaucracy contributed to the development of their major cities—Nishapur, Bukhara, Samarqand—as important centers of Islamic culture. In the Samanid case, however, this blossoming of Islamic culture was not only in Arabic but also, for the first time, in Persian. This was a momentous development in the history

Mahmud of Ghazna crossing the Ganges, as portrayed in the *Compendium of Chronicles* composed and illustrated for the Ilkhanid vizier Rashid al-Din in the early fourteenth century. The Ghaznavids, Turkish military governors for the Samanids, were renowned in later times as the first to extend Muslim power into northern India.

of Islamic civilization, which until then had been elaborated exclusively in Arabic. The development of a Persianate variant of Islamic culture broke this monopoly and opened the way for the development of other Islamic languages in later times, such as Ottoman Turkish and Urdu. (All the Islamic languages, however, adopted a modified form of the Arabic script, closely identified with Islam's sacred text, the Quran, as the symbol of their religious identity.) The Samanids patronized such renowned Persian poets as Rudaki and Firdowsi, whose *Shahnameh* (*Book of Kings*), or Persian national epic, emphasized the "eternal" struggle between Iran, which was settled and agricultural, and Turan (the Turkish steppe), which was pastoral. This epic poem echoed the tense conditions on the steppe frontier over which the Samanids themselves ruled while saying little about the economic interdependence between settled people and pastoral nomads that typified this frontier.

In the end the Samanids fell to just such a "Turanian" threat. The Qara-Khanids, a confederation of Turkish peoples living east of the Jaxartes River were the first political grouping of the inner Asian steppe to be led by Muslim rulers. Crossing the Jaxartes, they entered Transoxiana from the east, defeated the Samanids, and seized the province in 999. Khurasan and parts of Afghanistan remained in the hands of the Samanids' Turkish military governors of Ghazni, who thus began their existence as an independent state. The Ghaznavids were among the first to regularly call themselves *sultans*, a Quranic word that from the tenth century was used to refer to an Islamic secular monarch. (Other terms that came to be used in this way were the Persian *shah* and the Turkish *khan*.) The Ghaznavid sultans, although they maintained a cultured court that patronized some important authors (including, in his later years, Firdowsi), built a military regime intent on raising revenue through taxation and raiding. They frequently descended from Afghanistan into non-Muslim parts of Sind (modern Pakistan) to seize the rich booty available there, particularly from its many Hindu temples. After 1040, when they lost Khurasan to the Seljuks, the Ghaznavids were limited to Afghanistan and increasingly turned their attention to Sind. As a result of this reorientation, they contributed significantly to the spread in India of Sunni Islam, which had until then been restricted to relatively small communities that were remote from the rest of the Islamic world.

Some areas of the Iranian plateau were from the start beyond effective caliphal control because of their difficult terrain, and they remained so even when the caliphs were powerful. The main case of such inaccessibility was the jungle-like region along the slopes of the Elburz Mountains south of the Caspian Sea (Daylam, Gilan, Tabaristan, Mazandaran). Here local chieftains, who at best paid lip service to the caliphs, struggled with one another for primacy. This area, like Yemen, served as a natural refuge zone and received several fugitive Alid princes, who helped convert much of the population of Daylam, at least, to Shiism. This area also served as the initial base for the warlord Mardavij (d. 935), who made a short-lived attempt to restore an Iranian monarchy and Zoroastrianism, and then for the Shiite Buyid family, who emerged from Mardavij's entourage to gain power in much of central Iran—parts of Daylam, Jibal, and the rich province of Fars. By 945 one of the Buyid chiefs, Ahmad ibn Buyeh (later known as Muizz al-Dawlah), had moved his troops into Iraq and taken possession of Baghdad, where he was recognized by the Abbasid caliph as commander in chief (*amir al-umara*). In the process the caliphs were effectively reduced to figureheads, having significant religious authority but usually little real power.

The Buyids prevailed in central and western Iran and in central and southern Iraq for more than a century, and in their heyday they managed to exert their control also over Oman, across the Persian Gulf from Fars, and over Mosul (Al-Mawsil) and northern Iraq. Their domains, however, were not a unified state but rather a loose confederation of holdings called appanages, each granted to a different member of the Buyid family. At times, a single Buyid chief was unquestionably head of the family—the most notable example being the ascendancy of Adud al-Dawlah (r. 949–83)—but most of the time the

The Gunbad-i Qabus in northeastern Iran marks the grave of Qabus bin Washmgir, ruler of the local Ziyarid dynasty, who died in 1012. The flanged shaft soars 52 meters above the artificial hillock on which it stands.

Buyid brothers and cousins were in sharp competition with one another to extend their appanages at the expense of their relatives, or to oust their relatives and take over their appanages. The Buyid princes who held appanages in Iran usually established close relations with the local landholding classes, which provided a solid financial basis for their essentially military domination. The most prosperous of the Buyid appanages was Fars, which had a solid agrarian base and significant commercial activity. Its capital at Shiraz also was home to an extensive bureaucracy, a vestige of Abbasid times, and an important court that sponsored a brilliant literary culture (always, despite the Buyids' Iranian origins, in Arabic). Other Iranian appanages of the Buyid confederation, particularly Jibal and its capital Rayy, were relatively stable although less well developed than Fars.

Baghdad under the Buyids, by comparison, was an appanage of quite a different character. The presence of the caliph and his court gave Baghdad great prestige and made it important as a center of Arabic-Islamic culture, but it also meant that the Buyids and their Daylamite troops had to manage, and sometimes face the opposition of, the turbulent factions in the Turkish army there. Moreover, the continuing decline of Iraqi agriculture deprived the Buyid amir in Baghdad of the kind of agrarian base that contributed to the viability of Buyid appanages in Iran and southern Iraq. The Buyid era in Baghdad proved to be of great significance for the development of Shiite culture, however. Although the Buyids were often on good terms with the Abbasid caliphs, whose presence under their protection provided them with valuable Islamic legitimacy, as Shiites they allowed Baghdad's large Shiite population for the first time to openly observe the major Shiite holidays. For the same reason Shiite scholarship entered its first great flowering during the Buyid period, which saw the production of major works in Shiite law, theology, and other disciplines.

The Buyids further extended the use of iqta, an institution that had originated under the Abbasids as a way of paying troops while saving on administrative costs. By letting soldiers and commanders collect tax revenues directly from their iqta, the need for a costly tax bureaucracy was eliminated, and the troops got paid. But this system was prone to abuse by unscrupulous holders if not closely supervised. Its extension into new areas contributed both to a general decline in agrarian productivity and to a loosening of effective control by the ruler—whoever he was—over the districts assigned in this way. The spread of iqta was difficult to reverse, however, for it was the quickest way for a ruler to secure the soldiers' loyalty in the competitive and increasingly militarized politics of Iraq and Iran in the tenth and eleventh centuries. The Buyids would be ousted from most of their territories in Iran and Iraq by forces of the Seljuk Turks between 1040 and 1055, but the new masters—and their eventual successors—would rely even more firmly on the iqta system.

As the Abbasid caliphs' real power contracted, even the central provinces of their former empire—Iraq, Syria, and northern Arabia—fell beyond their grasp. Sometimes these areas fell under the sway of powerful rulers of Iran (such as the Buyids in Iraq) or of Egypt (such as the Tulunid occupation of Syria in the late ninth century). In other cases, these areas were held by a mosaic of local powers. Some of these were pastoral nomadic tribes that took advantage of the empire's collapse to establish their control over the key towns within or adjacent to their traditional grazing territories, and so enter the consciousness of the chroniclers as short-lived "dynasties." The most important were the Hamdanids of Mosul and Aleppo (935–1016), important players in Iraqi politics under the fading Abbasids and early Buyids, but they quickly outgrew their origins among the Tanukh tribe and acquired the crucial trappings of a settled state, including mercenary troops. The pastoral nomadic base was more essential to groups such as the Jarrahids of tenth-century Palestine, the Mirdasids of Aleppo (1023–79), the Uqaylids of Mosul, and the Mazyadids of Hilla in central Iraq. The Qarmatis—most of whom were bedouins of Syria, southern Iraq, or eastern Arabia (in the late ninth through the late eleventh centuries)—belonged to an activist branch of Shiism, the Ismailis, and established an Ismaili state in eastern Arabia. Meanwhile, in the nearby mountains of western Iran, Azerbaijan, eastern Anatolia, Armenia, and the Caucasus, Kurdish tribes in several instances established independent Muslim states, such as the Marwanids around Amida (modern Diyarbakir in Turkey) and the Hasanuyids around Hamadhan (in western Iran). In a few cases, groups with nontribal identities formed the basis of small polities. The most interesting case is that of the Zanj, African slaves who from 869 until 883 revolted against their masters and dominated parts of southern Iraq, including the city of Basra.

The Ismaili Challenge

The most effective ideological challenge to the Abbasid caliphate from within the Islamic community arose from developments in Shiism in the ninth and tenth centuries. The Shiites had articulated the doctrine that only a descendant of the Prophet's cousin and son-in-law, Ali ibn Abi Talib, could be imam or leader of the Muslim community. Some Shiites argued that the imam's leadership was crucial because he possessed a secret knowledge. In their view this secret knowledge, which each imam conveyed to his designated successor before his death, was vital to the proper guidance of the community. This group split into activist and quietist wings. The quietists, usually called Imami or "Twelver" Shiites, believed that the line of visible imams had ended in 874 when the twelfth imam, still only an infant, had gone into hiding in Samarra, from which he would return in the fullness of time as the *mahdi*, a millenarian figure expected to lead the Muslim community in righteous preparation for the Last Judgment. For many Twelvers, then, there was no longer any basis for political action after 874, because there was no longer any imam in whose name rebellion could be raised. A more activist group, however, the Ismailis, argued that the imamate had not ended as the Twelvers claim. Rather, it continued in a different line of Ali's descendants. In the Ismaili view, there never ceased to be a living imam among Muslims, even though his identity at a particular moment might not be generally known. Periodically individuals emerged who claimed to be the imam. Clearly, this version of Shiite doctrine was likely to appeal to those with an activist turn of mind. A third variant of Shiism, called the Zaydiyya, argued that the imamate did not proceed in a particular line of descendants. Rather, it resided in the Alid who was most capable of providing effective leadership for his generation. This variant became especially important in Yemen.

The Ismailis, who were initially a unified movement with a secret, centralized leadership, strove to win adherents by means of *dawa* (missionary work) carried out by agents highly trained in theological argument. Their aim was to establish small groups or communities of followers secretly pledged to follow the imam upon his appearance, even though his identity was for reasons of prudence not divulged. By the late ninth century, as the Abbasid caliphate's power was dwindling, Ismaili communities were established in many areas: Yemen, North Africa, Iran, southern Iraq, eastern Arabia, and Syria. One group of Ismailis, the Qarmatis, rebelled openly against the Abbasids in the 890s and in 899 established a small state in northeastern Arabia; this state lasted until the 1070s and was for much of the tenth century a power to be reckoned with in northern Arabia and Syria.

The most successful Ismaili movement, however, grew out of the missionary work of a Yemeni agent in North Africa, who during the 890s established a strong

Ismaili following among the Kutama Berbers, in opposition to the Abbasids' Aghlabid governors. By 899 a leader of the Ismailis in Syria, Ubayd Allah, had broken with the Qarmatis, proclaimed himself to be the imam, and in 902 made his way to Ifriqiya to lead the new state. Because Ubayd Allah, as imam, claimed descent from Ali's wife Fatima, he and his descendants are called Fatimids. Ubayd Allah was imprisoned for a time by the Aghlabids, but in 909 the Ismaili movement in North Africa succeeded in overthrowing the Aghlabids. Ubayd Allah was freed and assumed power, taking the regnal name al-Mahdi (r. 909–34) and the title amir al-muminin in defiance of the Abbasids. The Umayyads in Spain responded to the Fatimid claim by also assuming this title in 923. Ubayd Allah also founded a new capital at Mahdiyah, to symbolize his inauguration of a new order. For sixty years (909–69) the Fatimids carefully built up a powerful state in North Africa, first consolidating their power against the very propaganda movement that had brought them to power, then against widespread local opposition.

The Great Mosque at Mahdiyah is the most important structure to survive from the new capital established on the Tunisian coast by the first Fatimid caliph al-Mahdi (r. 909–34). The design of the portal was inspired by Roman triumphal arches and gateways in the region.

The Sunni religious establishment in Qayrawan and the Sunni population of Ifriqiya generally were unsympathetic to the Ismaili's Fatimid claims. Even more hostile were the large number of North African Berber tribes who had embraced Kharijism. These tribes mounted numerous rebellions against the Fatimids, including a major one in the 940s that nearly toppled the dynasty. In the central and western Maghreb (northwest Africa), the Fatimids had to face the resistance of the small Rustamid and Idrisid states as well as the challenge of the more powerful, but more distant, Umayyads of Spain. The Fatimids overcame all these challenges, particularly during the reign of the great caliph al-Muizz (r. 953–75), whose brilliant general, Jawhar, consolidated Fatimid rule as far as the Atlantic Ocean. Al-Muizz also oversaw the construction of a powerful navy, with which

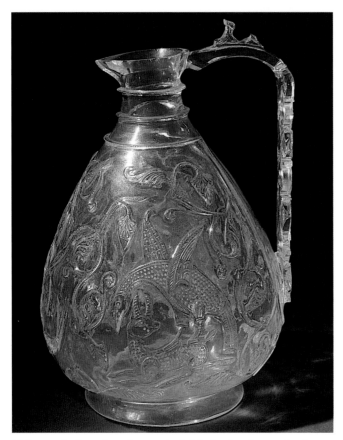

This ewer hollowed out from a single block of rock crystal epitomizes the luxury arts associated with the splendid court established by the Fatimids after they conquered Egypt in 969. Texts describe hundreds of such objects, but only a handful has survived.

the Fatimids established control over Sicily; it also played a crucial role in their conquest of Egypt.

As important as Ifriqiya was to them, the Fatimids never seem to have considered it as more than an interim station on the path to supreme power in the Islamic world. Almost immediately after their rise to power in 909, they tried unsuccessfully to conquer Egypt. Only after the Fatimids had built a strong base in Ifriqiya and engaged in extensive missionary work in Egypt was General Jawhar able to organize a successful conquest of Egypt in 969. Within a few years the Fatimid caliph left Ifriqiya in the hands of their Berber supporters, the Zirids, and took up residence in a new capital in Egypt at Cairo (from Arabic *al-Qahira*, meaning "the victorious"), a government and military complex that they founded beside Fustat. The splendid mosque of Al-Azhar was built in the new city to serve as the center of Ismaili worship. The extensive education that underlay the Ismaili dawa was carried out at many locations.

The Fatimids would govern Egypt for two centuries (969–1171). During the first century of their rule there, they made impressive gains on several fronts. They established a presence in Syria and intermittent control over its main towns, Damascus and Aleppo, but they continually faced opposition from the Qarmatis; from bands of Turkish mercenaries dislodged from Buyid Baghdad; from local tribal powers, the Jarrahids in Palestine and the Hamdanids in Aleppo; and from the Byzantine Empire, resurgent under powerful military emperors from 975 to 1025. Their power was recognized in the holy cities of the Hejaz and by some Ismaili groups in Yemen. From Yemen, Ismaili agents established communities of supporters among the Muslims of India. Despite persistent diplomatic and

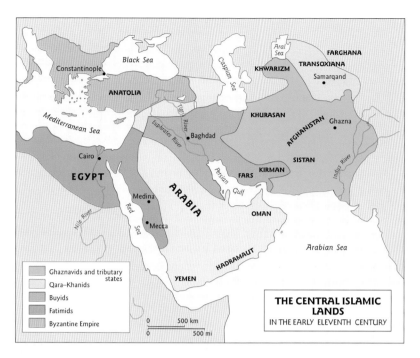

THE CENTRAL ISLAMIC
LANDS
IN THE EARLY ELEVENTH CENTURY

propagnda efforts, however, the Fatimids failed to gain recognition in Baghdad, then under control of (Twelver) Shiite Buyids.

Under the caliphs al-Aziz (r. 975–96), al-Hakim (r. 996–1021), and al-Zahir (r. 1021–36), the Fatimid caliphate in Egypt became the most powerful state in the Islamic world and displayed a durability that enabled it to weather numerous crisis—even the protracted chaos and terror unleashed by al-Hakim, whose repressions of Egypt's large Christian population, assassination of many of his key advisers and commanders, and many other unpredictable measures would have undone a less stable regime. Fatimid might was based on a prosperous economy, an efficient, centralized administration, a powerful army, and skilled use of military governors to manage complex provinces, particularly Syria. The economy burgeoned partly because of a fortuitous increase in international trade passing through Egypt. This quickening of trade was to some extent the result of increasing demand in Europe, which was reviving economically, but it was also fostered by the instability of Iraq at this time, which caused merchants coming from the east to favor the Red Sea route to the Mediterranean.

The Fatimids also had access to plentiful gold supplies in Nubia (along the Upper Nile), which helped them to pay their armies and to mount the ambitious program of missionary work aimed at spreading recognition of the Fatimid caliphate. Egypt's rich farmland provided a steady flow of tax revenues, thanks to careful management by the Fatimid bureaucracy, supervised by a series of talented viziers (some of whom were native Christians, and some, such as Yaqub ibn Killis and al-Jarjarai, were of Iraqi origin). The Fatimid army consisted of a core of Kutama Berber units—heritage of their North African origins and staunch Ismailis—and units of African slaves and "easterners," mainly Turks but also including Daylamis, Armenians, and others. Key military men became important pillars of the regime, such as the Turk Anushtakin al-Dizbari, who in the 1020s and 1030s helped contain the threat posed to Syria by the Jarrahids and other bedouin groups.

After about 1045 the power and stability of Fatimid rule slipped rapidly because of the rise of factional fighting between Berber and "eastern" cliques in the bureaucracy and among Berber, Turkish, and African contingents in the army. The earlier Fatimids had been careful to maintain a balance among different groups, but when this balance was lost, it proved impossible to restore. This internal strife caused the Fatimids to lose Syria to the Hamdanids and then, later in the eleventh century, to the Seljuk Turks, who had ousted the Buyids as protectors of the Abbasid caliphs in Baghdad. The Abbasids and their Seljuk guardians were also recognized in the Hejaz, including the holy cities of Mecca and Medina, by the end of the eleventh century. The Fatimids' weakening grip was symbolized by the decision of their Zirid vassals in Ifriqiya to repudiate the Fatimids and shift their formal allegiance to the Abbasid caliphs in 1044. The Zirids were in effect declaring themselves independent, because the Abbasids were too far away to have any real control over them. In retaliation, the Fatimid caliph al-Mustansir (r. 1036–94) sent the bedouin tribes of Hilal and Sulaym, who had proven troublesome in Egypt, to find new abodes in Ifriqiya. The long-term impact of the so-called Hilalian invasion has been hotly debated, but the arrival of these groups in Ifriqiya did disrupt the region politically (they sacked Qayrawan in 1057) and hastened the spread of Arabic as a spoken language in parts of the North African countryside.

In 1073 the caliph al-Mustansir, facing grave civil disorder in Cairo, called on his military governor in Syria, an Armenian named Badr al-Jamali, to restore order. Badr (r. 1073–94) and his son al-Afdal ibn Badr (r. 1094–1121) did restore order, but in the process they reduced the Fatimid caliphs to figurehead status, similar to that occupied by the Abbasids during the Buyid period. Henceforth, real power in the Fatimid domains was held by viziers and by key army chiefs, who were often engaged in complex intrigues and factional fighting. The presence of the Crusaders in Syria after 1099 only further complicated the situation of the Fatimids. Eventually, a desperate vizier called for support from Saladin (known in Arabic as Salah al-Din ibn Ayyub), a Kurdish military commander who had risen in the service of a Seljuk successor state in Syria, the Zangids. In 1171, Saladin himself acceded to the vizierate. One of his first acts after doing so was to renounce the Fatimids and recognize the Abbasids once again—in theory at least—as the overlords of Egypt.

Despite the Fatimids' concern for the Ismaili dawa, Ismailism made surprisingly little progress in Egypt during their rule. When the dynasty fell in 1171, Egypt's Muslim population was still staunchly Sunni, and Christian and Jewish communities were still strong. The Ismaili notion of the imamate as a linear progression made it prone to schism; several of these shook the Fatimid caliphate. One offshoot was the Druze faith, whose adherents considered the caliph al-Hakim to be divine; they established themselves (and are still to be found) in Lebanon and Syria. The so-called Assassins were another offshoot; in the eleventh and twelfth centuries they became the radical terrorists of the Islamic world, striking down selected political and cultural leaders to advance the cause of an Ismaili revolution. The positive accomplishments of the Fatimids, however, were significant. The brilliance and prosperity of Fatimid Cairo attracted many talented people in the arts, architecture, literature, administration, and military service. Consequently Fatimid Cairo replaced Baghdad as the most important cultural, and to some extent political, center of the eastern Arabic-speaking world, a position it has never relinquished.

Islamic Revivalism in the Maghreb

From the late eleventh to the early thirteenth century, the Maghreb (Islamic west) was dominated in succession by two states: the Almoravids (al-murabitun) and the Almohads (al-muwahhidun), both of which began as Sunni revivalist movements among the Berbers of North Africa. In about 1050 North Africa was politically fragmented among rival tribes in the wake of the collapse of Fatimid power and the Hilalian invasion, and Muslim Spain was divided into many small petty kingdoms. Furthermore, North Africa still displayed a great religious diversity; Sunni Islam was strong in the old bastion at Qayrawan, but Kharijism was still widespread, and many areas (particularly in the mountainous far Maghreb, where large towns were few) were still only nominally Islamized.

The Almoravids began as a Sunni reform movement among the lowland Sanhaja Berbers of the Sahara, sparked by a scholar who had become filled with an austere religious zeal from his pilgrimage to Mecca and his studies in Sunni Qayrawan. He returned to his people in the Sahara to reform their Islam, founding a "pure" Muslim community somewhere near the Senegal River in the 1040s. Alliance with Sanhaja tribal chiefs gave the Almoravid movement the military base needed to expand northward, with the aim of establishing proper Islamic practice as they understood it. Under their greatest leader, Yusuf ibn Tashfin (1061–1106), the Almoravids subdued semi-Islamized Berber groups, whom they viewed as heretical, as well as tribes who had been political rivals of the Sanhaja during the 1060s and 1070s. Ibn Tashfin thus conquered much of

Morocco and western Algeria. In about 1060 Ibn Tashfin established the settlement of Marrakesh as a kind of military camp; it grew rapidly and became the Almoravid capital.

Ibn Tashfin emerged as the most powerful figure in the western Islamic world, just when the petty kingdoms of Islamic Spain were confronted by the threat of the reconquista. The resurgent Christian kingdoms of northern Spain, led by Alfonso VI, had already seized Toledo and were pressing on the Muslim city-states of Andalusia. In desperation, several of the petty kings called on Ibn Tashfin to enter Spain and ward off the Christians. His decisive defeat of Alfonso's army at the Battle of Zallaqa in 1086 kept southern Spain out of Christian hands for the moment, but the various Muslim kings of Spain were gradually deposed and the area was incorporated into the sprawling Almoravid empire, which now extended from central Spain to the Senegal River. Further Almoravid victories on the battlefield helped to keep the Christian kingdoms of northern Spain at bay; yet many Spanish Muslims resented the hegemony of the Almoravids. In part, this reflected a long tradition of hostility to the Berbers in Spain, legacy of their frequent use as mercenaries; in part, it was because the Muslims of Spain considered the Almoravids culturally unsophisticated; and finally, in part it was because they were repelled by the Almoravids' harsh enforcement of Islam, which included persecution of Sufis and the burning of religious books deemed heretical. Widespread rebellions against the Almoravids in the 1140s heralded the collapse of their rule in Spain.

Meanwhile, in North Africa another revivalist movement, that of the Almohads, was already challenging the Almoravids by about 1125. The founder of the Almohad movement, Muhammad Ibn Tumart (ca. 1080–1130), was a highland Berber of the Masmuda tribe who, after study in Córdoba and the Islamic east, had returned to the Maghreb to preach a message of strict piety,

The mosque at Tinmallal (1153–4), located high in the Atlas mountains south of Marrakesh, is the sole vestige of the Almohad capital established there by Ibn Tumart around 1125.

declaring himself to be the *mahdi*, the eschatological just ruler, and claiming that the Almoravids were impious and corrupt. In about 1125 he established a base at Tinmallal in the Atlas Mountains (modern Morocco) and began to conquer nearby areas, having won many followers among the highland Masmuda Berbers. The speed with which Ibn Tumart won support may have been because his actions conformed to the traditional Berber concept of a charismatic holy man. His attack on the Almoravids and their Sanhaja supporters may also have articulated the highland Berbers' traditional disdain for lowlanders, such as the Sanhaja. In the 1130s and early 1140s Ibn Tumart's successor, Abd al-Mumin (1145–63), defeated the last Almoravids in battle and seized much of northern Morocco and western Algeria, taking Marrakesh in 1147.

The collapse of Almoravid rule resulted in a renewed period of political division among the Muslim city-states in Spain, which Alfonso VII, the king of Castile, attempted to exploit. But the Muslims invited Abd al-Mumin to send an army to relieve them, so that between 1147 and 1157 the former Almoravid domains were recovered from Alfonso by Almohad forces. Meanwhile, Abd al-Mumin organized two massive expeditions in the eastern Maghreb. The first, which began in 1151, brought Almohad rule to the central Maghreb, ending the reign of local powers such as the Banu Hammad, a family that had established a small state in the mountains of what today is Algeria. The second campaign was directed against Ifriqiya, which had been seized by the Normans of Sicily. By driving them out of Mahdiyah in 1160 and bringing the region under Almohad control, Abd al-Mumin unified the whole Maghreb from Tunisia to the Atlantic Ocean, as well as the Islamic regions of Spain.

During the last decades of the twelfth century the Almohads had to overcome the stubborn resistance mounted by the last Almoravid holdouts from the Balearic Islands (near the eastern coast of Spain), who had seized much of Ifriqiya. In Spain the Almohads were engaged in a continuing struggle against the Christian kingdoms, particularly those of Castile and Portugal. Despite promising offensives into Castilian territory in the 1190s, the Almohads were crushingly defeated in 1212 by a Christian coalition at Las Navas de Tolosa (in southern Spain), the battle that really sealed the fate of Islamic Spain. Almoravid control in Spain unraveled over the next two decades, and Christian forces seized in rapid succession the major cities of Andalusia: Mérida (1231), Córdoba (1236), Valencia (1238), Seville (1248), Murcia (1261), and Cádiz (1262). Virtually all that remained of Muslim Spain thereafter was the small, brilliant kingdom of Granada, which hung on until 1492, partly because of the skill of its rulers, the Nasrids, and partly because in 1244 one of the rulers had signed a treaty recognizing the vague overlordship of the kingdom of Castile.

Matters did not go better for the Almohads in North Africa, where their empire gradually devolved into several independent states. In Ifriqiya a former Almohad viceroy of Tunis, Muhammad ibn Hafs, became effectively independent by 1235, beginning the Hafsid dynasty; Ibn Hafs even dared to take for himself the title amir al-mu'minin. The Banu Marin nomads of the Sahara gradually seized eastern Morocco from the Almohads, occupying Marrakesh in 1269; their capital at Fez would become an important cultural center in their day. Southern Morocco saw the rise to power of the Zayyanid dynasty.

The Almoravids and the Almohads both demonstrated once again the power that could be built on a combination of tribally based military units and compelling Islamic religious ideologies. Their key leaders may also have won support among the Berbers because they fit the Berber tradition of miracle-working holy men (igur-ramen). The fact that the Almoravids, at least, sat astride important Saharan trade routes and controlled valuable sources of gold in western Africa also contributed to their ability to project their power. The seemingly evanescent nature of the Almoravid and Almohad empires should not mask the fact that they helped create the Maghreb—both as a political unit, which they unified for the first time, and as a distinct zone of Islamic culture. Despite the presence in their religious beliefs of numerous idiosyncratic features, both movements were staunchly Sunni, and their piety-mindedness and intolerance of other religious views caused them to repress many of the remaining Kharijite, Shiite, and other heterodox forms of Islam that were widespread in the Maghreb until the eleventh century. In cultural terms, too, their rule was important to the development of the Maghreb, which had been a cultural backwater before the eleventh century. After their occupation of Spain, with its richly developed Islamic culture, the Almoravids imported many scholars and learned men of religion from Spain to their North African cities, particularly their capital at Marrakesh, which became a new center for the elaboration of Islamic civilization on the highly sophisticated Andalusian model.

The Turks Enter the Mashriq

The eleventh century brought profound and enduring changes to the eastern Islamic lands, or mashriq (roughly Egypt and Islamic southwestern Asia). These changes were associated with the arrival of new populations of Turkish-speaking peoples, who migrated into the region from the Central Asian steppe that had until then been their homelands.

Turks had long been familiar in the eastern Islamic lands as slaves, soldiers, and military governors. By the early eleventh century some Turks had even succeeded in establishing military regimes that were essentially independent states, such as that of the Ghaznavids in Khurasan and Afghanistan. In the early eleventh century, however, another kind of Turkish presence began to make itself felt in eastern Iran: not individual slaves or soldiers, or even companies of soliders, but Türkmen—whole tribes of Turkish-speaking people, mainly nomadic or semisedentary, moving with their flocks and possessions. During the tenth century merchants, preachers, and border raiders from the Samanid domains had converted Turkish tribesmen on their frontiers to Islam, some of whom settled or migrated into Khwarizm (modern Khorezm) and Transoxiana. During the early eleventh century branches of the Oghuz tribe of Türkmen, facing desperate conditions in Transoxiana and the Central Asian steppe, began to migrate into Khurasan, across northern Iran, and into Jibal and Azerbaijan, many under the leadership of members of the Seljuk family. In Khurasan the Ghaznavids' field armies failed to stem the arrival of these unwelcome migrants, who disrupted the towns and countryside, and in 1040 the Seljuks' Türkmen followers decisively defeated the Ghaznavid army in battle at Dandanqan, near the old Muslim garrison town of Marv. The Seljuks were now not only tribal chiefs but masters of a settled state based in Khurasan.

After 1040 more nomadic or seminomadic Türkmen moved across Iran into the Jibal region, Azerbaijan, and Armenia; others migrated southward into Kerman and elsewhere in Iran. The migration of large populations of Turkish-speaking peoples into Iran and Anatolia, and the establishment of Seljuk rule in Iran, Iraq, Anatolia, and Syria, were two different but related historical processes. They were related because the Seljuks relied to some extent on the Türkmen for their armies, and because many Türkmen recognized the Seljuks as their "royal house." Seljuk sultans, however, continually faced the problem of trying to control, or at least influence, the rugged Türkmen, whose migrations and raiding often had a momentum of their own that generated unwanted political and diplomatic problems for the sultans. For this reason soon after 1040 the Seljuks acquired mercenaries (often slave troops) to serve as the core of their army. This freed them of the need to rely totally on the Türkmen, and gave them an instrument to control unruly Türkmen when necessary. Around this core they added groups of allies, including Türkmen and others, to construct large armies for specific campaigns. Seljuk control of an area therefore usually followed the migration into it by large numbers of Türkmen, as was the case in Khurasan, Kerman, Jibal, Azerbaijan, and much of Anatolia. In other cases the Seljuks strove to keep the Türkmen out of certain areas, such as prosperous farming districts or those near cities that became important centers of Seljuk power—Baghdad, Hamadan, Isfahan, and so on. They did this by encouraging the Türkmen to engage in raiding elsewhere, particularly in frontier zones (for example, against the Christian kingdoms of Armenia and Georgia).

As the Seljuks moved into western Iran, they overpowered or outmaneuvered

Church of the Holy Cross on Aghtamar, an island in Lake Van. Built between 915 and 921, the palace church of the Armenian king Gagik epitomizes the beautiful stone architecture encountered by the Seljuks when they conquered the region in the late eleventh century.

the Buyid amirs there. Staunch Sunnis, like most of the Türkmen they led, the Seljuks portrayed their struggle against the Shiite Buyids as a restoration of Sunni Islam. In 1055 sultan Toghril Beg (r. ca. 1040–1063) entered Baghdad and eliminated the Buyid "protectorate" of the caliphate. The caliph's "protector" was now the Sunni Seljuk sultan, who ruled over a loose empire stretching from Transoxiana to Iraq (known as the Great Seljuk domains).

Meanwhile, the Türkmen had continued pushing northwestward into Armenia, the Caucasus, and Anatolia, eventually provoking a reaction from the Byzantine Empire, which like the Ghaznavids found that their fixed border fortresses and armies were incapable of stopping the influx of nomads. The decisive defeat of the Byzantine emperor and his vast army at Malazgirt (formerly Manzikert) near Lake

Van in 1071 by the Seljuk army sent by sultan Alp Arslan (r. 1063–72) ended all hope of Byzantine resistance in eastern Anatolia and Armenia. Leaders from a rival branch of the Seljuk family, who came to be known as the Seljuks of Rum, established themselves in Konya, which by the 1070s had become the focus of a powerful state in western Anatolia. Princes of another Turkish family, the Danishmendids, formed another powerful Türkmen sultanate in central and eastern Anatolia. For the next seventy-five years Anatolia was the arena of a complex struggle for political supremacy among the Rum Seljuks, the Danishmendids, and the Byzantines, with lesser roles played by the Great Seljuks, local Kurdish, Turkish, and Armenian chieftains, and the European Crusaders, who arrived in Anatolia in the 1090s. By the middle of the twelfth century, however, the Rum Seljuks were becoming the dominant power in Anatolia. The Danishmendids

The portal of the madrasa known as the Ince Minareli ("Slender Minaret") in Konya. Built in the mid-thirteenth century, the building was one of many theological schools built there.

effectively collapsed, and the defeat of the Byzantine army at Myriokephalon in 1176 ended the threat of serious Byzantine intervention in central and southwestern Anatolia. Under sultan Kilij Arslan II (r. 1155–92), the Rum Seljuks built a prosperous state, commerce flourished, and Konya especially became an important center of Sufism (Islamic mysticism), fine arts, and literature—mainly in Persian, because the Turks' first intimate contact with refined Islamic culture had taken place in Iran. Above all, the chaotic century between the battles of Malazgirt and Myriokephalon saw Anatolia begin its decisive transformation from an area that was primarily Christian in faith and Greek or Armenian in language, to one that was primarily Muslim in faith and Turkish in language. The Kurdish populations of east-

ern Anatolia and the Zagros Mountains of western Iran, Muslim in faith and tribally organized, sometimes fought and sometimes allied themselves with the Turks,
but survived, with changes.

The Great Seljuk domains were conceived as constituting a collective Seljuk
family possession, parts of which were parceled out as appanages to individual
princes under the loose control of the sultan. As with the Buyids, however, the
appanage system led to intrigues and strife between rival princes. The early
Seljuk sultans—Toghril Beg, Alp Arslan, and Malik Shah (r. 1072–92)—made significant efforts to create a more centralized, bureaucratic regime by relying especially on skilled administrators from Khurasan who continued the Samanid and
Ghaznavid bureaucratic traditions. The great vizier Nizam al-Mulk (1018 or
1019–92, died at the hands of an Assassin), who wrote a famous Persian handbook on statecraft for sultan Malik-Shah, was the main architect of this effort. To
encourage the study of Islamic law and administration, the Seljuks and their
viziers also endowed special schools (madrasas), an institution they had discovered
in eastern Iran that soon spread throughout the Islamic world. Their goal in
doing so was partly to strengthen Sunni Islam against Shiism, but also to help
train administrators, and by dispensing patronage to make the religious elite
responsive to their wishes.

Despite these strivings toward centralization, by the early twelfth century the
various appanages of the Great Seljuk "empire"—particularly in its western
parts—were increasingly becoming independent states. This tendency to decentralization was reinforced by the Seljuks' heavy reliance on assignment of lands
as iqta to pay commanders and bureaucrats, and by the practice of appointing
minor sons as appanage holders under the protection of experienced military
men (atabegs, tutor-guardians). Frequently, the atabeg pushed his charge aside and
ended up ruling the appanage for himself. During the twelfth and first half of the
thirteenth centuries the territories once claimed by the Great Seljuks in Syria,
Mesopotamia, and the mountains bordering Mesopotamia on the north and east
were held by more than a half-dozen small atabeg states, such as the Urtuqids of
Amida (modern Diyarbakir) and Mardin and the Zangids of Mosul and Aleppo.
The European Crusaders, by their sheer good fortune, happened to arrive in the
Near East at a time when the eastern Mediterranean coast and hinterland were
fragmented in this way, a fact that facilitated their advance and ultimate conquest
of Antioch, Edessa, Tripoli, Acre, and Jerusalem in 1098 to 1099.

Toward the middle of the twelfth century the Zangids succeeded in consolidating their hold over Mesopotamia and most of Syria's interior against the
Crusader kingdoms. As the power of the Zangids grew, they became entangled
in the factional intrigues that marked the last years of the Fatimid caliphate in
Egypt. As a result of this involvement, a Kurdish officer in Zangid service,

Saladin (Salah al-Din ibn Ayyub, 1169–1193), seized effective control of Egypt in 1169 and abolished the Fatimid caliphate in 1171. Drawing on his power base in Egypt, Saladin was able to establish himself as master of the former Zangid territories in Syria and Mesopotamia. Then in 1187 he decisively defeated the Crusaders at the Battle of Hattin and reconquered Jerusalem. From this time until their virtual extinction a century later, the Crusader "kingdoms" typically led a tenuous existence in some towns along the Syrian coast. The Ayyubids, as Saladin's descendants are called, continued to dominate Syria until the mid-thirteenth century. Although of Kurdish origin, in politics and statecraft they were truly products of the environment in which they had risen, the Seljuk atabeg states, and so helped to bring many institutions typical of the Seljuks to Syria and Egypt, particularly heavy reliance on iqta, and the endowment of many madrasas. The appanage-type politics of the Ayyubids resulted in almost continuous internecine strife among Ayyubid princes. The last Ayyubid sultan built a powerful contingent of Turkish slaves, hoping thereby to give himself the military advantage, but upon his death in 1249 these slave troops seized power for themselves, marking the beginning of a powerful new regime based in Egypt— the Mamluks (1250–1517).

The one area of the Great Seljuk empire that for a time escaped the fragmentation of the early twelfth century was Khurasan, which under sultan Muizz ad-

The Citadel of Cairo, founded by Saladin in the late twelfth century, underwent its greatest expansion during the period of Mamluk rule (1250–1517). The citadel not only protected the capital but also symbolized the power of the military state.

Din Sanjar (r. 1118–57) enjoyed a period of relative stability and prosperity. However, Transoxiana fell under the control of the non-Muslim Kara-Khitai in the 1140s. This weakened Sanjar's rule and forced into Khurasan many restless Oghuz tribesmen, who overthrew Sanjar in 1153. In the vacuum that resulted there arose the meteoric "empire" of the Khwarizmshahs—Turkish amirs who had governed the rich Khwarizm basin for the Seljuks and now were independent. Using a large mercenary army, they conquered Transoxiana, Khurasan, central Iran, and much of Afghanistan in the second half of the twelfth century and first decade of the thirteenth; they even intervened in Anatolia and began to plan an invasion of Iraq. The empire of the Khwarizmshahs, even their army, was poorly integrated and overextended, however. It quickly collapsed before the Mongol forces of Genghis Khan (ca. 1162–1227), who arrived on the borders of Transoxiana in 1219.

As the real power of the Great Seljuk sultans in the western parts of their domains weakened, the Abbasid caliphs began to reassert themselves. In 1152 the caliph was able to eliminate the last vestiges of Seljuk control in Baghdad, and he ruled at least part of Iraq as independent monarch for the first time in over two centuries. The caliph al-Nasir (1180–1225), the most capable of the late Abbasid caliphs, became the most powerful political figure of his day in Iraq. His ineffectual successors did little to enhance the power of the caliphate, however. They proved utterly incapable of withstanding the most terrible threat the Islamic world had ever faced: the Mongols.

The Mongols and the End of the Caliphate in the East

In the early thirteenth century the Mongol leader Genghis Khan embarked on his career of world conquest, which would eventually bring inner Asia, China, Russia, Iran, Anatolia, and Iraq under his family's domination. The Mongols tolerated no opposition and were careful to destroy any centers of political power independent of their own. Moreover, for some time they clung to the pastoral traditions of the steppe and had little interest in, and no sympathy for, cities or agricultural areas, except as revenue sources. These factors, coupled with their perhaps intentional use of terror as a means of social control, may explain the destructiveness of the Mongol invasions, which saw the obliteration of many cities and their inhabitants and the destruction or neglect of many irrigation works on which the agrarian prosperity of the countryside depended.

The Mongol forces arrived in Transoxiana, on the steppe fringes of the Islamic world, in 1219. Shortly thereafter they conquered Khurasan and Khwarizm, after which they swept through northern Iran and the Caucasus Mountains, leaving devastation in their wake. The Mongols' consolidation of power in inner Asia led to a massive migration of Türkmen refugees into Anatolia, which upset the prosperity that the Rum Seljuks had overseen there. Sensing the Rum Seljuks' weakness, the Mongols then invaded Anatolia, defeated the Seljuks in 1243 at the Battle of Kösedag, and reduced the Seljuks to a protectorate of the Mongol Empire. In 1256 the Mongols, led by Genghis' grandson Hülegü (r. 1256–65), once again invaded Iran. After subduing eastern Iran and the Jibal region and systematically eliminating the Assassin centers in northern Iran, Hülegü seized Baghdad and had the last Abbasid caliph executed in 1258, along with a good part of the city's population. His armies then marched across northern Mesopotamia into Syria. Their advance in this direction was finally stopped when the newly established Mamluk regime defeated the Mongols in 1260 at the Battle of Ayn Jalut in Palestine. This victory spared Cairo, which was at this time the main center of Arabic culture, from Mongol devastation. But Hülegü's forces then controlled the majority of the Islamic east.

The advent of the Mongols marked a turning point in the history of the Islamic Near East in several ways. Their arrival accelerated the immigration of Turkish-speaking peoples from the steppes into Anatolia and parts of Iran. The strong nomadic orientation of the early Mongols at first dealt a severe blow to city life and to rural agriculture alike, both of which were slow to recover to former levels of prosperity. Recovery, when it came, often followed new patterns: different cities rose to prominence (such as Ardabil and Qazvin), while some formerly important ones languished or vanished (such as Baghdad and Nishapur). Some once important regions, such as Khurasan, also waned to relative insignificance. New patterns of commercial activity were established, some of which were related to the fact that the territories conquered by Hülegü were for a time part of the vast Mongol empire that extended from Russia to China. In intellectual terms, too, the Mongol invasions represented a watershed in the history of the Islamic world. It was the first time, since the establishment of the caliphate more than six hundred years earlier, that a significant part of the Islamic world had been subjected to the domination of a non-Muslim power— a fact that must have called into question the assumption made by many Muslims that God's favor for their community was revealed in its continuing political superiority. The Mongols brought new concepts of legitimacy, such as descent from Genghis Khan and the notion of the ruler's decree as law. These concepts were widely emulated by many later dynasties in the eastern Islamic world, even those that also appealed to Islamic traditions of legitimacy.

The Caliphate as Agent of Political and Cultural Change

The preceding pages have traced the simultaneous spread of the Islamic community from its origins to the thirteenth century and the rise and fall of the caliphate. Muhammad's community in Medina had been at once a small religious community and an embryonic state or political community. The political entity, under caliphal leadership, grew into a vast empire with explosive speed, but the religious community grew much more slowly. The early Believers were at first a small minority in the empire they ruled, but they were politically dominant. The caliphate thus provided the sheltering aegis and a political identity that enabled the small Islamic religious community to survive, along with the political and social conditions within the empire that attracted new converts to the faith. When the caliphs lost real power in the tenth century, moreover, the autonomous or independent states that sprang up in their former territories, from Spain to India, were also self-consciously Muslim regimes. Under these Muslim successor states, Islam continued to put down deep roots throughout the Near East and North Africa.

The caliphate also played another important role. By providing a political and social haven for Muslims, the caliphate also allowed the development of a rich new culture, of which the Islamic religion was the distinguishing element. The rise of Islamic culture was even more important than political and social factors in drawing new people to the Islamic community, which now began to spread beyond the confines of the caliphal empire.

With the political regionalism of the tenth and following centuries came cultural regionalism. Spain, North Africa, Egypt, Syria and Iraq, Iran, Anatolia, Yemen, and other regions developed distinctive variants of a recognizably common Islamic culture, focused particularly in the main cities: Córdoba, Cairo, Damascus, Baghdad, Isfahan, Samarqand, Konya, and others. Changes in demographic patterns and linguistic usage contributed to this cultural regionalism. The rise of the new Persian language in Iran, the flow of Turkish-speaking peoples from Central Asia through Iran into Anatolia, the interplay of Arabic and Berber in North Africa, and many other phenomena all played their part. Needless to say, this process of cultural evolution and diversification continued in the later Islamic centuries, as Islam spread to many new areas and as new cultural developments took place in the Islamic heartlands.

By 1258, when the Mongols executed the last Abbasid caliph, the caliphate had effectively spent itself as a physical symbol of Islam's unity and identity. Several other rulers—including the Fatimids, the Umayyads of Spain, one of the Almohads, and even the Hafsid governor of Ifriqiya—had taken for themselves the once coveted titles of *amir al-mu'minin* or caliph, and the Shiite development of the rival concept of imam (head of the Islamic community) had also called the caliphate's meaning into question. But by this time the Islamic community was no longer defined merely by political boundaries and hegemony. More important now were a common set of religious beliefs, an elaborate system of religious law and practice, and other elements of Islamic culture, and this identity was firmly enough established to survive even rule by non-Muslims such as the Mongols. Above all, it was this solid cultural basis, first fostered by the imperial caliphate, that made possible Islam's survival over fourteen centuries and its spread to every corner of the globe.

CHAPTER TWO

Fruit of the Tree of Knowledge

THE RELATIONSHIP BETWEEN FAITH
AND PRACTICE IN ISLAM

Vincent J. Cornell

Knowledge without practice is like a tree without fruit.

—The Moroccan Sufi Ahmad ibn Ashir of Salé

Faith in Islam is never blind. Although belief in the unseen is just as important in Islam as it is in other religions, there comes a point at which the spiritually aware human being transcends the level of simple faith. At this point the person is more than just a believer, for his or her spiritual consciousness has penetrated the fog of the unseen, leading to knowledge of the true nature of things. The Quran speaks of this progression from faith to knowledge as an inward metamorphosis in which belief (*iman*) is transformed into certainty (*yaqin*). This certainty is expressed in the Quran in terms of three types of knowledge of God, which were discussed by philosophers, mystics, theologians, and jurists during the Islamic Middle Period (the ninth through fifteenth centuries C.E.).

(Left) Thousands of Muslims gather for communal worship at the Badshahi Mosque in Lahore, Pakistan, to celebrate the Feast of the Sacrifice that commemorates the willingness of Ibrahim (the Biblical Abraham) to sacrifice his son and the end of the annual pilgrimage to Mecca.

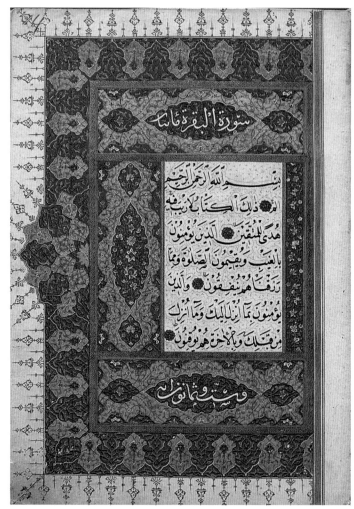

God's word, as revealed in the Quran, is the centerpiece of Muslim faith. Copying the Quran was the noblest of arts and luxury manuscripts were produced at all times. This copy, transcribed in 1491 by the noted Ottoman calligrapher Shaykh Hamdullah and lavishly decorated with arabesque designs, is a worthy testament to Muslim faith.

Modalities of Certainty

The most basic and fundamental type of knowledge is the "knowledge of certainty" (*ilm al-yaqin*, Quran 102:5). This type of certainty, which is analogous to Aristotle's concept of intellectual knowledge, refers to the knowledge that results from the human capacity for logical reasoning and the appraisal of what the Quran calls the "clear evidences" (*bayyinat*) of God's presence in the world. It is also the knowledge that comes from the study of Islam through the Quran, the

traditions of the Prophet Muhammad (*hadith*), and books of theology and exegesis. By nature, the "knowledge of certainty" is rational and discursive, a point
that the Quran acknowledges when it admonishes human beings to "travel
throughout the earth and consider how [Allah] initiated the Creation" (Quran
29:20). The same type of knowledge is involved when the Quran presents rhetorical arguments for the existence of God: "It is [Allah] who brings things to life
and causes them to die, and [Allah's] is the alteration of the night and the day.
Will you not understand?" (Quran 23:80).

Over time and under the influence of contemplation and spiritual practice, the
"knowledge of certainty" may be transformed into a higher form of knowledge
of God, which the Quran calls the "eye of certainty" (*ayn al-yaqin*, Quran 102:7).
This term, which broadly corresponds to Plato's concept of the "vision" of the
intellect, refers to the knowledge that is acquired by the spiritual intelligence,
which Islam locates metaphorically in the heart. Before attaining this type of
knowledge, the heart of the believer must first be "opened to Islam" (Quran
39:22). Once opened, the heart receives knowledge as a type of divine "light"
or illumination, which leads the believer toward remembrance of the Creator.
Just as with the "knowledge of certainty," with the "eye of certainty" the believer
apprehends God's existence through God's presence in the world. In this latter
case, however, what leads the believer to the knowledge of God are not arguments to be understood by the rational intellect, but rather theophanic "appear-
ances" (also called bayyinat) that strip away the veil of worldly phenomena to
reveal the divine reality beneath.

The metaphor of the "eye of certainty" is thus more than just a simple gloss
on the axiom "seeing is believing." From a spiritual perspective the one who
holds knowledge of God, who perceives reality in this way, is the true "intellectual." Unlike the scholar, who develops his or her skills through years of formal
study, the spiritual intellectual does not need book-learning to apprehend the
divine light. Although the Prophet Muhammad was barely able to read or write,
he has always been regarded by Muslims as the greatest intellectual of Islam. A
spiritual intellectual can be anyone, scholarly or otherwise, whose knowledge
extends both outward, to take in the physical world, and upward, to realize his
or her ultimate transcendence of the world through his or her link with the
Absolute. Without such a vertical dimension of the spirit, the scholar's knowledge, whatever its extent may be in academic terms, is of little worth. By being
blind to divine illumination, such a person is bereft of real wisdom, and according to a famous prophetic tradition amounts to little more than "a donkey carrying a load of books."

The third and most advanced type of knowledge builds on the transcendent
nature of knowledge itself. This highest level of consciousness is called the "truth

of certainty" (*haqq al-yaqin*, Quran 69:51). Also known as *ilm ladunni* ("knowledge by presence," Quran 18:65), this form of knowledge partakes directly of the divine reality and leaps across the synapses of the human mind to transcend both cognitive reasoning and intellectual vision at the same time. The "truth of certainty" refers to that state of consciousness in which a person knows the "real" through direct participation in it, without resorting to logical proofs and without objectifying either subject or object. Viewed in terms of Islamic sacred history, this type of knowledge characterizes God's Prophets and Messengers, whose consciousness of the truth is both immediate and participatory, because the knowledge on which it is based comes from direct inspiration.

Although Muhammad is the final Prophet of Islam, many scholars in the Islamic Middle Period were open to the possibility that divine inspiration could remain accessible to believers even after Muhammad's death. This possibility is symbolized in Islamic tradition by the figure of al-Khidr (Green One). Appearing first in the Quran as an unnamed servant of God and companion of the Prophet Musa (Moses), al-Khidr is endowed with a knowledge of the unseen that Musa himself lacks. The Quran describes this enigmatic sage, who is not a prophet yet partakes of divine inspiration, in the following way: "We have bestowed upon him a mercy from Ourself, and have taught him a knowledge from Our own presence" (Quran 18:65). Traditions of the Prophet Muhammad would later highlight the difference between al-Khidr's knowledge and the knowledge of prophets, while at the same time affirming its complementarity to prophecy. For example, in the *Sahih al-Bukhari*, or "sound collection" of prophetic traditions by Muhammad al-Bukhari (810–70), al-Khidr is depicted as saying to Musa: "Verily, I act on knowledge from the knowledge of Allah, which He has made known to me but has not made known to you, while you act on knowledge that He has made known to you but has not taught to me."

Thus, according to both the word of God as expressed in the Quran and the traditions of the Prophet Muhammad, faith in Islam has as much to do with what today would be called theoretical and experiential knowledge as it does with simple belief. This multidimensional conception of knowledge comprehends a reality that lies hidden within the phenomenal world yet can be revealed by the human mind and the vision of the spiritual intellect through the signs of God that are present in the world itself. In the Quran, God calls on humanity to "bear witness to what you see and what you do not see . . . a Message sent down from the Lord of the Worlds . . . verily this is the Truth of Certainty" (Quran 69:38–39, 43, 51).

The Quranic notion of religious belief as dependent on knowledge is actualized in practice in the term *Islam*. In Arabic *islam* is a verbal noun that is derived from the root *aslama*, which means "he gave up, surrendered, or submitted." In purely etymological terms, *islam* thus signifies the idea of surrender or submission. Following this logic, the religion of Islam can be characterized as the religion of self-surrender: Islam is the conscious and rational submission of the contingent and limited human will to the absolute and omnipotent will of God. Such a complete surrender of one's personal will clearly is not easy for everyone and is likely to be resisted by the human ego. Islam's advocacy of self-surrender should not be thought of as irrational, however, or dismissed as the product of a passive or fatalistic mentality. On the contrary, the type of surrender Islam requires is a deliberate, conscious, and rational act made by the person who knows with both intellectual certainty and spiritual vision that Allah, the God who is the subject of the Quranic discourse, is reality itself. This knower of God is the *muslim* (fem. *muslimah*), "one who submits" to the divine truth, and whose relationship with God is governed by *taqwa*, the consciousness of humankind's responsibility toward its creator.

But consciousness of God alone is not sufficient to make a person a Muslim. Neither is it enough to be merely born a Muslim or to be raised in an Islamic cultural context. The concept of *taqwa* implies that the believer has the added responsibility of acting in a way that is in accordance with the three types of knowledge previously discussed. The sincere believer must endeavor at all times to maintain herself in a constant state of submission to God. By doing so, she attains the honored title of "slave of God" (*abd Allah*, fem. *amat Allah*), for she recognizes that all power and all agency belong to God alone: "Allah has willed it. There is no power but Allah's" (Quran 18:39). Trusting in the mercy of her divine master, yet fearing God's wrath, the slave of God walks the road of life with careful steps, making her actions deliberate so that she will not stray from the path that God has laid out for her (Quran 1:5–7). Such is the epistemological "leap of faith" that Islam requires of its believers. It is an all-encompassing and highly personal type of commitment that has little in common with the academic understanding of Islam as a civilization or a cultural system. Rather, this "leap of faith" has much more in common with the spiritual perspective of the "born-again" Christian or the mystic within a traditional religion, whose heedless soul is "resurrected" or awakened by the light of the truth. This similarity between the spiritual knowledge of Muslims and the adherents of other religions is a reminder that religious experience is not limited to specific peoples or cultures; it is universally human in nature.

The universality of religious experience is an important premise of the Quran's argument against the profane or secular life. Taking a different tack from the hadith (the corpus of prophetic traditions that provides detailed instructions on how to act as a Muslim in specific ritual or moral contexts), the Quran is less concerned with defining creedal boundaries than with affirming the universal

When praying, worshipers separate themselves from the ground with a mat or rug. Wealthy people might use a beautiful prayer carpet, such as this exquisite wool and silk example made in the seventeenth century under the Mughal emperors.

obligation to believe in one God. The Quran thus speaks of broad verities of religious experience to which every human being can relate. Similarly, when dealing with religious practices, the Quran is less concerned with the details of ritual than with the meaning that lies behind the rituals it prescribes. The details of ritual practice, which serve to define Islam for most believers, are usually left for tradition to define. By speaking in a transcendental voice and presenting a discourse that is relevant to human experience in general, the Quran overcomes the cultural limitations of the Arab civilization in which it was originally revealed and makes its message accessible to peoples of different cultural backgrounds. This universalism has never been more important than in the present day, when the majority of Muslims are South or Southeast Asian in origin and when only one-fifth of them are Arabs.

Such a transcendence of culture is necessary for any religion that aspires to universal validity. As the vehicle for the word of God, it is necessary for the Quran to overcome linguistic and cultural differences and express itself in a metalanguage that can be understood even when its original Arabic is translated into a non-Semitic tongue such as

The majority of Muslims today live in south or southeast Asia. The universalism of Islam transcends the cultural boundaries of Arab civilization for these children studying the Quran in Malaysia.

English or Indonesian. An example of this metalanguage can be found in the tripartite model of knowledge previously discussed. Despite the exceptionalism of postmodern philosophy, which accentuates cultural boundaries by hypostasizing the notion of difference, the comparative study of human societies reveals that most people—whatever their experiences and regardless of variations in culture—think in similar ways and have similar wants and needs. Responding to this fact, the Quran seeks to establish a common foundation for belief that is based on such shared perceptions and experiences. Over and over again, the Quran reminds the reader to think about the truths that lie behind the familiar or mundane things of the world, such as the signs of God in nature, the practical value of virtue, and the cross-cultural validity of fundamental moral principles. What is good for Muslims is meant to be good for all human beings, regardless of gender, color, or origin. The Quran thus appeals to both reason and experience in determining the criteria for differentiating between truth and falsehood.

The most important theological point made by the Quran is that there is one God—Allah (The God)—universal and beyond comparison, who creates and sustains both the material universe and the world of human experience: "[Allah] has created the heavens and the earth in Truth; exalted is He above the partners they ascribe to Him!" (Quran 16:3). All other forms of so-called truth are either false in their initial premises or contingently true only in limited situations. The recognition of this fact produces an alchemical effect on the human soul that forever transforms the outlook of the believer. This is eloquently described in the following passage from Fi Zilal al-Quran (In the shade of the Quran), a commentary by Sayyid Qutb (1906–66), the Egyptian activist and chief ideologist of the Muslim Brotherhood:

> When a conception that sees nothing in the world but the reality of Allah establishes itself in the human mind and heart, it is accompanied by the vision of this genuine, permanent reality in every other being that has sprung from it. This is the stage at which the heart feels the hand of Allah in everything and beyond which it feels nothing but Allah in the whole universe. There would be no other reality to be felt.
>
> It is also accompanied by the attribution of every event and every movement in this life and in this universe to the first and only cause, that is, Allah, that brings other causes about and influences their effectiveness. The Quran takes great care to establish this truth in the Muslims' concept of faith. It has always put aside apparent causes and associated events directly with the will of Allah. It says, "When you threw (a handful of dust) it was not your act, but Allah's" [Quran 8:17]. "There is no triumph except that given by Allah" [Quran 8:10 and Quran 3:126]. "You have no will except as Allah wills" [Quran 76:30].

A faith such as Islam, based on certain knowledge, is both a liberation and a limitation. It is a liberation in the sense that certainty of the divine reality allows the human spirit to expand both outward and upward, so that the consciousness becomes three dimensional. But it is also a limitation, because with the knowledge of God comes a concomitant awareness of the limits and responsibilities imposed on the person as a created being. Unlike the secular humanist, the true Muslim who submits to God cannot delude herself by claiming that she is the sole author of her destiny. She knows that such a statement is absurd, for a person's fate is routinely influenced by factors beyond her control. This truth has even been recognized by some thinkers in the Western secular tradition. The German political philosopher Karl Marx, for example, acknowledged that a person's destiny is to a large extent dependent on external factors. For the Muslim, however, the "hidden hand" that guides a person's fate is not some idealized construct such as political economy, class, or ideology; rather, it is the divine will that governs both the social and the material universes. In Islam it is not religion that is the "opium of the masses" but the heedless arrogance of the human ego, which deludes itself by claiming that it can be all things to all people: "[Allah] created the human being from a tiny drop [of sperm]; yet see how he has become a brazen disputer!" (Quran 16:4).

A middle position between the limits and possibilities of human agency can be found in the doctrine of choice (ikhtiyar), which has become an important part of Shiite theology. According to this doctrine, the overall fate of the human being, like that of all creatures, is governed by the fore-knowledge (qada) of an all-powerful and all-just God. This does not mean that the believer must throw up his hands in resignation and do nothing on his own behalf, however. Quite the opposite. According to this perspective, God's determination of affairs is immutable only on the universal level, the level of the whole. On the level of the part, the necessity of a meaningful choice between good and evil demands that absolute predestination be replaced by the possibility of human agency, which allows the human being to choose between ethical alternatives. On the personal level, an individual's fate (qadar) is to a large extent dependent on the choices that he makes during his life. These may be moral choices such as seeking virtue rather than vice, political choices such as whom to regard (the family of the Prophet or subsequent dynasties of caliphs) as Muhammad's successors, or eschatological choices such as whether to believe that the Shiite "Hidden Imam" will return at the end of time. In other words, each person's fate is the result of an ongoing and continuous interaction, on many levels and over many years, between the human will and the will of God. Each individual makes his or her choices freely, but the options from which to choose are divinely determined, and thus beyond the individual's ability to control.

For the Muslim, belief in God's determination of affairs is not fatalism but common sense. A believer feels liberated in knowing his or her limits, because the acceptance of what can never be changed removes the worry and frustration of striving in vain and opens the door to constructive engagement with the possible. Just as knowledge of the truth compels a person to accept God as the Creator and Sustainer of the universe on the level of the macrocosm, the same knowledge requires him or her to accept the givens of material life on the level of the microcosm. Either a person puts her mind at ease by practicing what some Christians refer to as "letting go and letting God," or he suffers the endless frustration of the "secular fideist" or doctrinaire secularist, who vainly believes that humankind can overcome all obstacles, only to find that no strategy can save him from death. The Quran admonishes such people in the fol-

The doctrine of choice (*ikhtiyar*) plays an important role in the ethical philosophy of Shiite Islam. Shiism is prevalent in modern Iran, where clerics often meet to discuss religious affairs in local shrines, as at the Imamzada Sayyid Ali in Nain.

lowing verse: "Do not be like those who forgot God so that [God] made them forget their own souls" (Quran 59:19).

In this sense Frithjof Schuon, the noted writer on comparative religion, defines Islam in his work *Comprendre l'Islam* (Understanding Islam) (1976) as "the juncture between God as such and man as such." Schuon adds that when the Muslim conceives of God, it is not "in the sense that [God] can manifest Himself in a certain way and in a certain time, but independently from history in that [God] is what He is, and also that He creates and is revealed by His nature." Conversely, when the Muslim is conceived as a rational agent, it is not "in the sense that he is lost and is in need of a saving miracle, but in the sense that he is created after the image of God (*déiforme*), is given an intelligence capable of conceiving of the Absolute, and a will capable of choosing that which will guide it." If humankind is to be saved through faith, and the essence of faith is knowledge, then it is incumbent upon God as the source of all knowledge to provide humanity with the knowledge that will enable it to apprehend the truth and thus save itself. In this sense the message of Islam echoes that of the Gospel: "Ye shall know the Truth, and the Truth shall make you free."

From the Knowledge of God to the Practice of the Sunna

As a revealed text, the Quran is God's book, not the Prophet Muhammad's. Although one of the discourses (*surah*) of the Quran is named after Muhammad

(Quran 33) and the Prophet is often addressed directly by God in the Quran, he is mentioned by name only four times (Quran 3:144; 33:40; 47:2; 48:9). More often the Quran expresses itself in the first-person or imperative voice. In all such cases, the voice that speaks in the text is God's, not that of the Prophet. This first-person perspective imparts an immediacy to the Quranic discourse that is somewhat similar to the tone used in the New Testament. Also like the New Testament (and parts of the Hebrew Bible), the Quran is not only didactic but "autobiographical," because God is often depicted as speaking about God's own divine nature. Thus, to assert that the authorship of the Quran is anything but divine is to strip the Quran of the very reality that it claims for itself. Such a stance would never be acceptable to a believing Muslim.

While it would be a travesty of Islam's claim to the truth to call the religion "Muhammadanism" or to say that in the Quran "Muhammad says such-and-such," it is equally wrong to say that the Prophet had nothing whatsoever to do with the Quran. First, the Quranic revelation came out of the Prophet's mouth and in his own Arabic language, either as the result of a direct revelation from God or through the mediation of the angel Gabriel. In addition, during more than twenty-two years of revelation, the Prophet was the prime interpreter of the Quran, and his recorded statements about how its teachings are to be put into effect form the basis of the Sunna, the paradigm of behavior that every Muslim must follow. As God says to the Prophet: "We have revealed unto you the Remembrance, so that you may explain to people that which has been revealed for them" (Quran 16:44).

The concept of the Sunna is based on the belief that the Prophet Muhammad is a role model for all Muslims, both male and female. This is confirmed by the Quran in the following verse: "A good example you have in Allah's Messenger, for all whose hope is in Allah and in the Final Day and who remember Allah frequently" (Quran 33:61). Besides being the human vehicle of revelation, the Prophet is also mentioned in the Quran as the executor of God's laws. For this reason the Prophet's orders must be obeyed by Muslims as if those orders came from God Himself: "Obey Allah and the Messenger so that you may find mercy" (Quran 3:132). Finally, by extending the word of God through the process of Quranic interpretation, the Prophet acts as a legislator for the Muslim community: "[The Prophet] will make lawful for them all good things and prohibit them only the bad, and will relieve them of their burdens and the fetters which they used to wear" (Quran 7:157). These Prophetic roles of moral exemplarity, executive decision making, and legislative law making all have an important bearing on religious practice. Thus, it is not surprising to discover that there are more statements about practice in the Sunna than in the Quran.

During his lifetime the Prophet's authority was accepted without dispute, because it was already confirmed by God in the Quran and thus did not depend on the Muslim community's assent. The question of the Sunna's authority after Muhammad's lifetime, however, was not explicitly discussed in the Quran. In the first century after the Prophet's death, many Muslims preferred to follow local or regional interpretations of Islamic practice rather than uncertain accounts of Muhammad's behavior that were orally passed down through the generations. In the second and third centuries of Islam, tradition-minded legal scholars such as Malik ibn Anas (ca. 715–795) and Muhammad ibn Idris al-Shafii (767–820) argued through analogical reasoning that the collective example of the Prophet, his Companions (al-Sahabah), and their followers (collectively known as al-Salaf al-Salih, "The Virtuous Forerunners") was to be accepted along with the word of God as a primary and thus normative source of practice. This extension of the living authority of the Prophet and his Companions into future generations became so widely accepted in the Muslim world that all pious Muslims now see themselves as following the Sunna in one way or another. Today the Sunna enjoys near canonical status as a source of Islamic precedent—so much so that in the hands of politically motivated Islamists, those who follow the doctrines of the Wahhabis of Saudi Arabia, and other so-called Muslim fundamentalists, the Sunna has been denuded of all historical contextualization and stands nearly equal to the Quran as a source of truth.

The raw material of the Sunna is the corpus of hadith (pl. ahadith). This consists of collected accounts of the Prophet's deeds and sayings, which are at times supplemented by the actions and comments of the Prophet's Companions. The word hadith means "report or saying." In Sunni Islam this term most often refers to a consensually legitimated body of sayings and reports about Muhammad's behavior that was compiled in six major collections (the Six Books or al-Kutub al-Sittah) in the late ninth to tenth centuries, about two and a half centuries after the Prophet's death. These collections are seen today as primary sources of both juridical and moral precedent and are second only to the Quran in their practical significance and authority.

During the period in which they were compiled, the hadith were classified according to the soundness of their chains of transmission and the character, piety, trustworthiness, and reputation of their transmitters. The Six Books of Sunni hadith attained their status as normative sources because few if any of the traditions contained therein were found to be spurious. Two of these collections have been designated by a consensus of scholars as particularly sound (sahih). These works—Sahih al-Bukhari (mentioned earlier) and Sahih Muslim (named after Muslim ibn al-Hajjaj al-Nisaburi, ca. 817–875)—are the most authoritative books of Sunni hadith. The remaining books are also named after their compilers and are known either as collections of precedents (*sunan*)—such as the Sunan of Abu Daud al-Sijistani (817–88), the Sunan of Ibn Majjah al-Qazwini (822–87), and the Sunan of al-Nasai (830–915)—or as a collection (*jami*), such as *Jami al-Tirmidhi* (named after al-Tirmidhi, 824–92). Shiite Muslims consider the traditions of their imams (spiritual leaders descended directly from the Prophet Muhammad) to be equal in importance to those of the Prophet himself. The most significant collections of Shiite hadith are those of Abu Jafar Muhammad al-Kulayni (d. 940), Abu Jafar Muhammad ibn Babuyah, also known as Shaykh Saduq (ca. 923–91) and al-Hasan al-Tusi (995–1067).

In Sahih *Muslim* is a tradition known as the Hadith of Gabriel (*Hadith Jibril*), which has long been regarded by Muslims as one of the most important statements on Islamic faith and practice. Like other traditions of its kind, it originates with Umar ibn al-Khattab (ca. 586–644), a close companion of the Prophet Muhammad and the second *khalifa* (caliph or successor to Muhammad) of the Muslim community. For many Muslim scholars the Hadith of Gabriel constitutes the defining statement of the Islamic creed (*aqidah*), because it appears as a sort of catechism of Islamic dogma. Because it is not part of the Quran, this hadith is not fully equivalent to the word of God. It enjoys a particularly high status, however, because it depicts the Prophet as being tested on matters of doctrine by the angel Gabriel, God's messenger in the world of spirits and the main conduit of the Quranic revelation. Because of its importance to the definition of Islamic practice, the full text of this hadith is reproduced below, except for the last section (probably added at a later date), which discusses the signs and portents of the end of the world and the advent of the Day of Judgment:

> [Umar ibn al-Khattab reported:] One day, while we were sitting with the Messenger of God (may God bless and preserve him), there came upon us a man whose clothes were exceedingly white and whose hair was exceedingly black. No dust of travel could be seen upon him, and none of us knew him. He sat down in front of the Prophet (may God bless and preserve him), rested his knees against [the Prophet's] knees and placed his palms on [the Prophet's] thighs. "Oh Muhammad, tell me about Islam," he said. The Messenger of God (may God bless and preserve him) replied: "Islam means to bear witness that there is no god but Allah, that Muhammad is the Messenger of Allah, to maintain the [required] prayers, to pay the poor-tax, to fast [in the month of] Ramadan, and to perform the pilgrimage to the House [of God at Mecca] if you are able to do so."
>
> "You are correct," [the man] said. We were amazed at his questioning [of the Prophet] and then saying that [the Prophet] had answered correctly. Then

> he said, "Tell me about faith." [The Prophet] said: "It is to believe in Allah, His angels, His books, His messengers, and the Last Day, and to believe in Allah's determination of affairs, whether good comes of it or bad."
>
> "You are correct," he said. "Now tell me about virtue (ihsan)." [The Prophet] said: "It is to worship Allah as if you see Him; for if you do not see Him, surely He sees you." . . . Then [the man] left. I remained for awhile, and [the Prophet] said to me: "Oh, Umar, do you know who the questioner was?" "Allah and His Messenger know best," I replied. He said: "It was [the angel] Gabriel, who came to you to teach you your religion."

An important aspect of the Hadith of Gabriel is that the expected polarity between faith and practice is reversed. Instead of faith being a prerequisite for practice, it is practice that defines faith. This reversed polarity is a reminder that Islam is defined not only as a set of beliefs but also as a body of actions that reveal the inner convictions of the believer. This practice-oriented view of Islam is typical of the hadith genre in general. Each normative prescription or explanatory statement that one finds in these traditions acts as a complement to one or more verses of the Quran. Another way to describe the relationship between the hadith and the Quran is to say that traditions such as the Hadith of Gabriel express a "nomocentric" or law-centered perspective on Islam, in which knowledge of spiritual realities is less important than the performance of appropriate behavior. This stands in contrast to the Quran's more "logocentric" or word-centered approach to Islam, in which the divine word arouses knowledge of God in the human consciousness.

This shift in emphasis from inner belief to outward practice is less surprising when nomocentric traditions such as the Hadith of Gabriel are viewed in their historical context. The Hadith of Gabriel was originally passed down by Abdallah ibn Umar, the son of Umar ibn al-Khattab, some time after his father's death. The caliph Umar is a central figure in Islamic history, because it was he who initiated the Muslim conquests of Palestine, Syria, and Iran. Just before these conquests, the Muslim community was forced to undergo the so-called Apostasy (Ridda) Wars, in which Arab tribes used the death of the Prophet Muhammad as an excuse to reassert their independence from the Islamic state. During this time of transition, when former apostates were being taken back into the Islamic fold and many non-Muslims sought to avoid the social and economic disadvantages of conquest by converting to the new religion, it was imperative for the Islamic state to define the minimum requirements for becoming a believer. Once identified as a Muslim, the convert became exempt from the jizyah (the poll-tax levied against non-Muslims) and could claim a share of the stipends that were paid on an annual basis to participants in the jihad or war of Islamic expansion.

This need for a creedal definition of Islam is amply served by the Hadith of Gabriel, which defines Islam in three ways: (1) theologically, by asserting that Allah is the One God and not part of a pantheon; (2) historically, by asserting that the Prophet Muhammad is the messenger of God, thus separating the nascent era of Islam from the previous era of theological ignorance (Jahiliyyah); and (3) doctrinally, by mandating five basic and fundamental pillars of Islamic practice that formally differentiate Islam from Christianity, Judaism, and the other religions of the Middle East.

The Five Pillars of Islam

The Five Pillars of Islam (arkan al-Islam), which are presented systematically for the first time in the Hadith of Gabriel, are relatively simple to carry out and can easily be learned by the person who wishes to convert to Islam. The first pillar of Islam is to openly proclaim and bear witness that there is no god but Allah and that Muhammad is the messenger of Allah. This is known as the *Shahadah* (the act of bearing witness). It may also be called *al-Shahadatayn* (the two witnessings), because it consists of two separate acts of bearing witness. The first witnessing, "There is no god but Allah," affirms the acceptance of the divine reality by the human intellect. As a formal proclamation of divine singularity (*tawhid*), it is the creedal equivalent to the

Five fundamental tenets, often described as the pillars of Islam, distinguish Islam from other religions. The first is the *shahada*, or profession of faith, which attests that there is no god but God and that Muhammad is God's messenger. In this modern Moroccan calligraphic panel embroidered in gold thread, the words of the profession of faith have been given the form of a human figure at prayer.

"knowledge of certainty" discussed earlier. The second witnessing, "Muhammad is the messenger of Allah," affirms one's submission to God, which is the meaning of the word *islam* itself. Here, the human being responds to the divine will by acknowledging the Prophet Muhammad as both the vehicle of the Quranic revelation and the paradigmatic *muslim* or "submitter" to God. By stressing the sources of both the theoretical and the practical knowledge of religion (i.e., Allah and the Prophet), the "two witnessings" of the Shahadah thus reaffirm the complementarity of faith and practice in Islam.

The second pillar of Islam is to make the required five prayers each day in the direction of the Great Mosque (*al-Masjid al-Haram*) in Mecca. These prayers, collectively known as *al-Salat*, are performed just before dawn, at noon, at mid-afternoon, just after sunset, and in the evening, from an hour after sunset to around midnight. In the hadith, prayer is depicted as the quintessential act of submission to God and the main proof of Islam. In *Jami al-Tirmidhi*, the Prophet is quoted as saying: "Prayer is the proof [of Islam]." The central importance given to prayer

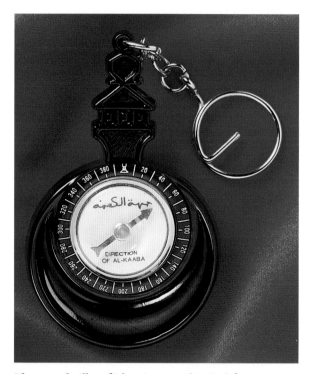

The second pillar of Islam is to worship God five times a day in the direction of the Kaaba in Mecca. To determine the direction of Mecca, known as the *qibla*, Muslims developed the science of astronomy. Twentieth-century worshipers can use this qibla compass.

in Islam is due to the recognition that the performance of al-Salat forces the human body to respond to the reality that has first been acknowledged by the heart and the tongue in the Shahadah. In addition, the essential contrast between the absolute independence of God and the ontological dependency of the human being is reaffirmed in the actions and attitudes of the prayer.

To perform the prayer, the believer must first put herself in a state of purity by performing either a ritual ablution (*wudu*) or a bath (*ghusl*). The symbolic nature of the ablution is illustrated by the fact that either clean water or clean sand may be used to perform this ritual. The full bath, in which water is poured over both the body and the head, is needed only in cases of serious ritual pollution or after sexual intercourse. In general, the ablution should be seen as an expression of respect for God's majesty and as a means of preparing the believer for meeting and addressing the Lord and Creator.

The movements of the Muslim prayer are patterned after attitudes of obeisance that were associated in late antiquity with entering into the presence of a great ruler. To visualize how the prayer movements correspond to the act of greeting such a ruler, imagine a petitioner standing outside a king's throne room. The first thing that the petitioner is likely to do before entering the royal presence is to summon the resolve to enter the throne room. This corresponds to the act of affirming the intention (*niyyah*) that precedes not only the canonical prayer but all other ritual observances in Islam as well. Next the petitioner enters the throne room itself. After stepping over the threshhold she stops, raises her hands to her ears, and proclaims the glory and majesty of the ruler for all to hear. This corresponds to the act of "magnification" (*takbir*), which begins the prayer. To perform the takbir, the Muslim worshipper raises her hands to her ears and proclaims in Arabic, "Allah is most great!" (*Allahu akbar!*).

The petitioner then bows before the king in an attitude of reverence and uses a ritual formula to address the king. This corresponds to the next stage of the prayer,

Before worship, Muslims must put themselves in a state of ritual purity, and many mosques, such as the Kairouiyyin in Fez, Morocco, provide fountains for ablution.

in which the worshipper recites Surat al-Fatihah, the Quran's opening discourse. This surah, which is translated below, has often been described by Muslim theologians as summarizing in a few lines the essential message of the Quran:

> Praise be to Allah, Lord of the Worlds; the Beneficent, the Merciful; Master of the Day of Judgment. You alone do we worship and from You alone do we seek aid. Show us the Straight Way, the way of those upon whom You have bestowed Your grace, not of those who have earned Your wrath or who go astray (Quran 1:1–6).

After reciting the Fatihah, the worshipper recites another verse from the Quran, which is chosen at her individual discretion. Although any verse from the Quran may be used, this second recitation is often used by Muslims to further magnify God by recounting some of the divine attributes. After greeting the king from the threshhold of the throne room, the petitioner next approaches halfway to the throne itself. At this points, she stops, bows, and utters another ritual formula. This corresponds to the third part of the prayer, which is called the "bowing" (ruku). After again saying "Allah is most great!" the worshipper bows from the waist and proclaims three times, "Glory to the Greatest Lord!" After raising herself to an upright position, she next utters: "Allah hears the one who praises Him." After this the worshipper immediately adds, "Our Lord, all praise belongs to You!"

In the final act of approaching the king, the petitioner is summoned to the foot of the throne and falls prostrate before the ruler. This expression of submission—which the secular individualist often sees as both repellant and antithetical to the concept of personal dignity—was common practice in late antiquity. When Islam first appeared in the Middle East, petitioners were expected to prostrate themselves before both the Byzantine emperor (a Christian) and the Shah of Persia (a Zoroastrian). This was because these rulers performed the dual role of king and high priest, exercising political authority as heads of state and religious authority as heads of their respective religious institutions. In both cases as well, they were thought to be the vicegerents of God on earth: the Byzantine emperor ruled over the lands of "New Rome" (the only "Rome" known to Muslims) as both Caesar and Vicar of Christ, while the Shah of Persia ruled over his kingdom as the semidivine representative of the god Ahuramazda.

In Catholic Christianity it is still required for those joining monastic orders to prostrate themselves before the altar of Christ. This religious attitude of humility is in full agreement with the perspective of the Islamic prayer. If a person is willing to humble himself before the secular kings of the world, is it not more fitting to humble himself before God, who is the King of Kings? Because Muslims readily prostrate themselves before God, however, it does not mean that they are

After raising his hands in *takbir*, the petitioner bows his head in an attitude of reverence while reciting the *fatiha*, the opening chapter of the Quran. The final two steps are bowing (*ruku*) and prostration (*sajdah*).

similarly inclined to submit to worldly authority figures. In the first century of Islam, Muslims were notably stubborn in their refusal to prostrate before anyone or anything but Allah. The arrival in the mid-seventh century of a Muslim delegation to the emperor of China was recorded as a remarkable event in T'ang dynasty chronicles, because these Arab or Persian visitors (called *Ta-Shih* by Chinese historians) refused to prostrate themselves before the emperor, who was believed to be the "Son of Heaven."

Before commencing the act of prostration (*sajdah* or *sujud*), the worshipper must first repeat the takbir, "Allah is most Great!" At this point she falls to her knees and prostrates herself before God, placing both hands flat on the ground and touching her forehead between them. While in the bowing position she recites three times, "Glory to the Lord Most High!" After once again saying "Allah is most Great!", the worshipper sits back on her heels and asks for God's mercy, saying, "Oh God, forgive me and show me mercy." Repeating the formula "Allah is most Great!" one more time, she again resumes the attitude of prostration and recites three times, "Glory to the Lord Most High!" After this, she stands up and repeats the entire cycle of prayer, starting with another magnification of God.

The third pillar of Islam is to pay a yearly poor-tax (*zakah*) to a religious official or a representative of the Islamic state. Personal charity, such as almsgiving to this blind beggar in Gambia, is an important article of faith.

Each cycle of the Muslim prayer—from the initial takbir through the recitation of the Quran, the bowing, the prostration, the sitting, and the second prostration—is known as a *rakah* (pl. *rakat*). Every canonical prayer requires from two to four rakat to complete: two for the dawn (*fajr*) prayer, four for the noon (*zuhr*) prayer, four for the mid-afternoon (*asr*) prayer, three for the sunset (*maghrib*) prayer, and four for the evening (*isha*) prayer. In all, the total number of cycles performed for the prayers is seventeen. After every two cycles and after the third cycle of the sunset prayer, the worshipper sits back on her heels in an attitude known as the "sitting" (*jalsah*). While in this position, she addresses God with a formula known as the "greeting" (*tahiyyah*). At this time she also calls forth God's blessings on the Prophet Muhammad. Although the actual words of this greeting vary slightly according to the different schools of Islamic law, the meaning is essentially the same in all cases.

After all of the cycles of the canonical prayer have been completed, the worshipper sits back on her heels once again and recites a formula known as the "witnessing" (*tashahhud*), because it contains the words of the "profession of faith" (Shahadah). Outwardly, this witnessing acts as a formal reaffirmation of the truth of Islam. Inwardly, it is the point at which the worshipper engages in her most direct communication with God. Muslim scholars consider this to be the most intimate part of the canonical prayer, where the worshipper privately petitions the favor of her lord, who responds by sending down divine mercy as a relief for her worldly cares.

The witnessing is followed by a formal supplication that asks God's blessings for the Prophets Muhammad and Ibrahim (Abraham), the last and first of Allah's messengers, whose purpose was to bring salvific truth to humanity through a revealed book. Finally, the prayer is ended with an invocation of peace (*salam*). To make this invocation, the worshipper turns her head first to the right and then to the left, uttering, "May the peace, mercy, and blessings of Allah be upon you." Although the most

The fourth pillar of Islam is to fast during the month of Ramadan, the ninth month according to the Islamic lunar calendar. Muslims abstain from food and drink during the daylight hours. Here a family in Bahrain breakfasts in the predawn darkness.

probable objects of this invocation are the fellow believers who sit at the worshipper's right and left during the congregational (jamaa) prayer, Muslims have long believed that with this formula they are also addressing their guardian angels, who hover over their shoulders as they pray.

The third pillar of Islam is to pay the yearly tithe to a religious official or a representative of the Islamic state. This tithe is known as al-zakah (the purification) and is levied on each individual believer. The official level of this tithe, which is set at one-fortieth (2.5 percent) of the value of all liquid assets and income-generating properties in the worshipper's possession, is based on a hadith text and was confirmed by Muslim scholars following the usage of the Prophet's Companions and their successors. According to the Quran, the tithe may be used to feed the poor, to encourage conversion to Islam, to ransom captives, to relieve debtors of their burden, to help wayfarers, and to support those who devote themselves to the cause of God (Quran 9:60). It may also be used in defense of the faith and for any other purpose deemed appropriate by the ruler of an Islamic state. In Shiite Islam another tithe, called "the fifth" (khums), is also required of believers. This consists of a 20 percent tithe on all new income for the year and is used to support the juridical and educational institutions of the Shiite community.

The fourth pillar of Islam is to observe the month-long fast of Ramadan, the ninth month of the Islamic lunar calendar. During the twenty-nine or thirty days

وَكَذَا يَنْزِعُ الجِمَالِ الشَّرعَ وَأَنْشَدَ
مَا الحَجُّ يَبْرُكُ نَا وِنَا وَلَا جِنَا وَلَا صِيَامَ إِنَّ لَهُمَا وَاحِدَا

الحَجُّ أَنْ تَصِدَ البَيْتَ الحَرامَ عَلَى حُكْمٍ يَنْزِعُ الحَجُّ لَا تُبْوِبَهُ جَاءَ اجَا
وَ عَلَى كَامِلٍ مِنَ الإِنْسَانِ يَتَنَزِّهُ رَدْعَ الهَوَى هَادِبَاوَا الجُوَّى بَيْنَهَا جَا

The fifth pillar of Islam is the pilgrimage to Mecca, which takes place during the first ten days of the twelfth month in the lunar year. In medieval times pilgrims traveled together to Mecca in caravans, as depicted in this illustration from a thirteenth-century manuscript of al-Hariri's *Maqamat*.

of the fasting period, the believer must abstain from food, drink, and sex during daylight hours. This pillar is known as *al-Sawm* or *Siyam Ramadan* and is seen by Muslims as both a purificatory act of sacrifice and an affirmation of ethical awareness. The sacrificial aspect of Ramadan is reflected in the *Sahih Muslim* hadith mentioned earlier. Just after stating that prayer is the proof of Islam, the Prophet Muhammad adds that "fasting is [the key to] heaven." The Ramadan fast is a key to heaven because it involves the sacrifice of a person's bodily desires and is performed for the sake of God alone. By also denying himself drink, the believer further ensures that the sacrifice will be felt by the body. The pain that is felt by the believer during the Ramadan fast acts as a bridge that links the sacrifice to a larger sense of social responsibility. Inwardly, the believer purifies the body by consecrating it to God. Outwardly, the believer uses the fast to recall the responsibility that must be felt toward his fellow human beings. By undergoing the pain of hunger and thirst for an extensive yet limited period of time, the believer recalls the pain of the person whose "fast" never ends because his stomach is never free from want.

The fifth pillar of Islam is the pilgrimage to Mecca. This takes place in the first ten days of the month of Dhul-Hijjah (the twelfth month of the Islamic calendar) and is obligatory for every believer who is physically and financially able to make the journey and perform the prescribed rites. This pillar of Islam is called *al-Hajj*. Its nine essential rites are as follows:

1. To put on the "garment of consecration" (*ihram*), which consists of two pieces of unsewn cloth for men and covers all parts of the body except the face, hands, and feet for women. While in the state of

ihram, it is not permissible to
have sexual relations, to kill
animals or insects, or to
remove any hair from the body.

2. To circumambulate the Kaaba
(literally, "cube"), also known
as the House of God (*Bayt Allah*),
at the center of the Grand
Mosque of Mecca. This is done
seven times in a counterclockwise direction. While circum-
ambulating the Kaaba, many
pilgrims also attempt to touch
the "Black Stone" (*al-Hajar al-
Aswad*), a meteorite considered
to be sent from heaven and
originally placed by the
Prophets Ibrahim and Ismail
(Ishmael) in one of the corners
of the Kaaba. Pilgrims may also
perform the act of "running" (*say*) seven times along a corridor of
the Grand Mosque, in commemoration of the Prophet Ibrahim's slave
woman Hajar (Hagar), who searched for water for her infant son, the
Prophet Ismail. Although these last two rites are performed by many
if not all pilgrims, they are not official parts of the pilgrimage.

The pilgrim arriving in Mecca dons a special garment of consecration (*ihram*), worn throughout the pilgrimage. For men
this comprises two seamless lengths of white cloth; women
must cover the entire body except hands, face, and feet.

3. To stand at Arafat, a plain southeast of Mecca, on the ninth day of the
month of Dhul-Hijjah, even if it is only for a short time. Those who
have staked out a place for themselves and are able to remain for a
longer period listen to a sermon delivered from the heights of Mount
Arafat. This commemorates the final pilgrimage of the Prophet
Muhammad, who delivered his farewell sermon from this site.

4. To spend the night at an encampment near Mecca called
Muzdalifah.

5. To throw stones at the three places where, according to Muslim tradition, Satan tried to tempt the Prophet Ismail. This is to be done
once before the sacrifice at Minah, and then again on the two days
following the sacrifice.

6. To sacrifice an animal (usually a sheep or a goat, but sometimes a

cow or a camel) at the place called Minah. This commemorates God's acceptance of a sheep as a sacrifice in place of the Prophet Ismail. Muslims disagree with Biblical traditions about Ismail, which assert that this ancestor of the Arabs could not have been the "first-born" son and heir of the Prophet Ibrahim because he was born from Hajar the slave rather than from Ibrahim's free wife Sarah. In Islam, unlike either Christianity or Judaism, the child of a female slave and the child of a free woman are equally legitimate and both can claim shares of their father's inheritance. For this reason Muslims believe that it was Ismail, the Prophet Ibrahim's first-born son, and not his second son Ishaq (Isaac), whom Ibrahim intended to consecrate to God as a sacrifice. They further believe that the Kaaba was a temple that Ibrahim and Ismail built for God in Mecca when Ismail had reached adulthood.

7. To repeat the circumambulation of the Kaaba seven more times.

8. To drink the water from the well called Zamzam (literally, "bubbling") in the precincts of the Great Mosque of Mecca, where Muslims believe God provided water for Hajar and her infant son Ismail during their wanderings in the desert.

9. To perform two cycles of the canonical prayer at a place known as the Station of Abraham (*Maqam Ibrahim*), where the Prophets Ibrahim and Ismail are believed to have prayed together after building the Kaaba.

The rites of the pilgrimage take the pilgrim to several sites in and around Mecca. Here, on the stony slopes of Mount Rahma overlooking the plain of Arafat, where the Prophet gave his farewell sermon, an Iranian pilgrim beseeches God while others shelter from the blazing sun.

While on the pilgrimage to Mecca, most pilgrims include a visit to the city of
Medina, where Muhammad emigrated in 622. The most important spot there is
the Prophet's mosque and tomb, represented here in a sixteenth-century religious
text from Morocco.

The minimum requirements of the Hajj are the wearing of the ihram, the
standing at Arafat, and the second circumambulation of the Kaaba. Although the
Hajj may be completed without performing the remaining rites, the pilgrim is
required to pay expiation (*kaffarah*) for his failure to complete them. During the
entire Hajj the pilgrim must avoid thinking about anything other than the
remembrance of God and the rites of the pilgrimage itself. This is because cir-
cumambulating the Kaaba, like the canonical prayer, symbolizes the believer's
entry into the divine presence. The earthly House of God (*Bayt Allah*) that the pilgrim visits in Mecca is believed by many Muslims to replicate the cosmic House
of God in the Seventh Heaven, which contains the divine throne and is circum-
ambulated by the angels and all of the archetypes of creation.

The Six Pillars of Faith

The Five Pillars of Islam are followed in the Hadith of Gabriel by another group
of creedal principles known as the Six Pillars of Faith (*arkan al-iman*). Despite the
Quranic link between knowledge and faith, these pillars of faith are not associ-

ated with the highest levels of knowledge that were discussed earlier. Like the Pillars of Islam, they instead comprise a practice-oriented approach to religion because they are meant to be ritually affirmed at the time of conversion or whenever one's doctrinal orientation is called into question by the religious authorities of the Islamic state. Like the pillars of Islam, the pillars of faith are thus associated only with the most primary level of knowledge mentioned in the Quran—*ilm al-yaqin* (the rational or doctrinal knowledge of the truth)—and do not involve the most advanced states of knowledge (*ayn al-yaqin* and *haqq al-yaqin*). The Six Pillars of Faith in Islam are as follows:

1. To believe in God (Allah).

2. To believe in Allah's angels.

3. To believe in Allah's revealed books, which include the Quran, the New Testament, also known as the Evangel (al-Injil), the Psalms of David (al-Zabur), the Torah (al-Tawrat), and the Pages of Abraham (Suhuf Ibrahim).

4. To believe in Allah's messengers, which include many of the prophets of the Hebrew Bible as well as Jesus (Isa), John the Baptist (Yahya), and such previous Arab prophets as Hud and Salih.

5. To believe in the Last Day (*al-Yawm al-Akhir*, also known as *Yawm al-Qiyama*). Islamic eschatology is close to that of Christianity and even includes an intercessory role for Jesus. Many Muslims also believe in a quasi-prophetic figure called the Mahdi (Guided One), who will come after Jesus and usher in a period of peace and justice that will last until the Day of Judgment. This figure does not appear in the Quran but is a later addition from the hadith. Significantly, the Mahdi's first appearance in the hadith is to be found, like the Hadith of Gabriel, in Sahih Muslim.

6. To believe in Allah's determination of affairs, whether good or bad. This is a reaffirmation of the concepts of divine fore-knowledge (*qada*) and fate (*qadar*) discussed earlier.

Were it not for the details added to the Six Pillars of Faith in the hadith, it would be theoretically possible for most Christians or Jews to affirm the Islamic pillars of faith and still remain within their own religions. This is why the public affirmation of the pillars of faith is not accepted by most Muslim jurists as a sufficient proof of Islam without also being accompanied by the Five Pillars of Islam. The first of the five pillars, the witnessing or Shahadah, unequivocally requires the believer to accept the prophet Muhammad as the messenger of Allah. In doing so, the prospective believer must also acknowledge the truth of the Quranic revelation as well as the normative nature of the Sunna. Whenever the teachings of the Quran or the Sunna differ from those of the Hebrew Bible or the New Testament, Muslims are required to favor the later Islamic interpretation over the earlier doctrines of Judaism or Christianity.

The primacy of practice over faith that is reflected in such traditions as the Hadith of Gabriel is so widely accepted in the Muslim world that some Western scholars have erroneously asserted that Islam has no orthodoxy. In their view, there is no single creed or body of doctrine—apart from the Shahadah—that all Muslims regard as normative. In the absence of such a doctrine, these scholars posit an orthopraxy, a form of Islam that is defined almost entirely in terms of ritual observance.

From a comparative perspective, however, this stance is difficult to justify. First, all Muslims do not pray in exactly the same way. The schools of Islamic jurisprudence differ on minor points of what is to be said or done in the canonical prayer. Second, no orthodoxy is static; all orthodoxies are "orthodoxies in the making." Official interpretations of doctrine tend to fluctuate over time and may be transformed in response to changing social conditions or relations of power. This can even happen in a highly centralized institution such as the Catholic Church. It is no coincidence, for example, that the doctrine of papal infallibility was promulgated in the mid-nineteenth century, at the very time when the ideals of nationalism and participatory democracy were undermining the papacy's influence. Likewise, it is no coincidence that the official doctrine of the Virgin Mary is currently undergoing a review process in the Catholic Church, at a time when feminism has revolutionized the status and role of women in Western society.

Islamic orthodoxies are no different. Doctrines have changed repeatedly in the fourteen hundred years of Islamic history. For example, the theological rationalism of the Mutazilite school of theology—a dogma that was officially imposed on Muslims by the caliph and enforced by an inquisition—was replaced as "orthodox" doctrine after less than a century by its antithesis, the tradition-based fideism of the Ahl al-Sunnah wal-Jamaa (the people of the Sunna and the majority). One may also recall how the mystical interpretations of Sufism, once widely accepted as an alternative approach to Islamic theology, have recently been replaced and even anathematized by the hadith-driven scripturalism of Wahhabism (a practice-oriented sect from Saudi Arabia that advocates a literal interpretation of the Quran and hadith) and other movements of Islamic reform. Today, the more innovative aspects of Sufism have been driven so far off the historical stage that even many Sufis themselves now differ little from their reformist opponents in adhering to a hadith-based approach to theology and Quranic exegesis.

Yet to give the advocates of orthopraxy their due, it must be admitted that the outcome of both of these doctrinal disputes depended to a large extent on the belief, implied in the Hadith of Gabriel, that practice is the criterion of faith and not the other way around. Despite the Quran's emphasis on the primacy of knowledge, the Sunna's emphasis on the primacy of practice has clearly prevailed among most Muslims. Today, "orthodox" Islam is more than anything else a "nomocentric" or law-centered religion. As the Hadith of Gabriel illustrates, this trend began quite early in Islamic history. Another early example can be found in the thousand-year-old creed of the Tunisian jurist Abu Muhammad ibn Abi Zayd al-Qayrawani (922–96). This creed, which appears in the introductory section of ibn Abi Zayd's *Risalah*, or treatise on Islamic law, is now regarded as dogma by the adherents of the Maliki school of jurisprudence in North and West Africa. If a Maliki Muslim from this region is asked to discuss the subject of faith and practice in Islam, he or she is likely to respond by reciting one or more passages from the *Risalah*. In the passage reproduced below, a strong echo of the Hadith of Gabriel can be found in ibn Abi Zayd's contention that faith is subject to increase and decrease according to the level of a person's practice:

> Faith consists of a declaration by the tongue, sincerity in the heart, and practice through the limbs. It increases through an increase in practice and decreases through its decrease. Thus, both decrease and increase pertain to it. The declaration of faith is not completed except through practice. Also, neither the declaration [of faith] nor practice [is sufficient] except through the mediation of intention, and neither declaration, practice, nor intention [is sufficient] unless it is in agreement with the Sunna.

The Institutionalization of Islamic Practice in the Shariah

In creeds such as that of ibn Abi Zayd al-Qayrawani, the concept of practice becomes more than just a matter of doctrine; it also becomes a matter of law. The notion of the law in Islam is expressed by two different but semantically related terms: *shariah* (the "way" or method set out by God) and *fiqh* (the "understanding" or application of this method in specific cases). In theory, all Islamic law is divine in origin because it is rooted in God's commandments in the Quran. In practice, however, most of the precedents for Islamic legal decisions are found not in the Quran but in the Sunna—particularly in that portion of the hadith that reflects the prophet Muhammad's interpretations of Quranic rulings. Despite this apparent discrepancy, it is not correct to assume that Islamic law is extrascriptural like the Western system of secular laws. Although not all of the content of Islamic law comes directly from the Quran, the Quran still retains its scriptural nature for Muslims because the Prophet's precedent-setting judgments are believed to be divinely inspired.

When speaking about Islamic law, informed Muslims use the term shariah to connote the sacred law as a global concept or ideal, while fiqh is used to connote the ongoing interpretation of the law through the schools (four Sunni and one Shiite) of juridical practice (madhhab, pl. madhahib). From the earliest days of Islamic history, knowledge of the law was regarded by Muslims as essential knowledge, the very epitome of "science" (ilm) itself. But the science of the law, like any other science, does not stand still. Ideal principles are useless unless they are put into practice, and the changing conditions of Islamic society demanded new interpretations and applications of the way set forth by God and the Prophet Muhammad. For this reason the interpretive science of fiqh was developed in the first Islamic century. From an historical perspective the relationship between shariah and fiqh can be summarized by saying that the shariah developed as the paradigm or model of the Islamic way of life, whereas fiqh, the application of the shariah to specific cases, developed as the paradigm of Islamic reasoning. In these two concepts, one normative and ideal and the other hermeneutical and practical, a true complementarity between theory and practice is achieved. Without the open-ended interpretive process of fiqh, the shariah is no more than an immobile edifice, unresponsive to changing times. Without the anchor of tradition embodied in the shariah, the interpretive process of fiqh is liable to cut itself off from its scriptural roots and reduce Islamic law to a system of situational ethics.

As an institution, Islamic law has been weakened considerably over the past century. A combination of debilitating factors, including the substitution of Western notions for Islamic conceptions of justice under colonialism, attempts by authoritarian regimes to bypass the judicial process, the rise of Islamic populism under various forms of Islamic modernism, and the trivialization of religious training in modern secular education have conspired to undermine the status of the four Sunni schools of fiqh. Today, few Muslims can claim to be true scholars of the law (fuqaha, sg. faqih), and most believers are confused about what the shariah really means. A common belief fostered by modern political Islamists is that only the shariah—but not fiqh—constitutes the true law of God. According to this perspective, the content of the shariah is to be found in the Quran, the Sunna, and in cases in which consensus has been reached among the four Sunni schools of fiqh. However, the interpretive methodologies of these schools—their very reason for being—are to be eliminated as sources of dissension that undermine Muslim unity. This negative view of Islamic jurisprudence—which is advocated by such groups as the Muslim Brotherhood, the Jamaat-i-Islami of Pakistan, and the Taliban of Afghanistan— ignores the essential complementarity of shariah and fiqh and threatens to deny Islamic law the ability to adapt to changing conditions. Even worse, the refutation of fiqh has often led to a travesty of the Islamic practice of justice by opening the process of legal reasoning to the influence of political demagoguery.

Partisans of hadith and other scriptural literalists see fiqh as an extrascriptural (and hence, invalid) form of law because it entails the extension of rulings from the Quran and Sunna into new domains on the basis of analogical reasoning. Some rulings in Islamic law come directly from the Quran; these are seldom disputed. Others come from the hadith and are usually held to be binding if they are transmitted from reliable sources. Still other rulings, however, are found neither in the Quran nor in the hadith but are analogically derived from similar or comparable cases found in these primary texts. This last category of rulings provides most of the differences of opinion that separate the schools of Islamic jurisprudence from one another. This is also where culture and hermeneutical methods play their most significant roles in the process of interpretation.

The methodology of each school of fiqh is founded on the concept of living tradition, which consists of a combination of the Sunna of the Prophet and the practice (amal) of a particular legal school. The methodological perspective of each school has been refined over centuries of legal research and dialectical disputation and holds the status of a canon to which all jurists in a particular school adhere. This canon, or "imitation" (taqlid) of the decisions and interpretive methodology of a particular legal school, should not, however, be thought of as a formal law code. Very few decisions of Islamic jurists attain the status of binding consensus (ijma). Instead, juridical opinion (ijtihad) is likely to coalesce around a majority interpretation or ruling, while minority positions continue to exist as alternative interpretations. Although the opinion of the majority may attain the status of de facto consensus in certain regions, the fiqh system, as traditionally applied, remained open to differences of opinion and even allowed later revisions of the majority opinion. Cases even exist in which practices permitted by the Quran or the Sunna were abandoned by Muslims in later generations, according to the needs of equity (istihsan) or legitimate public interest (maslahah mursalah). Such is the case, for example, with the practice of slavery. Although the effects of slavery are clearly mitigated in the Quran, the practice itself was never abolished in Islam. Slavery has become so abhorrent to modern sensibilities, however, that no Muslim country officially allows it within its borders. To justify this change of opinion, Muslim jurists used the concept of gradualism to argue that the mitigation of slavery's cruelty in the Quran implied God's intention that the practice be ultimately abolished.

The actions of individuals in Islamic law are judged on the basis of five valuations, which rate each act according to its permissibility in a specific context. Most religious obligations, such as the Five Pillars of Islam, are regarded as obligatory (fard or wajib). These are acts whose commission is rewarded by God and whose omission may be punished by God, the Islamic state, or both. In many Muslim countries, for example, willful neglect of the fast of Ramadan may result in fines or even imprisonment. In some countries, such as Saudi Arabia, parajudicial organizations exist whose purpose is to ensure that people make their five daily prayers at the proper times and adhere to consensual standards of decency. Most acts in Islamic law, however, although still ethically valued, are not considered obligatory. Instead, they fall under the three central categories of moral valuation: approved (*mandub* or *mustahabb*), morally neutral (*mubah*), and morally reprehensible (*makruh* or *mahzur*). Although the omission of obligatory acts may bring about punishment from the state, this is not the case for acts that are merely approved; conversely, the commission of acts that are disapproved is not likely to bring about punishment. In such cases, whatever reward or punishment accrues from the act is a matter for God to decide, while the commission or omission of an act is a matter for each person's conscience. The neutrality or permissibility (*ibaha*) of an act means exactly what it says: neither reward nor punishment accrues to the perpetrator.

At times, members of the public may seek an opinion (*fatwa*) about the permissibility of an act from a specialist in Islamic law (*faqih* or *mufti*). In coming up with his opinion, the legal expert is likely to collapse the three middle categories of moral valuation into two: permissible (*jaiz*) for acts that are either approved or neutral, and impermissible (*ghayr jaiz*) for acts that are either disapproved or forbidden (*haram*). For the most part, acts that are clearly forbidden are mentioned in the Quran and include such vices as murder, sexual license, cheating, gambling, eating pork, consuming alcohol, and taking usury. In such cases the opposite of the rule applied to obligatory acts pertains: the comission of a forbidden act is likely to be punished by both God and the state, while its omission is rewarded by God. Forbidden acts of a particularly severe nature, which threaten the social and moral order of the Muslim community, are seen as transgressing the limits (*hudud*, sg. *hadd*) set by God Himself and thus have punishments that are mandated in the Quran. In such cases, which include the crimes of murder, theft, and (by analogy) adultery, not only the rights of the victim but also the "rights of God" (*huquq Allah*) are violated.

The "five values" of Islamic law were never meant to be abstract ideals, totally divorced from the contexts in which they occurred. This point is often forgotten by contemporary Muslim politicians, who seek to create legal mandates for moral or ethical ideals without the benefit of juridical training or experience. In earlier, more judicious times a number of important questions were asked about human actions before they were assigned a specific status in the hierarchy of values. Such questions included: Which is the primary valuation to be used when judging an act: permissibility or prohibition? If an act is not explicitly prohibited in the Quran or the Sunna, is it automatically permissible? Or should it be deemed forbidden until proven otherwise? Which actions are obligatory for every Muslim (*fard ayn*) and which are obligatory only for the community in general (*fard kifayah*)? If an act is fard kifayah, what is the minimum number of people required to perform it? Questions such as these were often asked about Islamic rituals. For example, the five canonical prayers are required for every Muslim and thus are considered fard ayn. But the two festival (*Id*) prayers, which are performed in commemoration of the end of Ramadan and the sacrifice made by the hajj pilgrims after the "standing" at Arafat, are fard kifayah. Although both prayers are to be held congregationally, it is not required that every Muslim attend them. Similarly, while attendance at the Friday congregational prayer (*salat al-jumu ah*) is fard ayn for all Sunni men, for women it is fard kifayah. For Shiite Muslims the Friday prayer is fard ayn for men only when the Imam is present. In the absence of the Imam (who is presently believed to be in a state of occultation), it is fard kifayah. This is why in a Shiite country such as Iran the Friday prayer is often held in only a single location in each city.

Furthermore, is *forbidden* the opposite of *lawful*? Does a rule apply in all cases or must the jurist first investigate the merits of each case before making a decision? Is it possible to forbid an act because of its consequences, even if it is not forbidden per se? What makes a thing forbidden? Is it forbidden intrinsically, in that it is bad in and of itself, or is it forbidden extrinsically, in that it is bad only because of the way in which it is used? Such questions are often asked about such forbidden substances as pork or alcoholic beverages. Many Indian and Pakistani Muslims, who still preserve the notions of intrinsic purity and impurity held by the Hindu religion, consider not only the flesh but all other parts of the swine to be forbidden. Thus, they forbid the use of such products as pig-bristle hairbrushes or pigskin footballs. In the Middle East and North Africa, however, it was usually not the pig itself that was deemed forbidden but only the act of eating its flesh. In these regions grafts made of pig skin might even be used to treat head wounds. At what point do circumstances change the valuation of an act? Although the flesh of swine and carrion are forbidden for Muslims, it is permissible to eat them if the alternative is starvation. But what about the Quranic order to "command the good and forbid evil?" (Quran 3:104). When should this be applied? And might the imperative to enforce the good cause an even greater evil than the original sin itself if this leads to social unrest, terrorism, or revolution? Such questions are all too pertinent today in such countries as Algeria and Egypt, where this injunction has been applied by Muslim insurgents in an especially severe and uncritical manner.

The answers to such questions lie at the heart of the differences between Islamic schools of law. Other differences are methodological in nature and revolve around the assessment of tradition. The Hanafi school of jurisprudence, for example, founded by the Iraqi jurist Abu Hanifa (699–767), tends to be somewhat distrustful of the hadith as a source of law and gives greater weight to the analogical reasoning (ray or qiyas) of jurists in the formation of legal opinions. This stance has led to both a greater flexibility in decision making and a potential for political abuse. The Maliki school of jurisprudence, founded by the Medinan scholar Malik ibn Anas (ca. 715–795), is also somewhat critical of the hadith but still prefers to ground its decisions in tradition. Malik chose to take the collective tradition of the Prophet's city of Medina as his main source of precedent, while later Maliki scholars saw this tradition continued in the decisions made by Maliki jurists in North Africa and Muslim Spain. Although it was respected for its consensual approach to tradition, the Maliki school of law was often criticized for going its own way in the Muslim West and ignoring a wider consensus that may have formed in other parts of the Muslim world.

The Shafii school of law—founded by the successors of Muhammad ibn Idris al-Shafii (767–820), the first systematic legal theorist in Islam—sought to balance reason and tradition by prioritizing sources of knowledge. For al-Shafii the primary source of legal decisions is the Quran, followed by the Sunna of the Prophet, analogical reasoning, and binding consensus. This model is now accepted by all schools of jurisprudence in Sunni Islam. The Hanbali school, founded by al-Shafii's student Ahmad ibn Hanbal (780–855), also adheres to this method, but it depends more on tradition and uses analogical reasoning only as a last resort. The dominant Shiite school of jurisprudence, the Jafari, named after the sixth Shiite imam Jafar al-Sadiq (ca. 699–765), adheres for the most part to the methodology associated with the Hanbali school of law, but it includes traditions of the twelve Shiite imams among its corpus of hadith. Each of these last three schools of law can be criticized for reifying and idealizing tradition to such a degree that the corpus of hadith is not subjected to rational analysis or content criticism. Individual ahadith are accepted as true by these schools even if only one transmitter links these traditions to either the Prophet or an imam and regardless of whether they agree or disagree with an apparent ruling in the Quran.

From Shariah to *Taqwa*: Islam and Ethics

The Islamic notion of human responsibility is epitomized in the Quran by a covenant struck between God and humanity before their placement on earth. In this Quranic covenant the archetypal (or "Adamic") human being—prideful of human superiority over all other creatures but unmindful of human limitations as a created being—assumes the responsibility of the heavens and the earth and all that they contain: "We offered the trust of the heavens, the earth, and the mountains [to the jinn and angels], but they refused to undertake it, being afraid [of the responsibility thereof]; but the human being undertook it; however, he was unjust and foolish" (Quran 33:72).

The state of moral responsibility that is implied in this primordial covenant is referred to in the Quran as the vicegerency (*khilafah*) (Quran 2:30–33). Those who uphold the requirements of the covenant are known as God's vicegerents (*khulafa*, sing. *khalifah*) on earth. In the Quran they are described as those who must "Fear Allah [*ittaqu Allah*] and speak the appropriate words, so that He may make your conduct sound and forgive your sins" (Quran 33:70–71). The society that is made up of such God-fearing people (*muttaqin*) constitutes a "middle nation" or "axial community" (*ummah wasat*), whose collective responsibility is to bear witness to the truth and act as an example for the rest of humanity (Quran 2:143). This community maintains itself in a permanent state of surrender to God (*ummah muslimah*) and is exemplified historically by the polity founded by the prophet Muhammad and his companions in Medina between 622 and 632 C.E.

Evident in the previous discussion of the Sunna, the relationship between faith and practice in Islam is exemplified by the judgments, interpretations, and personal behavior of the prophet Muhammad. This example is canonized in the Sunna and codified in the shariah. Yet despite the often obsessive attention that is paid to the outer form of the Prophet's behavior by contemporary Muslims, the inner state that influences this behavior is often overlooked. This subtle but crucial aspect of the Sunna warrants further examination. This aspect is epitomized in what the Prophet's wife Aishah once said when summing up her husband's character. "His nature was the Quran [*khuluquhu al-Quran*]; he approved what it approved and he hated what it hated."

In this famous hadith the idea of practice in Islam intersects with the concepts of God-consciousness (*taqwa*) and ethics. All ethical systems, whether religious or philosophical in nature, must start by explaining what is meant by "the good." As with so much else in Islam, the ultimate definition of the good is seen to reside in the Quran. Although the Quran refers to the good in many ways, only a few Quranic terms, such as *al-khayr* (the good) and *al-haqq* (the truth), deal with what might be called philosophical principles. For the most part the Quran does not so much define the good as illustrate it with repeated examples of virtuous behavior. This indicates that from the Quranic perspective, ethics is more a matter of practice than of philosophy.

One of the most important terms used to describe the practice of "good" in the Quran is *maruf* (virtue). This is expressed most significantly in a Quranic verse that was previously alluded to in the discussion on Islamic law: "Let there be among you a community that calls to the good (*al-khayr*), commanding virtue (*yamuruna bi-l-maruf*) and forbidding vice (*yanhawna an al-munkar*); these are the ones who have attained felicity" (Quran 3:104). In Arabic, the meaning of *maruf* is essentially social in nature. It derives from the root *arafa* (to know) and literally means "that which is known." As an ethical term, it signifies "known" or virtuous acts that are performed in the full light of day and thus do not need to be hidden away from a neighbor's sight. This socially contextualized definition of the good comes quite close to a practice that can be found in Mexico and parts of Central America, where the doors to village houses are left open so that neighbors can see that nothing shameful is going on inside. The antithesis of maruf, the semantic domain of secrecy and hypocrisy, is expressed by the Quranic term munkar (vice). Literally meaning "that which is hated or despised," munkar connotes those behaviors that would ruin a person's reputation if they were performed in the open.

Another important ethical term in Islam is salah (social virtue). Although the word itself does not appear in the Quran, there are numerous references to this concept, as in the verse that depicts morally upright Muslims as residing "in the company of those whom Allah has favored: the prophets, the truthful [siddiqin], the martyrs, and the virtuous [salihin]" (Quran 4:69). The practitioner of salah is referred to in the Quran as a salih (fem. saliha) or a muslih, a morally upstanding individual who works for the betterment (islah) of himself and his fellow Muslims. By upholding the Sunna, he stands in opposition to the fasid (the "ruiner") or selfish individualist, who jeopardizes the moral integrity of the Muslim community by undermining the standards of virtue that the salih seeks to establish. In Islam this moral distinction between socially conscious virtue and asocial individualism replicates the dichotomy between faith and unbelief that separates the social environment of Islam from that of non-Muslims. Although most Muslims would hesitate to repudiate the faith of a fellow believer simply because he or she has sinned, the venal sinner or social deviant might well be ostracized from the community as a "ruiner." The sinner would still theoretically retain the option of returning to the fold, however, once he or she had stopped sinning and had sincerely resolved never to sin again.

Much of the appeal of contemporary reformist movements in Islam is a result of their advocacy of social virtue. Indeed, the Arabic term for "reformist" (islahi) is related to the concept of salah. Throughout the Muslim world reformist organizations, such as the Muhammadiyah of Indonesia, devote a considerable percentage of their budgets to social welfare projects, such as building hospitals and medical centers and providing various kinds of family and social services. In Egypt the Mustapha Mahmoud Society, founded by a reformist physician, provides some of the best medical care in Cairo; the fee charged is based on the patient's ability to pay. In countries in which state-supplied services are either lacking or inadequate, the honesty, selflessness, and dedication to the common people displayed by such reformist activists count for much more than the theological or philosophical deficiencies that may exist in their doctrines.

Ethical terms such as *maruf* and *salah* recall the third dimension of Islamic practice that was mentioned earlier in the discussion of the Hadith of Gabriel: the doing of good or active virtue (*ihsan*). Although this term has been interpreted in many different ways, in the Quran the concept of active virtue is specifically linked to the concept of justice (*adl*). This connection between virtuous and just forms of action is clearly expressed in one of the most famous ethical verses of the Quran: "Verily Allah commands justice [*adl*], the doing of good [*ihsan*], and giving to one's near relatives; He forbids acts of wickedness, vice [*munkar*], and lust [*bagha*]" (Quran 16:90). In a later verse of the Quran, the concept of justice is expanded to include the notion of epistemological truth. This occurs in a discussion of the ends for which God created the universe: "Not but for just ends [*illa bi-l-haqq*] did Allah create the heavens and the earth and all that is between them" (Quran 30:8). In this verse *al-haqq* not only expresses the idea of truth in an abstract sense, but it also implies the notion of collective and individual rights (*huquq*), as in "human rights" (*huquq al-insan*) or even "divine rights" (*huquq Allah*). Therefore, when the Hadith of Gabriel defines active virtue as worshiping God "as if you see Him; for if you do not see Him, surely He sees you," it is clear that this involves much more than mere perfection in the ritual observances of Islam. In this statement the epistemological and behavioral complementarity of faith and practice coincides with the moral complementarity of truth and justice. This is one of the main reasons why both Sufis and politically active Islamic reformists have taken the term ihsan to connote the highest degree of Islamic practice.

One Sufi social critic was so impressed by the complementarity of truth and justice that he chose to conceptualize nearly all of Islam around it. This was Abu-l-Abbas al-Sabti (d. 1204), the patron saint of Marrakesh and the North African equivalent of Mother Theresa or St. Francis of Assisi. In a hagiographic work that was written by one of his disciples, al-Sabti discusses the social meaning of *ihsan* and its importance to the spiritual life of Muslims:

> I found a verse in the Book of God that had a great effect on both my heart and my tongue. It was, "Verily, God commands justice and *ihsan*." I pondered this and said [to myself], "Perhaps [finding] this is no coincidence and I am the one who is meant by this verse." I continued to examine its meaning in the books of exegesis until I found [a work] which stated that [the verse] was revealed when the Prophet established brotherhood between the Emigrants and the Helpers [upon moving to Medina]. They had asked the Prophet to establish a pact of brotherhood between them, so he commanded them to share proportionately among themselves. In this way, they learned that the justice commanded [by God] was to be found through sharing . . . I understood that what [the Prophet] and his Companions adhered to were the practices of sharing in proportionate measure (*mushatara*) and selfless devotion to others [*ithar*]. So I vowed to God Most High that when anything

Islamic law was initially taught in mosques, but with time a new institution, known as a *madrasa*, or theological college, developed. This madrasa built in late fifteenth-century Cairo combined spaces for teaching with a small mosque where students and teachers could perform daily prayers.

came to me, I would share it with my believing brethren among the poor. I followed this practice for twenty years, and this rule affected my ideas to the point where nothing dominated my thoughts more than [the concept of] absolute sincerity [sidq].

After reaching forty years of age, another idea occurred to me, so I returned to this verse and [again] meditated upon it, and discovered that justice was [indeed] in sharing but that ihsan went beyond that. I thought about it a third time and vowed to God that if anything, small or large, came to me, I would keep one-third of it and expend two-thirds for the sake of God Most High. I followed this practice for twenty years, and the result of that decision among humankind was [both] respect and repudiation; I was respected by some but repudiated by others.

After twenty [more] years, I meditated on the first requirement of the station of ihsan required by God Most High for His servants, and found it to be gratitude for His bounty. This is proven by the emergence of the instinct toward good at birth, before the acquisition of either understanding or intellect. I then found that eight grades of behavior were required for charity and that seven other grades [were required] for ihsan in addition to [what was required for] justice. This is because there is a right for oneself, a right for the wife, a right for what is in the womb, a right for the orphan, and a right for the guest [these rights are detailed in the Sunna]. . . . Once I arrived at [the station of ihsan], I vowed to God that whatever came to me, whether it be little or much, I would keep two-sevenths of it for myself and my wife and [give up] five-sevenths to the one for whom it was due [i.e., the poor].

Toward the end of his life, after al-Sabti had become a widely revered advocate for the poor and enjoyed the patronage of the ruler of Marrakesh, he refined his practice of ihsan even further.

I divide everything that comes to me into seven portions. I take one seventh for myself and the second seventh for that which I am required to spend on my wife and the small children under her care, as well as the slaves and slave girls [in our household], all of whom number thirty-two individuals. Then I look after those who have lost their sustenance; they are the neglected orphans who have neither mother nor father. I take them in as my own family and see to it that not one of them lacks a [proper] marriage or a burial, unless someone else provides it for them. Then I look after my kinfolk, who number eighty-four individuals. They have two rights: their right as family members and their right as residents [in my household]. Then come those who have been deprived of their support as mentioned in the Book of God Most High. They are the poor who have fallen into hardship on the Way of God—those who are unable to work the land

and are thought of as ignorant but who are rich in patience and restraint; they are the ones unable to manage their own affairs . . . I take them in as if they are my own relatives, and when one of them dies, I replace him with another. I carried out these obligations for fourteen years without respite.

It is important to reproduce al-Sabti's comments in detail because his discussion of ihsan so clearly illustrates the interrelationship in Islam between truth and knowledge on the one hand and justice and practice on the other. Although many other Muslims, both Sufi and non-Sufi, also discussed the Quranic notions of truth and knowledge and how they related to both inward and outward practices, few were as single-minded as this Sufi of Marrakesh in following the relationship between knowledge and practice to its logical conclusion in the domain of social action. In this regard, the trivialization by many Sufis of the social aspect of Islam comes as something of a surprise, because Islamic law clearly recognizes that religious practice involves both acts that are ritual in nature (*ibadat*) and those that have a bearing on social life (*muamalat*). For al-Sabti, ritual acts could never be performed correctly if they were divorced from their larger ethical and social contexts. Therefore, he set out to reestablish the connection between the ritual aspects of the five Pillars of Islam and their ethical implications.

When dealing with the first pillar of Islam, al-Sabti passes over the ritualized aspect of the Shahadah in favor of the main point of the declaration of faith—the concept of the oneness of God (*tawhid*). As the witnessing of the Shahadah is seen as the formal means of entry into Islam and the prerequisite for each of the four other pillars, a full understanding of tawhid is seen by al-Sabti as the essential prerequisite for ihsan. For al-Sabti, tawhid as an ethical concept involves more than anything else the relinquishing of all sense of personal ownership or possession. This is because the affirmation of divine reality that is expressed in the declaration of God's oneness implies the negation of all forms of contingent exis-

Prayers held to commemorate the end of Ramadan and the sacrifice made by hajj pilgrims are traditionally celebrated in an outdoor praying place know as a *musalla* or *idgah*. Like this twelfth-century example from Bukhara, these were normally located on the outskirts of cities in order to hold all the men who were old enough to engage in prayer.

tence. If the goods of the material world become the goals of a person's life, they are functionally equivalent to idols. The material world thus becomes an object of worship whose mastery of the human being increases in direct proportion to the importance it is given. "Everything that masters a person is his god," says al-Sabti. For this reason to be a true *muwahhid* or affirmer of God's oneness, the human being must divest himself of everything but Allah—the One God, Absolute and Unique.

Al-Sabti gives a similarly ethical interpretation of the concept of prayer. Like the Shahadah (the act of bearing witness), the performance of al-Salat (the required five prayers) is more than a mere ritual. It is also a symbolic act of divestment in which a worshiper renounces before the Creator everything that he or she has vainly acquired and presumes to own. "He who does not understand the [ethical] meaning of prayer has not prayed," says al-Sabti. "The beginning of prayer is the 'Magnification of Consecration,' which involves raising your hands and saying, 'God is Most Great.' The meaning of 'God is Most Great' is that you do not begrudge God anything. When the person considers a certain aspect of the material world to be most important for him, he has not consecrated himself and thus has not magnified God in his prayers. The meaning of raising one's hands to magnify God is that you have been emptied of everything and are saying, 'I possess neither much nor a little.' " Such a person, who knows with certainty that the human being in reality possesses nothing of one's own, is the true "slave of God."

What is true for the canonical prayer is even more true for the Ramadan fast: "The secret of fasting is that you are hungry," says al-Sabti. "When you are hungry you remember the one who is always hungry and know the strength of the fire of hunger that afflicts him, so that you become charitable toward him. Thus, if you deny yourself food but have no compassion for the hungry and your fasting does not cause this idea to occur to you, you have not [truly] fasted and have not understood the intended meaning of the fast." The same is the case for the poor-tax (*al-Zakah*), a pillar of Islam that is ethical by its very definition. Here, al-Sabti agrees with the majority of Muslim scholars, who hold that the poor-tax is made obligatory for Muslims every year so that they become accustomed to spending on others instead of themselves. Also pertinent are al-Sabti's interpretations of the pilgrimage to Mecca and what Islamic activists often call the sixth pillar of Islam: the concept of struggle or jihad. For al-Sabti the point of the hajj pilgrimage is not the circumambulation of the Kaaba. Instead, it is that the pilgrim "appear in the dress of the poor, with a shaved head, unkempt, and wearing sandals, [after] having divested himself of fine clothing, expending his efforts for the sake of God Most High, and showing worshipfulness [toward Him]." As for the term *jihad*, its real meaning is not holy war against the unbelievers, as

Muslim exoterists believe, but rather, as al-Sabti says, "the expenditure of oneself for the pleasure of God Most High, emptying oneself of everything for His sake, and divesting oneself of reliance on the material world."

Al-Sabti's interpretation of the Five Pillars of Islam through the conceptual lens of ethics was meant to restore a sense of balance to what scholar Charles Eaton has termed the "human paradox." Although the human being was created as the

In addition to upholding the Five Pillars of Islam, Muslims are exhorted to go beyond the miminum. For example, they should practice good deeds or active virtue (*ihsan*) to enrich their spiritual lives. In 1905 beggars gathered near the tomb of the great Persian poet Saadi in Shiraz in the expectation of receiving munificence from their brethren.

vicegerent of God on earth, more often than not she fails to live up to the responsibilities of the vicegerency because of heedlessness or vice: "And when your Lord said to the angels, 'Verily I shall place on the earth a vicegerent,' they said, 'Will You place upon it one who will make mischief therein and shed blood while we praise You and glorify You?'" (Quran 2:30). Al-Sabti reminded his audience through his teachings that by ignoring the ethical dimension of Islamic practice, the salvation of both society and the individual may be lost and its antithesis, social discord or perdition, may be found. In addition, through his selfless devotion to the poor, he shamed those who neglected their responsibility to their fellow Muslims and reminded them through his acts of charity that the greatest losers by their works are "those whose effort is wasted on the life of the world, although they believe that they are doing good" (Quran 18:104). For those who did not heed his warning, al-Sabti reiterated the Quran's stern admonition: "Those who desire the life of the world and its glitter will pay the price of their deeds in [this world] without any alleviation" (Quran 11:15).

One can therefore conclude—from the discourses of the Quran to the Sunna of the Prophet, the laws of the shariah, and the ethical teachings of al-Sabti and other Islamic reformers—that the truest means to happiness is to be found in the proper balance between knowledge (ilm) and practice (amal). This applies equally to acts that are purely religious in nature and to those that are essentially social. Faith, like speech, is both social and individual. Acts of faith always involve a dialogue—either between the worshiper and the object of her worship, or between the actor and his fellows in a religious community. This is why, for both the Sufi Abu-l-Abbas al-Sabti and the non-Sufi jurist ibn Abi Zayd al-Qayrawani, a faith that is not expressed in the context of structured social relationships is no faith at all.

According to the noted Muslim theologian Abu Hamid al-Ghazali (1058–1111), moral character (khuluq) is not to be found in the knowledge of good or evil or even in the capacity for good or evil; rather, it is a state of the human spirit (nafs). Character thus precedes action for al-Ghazali and is a sort of gestalt that enables morally valued acts to occur immediately, without the need for reflection or deliberation. This gestalt of the soul reflects the vision of the heart and is good or bad to the extent that the heart "sees" with the Quranic "eye of certainty."

Herein lies the importance of Aishah's statement that the prophet Muhammad's character "was the Quran." If character refers to an inner state or condition of the human being, then each person inclines toward good or evil to the extent that his inner self has assimilated the moral outlook of the Quranic concept of vicegerency. To say that a Muslim's character "is the Quran" is to say that he is a complete vicegerent of God: his intellect understands reality through the "knowledge of certainty," his eyes comprehend both himself and God's creation through the "eye of certainty," and his spirit finds its center through the "truth of certainty." This assimilation of the Quranic perspective is the practical essence of the prophetic Sunna and the basis of Islamic ethics. Because it is rooted in God's own "knowledge from the divine presence," it is the tree of knowledge out of which all ritual and ethical practices grow.

CHAPTER THREE

Law and Society

THE INTERPLAY OF REVELATION
AND REASON IN THE SHARIAH

Mohammad Hashim Kamali

This chapter is divided into several sections, each addressing an aspect of Islamic law that relates to the concerns of Muslim society. The chapter begins with an explanation of the two terms, Shariah and fiqh, which are often used interchangeably but are not identical. A brief explanation of the differences between these terms sets forth the context for the rest of the chapter. The next section discusses the history and sources of Islamic law. A review of the distinctive contributions of the leading schools of law to the development of fiqh follows. Next is a general characterization of the Shariah, beginning with a discussion of its religious and moral dimensions, followed by explorations of continuity and change, the scope of interpretation, and rational analysis (talil). The Shariah is also characterized as pragmatic, and the doctrine of siyasa shariyya (Shariah-oriented policy) is explained as an instrument of pragmatism in Shariah. This is followed by a discussion of the status of the individual and the community in Shariah. The chapter ends with a survey of recent reforms in Muslim countries that are seeking to adapt Islamic law to the concerns of modern society.

Shariah and Fiqh: The Duality of Islamic Law

Islamic law originates in two major sources: divine revelation (wahy) and human reason (aql). This dual identity of Islamic law is reflected in its two Arabic desig-

(Left) The Imam al-Shafii (d. 820) founded one of the four major Sunni schools of law. His tomb in the southern cemetery of Cairo became a focus of veneration; a large mausoleum, covered with a wooden dome, was erected over it in the early thirteenth century. The Shafii school of law is prevalent in Lower Egypt, southern Arabia, East Africa, Indonesia, and Malaysia.

nations, *Shariah* and *fiqh*. Shariah bears a stronger affinity with revelation, whereas fiqh is mainly the product of human reason. Shariah literally means "the right path" or "guide," whereas fiqh refers to human understanding and knowledge. The divine Shariah thus indicates the path to righteousness; reason discovers the Shariah and relates its general directives to the quest for finding solutions to particular or unprecedented issues. Because the Shariah is mainly contained in divine revelation (that is, the Quran and the teachings of the Prophet Muhammad or the Sunna), it is an integral part of the dogma of Islam. Fiqh is a rational endeavor and largely a product of speculative reasoning, which does not command the same authority as Shariah.

To say that the Shariah is contained in the Quran and Sunna, however, would exclude the scholastic legacy of fiqh and its vast literature from the Shariah. In fact, it is the clear injunctions of the Quran and the Sunna that provide the nucleus of the Shariah. The parts of the Quran that consist of historical data and parables, for instance, are not included. The specific rules of the Quran and the Sunna—collectively known as the *nusus*, which are relatively small in number—represent the core of the Shariah. Shariah is a wider concept than fiqh, however; it comprises the totality of guidance that God has revealed to the Prophet Muhammad relating to the dogma of Islam: its moral values and its practical legal rules. Shariah thus comprises in its scope not only law but also theology and moral teaching. Dogmatic theology (*ilm al-kalam*) is primarily concerned with liberating the individual from belief in superstition and inculcating faith in God and a sense of enlightened conviction in the values of Islam. Morality (*ilm al-akhlaq*) educates the individual in moral virtue, the exercise of self-discipline and restraint in the fulfillment of natural desires. Fiqh is concerned with practical

The Shariah provides clear rulings on the fundamentals of faith and practice, including prayer, fasting, and other devotional matters. At the Haydar Mosque in Kuliab, Tadjikistan, devout Muslims prostrate themselves in prayer towards the Kaaba in Mecca.

legal rules that relate to an individual's conduct. Fiqh is thus "positive" law, and although much of it is in common with the Shariah, it does not include general guidelines on morality and dogma that are not legally enforceable. Yet jurists agree about the primacy of morality and dogma in the determination of basic values. By comparison, fiqh is described as a mere superstructure and a practical manifestation of commitment to those values.

The Shariah provides clear rulings on the fundamentals of Islam: its basic moral values and practical duties, such as prayers, fasting, legal alms (*zakah*), the *hajj* (pilgrimage to Mecca), and other devotional matters. Its injunctions on what is lawful and unlawful (*halal* and *haram*) are on the whole definitive, and so are its rulings on some aspects of civil transactions (*muamalat*). But the Shariah is generally flexible with regard to most civil transactions, such as criminal law (with the exception of the prescribed punishments or *hudud*), government policy and constitution, fiscal policy, taxation, and economic and international affairs. In many of these areas the Shariah provides only general guidelines.

Fiqh is defined as the knowledge of the practical rules of the Shariah, which are derived from the Quran and the Sunna. The rules of fiqh are thus concerned with the manifest aspects of individual conduct. The practicalities of conduct are evaluated on a scale of five values: obligatory, recommended, permissible, reprehensible, and forbidden. The definition of fiqh also implies that the deduction of the rules of fiqh from the Quran and the Sunna is through direct contact with the source evidence and necessarily involves a certain measure of independent

Other devotional matters covered by the Shariah include burial. Outside a small mosque at Marbat, Oman, the graves of pious Muslims are aligned so that the deceased can rise and face Mecca on the Day of Final Judgment.

reasoning and intellectual exertion (*ijtihad*). The ability to use the Quran there-fore necessitates the knowledge of Arabic and a certain degree of insight and eru-dition that an "imitator," or one who memorizes the rules without understanding their implications, could not achieve. A jurist (*faqih*) who fulfills these requirements and has the ability to deduce the rules of the Shariah from their sources is a *mujtahid*, one qualified to exercise independent reasoning.

The rules of fiqh may be divided into two types. First, there are rules that are conveyed in a clear text, such as the essentials of worship, the validity of mar-riage outside the prohibited degrees of relationship, the rules of inheritance, and so forth. These are self-evident and therefore independent of interpretation. This part of fiqh is simultaneously a part of the Shariah. Second, there are rules that are formulated through the exercise of independent reasoning in that part of the Quran and the Sunna that is not self-evident. Because of the possibility of error, the rules that are so derived are not immutable. They are not necessarily an inte-gral part of the permanent Shariah, and the mujtahid who has reason to depart from them in favor of an alternative ruling may do so without committing a transgression. Only when juristic opinion and independent reasoning are sup-ported by general consensus (*ijma*) does that reasoning acquire the binding force of a ruling (*hukm*) of Shariah.

The schools of law vary in their treatment of the contents of fiqh. Broadly speaking, the body of law is divided into two main categories: devotional mat-ters (*ibadat*) and civil transactions (*muamalat*). The devotional matters are usually studied under the six main headings of cleanliness, ritual prayer, fasting, the hajj, legal alms, and *jihad* (holy struggle); the schools of law do not vary much in their treatment of these subjects. Juristic differences among the schools occur mainly in the area of the civil transactions, which are generally studied under the five headings of transactions involving exchange of values, equity and trust, matri-monial law, civil litigation, and administration of estates. Crimes and penalties are often studied under a separate heading (*uqubat*) next to these two main cate-gories. The most detailed exposition of the entire range of fiqh remains the thirty-volume *Kitab al-Mabsut* by Shams al-Din al-Sarakhsi (d. 1083).

The History of Islamic Law

Islamic legal history is in a sense the history of fiqh rather than of the Shariah. The Shariah had a short history, as its development began and ended in just over two decades during the Prophet's mission in Mecca and Medina. Only the rudi-ments of fiqh were laid down during this period, and there was no distinction between the legal subject matter of Islam and its other parts at this early stage. *Fiqh* in this period referred to the knowledge of religion in general; the distinction that confined fiqh to practical legal rules was made by the *ulama* (religious scholars) of later periods. This was to a large extent stimulated by the documentation of *hadith* (a verified account of a statement or action of the Prophet Muhammad) and the extensive materials that were consequently made available for fresh inquiry and research. Legal historians have distinguished six periods in the development of fiqh. In the initial phase—the prophetic period (ca. 610–32 c.e.)—the Quran was revealed and the Prophet explained and reinforced it through his own teaching and practice, the Sunna. There was a general preoccupation with the Quran and the emphasis was not as much on law as on the dogma and morality of Islam. The legal rulings of the Quran, which were mainly revealed during the second decade of the prophetic mission, were primarily issue-oriented and practical. There was no need for speculative legal reasoning (*ijtihad*) simply because the Prophet himself provided definitive rulings on issues as and when they arose.

The second period of the development of fiqh—the era of the Prophet's Companions (ca. 632–61)—is one of interpretation and

Devotional matters (*ibadat*), including cleanliness and ritual prayer, are treated much the same by all schools of law. For example, everyone must remove shoes before prayer. Here, a group of Muslim men put their shoes back on outside a London mosque as they return to their daily lives.

supplementation of the textual subject matter of the Shariah. In this period fiqh and ijtihad find their historical origins. The Companions of the Prophet took a rational approach toward the textual materials—the Quran and the Sunna. Their understanding and interpretation of the texts were not confined to the meaning of words; rather, the Companions sought to understand their underlying rationale, effective cause, and purpose. The Companions' interpretations are generally considered authoritative, not only because they were the direct recipients of prophetic teachings but also because of their participation and insight into the Quran's phenomenology (*asbab al-nuzul*). The Companions frequently resorted to personal reasoning and consultation in the determination of issues. The first four caliphs—Abu Bakr, Umar ibn al-Khattab, Uthman ibn Affan, and Ali ibn Abi Talib, collectively known as the "rightly guided caliphs"—are particularly noted for their interpretations.

The third phase in the development of fiqh, known as the era of the successors, began with the Umayyads coming to power around 661 and ended with that dynasty's demise in 750. Because of the territorial expansion of the Umayyad state, new issues arose that stimulated significant developments in fiqh. This period is marked by the emergence of two schools of legal thought that left a lasting impact on the subsequent development of fiqh: Traditionists (Ahl al-Hadith), who were centered mainly in Mecca and Medina in the Hejaz, and the Rationalists (Ahl al-Ray), who were active in the Iraqi cities of Kufa and Basra. Whereas the Traditionists relied mainly on textual authority and were averse to the use of personal opinion (ray), the Rationalists were inclined, in the absence of a clear text, toward a more liberal use of personal reasoning. Although the Traditionists opposed the approach, the Rationalists maintained that the rules of the Shariah, outside the sphere of devotional matters, pursued objectives and were founded in causes that provided the jurist and *mujtahid* with guidelines for further inquiry and research. The secession of the Shiites from the main body of Muslims, the Sunnis, which took place as a result of disagreement over political leadership, led to the emergence of the Shiite school of law during this period. The Shiites maintained that Ali, the cousin and son-in-law of the Prophet, was the rightful caliph and leader, but that his predecessors, Abu Bakr, Umar, and Uthman, denied Ali that right. The Shii school advocated doctrines that are significantly different from those of their Sunni counterparts.

The next two centuries (ca. 750–950), known as the era of independent reasoning, marked the fourth phase in the history of fiqh. This phase saw major developments that were later manifested in the emergence of the legal schools

All schools require ritual ablution (*wudu*) before prayer, and the Muslim must wash the face, hands and arms, head, and feet. Most congregational mosques provide water for washing. Here men are washing before entering the mosque.

Civil transactions (*muamalat*), including matrimonial law and civil litigation, vary significantly according to the different schools of law. This scene shows the bride carried to the groom's car in a traditional doli as she begins her married life with his family in Kashmir.

that have survived today: the Hanafi, Maliki, Shafii, and Hanbali. The Hanafi school, named after Abu Hanifah al-Numan ibn Thabit (699–767), presently has the largest following of all the surviving schools, in part because of its official adoption by the Ottoman Turks in the early sixteenth century. Abu Hanifah advocated legal reasoning by analogy (*qiyas*), which gained general acceptance over time, but his liberal recourse to personal opinion and juristic preference (*istihsan*) were criticized by the Traditionists. To this day the Hanafi school has retained its relatively liberal stance. The Maliki school, founded by Malik ibn Anas al-Asbahi (ca. 715–95), led the Traditionist movement in Mecca and Medina and advocated the notion that the Medinan consensus (*ijma*) was the only valid consensus. Despite its traditionalist leanings, however, the Maliki school over time has embraced a number of important doctrines that are inherently versatile, and its jurisprudence is in many ways more open than that of the other legal schools. It is the only school, for instance, that has accepted almost all the subsidiary sources and proofs of the Shariah, about which the other schools have remained selective (accepting some and rejecting or expressing reservations about others). The Maliki school is predominant today in Morocco, Algeria, Tunisia, northern

Egypt, Sudan, Bahrain, and Kuwait; the Hanafi school prevails in Turkey, Pakistan, Jordan, Lebanon, and Afghanistan.

Muhammad ibn Idris al-Shafii (767–820) is also a leading figure in the Traditionist camp, but he tried to reconcile the various trends and strike a middle course between the Traditionists and Rationalists. The controversy between the Traditionists and Rationalists had by al-Shafii's time accentuated the need for methodology. Al-Shafii saw the need to articulate the broad outline of the legal theory of the sources, the *usul al-fiqh*. He spent the last five years of his life in Egypt, where he found the customs of Egyptian society so different from those of Iraq that he changed many of his legal verdicts. The Shafii school is now prevalent in southern Egypt, the Arabian Peninsula, East Africa, Indonesia, and Malaysia, and it has many followers in Palestine, Jordan, and Syria. Even al-Shafii's degree of emphasis on tradition and his strong advocacy of the Sunna did not satisfy the uncompromising Traditionists, who preferred not to rely on human reason and chose instead to base their doctrines as much as possible on the precedents established in the Quran and the hadith. This was the avowed purpose of the two new schools that emerged in the ninth century. The first (and the only successful) of these was the Hanbali school, founded by Ahmad ibn Hanbal (780-855). The other was the Zahiri school of Dawud ibn Ali al-Zahiri (819-91), now extinct. The number of ibn Hanbal's followers declined until the eighteenth-century Wahhabi puritanical movement (named after the scholar Muhammad ibn Abd al-Wahhab) in the Arabian Peninsula gave it a fresh impetus. The Hanbali school is now predominant in Saudi Arabia, Qatar, and Oman.

The fifth phase in the formative history of fiqh began around 950. This period is characterized by the institutionalization of the dominant schools, with emphasis not on new developments but on following precedent (*taqlid*). The jurists

During the era of independent reasoning (*ijtihad*), four major schools of Islamic law developed—the Hanifi, Maliki, Shafii, and Hanbali. Most *madrasas*, or theological colleges, are devoted to a single school, but occasionally all four were included in a single building. The huge funerary complex founded by the Mamluk Sultan Hasan in the mid-fourteenth century in Cairo, seen in David Roberts' nineteenth-century lithograph, has a cruciform congregational mosque with a madrasa for each of the four schools in the corners of the courtyard.

occupied themselves with elaboration and commentaries on the works of their predecessors. By far the longest phase, this period lasted for about nine centuries and witnessed the downfall of the Abbasid and Ottoman Empires, the expansion in the military and political powers of the West, and the industrial revolution and colonial domination of Muslim lands by European powers. The colonial powers propagated their own doctrines and legal codes in almost every area of the law. As a result, fiqh lost touch with social reality and underwent a sustained period of stagnation. Original thinking and direct recourse to the sources of the Shariah, which had characterized the first three centuries of development, were no longer encouraged. A climate of opinion prevailed that the early predecessors had exhaustively used and developed the resources (the Quran and the Sunna), and the digested version of fiqh that they had produced was to be strictly followed. Imitation and following precedent thus gained ground, and the so-called "closure of the gate of ijtihad" followed.

Madrasas were initially established by Sunnis to combat the spread of Shiism, but with time, Shiites established madrasas of their own. The Madar-i Shah Madrasa in Isfahan, seen in this early photograph by Captain G. C. Rigby, was built by the Safavid Shah Husayn (1694–1722). Since the Islamic Revolution, it has been returned to its original function as a theological college.

The sixth and final phase in the development of fiqh began at the turn of the twentieth century. It is marked by less emphasis on precedent and greater emphasis on original thinking and the quest to make the Shariah once again relevant to the social reality and experience of contemporary Muslims. The revivification of fiqh and its necessary adjustment to respond to the prevailing needs of society is generally seen as an important component of the Islamic resurgence of the recent decades.

A large number of Sunni jurists have acknowledged the so-called "closure of the gate of ijtihad" and the onset of imitation around the mid-tenth century. The Shiite jurists have held, alternatively, that ijtihad is a collective obligation of all Muslims in the absence of the imam (the divinely appointed leader and successor of Muhammad). Independent reasoning is thus viewed not simply as a meritorious endeavor that might succeed or fail but as an effort to reach the highest possible degree of objective truth in the absence of the infallible imam. This effort must constantly be renewed in the hope of coming ever closer to objective truth. Intellectual exertion thus remains an open process until the return of the imam, who alone can offer certainty and truth. Furthermore, the Shiite imams have gone on record to instruct their disciples to remain diligent in ijtihad, especially regarding the implementation of the general principles of Shariah. In time, Shiite jurisprudence adopted the notion that a fully qualified *mujtahid* (one qualified to exercise independent reasoning) is a representative (*naib*) of the imam and performs the functions of the imam

Before the establishment of *madrasas*, mosques were the traditional setting for teaching and learning, and much instruction still takes place in mosques. Traditionally, the teacher sits against a column or wall surrounded by his students, as here at the al-Aqsa Mosque in Jerusalem.

The mosque of al-Azhar in Cairo, founded under the Fatimids in the tenth century, became a major center of learning in the Arab world. The curriculum there was reformed at the turn of the twentieth century, the time depicted in this photograph, and legal opinions issued by the shaykh there exemplify one type of independent reasoning (*ijtihad*).

regarding judgment and administration of the people's affairs. The leading Shiite mujtahids who expounded Shiite principles included Seyyed Morteza Alam al-Huda (d. 1060), Abu Abd Allah al-Mufid (d. 1044), Muhammad ibn Hassan al-Tusi (d. 1067), and Morteza al-Ansari (d. 1864). Morteza al-Ansari's two major words, *Faraid al-Usul* and *Makasib*, are currently used as textbooks on Shiite law.

In modern times legal interpretation or reasoning has occurred in the following three ways: statutory legislation, judicial decision and learned opinion (*fatwa*), and scholarly writings. Instances of legislative interpretation, which Noel Coulson referred to as "neo-ijtihad," can be found in the modern reforms of family law in many Muslim countries, particularly with reference to polygyny and divorce, both of which have been made contingent upon a court order, and therefore are no longer the unilateral privilege of the husband. Current reformist legislation on these subjects derives some support from the jurists' doctrines of the Maliki and Hanafi schools, but these reforms are essentially based on novel interpretation of the Quran's relevant portions. Numerous instances of independent reasoning are also found in the views of the ulama, such as the collections of published opinions of Muhammad Rashid Rida in the 1920s and those of the late shaykh of Azhar, Mahmud Shaltut, in the 1950s. In the 1967 case of *Khursid Bibi* vs. *Muhammad Amin*, the supreme court of Pakistan's decision to validate a form of divorce, known as *khula*, that can take place at the wife's initiative, even without the consent of the husband, can be cited as an example of judicial ijtihad. Another example of ongoing reinterpretation is the scholarly contribution of the Egyptian scholar Yusuf al-Qaradawi, who validated air travel by women unaccompanied by male relatives. According to the rules of fiqh that were formulated in premodern times, women were not permitted to travel alone. Al-Qaradawi based his conclusion on the analysis that the initial ruling was intended to ensure women's physical and moral safety, and that modern air travel fulfills this requirement. He further supported this view with an analysis of the relevant hadiths on the subject and arrived at a ruling better suited to contemporary conditions.

Sources of Shariah: The Quran, the Sunna, and Independent Reasoning

As noted earlier, the sources of the Shariah are of two types: revealed and non-revealed. There are only two revealed sources—first, the Quran; second, the teaching and exemplary conduct (Sunna) of the Prophet Muhammad, including his sayings, acts, and tacit approval (or lack of condemnation) of the conduct of his Companions and some of the customs of Arabian society. The authority of the Sunna as a source of Shariah as next to the Quran is indicated in the Quran itself. Some disagreement, however, prevailed over the precise meaning and authority of the Sunna until the theologian and jurist al-Shafii addressed the issue in the early ninth century. The legal theory that al-Shafii articulated underscored the normative status of the Sunna as a source of revelation that explained and supplemented the Quran. The nonrevealed sources of Shariah are generally founded in juristic reasoning (*ijtihad*). This reasoning may take a variety of forms, including analogical reasoning (*qiyas*), juristic preference (*istihsan*), considerations of public interest (*istislah*), and even general consensus (*ijma*) of the learned, which basically originates in ijtihad and provides a procedure by which a ruling of juristic reasoning can acquire the binding force of law. Analogy and consensus have been generally recognized by the vast majority of ulama, but there is disagreement over the validity and scope of many of the rational proofs that originate in ijtihad.

The Quran, by its own testimony, consists of the words of God as recited in Arabic to the Prophet Muhammad through the angel Gabriel (Quran 26:193). Much of the Quran was revealed through actual events encountered by the Prophet, and questions asked and answered by him. The Prophet also used the Quran as a basis of his own teaching and adjudication. Nevertheless, the Quran

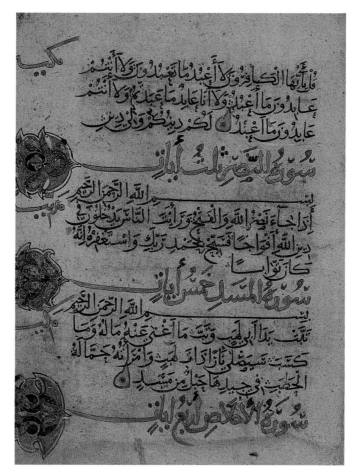

The Quran, God's word as revealed to the Prophet Muhammad, is
the basis of Muslim law. The text is divided into 114 chapters of
unequal length. Eighty-five chapters, mostly short, were revealed in
Mecca, as shown by the word Mecca written in gold in the margin
near the gold chapter heading in this copy of the Quran transcribed
by the famous calligrapher Ibn al-Bawwab at Baghdad in 1000–1001.

is neither a legal nor a constitutional document, although legal materials occupy
a small portion of its text; less than 3 percent of the text deals with legal matters.
The legal contents of the Quran were mainly revealed following the Prophet's
migration from Mecca to Medina, where he established a government and the
need therefore arose for legislation on social and governmental issues. The contents of the Quran are not classified according to subject. Its pronouncements on
various topics appear in unexpected places and in no particular thematic order.
This fact has led many thinkers to conclude that the Quran is an indivisible

whole, and its legal parts should not be read in isolation from its religious and moral teachings.

Of the 350 legal verses in the Quran, known as *ayat al-ahkam*, close to 140 relate to dogma and devotional matters, including such practical religious duties as ritual prayer, legal alms and other charities, fasting, pilgrimage, and so forth. Another seventy verses are devoted to marriage, divorce, paternity, child custody, inheritance, and bequests. Rules concerning commercial transactions, such as sale, lease, loan, usury, and mortgage, constitute the subject of another seventy verses. There are about thirty verses on crimes and penalties, another thirty on justice, equality, evidence, citizens' rights and duties, and consultation in government affairs, and above ten on economic matters. The ulama are not, however, in agreement on these figures, as calculations of this nature tend to differ according to the criteria and approach of one's inquiry. It is possible, for instance, to derive a legal ruling from the parables and historical passages of the Quran. Some of the earlier rulings of the Quran were also abrogated and replaced because of new circumstances, although the scope of these abrogations and their precise import is a matter of disagreement among scholars.

As previously noted, the ulama unanimously believe that the normative teachings (the Sunna) of the Prophet are a source of Shariah and that the Prophet's ruling on what is lawful and unlawful (*halal wa haram*) stands on equal footing with the Quran. The words of the Prophet, as the Quran declares, are divinely inspired (Quran 53:3), and obedience to them is every Muslim's duty (Quran 4:80; 59:7). Thus the Prophet's words were normative for those who actually heard them. Subsequent generations of Muslims, who have received the Prophet's words through various verbal and written records, however, had to ascertain their authenticity before accepting them as normative. The evidence of authenticity may be definitive, because it relies on numerous sources of recurrent and continuous testimony (*tawatur*), or it may consist of solitary reports that may not appear to be entirely reliable. One of the first kind of hadith (known as *mutawatir*) is a verbal mutawatir, a word-for-word transmission of what the Prophet said. This is very rare. There are no more than ten such hadiths. Another kind of hadith is known as the *conceptual mutawatir*, wherein the concept is taken from the Prophet but the words are supplied by a narrator. When the reports of a large number of transmitters of hadith concur in their purport but differ in wording, this is considered as mutawatir. This kind of mutawatir is quite frequent and is found in reference to the acts and sayings of the Prophet that explain the essentials of the faith, the rituals of worship, the rules that regulate the application of certain punishments, and so forth. The Companions of the Prophet and subsequent generations of Muslims have complied with the Prophet's teachings on these matters, and vast numbers of people throughout the ages have consistently adhered to them. Many hadiths on what is lawful and unlawful, as well as those that explain and supplement the injunctions of the Quran, are also classified as this type of mutawatir.

The Sunna relates to the Quran in various capacities. It may consist of rules that merely corroborate the Quran, it may clarify ambiguous parts of the Quran, or it may qualify and specify general rulings of the Quran. These three varieties comprise among them the bulk of the Sunna, and the ulama are in agreement that they are integral and supplementary to the Quran. The Sunna may also consist of rulings on which the Quran is silent, in which case the Sunna represents an independent source of Shariah. There are a number of hadiths that fall under this category; this type of Sunna, known as "Founding Sunna" (*Sunna muassisa*), is the main argument in support of the generally accepted view that the Sunna is not only an explanation and supplement to the Quran, but it is also an independent source of the Shariah.

For the Sunnis, the possibility of divine revelation (*wahy*) ended with the death of the Prophet. For the Shiites, however, divine revelation continued to be transmitted after the Prophet's death, through the line of their recognized leaders or imams. Shiite jurists have thus maintained that in addition to the Quran and the Sunna, the pronouncements of their imams constituted divine revelation and therefore binding law. This is reflected in the Shiite definition of *Sunna*, which under Shiite law includes the sayings, acts, and tacit approvals of the Prophet *and* the imams. The same doctrinal outlook is reflected in the Shiite perception of *ijma* (consensus), which is not possible without the imam's approval. In other words, the consensus of the jurists demonstrates the views of the imams. Consensus thus becomes a part of the Sunna as well as a means of discovering it. In some cases, this means that consensus becomes a carrier of the decrees of the imam. These are undoubtedly important doctrinal differences, yet since the last imam (according to the majority of Shiites) went into occultation and "disappeared" in 874, Shiite jurists have carried the imam's mantle and have played a similar role to that of their Sunni counterparts in expounding and interpreting the Quran and the Sunna.

Another source of Shariah is *ijtihad*, which literally means "striving." It is defined as exertion by a qualified scholar to the best of his or her ability to deduce the ruling of a particular issue from the evidence found in the sources. Unlike the revelation of the Quran and the Sunna, which ended with the Prophet's death, juristic reasoning continues to be the principal source and instrument that keeps the law consistent with the realities of social change. It is a collective obligation (*fard kifai*) of the Muslim community, meaning that the obligation has been met if performed sufficiently by at least one jurist (*mujtahid*) qualified to exercise independent reasoning. It becomes a personal obligation (*fard ayn*) of all mujtahids when it appears that the obligation has not been met and there is fear that justice may be lost if ijtihad is not immediately attempted.

Historically, analogical reasoning (*qiyas*) represented the most common—according to the theologian al-Shafii, the only valid—form of ijtihad. As a principal mode of ijtihad, analogy ensured the conformity of juristic opinion with the textual rulings of the Quran and the Sunna, which it sought to extend to similar cases. Personal reasoning plays a role in the construction of analogy through the identification of an effective cause (*illah*) between an original case and a new case. For example, the Quran (24:4) calls for penalizing anyone who slanderously accused chaste women of adultery by eighty lashes of the whip. This punishment was then analogically extended to those who accused innocent men of the same offense because of the commonality of the effective cause—namely of defending the honor of an innocent person—between the original case (women) and the new case (men).

Analogy was thus seen to be the surest way of developing the law within the guidelines of the text. But analogy was not altogether devoid of difficulty, especially in cases in which the analogical extension of a given ruling to a similar but not identical situation could lead to undesirable results. Therefore, some felt the need for a new formula to overcome the rigidities of analogy. The Hanafis developed the doctrine of juristic preference (*istihsan*), which enabled the jurist to search for an equitable solution in the event in which strict analogy compromised the ideals of fairness and justice. Al-Shafii, while strongly in support of analogy, totally rejected the notion of juristic preference, considering it to be no more than an arbitrary exercise in questionable opinions.

Shiite law does not recognize analogy as a source of law. The sixth Shiite imam, Jafar al-Sadiq (699–765), equated such analogical reasoning with pure conjecture and thus rejected it. Shiite law recognizes human reason as a source of law and a means of discovering the Shariah. Reason can thus determine that for certain issues a permissive or prohibitive law necessarily exists. For example, if the revealed law is silent on a certain matter, reason may determine, by reference to the general principles of Shariah and the best interest of human beings, that a certain law exists concerning that matter, especially when jurists realize that the Shariah simply cannot remain indifferent concerning the matter. Addiction to opium was not an issue during the time of the Prophet, for example, and no ruling was issued on it. Yet experience shows with certainty that addiction to opium causes harm and corruption. Because the Shariah forbids corruption, through the application of reason, consumption of opium is therefore considered forbidden. In this manner, reason tells Muslims that when something is forbidden by law, the means toward procuring it is also forbidden. Human reason thus becomes a proof and source of the Shariah and an important tool in the service of interpretation and ijtihad. Compared with analogical reasoning, human reasoning is a more open concept—it is not encumbered by the sort of technicalities that are involved in analogical reasoning. Analogies cannot be constructed without the prior existence of an original case, a ruling (hukm) in the sources, and an effective cause that links the original case to the new case. Human reasoning basically consists of unrestricted reasoning, which does not depend on such requirements. For example, the Quran prohibits alcohol because it is an intoxicant. This prohibition can be extended, by analogy, to narcotic drugs. But no such analogy can be extended to a drug that only causes lapse of memory or blurs the eyesight, for want of the effective cause, intoxication. But these can be prohibited by recourse to human reasoning.

Although the leading schools have also recognized considerations of public interest (istislah) as a source of law, they have generally tended to impose a variety of conditions on it because of its strong utilitarian leanings. Only the theologian Malik advocated it as a source of law in its own right, which is why the considerations of public interest are seen as a Maliki contribution to the legal theory of the sources, the usul al-fiqh. Whereas analogy operated within the given terms of the existing law, and juristic preference basically corrected the rigidities of analogy, public interest was not bound by such limitations. Furthermore, it vested the ruler and mujtahid with the initiative to take all necessary measures, including new legislation, to secure what he considered to benefit the people.

Almost every major school of law proposed a principle or method to regulate independent reasoning and to ensure its conformity with the overriding authority of divine revelation. Whereas some ulama, such as the Zahiris, confined the sources of law to the Quran, the Sunna, and consensus, the Hanafis added analogy, juristic preference, and custom, and the Malikis added public interest and the notion of "blocking the means" (sadd al-dharai), which ensured the consistency of means and ends with the Shariah by blocking the attempt to use a lawful means toward an unlawful end. Examples of this include banning the sale of arms at a time of conflict or forbidding a sale that may merely disguise a usurious transaction. This practice also provides preventive measures that are taken even before the actual occurrence of a feared event, such as banning an assembly that is likely to lead to violence. Although some of the obvious applications of this doctrine were generally accepted, the Maliki school has applied it more widely than most. The Shafii school contributed the doctrine of istishab (presumption of continuity), which safeguards continuity and predictability in law and in court decisions by proposing that facts and rules of law and reason are presumed to remain valid until there is evidence to establish a change. For example, certainty may not be overruled by doubt, and an unproven claim should not affect the basic presumption of innocence and continuity of the existing rights of the people under the Shariah. These doctrines are all designed, each in its respective capacity, to regulate independent reasoning and to provide formulas for finding solutions to new issues. The methods proposed by these doctrines also ensure the conformity of human interpretation and application to the basic principles and objectives of the Shariah. The idea that the law must evolve and develop within the framework of a certain methodology lies at the root of these doctrines.

Historically, ijtihad has been perceived as a concern primarily of the individual scholar and mujtahid. But in modern times, ijtihad has become a collective endeavor that combines the skills and contributions not only of the scholars of Shariah, but of experts in various other disciplines, because acquiring a mastery of all the skills that are important to society is difficult for any one person. Ideally, independent reasoning should be combined with the Quranic principle of consultation (shura), making it a consultative process, preferably as an integral part of the workings of the modern legislative assembly. Ijtihad has also been seen in the past as a juristic concept, a preserve of the jurist to the exclusion of specialists in other disciplines. But as a method by which to find solutions to new issues, ijtihad should be exercised by the scholars of Shariah as well as by experts in other disciplines, provided that those who attempt this independent reasoning acquire mastery of the relevant data, the Quaran, and the Sunna. There is thus no reason why experts in Islamic economics and medicine, for example, could not carry out ijtihad in their own fields.

Scholastic Contributions to Legal Thought

Hanafi application and interpretation of law is distinguished by its rationalist tendency and to some extent by its theoretical leanings in that it deals not only with actual issues but also with theoretical problems that are based on mere supposition. Because he was a merchant, Abu Hanifah's contributions to the law of commercial transactions are particularly noted. Abu Hanifah's legal thought is also distinguished by his emphasis on personal liberty and his reluctance to impose unwarranted restrictions on it. He thus maintained that neither the community nor the government is entitled to interfere with the personal liberty of the individual as long as the individual has not violated the law. Hanafi fiqh thus entitles a woman to conclude her own marriage contract without the consent of a guardian, whereas the other schools have stipulated the consent of a guardian as a requirement of valid marriage. The Hanafis have reasoned that the Quran (4:6) has endowed the adult female with full authority to manage her own financial affairs. This ruling has been extended by way of analogy to marriage. The majority of jurists of the leading schools, however, have considered this an "analogy with a difference" (qiyas ma al-fariq), which treats two different things (property and marriage) on the same footing, and therefore invalid. But Abu Hanifah called for equality (kafaa) in marriage and entitled the woman's guardian to seek annulment of a marriage in the event of a wide discrepancy in the socioeconomic status of the spouses. Equality is not a requirement according to the other leading legal schools simply because the guardian's consent is, according to them, a prerequisite of a valid marriage contract. Moreover, Abu Hanifah refused to validate interdiction of the foolish (safih) or the insolvent debtor on the analysis that restricting the freedom of these individuals is a harm greater than the financial loss that might otherwise occur. Abu Hanifah also held that no one, including a judge, may impose restrictions on an owner's right to the use of his or her property, even if that property inflicted harm on another person, provided that the harm is not exorbitant. Furthermore, because the judge cannot restrict the owner's liberty, the owner would not want to restrict his or her own liberty either. A charitable endowment (waqf) of one's personal property is consequently not binding on the owner, nor on his or her legal heirs. In other words, the owner or dedicator of endowed property is at liberty to revoke the endowment and thereby remove the self-imposed restriction on his or her right of ownership. The other legal schools disagree, mainly because they consider a charitable endowment as a binding commitment that the dedicator of the property must observe, once it has been duly instituted.

In one of his widely quoted statements, which represents a defining principle of the Hanafis, Abu Hanifah declared: "Whenever the authenticity of a hadith is ascertained, that is where I stand." A more general statement, also attributed to Abu Hanifah, is: "When you are faced with evidence, then speak for it and apply it." Consequently, it is evident that on occasions Abu Hanifah's disciples have differed with some of the rulings of the imam on the basis of newly uncovered evidence, often stating that the imam himself would have followed it had he known of it. A ruling by a disciple that differs from that of the imam is thus still regarded as a ruling of the school, sometimes in preference to that of the imam. Another saying of Abu Hanifah that represents another Hanafi principle is: "No one may issue a verdict on the basis of what we have said unless he ascertains the source of our statement." These eminently objective guidelines were upheld during the era of ijtihad, but the ulama of subsequent periods departed from the spirit of that guidance. The early nineteenth-century Hanafi jurist Ibn Abidin thus stated the new position of the school in the following terms: "A jurist of the later ages may not abandon the rulings of the leading imams and ulama of the school even if he sees himself able to carry out ijtihad, and even if he thinks that he has found stronger evidence. For it would appear that the predecessors have considered the relevant evidence and have declared their preference." The only exception here is made for "situations of necessity," in which case the jurist may give a different verdict to that of the established ruling of the school, if this provides a preferable solution to an urgent issue that is not adequately covered by an established precedent of the school.

The renowned work *Al-Muwatta* (The Straight Path) of the eighth-century theologian Malik ibn Anas al-Asbahi is the earliest complete work of fiqh on record. It relies heavily on the hadith, so much so that many have considered it to be a work of hadith. Because it uses the hadith as basic evidence for juristic conclusions, however, it is rightly classified as a work of fiqh. Notwithstanding his leading position in the Traditionist camp (Ahl al-Hadith), Malik relied extensively on opinion (*ray*)—in some cases he did so even more than representatives of the other leading schools. Malik is the chief source of the two important doctrines of public interest and blocking the means, both of which are eminently rational and rely mainly on personal reasoning. Maliki jurisprudence also attempted to forge a closer link with the practicalities of life in Medina and attached greater weight to social customs than other jurists did. This is borne out by its recognition of the Medinan consensus as a source of law, a concept that is advanced only by the Maliki school. Malik thus validated, on this basis, using the testimony of children in cases of injury, provided they have not left the scene of the incident. He also held that the wife of a missing husband may seek judicial separation after a four-year waiting period. Maliki law also recognized judicial divorce on the grounds of a husband's injurious treatment of his wife. The majority ruling entitles the wife to judicial relief, whereby the court may punish the husband; Maliki law ruled that if the treatment in question amounted to injury (*darar*), the wife could request dissolution of the marriage on that basis. Another Maliki contribution in this area is a type of divorce known as *khul*, in which the wife proposes dissolution of marriage against a financial consideration, usually by returning the dowry she received from her husband. Because the Quran validates khul (2:229), it is recognized by all the legal schools, but it can only be finalized with the husband's consent. Maliki fiqh took this a step further by ruling that if there are irreconcilable differences the court may finalize the divorce even without the husband's consent. By the late twentieth century the Maliki law of divorce had generally been adopted in the reformist legislation of many Muslim countries.

Muhammad ibn Idris al-Shafii's impact, as founder of the Shafii school of law, on the development of Shariah is most noticeable in the area of the methodol-

The Maliki school of law, which is prevalent in North Africa, prohibits an individual from appointing himself the administrator of a pious endowment, and most madrasas there were sponsored by the ruler, the only person who could afford such large sums. The Ben Yusuf Madrasa at Marrakesh, the largest in the Maghreb, was founded by the Saadian ruler Abdallah al-Ghalib in 1564–65.

ogy of law. His contribution is manifested by his pioneering work, the *Risalah*, in which he articulated the legal theory of *usul al-fiqh*, which consequently emerged, around the early ninth century, as one of the most important disciplines of learning in the history of Islamic scholarship. Al-Shafii's role in articulating the methodology of law has often been compared with that of Aristotle in logic. He maintained that the Sunna was a logical extension of the Quran and vindicated the exclusive authority of the prophetic Sunna as a source of Shariah next to the Quran. Al-Shafii's vision of the basic unity of the revealed sources came close to saying that rejecting the Sunna also amounted to rejecting the Quran, and that accepting the one and rejecting the other was untenable. He took his teacher, the theologian Malik, to task for placing undue emphasis on the Medinan consensus and the precedent of the Prophet's Companions at the expense of the Sunna of the Prophet.

In its general orientation Shafii law takes an intermediate posture between the Traditionist stance of the Maliki school and the pragmatism of the Hanafis. Al-Shafii took an objective stand on issues at a time when the Traditionists and Rationalists were engaged in bitter controversies. He was critical of Malik's validation of unrestricted public interest and of Abu Hanifah's frequent concession to specific at the expense of general principles. Al-Shafii's approach to the interpretation of contracts and verification of their validity was almost entirely based on the form rather than the intent of a contract. He thus overruled inquiry into the intention of the parties, even in circumstances that might arouse suspicion. For example, a man is thus within his rights in buying a sword, even if he intends to kill an innocent person with it. A man may likewise buy a sword from someone he saw using that sword as murder weapon. Contracts and transactions are therefore to be judged by their obvious conformity to the law, not by a mere suspicion that they may have violated it. Al-Shafii thus understood the Shariah to be concerned with the evident manifestation of human conduct and maintained that the judge and jurist were not under duty to inquire into the hidden meaning of the text or into the thoughts and motives of individuals. This reliance on the manifest form of conduct, contracts, and transactions is not peculiar to al-Shafii, as the Hanafis have also shown the same tendency, but al-Shafii exhibited it more frequently than most.

Al-Shafii maintained that a jurist should not hesitate to change his previous verdict (*fatwa*) if that would make a better contribution to the quest for truth. Thus, it is noted that he frequently changed his verdicts, and he sometimes recorded different rulings on the same issue. If, for example, a man deceives a woman by presenting her with a false family pedigree, the man is liable to a deterrent (*tazir*) punishment, such as being whipped, imprisoned, or fined. Then two additional views are recorded on the same issue from the imam and neither is given preference. The first view entitles the wife to choose either to continue the marriage or to separate. The second view says that the marriage is null and void.

Notwithstanding the common perception or stereotype of the Hanbali school as the most restrictive of the leading legal schools, Hanbali jurisprudence is in some respects more liberal than most. This is indicated by its extensive reliance on considerations of public interest. The imam ibn Hanbali issued a verdict, for example, that permitted compelling the owner of a large house to give shelter to the homeless. He also validated compelling workers and crafts-people who join together to deprive the public of their services to continue to provide those services at a fair wage to avoid inflicting hardship on society. The Hanbali school also takes a considerably more open view of the basic freedom of contract than other schools do. The legal schools differ on whether the norm in contract is permissibility, prohibition, or an intermediate position between the two. The majority tend to be restrictive in maintaining that the agreement of parties creates the contract, but the contract's requirements and consequences are independently determined by Shariah. The parties therefore are not at lib-erty to alter the substance of these nor to circumvent them in a way that would violate their purpose. The parties making the contract do not create the law but only a specific contract; their stipulations and terms of agreement should there-fore be in conformity with the provisions of Shariah. The schools differ over details, however. The Malikis and Hanafis tend to take a moderate position by making many exceptions to the basic norm of prohibition. Similarly, the Shafii position, like that of the Zahiris, tends to proscribe altering the basic postulates and attributes of contracts through mutual agreement. The Hanbalis maintain that the norm regarding contracts is permissibility (ibaha), which prevails in the absence of a clear prohibition in the Shariah. The reason is that the Quran has only laid down the general principle that contracts must be fulfilled (Quran 5:1), and that they must be based on mutual consent (Quran 4:19). Because the Lawgiver (God) has not specified any requirements other than consent, consent alone is the validating factor. The will and agreement of the parties can there-fore create binding rights and obligations.

The principle of permissibility under Hanbali law can also form the basis for unilateral obligation, which means that the individual is free to commit himself or herself in all situations in which this principle can apply. Thus a man may validly stipulate in a marriage contract that he will not marry a second wife. Because polygyny is only permissible (that is, it is not required) under the Shariah, the indi-vidual is free to make it the subject of stipulation. The other legal schools disallow this, saying that the Shariah has made polygyny lawful, a position that should not be circumvented or nullified through contractual stipulation. Therefore, any stip-ulation that seeks to do so is not binding. Ibn Hanbal stated that stipulations in a marriage contract must be strictly observed, even more so than in other contracts. Consequently, when one spouse fails to comply with the terms of the agreement, the other spouse is entitled to seek the annulment of the contract.

Shiite law permits temporary marriage (mutah) for any period of time up to the maximum of ninety-nine years. Under Shiite law, temporary marriage is a contractual arrangement whereby a woman agrees to cohabit with a man for a specified period of time in return for a fixed remuneration. This arrangement does not give rise to any right of inheritance between the spouses, but the children are legitimate and entitled to inheritance. Sunni law prohibits temporary marriage altogether. The differential rulings of Sunni and Shiite law relate to the interpretation of verses in the Quran (2:236; 4:24); because mutah can mean both "temporary marriage" or a "gift of consolation" given to a divorced woman, the Sunnis have upheld the latter meaning and the Shiites the former. The Prophet himself permitted mutah in the early years of Islam, but he later declared it forbidden, according to Sunni but not according to Shiite reports in the Prophetic hadith.

Another area in which Shiite law differs significantly from its Sunni counterpart is the system of priorities in inheritance. Male agnates—such as the father's father, germane brothers (who share both parents) and consanguine brothers (who share a father but have different mothers), and paternal uncles of the deceased—are often entitled to a share of the inheritance, even if there are closer female relatives, under Sunni law, but they are likely to be excluded from inheritance under Shiite law. Whereas Sunni law tends to uphold the basic concept of the extended family, Shiite law rests on the notion of the nuclear family, consisting of parents and lineal descendants. Under both systems the son of the deceased enjoys the same entitlement, but all other male relatives, particularly the collaterals, are often much less favorably placed under the Shiite law. The divergent systems of Sunni and Shiite succession are premised on their respective political and theological doctrines. For example, the principle of Shiite succession that any lineal descendant, particularly the child of a daughter, has complete priority over all collaterals reflects the Shiite view that the political title of the Prophet was properly inherited by his lineal descendant, through his daughter Fatima, not by the agnate collaterals through the Prophet's uncle al-Abbas ibn Abd al-Muttalib (566-ca. 653).

Salient Features of the Shariah:
Religious and Moral Dimensions and Continuity and Change

This section draws attention to some of the characteristic features of the Shariah, such as its identity as a religious law and its capacity to adapt through interpretation and rational analysis. The Shariah is characterized as pragmatic, especially in the area of public policy, and it favors a gradual approach to social reform. The Shariah advocates the moral autonomy of the individual and visualizes a basic harmony between private and public interests, and so the Shariah's orientation toward the concerns of the individual and those of the community as a whole is also discussed.

To say that Islamic law is God-given and an integral part of the religion is to say that adherence to its rules is both a legal and a religious duty of Muslims. Related to this are the concepts of *halal* and *haram*, the permissible and the prohibited. These are legal and religious categories that involve duty toward both God and fellow human beings. The religious and civil aspects of the Shariah tend to enforce one another in that legal compliance, as far as Muslims are concerned, is a religious duty. But for non-Muslims living under Islamic law, the law takes on a civilian character. It is of interest to note, however, that even with regard to Muslims, the jurists have drawn a distinction between the religious and the civilian aspects of the Shariah, especially in the area of civil transactions. In this area the rules of the Shariah are enforced on the basis only of what is apparent, whereas religion decrees based on true reality and intention. Thus the legal status of one act may differ in the judicial context from what it might be in a religious perspective. Judges do not issue judgments on religious considerations alone. This is why Muslim jurists often define their legal status in relationship to particular cases, but religiously it is the reverse.

For example, assume that someone denies that he is a debtor, and the creditor is unable to prove the debt in the court of law. If some property of the debtor comes into the creditor's possession, religion would entitle the creditor to take the equivalent of what is due to him without the debtor's permission. But if the matter is brought before the court, the creditor will not be allowed to take anything unless he proves the claim through legal methods. Consider a situation in which the creditor first waives the debt by giving it to the debtor as charity without actually informing the debtor of the decision, and then changes his mind and sues the debtor for the gift. In this case the creditor is entitled to receive payment judicially but not on religious grounds, as charity may not be revoked and the debtor does not owe the creditor anything in the eyes of God. The distinction here between religious and juridical obligations (*wajib dini* and *wajib qadai*) also signifies the difference between adjudication (*qada*) and a juristic opinion (*fatwa*). The judge (*qadi*) must adjudicate on the basis of apparent evidence and disregard the religious position of the dispute before him, whereas a *mufti* investigates both the apparent and the actual positions and both are reflected in the verdict. If there is a conflict between the two positions, the mufti pronounces his opinion on religious considerations, whereas the judge considers objective evidence only, regardless of the religious motives or personal disposition of the litigants. A pious individual in a court case is not to be treated differently from one of questionable piety or of no apparent dedication to religion.

The scholastic manifestation of this dual approach to rights and duties can also be seen in the different orientations of the legal schools with regard to externality and intent, and the question of the relative value that is attached to the manifest form as opposed to the essence of conduct. As previously noted, the Shafiis and Hanafis tend to stress the externality of conduct without exploring the intent behind it, whereas the Malikis and Hanbalis are inclined toward exploring the intent. These different approaches can be illustrated with reference to the intention behind a marriage contract. If a man marries a woman with the sole intention of sexual gratification followed by a quick divorce, the marriage is invalid according to the Malikis and Hanbalis but lawful according to the Hanafis and Shafiis. When the legal requirements of a valid marriage contract are objectively fulfilled, that is all that is necessary according to the Hanafis and Shafiis, whereas the Malikis and Hanbalis base their judgments on the underlying intent and maintain that evil and abuse should be obstructed whenever they become known.

A consequence of this attitudinal difference can also be seen in the approval or disapproval of legal stratagems (al-hiyal al-fiqhiyyah) in such cases as a catalyst marriage (tahlil) and usurious sale (inah). The former involves a man marrying a woman who has been divorced in order to allow her to remarry her first husband. This is a perversion of the requirement that there be a genuine intervening marriage before a divorced couple can remarry. In usurious sale, person A sells a piece of cloth to person B for $100, payable in one year, and then immediately buys the cloth back for $80, paid then and there. The difference is a disguised usury (riba), as it amounts to charging an interest of $20 for a loan of $80 for one year. In both examples, the acts are designed to circumvent the rules of Shariah by violating their intention. Malikis and Hanbalis reject such stratagems altogether, but the Hanafis and Shafiis have upheld them and recognize the legal consequences that flow from them. The Maliki jurist Abu Ishaq Ibrahim al-Shatibi (d. 1388) stated the Maliki position as follows: "Anyone who seeks to obtain from the rules of Shariah something which is contrary to its purpose has violated the Shariah and his actions are null and void."

The Hanbali scholar Ibn Qayyim al-Jawziyyah (1289–1349) held substantially the same position. Al-Shatibi added that the rulings of Shariah regarding what is permissible and prohibited generally consider both the acts and their underlying intention. The Maliki-Hanbali position is also upheld in a hadith-cum-legal maxim that declares, "Acts are judged by the intentions behind them." A Muslim therefore must not seek to legalize for himself or herself something that is prohibited even if he or she obtains a judicial decree to that effect. This conclusion is based on the hadith in which the Prophet adjudicated a case on the basis of apparent evidence, but then said:

> I am but a human being. When you bring a dispute to me, some of you may
> be more eloquent in stating your cases than others. I may consequently

According to Muslim law, a market supervisor, known in Arabic as *muhtasib*, is in charge of monitoring business transactions in the market. He was authorized, for example, to intervene and stop instances of cruelty to animals. Markets like this one in Kirman in central Iran were typically housed in vaulted structures that protected produce and people from the strong rays of the sun.

> adjudicate on the basis of what I hear. If I adjudicate in favor of someone something that belongs to his brother, let him not take it, for it would be like taking a piece of fire.

This hadith is premised in the binding force of judicial orders in that no one is at liberty to defy them on the basis merely of a moral argument. If a miscarriage of justice is due to false evidence, however, the person who wins the case because of the false evidence bears a moral responsibility not to insist on enforcement. The Shariah also contains provisions on expiations (*kaffarat*), which are self-inflicted punishments of a religious character that the courts are not authorized to enforce. If a person breaks a solemn oath, for example, he may expiate for it by giving charity sufficient to feed ten poor people or fasting for three days. Other expiations have been provided for in the Quran, but none are legally enforceable.

Morality and religion are thus closely interrelated. The Prophet declared in a hadith that "I have not been sent but to accomplish moral virtues." The moral overtones of the Shariah are clearly seen in its propensity toward duty (*taklif*), so much so that some commentators have characterized the Shariah as "a system of duties" as compared with statutory law, which often speaks of rights. The Shariah clearly recognizes both duty and right, but it is nevertheless indicative of the moral underpinnings of the Shariah that it speaks mainly of duty rather than right. The fact that the Shariah proscribes usury, wine drinking, and gambling, proclaims legal alms as one of its major duties, and encourages "lowering of the gaze" between members of the opposite sex, as well as declaring divorce as "the worst of all permissible things" all reflect the Shariah's moral outlook. This is also evident in the rules pertaining to war, in which the Shariah forbids maiming, injuring children, women, and the elderly, as well as damaging animals, crops, and buildings. The Prophet and the early caliphs condemned cruelty to animals and took to task those who caused hardship to animals and neglected their needs. Although these are not justiciable in the court of law, the market controller (*muhtasib*) is nevertheless authorized to intervene and to stop instances of cruelty to animals. The muhtasib, who became known in the Abbasid period (749–1258) as market controller, mainly in charge of price regulations, was initially the officer in charge of the moral and religious duties of Islam, including the *hisba* (that is, commanding good and forbidding evil). Some of the hisba functions—such as those relating to the observance of religious duties in the fasting month of Ramadan, attendance of Friday congregational prayer, and so on—were gradually abandoned or taken over by other government agencies.

This distinction between the Shariah's moral and legal precepts is also reflected in its scale of five values—obligatory, desirable, neutral, reprehensible, forbidden. Only the two extremes—the obligatory (*wajib*) and the forbidden (*haram*)—are legal categories. The remaining three categories, which cover a much larger area, are basically moral and not justiciable. A substantive distinction between the religious and legal aspects of conduct can be seen even within the two categories of obligatory and forbidden. Religious obligations, such as prayer, fasting, and the hajj, are classified as "pure right of God" (*haqq Allah*) and are normally not justiciable. They differ in that respect from those obligations that fall under the right of human beings (*haqq al-adami*), such as debt repayment or spousal support. These rights *can* be made the subject of a judicial order.

It is often said that Islamic law is immutable because it is divinely ordained. Yet, in its philosophy and outlook, divine law itself integrates a certain amount of adaptability and change. Some of the basic principles of the Shariah, such as justice, equality, public interest, consultation, enjoining good, and forbidding evil, are inherently dynamic. They are therefore immutable in principle, but they remain open to adaptation and adjustment on the level of implementation. The fundamentals of the faith and the practical pillars on which those fundamentals stand—the basic moral values of Islam and its clear injunctions—are on the whole permanent and unchangeable. But in many other areas of the law, the Shariah only provides general guidelines, the details of which may be adjusted and modified through the exercise of human reasoning.

The overriding objectives of Shariah are the promotion of human dignity, justice, and equality; the establishment of a consultative government; the realization of the lawful benefits of the people; the prevention of harm (*darar*); the removal of hardship (*haraj*); and the education of the individual by inculcating in him or her a sense of punctuality, self-discipline, and restraint. In their broad scope these objectives are permanent and unchangeable. When the Quran and the Sunna identify a certain objective to be of overriding importance, then all measures that can be taken toward its realization are automatically protected by the Shariah, provided that they are clear of distortion and abuse. In other words, the means toward attaining those ends are of as much value as the ends themselves. The ulama have attempted to classify the basic benefits (*masalih*) into the three broad

The basic objectives of the Shariah are conveyed in the Quran and the Sunna. They include establishing a consultative government. Many modern Muslim states have parliaments. The Kuwait Parliament building was designed by the Danish architect J. Utzon.

yet interrelated categories: essential interests (*daruriyyat*), complementary interests (*hajiyyat*), and desirabilities (*tahsiniyyat*). The contributions of the Maliki jurist al-Shatibi to these, and to the philosophy of Shariah in general, are particularly noted. Only the main categories of benefits are predictable in advance; their details are changeable according to the circumstances of time and place, however. They need therefore to be identified and pursued as and when they arise.

The means toward securing the Shariah's recognized objectives are flexible, as they are not specified in the sources and therefore remain open to considerations of public policy and justice. For example, vindicating the truth is an objective in its own right. Truth may be established by the testimony of upright witnesses or by other means as they become available, such as sound recording, photography, and laboratory analysis, which are perhaps even more reliable than verbal testimony. The Shariah only specifies the end that must be sought, but it leaves open the means by which the ends are achieved. Another example is the issue of female witnesses and the fiqh rule that the testimony of two females is equal to that of one male. This was the conclusion of the ulama of the past, whose reading of the Quranic text in light of the prevailing conditions of earlier times was generally accepted and perhaps also justified in the Quran. There is a reference in the Quran that validates the testimony of men and women, in that order, but the text does not preclude the testimony of female witnesses. The reading of the Quran should be goal-oriented and responsive to the realities of contemporary Muslim society. If the overriding objectives of the Quran, truth and justice, are now better served by admitting equally the testimony of female witnesses, especially when they might be the only witnesses available in a particular case, the judge would not hesitate to admit them; the rules of fiqh on this subject may also be adjusted in the future to that effect.

The Scope of Interpretation and Reasoning

There are two types of rules of Shariah that occur in the Quran and the Sunna: definitive (*qati*) and speculative (*zanni*). Definitive rules refer to injunctions that are self-evident and need no interpretation. Some of the injunctions of the Quran are conveyed in this form; they are definite and self-contained. There are also instances in which the Quran lays down a basic rule, which, however definitive, needs to be supplemented; in this case, the necessary details are often supplied by the Sunna. The definitive injunctions of the Quran and the Sunna constitute the common core of unity among the various legal schools and among Muslims in general. It is thanks mainly to definitive injunctions that the Shariah is often described as a diversity within unity: unity in essentials but diversity in details; unity on matters of belief, on what is permitted or prohibited, but diversity in values that fall below these categories. A legal text is classified as speculative when it is conveyed in a language that leaves room for interpretation and human endeavor.

Also in the Quran and the Sunna are instances in which a legal text may be definitive in some respects but speculative in others. For example, the Quran injunction "forbidden to you (in marriage) are your mothers and your daughters . . ." (4:23) conveys a definite meaning on the basic prohibition it contains, but questions arise about whether the word *daughters* includes, in addition to legitimate biological daughters, illegitimate daughters, stepdaughters, granddaughters, and foster daughters. And if so, are they all entitled to inheritance? Because *daughters* is a general word, it includes all of its possible meanings; this is the Hanafis' interpretation. But the majority of legal scholars maintain that this is conjectural and the application of all of its possible meanings is not a matter of certainty. Although the Hanafis conclude that *daughters* includes all daughters, the majority of legal scholars do not, for example, include illegitimate daughters in that meaning. There is a similar debate with regard to the ablution (*wudu*) for ritual prayer. This is necessary, as the Quran says, when one touches (*lamastum*) a member of the opposite sex (Quran 4:43). The precise meaning of the word—whether it means merely touching or sexual intercourse—is a matter of disagreement among the leading legal schools. The scope of such interpretations is not confined to words but extends to entire sentences and the meaning conveyed in a particular context. Even with regard to such basic prohibitions as murder and theft, questions arise as to the precise definition in the Quran. For example, does stealing from a deceased person or picking pockets fit the standard definition of theft? By far, the larger portion of the Quran's legal content is speculative in this sense, although the whole of the Quran is definitive in respect of authenticity.

The jurists have differed in their approach to interpretation. Although some schools like the Zahiris took a literalist approach to interpretation, the majority have included allegorical interpretation (*tawil*) in addition to interpretation proper (*tafsir*). They have validated interpretation based on personal opinion (*tafsir bil ray*) in addition to interpretation founded on valid precedent (*tafsir bil mathur*) in their understanding of the Quran and the Sunna. Whereas interpretation proper signifies interpretation based on the actual words of the text, allegorical interpretation includes the more remote interpretations, such as the implied and metaphorical meanings that fall beyond the confines of the text.

Because the Quran is characteristically devoted to broad guidelines and principles, its language is often versatile. Because of this versatility, "every scholar who has resorted to the Quran in search of solution to a problem," commented the jurist al-Shatibi in *Muwafaqat*, "has found in the Quran a principle that has provided him with some guidance on the issue." Al-Shatibi also observed that the specific rulings of the Quran are often related to a better understanding of its general principles. For example, the following proclamations in the Quran lay down basic values rather than specific rules and procedures: "God permitted sale and prohibited usury" (Quran 2:275); "God does not intend to impose hardship upon people" (Quran 5:6); the charge to believers to "cooperate in pursuit of good works and piety and cooperate not in hostility and sin" (Quran 5:2); another charge to believers to "obey God and obey the Messenger and those who are in charge of affairs" (Quran 4:59), or the preceding text in the same chapter (Quran 4:58), addressing believers to "render the trust *al-amanat* to whom that they belong and when you judge among people, you judge with justice"; and the proclamation regarding punishment "and the recompense of evil is an evil equivalent to it, but one who forgives and makes reconciliation, his reward is with God" (Quran 42:40). (*Amanat* here include a variety of public functions—a witness in court, a judge, the guardian of a minor, or a holder of public office—and also an object that is borrowed on trust. Because a reference to justice immediately follows in the verse, justice is understood to be one of the most important amanat.) In each case, the text is concerned with laying down a basic norm and a general principle, which may well relate to new developments and be given a fresh interpretation in light of unprecedented issues. This is evident in the following commands and statements: to "consult them [the community] in their affairs" (Quran 3:159), to "fulfill your contracts" (Quran 5:1), to "devour not each other's property in vain, unless it be through lawful trade by your mutual consent" (Quran 4:29), and the statements that everyone is responsible for his own conduct and "no soul shall be burdened with the burden of another" (Quran 6:164), the statement that "God commands justice and fairness" (Quran 16:90), the statement that "one who is compelled without intending to violate or revolt is not to be blamed" (Quran 2:173), and so forth.

Ratiocination (exact reasoning) is a step beyond interpretation in that interpretation is confined to the words and sentences of the text, while ratiocination looks into the text's rationale and purpose. When the Quranic legislation is compared with modern statutes, it is notable that the textual rulings of the Quran are not confined to a series of commands and prohibitions; rather, they are an appeal to the reason and conscience of its audience. The Quran on numerous instances expounds the rationale, cause, objective, and purpose of its rulings, the benefit or reward that accrues from conformity to its guidance or the harm and punishment that may follow from defying it. This aspect of the Quran, known as *talil* (rational analysis), is also manifested in the affirmative stance that the Quran takes to the exercise of reason and in the frequent references that it makes to those who think, who inquire into the world around them and investigate, those who possess knowledge and draw rational conclusions from their observations. Rational analysis is an essential component of analogical reasoning in that analogy cannot be constructed, as previously noted, without the identification of an effective cause that is in common between the original case and the new case. Rational analysis is not valid with regard to devotional matters, but outside this sphere the Shariah encourages investigation and inquiry into its rules. Ratiocination in the Quran means that the laws of the Quran are not imposed for the sake of mere conformity to rules, but that they aim at the realization of certain benefits and objectives. When the effective cause, rationale, and objective of an injunction are properly ascertained, they serve as basic indicators of the continued validity of that injunction. Thus when a ruling of the Shariah outside the sphere of worship no longer serves its original intention and purpose, it is the proper role of the scholar to substitute a suitable alternative.

In the precedent of the Companions of the Prophet, instances can be found in which some of the rulings of the Quran and the Sunna were suspended or replaced because they no longer served the purpose for which they were initially introduced. Thus the second caliph, Umar ibn al-Khattab, suspended the share of the *muallafah al-qulub* (friends of the faith) in the tax revenues of *zakah*. These friends were people of influence, not necessarily devout Muslims, whose cooperation was important for the victory of Islam. The Quran (9:60) had assigned a share for them, which the caliph discontinued on the ground that "God has exalted Islam and it is no longer in need of their support." The caliph thus departed, on purely rational grounds, from the letter of the Quran in favor of its general purpose, and his ruling is generally held to be in harmony with the spirit of the text. Also noted in the hadith is a case in which the Prophet declared a request by some Companions, made at a time of price hikes in commodities, to introduce price control in the Medinan market on the ground that this might amount to an unfair imposition on the traders. But changed circumstances some sixty years later prompted the Medinan ulama to validate price control, coming to the opposite conclusion based on the same concerns the Prophet had expressed—to prevent unfair trading and abuse—although this time the harm was likely to affect the community as a whole. According to another report, the Prophet's widow Aishah reversed the ruling of the hadith that had allowed women to attend the mosque for congregational prayers, stating that owing to the spread of corruption, the Prophet would have done the same were he alive. Because of changing conditions in modern times, the prevailing custom permits women's participation in almost all walks of life, and it would not make sense now if the mosque were to be the only place where women could not go. The specific cause and argument may vary in each case, but the basic rationale in these examples is the concern that the people benefit and the aversion to irrational conformity to rules that is at the root of the idea of talil. Rational analysis is therefore indispensable to the notion of independent reasoning. Only the Zahiris opposed it, but the majority of jurists upheld it on the analysis that a mechani-

According to one report, the Prophet's widow Aishah reversed the practice that had allowed women to attend the mosque for congregational prayer. In many places, including this mosque in Regent's Park, London, women still pray in a separate area.

cal reading of the Quran, oblivious of public welfare and driven only by considerations of conformity and imitation, should be avoided.

Graduality and Pragmatism: Shariah-Oriented Policy

Islamic law favors a gradual approach to social reform to avoid hardship that may be caused by confrontation with the existing reality and customs. This is illustrated by the fact that the Quran was revealed over a period of twenty-three years, and much of it was revealed in relation to actual events. The Meccan portion of the Quran was devoted mainly to moral teaching and instruction in the new religion, and it contained little legislation. Legislation in social affairs is almost entirely a Medinan phenomenon. Even in Medina, some of the Quran's laws were revealed in stages. The final ban on drinking wine, for instance, was preceded by two separate declarations—one merely referred to the adverse effects of intoxi-

The rules governing the dress appropriate for women vary according to different interpretations of the Shariah by the various schools of law. In the Islamic Republic of Iran, for example, women must cover their entire bodies except their faces, and many women there wear a *chador* or full veil.

cation and the other proscribed drinking during ritual prayer. Both measures pre-pared the ground for the final step that banned drinking altogether. This man-ner of legislation can also be seen in reference to the five daily prayers, which were initially fixed at two and later were raised to five, and the legal alms, which was initially an optional charity and became obligatory after the Prophet's migra-tion to Medina; fasting was also optional at first and was later made into a reli-gious duty. Some of the Quran's earlier rulings were subsequently abrogated and replaced in light of new circumstances that the community experienced.

Islamic law therefore advocates realistic reform, but it does not favor abrupt revolutionary change. This is conveyed in the response, for example, that the Umayyad caliph Umar ibn Abd al-Aziz (682 or 683–720) gave to his ambitious son Abd al-Malik, who suggested to his father that God had granted him the power to decisively fight corruption in society once and for all. The caliph advised his son against such a course, saying that Almighty God Himself denounced wine drinking twice before he banned it. The caliph said: "If I take sweeping action even in the right cause and inflict it on people all at once, I fear revolt and the possibility that they may also reject it all at once." Commenting on this, Yusuf al-Qaradawi wrote: "This is a correct understanding of Islam, the kind of understanding that is implied in the very meaning of fiqh and would be unquestionably upheld by it."

The pragmatism of the Shariah is also manifested in the frequent concessions it makes concerning those who face hardship—for instance, difficulties the sick, the elderly, pregnant women, and travelers might find in daily prayers and fast-ing. It also makes provisions for extraordinary and emergency situations in which the rules of Shariah may be temporarily suspended on grounds of neces-sity. Thus, according to a legal maxim, the verdict of the mufti must take into consideration the change of time and circumstances. For instance, people were not allowed in the early days of Islam to charge a fee for teaching the Quran, as this was considered an act of spiritual merit. But when people did not volunteer and the teaching of the Quran suffered a decline, the jurists consequently issued a verdict that reversed the position and allowed teachers to be paid. Another example is the pragmatic verdict of Imam Malik that permitted the pledging of allegiance (bayah) to the lesser qualified of two candidates for leadership, if that were deemed to be in the public interest. The normal rule required, of course, that allegiance should only be given to the best qualified candidate. Similarly, normal rules require that a judge must be a qualified jurist and scholar, but a per-son of lesser qualification may be appointed should there be a shortage of qual-ified people for judicial posts. This also applies to a witness, who must be an honest person. If, however, the only witness in a case is a less-than-honest per-son the judge may admit the witness and adjudicate the case if this is the only reasonable alternative available. Finally, the Prophet's widow, Aishah, reported that "the Prophet did not choose but the easier of two alternatives, so long as it did not amount to a sin." Thus the judge, jurist, and ruler are advised not to opt for more onerous decisions if easier options could be equally justified.

In its broad scope, Shariah-oriented public policy (*siyasah shariyyah*) authorizes government leaders to conduct government affairs in harmony with the spirit and purpose of the Shariah, even at the expense of a temporary departure from its specific rules. The two most important objectives of this policy are the realization of social benefit and the prevention of evil. Shariah-oriented policy is an instrument of good government, and it applies both within and outside the parameters of the established Shariah, although some ulama have held that there is no policy outside the Shariah itself. According to the Hanbali scholar Ibn Qayyim al-Jawziyyah in *Al-Turuq al-Hukmiyyah* (Methods of Judgment):

> *Siyasah shariyyah* includes all measures which bring the people closer to beneficence and furthest away from corruption, even if it has not been approved by the Prophet (peace be upon him) nor regulated by divine revelation. Anyone who says that there is no *siyasah shariyyah* where the Shariah itself is silent is wrong. . . .

Any measures taken by a lawful ruler that in his judgment secure a benefit or repel a mischief fall within the ambit of siyasah. The scope of public policy (*siyasah*) is therefore exceedingly wide, as it encompasses matters of concern not only to law but also to economic development, administration, and politics. The Quranic authority for siyasah is found in its principle of enjoining good and forbidding evil, which is enunciated in several places in the Quran. There are also numerous instances of siyasah in the Sunna of the Prophet and in the precedent of the pious caliphs (the four caliphs who ruled during the forty years immediately after the Prophet's death). Siyasah thus enables government leaders and judges to be effective in responding to circumstances, both under normal conditions and in emergency situations. Ibn Qayyim thus observed that whoever sets free the accused for want of witnesses after he takes an oath swearing his innocence, even though he has the reputation for corruption and robberies, verily acts contrary to siyasah. Conversely, it would be contrary to siyasah for a judge to treat a first offender with the same degree of severity as a recidivist who has an established record of criminality and violence.

Shariah-oriented policy may operate in any of the following four ways: First, it can restrict what is permissible in order to secure a benefit or to prevent harm. An example of this is the caliph Umar ibn al-Khattab's decision to ask the people not to consume meat on two consecutive days in a week at a time when meat was in short supply in Medina. Other examples might be to specify a maximum acreage for certain agricultural crops or to restrict imports of certain items in order to protect national industries.

Second, it can legislate both within and outside the Shariah-regulated areas. This is an extensive field in which policy can be used to great advantage, not only in the sense of administering the existing Shariah but also in initiating new law in other areas. Legislation may be introduced to implement the Quranic injunctions on consultation, equality, and justice—subjects on which basic guidelines are found in the Quran but that must be adequately regulated in light of prevailing conditions. The ruler may also initiate new legislation. An example of this is the precedent set by the caliph Umar, who was once making one of his night tours of Medina when he heard the persistent cries of a child. He alerted the child's mother but later he heard that the infant was still crying. Upon further inquiry, it turned out that the woman had weaned the child too early, because the caliph had allowed only children who had been weaned to obtain welfare assistance. Consequently, the caliph issued orders that entitled children of all ages to welfare assistance.

Third, there is the possibility of selecting one of several available solutions. Should there be several juristic views on a certain issue, the ruler may select one that he considers to be most suitable. When he does so, his ruling becomes the authoritative ruling of the Shariah to the exclusion of all other interpretations. This is the subject of a legal maxim that reads: "The command of the imam puts an end to disagreement."

And finally, in the area of penal law, applying the deterrent punishment (tazir), which is an instrument of siyasah, enables the judge to exercise flexibility in selecting both the type and the quantity of punishment that might seem suitable in a case before him. This punishment may vary from a mere verbal admonition to corporal punishment to imprisonment and fines. It may be ordered only by competent authorities and only as a result of conduct that amounts to a violation. In other words, the judge may not create the offense and may only penalize what is a violation under Shariah in the first place.

The Community Versus the Individual

Many commentators have held the view that the divine Shariah does not relate to the concerns of society in the way that human-made laws are expected to do. Instead of taking its origin from the needs and aspirations of society, Islamic law expects the society to conform with its mandate. In this view, Islamic law is shown to be nonparticipatory and authoritarian. But attention must be given to a different side of this picture: Islamic legal theory also incorporates general consensus (ijma), considerations of public interest (istislah), and social custom (urf) among the recognized sources of Shariah. Consensus is particularly important because it is the binding source that ranks in authority next to the Quran and the Sunna. Furthermore, the Quran proclaims consultation as a principle of government and a method that must be applied in the administration of public affairs. Islamic legal theory thus recognizes a number of nonrevealed sources that are eminently participatory and founded in social need and consensus. From this perspective, Islamic law responds positively to the prospect of legislation on rationalist and utilitarian grounds that accommodate social change.

The populist base of Islamic law is strong enough to persuade many Muslim commentators to embrace the minority view that sovereignty in an Islamic state belongs to the Muslim community (ummah). This is because in the constitutional theory of the Shariah, the head of state acts in his capacity as the representative (wakil) of the people, and he may be deposed by the people in the event of a flagrant violation of the Shariah. Legal theory recognizes general consensus as a binding source of law, and the government is also bound by the Quranic mandate to consult the community in public affairs. The conclusion is that the Muslim community is the repository of what is known as executive sovereignty. The majority view, however, is that sovereignty in the Islamic state

Muslim law extends into many areas of finance and banking. Muslims are obliged to pay alms and are forbidden to practice usury. Islamic banks, as in this example from Doha, in Qatar, combine modern finance with the requirements of Muslim law.

belongs exclusively to God, whose will and command, which is the Shariah, binds the community and state. The dignified status of the community finds support in its Quranic designation as the vicegerent of God in the earth (Quran 22:31) and the declaration that God has subjugated the earth and the entire created universe for the benefit of human beings (Quran 45:12).

Public interest is not only recognized as a source of law, but Islamic law further requires that governmental affairs must be conducted in accordance with public interest. This is the subject of a legal maxim that declares: "The affairs of the imam are determined by reference to public interest." According to another legal maxim, instances of conflict between public and private interests must be determined in favor of public interests. Public interest is thus the criterion by which the success or failure of government is measured from the perspective of the Shariah.

Furthermore, the Quran and the Sunna are emphatic on solidarity with the vast majority of the community of believers (jamaa). In a number of places the Quran simultaneously praises and defines the Muslim community as "a mid-most nation" (2:143), a nation of moderation that is averse to extremism; "it enjoins good and forbids evil" (3:109); a community that is committed to the truth and administers justice on its basis (7:181); a community that advocates unity and shuns separation (3:102 and 21:92); and a community that in its advocacy of truth is a witness unto itself and over mankind (16:89 and 2:143). The jurists have consequently formulated the doctrine of the infallibility of the collective will of the community, which is the doctrinal basis of consensus. Although consensus consists of the agreement of the jurists, they must act in the capacity of the representatives of the community. Representation as such does not change the original locus of authority, which still remains the Muslim community. The Sunna is also emphatic on solidarity with the community, which is the subject of numerous hadiths, including the following: "Whoever separates himself from the community and dies, dies the death of ignorance [jahiliyyah]"; and "Whoever boycotts the community and separates himself from it by the measure of a span is severing his bond with Islam."

Notwithstanding the concern of the Shariah for social well-being, the Shariah is also inherently individualist. Religion is a matter primarily of individual conscience. As religious law, the Shariah exhibits the same tendency. The individualist orientation of the Shariah is manifested in a variety of ways, including the fact, for instance, that the rules of Shariah are addressed directly to the legally competent individual. The Shariah's focus on the individual was evidently strong enough to persuade the Kharijites (literally, "outsiders"), who boycotted the community in the early decades of Islam, and the Mutazilite followers of Abu Bakr al-Asamm in the late eighth-century emigration to embrace the minority view that forming a government was not a religious obligation. For the Shariah addresses the individual directly; if every individual complied with the Shariah, justice and peace would prevail even without a government. These and similar views were expressed within a context that assumed basic harmony between the interests of the individual and those of the community. This is a corollary of the Quranic doctrine of monotheism (tawhid), that is, the oneness of being that encourages unity and integration in Islamic thought and institutions and discourages duality and conflict: God created the universe and every part of it is reflective of the unity of its source and consequently synchronized with every other part. Religion is inseparable from politics, morality, and economics, just as the human personality cannot be compartmentalized into religious, political, and economic segments.

Broadly speaking, Islam pursues its social objectives through reforming the individual. The ritual ablution before prayer, the five daily prayers, fasting during the month of Ramadan, and the obligatory giving of charity all encourage punctuality, self-discipline, and concern for the well-being of others. The individual is also seen not just as a member of the community and subservient to the community's will, but also as a morally autonomous agent who plays a distinctive role in shaping the community's sense of direction and purpose. This can be seen, for example, in the conditions that the Quran and the Sunna have attached to the individual's duty of obedience to the government, and the right the individual is simultaneously granted to dispute with the rulers over government affairs (Quran 4:59). The individual obeys the ruler on the condition that the ruler obeys the Shariah. This is reflected in the declaration of the hadith that "there is no obedience in transgression; obedience is only in righteousness." The citizen is thus entitled to disobey an oppressive command that is contrary to the Shariah. The hadiths convey a general ruling that applies to all contexts, military or otherwise. But the general ruling of the Quran and the Sunna, according to the majority (excluding the Hanafi school), is speculative and may be specified or qualified on rational grounds. Other hadiths substantiate the moral autonomy of the individual. One of these instructs the believers to "tell the truth even if it be unpleasant"; the other declares that "the best form of jihad [holy struggle] is to tell a word of truth to an oppressive ruler." Because these hadiths are also conveyed in general terms, their messages are not confined to moral teaching; rather, they may be adopted into legal rules.

The dignity of the human being is a central concern of Islamic law. This is the clear message of many of God's proclamations in the Quran: "We have bestowed dignity on the progeny of Adam" (17:70), "We created humans in the best of forms" (95:17), and in the affirmation that "I breathed into Adam of My spirit" (38:71) and "endowed him with a spiritual rank above that of the angels" (2:30 and 17:70). The five essential values of Shariah, on which the ulama are in agreement—faith, life, intellect, property, and lineage—are premised on the dignity of the human being, which must be protected as a matter of priority. Although the basic interests of the community and those of the individual may be said to coincide within the structure of these values, the focus is nevertheless on the individual.

The Quranic principle of enjoining good and forbidding evil is supportive of the moral autonomy of the individual. This principle authorizes the individual to act according to his or her best judgment in situations in which his or her intervention would advance a good purpose. The individualist moorings of this principle can be seen in a hadith that addresses the believers in the following manner: "If any of you sees an evil, let him change it by his hand, and if he is unable to do that, let him change it by his words, and if he is still unable to do that, then let him denounce it in his heart, but this is the weakest form of belief." This principle assigns to the individual an active role in the community in which he or she lives. It also validates in principle the citizen's power of arrest, but it is only on grounds of caution that the police have been made the exclusive repository of this power. The jurists have dealt with the details of this concept at length. Suffice it to say that a person must act out of conviction when he believes that the initiative taken is likely to achieve the desired result. He is advised not to do anything if he is convinced that his intervention, however well intended, might cause a harm equal to or greater than the one he is trying to avert.

Another Quranic principle that supports moral autonomy of the individual is that of sincere advice (nasihah), which entitles everyone to advise and to alert a fellow citizen, including the head of state and his officials, to what she considers to be of benefit or to what may rectify an error on her part. The main difference between the principle of enjoining good and forbidding evil and that of sincere advice is that the former is concerned with events that are actually witnessed at the time they occur, but the latter is not confined to the actual moment of direct observation. Therefore it is more flexible. The broad scope of sincere advice is clearly depicted in a hadith in which the Prophet declared that "religion is good advice." Religion, in other words, is meant to be the agent of benefit and a reminder to good. These individualist leanings of the Shariah are also evident from the familiar tone of the Quranic address to the believers to "take care of your own selves. If you are righteous, the misguided will not succeed in trying to lead you astray . . ." (Quran 5:105). Within the context of matrimony, for example, the Shariah opts for the separation of property, and the wife's right to manage her own financial affairs remains unaffected by her marriage. Once again, although Islam encourages the call to religion (dawa), it proclaims nevertheless that "there shall be no compulsion in religion" (Quran 2:256). For example, a husband is required to respect the individuality of his non-Muslim wife; he is therefore not allowed to press her into embracing Islam.

The individualist propensities of Islamic law can also be seen in the history of its development. For instance, Islamic law is often characterized as the jurists' law, developed mainly by private jurists who made their contributions primarily as pious individuals rather than as government functionaries and leaders. This aspect of Islam's legal history is also seen as a stabilizing factor in that it was not particularly dependent on government participation and support. Governments came and went but the Shariah remained as the common law of the Muslims.

Another dimension of Islam's individualist propensities is that relations between governments and the ulama remained generally less than amicable ever since the early years of the Umayyad rule (661-750). The secularist tendencies of the Umayyad rulers marked the end of the "Righteous Caliphate"; the ulama became increasingly critical of this change of direction in the system of government. The ulama retained their independence by turning to prominent individuals among them, which led eventually to the formation of the schools of law that bore the names of their founders (Hanafi, Maliki, and so on). One of the consequences of this pattern of development was that Islamic law made few concessions to the government. The immunities against prosecution, for example, which are enjoyed to this day by the monarch, the head of state, state assemblies, and diplomats in other legal systems, are totally absent in Islamic law. No one can claim any immunity for his or her conduct merely on account of social and official status. Trial procedures in the courts of Shariah consequently did not permit the judge to treat the head of state, if he were involved in a dispute, any differently than other citizens. There have been many instances of this in legal history.

The schools of law functioned as guilds and professional associations in which outstanding contributions found recognition and support, even if they went against official policy. The two most important principles of Islamic law—personal reasoning (ijtihad) and general consensus (ijma)—can be conducted by jurists without depending on the participation of the government in power. These two principles manifested the nearest equivalent of parliamentary legislation in modern times. Personal reasoning has almost always been practiced by individual jurists. General consensus is broadly described as the unanimous consensus of the qualified scholars (mujtahidun) of the Muslim community on the ruling of a particular issue. As such, consensus can be initiated by individual jurists, concluded, and made binding on the government even without the latter's participation. Neither ijtihad nor ijma were institutionalized and have remained uninstitutionalized to this day. The jurist who carries out independent reasoning in theory enjoys complete independence from government and is only expected to act on the substantive merit of each case in line with the correct procedure of ijtihad. It is not surprising therefore to see that commentators have described Islamic law and its main advocates, the ulama, as champions of the rights of the individual and bulwarks against arbitrary exercise of official power.

Consolidation, Reform, and the Current Status of Islamic Law

Poor access to Islamic law has been one of the problems that has hampered efforts toward the revival of rational and independent reasoning. The bulk of scholastic Islamic law is contained in voluminous works of medieval origin in Arabic, which are poorly classified and difficult to use; this scholarship tends toward scholastic exclusivism and isolation. The 1876 Ottoman work entitled *Mejelle* was an attempt by the Turkish government and the ulama to codify the Hanafi law of civil transactions. It contains 1,851 articles that primarily address contracts and transactions, evidence and court procedures, but it excludes family law. It was followed in 1917 by the promulgation in Turkey of the Law of Family Rights. This law used Hanafi fiqh as well as that of the other three legal schools more widely than the *Mejelle*. Although Turkey itself abandoned these laws, the works remained influential nevertheless. The 1929 Egyptian Law of Personal Status drew not only from the justice legacy of the four leading schools but also from the opinions of individual jurists, when these issues were deemed to be conducive to public interest. The 1953 Syrian Law of Personal Status was another step in the direction of attempting independent reasoning through the modality of statutory legislation. This neo-ijtihadi approach to legislation was followed by similar attempts in Morocco, Tunisia, Iraq, and Pakistan, where statutory reforms were introduced in the traditionally Shariah-dominated laws of marriage, polygyny, and divorce.

The Islamic Law Conference that was held in Paris in 1951 called for the compilation of a comprehensive encyclopedia of fiqh, and several projects were undertaken toward that end. The University of Damascus began a project in 1956, and the governments of Egypt and Kuwait started their own projects in 1951 and 1971, respectively. The Egyptian and Kuwaiti encyclopedias, both bearing the title *al-Mawsua al-Fiqhiyya*, have each exceeded thirty volumes. The Kuwaiti edition is soon to be completed, but its Egyptian counterpart is far from ready. These and other compilation projects have shown latitude by treating the major schools of fiqh strictly on the merit of their contributions. The information compiled is relatively free of sectarian bias. Yet by the very terms of their reference, the encyclopedic collections were designed to consolidate rather than to reform existing Islamic law. Undoubtedly they provide valuable resources, but they consist basically of an uncritical description of the scholastic heritage of fiqh.

The need was then felt to supplement and enrich the scope of these endeavors by establishing a forum to facilitate collective interpretation on new issues. A project was undertaken by the Organization of Islamic Conference, which led to the formation of the Fiqh Academy in Jidda, Saudi Arabia, in 1981 and another Fiqh Academy in Mecca by the Muslim League. India and Pakistan have each established fiqh and Shariah academies of their own. There are also a number of international institutes and organizations that undertake specialized research in Islamic legal themes. An even earlier attempt along these lines was made by al-Azhar University in Cairo, which set up the Islamic Research Academy in 1961.

Following that, King Abdul Aziz University in Jidda established its International Center for Islamic Economic Research in 1977. The International Islamic University of Malaysia and that of Islamabad started operations in the early 1980s and both institutions are currently building a stronger and more balanced infrastructure for specialized research efforts in Islamic law.

Islamic law relates to society more effectively in some areas than others. In the areas of matrimonial law and inheritance, the Shariah has remained in force with revisions and has been adopted by statutory legislation in almost every Muslim country. Saudi Arabia and Afghanistan have generally retained the Shariah. In most other areas, however, the Shariah has been marginalized for many reasons. Some of the earlier distortions, such as the closing of the door of ijtihad and the ensuing prevalence of the imitative tradition of taqlid, were exacerbated by persistent alienation between the ulama and government. This was condoned and reinforced by the subsequent domination of Western colonialism and the ascendant secularity that came with it. Western law dominated almost every aspect of the law, from constitutional to commercial law, to civil litigation, criminal procedure, and evidence. The abolition of Shariah courts in Egypt in the late nineteenth century was followed by similar developments in other countries and the prevalence of national courts that often combined elements of both Western and Shariah laws. This pattern is currently prevalent in most Muslim countries, although some countries, such as Malaysia, operate a dual system of national and Shariah courts, each having separate jurisdictions. In recent decades many Muslim countries have attempted to revive the Shariah on a selective basis and in varying degrees. Only Iran has adopted it generally. Measures have also been taken in Middle Eastern countries, Pakistan, Sudan, Egypt, and elsewhere to confirm that their constitutions and laws of court procedure, property, and evidence are acceptable to the Shariah. The latest development in Malaysia was the government's announcement in early 1997 that they would raise the status of the Shariah courts, to bring them up to that of the civil courts. Islamic laws of transactions have also seen a concerted revivalist effort in the wake of successful experiments in Islamic banking. Considerable interest is also taken by Islamic institutions of higher learning in the Islamization of disciplines, with a view to harmonizing the teaching of social sciences and humanities with Islamic values and outlook.

These efforts continue, but they have not been devoid of difficulties because of political upheavals and unrest that have been a feature of the Islamic resurgence movement in recent decades. Governments in Muslim lands are apprehensive of these movements and the prospect of the ulama and Islamist ascendancy to power. The Algerian experience in the mid-1990s, which has involved violent confrontation between the religious strata and government, and the collapse in June 1997 of the Islamist government in Turkey are cases in point. Iran's example of Islamic revolution evidently has not been followed in other Muslim countries. To a large extent, this revolution has remained a significant but nonetheless exceptional development.

The individualist propensities of the Islamic legal theory have already been discussed in this chapter. The question now is whether the contemporary Muslim community has inherited a legacy that is often at odds with their prevailing political reality and experience. Perhaps Islamic legal thought has traveled too far in its individualist, even antigovernment, orientation to offer easy options in an era in which the nation-state and its legal machinery have become increasingly collectivist and representative. Unless reformist measures are introduced to make independent reasoning a concern of the legislative assembly and parliament, its practice by the private jurist is no longer a realistic alternative. Regarding the principle of consensus, it basically envisioned the agreement of private jurists who are relatively uninvolved in state affairs. As such, the main issue is also one of institutionalization and the prospect of making it a part of the normal function of the state machinery, measures that

The community of believers is exemplified by the gathering of Muslims for communal prayer in the congregational mosque at noon on Fridays and for major religious holidays.

have been suggested more than half a century ago but that have remained unfulfilled. The secularist orientations of the nation-state in present-day Muslim countries are not particularly conducive to the revival of consensus and independent reasoning as the principal modes of statutory legislation. But even so, a basic change of direction appears to have taken place, as there is now greater awareness of Islamic values. Furthermore, the pressure of public opinion in countries with majority Muslim populations is likely to influence government policy in making the Shariah a reality of Muslim life. The era of revolution seems to be waning, and it is increasingly giving way to selective and gradual restoration of the Shariah through the recognized channels of legal reform.

CHAPTER FOUR

Science, Medicine, and Technology

THE MAKING OF A SCIENTIFIC CULTURE

Ahmad Dallal

Science was an extensive cultural undertaking that occupied the minds and energies of many of the leading intellectuals in medieval Muslim societies. Indeed, science was practiced on a scale unprecedented in earlier or contemporary human history. In urban centers from the Atlantic to the borders of China, thousands of scientists pursued careers in diverse scientific disciplines. Countless artifacts, ranging from architectural monuments to intricate automata and instruments provide a vivid testimony to the scientific and technological achievements of these scientists. Their written contributions are equally compelling: thousands of scientific manuscripts, from various regions of the medieval Islamic world, are scattered in modern libraries all over the globe. Considerable resources were also devoted for the support of scientific activity in Muslim societies. Until the rise of modern science, no other civilization engaged as many scientists, produced as many scientific books, or provided as varied and sustained support for scientific activity.

The study of the history of Islamic science is itself an extensive endeavor: it calls for an examination of wide-ranging cultural activities, in a vast geographical area, under different historical conditions, and for a period of at least seven centuries. The sources for the study of this subject are equally daunting, even when only written evidence is examined. Historians of Islamic science are fortunate to have a large number of extant scientific manuscripts that promise to shed light on its history. This abundance gives rise to a number of methodological difficulties, however. Earlier

(Left) Astronomy, one of the oldest and most esteemed exact sciences in antiquity, flourished in the Islamic lands from the ninth century, when major Greek astronomical texts were translated into Arabic. Many astronomers served the court, as in this depiction of the observatory established by the Ottomans in 1575 at Istanbul.

surveys of the history of Islamic science were based on a handful of random studies of scientific treatises. Some of the actual studies were of a high quality; yet ironically, the paucity of hard evidence available to early scholars often enabled them to cover all the fields of science in all-inclusive and often reductive narratives. In the past few decades many more scientific treatises have been critically examined, with the dual effect of providing detailed information about the various scientific disciplines and highlighting the peculiarity of the history of each separate discipline or even fields within disciplines.

The Cultural Context of Early Muslim Science

Despite the significant increase in studies of Islamic science, the vast majority of scientific manuscripts remain unexamined. Consider the example of al-Biruni (973–1048), one of the greatest Muslim scientists of all time. Al-Biruni wrote more than 150 works, of which only a third are extant. Although he is the most studied of all Muslim scientists, about half of his works have yet to be edited or to receive thorough analysis. Other scientists are less fortunate, and many are known only by name. This shortcoming notwithstanding, the recent accumulation of studies has enabled several historians of Islamic science to provide more informed and differentiated accounts of the scientific disciplines. Drawing on these historical overviews, this chapter provides an account of the scope and cultural significance of scientific activity in Islamic societies, and of the main trends in the development of specific scientific disciplines.

Like most histories of science, this chapter traces scientific developments under a succession of famous scientists. The focus on individuals may give the misleading impression of a linear course of forward progress that connects the various individuals under examination. The advance of science, however, is seldom orderly or predictable: new theories often coexist with old ones for long periods of time before they succeed in replacing the old theories; the importance of a new idea may sometimes go unnoticed for decades or even centuries before it is revived and adopted; and scientific progress in general seems to occur in leaps rather than in a smooth forward flow. It would be more misleading to suggest that the scientific developments in Islamic societies were isolated occurrences, however, or to attribute such advances simply to the personal genius of individual scientists. For every celebrated scientist known to have conducted rigorous research in any field, there are many more practitioners who—although they may not have made significant advances in their fields—provided the context without which such advances would have been impossible. Therefore, it is essential to recognize the existence of a scientific culture that enabled seemingly disjointed leaps from one invention to another, and of communities of scientists that provided temporal and spatial continuity for the culture of science.

Recent research has provided compelling evidence for the continuity and coherence of Arabic scientific traditions. Examples can be found in the tradition of reforming Ptolemaic astronomy that started in the eleventh century and continued until at least the sixteenth, and that spanned most of the Islamic world. Similarly, research on the various disciplines of Arabic mathematics has revealed that for each instance of seemingly isolated scientific breakthrough, there are in fact precedents and successors as well as a community of interested scholars and intellectuals. Almost invariably, original contributions emerge from and enhance a large body of methodical research generated within different traditions. In some cases certain scientists may have been accorded a privileged position simply because they were accidentally discovered by modern scholars, or because their works happened to be translated into European languages. Moreover, certain works may not be impressive when considered in isolation, while their real significance lies in triggering new trends of research or in laying the foundation for future developments within a particular discipline. Such is the importance of al-Khwarizmi's (ca. 780–850) *Kitab al-Jabr wal-Muqabala* (The book of compulsion and comparison), which introduced the term *al-jabr* (algebra). Despite its lack of sophistication in comparison to later works of Arabic algebra, this treatise was the indispensable prerequisite for advanced future research in the field.

The cultural coherence of scientific traditions is not merely a factor of their own internal workings. Science flourished in the heart of Islamic urban centers, not only as an integral part of Islamic civilization but also as one of its social institutions. In this sense it would be accurate to call this science "Islamic science." Although Islam played a role in defining the position and role of science in society, it did not define the cognitive content of the sciences. Religious discourses on science advocated its separateness from religion. As a result, a concept of value-free or ethically neutral scientific knowledge that is not specific to any one particular culture was able to develop. In distinction from religious knowledge, the exact sciences were often called "the sciences shared among all the nations." In his masterly work, the *Muqaddima* (Introduction [to the science of history]), the Arab historian Ibn Khaldun (1332–1406) eloquently summed up this universal conception of science:

> The intellectual sciences are natural to man, inasmuch as he is a thinking being. They are not restricted to any particular religious group. They are studied by the people of all religious groups who are all equally qualified to learn them and to do research in them. They have existed (and been known) to the human species since civilization had its beginnings in the world.

This ideal of cultural neutrality was greatly enhanced by the use of Arabic as the language of a new universal scientific culture. Science in Islamic societies was international; it inherited all the earlier scientific traditions and fused them into one new whole. The large geographic area under Islamic rule during this period enjoyed a high degree of cultural unity. Within this area, scientists from diverse ethnic and religious backgrounds participated in the production, exchange, and dissemination of scientific knowledge. The most important factor contributing to the universality of this Islamic scientific culture was the emergence of Arabic as the universal language of communication, not only for the elites but for all peoples within the Islamic empire. Most important, this enabled a level of scientific exchange unprecedented in earlier civilizations.

Many of the scientists who wrote in Arabic were not themselves Arabs. In later periods a few scientists wrote some of their scientific works in their national languages, most notably Persian. In such cases, these scientists also often produced Arabic translations of their works. Still, the vast majority of scientific works produced in the period between the ninth and sixteenth centuries were written in Arabic. Because of the preponderance of Arabic scientific works, and because of the crucial role played by the Arabic language in the subsequent development of the scientific tradition, it is perhaps more accurate to call the scientific traditions of Islamic societies "Arabic sciences" rather than Islamic. In fact, the first main cultural transformation that occurred after the establishment of the Islamic empire had more to do with language than with religion. After the early conquests most of the regions and peoples of the ancient world came under Islamic political rule. Outside Arabia, conversion to Islam was gradual and preceded at a slow pace. The linguistic conversion of the conquered lands was much faster, however. Within one century, Arabic became the official language of the state and its bureaucracy, either completely replacing older languages or coexisting with them as the universal language of communication within the empire's vast domains. References in this chapter to Arab scientists are not necessarily to ethnic Arabs (or even Muslims); rather, these references are to scientists who adopted Arabic as a language of scientific expression and communication.

In addition to religious works, the earliest scholarly contributions among Muslims were of a linguistic nature. Of particular relevance to the later development of science was the extensive compilation efforts by Arabic philologists and lexicographers. The specialized lexicons that were produced in the eighth and ninth centuries represent a large-scale attempt at collecting and classifying Arabic knowledge. These attempts were not always "scientific," and they were eclipsed by later, more systematic achievements. Nonetheless, these encyclopedic efforts provided a linguistic foundation that fostered the development of various intellectual disciplines.

While the peoples of the Byzantine and Sasanid (Persian) empires were undergoing a gradual linguistic conversion under the new Islamic rule, a deliberate effort was made to appropriate the cultures of these ancient civilizations. In its most obvious manifestation, this effort, once again, was linguistic. As early as the eighth century, but primarily in the ninth, scientific works were translated into Arabic. The main reason often adduced for the rise of Arabic science is the translation into Arabic of scientific works from Persian, Indian, and Greek (in this order of occurrence and importance). Quite the reverse is true, however: translation was not the source of the growing interest in science at the time but a consequence of this interest. Like all emerging social phenomena, the rise of science in Islamic societies is historically contingent, owing as much to active agency as to external determinants. The most influential body of scientific knowledge was undoubtedly the Greek. Yet before the rise of Islam, the existence of the same Greek scientific works among a Greek-speaking population was not in itself sufficient to preclude a period of several centuries of steady decline in scientific activity. Therefore, other factors must have contributed to the emergence of Arabic science. One factor was the growing awareness in the new society of the status of Islamic civilization as heir to world civilizations. At a more tangible level, the increasing complexity of social organization and the subsequent social demand for professional expertise provided opportunities and incentives for aspiring professionals to cultivate scientific knowledge. The foundational philological work done by the early lexicographers was itself a first step in the production of a scientific culture. This work also enriched Arabic technical diction and effectively transformed Arabic into a language of science.

Evidence from the earliest extant scientific sources indicates that the translation movement was concurrent with, rather than a prerequisite for, scientific research in the Islamic world. Simultaneous research and translation did not take place in just one field; rather, such research was the driving force behind the translation of numerous astronomical, mathematical, and medical texts. The massive transfer of scientific knowledge into Arabic is a complex phenomenon that cannot be reduced to a mechanical process of translation. The translation movement was itself an aspect of the emergence of Arabic science rather than its sole cause. This emergence was not accidental; it was a result of deliberate and persistent efforts undertaken by professionals who were responding to the demands of their society—efforts that were supported by different segments of society and stimulated by the internal needs of scientific research.

Most of the translations were produced in Baghdad in the course of the ninth century. During the reign of the Abbasid caliph al-Mamun (r. 813–33), translation activities gained considerable momentum, and they continued under several of his successors. Translations were frequently produced at the request of patrons who commissioned and financed them. In addition to such rulers as al-Mamun, these patrons included government officials and civil servants as well as scientists and physicians often employed by members of the political elite. Some of the officials who commissioned translations were involved in court politics as well as large-scale development projects undertaken in the rapidly growing urban centers. The most famous example of this group are the Banu Musa brothers, who in addition to their political involvement were among the leading practicing scientists of the time. Some translations were also prepared for various members of the social elite. An official library named the *Bayt al-Hikma* (the house of wisdom) was established in Baghdad under the Abbasid caliph Harun al-Rashid (r. 786–809), but gained its reputation in the context of the translation movement during the reign of his son al-Mamun. Many of the acquired and translated scientific and philosophical works were collected in this library, and they were in turn made available to the researchers and translators of the period.

The most famous of these translators was a Nestorian (Christian) Arab by the name of Hunayn ibn Ishaq al-Ibadi (808–73). Together with a handful of students, he is responsible for the translation of most of the Galenic medical corpus, as well as many other Greek philosophical and scientific treatises. Hunayn left an autobiography in which he lists a large number of the works that he translated from Greek into Syriac or Arabic. He also describes some of the circumstances of his early career. Hunayn started as a disciple of a Baghdad-based Nestorian physician named Ibn Masawayh. Ibn Masawayh belonged to a group of Nestorian families, originally from the city of Gundishapur, that effectively monopolized the practice of medicine in the Abbasid court. The ambitious Hunayn—who at the time knew only Arabic and Syriac—was rebuffed by his teacher when he inquired about Greek medical texts. Disheartened by this experience, Hunayn set out to study Greek on his own to gain access to this medical knowledge. In due time he mastered Greek and was able to outdo his teacher Ibn Masawayh with newly acquired linguistic skills. Thus it was professional competition that dictated the course of Hunayn's career. When he demonstrated the use of this new skill, even members of the small group of Syriac-speaking physicians started requesting translations of new Greek medical texts. These physicians could no longer maintain their privileges by simple monopoly; to survive in an increasingly competitive environment, they had to raise their standards. To do so they needed more books. Some of the Syriac translations were also used as stepping stones for the preparation of Arabic translations. When the Arabic translations were produced, the Syriac intermediaries rapidly fell into disuse. It was the professional demands of the expanding Islamic society, therefore, that gave rise to this sudden and brief surge in Syriac scientific activity in the ninth century.

The context for ninth-century scientific translations from Greek into Syriac was decidedly Islamic. The rise of Arabic science cannot be attributed to the agency of a Syriac scientific culture; rather, this Syriac scientific culture itself received a significant—albeit brief—impetus from the emergence of Arabic scientific activity. Despite the paramount importance of Greek traditions in the development of the Arabic sciences, Arabic science was not a mere museum of Greek scientific knowledge. Arabic science did more than simply preserve the Greek scientific legacy and pass it to its European heirs. The complex process of cultural transmission necessitates that this legacy, even as its texts were being translated, was reformulated and transformed. The final outcome of this transformation was a new science that was informed by (but not reducible to) its individual components. To appreciate the significance of the emergence of this new scientific tradition, the remaining part of this chapter examines some episodes in the development of various Arabic scientific disciplines.

Astronomy

Astronomy was one of the oldest, most developed, and most esteemed exact sciences of antiquity. Many of the mathematical sciences were originally developed to facilitate astronomical research. Initial interest in astronomy had its roots in astrology and the fascination with the powers and mysteries of the heavens. Practical considerations, such as finding one's direction during night travel or understanding the correlation between the seasons of the year and the positions of the planets, provided additional incentives for the study of astronomy. The Babylonians, Greeks, and Indians had devised elaborate systems for the study of astronomy that went beyond simple empirical observation and were characterized by various degrees of mathematical rigor and sophistication. Before Islam, however, the Arabs had no scientific astronomy. Their knowledge was empirical, and it was limited to the division of the year into precise periods on the basis of the rising and setting of certain stars. This area of astronomical knowledge was known as *anwa*; it continued to attract attention under later Arab astronomers after the rise of Islam, and its study gained much from the mathematical methods employed by these astronomers.

From its beginnings in the ninth century through its maturity in the sixteenth century, astronomical activity was widespread and intensive. This activity is reflected in the large number of scientists working in practical and theoretical astronomy, the number of books written, the active observatories, and the new observations. Astronomy, it should be noted, was unambiguously differentiated from astrology. Astrology continued to be practiced and to draw on and encourage astronomical knowledge. In fact, a good portion of the funding for astronomical research was motivated by the desire to make astrological predictions. Nevertheless, a clear line was drawn between the two disciplines. The vast majority of the thousands of written works are on astronomy, whereas only a handful deal with astrology. Many astronomers served as court astrologers, but many more condemned astrology and distanced themselves from it. Distinct terms were also used to refer to either field: *ilm ahkam al-nujum* or simply *tanjim* referred to astrology, whereas *ilm al-falak*, *ilm al-haya*, or *ilm al-azyaj* referred to the science of the celestial orb, the science of the configuration of the heavens, and to major astronomical treatises containing tables for the motion of the stars and instructions on using these tables.

The first astronomical texts that were translated into Arabic in the eighth century were of Indian and Persian origin. The earliest extant Arabic astronomical texts date to the second half of the eighth century. Two astronomers, Muhammad ibn Ibrahim al-Fazari (d. a. 777) and Yaqub ibn Tariq (eighth century), translated an eighth-century Indian astronomical work known as *Zij al-Sindhind* (a *zij* being an astronomical handbook with tables). Sources indicate that they produced this translation after 770, under the supervision of an Indian astronomer visiting the court of the Abbasid caliph al-Mansur (r. 754–75). Extant fragments of the works of these two astronomers also reveal a somewhat eclectic mixing of Indian parameters with elements of Persian origin as well as some from the Hellenistic pre-Ptolemaic period. These fragments also reflect the use of Indian calculation methods and the use of the Indian sine function in trigonometry, in place of the cumbersome chords of arc used in Greek astronomy. Late Arabic sources also contain references to *Zij al-Shah*, a collection of astronomical tables based on Indian parameters, which was compiled in Sasanid Persia over a period of two centuries.

Arab astronomers were first exposed to Persian and Indian astronomy, and they continued to use some of the parameters and methods of these two traditions, yet the greatest formative influence on Arabic astronomy was undoubtedly Greek. In the early ninth century astronomers realized that the Greek astronomical tradition was far superior to that of Persia or India, in both its comprehensiveness and its use of effective geometrical representations. One particular second-century Greek author, Ptolemy, and more specifically one work by this author, the *Almagest*, exerted a disproportionate influence on all of medieval astronomy through the Arabic period and until the eventual demise of the geocentric astronomical system. That this text exerted so much influence is neither accidental nor surprising, for it is the highest achievement in Hellenistic mathematical astronomy and one of the greatest achievements of all of Hellenistic science. Other works by Ptolemy, commentaries on his works, and several treatises by other authors were also used in conjunction with the *Almagest* and as introductions to it. These include eleven short treatises in Greek, by different authors, called the "Small Astronomy Collection," which were all translated into Arabic during the ninth century.

In the *Almagest*, Ptolemy synthesized the earlier knowledge of Hellenistic astronomy in light of his own new observations. The book's main purpose was to establish the geometric models that would accurately account for observational phenomena. A large part of the work is dedicated to the methods for constructing various models and for calculating their parameters. Ptolemy also provided tables for planetary motions to be used in conjunction with these models. Of all the books of antiquity, the *Almagest* represents the most successful work of mathematical astronomy: its geometric representations of the universe provided the most accurate and best predictive accounts for the celestial phenomena. The Greek tradition of physical astronomy is reflected in the *Almagest* and in Ptolemy's other influential work, *Planetary Hypothesis*. According to this predominantly Aristotelian tradition, the universe is organized into a set of concentric spheres, each carrying a star and rotating around the stationary earth at the center of the universe. Ptolemy adopted, at least in theory, these two basic Aristotelian principles: that the earth is stationary at the center of the universe and that the motion of heavenly bodies ought to be represented by a set of perfectly uniform circular motions. In practice, however, mathematical considerations often forced Ptolemy to disregard these principles.

Arabic sources report at least four Arabic translations of the *Almagest*, of which two are extant. The first is a translation by al-Hajjaj ibn Matar in the first half of the ninth century. The second is a translation by Ishaq, the son of the famous translator Hunayn; this second translation was revised by Thabit ibn Qurra toward the end of the ninth century. Separated by more than fifty years, the second translation reflected the maturity of Arabic technical terminology; whereas certain parts of the first translation lacked full clarity, the second translation provided a coherent text that eliminated any need for further reference to the Greek original.

The first extant original work of Arabic astronomy is al-Khwarizmi's (fl. 830) *Zij al-Sindhind* (which is unrelated to the translation of the Indian text mentioned earlier with same name). This work contains tables for the movements of the sun, the moon, and five planets, with explanatory remarks on how to use these tables. Most of the parameters used by al-Khwarizmi are of Indian origin, but some are derived from Ptolemy's *Handy Tables*, and no attempt is made to harmonize the two sources. This work is significant not only for its content but also because it was written simultaneously with the earliest translations of the *Almagest*. The first introduction of Ptolemaic astronomy into Arabic science thus occurred in the context of two significant trends. First, research in Arabic astronomy went hand in hand with translation; despite its manifest superiority, Ptolemaic astronomy did not exclusively set the agenda for future research in Arabic astronomy. The second trend was the selective use of parameters, sources, and methods of calculation from different scientific traditions. As a result, the Ptolemaic tradition was rendered receptive from the beginning to the possibility of observational refinement and mathematical restructuring. These revisionist tendencies characterize the first period of Arabic astronomy.

A significant part of the intensive ninth-century astronomical research was dedicated to the dissemination of Ptolemy's astronomy, not just by translating parts or all of his work into Arabic, but also by composing summaries and commentaries on it. Ptolemy's work was thus made available and accessible to a large audience among the educated classes. In the first half of the ninth century, al-Farghani (d. ca. 850), for example, wrote *Kitab fi Jawami Ilm al-Nujum* (A compendium of the science of the stars). This book was widely circulated in the Arabic version and also in later Latin translations. This work provided a brief and simplified descriptive overview of Ptolemaic cosmography, without mathematical computations. Unlike the *Almagest*, however, it started with a discussion of calendar computations and conversions between different eras. Although its primary purpose was to introduce Ptolemaic astronomy in a simplified way, it also corrected Ptolemy based on findings of earlier Arab astronomers. Al-Farghani gave revised values for the obliquity of the ecliptic, the precessional movement of the apogees of the sun and the moon, and the circumference of the earth. This critical approach, thus far restricted to the correction of constants and parameters, had already been set by earlier astronomers at the beginning of the ninth century.

Under the Abbasid caliph al-Mamun, a program of astronomical observations was organized in Baghdad and Damascus. Like any organized research project, this program endowed astronomical activity in the Islamic world with formal prestige. It also set a precedent for future support of scientific activity by other rulers and established patronage as one of the modes of supporting such activities. The professed purpose of this program was to verify the Ptolemaic observations by comparing the results derived by calculation, based on Ptolemaic models, with actual observations conducted in Baghdad and Damascus some seven hundred years after Ptolemy. The results were compiled in *al-Zij al-Mumtahan* (The verified tables), which is no longer extant in its entirety but is widely quoted by later astronomers. The most important correction introduced was to show that the apogee of the solar orb moves with the precession of the fixed stars. On a more general note, this program stressed the need for continuing verification of astronomical observations and for the use of more precise instruments. The program also represented the first recorded instance in history of a collective scientific undertaking.

From its beginnings, Arabic astronomy set out to rectify and complement Ptolemaic astronomy. Having noted several discrepancies between new observations and Ptolemaic calculations, Arab astronomers then proceeded to reexamine the theoretical basis of Ptolemy's results. This critical reexamination took several forms. One example of the critical works of the ninth century is *Fi Sanat al-Shams* (The book on the solar year), which was wrongly attributed to the mathematician Thabit ibn Qurrah, but was produced around his time. This work corrected some of Ptolemy's constants, and although it retained Ptolemy's geometrical representations, it questioned his observations and calculations. Other astronomers devised enhanced methods of calculation. New mathematical tools were introduced to modernize the computational procedures. For example, in his *al-Zij al-Dimashqi* (The Damascene zij) written around the middle of the ninth century, the mathematician Habash al-Hasib (d. between 864 and 874) introduced the trigonometric functions of sine, cosine, and tangent, which were at that time unknown to the Greeks. Habash also worked on a problem that was not treated in the Greek sources: he examined the visibility of the crescent moon and produced the first detailed discussion of this complicated astronomical problem. Habash is an example of an astronomer who undertook his study to verify the results of the *Almagest*, but in the process he expanded these results and applied them to new problems. Although the general astronomical research of this period was largely conducted within the framework of Ptolemaic astronomy, this research reworked and critically examined the observations and the computational methods of Ptolemaic astronomy and in a limited way was able to explore problems outside its framework.

One of the main ninth-century scientists from whom several extant astronomical manuscripts exist today is Thabit ibn Qurra (ca. 836–901). Thabit was a pagan from Harran (in southeast Turkey); his native language was Syriac, but he was fluent in Greek and his working language was Arabic. Thabit joined the Banu Musa circle in Baghdad, and produced numerous works on several scientific disciplines. Of about forty treatises on astronomy, only eight are extant. All the treatises reflect Thabit's full command of Ptolemaic astronomy and illustrate the level to which this astronomy was thoroughly absorbed by Arab astronomers. A few of these are of particular interest. In one treatise, for example, Thabit analyzed the motion of a heavenly body on an eccentric, and the model he used was Ptolemaic. In contrast to Ptolemy's description, which was stated without proof, Thabit provided a rigorous and systematic mathematical proof with the aid of the theorems of Euclid's *Elements*. In the course of this proof, Thabit introduced the first known mathematical analysis of motion. For the first time in history, he also referred to the speed of a moving body at a particular point. In another work, Thabit provided general and exhaustive proofs for problems that Ptolemy examined only for special cases or for boundary conditions. Another work is exclusively devoted to lunar visibility. Thabit's solution, which was far more complex than that of Habash, exhibited the same mathematical rigor apparent everywhere in his work: he proved the general law that applies to the visibility of any heavenly body, then he applied this law to the special case of the crescent moon. Thabit's work is significant because it illustrates the high creativity of Arabic astronomy in its earliest periods. The roots for this creativity lie in the application of diverse mathematical disciplines to each other. This application had the immediate effect of expanding the frontiers of various disciplines and introducing new scientific concepts and ideas. The use of systematic mathematization transformed the methods of reasoning and enabled further creative developments in the diverse branches of science.

Another famous astronomer of this early period is Abu Abd Allah Muhammad ibn Jabir al-Battani (ca. 858–929), who originally came from Harran but lived in Raqqa in northern Syria. At Raqqa, al-Battani conducted observations for more than thirty years. The results of his research were recorded in *al-Zij al-Sabi* (The Sabian tables), which was translated into Latin in the twelfth century and into Spanish in the thirteenth. Although al-Battani did not contribute significantly to theoretical astronomy, his meticulous observations enabled him to make some important discoveries. For example, he noted the variations in the apparent diameters of the sun and the moon and deduced, for the first time in the history of astronomy, the possibility of an annular eclipse of the sun.

In the ninth century, then, Arabic astronomy had already struck deep roots. It integrated all the knowledge there was to integrate from earlier traditions and was justly positioned to surpass this knowledge. The achievements of the ninth century laid the foundation for the high-quality work in the following two centuries. The tenth and eleventh centuries witnessed important developments in trigonometry, with dramatic effects on the accuracy and facility of astronomical calculations. In this period steps were taken toward the formal establishment of large-scale observatories. Although the information from these two centuries is spotty and fragmented, several extant sources provide evidence for significant attempts to reevaluate Ptolemaic astronomy. In the tenth and eleventh centuries the earlier examinations of Ptolemaic astronomy led to systematic projects that rather than addressing the field in its totality, focused on specific aspects of astronomy. The work of Abd al-Rahman al-Sufi (who was born in Rayy and worked in the Iranian centers of Shiraz and Isfahan, 903–86) illustrates this tendency. In his famous book, *Kitab Suwar al-Kawakib al-Thabita* (Book on the constellations), al-Sufi reworked the star catalog of the *Almagest* on the basis of a corrected value of 1°/66 years for the precessional movement (in the place of Ptolemy's 1°/100 years), as well as

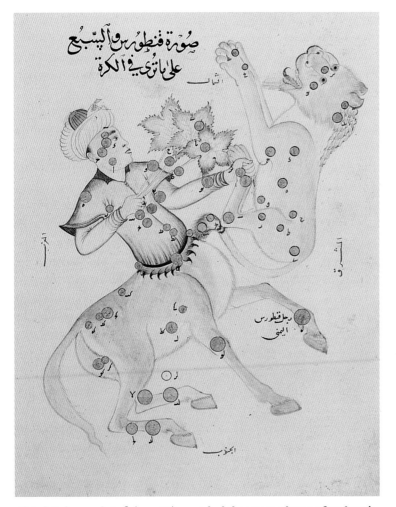

Abd al-Rahman al-Sufi (903–86) reworked the star catalogue of Ptolemy's *Almagest*, and his book on the fixed stars, *Kitab Suwar al-Kawakib al-Thabita*, became a standard work. This illustration of the constellation Centaurus, from a copy of the text made for the Timurid prince Ulughbeg ibn Shahrukh, probably in Samarqand in the 1430s, transforms the centaur of classical mythology into a turbaned man-horse.

several other new observations and verifications. Al-Sufi produced an accurate representation of the constellations and their coordinates and magnitudes. His work was translated into Latin and is the source of many Latin star names of Arabic origin. Another example of the tendency to synthesize is Abu al-Hasan Ali Ibn Yunus' (Cairo, d. 1009) *al-Zij al-Hakimi al-Kabir* (The Hakimi zij), a monumental work in eighty-one chapters, of which only about one-half is preserved. The book is a complete treatise on astronomy, which contains tables for the movement of the heavenly bodies, their various parameters, and instructions on the use of these tables. Here, too, the objective of the work was to provide an exhaustive documentation of previous observations, subsequent verifications or corrections of these, and new observations recorded by the author.

Some of the astronomers of this period were known as instrument builders and for their association with observatories. The astronomer Abu Mahmud Hamid al-Khujandi (d. a. 1000), for example, wrote several works on scientific instruments and built a large sextant at Rayy. The astronomer Abu al-Wafa al-Buzjani (940–98) worked in a large observatory built by the Buyid ruler Sharaf al-Dawla in the gardens of the royal palace in Baghdad. Like Abu Nasr Mansur ibn Iraq (d. a. 1036) of Ghazna, al-Buzjani was a mathematician-astronomer who made great contributions in the field of trigonometry. Although much of the trigonometric works of these early scientists is lost, ample information exists from the extensive discussion on these works by the illustrious scientist al-Biruni.

Al-Biruni was born in 973 in Khwarizm (modern-day Khorezm) and died in 1048 in Ghazna (in eastern Afghanistan). Among other places, he worked in Rayy, where he collaborated with al-Khujandi. He also studied with Abu Nasr Mansur ibn Iraq, who was a student of al-Buzjani. Al-Biruni considered these two scholars as his teachers, and with them he shared a focused interest in trigonometry and its application to astronomy. Al-Biruni's native language was Persian, but he composed the vast majority of his works in Arabic. He also knew Sanskrit, and as a result he had full command of Indian astronomy in addition to the well-established Greek and Arabic traditions. Al-Biruni wrote more than 150 works on most of the known sciences of his time, including astronomy, mathematics, mathematical geography, mineralogy, metallurgy, pharmacology, history, and philosophy. Although only a third of his works are extant, these contain a wealth of scientific and historical information. His *al-Oanun al-Masudi* (Canon Macudicus) is a veritable treasure, which, as a great synthesis of the Greek, Indian, and Arabic astronomical traditions, has been compared to the synthesis produced in the *Almagest* by Ptolemy. The book is also a history of Arabic astronomy through the early eleventh century, and it provides the only extant source of information on many of the contributions of earlier astronomers. The value of this and other historical works by al-Biruni is further enhanced by his keen historical consciousness and cultural sensitivity.

Advances in trigonometry resulting from the full integration of the Indian achievements in the field, as well as from new discoveries in the tenth and eleventh centuries, played a central role in the development of Arabic astronomy. This tendency is itself part of a larger phenomenon whereby the systematic mathematization of disciplines contributed to the expansion of their frontiers. Equipped with new and more rigorous mathematical tools, al-Biruni, like many of his predecessors and contemporaries, provided exhaustive studies of specialized topics within astronomy. His "exhaustive" treatises cover such topics as shadows; the theory, construction, and use of astrolabes; the coordinates of geographical locations; and many more. In most of these monographs, al-Biruni starts with a thorough critical overview of older theories and mathematical methods for solving the particular problems in question; he then proceeds either to choose one of these theories or to propose his own alternative theory. Al-Biruni's work as a whole represents a critical assessment of the state of mathematical astronomy through the early eleventh century. Such comprehensive surveys of earlier knowledge exhausted the possibilities of expanding the astronomical disciplines from within; to achieve further progress, scientists needed to move in new directions, devise new strategies, and explore new research programs.

Another characteristic of this period is the seemingly random use of old as well as new mathematical methods in the solution of astronomical problems. Thus the same author may have used an archaic method in one place and an advanced method in another. Al-Biruni, for example, used both the old, cumbersome Menelaus theorem as well as the new, elegant sine rule in several solutions to the problem of determining the qibla, the direction that Muslims have to face in prayers. This simultaneous use of different mathematical procedures cannot be attributed to the slow dissemination of scientific knowledge or to the limited circulation of this knowledge. There is ample evidence for a high level of mobility and of efficient and speedy communication among scientists working in various regions of the Muslim world. Al-Biruni himself did not travel to Baghdad, but he apparently corresponded with scientists there and was fully aware of scientific developments there and elsewhere. The use of different methods is likely a result of the increasing diffusion of scientific knowledge among large segments of the educated elites. Within the broad ranks of these elites, "full-time" scientists were expected to keep up with the latest research in their fields, while scholars with partial interest in science would be familiar only with older theories and methods. The use of a variety of mathematical methods is thus an indication of the degree to which scientific culture had filtered into society, and the extent to which it became available to average members of the educated class.

Expanding the Frontiers of Theoretical Astronomy

A third, less noted aspect of al-Biruni's work attests to the emergence of a new understanding of the relationship between science and other forms of knowledge. A book entitled al-Asila wal-Ajwiba (Questions and answers) preserved an exchange between al-Biruni and his contemporary Ibn Sina (980–1037), the most celebrated Muslim philosopher of all time. In this exchange, al-Biruni presented Ibn Sina with a set of questions in which he criticized Aristotle's physical theory, especially as it pertained to astronomy. Ibn Sina responded and a lively debate ensued. In the course of this debate, al-Biruni questioned almost all of the fundamental Aristotelian physical axioms: he rejected the notion that heavenly bodies have an inherent nature, and he asserted that their motion could very well be compulsory; he maintained that there is no observable evidence that rules out the possibility of vacuum; he further asserted that although observation corroborates Aristotle's claim that the motion of heavenly bodies is circular, there is no inherent "natural" reason why this motion cannot be, among other things, elliptical. What is more significant than the actual objections al-Biruni raised is the argument he employed in the course of the debate. He drew a sharp and unambiguous distinction between his profession and that of Aristotle and Ibn Sina as philosophers. He argued that the metaphysical axioms on which philosophers build their physical theories do not constitute valid evidence for the mathematical astronomer. In other words, al-Biruni clearly distinguished between the philosopher and the mathematician, the metaphysician and the scientist. He conceived himself as a mathematical astronomer for whom the only valid evidence is observational or mathematical. Al-Biruni's example illustrates how the systematic application of rigorous mathematical reasoning led to the mathematization of astronomy and, by extension, to the mathematization of nature. Rather than subsuming the various sciences under the all-encompassing umbrella of philosophy, many scientists considered their professions as autonomous mathematical enterprises, separate from and on par with philosophy.

To be sure, not every exact scientist conformed to this view. There existed a plurality of viable possibilities that allowed scientists more freedom to question the fundamental assumptions of their disciplines. Philosophy, for such scientists, was not discarded: rather, it was no longer sacred. After the eleventh century the efforts of most theoretical astronomers were directed toward providing a thorough evaluation of the physical and philosophical underpinnings of Ptolemaic astronomy and proposing alternatives to it. The emergence of this tendency in astronomical research did not represent a move away from the thorough mathematical examination of astronomy, but it was an outcome of this increasing mathematization. Between the ninth and eleventh centuries Arab astronomers moved back and forth between mathematical theory and observation. Using rigorous mathematical reasoning, they systematically examined every possible aspect of Ptolemaic astronomy; they recorded numerous anomalies and attempted to rectify them or to eliminate their causes. In the course of this activ-

ity, these astronomers amassed a large number of critiques of Ptolemaic astronomy. Armed with a thorough mathematical conceptualization of their discipline,
Arab astronomers were now ready to boldly question its fundamental philosophical framework.

This line of research was pursued by several eleventh-century scientists. In his
book *Tarkib al-Aflak* (Composition of the heavenly spheres), Abu Ubayd al-Juzjani
(d. a. 1070) indicated that both he and his teacher, Ibn Sina, were aware of the
so-called equant problem of the Ptolemaic model. Al-Juzjani even proposed a
solution for this problem. The anonymous author of an Andalusian astronomical manuscript referred to another work that he composed entitled *al-Istidrak ala
Batlamyus* (Recapitulation regarding Ptolemy), and indicated that he included in
this later book a list of objections to Ptolemaic astronomy. The most important
work of this genre, however, was written in the same period by Ibn al-Haytham
(965–1039). In his celebrated work *Al-Shukuk ala Batlamyus* (Doubts on Ptolemy),
Ibn al-Haytham summed up the physical and philosophical problems inherent
in the Greek astronomical system and provided an inventory of the theoretical
inconsistencies of the Ptolemaic models. Building on the cumulative achievements of Arabic astronomy, the eleventh century witnessed the emergence of a
new tradition of astronomical research, a tradition that thrived in the thirteenth
century, climaxed in the fourteenth, and continued well into the fifteenth and
sixteenth centuries.

Most astronomers of this period took up the theoretical challenge outlined
by Ibn al-Haytham and attempted to rework the models of Ptolemaic astronomy and to provide, with varying degrees of success, alternatives to these models. The list of astronomers working within this tradition comprises some of
the greatest and most original Muslim scientists. Most of the current information on these scientists derives from studies that were produced in the past few
decades; further research will undoubtedly expand the list of reformers and
provide a more detailed picture of their tradition of reform. The astronomers
who have received modern scholarly attention include: Muayyad al-Din al-
Urdi (d. 1266), Nasir al-Din al-Tusi (1201–74), Qutb al-Din al-Shirazi (d.
1311), Sadr al-Sharia al-Bukhari (d. 1347), Ibn al-Shatir (d. 1375), and Ala al-
Din al-Qushji (d. 1474).

In his *Almagest*, Ptolemy used the results of earlier Hellenistic astronomy and
incorporated them into one great synthesis. Of particular geometrical utility was
the concept of eccentrics and epicycles developed in the second century B.C.E. by
Hipparchus and adopted by Ptolemy. In an astronomical representation employing the eccentric model (figure 1), a planet, P, is carried on the circumference of
an eccentric circle that rotates uniformly around its own center, G. This center,
however, does not coincide with the location, O, of an observer on the earth. As

a result, the speed of the planet appears to vary with respect to the observer at point O. In an epicyclic model, the planet is carried on the circumference of an epicycle, whose center is in turn carried on a circle called the deferent, which rotates uniformly around the center of the universe, the earth. Viewed by an observer at point O, the combination of the two uniform motions of the deferent and the epicycle produces a nonuniform motion that is mathematically equivalent to the motion of the eccentric model.

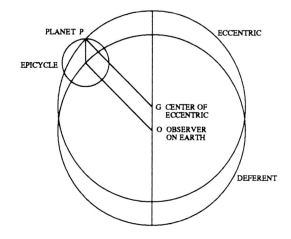

Ptolemy's model for the sun employing either an eccentric or a deferent and an epicycle.

The Ptolemaic model for the motion of the sun utilized either a simple eccentric model or the equivalent combination of a deferent and an epicycle. Other Ptolemaic models for planetary motions were considerably more complex. For example, in the model for the longitudinal motion of the upper planets, Mars, Jupiter, and Saturn (figure 2), the center, G, of the deferent circle no longer coincides with the earth, O. Moreover, the uniform motion of the center of the epicycle on the circumference of the deferent is measured around the point E, called the equant center, rather than the center, G, of the deferent. Ptolemy proposed this model because it allowed for fairly accurate predictions of planetary positions. However, circle G in this model is made to rotate uniformly around the equant E, which is not its center. This represented a violation of the Aristotelian principle of uniform circular motion that Ptolemy had adopted. In other words, for the sake of observation, Ptolemy was forced to breach the physical and philosophical principles on which he built his astronomical theory. Still other Ptolemaic models were even more complex, and with each additional level of complexity, new objections were raised against Ptolemaic astronomy.

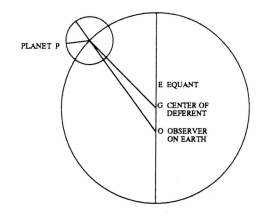

Ptolemy's model for the longitudinal motion of Mars, Jupiter, and Saturn.

Other objections raised by Ibn al-Haytham and taken up by later astronomers include the problem of the prosneusis point in the model for the longitudinal motion of the moon; the problem of the inclination and deviation of the spheres of Mercury and Venus; the problem of planetary distances, and so on. In the case of the moon, additional difficulties arise because Ptolemy's model has a deferent center that is itself moving. Moreover, the motion of the center of the epicycle on this deferent is not uniform around the deferent's center; rather, it rotates uniformly around the center of the universe. To complicate matters further, the anomalistic motion on the epicycle is measured away from the mean epicyclic apogee, which is aligned with a movable point called the prosneusis point, rather than being measured from the true apogee, which is aligned with the center of the universe. This prosneusis point is the point diametrically opposite to the center of the deferent on the other side of the center of the universe. The model for the longitudinal motion of Mercury contained complex mechanisms that were equally objectionable.

Additional complications also resulted from the motion of the planets in latitude: the motion in longitude is measured on the plane of the ecliptic, which is the great circle of the celestial sphere that traces the apparent yearly path of the sun as seen from the earth. The deferents of the Ptolemaic models, however, did not coincide with this plane. The least problematic is the case of the lunar model, in which the deferent has a fixed inclination with respect to the ecliptic, and the epicycle lies in the plane of the deferent. The epicycles of the upper planets do not lie in the plane of the deferent, however, and they have a variable deviation with respect to it. In the case of the lower planets, both the inclination of the deferent with respect to the ecliptic and that of the epicycle with respect to the deferent are variable. It is easy to imagine the complexity and potential problems of the Ptolemaic models that attempted to account for these seesaw and oscillation motions.

The astronomers who attempted to solve these problems are classified into two general schools: a mathematically oriented school predominantly based in the Muslim world's eastern parts, and a philosophically oriented school based in the Muslim empire's western regions. The Maragha school is the name often given to the eastern reformers, in recognition of the achievements of a number of astronomers working in an observatory established at Maragha (near Azerbaijan). The contributions of these astronomers were no doubt monumental, but the reform of Ptolemaic astronomy started before the establishment of the Maragha observatory in the thirteenth century. This reform reached its highest point in the fourteenth. In fact, some of the astronomers of the Maragha group seem to have started their reform projects even before they joined this observatory; perhaps they were invited to join the observatory team because they were already engaged in such research. The eastern reform tradition was too diffused to be associated with any one geographical area or period; rather, it includes several centuries of Arabic astronomical research throughout the eastern domains of the Muslim world.

Astronomers of the eastern reform tradition adopted several mathematical strategies in their attempts to solve the theoretical problems of the Ptolemaic models. One of their main objectives was to come up with models in which the motions of the planets could be generated as a result of combinations of uniform circular motions, while at the same time conforming to the accurate Ptolemaic observations. Two useful and extremely influential mathematical tools were invented by the thirteenth-century astronomers al-Tusi and al-Urdi. The first tool, known in modern scholarship as the *Tusi couple*, in effect produced linear oscillation as a result of a combination of two uniform circular motions. This tool was used in various ways by many astronomers, including the Polish astronomer Nicolaus Copernicus. The *Urdi lemma* was an equally versatile mathematical tool used by al-Urdi and his successors. To apply this lemma to the model of the upper planets, for example, al-Urdi reversed the directions of motion and divided the eccentricities of the Ptolemaic model. He was thus able to produce uniform motion around the geometric center of the sphere, while at the same time reproducing the uniform motion around the Ptolemaic equant center. To produce optimal representations that are physically and mathematically sound, other astronomers used various combinations of these two tools and devised additional tools of their own invention. The most comprehensive and successful models were introduced in the fourteenth century by the Damascene astronomer Ibn al-Shatir; his models for all the planets use combinations of perfect circular motions in which each circle rotates uniformly around its center. Ibn al-Shatir was also able to solve problems of planetary distances and to provide more accurate accounts for observations. A number of Ibn al-Shatir's models were reproduced a century and a half later by Copernicus, clearly situating the latter within the eastern Arabic tradition of astronomical reform.

The development of Arabic astronomy in the Muslim states of Andalusia and North Africa followed different routes. The beginnings of significant scientific activity in Andalusia started in the ninth century, yet this activity was almost completely dependent upon and lagging behind the sciences of the eastern part of the Muslim world. Between the ninth and eleventh centuries, however, a full-fledged scientific tradition emerged. Many scientists traveled east to study science; scientific books were systematically acquired and large private and public libraries were established. According to tradition, under the patronage of al-Hakam II (r. 961–76), the Umayyad caliph of Córdoba, one royal library is said to have amassed four hundred thousand books. A solid familiarity with the eastern astronomical tradition led, in the eleventh century, to intensive and at times original astronomical activity in Andalusia. The main astronomers of this period include Maslama al-Majriti (d. 1007) of Córdoba, his student Ibn al-Saffar, and al-Zarqiyal (known as Zarqallu, d. a. 1100). Zarqallu, was one of the main contributors to the compilation of the celebrated *Toledan Tables*, which greatly influenced the development of Latin astronomy. The emphasis of the activity of these and other astronomers was focused on the compilation of tables and on spherical astronomy. Their primary original contributions included some new observations, but most of their work concerned the mathematics of the trepidation movement of the stars and the invention of highly sophisticated astronomical instruments. During this period, however, little work of significance was devoted to planetary theory.

In the twelfth century, however, the focus of astronomical research in Andalusia shifted to planetary theory. The names associated with this research include the Andalusian philosopher Ibn Bajja (ca. 1095–1138), the Andalusian astronomer Jabir ibn Aflah (fl. 1120), the Andalusian philosopher and physician Ibn Tufayl (d. 1185), the Islamic philosopher Ibn Rushd (1126–98, known in the west as Averroës), and the Andalusian astronomer Abu Ishaq al-Bitruji (fl. 1190). Of these, al-Bitruji was the only one to formulate an alternative to Ptolemaic astronomy, while the others produced philosophical discussions of this astronomy. These discourses on Ptolemaic astronomy, as well as al-Bitruji's actual proposed model, conceived of astronomical reform in reactionary terms—that is, in terms of adopting older and mathematically inferior models in place of the ones used since Ptolemy. The aim of this western school of astronomical reform was to reinstate Aristotelian homocentric spheres and to completely eliminate any use of eccentrics and epicycles. In accordance with the most stringent and literal interpretations of Aristotelian principles, the western researchers demanded that the heavens be represented exclusively by nested homocentric spheres and perfectly uniform circular motions. Even epicycles and deferents that rotated uniformly around their centers were not tolerated, because their use entailed an attribution of compoundedness to heavenly phenomena, while according to Aristotelian principles, the heavens are perfectly simple. Because the predictive power of the Ptolemaic models and their ability to account for the observed phenomena relied on the use of epicycles and eccentrics, however, the western models were strictly qualitative and philosophical and were completely useless from a mathematical perspective. These models were neither numerically verifiable, nor could they be used for predicting planetary positions. It is no wonder, therefore, that all but one of the western philosophers did not bother to produce actual geometrical models.

The significance of the difference between the eastern and western reform traditions of Arabic astronomy cannot be overemphasized. The prevalent view in contemporary scholarship attributes the steady decline of the intellectual sciences in Andalusia and North Africa to the rise of the so-called fundamentalist states of the Almoravids (1091–1144) and Almohads (1147–1232). Precisely during this period, however, the greatest Andalusian philosophers worked under the patronage of the rulers of these two states. What transpired, therefore, was not a steady decline of the intellectual disciplines but the rise of some disciplines at the expense of others. The decline of mathematical astronomy had nothing to do with the Almoravids or the Almohads or with an alleged theological counterrevolution. Rather, the decline was a result of the adoption of a specific research program of astronomical research, a program that was driven by the untenable, and by then outdated, Aristotelian philosophical concerns that proved incompatible with astronomy's advanced mathematical and scientific aspects.

Unlike the western school, the eastern school of Arabic astronomy did not favor philosophy at the expense of mathematics. The objections of the eastern school were mathematical and physical, and as the comparison with their western counterpart clearly illustrates, these objections were certainly not philosophical. A common view prevalent in earlier studies maintains that the eastern reform tradition of Arabic astronomy was driven by philosophical considerations, a notion that is often used to undermine the mathematical and scientific significance of this tradition. Given the overwhelming evidence of detailed research on this tradition, such a view is no longer tenable. The alternative solar model proposed by Ibn al-Shatir is an example in which reform was motivated purely by observational considerations, even though the Ptolemaic model was completely unobjectionable from a physical or philosophical perspective. More generally, the eastern tradition of astronomical reform had its roots in the systematic mathematization of astronomy, and to some extent of nature itself. A recent study of *al-Takmila fi Sharh al-Tadhkira* (The complement to the explanation of the memento) of Shams al-Din al-Khafri (d. after 1525) clearly illustrates one of the main characteristics of this tradition. Al-Khafri was primarily a religious scholar who wrote a highly sophisticated commentary on al-Tusi's *Tadhkira*, one of the classics of the eastern reform tradition. In this work Al-Khafri presented thorough accounts for the various alternative models proposed by earlier astronomers. The purpose of this work, however, was not to look for a correct model, nor to decide which model conformed with an ideal or preferred cosmology, but to establish the mathematical equivalence of all of these models.

Practical Astronomy

Although the most important contributions of Arabic astronomy were in the field of theoretical astronomy, practical astronomical problems occupied a great many astronomers, who were responsible for significant advances in the field. Some of these problems had a specific Islamic character; other problems had to do with society's practical needs, including such problems as finding the direction of one locality with respect to another, a problem that required determining the longitudes and latitudes of these localities as well as other aspects of mathematical geography. The "Islamic" problems were those related to Islamic worship, such as determining the times of prayer; the time of sunrise and sunset in relation to fasting; the direction of the qibla; crescent visibility in connection with the determination of the beginning of the lunar month; and calendar computations. The methods employed to solve these problems varied from simple approximative techniques to complex mathematical ones. For the more complex mathematical method, studies often occasioned complex theoretical analysis that far exceeded the initial scope of the examined problems.

One of the main topics addressed in various astronomical treatises is the problem of crescent visibility. The official Islamic calendar is a lunar calendar, with the first year coinciding with the year 622 C.E. The lunar month begins right after sunset with the sighting of the crescent. The visibility of this crescent, however, is itself a function of many variables, some of which are more relevant than others. These variables include, for example, the celestial coordinates of the sun and the moon, the latitude of the place at which the crescent is sighted, and the brightness of the sky. Various methods were devised to determine the conditions under which the crescent would be visible. Some of these methods accounted for a limited number of variables in the special case of the moon, while other methods exhausted all possible factors that affect the visibility of any heavenly body on the horizon just after sunset and treated the problem of crescent visibility as a special case.

Muslims use a lunar calendar, and the new month starts just after sunset with the sighting of the new crescent moon. This illustration from a sixteenth-century poetical text shows the sighting of the new moon that marks the feast of Id al-Fitr and celebrates the end of the monthlong fast of Ramadan.

Finding the direction of the qibla is another case in which complex mathe-matical methods were employed. Muslims are enjoined to face Mecca during their five daily prayers, and at least in theory all mosques are supposed to be oriented toward the Kaaba, in Mecca. Before mathematical methods were available, Muslims determined the direction of the qibla based on the practices of Muhammad's early Companions and their successors. They also made use of tra-ditions of folk astronomy and of the fact that the Kaaba itself is astronomically aligned. Many early Muslims, therefore, used the same astronomical alignment adduced for the Kaaba to orient themselves during prayers. This method provided a reasonable approximation in locations close to Mecca, but it was quite inaccu-rate in such far-away places as North Africa and Iran. Many of the mosques that were built in the early period were misaligned, and although some retained their orientation, others were rebuilt to face the correct direction of Mecca. Numerous simple, nonmathematical methods were employed in the early period and con-tinued to exist even after the emergence of mathematical sciences. With this emer-gence, however, new methods were devised to compute the qibla for any locality on the basis of the geographical coordinates of that locality and Mecca.

The problem of determining the direction of the qibla was treated as one of mathematical geography: the purpose is to find the direction of Mecca along the shortest arc of the great circle joining the locality of Mecca to the locality from which the measurement is made. To solve this problem, it is necessary to know the geographical coordinates of both Mecca and the locality in question. Various methods could then be used to calculate the direction of the qibla. Most astro-nomical handbooks contained chapters on finding this direction by one or more approximative or accurate methods. Separate treatises were also composed on the subject. Approximative methods involved the use of cartography to represent on a plane orthogonal grid of latitude and longitude the relative location of Mecca with respect to a particular locality. The analemma solutions are accurate projec-tion methods in which the meridian, celestial equator, and horizon planes are rep-resented on one plane, and the problem is solved by a series of rotations of these planes. In the accurate solution, the problem is transferred to the celestial sphere where the position of the zenith of Mecca relative to the zenith of the locality is determined. The direction of the qibla is then calculated as the azimuth (arc) of the zenith of Mecca on the local horizon. As in many other fields of astronomy, attempts were made at devising universal solutions for all possible cases, and mathematical procedures of considerable sophistication were used.

Starting in the ninth century, tables were computed displaying the direction of the qibla as a function of terrestrial longitude and latitude. These computa-tions were based on both approximate and accurate methods. In addition to the qibla tables, different tables were compiled in connection with timekeeping and

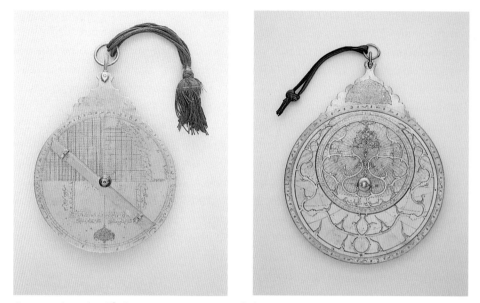

Constructing scientific instruments was particularly important to Muslim astronomers who needed to pinpoint the location and movement of the heavenly bodies in order to determine the direction of Mecca and the times of prayer. The astrolabe, a versatile observational instrument and calculator, was particularly useful in this respect. Some of the most beautifully decorated examples were made for the Safavid rulers of Iran, such as the one on the left, made for Abbas II in 1647–48. The astrolabe on the right was made by Abu al-Aimma in 1712–13.

other astronomical functions. Timekeeping received particular interest because of its relevance to the regulation of the times of prayer. Each of the five daily prayers that are required of Muslims could be performed within set time limits, which vary throughout the year and in different localities. These limits are defined in terms of the apparent position of the sun in the sky relative to the local horizon. In other words, they vary as a function of the solar altitude and longitude as well as the latitude of the locality. In the attempt to compute the times of prayers, extensive literature was generated on various aspects of timekeeping and on the theory and construction of sundials.

The earliest known text on timekeeping was composed by al-Khwarizmi in the early ninth century, and a comprehensive work on sundial theory was composed by the mathematician Thabit ibn Qurrah. Standard works on timekeeping, such as the famous *Jami al-Mabadi wal-Ghayat fi Ilm al-Miqat* (The comprehensive principles and objectives of the science of timekeeping) written in Cairo by Abu Ali al-Marrakushi around 1280, often included theoretical treatments of spherical astronomy and sundial theory, discussions of the construction and use of various instruments, and extensive tables. Several such tables were universal, and they were compiled for all terrestrial latitudes. These tables were often augmented with auxiliary trigonometric tables to facilitate the solution of problems of spherical trigonometry. The tables of the fourteenth-century Damascene timekeeper al-Khalili are examples of the finest accomplishments within this tradition. They are the most accurate and exhaustive numerical solutions for all timekeeping problems and for the direction of the qibla.

Such problems gave a great impetus to the science and art of instrument building. Astrolabes, quadrants, compass boxes, and cartographic grids of varying degrees of sophistication were designed and introduced to solve some of these problems. Many of these instruments were also used for other astronomical observations and computations. The most important of these is the astrolabe, which was a versatile medieval observational instrument and calculator. Eleventh-century Andalusian astronomers in particular contributed important innovations in the field of astronomical instruments. The invention of the universal astrolabe and the simpler Shakkaziyya plate are rare examples of creative activity that started in Andalusia and later influenced the eastern part of the Muslim world. Instruments of different sizes

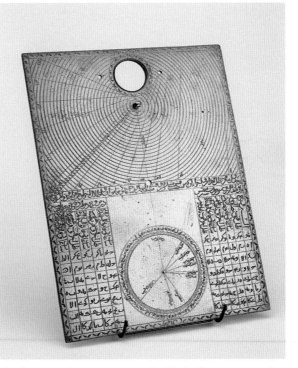

This horizontal pin gnomon and qibla indicator was used to determine the direction and times of prayer.

were also designed and used in connection with programs of astronomical observation and within the confines of organized observatories. The earliest planned and programmed observations were produced in Baghdad and Damascus during the last years of the reign of the Abbasid caliph al-Mamun (r. 813–33). Since then, many other observations were recorded. Many of these were conducted in private observatories, where relatively small instruments were often used. Official observatories that enjoyed financial support tended to use larger instruments, which had the advantage of producing more accurate observations. Toward the end of the tenth century in Rayy, for example, under the patronage of the Buyid ruler Fakhr al-Dawla (r. 978–97) the astronomer al-Khujandi designed and built a large sextant that had a radius of twenty meters. A degree of arc on this sextant measured about thirty-five centimeters, enabling much more accurate solar observations. Another large instrument is described by the Muslim philosopher Ibn Sina; a modified version of this instrument was later used in the Maragha observatory.

An important development took place in eleventh-century Isfahan, where a large and highly organized observatory was established under the patronage of

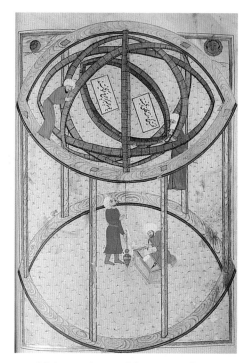

In addition to the astrolabe, many other instruments were constructed for astronomical observations and computations. This illustration to an Ottoman manuscript from the second half of the sixteenth century shows four scientists taking observations using a giant armillary sphere made of wood.

the Seljuk ruler Malikshah (r. 1072–92). The observations there were planned over a thirty-year period, which is the time taken by Saturn, the furthest planet from the earth, to complete one full revolution. The observatory functioned for only eighteen years, however, and was shut down when its founder died. Nonetheless, this represented the first official observatory to last for such a long period of time. The observatory thus acquired the status of a long-living scientific institution.

The most famous of these institutionalized observatories was established in the thirteenth century in Maragha under the patronage of the Ilkhanid Hulagu and the directorship of Nasir al-Din al-Tusi. It was built on a large piece of land and was financed by assigning *waqf* (revenue-yielding source often endowed for a religious institution or charity) revenues to support it. Because of its financial autonomy, the observatory was able to survive after the death of its founder Hulagu, and it was active for more than fifty years. The Maragha observatory served as a center of astronomical research and attracted a large team of astronomers from all over the Muslim world. These were the most talented astronomers of the time, and their collaboration, despite their diverse regional backgrounds, is a compelling illustration of the high mobility of scientists and the universality of Arabic scientific culture. The Maragha astronomers engaged in various kinds of scientific research, including the building of specialized observational instruments and the compilation of new tables (*Ilkhanid Zij*), as well as the most advanced work on planetary theory. The Maragha observatory also served as a model for the organization of the large fifteenth-century Ulegh Beg observatory in Samarqand, the sixteenth-century Taqi al-Din observatory in Istanbul, and the eighteenth-century Jai Singh observatory in Jaipur.

Several sciences were methodologically allied to astronomy. Mathematical geography, for example, required the determination of latitudes as well as longitude differences between localities; the longitude difference was often calculated by measuring the difference in the two places between the respective local times of occurrence of the same astronomical phenomena, such as a lunar eclipse. Numerous sources give lists of place names and their terrestrial coordi-

The most famous observatory founded by the Muslims was established in the thirteenth century in Maragha under the directorship of Nasir al-Din al-Tusi. It served as a model for the large observatory that was built by the Timurid prince Ulugh Beg in Samarqand in the early fifteenth century and has been recently restored.

nates. Another aspect of mathematical geography is cartography. Advanced research on projection theory was conducted by Arab scientists; as a result, several new theories were introduced. It seems, however, that there was little systematic application of these theories in the construction of world maps. The extant examples of such maps—including the famous twelfth-century map of the Arab geographer and cartographer Abu Abd Allah Muhammad al-Idrisi (1100–66) that was commissioned by the Norman King Roger II (1095–1154) of Sicily—are highly schematized. The nautical sciences were also dependent on astronomy. In addition to the experience of the navigators, these sciences drew on knowledge of astronomy, geography, and measuring and observational instruments. The only surviving texts in this field were written by Ibn Majid and Sulayman al-Mahri toward the end of the fifteenth and beginning of the sixteenth centuries. The real nautical knowledge, however, was more dependent on ship-making technology and practical experience in navigating the Indian Ocean than on purely scientific knowledge.

Mathematics

The Arabs inherited and developed several arithmetic numeration systems. Finger reckoning was used by the Arabs before Islam. It is also known as *hisab al-jummal* (sentence arithmetic), in reference to the use of a fixed order of the letters of the Arabic alphabet to denote numerals. Because it is primarily mental, addition and subtraction in this system are fairly simple, whereas various cumbersome schemes are employed for multiplication, division, and ratios—complicated computations are especially difficult to perform. This is why finger reckoning started to disappear with the introduction of Hindu arithmetic, the base for the current scheme of numeration and calculation. In the Hindu arithmetic system, any number can be denoted using only nine digits and a zero. Its great versatility derives from the use of the decimal scale and the idea of a place value. The sexagesimal system is also a place-value system, but it is based on a scale of sixty. Of ancient Babylonian origins, this system was used extensively in connection with astronomy. Even after the introduction of decimal fractions, Arabic computations often mixed bases and systems. In astronomy the common practice was to use the decimal system for integers and the sexagesimal system for fractions; for both integers and fractions the letters of the Arabic alphabet were normally used instead of numerals. Numerals took different forms in different regions, with a marked difference between the eastern and western parts of the Muslim world. These numerals were known among Arabs as Indian numerals; the western version of these numerals passed into Europe and became known as Arabic numerals.

The phenomenon of the reorganization and reconstruction of disciplines by cross-application was as true of the fields of mathematics as it was for astronomy. The foundations of each discipline were thoroughly reorganized by systematically applying other fields to it and by generalizing its concepts and methods. The three mathematical disciplines that interacted in this generative way were arithmetic, algebra, and geometry. The new Arabic discipline of algebra played a central role in this process. Older mathematical traditions provided case-by-case solutions for specific equations. The equations themselves, however, were never the autonomous object of study. The first work to consider algebraic expressions irrespective of what they may represent was al-Khwarizmi's *Kitab al-Jabr wal-*

The tradition established by the Maragha observatory continued into the eighteenth century, as shown by the one Jai Singh established in Jaipur, India. He modeled some of his instruments after those of Maragha, including hemispherical and equinoctial sundials.

Muslims developed several sciences related to astronomy, such as mathematical geography and cartography. One of the most important world maps of medieval times was drawn by al-Idrisi for the Norman King Roger II of Sicily (r. 1095–1154). The original has been lost, but this twentieth-century re-creation shows how sophisticated it was, with seventy sectional maps covering the seven climes in ten columns. Like most maps made in the Islamic lands, this one has south at the top.

Muqabala (known as The book of algebra, literally "the book of compulsion and comparison"). Written in the first quarter of the ninth century, this work was considered by Arab mathematicians as well as by early and late historians as an outstanding achievement in the history of mathematics. Al-Khwarizmi himself was aware of the novelty of his work: he used a title never used before in earlier disciplines, and he provided an innovative technical terminology often without parallel in earlier traditions. The objectives of al-Khwarizmi's work were equally original: to provide, for the first time, a theory for the solution of all types of linear and quadratic equations by radicals, without restricting the solution to any one particular problem. Thus, the subject of al-Khwarizmi's new discipline was equations and roots: all geometric or arithmetic problems were reduced, through algebraic operations, to normal equations with standard solutions.

The work of al-Khwarizmi was only the first in a long and increasingly more sophisticated tradition of algebraic research. Almost immediately after the emergence of this new field, other mathematicians started developing it and exploring the possibilities for applying it to other mathematical disciplines. In the tenth and eleventh centuries Abu Bakr Muhammad al-Karaji (fl. 1010) introduced new research focused on the systematic application of the laws of arithmetic to algebraic expressions. In the second half of the ninth century, the Arab scientist Qusta ibn Luqa al-Balabakki (d. a. 912) had translated the first seven books of Diophantus' *Arithmetica* into Arabic. Significantly, the Arabic translation was given the title *The Art of Algebra*. The translator's use of the language and conception of the new field of algebra reoriented the *Arithmetica* and provided instead an algebraic interpretation of this arithmetic. In this particular instance, the translation from Greek into Arabic was both motivated and conditioned by the earlier original research in Arabic algebra. Thus, the Greek arithmetic that al-Karaji applied to

Al-Khwarizmi's book *Kitab al-Jabr wal-Muqabala*, written in the first quarter of the ninth century, is the oldest Arabic work on algebra. In it, al-Khwarizmi tried to provide a theory for the solution of all types of linear and quadratic equations. Partially translated into Latin by Robert of Chester, the text served to introduce the science of algebra to Europe.

algebra had already been modified, even as it was being translated, under the influence of the work of al-Khwarizmi and his successors. After al-Karaji's work, the central efforts in algebraic research focused on the arithmetization of algebra, a genre of research that was new both in its contents and in its organization. For six centuries most of the important mathematicians continued to build on and to develop the work of al-Karaji. The work of Ibn Abbas al-Samawal al-Maghribi (d. a. 1175) is of particular importance within this tradition. In his *al-Bahir fi al-Jabr* (The splendid on algebra), al-Samawal defined algebraic power, studied arithmetical operations on polynomials, and examined the multiplication, division, addition, subtraction, and extraction of roots for irrational quantities.

While the application of arithmetic to algebra occupied center stage in algebraic research, the theory of algebraic equations also continued to develop. The mathematician Thabit ibn Qurra, for example, provided systematic geometrical interpretations of algebraic procedures and explained quadratic equations geometrically. Other mathematicians attempted to do the reverse and explain geometrical problems in algebraic terms. Aware of the difficulty of solving cubic equations by radicals and demonstrating such solutions geometrically, Abu Abd Allah Muhammad ibn Isa al-Mahani (d. a. 880) introduced the first algebraic formulation of a solid problem. Mathematicians then increasingly resorted to conic sections to solve cubic equations that could not be solved by radicals. Unlike earlier attempts to geometrically demonstrate equations whose roots are known through algebraic solutions, the objective of this last research was to find, with the help of geometry, the roots of equations that are not solvable numerically. A continuous tradition of partial contributions to this field began in the ninth century and culminated in the systematic work of the Persian mathematician Umar al-Khayyam (1048–1131). Al-Khayyam elaborated a geometrical theory for equations of degree equal to or less than three. For all types of third-degree equations, he provided a formal classification according to the number of terms; he then solved these equations by means of the intersection of two conic sections. These solutions, as well as al-Khayyam's method of using auxiliary curves and geometric figures to solve third-degree equations, are often wrongly attributed to the French mathematician and philosopher René Descartes (1596–1650).

Al-Khayyam's monumental contributions to the theory of algebraic equations were not isolated, as general surveys of the history of mathematics often assert. In fact, his work constituted only the beginning of a long and continuous tradition that was further transformed, a half century later, by Sharaf al-Din al-Tusi (born before 1135–d. a. 1213). In its analytic approach, al-Tusi's work on equations marks the beginning of the discipline of algebraic geometry: the study of curves by means of equations. Like al-Khayyam, al-Tusi continued to solve equations by auxiliary curves; unlike his predecessor, however, al-Tusi algebraically proved the

Al-Khwarizmi is often considered the founder of algebra, and his name gave rise to the term algorithm. This page is from a manuscript of his treatise on algebra.

intersection of curves by means of their respective equations. Before al-Tusi, al-Khayyam had already noted, in his classification of third-degree equations, that some of these equations are impossible; that is, they have no positive solutions. Al-Khayyam only examined the equations that allow possible cases, however. Al-Tusi also examined these cases, but in the course of his treatment of the impossible cases, he introduced new concepts and methods and charted even more new directions for mathematical research. Several new concepts usually attributed to later European mathematicians were introduced by al-Tusi. For the first time in history, he formulated the concept of a maximum of an algebraic expression, which is often wrongly attributed to the French mathematician François Viète (1540–1603): to find the value of an unknown x for which a cubic function of that unknown is a maximum. To do this, al-Tusi calculated the value of the variable x for which the derivative of the above function is equal to zero. Al-Tusi did not use the Arabic equivalent for the word *derivative*, but he clearly introduced local analysis, the study of maxima, and the notion of a derivative—all of which were crucial concepts for the development of algebraic geometry.

Starting with al-Khwarizmi, and on to al-Khayyam and al-Tusi, these mathematicians were fully aware of the novelty of their work. They concocted unfamiliar titles for their books, coined technical terminology unique to their disciplines, organized their works in decidedly different ways, and invented original mathematical algorithms to solve the problems of their disciplines. Above all, they conceived of totally new subjects and mathematical concepts. Such innovations were made possible by the deliberate and systematic application of three mathematical disciplines to each other: algebra, arithmetic, and geometry. The effect of these trends was not restricted to the restructuring of Hellenistic mathematical knowledge; rather, it extended to the creation of new mathematical disciplines. The professional contexts for the emergence of these disciplines are wide and diverse. Outside the three mathematical disciplines, scientists were informed by the results of research in a wide array of fields. In certain cases, momentum for scientific research derived from interests totally unrelated to the exact sciences. Combinatorial analysis, for example, was one such field; it developed not just in connection with algebraic research but also linguistics. To compile an exhaustive Arabic lexicon, al-Khalil ibn Ahmad (718–86), one of the earliest Arab lexicographers, enumerated for all the letters of the Arabic alphabet all the possible combinations of words with a maximum number of five letters. Of these possible words, the actual lexicon includes only those that are empirically verifiable.

Communities of scholars that include not only first-class mathematicians but also commentators of lesser reputation, as well scholars working in other fields, contributed to the creation and diffusion of a multitude of mathematical traditions. Methods used for the solution of certain kinds of problems became in themselves subjects for further examination and systematization. In addition to these disciplines, new fields of research developed, including intermediate analysis, integer Diophantine analysis, and the study of asymptotic behavior and of infinitesimal objects, among others. Even in geometry, which was the most advanced branch of the inherited Hellenistic mathematical sciences, Arabic geometry acquired its own characteristic features at an early stage in its development. This too was a result of combining geometry with algebra and arithmetic. Although most advances in geometry were deliberate and programmatic, some were unintended. The most notable example is the long tradition of examining Euclid's theory of parallels (the fifth postulate of Euclid's *Elements*), which was initially aimed at providing better proofs for Euclid's theory. Ibn al-Haytham, al-Khayyam, and al-Tusi were among the many mathematicians who tried to provide such proofs. In the course of these attempts, some of the theorems of non-Euclidean geometry were proved. Although Muslim mathematicians did not finally formulate such a geometry, they established a tradition of research that was central to its later discovery.

Trigonometry was another hybrid mathematical discipline in which Arab scientists enriched, and eventually reoriented, earlier scientific knowledge. Initially developed in conjunction with research in astronomy, trigonometry finally became an independent mathematical discipline in its own right. While Ptolemy's astronomy was superior in its models, it rested on elementary geometrical propositions. Ptolemaic astronomical computations were based on a single function, the chord of a circular arc. Moreover, the only tool for spherical computation was Menelaus' theorem—a cumbersome formula for the relationship between the six segments that result from the intersection of four arcs in a complete quadrilateral. Soon after translating Ptolemy and adopting his models, Arab astronomers augmented his geometry with the powerful sine function of Indian trigonometry. In the ninth century the tangent function was also introduced. The emergence of trigonometry as an independent science, however, required two additional developments: first, identifying the spherical triangle as the object of study as opposed to the calculus of chords on the spherical quadrilateral; and second, including the angles of triangles in this calculus and not restricting it to the sides. The first accounts of the spherical triangle appeared by the end of the tenth century. In a testimony to the universality of the scientific culture of the time, the general theorem of sines, known as the Rule of Four Quantities, was discovered simultaneously and independently by three astronomers from Khwarizm, Baghdad, and Rayy (Abu Nasr Mansur ibn Iraq, Abu al-Wafa al-Buzjani, and Abu Mahmud Hamid al-Khujandi). In the eleventh century all six relations of the right-angled triangle appeared in various texts, including, among others, al-Biruni's *Maqalid Ilm al-Haya*. In the thirteenth century Nasir al-Din al-Tusi wrote the first independent treatise on trigonometry without reference to astronomy, thus sealing the process by which another independent discipline was created.

Optics

The Arabs also inherited a large body of Hellenistic optical knowledge, which covered the physical as well as geometric study of vision, the reflection of rays on mirrors (catoptrics), burning mirrors, and atmospheric phenomena such as the rainbow. Within two centuries, however, the field of optics was radically transformed, and Arabic optics acquired the characteristics of a new field of study with distinct methods and approaches. As in other scientific disciplines, the first Arabic translations of Greek optical texts were produced at the same time as the first research in Arabic was being conducted. Arabic compositions in optics started in the eighth century and continued through the ninth with the works of Ibn Masawayh, Hunayn ibn Ishaq, Qusta ibn Luqa al-Balabakki, and Thabit ibn Qurra. In addition to its primary focus on physiological optics, ninth-century works also treated, in separate studies, the subject of burning mirrors, reflection on mirrors, and geometrical and physical optics. Yaqub ibn Ishaq al-Kindi (ca. 801–ca. 866) is said to have produced ten treatises in the latter fields, of which at least four are extant. Both Qusta ibn Luqa and al-Kindi adopted a deliberate strategy in their research: To rectify the results of one particular subfield of Hellenistic optics, they drew on other subfields of this research, with the intention of combining the geometry and the physiology of vision. One of the most immediate results of this innovative approach was to integrate catoptrics, the study of the reflection of visual rays on mirrors, into the mainstream of optical research.

The greatest work of Arabic optics is undoubtedly Ibn al-Haytham's *Kitab al-Manazir*. In the tenth century the earlier work of Abu Sad al-Ala ibn Sahl (fl. 970–90) expanded the horizons of optics and provided an important link in the line of research that culminated in Ibn al-Haytham's seminal contributions in the eleventh century. One of Ibn Sahl's own additions was the creation of the field of dioptrics, in which the study of burning instruments was no longer restricted to mirrors but also included lenses. Ibn Sahl produced a systematic theoretical study of refraction in lenses, in which he included an examination of various kinds of curves and of geometrical methods of drawing them. He also introduced the notion of a constant ratio, which is the inverse of what is now called the index of refraction. This ratio measures the refraction of a visual ray in a particular medium with respect to air. Its discovery represents the first instance of a fundamental principle of dioptrics, which is often referred to as the law of Snellius (in reference to the 1621 discovery in Europe of the same law).

The creative trend of expanding optical research in all of its subfields reached a peak under Ibn al-Haytham (known as Alhazan in the west), who covered in an integrated research project all of the traditional themes of optics as well as those invented by his forerunners. This project effectively undermined the basic premise and structure of Greek optical research. At a basic conceptual level, Ibn al-Haytham rejected the Hellenistic theories of vision and introduced a radically different theory. Vision, according to earlier theories, is considered a result of contact between the eye and the object, either through a ray emitted from the eye to the object (as in the extramission theories of Euclid and Ptolemy) or through the transmission of a "form" from the object to the eye (as in the intro-

Ibn al-Haytham (d. 1039), known in the West as Alhazan, was a leading Arab mathematician, astronomer, and physicist. His optical compendium, *Kitab al-Manazir*, is the greatest medieval work on optics.

mission theories of Aristotle and the atomists). Ibn al-Haytham's remarkable insight was to argue that what is sensed is not the object itself and that an image of the object is formed as a result of the reflection of light from the object to the eye. Ibn al-Haytham could thus proceed to study the geometric aspects of the visual cone theories without having to explain at the same time the psychology of perception. He also benefited from advances in the study of the eye's physiology, thus integrating into his theory of vision the cumulative results of mathematical, physical, and medical research. This comprehensive theory enabled Ibn al-Haytham to provide various levels of explanation. For example, the conditions of the propagation of light could be studied in separation from physical theories of vision. Ibn al-Haytham built on the already rich Arabic tradition and proceeded to examine various aspects of the rules of propagation of light. In the course of his systematic and integrated research, he conceived of new problems that were not addressed in earlier optical research. One such famous mathematical problem is known as Alhazan's problem: to find the point of reflection on the surface of a concave or convex spherical mirror, given the fixed positions of the visible object and the eye.

Ibn al-Haytham's innovative conceptualization and approach also led to the adoption of controlled experimentation as a practice of investigation as well as the norm for proofs in optics and more generally in physics. More systematic experimentation was employed by Kamal al-Din al-Farisi (d. 1319), who pursued Ibn al-Haytham's project of reforming optics and wrote commentaries on a number of his works. To explain the formation of rainbows, al-Farisi introduced an experimental setup in which a glass sphere filled with water simulated the water droplets suspended in the atmosphere. He then proceeded to mathematically justify the analogy between this artificial model and nature by arguing that a sufficiently thin glass sphere would produce negligible additional refraction. By controlling the medium in which the experiment was conducted, al-Farisi was successful in explaining the shapes of the principal arc and the secondary arc of the rainbow as resulting from two refractions and one or two reflections inside the sphere.

It has often been argued that Ibn al-Haytham's work had no effect on Arabic optical research and was only appreciated in later European scholarship. Yet the work of al-Farisi, in addition to recent evidence for an eleventh-century Andalusian version of Ibn al-Haytham's *Manazir*, seems to illustrate a continuity in the creative activity in optical research not just before Ibn al-Haytham but also after him. As in all of the other sciences considered thus far, communities of scientists always existed within which normal science was practiced. These normalized practices provided the social and intellectual contexts for the exceptional moments of creativity in the history of Arabic science.

Engineering and Technology

In addition to the classical scientific disciplines, great energies—commensurate with the immensity and eminence of the Islamic empire—were brought to bear on technological developments. These developments contributed significantly to the material prosperity of medieval Islamic societies and to the increased production of raw materials as well as finished commodities. For most of these technologies, only samples exist of the final products of Arabic technological knowledge. Buildings and fabrics, for example, provide living evidence for a fine architectural tradition as well as a developed textile industry. Yet there is little written material that describes the technological knowledge used in such industries. As the field of technology is a vast subject, this section provides only a brief and selective overview, emphasizing technologies about which there are existing written documents.

The Arabs inherited a number of Hellenistic theoretical studies on geometrical statics, including, among other subjects, the mathematical study of the laws of equilibrium, the concept of a center of gravity, and hydrostatic studies of the equilibrium of bodies in liquids. They also inherited practical studies of simple machines for lifting and moving objects. The most famous Greek work in this field was that of the mathematician and inventor Archimedes. Building on this legacy, Arabic research in statics was pursued on three fronts. The first can be called practical statics, and it includes the Arabic science (or art) of designing ingenious mechanical devices (ilm al-hiyal). Several works were composed on this subject, the most famous of which are those of Banu Musa (ninth century) and ibn al-Razzaz al-Jazari (fl. a. 1200). These works described several mechanical devices and automatic machines and provided diagrams illustrating how these devices operated. Some of these machines had an obvious use, apparently designed in response to general social needs; such devices include, for example, water-lifting machines. Other machines had a narrower use, designed at the demand of smaller sectors of society. Fine machines, water clocks, fountains, and various kinds of automata were designed either for the entertainment of affluent segments of society, or to respond to the specialized needs of professional groups.

The second field of research focused on theoretical statics and hydrostatics and is best exemplified by Abd al-Rahman al-Khazini's twelfth-century encyclopedia of medieval statics, Kitab Mizan al-Hikma (The book of the balance of wisdom). The third area focused on the determination of the specific weights of metals and minerals. Scientists like al-Biruni and al-Khazini provided thorough theoretical treatment of this problem. They also invented practical machines and tools to easily determine the specific weights of metals as well as the relative compositions of compounds and alloys.

One of the main trends in Arabic statics was the systematic use of inherited as well as new mathematical techniques, particularly algebra. This trend enabled both a generalization of Greek statics and the invention of new fields within the discipline. This dynamic approach to the study of statics—itself a result of the systematic application of new mathematical skills—led to the emergence of the science of mechanics. The application of this dynamic approach to hydrostatics, as reflected in al-Khazini's study of the motions of bodies in fluids, led to the emergence of the new field of hydrodynamics. The discipline of statics as a whole represents a domain in which theoretical science and technology clearly interacted. The findings of the various theoretical sciences were continuously applied to develop innovative technologies and thus contributed in the process to the development of modern engineering, the art through which the results of science are put to practical use.

Many of the contributions of early Arabic statics were central to the development of what is known today as mechanical engineering. Many new mechanisms and machines were introduced during this time. To name only a few, these included the invention of conical valves, the use of complex gears to transmit high torque, the introduction of double-acting pumps with suction pipes, the use of a crank mechanism in a machine, and the invention of sensitive control mechanisms. The emergence of mechanical engineering was equally dependent on developing the procedures and techniques used in the production of these

Al-Jazari's book on automata is the first mechanical engineering handbook that provides full information for the construction of machines as well as illustrations of how they work. This artistic illustration from a copy of his text made in Syria in 1315 shows a handwashing device in the form of a servant pouring water from a ewer. When the water is poured, the servant offers the towel in his left hand.

The technology to handle and control water was of great importance in the arid regions where Islam flourished. In certain regions, such as Iran and Morocco, people tapped into underground aquifers to create conduits known as *qanats* or *khattaras*, which are visible above ground by their crater-like cleanout holes.

new machines. Early descriptions of mechanical devices were strictly schematic: diagrams were used to illustrate the theory underlying a device, not to provide information on its construction or relative dimensions. The first mechanical engineering handbook was al-Jazari's *Kitab fi Marifat al-Hiyal al-Handasiyya* (The book of knowledge of ingenious mechanical devices). In addition to schematic illustrations of how machines work, the book provided detailed instructions on the dimensions of their various parts; the materials to be used and their treatment; casting techniques; and information on finishing, calibration, and priming procedures. In short, this handbook provided all the information needed to manufacture a machine as well as to understand its workings.

Relatively elaborate and detailed guidelines for the application of technological knowledge are preserved in the field of irrigation engineering. Many irrigation methods were inherited from the practices of agrarian-based ancient Near Eastern societies. The Muslims also supported intensive agricultural development projects. Arabic chronicles provide considerable information on the scale and significance of such projects initiated by the Umayyads (661–750), the Abbasids (750–1258), and others. These projects were crucial to the development of the economies of Muslim societies and for providing the needs of newly established cities or expanded older ones. Many irrigation projects were of a massive scale: they often involved the building of dams to control and regulate the flow of rivers; the use of water-raising machines to transfer water for irrigation and water supply; and the building of extensive networks of canals and *qanats* (underground conduits) to divert water as necessary. Highly advanced technical and administrative skills were needed to regulate large-scale irrigation and water supply projects. For example, Arabic chronicles report that a tenth-century supervisor of the irrigation system of the city of Marv and its environs was in charge of more than ten thousand workers who were employed in the building, maintenance, and control of the irrigation system. Specialized technical skills, such as the surveying and excavation of canals, were also developed in connection with irrigation. Several treatises were written during this time on quantity surveying methods, providing detailed instructions for the management of the construction of large-scale irrigation systems.

Of particular importance was *qanat* irrigation, which required the careful application of standardized technologies. A *qanat* is an underground conduit that runs almost horizontally and transfers water from an aquifer to a specific location. This system was used extensively in Iran and North Africa. According to some estimates, 70 percent of all water use in Iran until the modern period came from qanats, spanning a length of more than one hundred thousand miles. The digging of an underground conduit represented a major engineering undertaking that involved locating an underground source, estimating its potential yield, surveying the land between the source and the surface outlet to determine the route, digging vertical ventilation and cleaning shafts every thirty to fifty yards along the desired route, and finally excavating the sections between these shafts at very slight inclinations to ensure smooth water flow between the source and the outlet. The procedure also required the application of techniques to align the underground tunnels and to test air quality for the safety of workers.

Other technologies were also used to handle, control, and divert water. Dams of different designs, sizes, and purposes were constructed and often used to provide power for milling or to drive waterwheels, which would raise the water to an elevated reservoir level so that it could be used to supply a surrounding region. The large

Large waterwheels, known as *norias*, were used to raise water from rivers to a reservoir level from which it would be distributed to surrounding regions. The Syrian city of Hama on the Orontes River was famous for its enormous wooden waterwheels.

wheel known as the *noria* was such a water-raising machine. It was used in the ancient Near East, but its hydrodynamic features were enhanced in the Islamic period and it was used extensively in such places as Andalusia and Syria. The most popular of these machines was the *saqiya*, which was driven by animals. Many of these machines are detailed in al-Jazari's work. The work of the sixteenth-century mechanical engineer Taqi al-Din is also of particular importance. He provided a description of a six-cylinder pump, equipped with one-way valves, pistons, and cams, which resembled, and may have influenced, later European machine technologies.

Among the most important of the many technologies that developed in the Muslim world are shipbuilding, mining, and metallurgy as well as paper, textile, and military industries. The technological knowledge and practical skills amassed in these crafts was not always recorded, but fortunately in several cases written records exist. For example, many treatises discuss aspects of the military technologies, including such diverse topics as fortification, siege machines, weapons, sword making, gunpowder recipes, firepots and grenades, fuses for rockets and torpedoes, canons, and so on. Many of these technologies required an advanced level of chemical knowledge. Yet chemistry, or rather alchemy, was not clearly and exclusively an exact science. At least in part, it was an occult discipline with metaphysical and spiritual concerns. Despite its ambiguous status, the field of alchemy also had a strong technological dimension. Aside from such questions as the transformation of the spirit, a significant part of alchemy dealt with pure technological matters, including the preparation of compounds and chemical products, chemical operations like distillation and crystallization, and the invention of technical apparatus for laboratory use. Most of the known works of alchemy, including those of the celebrated Jabir ibn Hayyan (ca. 721–815) and Abu Bakr al-Razi (ca. 865–between 923 and 935), contain considerable sections on practical chemistry. This aspect of alchemy justifies its inclusion as one of early Arabic technology's main areas of achievement.

Medicine

Because of its immediate social significance, medieval sources provide a wealth of information on the theory and practice of Arabic medicine. In addition to numerous medical treatises, many sources also shed light on the lives of scientists, the professional medical communities, the social practice of medicine, the various healing institutions, and the regulation of the medical profession. Both the area and the period in which the Arabic medical tradition evolved are immense. In the ninth century Baghdad was the dominant center for the production of the Arabic medical tradition. In the tenth and eleventh centuries, however, many regional centers competed with Baghdad. In the thirteenth and

The apparent uniformity of Arabic medicine can be traced to a shared Hellenistic heritage. This page from a thirteenth-century copy of Yahya al-Nahwi's summary of Galen's treatise show Andromachos and the eight Greek doctors of antiquity.

fourteenth centuries, Syria emerged as the leading center in medical activities. During this period many medical institutions were built there, and a large number of physicians traveled from all over the Muslim world to seek employment in its institutions.

A shared Hellenistic medical legacy accounts for the apparent uniformity of Arabic medicine. The actual practice of medicine produced diverse and at times competing tendencies within this tradition. Insights into the rise of such tendencies can be pieced together from a variety of sources, including medical treatises, specialized and general biographical works, *waqf* charters, and market supervision manuals, as well as many anecdotes in literary and historical sources. These sources contain references to rudimentary medical practices among the Arabs before Islam, but an Arabic medical tradition per se, or even quasi-scientific medicine, did not exist.

The first references to learned medicine are under the Umayyad caliphate, which employed physicians trained in the Hellenistic tradition. In the eighth century a member of the Umayyad family is said to have commissioned the translation of medical and alchemical texts from Greek into Arabic. Various sources also indicate that the Umayyad caliph Umar ibn Abd al-Aziz (r. 717–20) commissioned the translation from Syriac into Arabic of a seventh-century medical handbook written by the Alexandrian priest Ahrun. As in the case of the other sciences, these early activities increased dramatically under the Abbasid caliphs of Baghdad, who employed Nestorian physicians from the city of Gundishapur. In particular, eight successive generations of the Bakhtishu family were favored physicians in the Abassid court well into the eleventh century. In addition to the learned practice of medicine, translations of medical texts and new medical writings started to appear in the ninth century. Most of these writings were based on Hellenistic medicine, but even in the very early period some new treatises contained original features that were not found in the earlier Greek sources. The most famous of the early translators and physicians are Yuhanna ibn Masawayh (d. 857), the head of Bayt al-Hikma, and Hunayn ibn Ishaq (808–873). With his students, Hunayn translated almost all of the then-known Greek medical works into either Syriac or Arabic.

At the same time these translations were made, original works were composed in Arabic. Hunayn, for example, composed a few medical treatises; of these, *al-Masail fi al-Tibb lil-Mutaallimin* (Questions on medicine for students) and *Kitab al-Ashr Maqalat fi al-Ayn* (Ten treatises on the eye) were both influential and considerably innovative. Although Hunayn's works included very few new observations, their creativity lies in a new organization, and in the case of the second book, in its deliberate attempt to exhaust all questions related to the eye. In any event, a solid command of medical knowledge was needed to produce these works. The most famous work of the early period was composed by Ali ibn Sahl Rabban al-Tabari (ca. 783–ca. 858), a Christian convert to Islam from Marv. Al-Tabari's book *Firdaws al-Hikma* (Paradise of wisdom) was the first comprehensive work of Arabic medicine that integrated and compared the various medical traditions of the time. This work adopted a critical approach to enable readers to choose between different practices. A section on Indian medicine provided valuable information on its sources and practices. Indian medicine was far less crucial than Hellenistic medicine in shaping the Arabic medical tradition, although occasionally physicians would compare Greek and Indian medicine and opt for the latter. This was the exception rather than the rule, however. The main role of Indian medicine was not to define the contours of the Arabic medical tradition but to set the tone for some of its initial interests and curiosities. Although the Greek scientific legacy was dominant, a mere awareness of more than one tradition encouraged a critical and selective approach that pervaded all fields of early Arabic science.

By the end of the ninth century the Galenic humoral system of pathology was completely integrated into Arabic medicine. Although extensive use was made of the writings of Hippocrates (fourth century B.C.E.), they were used within the more systematic theoretical framework of Galenic medicine. Humoral pathology was based on the notion of four humors (blood, phlegm, yellow bile, and black bile) and their relation to the four elements (air, water, fire, and earth), as well as to the four qualities (hot, moist, cold, and dry). The balance or equilibrium (*itidal*) of these humors and qualities amounted to health; imbalance, therefore, was considered to be the cause of illness and disease. Emphasis in treatment was placed on maintaining or reestablishing equilibrium by controlling the environment and the internal constitution of the body through the use of certain kinds of foods or medicines as well as through bleeding and purgatives. This system of medicine employed a significant degree of logical reasoning along with medical observation to explain illness and to devise treatment. Theoretical discourse was thus superimposed on clinical observation, and theoretical considerations played a major role in the structuring and organization of medical knowledge. Arabic medicine further developed this tendency to systematize and rationalize. For the first time, attempts were made to organize the vast body of medical knowledge in all branches of medicine into one comprehensive and logical structure.

An equally important trend focused on expanding empirical medical knowledge—with emphasis on clinical or case medicine—and on practical procedures for treatment, as opposed to the theoretical reflections on illness and health. One of the greatest representatives of this trend is the ninth-century scientist Abu Bakr al-Razi. In his prolific writings, al-Razi generated various theoretical criticisms of the body of inherited medical knowledge. More important than these criti-

The Greek scientific tradition remained strong in Islamic times, and the theoretical framework of Galenic medicine of classical antiquity was integrated into Islamic practice. This illustration from a thirteenth-century Arabic translation of Dioscorides' *Materia Medica* shows a pharmacist preparing drugs.

cisms, however, was his focus on method and practice. Throughout his work, al-Razi put more emphasis on observational diagnosis and therapy than on the theoretical diagnosis of illnesses and their cures. Al-Razi surveyed all of the available medical knowledge and then provided a critical review of this inherited knowledge on the basis of his own practice. His experience as a clinician was undoubtedly wide and rich; it was acquired in a long career as the head of hospitals in Rayya and Baghdad. Some of al-Razi's most original works also derived from this position. His *Kitab fi al-Jadari wal-Hasba* (On smallpox and measles) is the first thorough account of the diagnosis and treatment methods of these two diseases and the differences between their symptoms. A focus on clinical rather than theoretical issues is what characterizes this work and perhaps what makes it original. Al-

Razi wrote many other medical treatises of considerable originality, covering such subjects as diabetes and hay fever. He also wrote an influential general textbook of medicine entitled *Kitab al-Tibb al-Mansuri* (The Mansuri book of medicine), which filled a vacuum because it provided a concise overview of medical theory that could be consulted by students and practitioners of medicine. The reputation of this book, however, has less to do with its original content than with its brevity and organization.

Al-Razi's most important work is his often mentioned but poorly studied book *al-Hawi fi al-Tibb* (The comprehensive book on medicine), an enormous work that in one incomplete copy fills twenty-three volumes. The book is not organized according to formal theoretical paradigms; rather, it is an encyclopedia of clinical medicine, including earlier writings on diseases and treatments as well as al-Razi's own clinical observations. In several places, al-Razi criticized Galen and stated that the reason for this criticism was that his own clinical observations did not conform with Galen's assertions. Al-Razi's meticulous documentation of his sources added to the merit of this work and made it a veritable treasure for the history of medicine. Al-Razi's primary interest was therapeutics, not the theoretical classification of medical knowledge. He did not devise treatments on the basis of logical inferences; rather, he conducted what often amounted to controlled experimentation. In the first volume of the book, for example, he traced the exact effects of bloodletting on treating brain tumor (*sarsam*). To do this, al-Razi divided his patients into two groups; he treated one with bloodletting and did not apply this treatment on the other. He then recommended a treatment method simply on the basis of the results of his observations. This and other examples illustrate that although al-Razi proposed no alternative theoretical framework, a considerable part of his research seems to have proceeded in practical neglect of Galenic theory. Theoretical medicine was simply irrelevant to al-Razi's rigorous research in clinical medicine. His most original contributions are undoubtedly in this field of clinical medicine.

The great *al-Hawi* of al-Razi was not without fault, however. Its main weakness was its enormous size and poor organization, which made the work inaccessible even to expert physicians. Because of these reasons, the work was not able to fill the demand for comprehensive but structured medical handbooks. Later in the tenth century Ali ibn Abbas al-Majusi (ca. 925–94) wrote *Kitab al-Kamil fi al-Sinaa al-Tibbiya* (The complete book of the medical art), also known as *Kitab al-Malaki* (The royal book), with the explicit intention of filling this gap. Al-Majusi praised al-Razi's work for its clinical comprehensiveness, but he noted its lack of a theoretical framework that could have provided structure and an organizational principle. Al-Majusi thus set out to write an accessible book that people could easily copy, buy, read, and use. His work was influential both in the Muslim world and later in Latin Europe.

In the same period an equally influential work was independently produced in Córdoba by Abu al-Qasim al-Zahrawi (936–1013); *Kitab al-Tasrif li man Ajiza an al-Talif* (Manual for medical practitioners), a large medical encyclopedia in thirty books, was intended as a synthesis of medical knowledge available at the time. The largest part of this work deals with symptoms and treatment, which reflects once again the increased interest among many Arab physicians in clinical medicine. The most popular and influential part of this work, however, is on surgery; this part, which was often copied separately from the rest of the book, provided detailed descriptions of medical operations, as well as illustrations of numerous surgical instruments. Further illustrating the practical trends in Arabic medicine, al-Zahrawi maintained in his work that the active practice of surgery was a prerequisite for theoretical knowledge of the field.

Although al-Majusi's work served as a popular handbook of medicine, it was soon replaced by what became the single most influential book on theoretical medicine in the middle ages and until the seventeenth century: *al-Qanun fi al-Tibb* (The canon of medicine) by the celebrated Muslim philosopher and physician Ibn Sina (981–1037). Ibn Sina composed several short treatises on medicine, including a popular didactic poem. His magnum opus *Canon* was written with the intention of producing the definitive canonical work on medicine, in terms of both comprehensiveness and theoretical rigor. In this book, Ibn Sina provided a coherent and systematic theoretical reflection on the inherited medical legacies, starting with anatomy, followed by physiology, then pathology, and finally therapy. Although he included many bedside observations and a few original contributions of a purely practical nature, Ibn Sina's main achievement was not primarily in the clinical domain. Rather, he produced a unified synthesis of medical knowledge, which derived its coherence from the relentlessly systematic application of logical and theoretical principles.

The fame of Ibn Sina's school of medical research often overshadows a significant tradition in Arabic medicine that although not completely innocent of philosophy practiced medicine essentially as a practical art. Medicine, according to this second tendency, was not primarily a matter of reflection on general rules and the deduction of particulars from them. Rather, for many Arab physicians, practice was the central concern of medicine. It is hard to find a physician during this time who promoted purely theoretical medicine without accounting for practical knowledge; it is equally hard to find advocates of pure empirical medical knowledge who were free of theoretical reflection. It is possible, however, to isolate tendencies that weigh in favor of either theoretical or practical medical knowledge. The careers of many physicians seem to have been disproportionately devoted to the cultivation of medicine as a practical scientific discipline. In Andalusia and North Africa, for example, after the end of the tenth century many physicians were also pharmacol-

ogists. This was the case of such famous physicians as Ibn al-Jazzar (d. 980) and
Abu Marwan ibn Zuhr (ca. 1090–1162). In fact, the first criticism of Ibn Sina's *Canon*
was written in Andalusia by another Abu al-Ala ibn Zuhr (d. 1131) of the same family of physicians, who objected mainly to the section that dealt with pharmacology because its exclusive theoretical nature reduced its practical usefulness. Abu
Jafar al-Ghafiqi (d. 1165), another famous physician and pharmacologist, mentioned in one of his works that most physicians of this period prepared medicines
themselves, suggesting that such practical know-how was part of what constituted
appropriate medical knowledge. In contrast to abstract reasoning, experimenting
with medicines as well as bedside observations was a common occupation among
a significant number of physicians.

Anatomy was another field in which strong empirical tendencies were manifest.
Quite understandably, the approach to surgery among most Arab physicians was
cautious. Despite this caution, new surgical techniques were introduced in many
fields; in ophthalmology, in particular, entirely new methods were adopted. Yet this
advanced status of surgery does not in itself constitute evidence for the existence
of a tradition of experimental anatomical discovery. Modern studies on Islamic
medicine often assert that because of cultural taboos and religious restrictions
anatomy was not pursued by Arab physicians, and that the notable anatomical
observations were mere theoretical speculations on inherited anatomical knowledge. The most debated example of Arabic anatomy is the thirteenth-century discovery by the Muslim physician Ala al-Din Ali ibn al-Nafis (d. 1288) of the
pulmonary circulation of blood. After obtaining his early education in Syria, Ibn al-
Nafis moved to Cairo, where he pursued a career in Islamic law and medicine. Ibn
al-Nafis wrote several commentaries on Ibn Sina's *Canon*. In his book *Sharh Tashrih al-
Qanun* (Commentary on the anatomy of the Canon), he noted that Galen's and Ibn
Sina's assertions that blood moves between the right and left ventricles of the heart
through a hole between them was not correct. Anatomy, Ibn al-Nafis maintained,
refutes this assertion because no such hole is detectable through anatomical observation. Ibn al-Nafis then argued that blood reaches the left ventricle through the
lungs, thus providing the first explanation of the minor circulation of blood.

Despite some earlier reservations in modern scholarship on Islamic medicine, there now seems to be no doubt that the discoveries of Ibn al-Nafis had a
definitive and decisive influence on the later European anatomical theories
regarding blood circulation. A more controversial question is whether these discoveries are scientifically significant. Many studies (including those of the historian of Arabic medicine Max Meyerhof) have argued that Ibn al-Nafis'
discovery was a "happy guess" and could not have been the result of scientific
anatomical experimentation. The basis for this argument is that because Islam
prohibits dissection, Ibn al-Nafis must have relied on pure speculation. Yet even

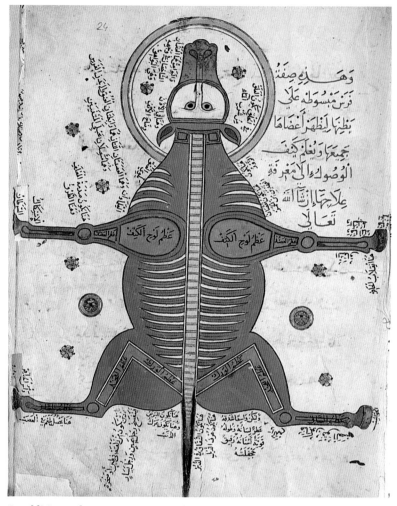

In addition to human anatomy, Muslim scientists also studied animals for practical and medical reasons. This illustration, from a fifteenth-century Egyptian manuscript, shows the skeleton of a horse.

a cursory reading of Ibn al-Nafis' work suffices to disprove this claim. In the introduction to his commentary on the anatomy of Ibn Sina's *Canon*, Ibn al-Nafis stated that both religion and general morality prevent him from conducting dissection. Yet the second chapter of this same book was devoted to the theoretical and practical benefits of dissection, and the fifth chapter discussed the methods and tools of performing dissection. More important, Ibn al-Nafis recurrently rejected or confirmed earlier assertions by referring to the results of anatomical observation, using such expressions as "anatomy (*tashrih*) falsifies what they say" or "anatomy confirms our findings and falsifies their view."

Furthermore, as an indication that he is not referring merely to inherited anatomical knowledge, Ibn al-Nafis often said that he observed certain things recurrently and did not find them in conformity with earlier accepted theories. There seems to be no doubt that despite some restrictions, early Arab physicians performed dissection, and used it to develop medical knowledge.

In addition to Ibn al-Nafis, there are many other references to practical anatomical observations. Disagreements with Galenic accounts of muscle and bone anatomy, for example, could not have derived from philosophical speculation. In the twelfth and thirteenth centuries Abd al-Latif al-Baghdadi provided yet another model through which ancient anatomy was criticized and developed. Al-Baghdadi wrote a description of a famine that occurred in Egypt in 1200. In that description he reported that after examining a large number of skeletons, and after asking other people to conduct their own independent examinations on other skeletons, he arrived at the conclusion that Galen's description of the bones of the lower jaw was erroneous. Although this correction did not amount to a complete rejection or reformulation of Galenic anatomy, it does demonstrate a readiness to question this anatomy on the basis of experimental anatomical examination.

The significant contributions of al-Baghdadi and Ibn al-Nafis did not occur in a vacuum. The twelfth and thirteenth centuries witnessed a surge in medical activity, as physicians from all over the Muslim world sought careers in the medical institutions at Damascus and Cairo. At the social level, physicians were closely integrated with the rest of society, and many of them were leading authorities in the religious disciplines as well, especially law. Ibn al-Nafis, for example, was a scholar of *hadith* (the verified accounts of the actions and sayings of the Prophet Muhammad). Diya al-Din ibn al-Baytar (ca. 1190–1248), one of the leading physicians and botanists of the period, was also a leading jurist who collaborated in his medical research with a circle of Syrian and Egyptian Hanbali scholars (one of four schools of law of Sunni Islam). In Cairo this circle included Abu al-Faraj Abd al-Latif ibn Abd al-Munim al-Harrani, the leading Hanbali jurist of the time. Such profiles suggest the increasing social prestige of larger numbers of physicians and a higher degree of participation in the profession by larger and more representative sectors of society. The first references to a *madrasa*-like institution (a college whose primary purpose is the teaching of Islamic law) for medical learning also came from this period. In thirteenth-century Damascus, Muhadhdhab al-Din al-Dakhwar endowed a school for the exclusive teaching of medicine. The school was inaugurated by the city's leading religious authorities and attracted many religious scholars as students; leading religious figures filled the prestigious position of head administrator of this school. There are also several references to medical instruction in religious schools. Al-Dakhwar himself was a distinguished teacher of a generation of accomplished physicians including Ibn al-Nafis. As a result of the enhanced social status of physicians in this period, another student of al-Dakhwar, Ibn Abi Usaybia, decided to compile a bibliographical dictionary for physicians, who were now fully recognized as members of the social elite.

The prestige of the medical profession increased but did not start in the twelfth and thirteenth centuries. This prestige was closely dependent on mechanisms of social and professional integration, most notably through hospitals. The hospital is one of the greatest institutional achievements of medieval Islamic societies. Between the ninth and tenth centuries five hospitals were built in Baghdad, and several others were built in other regional centers. The most famous of these was the Adudi hospital established under Buyid rule in 982. After this period the number of hospitals increased significantly, when such famous institutions as the Nuri hospital of Damascus (twelfth century) and the Mansuri hospital of Cairo (thirteenth century) were built along with others in Qayrawan, Mecca, Medina, and Rayy, to name a few.

These institutions were open to everyone who needed medical care, regardless of gender, religion, age, or social class and wealth. Medical care was also provided to prisoners, and mobile clinics were regularly dispatched to remote villages. Many of these hospitals were divided into different sections: men and women were treated in separate halls; special areas were reserved for the treatment of contagious diseases; there were also separate areas for surgical cases, and others for the mentally ill. The hospitals also had living quarters for the physicians in attendance as well as for other members of the service team. Some hospitals had their own pharmacies and libraries that could be used for medical instruction. Clinical training and bedside instruction were often provided in these hospitals. A chief administrator, who usually was not a physician, was in charge of hospital administration, while a chief of staff, who was also the head physician, was in charge of running the medical operations. Many of these hospitals had enormous operating budgets, which were usually derived from the

The hospital is one of the greatest institutional achievements of medieval Islamic societies. Hospitals were often part of pious foundations endowed by rulers, as in the one attached to the mosque complex built for the Ottoman Sultan Bayezit II in Edirne between 1484 and 1488.

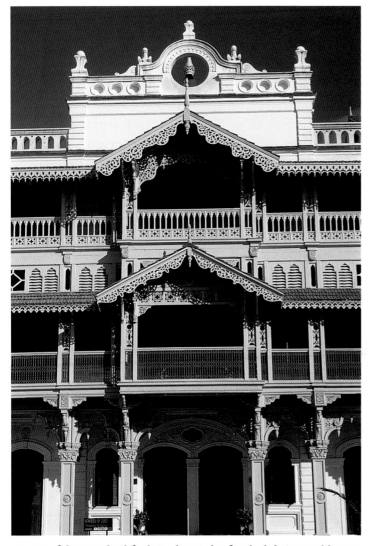

As part of their medical facilities, hospitals often had their own libraries
and pharmacies. This old dispensary in Zanzibar has recently been
restored by the Aga Khan Foundation.

revenues of *waqf* properties dedicated for hospitals. Such revenues were spent on
the maintenance of the premise and the staff, as well as on the cost of treatment,
which was provided to patients free of charge.

Although hospitals provided the most structured framework for the regulation
of the medical practices, there were other means through which such regulation
was attempted. The *muhtasib* (market supervisor) was a public officer, who was
in charge of guarding against fraudulent practices and cheating in all public pro-

Medicines were often stored and shipped in glazed cylindrical jars with concave sides and a rim for securing the cover. These jars were particularly popular in Syria, and many were exported to the West, hence their name *albarelli* (s. *albarello*). They were decorated like other Islamic ceramics. This example, made in the fourteenth century, is decorated with pseudo-Arabic in yellowish-green luster on blue.

fessions and crafts, including medicine, surgery, and pharmacology. *Hisba* (market supervision) manuals were compiled, outlining the duties of the muhtasib. References in such manuals to the medical profession appear only after the eleventh century, but other sources refer to earlier instances of testing of medical doctors by a chief physician (*Ra'is al-Attiba*) who worked in collaboration with the state authorities. Several treatises that outlined the subjects in which the physicians ought to be tested were also composed. Although the sources do not mention many actual cases of testing and examining, it is likely that at least some such testing must have taken place to generate the considerable literature on this subject. Although this testing did not amount to an organized system of licensing, it certainly provided theoretical norms, the systematic application of which depended on the general stability of social institutions at any particular historical moment. An even less organized form of regulation was provided through the abundant literature on medical ethics. Influenced by Hippocratic and Galenic writings, this literature dealt with appropriate codes of professional conduct. Such nonenforceable but highly normative codes were also passed on through teaching in hospitals, special schools, madrasas, and mosques, and within families of physicians. Taken together, these social practices afforded Arabic medicine a level of organization unprecedented in history that contributed to the further development of the Arabic medical tradition.

The Life Sciences: Botany and Pharmacology

Any discussion of the Arabic life sciences would be incomplete without reference to botany and pharmacology. Initially botany was linked to agronomy, as were discussions of nourishment to the healing effects of plants. The most influential ancient work in this genre was *al-filaha al-Nabatiyya* (Nabatean agriculture), which was translated from Syriac to Arabic at the end of the eighth century. Under the influence of two Greek works, botany was separated from agronomy. Of these two works only the *Materia Medica* of the first-century physician Dioscorides is extant. It was first translated under the Abbasid caliph al-Mutawakkil (r. 847–61) but was subsequently revised and retranslated. At the same time, these treatises were being translated, the Persian botanist Abu Hanifa al-Dinawari (ca. 815–95) was compiling his botanical lexicon *Kitab al-Nabat* (The book of plants), which represented the culmination of a tradition in which autonomous botanical writings were part of the sciences of the Arabic language.

The later development of Arabic botany was to a great extent a result of medical and pharmacological research. Andalusia in particular was ahead of other regions in the fields of agronomy, botany, and pharmacology. In the middle of the tenth century the Umayyad caliph Abd al-Rahman III (r. 891–961) received an illustrated manuscript of Dioscorides' *Materia Medica* from the emperor of Byzantium. With the help of a Byzantine monk, a group of Andalusian physicians set out to revise the earlier eastern translation of this book by Istifan ibn Basil. The team successfully identified all but a handful of the simple uncompounded drugs (called simples) described in *Materia Medica*. After this achievement, Andalusia witnessed a rapid and sustained expansion of research in pharmacology and botany. In addition, theoretical efforts were undertaken to make agronomy a "true" science by reference to the more developed sciences of botany, pharmacology, and medicine. Andalusian agronomy thus achieved a high technical level that was not surpassed until the nineteenth century.

This albarello, made in Syria in the fifteenth century, is decorated with flowers underglaze-painted in blue. This is a local Syrian interpretation of a popular type of Chinese blue-and-white ware. The surface is slightly cloudy and iridescent because it was buried for a long time.

An equally important development in the Muslim west was in the field of pharmacology. In the twelfth century several pharmacological encyclopedic works were compiled by such scientists as Abu Jafar al-Ghafiqi and Abu al-Abbas al-Nabati. These works attempted to integrate the known traditions of pharmacology and eventually culminated in the great synthesis of Ibn al-Baytar, *al-Jami li-Mufradat al-Adwiya wal-Aghdhiya* (The dictionary of simple medicines and foods). This is the most complete treatise of applied botany produced in the Middle Ages; it drew information from more than 150 sources and listed more than two thousand simples in alphabetical order. Ibn al-Baytar brought together the accumulated knowledge of numerous inherited traditions in addition to his own experiences. He gave the names of simple medicines in all the written languages he knew as well as in several local dialects. He also succeeded in finding the Arabic names of almost all of the simples listed in the work of Dioscorides. Ibn al-Baytar's method of research is as significant as the results of this research: Following the lead of several Arab botanists including his own teacher, Ibn al-Baytar traveled to conduct on-site research in North Africa, Greece, Anatolia, Iran, Iraq, Syria, Arabia, and finally Egypt. He then settled in Egypt, where he was appointed as the country's head pharmacist. Even after he settled, he continued to conduct field trips to Syria to collect new data and examine or verify earlier findings. Together with many other contributions in this field, Ibn al-Baytar's dictionary illustrates the tendency to simultaneously synthesize and to rely on observation for the expansion of scientific knowledge. Ibn al-Baytar's descriptions were extremely accurate, but the primary purpose of his book was medical.

Of special interest is a work by Abu al-Abbas al-Ishbili (d. 1239), *al-Rihla al-Mashriqiyya* (The eastern journey). This book is lost, but Ibn al-Baytar quoted it in full in more than one hundred entries. Unlike other works that contained botanical information but were ultimately interested in the medical use of plants, the interests of al-Ishbili's book were purely botanical. Although he was a famous physician, al-Ishbili provided meticulous descriptions of plants as plants, not for their potential medical use. As in many of the subfields of mathematics, al-Ishbili's work illustrated the familiar process through which new disciplines emerged as a result of the expansion and systematization of older ones.

The Arabic Sciences: Syntheses and New Creations

By nature, theories that synthesize and supplant earlier knowledge have to be comprehensive and conceptually distinct, not just anomalies within the older systems of knowledge. The characteristics of any new synthesis cannot be explained merely in terms of some revived archaic traditions, but ought to be sought in the historical details that account for the emergence of this synthesis. The inherited traditions of Galenic medicine, Ptolemaic astronomy and optics, Euclidean geometry, and Diophantine arithmetic were all conceptually situated within the unifying context of Aristotelian physics. In these fields the Arabic sciences simultaneously refined, deconstructed, expanded, and superseded the Greek traditions. The most notable characteristics of the Arabic sciences are the generation of syntheses and the related creation of new sciences. With many more disciplines that correspond to a much larger range of research interests, the Arabic sciences were not bound by the rigid categories of scientific thinking that prevailed in the older traditions. These older traditions were transformed at the hands of the scientists of the Muslim world, not so much through abrupt revolutions but by means of enlarging the scope and transforming the methods of earlier sciences. The transformation process was accelerated by the extension and systematic application of empirical research. In a sea of changes the strict hegemony of Aristotelian physics over the large number of old and new scientific disciplines was simply lost.

Religion did not play a direct role in this process of transformation. It neither shaped the cognitive content of the sciences nor did it impede their development. The overall outcome of the religious discourse on science was not to subjugate science to religion but to separate the two enterprises. This meant that the criteria of one were not to be used to judge the other. It was precisely through this separation that Islam played a role in shaping the destiny of science in the medieval Muslim world. Two immediate results of this separation were of great consequence for the later development of science. First, science was considered a value-free undertaking that needed no ethical or religious justification. That is, scientists could pursue their specialized professional interests and at the same time be fully integrated within the institutions of society. And so it was, for example, that most of the distinguished physicians and astronomers of twelfth- and thirteenth-century Syria and Cairo were employed as jurists, teachers in madrasa-like medical institutions, or timekeepers in the region's major mosques. The second important consequence of the separation of religious and sci-

Following Greek precedent, Muslim scientists separated botany from agronomy. Dioskorides' treatise was translated during the ninth century and later revised. This page, from one of the oldest surviving copies, made in the eleventh century, has brief descriptions of the individual plants accompanied by schematic representations.

entific knowledge was to dilute the hold of philosophical systems on the specialized sciences, which in turn resulted in the fragmentation and professionalization of scientific activity. The ultimate meaning of any particular science was no longer sought by necessity in a higher philosophical truth but mostly within its own disciplinary confines.

In many ways science in the Muslim world was a secular enterprise, and religion neither made an enemy of science nor championed its cause to the extreme. The locus of science was society: as long as general learning flourished in society, so did scientific learning, and the decline of one usually ushered the decline of the other. To be sure, with the absence of definite religious guidelines regarding the scientific disciplines, there were diverse independent attitudes toward the sciences. Some religious scholars opposed the sciences, while others sanctioned them on religious grounds. These views were personal, however, and they lacked the normative authority that would either pitch religion against science or subsume science under religion. Fortunately for the Arabic sciences, neither of these scenarios prevailed.

فقال الرب ليجوز أن يبيع وللصدق وخفي ن أن يبيع أنه بانه ليحيكم وللذ اليوم فال فكان الجماعة

إن ثابت بيع قوة وأبت نصديو دعوتو فنوجس ما هم في أفكارهم وفطن لما بطن من أشتكاثم وحاذران

... بعض الغز أثم ... ثم فال يا ودأة الفبض وأشأه الفول المبقر أن طأضة الجوهن

... الشك وقد قياياعر نم ... ن الزمان عبد الامتحان يكم عن الرجال أوهان

CHAPTER FIVE

Art and Architecture

THEMES AND VARIATIONS

Sheila S. Blair and Jonathan M. Bloom

All cultures throughout history have expressed themselves visually, and Islamic civilization was no exception. One need think only of oriental rugs, Persian miniatures, and Moroccan tiles, not to mention the Dome of the Rock, the Alhambra palace, the Selimiye Mosque, and the Taj Mahal, to see the great range of visual expression in the Islamic lands over the centuries. Islamic art encompasses all these and much more. As used in this chapter, the term *Islamic art* refers to all the visual arts produced in the lands in which Islam was the dominant religion, regardless of the confessional affiliations of the individuals who made the art or the purposes for which it was made. Unlike the term Christian art, the term Islamic art is not restricted to works made only for religious situations and functions, and many of the most cherished examples of Islamic art have little, if anything, to do with the religion of Islam. A page from a parchment manuscript of the Quran is obviously considered a work of Islamic art, but so is a bronze bowl inlaid with Christian scenes from thirteenth-century Syria.

What Is Islamic Art?

Islamic art could not have begun, of course, before the rise of Islam in early seventh-century Arabia, but it was nearly a century after that before Muslims began to be great and sophisticated patrons of the arts. Athough Muslims began erect-

(Left) A typical medieval library, as depicted in a manuscript of al-Hariri's *Maqamat* (Assemblies), transcribed in Baghdad in 1237. The leather-bound volumes were stacked flat in niches cut into the wall.

The broadest definition of Islamic art would include this life-size oil portrait of the nineteenth-century Qajar ruler Fath Ali Shah, although it can also be considered to represent a distinctly Persian style of painting.

ing structures soon after the revelation of Islam, the first example of Islamic architecture is generally considered to be the magnificent Dome of the Rock in Jerusalem, ordered in 692 by the Umayyad caliph Abd al-Malik ibn Marwan (r. 685–705). Following this broad definition, Islamic art continues to be produced to this day; artists continue to work in a variety of media in all Muslim countries. Nevertheless, the emergence of national identities, especially in the nineteenth and twentieth centuries, has changed the ways in which people think about works of art produced in the Islamic lands in modern times. Thus, a portrait of the Qajar ruler Fath Ali Shah (r. 1797–1834) is more often considered to exemplify a distinctly Persian style of painting rather than to illustrate Islamic or Iranian attitudes toward representation in the nineteenth century. In current usage concerning modern art, the term *Islamic* generally refers to purely religious expressions such as calligraphy.

Today, many museums in North America, Europe, and the Islamic lands proudly display their masterpieces of Islamic art, but traditionally the visual arts played a relatively minor role in Islamic civilization, especially compared with the important arts of poetry and music. For example, there is no word for art per se in classical Arabic. The word most commonly used today, *fann*, is a neologism because it traditionally meant "craft" or "skill." The same is true of the Persian and Turkish words *hunar* and *hüner*. In addition, artists did not usually enjoy high status in Islamic society, and there were few if any Michelangelos or Rembrandts, whose lives became the stuff of legends.

Of all the visual arts, the only one that was widely appreciated within its own culture was calligraphy, the art of beautiful writing. The names and biographies of calligraphers were collected and preserved, and treatises were written on the aesthetics of calligraphy. Calligraphy was the exception rather than the rule, however, and there was no Islamic equivalent to the first-century B.C.E. Roman architect Vitruvius or the fifteenth-century Italian architect Alberti, who wrote treatises on the theory of architecture. Nor did Islamic civilization produce figures comparable to the Chinese literati, who wrote treatises on the aesthetic appreciation of Chinese painting as early as the period of the Six Dynasties (229–589 C.E.). Because Muslims wrote so little about the aesthetic appreciation of their own visual culture, the study of Islamic art dictates a positivist approach. It must be based on the examination of the remains themselves. Some present-day scholars have tried to derive aesthetic principles for all Islamic art, but these principles tend to reflect modern preoccupations, as they were not generated by traditional Islamic society itself.

This bowl, probably made in Iran or Central Asia in the tenth century, is inscribed with the phrase "Blessings to the owner," followed by a proverb, "It is said that he who is content with his own opinion runs into danger."

Islamic art comprises an unwieldy grab bag of media, techniques, styles, periods, and regions. Its study, a relatively new discipline, developed not in the Islamic lands but in western Europe as an offshoot of studying the history of European art. From the European perspective, Islamic art evolved in the Near East out of the remains of ancient Near Eastern and late antique artistic traditions and bridged the gap between late classical and early medieval art. As Islam spread far beyond the geographical confines of the Near East to western and Sub-Saharan Africa, Central Asia, India, and Southeast Asia, and beyond the temporal confines of the Middle Ages, so did its visual expressions. The models created to understand the arts of the Mediterranean region in the eighth century thus are not necessarily valid for understanding the Islamic arts of Indonesia or Mali.

The arts of western civilization are traditionally understood in a hierarchy, in which architecture and the representational arts of painting and sculpture have dominated the artistic landscape to this day. This hierarchy does not hold for Islamic art. Although architecture is equally important in Islamic culture, Islam produced few sculptures or panel paintings. In Chinese civilization, another long tradition of artistic production, there was a clear division between artists (painters, calligraphers, and poets) and craftsmen (sculptors, potters, metalworkers, and so forth), and therefore between art and craft. This division does not hold in Islamic art, because there was no such distinction between art and craft. Indeed, a distinguishing feature of Islamic art was the transformation of utilitarian objects into sublime works of art. Looking at Islamic material culture, therefore, one should be prepared to find artistic expression in a vast range of situations, from the humblest oil lamps to the most monumental tombs. Nevertheless, Islamic art remains a useful rubric under which to consider the visual cultures of the past fourteen centuries in much of Eurasia and Africa, because it allows certain connections and relationships to be established.

Architecture was universally the most important form of Islamic art. It cost the most, lasted the longest, and was seen by the widest audience. Buildings built for religious purposes, such as mosques and *madrasas* (theological colleges), are often the best known and best preserved because they continued to be used and maintained over the centuries. Religious buildings may provide the framework for tracing the development of Islamic architecture, but the conservatism inherent in religious architecture means that these structures would have been slow to present innovations. It is more likely that architectural innovation was introduced in secular buildings—such as palaces, houses, caravanserais (medieval motels for caravans), bathhouses, markets, and the like—because they were constructed at the whim of a particular person to meet his own needs. Far fewer of these buildings, however, have survived: some literally have been worn to ruins, while others were deliberately destroyed. Few rulers, for example, saw any purpose in preserving the personal fantasies of their predecessors. Thus, the architectural sample available for study is skewed; in attempting to reconstruct the shape of the past, it is important to remember that what survives is not all that was made.

As calligraphy and calligraphers were revered in all Islamic societies, the arts of writing—and by extension all the arts of bookmaking—were given extraordinary importance in Islamic culture. In the age before printing, all manuscripts, from copies of the Quran to popular tales and scientific works, had to be laboriously transcribed by hand, first on sheets of papyrus and parchment and later on paper. From an early date, the works of gifted calligraphers were particularly appreciated and collected. The individual sheets were often embellished with elegant decoration and, where appropriate, beautiful paintings, and then gathered together in boxes or bindings made of tooled and gilded leather. Books were preserved in libraries attached to mosques and palaces. At a time when European monasteries might treasure a few dozen volumes, libraries in the Islamic lands regularly contained hundreds, if not thousands, of volumes.

A third medium that achieved preeminence in Islamic art was cloth. The production and trade of fibers, dyes, and finished goods was a major source of revenue in many places. One modern historian has likened the textile industry in medieval Islamic times to the heavy industries of modern industrial states, because textiles laid the economic foundations of medieval Islamic society. The two major fibers were wool, produced from sheep, and linen, produced from the flax plant. Silk and cotton were also important because they, like wool, could be

Textiles permeated the lives of nomads and urbanites alike, covering floors and defining living spaces. The ubiquitous role of textiles is seen in a painting of a nomadic encampment, attributed to the sixteenth-century Persian painter Mir Sayyid Ali.

A growing taste for abstract motifs was already apparent by the ninth century, as in this bowl decorated with a flowering plant painted in four colors of luster.

dyed relatively easily with brilliant colors. Many other fibers were used where available. Perhaps the most telling image of the centrality of textiles in Islamic culture is the *kiswa*, the cloth veil covering the Kaaba in Mecca, which may represent a vestige of the sacred tent—similar to the Israelites' tent for the Ark of the Covenant (2 Sam. 6:17)—in which God dwelled. Although today the kiswa is always black and embroidered in gold with quotations from the Quran, in the past it could be of virtually any color, including white, green, or even red.

As in many societies, clothing made the man or woman. Dress distinguished not only men from women and rich from poor but also nomads from townspeople and Muslims from non-Muslims. Dress was also used to make countless other social and religious distinctions: green turbans were worn by descendants of the Prophet Muhammad, turbans wrapped around a red baton signified followers of the Safavid rulers of Iran. A coarse cloak of wool (*suf* in Arabic) was often worn by mystics, whose very personal approach to religion became increasingly important alongside the communal practice of Islam. These mystics became known as Sufis.

Textiles were also used for furnishings. There was little or no need for the tapestries that kept down the drafts in the cold castles of the medieval north, just as there was no need in the relatively dry and warm climate that prevails in most of the region for wooden furniture to raise people off damp and cold floors. Most people sat on mats or carpets spread on the ground, leaned against pillows or cushions, and slept on rugs on the floor. Meals were normally communal affairs; spread on the carpet or floor was a washable cloth on which diners would sit and serve themselves off communal trays laden with food, which were sometimes set on a low stand.

Perhaps most distinctively, textiles were also used for portable architecture in the Islamic lands. The area in which Islam originally spread encompassed the two great traditions of tent construction. The bedouins of the Arabian deserts used tents made from long strips of woven cloth supported by posts and tied down with strings and pegs. By contrast, the Turkic nomads of Central Asia used tents made from self-supporting wooden frames covered with felts. Under Islam both types of structures, the Arab tensile structure and the Turkic compression structure, spread into the traditional regions of the other group, and characteristic features were exchanged. Because of the important and often powerful roles played by nomads in sedentary

Islamic society, these humble dwellings were adopted by rulers, who transformed the utilitarian structures with luxurious accoutrements made of the finest and most costly materials.

In the study of Islamic art, many of its other aspects—such as metalwork, ceramics, and glassware, and carved wood, ivory, and rock crystal—are usually encompassed under the rubric "decorative" or "minor" arts. In Western art these terms have somewhat derogatory connotations because these media are considered less noble than the major arts of painting and sculpture. This is simply not true in Islamic art. As in many other cultures, craftsmen working for rich patrons transformed expensive materials, such as elephant tusks, gold, and precious stones, into luxury items. In the Islamic lands, however, craftsmen also transformed the humblest materials, such as clay, sand, and ores, into brilliantly glazed ceramics, limpid glasswares, and glimmering metalwares used by many classes of society.

Muslim artists transformed everyday objects into artistic masterpieces. The Bobrinksi Bucket, cast of brass and inlaid with copper and silver, was a bathpail made in 1163 as a gift to the man who had everything.

These objects were often utilitarian, such as pitchers and basins for washing and trays and bowls for serving. It takes a great leap of imagination to transport an earthenware bowl, austerely displayed in a museum case, to its original setting as a serving dish at a medieval meal.

The Bobrinski Bucket, one of the masterpieces of Islamic art, exemplifies many of these characteristics. Bought in Bukhara (now part of Uzbekistan) in 1885, it was later acquired by the Russian count A. Bobrinski, from whom the piece gets its name. The round cast-brass body is inlaid in copper and silver with horizontal bands of inscriptions and figural scenes. According to the dedicatory inscription on the rim, the bucket was ordered by Abd al-Rahman ibn Abdallah al-Rashidi, formed by Muhammad ibn Abd al-Wahid, and inlaid by Masud ibn Ahmad, the designer from Herat (in present-day Afghanistan), for the merchant Rashid al-Din Azizi ibn Abul-Husayn al-Zanjani. The handle is inscribed with the date Muharram 559 of the Islamic calendar, corresponding to December 1163. None of the people mentioned in the inscription is known from other sources, and the function of the bucket is somewhat of a puzzle. It was once called a "kettle" or "cauldron," but it is too fancy to have been used for cooking. Nor could it have been intended for carrying food or liquids, because contact with the interior might have caused food poisoning from verdigris (corroded copper). The most likely explanation is that the bucket was a bath pail, intended to hold water for washing when the merchant went to the bathhouse. In short, the Bobrinski Bucket was a present for the man who had everything in 1163, the medieval equivalent of a costly gadget from an expensive catalog store.

Despite the enormous variety in Islamic art, which can range from great structures to tiny objects produced between the Atlantic coast of Africa and the islands of Indonesia from the eighth century to the present, several themes have had universal and perennial appeal. In the limited space available in this volume, it would be impossible to recapitulate the long and varied history of Islamic art over fifteen centuries and three continents. Furthermore, this approach tends to emphasize regional and chronological divisions. Instead, this chapter takes a thematic approach that emphasises common features that unite much Islamic art over the continents and centuries. Five themes have been chosen: the art of writing; aniconism, the absence of figures; the decorative themes of arabesque and geometry; the exuberant use of color; and the notion of willful ambiguity. Each of these themes may not appear in every work of Islamic art, but collectively they define an aesthetic approach that makes Islamic art distinct from the artistic traditions of surrounding regions and cultures.

The Art of Writing

Writing is the most important theme to run through all Islamic art. The use of inscriptions is not unique to Islamic culture; the Islamic tradition developed in part from precedents in the region in which Islamic civilization first developed. There was, for example, a long tradition in the classical world of using inscriptions, particularly to decorate the fronts of building as well as monuments, such as triumphal arches. In turn, this tradition passed to the Christian world, and Byzantine art was often decorated with inscriptions (although pictures eventually became more popular). Similarly, in the ancient Near East inscriptions were often used, as on the wall reliefs at Bisitun (or Behistun) in western Iran, where a trilingual inscription in Old Persian, Elamite, and Babylonian lauding the great Achaemenid king of Persia, Darius I (r. 522–486 B.C.E.), surrounds a monumental relief showing his triumph over the usurper Gaumata and the rebels. In all these cases, however, writing supplemented and explained the image. What is different about Islamic art is that writing became the main, and sometimes the only, element of decoration.

This fundamental change was due, in large part, to the pivotal role of writing in the religion of Islam. The first words that God revealed to Muhammad were the five verses opening chapter ninety-six of the Quran:

> Recite in the name of thy lord who created,
> Created man from a clot;
> Recite in the name of thy lord,
> Who taught by the pen,
> Taught man what he knew not.

In other words, the knowledge of writing distinguishes man from God's other creatures. The importance of writing is stressed throughout the Quran. Chapter sixty-eight, another early revelation known either as *surat al-Qalam* (The pen) or *surat al-Nun* (The letter nun), opens with the words "Nun. By the pen and what they write." According to another pair of verses revealed slightly later (Quran 50:17–18), two noble recording angels sit on man's shoulders to register his every action and thought. The one on the right writes down good deeds, the one on the left evil ones. On Judgment Day man's every deed will be tallied for the final accounting in the Book of Reckoning (Quran 69:18–19).

Given the importance of writing in revelation, it is no surprise that writing became such an important feature of Islamic culture. Books and book production became major art forms, and beautifully written words became a major decorative motif. Because the Quran was revealed in Arabic, the Arabic language and script quickly came to

Writing was one of the most common themes of Islamic art. Since Umayyad times, when the first Islamic coins were struck, almost all coins minted in the Islamic lands have been decorated exclusively with writing, as with this gold dinar minted for the Umayyad caliph Abd al-Malik in 696.

dominate the languages that had been used in the region, becoming the lingua franca that united the vast area. By the late eighth century calligraphers were responsible for making the Arabic script more legible and beautiful, and their efforts can be seen in surviving examples ranging from coins and milestones to buildings.

Byzantine and Sasanian coins bore pictures of the emperors under whose auspices the coins were struck. After a brief period of experimentation, Muslim rulers rejected this type of figural coin in favor of one purely dependent on words. Beginning in 692, under the Umayyad caliph Abd al-Malik, virtually all coins were exclusively decorated with writing. This is true, for example, of early gold coins, known as *dinars*. On the obverse or front, the center is filled by the

The first great monument of Islamic architecture, the Dome of the Rock in Jerusalem, erected by the Umayyad caliph Abd al-Malik in 692, was decorated with writing. The top of the mosaic panels on the interior has texts from the Quran in gold letters set against a blue ground.

profession of faith, which continues along part of the edge; the rest of the space contains a verse from the Quran (9:33) about the prophetic mission. On the reverse the coin is inscribed in the center with a Quranic verse (112) stating God's oneness and refuting the Trinity; the text around the edge contains the invocation, mint, and date. All of this appears on a coin less than twenty millimeters in diameter (smaller than a quarter). Although the style of script changed in various locales and periods, this type of epigraphic coin remained characteristic of virtually all Islamic coinage to modern times.

Inscriptions are found in all media and materials, even those in which the technical limitations of the medium made it extremely difficult to incorporate a running text. This is the case, for example, with textiles. It is relatively easy to weave symmetrical patterns of repeating motifs on a loom, but much more difficult to set up a directional design that reads in one direction. By the tenth century, however, Persian weavers had overcome the limitations of the medium and figured out how to incorporate long bands of inscriptions on their elaborately patterned silks. A good example is the fragmentary silk textile known as the Shroud of St. Josse, because it was used in medieval times to wrap the bones of St. Josse in the abbey of St. Josse-sur-Mer, near Caen in northwestern France, where it was probably brought by a Crusader returning home from the Holy Land. It shows how Islamic textiles were considered precious both at home and abroad. From the two surviving pieces, the textile can be reconstructed as a large square measuring one and a half meters (five feet) on a side, with a carpet-like design of several borders surrounding a central field. The borders contain a train of two-humped or Bactrian camels, and the field would have had two identical bands of elephants. Beneath the elephants' feet is an inscription band written in Arabic. The animals are arranged symmetrically, but the inscription band can be read only from right to left. The text invokes glory and prosperity to the commander, Abu Mansur Bakhtikin, who is identified in medieval texts as a Turkish commander in northeastern Iran. He was arrested and executed on orders of his Samanid sovereign Abd al-Malik ibn Nuh around 960. The silk had to have been made before that, however, because it invokes good wishes on a living person. Although it is the only example to survive, this silk must have been one of many identical pieces. It was extremely time-consuming and expensive to set up a drawloom to weave this complicated design in seven colors, but by weaving multiple copies of the silk squares the costs would have been spread more reasonably. It is not known exactly how the St. Josse silk was originally used, but it probably was woven to be a saddlecloth for the troops serving under Bakhtikin's command.

The St. Josse silk is just one example of how artists in medieval Islamic times used inscriptions to decorate works of art. On objects made from expensive materials, such as silk textiles or jade cups, the inscriptions often name the patron or user who commissioned the object. On objects of more humble materials or those made for the market, however, the inscriptions contain more generalized texts. This is the case with a bowl with flaring sides, produced, like the St. Josse silk, in northeastern Iran in the tenth century. Made of buff-colored earthenware covered with a fine white slip, painted in red and dark brown slips, and covered with a transparent colorless glaze, the deep bowl is notable for its size and fine decoration on the interior.

In the center the bowl has an abstract plant motif of a single stem with five leaves, but the major decoration is a wide band of elegant angular script encircling the walls. Assuming that the bowl was meant to hold food, only the scallops on the edge would have been visible when the bowl was full. As the food was eaten, however, the inscription would have become more and more visible until all the decoration was revealed when the bowl was empty. The Arabic text inscribed on the bowl begins after a small decorative motif set at about four o'clock, with the phrase "blessing to its owner." After a small teardrop motif set at about eight o'clock, the text continues with the proverb, "It is said that he who is content with his own opinion runs into danger." Assuming that the bowl was intended to be held and appreciated with the stem of the plant at the bottom, closest to the viewer, then the most important part of the inscription, the blessing to the owner, is immediately legible below it. To read the proverb, the reader must turn the bowl around in a counterclockwise direction.

Other bowls and plates made in the same milieu are decorated with similar aphorisms, such as "Planning before work protects you from regret; patience is the key to comfort," or "Knowledge is an ornament for youth and intelligence is a crown of gold." The inscriptions on these ceramics are thought out extremely carefully, and the stylized script, quite distinct from contemporary handwriting known in manuscripts from that time, justly deserves to be called calligraphy. Modern viewers, even those who know Arabic well, find these inscriptions difficult to decipher. It is likely that even in their own time they were meant to be entertaining puzzles for a sophisticated clientele, who not only appreciated having their dinnerware decorated with stylized writing but also knew the Arabic language well enough to understand the moralizing aphorisms. In tenth-century Iran and Central Asia, New Persian was coming to the fore as a popular language, but Arabic was more appropriate for writing. The earliest surviving manuscript written in Persian dates only from the eleventh century.

These two inscribed wares—the shroud and the bowl—both date from the tenth century, but inscriptions are found on objects created throughout the history of Islamic civilization, from the earliest times to the present. The earliest work of Islamic architecture, the Dome of the Rock in Jerusalem, shows a sophisticated use of inscriptions executed in glass mosaic. In the sixteenth century the Ottoman sultan Süleyman (r. 1520–66) had the mosaics on the outside of the

The Dome of the Rock in Jerusaleum was extensively decorated with glass mosaics like those that survive on the interior. Those on the exterior were replaced with tiles first in the sixteenth and again in the twentieth century, but it may well have had inscriptions like those on the interior.

dome replaced with tiles, which were themselves replaced again in the twentieth century, so it is impossible to say anything about the original role of inscriptions there. The interior, however, preserves most of its original aspect and is the most lavish program of mosaics to survive from ancient or medieval times. Two long bands of inscriptions, written in gold letters that sparkle against the deep blue ground, encircle the inner and outer faces of the octagonal arcade. The texts contain pious phrases and verses from the Quran about God's omnipotence and Muhammad's prophetic mission as well as the name of the patron, the Umayyad caliph Abd al-Malik, and the date of construction.

Writing remains a potent theme in modern Islamic art. The dome around the King Khalid International Airport, built in Riyadh, Saudi Arabia, in 1984, is inscribed with verses from the Quran about God's glory.

As on coins, the script used on the Dome of the Rock is carefully thought out and planned to fit the available space. The inscriptions there provide the first dated evidence for the writing down of the Quran, and they show that there were already calligraphers trained in exploiting the decorative possibilities of the Arabic script. No manuscripts of the Quran have survived from this early date, and some scholars have used this lack of evidence to suggest that Arabic script evolved rather slowly over the centuries. Judging from the inscriptions on the coins and the Dome of the Rock, there can be no question that the art of writing in Arabic was already well developed by the end of the eighth century.

Inscriptions remain an important theme of decoration in modern Islamic architecture. They are prominent, for example, inside the mosque erected in 1984 at King Khalid International Airport in Riyadh, Saudi Arabia. As at the Dome of the Rock, the inscription in this mosque is written in a large band around the dome's base, but in this instance the text is entirely from the Quran (57:1–7). The verses state that whatever is on the earth or in the heavens declares the glory of God, the Almighty who has power over all things. The verses conclude with the statement that whoever spends money on a pious work will be justly rewarded. The text was clearly chosen as a reference to the motives of the patron in founding a mosque.

Medieval masons evolved sophisticated methods of laying bricks in patterns. Contrasting light and shadow, these designs sometimes spelled out words and phrases. The minaret built around 1100 by the Ghaznavid sultan Masud III in Ghazna, Afghanistan, is the first surviving example of this script.

At all times and in all places, Quranic verses were carefully selected to fit a particular situation. Closely examining the chosen verses can provide clues about the original function or meaning of a work of art. Tombs were often decorated with verses referring to death and paradise, such as "All that dwells on the earth will perish, except the face of thy Lord" (55:26–27). Doorways might be inscribed with the verse asking God for a "just ingoing and a just outgoing" (17:80). Other Quranic texts were chosen because certain words had particular resonance. For example, the front of the tomb in the Shifaiye madrasa erected in 1220 at Sivas by the Rum Seljuk ruler Kaykaus is inscribed with a Quranic verse (69:28–29) that ends with the word *sultaniya* (power), undoubtedly chosen as a pun on Kaykaus' most important title, sultan.

Writing in Arabic was also the means by which non-Islamic forms were made Islamic. This can be seen in the arched screen that the Muslim ruler of Delhi, Qutb al-Din Aybak (1206–10), added to the congregational mosque there in 1198. Known as Quwwat al-Islam ("Might of Islam"), the mosque had been built less than a decade earlier, following the Islamic conquest of the region. The screen, which stands in the courtyard in front of the prayer hall, serves no structural purpose and was apparently added to the hypostyle building for aesthetic reasons, to mask what lay behind and to make the new building look more attractive. The screen is richly decorated with bands of naturalistic vine scrolls and inscriptions. The vine scrolls belong to the local tradition of stone carving that can be seen on Hindu and Jain temples. There, the scrolls are usually accompanied by exuberant figural sculpture depicting the activities of innumerable gods and goddesses with multiple arms and legs. The new Muslim patrons found this idolatry horrific and had the local masons replace the figures with Arabic texts from the Quran.

The desire to use writing to decorate buildings and objects in the Islamic lands was overwhelming, and builders and designers, particularly in medieval times, vied to create new styles and methods of writing out their messages on buildings. In some cases they added flowers and leaves around and among the letters. This style was particularly popular in Cairo, and many of the stone buildings erected under the patronage of the Fatimid dynasty, wealthy and sophisticated rulers there from 969 to 1171, have beautifully sculpted texts in the style known as floriated Kufic. These are some of the finest architectural inscriptions known from the Islamic lands, because they judiciously balance the demands of decoration and readability.

In Iran and the adjacent region, where baked brick was the most common material of construction, designers evolved other types of script, particularly those with knots and other geometric elements of decoration. One of the architectural styles that lasted the longest is known in Persian as *bannai* or builder's technique. The script developed out of the techniques of bricklaying, as bricks and other elements of construction were set in relief to spell out words and simple phrases. The earliest example of this script survives on the minaret erected at Ghazni (in eastern Afghanistan) about 1100 by the Ghaznavid ruler Masud III (r. 1098–1115). The panels on the minaret's shaft spell out the ruler's name and various titles. The text is unusual, as it is one of the only examples known of an inscription in this technique containing historical information. The text is also very difficult to read, because the letters are formed by small pieces of terra-cotta sandwiched between larger bricks that are laid vertically in stepped bond.

Designing and setting out this inscription must have been extremely labor-intensive (and therefore expensive), and builders and designers soon figured out how to adopt the technique to faster methods of production. They simplified the text itself, so that instead of having the names and titles of a specific ruler, the text contained sacred names or a common pious phrase, such as "There is no prophet after Muhammad" or "Dominion belongs to God." Builders and designers also

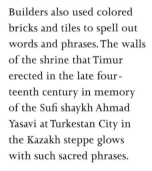

Builders also used colored bricks and tiles to spell out words and phrases. The walls of the shrine that Timur erected in the late fourteenth century in memory of the Sufi shaykh Ahmad Yasavi at Turkestan City in the Kazakh steppe glows with such sacred phrases.

simplified the technique. Instead of setting pieces of terra-cotta in relief, they used the bricks themselves to spell out the text. They first exploited the spaces between the bricks so that the shadows cast in the voids would form the words or phrases. It was a short step for designers to fill the spaces between the bricks with glazed elements, so that the words were spelled out by glittering surfaces that were flush with the brick bonds and contrasted with the matte surface around them.

This technique became widespread in the eastern Islamic lands from the thirteenth century, because it was an ideal way of covering large surfaces of brick buildings. A good example is the shrine that the Turkic conqueror Timur (1336–1405) built for the Sufi shaykh Ahmad Yasavi north of Samarqand. The shrine is a huge rectangular block that floats above the flat, dusty steppe. The expanse along the side walls is divided into a grid of cross shapes outlined in bricks glazed dark blue. Each cross is filled with light blue glazed bricks that spell out the names God, Ali, and Muhammad. The technique was not only visually effective but also religiously resonant, because anyone staring at the building from afar could repeat the sacred names, just as a pious believer would repeat sacred names as part of his or her devotions. The building was literally wrapped with sacred writing.

Aniconism: The Absence of Figures

It is often said that the depiction of living things is forbidden in Islamic art, but this is simply not true. The Quran has very little to say on the subject of figural representation, although it does explicitly forbid idolatry, divination, drinking, gambling, and other vices, which seem to have been commonly practiced at the time of the revelation. Making pictures of people was apparently not a topic of paramount importance in Arabia in the late sixth and early seventh centuries. Furthermore, there is no reason to depict people in Islamic religious art, because Muslims believe that God is unique and without associate and therefore that He cannot be represented, except by His word, the Quran. God is worshiped directly without intercessors, so there is no place for images of saints as there is in Christian art. Muhammad was God's messenger, but unlike Christ, Muhammad was not divine. His deeds—not his person—represent the ideal to which Muslims aspire. Unlike the Bible, little of the Quran is narrative, so there was little reason to use illustrated stories to teach the faith.

In time, this lack of motive and opportunity hardened into law, and the absence of figures (technically known as *aniconism*) became a characteristic feature of Islamic religious art. Thus, few, if any, depictions of people can be found in mosques and other buildings intended for religious purposes. Palaces, bathhouses, and locales designed for other activities, however, may well have had figural decoration, although in later periods the aniconism of the religious milieu often spilled over into the secular realm. According to the *hadith* (traditions of the Prophet), even Muhammad was aware of the difference; he ordered all the idols removed from the Kaaba in Mecca, but he is recorded to have used curtains and cushions decorated with figures in his house.

Representations of people and animals were used, often exuberantly, within private settings. One example from early Islamic times can be seen in the ruins of the Umayyad palace known as Khirbat al-Mafjar near Jericho. Destroyed in an earthquake in the 740s, the building was the retreat of the playboy prince al-Walid ibn Yazid, who partied with his friends for two decades waiting to succeed his elderly uncle, the Umayyad caliph Hisham ibn Abd al-Malik (r. 724–43). The palace contained an elaborate music hall, complete with swimming pool, hot bath, and private audience room. All that remains intact is the enormous mosaic floor, decorated with an extraordinary array of geometric patterns that resemble stone carpets. From the many fragments of stone and stucco that litter the site, the excavators were able to reconstruct much of the building's superstructure. The doorway, for example, was elaborately decorated with a stucco statue, presumably representing the patron, and inside the portal more stucco statues of half-naked voluptuous dancers suggested the plea-

Muslims disdained pictures or sculptures of living beings in religious settings, but they often used them in palaces and other secular settings. The entrance to the bath at Khirbat al-Mafjar near Jericho, a palace erected for the Umayyad prince al-Walid II in the eighth century, was decorated with stucco statues of bare-breasted dancers.

sures that lay within. The dome over the small audience room culminated in a cap of luscious acanthus leaves from which protruded heads of handsome young men and women, who peered down over other carvings of birds and winged horses. Clearly, what one did in private could be quite different from what one did in public.

In the same vein, German excavators in the early twentieth century found thousands of fragments from wall paintings that once decorated the houses, bathhouses, and palaces at Samarra, the site north of Baghdad that served as the

Paintings of people decorated the walls of the ninth-century palaces at Samarra, the Abbasid capital north of Baghdad. Excavators found one mural in the caliph's private quarters that shows two dancing girls with interlocked arms, pouring wine.

Abbasid capital in the mid-ninth century. The excavators were able to reconstruct some of the scenes from the palace, which included cornucopia scrolls inhabited with wild animals and naked ladies, hunting scenes, and one mural showing a pair of dancing girls. The two figures have interlocked arms; while they dance, each pours from a long-necked bottle into a cup held by the other. The liquid must surely be wine, because fragments of painted wine bottles also littered the site. Official histories may chronicle the official acts of the great and powerful, but art, like poetry and song, often shows aspects of private life that are at variance with the official ideal.

The same distinction between the religious and the secular stands for book decoration. Manuscripts of the Quran were often embellished with geometric or floral designs. Scholars do not know of any Quranic manuscript that was decorated with paintings of people, as were contemporary Christian manuscripts of the Bible. By contrast, pictures were often included in other kinds of books made in the Islamic lands, including scientific treatises, literary works, epic poems, and histories. In some cases these pictures were necessary to make the text understandable, in others, they made it pretty.

Only fragments of illustrated books survive from the period before 1000 C.E., but there is no reason to doubt their existence, particularly because they are described in other books. One of the earliest illustrated manuscripts to survive is a copy of Abd al-Rahman al-Sufi's treatise on the fixed stars. The work, ultimately derived from classical writings, particularly Ptolemy's *Almagest*, was composed around 965 by the astronomer al-Sufi (903–86) of Rayy for the Buyid ruler Adud al-Dawla (r. 949–83). The oldest suriving copy was made from the original by al-Sufi's son, and its illustrations show how classical traditions of representing the constellations were adapted to Muslim taste. The figures, for example, wear turbans and robes with long flowing drapery.

From this time, books of all kinds, including illustrated ones, have survived in greater numbers and represent a wider range of subject matter. One of the

كوكبة المسلسلة مع كوكبة السمكة
الشمالية التى وصفها بطلميوس

This copy of al-Sufi's treatise on the fixed stars is one of the earliest Islamic manuscripts with illustrations to survive. It was transcribed from the original by the author's son in 1009. This illustration of Andromeda wearing a long flowing robe shows how classical traditions of representing the constellations were adapted to Muslim taste.

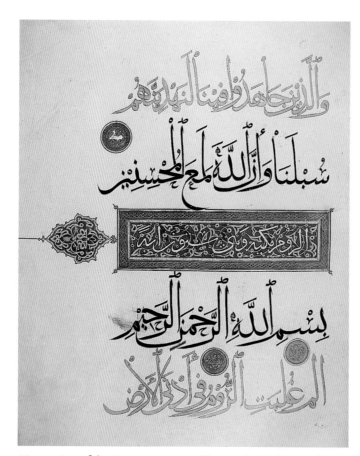

Manuscripts of the Quran were never illustrated with human figures, but in addition to the beautiful calligraphy used to transcribe
God's word, many manuscripts are decorated with plant and geometric designs, as with this fabulous thirty-volume copy made for
the Ilkhanid ruler Uljaytu at Hamadan in 1313.

most unusual is the *Maqamat* (Assemblies), written by the Arab writer al-Hariri (1054–1122), who lived in Basra. The *Maqamat* contains the merchant al-Harith's witty account of the rogue Abu Zayd's fifty adventures throughout the Islamic lands. Linguistically inventive and punning in style, the work was immensely popular among the educated bourgeoisie of the Arab lands. The verbal pyrotechnics of the text did not lend themselves easily to illustration, but the demand for illustrated books was so strong that the work was repeatedly illustrated. Eleven illustrated copies produced before 1350 have survived, suggesting that there were once many more. The illustrations provide rare glimpses of daily life in medieval times, showing such scenes as markets and libraries.

While books such as the *Maqamat* would have been an appropriate possession for a bourgeois bibliophile, under the Mongol rulers of Iran who were known as the Ilkhanids, books were transformed into a major art form for royalty, particularly after the Mongol rulers converted to Islam at the very end of the thirteenth century. Books became physically much bigger, probably because larger sheets of finer and whiter paper were available, and these large surfaces provided more room for elaborate decoration. Sumptuous manuscripts of the Quran were produced. These were often presentation sets comprising thirty volumes, which would have been given to a mosque, shrine, or tomb complex, where one volume would have been read aloud each day during the holy month of Ramadan. The largest manuscript to survive (each page measures 72 x 50 centimeters) was copied at Baghdad and endowed to the mausoleum of the sultan Muhammad Khudabanda Uljaytu (r. 1304–16) at Sultaniyya. It took eight years to copy; each page has three lines of majestic *muhaqqaq* script in gold outlined in black, alternating with two lines of a more fluid *thuluth-muhaqqaq* script in black outlined in gold—one of the most spectacular examples of monumental Quranic calligraphy. Like the other thirty-volume sets, it has magnificent double frontispieces containing geometric designs.

Large manuscripts of other works were produced in the Ilkhanid period. Histories, for example, were extremely popular, probably because the foreign Mongol rulers were interested in fitting themselves into the long traditions of Islamic and Persian history. The Mongol sultan Mahmud Ghazan (r. 1295–1304) commissioned his vizier Rashid al-Din to write a history of the Mongols, and Ghazan's successor Uljaytu expanded the commission to make it a universal history, the first known of its kind. Rashid al-Din's *Jami al-tawarikh* (Compendium of chronicles) was a multivolume work, comprising histories of the Mongol and the non-Mongol Eurasian peoples, a genealogy of ruling houses,

Islamic art transformed many of the subsidiary elements of pre-Islamic art into major themes. The mosaics on the walls of the Great Mosque of Damascus, erected by the Umayyad caliph al-Walid in the early eighth century, show a paradisial riverside landscape of fantastic buildings separated by trees. In earlier times, such landscapes would have been peopled with figures.

and a geography. To make his book more attractive and comprehensible, Rashid al-Din had it illustrated. His painters drew from the wide range of sources available in this cosmopolitan society. Sections on Chinese history, for example, were illustrated following Chinese models, and sections on biblical history followed Byzantine manuscript prototypes.

Perhaps most interesting and unusual in this multivolume work is the set of illustrations showing events from the Prophet's life. As there was no earlier tradition of representing Muhammad in Islamic art, and as Rashid al-Din's text provided only the most skeletal details of events in Muhammad's life, the painters had to look elsewhere for inspiration. One painting from the work shows Muhammad mounted on a horse leading the Muslims in battle against the Banu Qaynuqa, a Jewish tribe of Arabia. The Prophet is depicted against a ultramarine blue background and surrounded by white clouds and angels. Behind him are the Muslim forces, including his uncle Hamza, identifiable because he has a red beard and carries the Prophet's banner. The angels have bare heads with tight curls and wear long garments derived from the chiton, the basic garment worn by Greek men and women. In Mongol Iran, there seems to have been quite a bit of interest in depicting the Prophet, and several surviving manuscripts illustrate scenes from his life. These depictions of Muhammad are not religious images; they are historical illustrations not intended for devotional use. Somewhat unusual in the larger scheme of Islamic art, these images never-theless show the continuing distinction between the religious and secular realms of Islamic art.

The Decorative Themes of Arabesque and Geometry

Because figural imagery was unnecessary in Islamic religious art, other themes of decoration became important. Several of these themes had been subsidiary elements in the arts of pre-Islamic times. In Byzantine art, for example, depictions of people had been set off, framed, or linked by geo-metric elements (shapes and patterns) and vegetal designs (that is, stylized fruits, flowers, and trees). In early Islamic times these subsidiary elements were transformed into major artistic themes. Thus, the mosaics decorating the Great Mosque of Damascus, erected by the Umayyad caliph al-Walid (r. 705–15) in the early eighth century, were clearly derived from the traditions of late antiquity. The panel that survives along the west wall of the mosque shows a continuous landscape of fantastic buildings separated by trees and set above a flowing river. In classical and Byzantine art these subjects would have been background elements for large figures, but in this panel the landscape itself is the subject, probably meant to depict the garden paradise promised to Muslims in the Quran and described as a place of lofty chambers beneath which rivers flow.

In the Damascus mosaics the trees and buildings are still readily recognizable, but with the growing reluctance to depict figures, such specific representations were replaced by more stylized, abstract, and geometric motifs. This style was already popular by the ninth century, evident in a small ceramic bowl from this period that is decorated with four colors of luster. The main motif shown in the center of the bowl is a plant with a central stalk and paired leaves. The basic design is quite simple, but it has been elaborated with many different geometric patterns—spots, herringbones, blots, peacock's eyes, and so forth—that cover as much of the surface as possible and negate the organic quality of the main motif. In short, naturalistic elements, such as the flowers and leaves, were becoming increasingly stylized and subjected to the laws of geometry.

Little of the decoration has survived from the mosques in the Abbasid capital at Samarra, but one can get an idea of the abstract style of decoration that might have been used on the mosques there by looking at copies erected elsewhere. The mosque in Cairo, completed in 879 on the orders of the Abbasid governor Ahmad ibn Tulun (835–84), for example, is said to have been a close copy of a mosque in Samarra. In contrast to the earlier Damascus mosque, the decoration at the mosque of Ibn Tulun is restrained. A long wooden inscription runs around the building under the ceiling, and the undersides and borders of the heavy brick arches are embellished with stucco carved with simple elements to create patterns that combine geometric and floral elements. The decorated surface is totally filled so that there is no distinction between the background and the subject. This decoration, in which organic elements are subjected to the rules of geometry, can be extended infinitely in any direction.

A similar type of decoration was used in a small mosque at Balkh in northern Afghanistan, datable on stylistic grounds to the ninth century. Although badly ruined, the small square building has four massive cylindrical piers that once supported the nine covering domes. Most of the upper part was covered with

An original style of Islamic art evolved in the ninth century, when artists abstracted organic forms into a geometric style, in which there is no distinction between subject and background. This style was first developed in ninth-century Iraq, as exemplified in the plaster panels discovered at Samarra.

A more evolved stage in the abstraction of vegetal motifs can be seen in the plaster decorating the arches of the mosque of Ibn Tulun (879) in Cairo.

stucco, carved in geometrical and vegetal patterns with a distinctive slanted cut. The use of a similar style, documented from Cairo to eastern Iran in the ninth century, suggests that it must have had a common source, undoubtedly in the Abbasid capitals in Mesopotamia. Its widespread use shows how styles could be disseminated over wide areas during this period of centralized power.

This type of design, which is based on such natural forms as stems, tendrils, and leaves rearranged to form infinite geometric patterns, became a hallmark of Islamic art and architectural ornament from the tenth to the fifteenth centuries. To describe it, Europeans coined the term *arabesque*, first used in the fifteenth or sixteenth century, when Renaissance artists incorporated Islamic designs in book ornament and decorative bookbindings. Over the centuries the term has been applied to a wide variety of winding, twining vegetal decoration in art and meandering themes in music and dance, but properly it applies only to Islamic art. The nineteenth-century Viennese art historian Alois Riegl laid out the principal features of the arabesque: The tendrils of its vegetation are heavily geometricized and do not branch off as in nature from a single continuous stem; rather, the tendrils grow unnaturally from one another. Furthermore, the arabesque has infinite correspondence, meaning that the design can be extended infinitely in any direction. The structure of the arabesque gives sufficient information so that the viewer can extend the design in his or her imagination.

Like the Samarra style of ornament, the arabesque was probably disseminated from Iraq, the capital province of the Islamic world in the tenth century, and quickly spread to all Islamic lands. An early stage of this distinctive and original development may be found in carved marble panels flanking the *mihrab* (the niche in the wall facing Mecca) of the Great Mosque of Córdoba, which was completed in 965. A central stem, itself patterned, has tendrils growing unnaturally from its base and tip; the stem provides the armature for a symmetrical interlacing of tendrils, leaves, and flowers that seems to press out against the confines of the similarly patterned frame. In Islamic art the arabesque's popularity lasted until the fourteenth century, when it was slowly displaced by designs using the Chinese-inspired chrysanthemum, peony, and lotus motifs that became popular in Iran and by the fantastic naturalistic foliage of the *saz* style that became popular under the Ottomans. Even these designs retain some of the arabesque's geometric underpinnings, however.

The popularity of the arabesque was due no doubt to its adaptability, because it was appropriate to virtually all situations, from architecture to the illuminated pages that were added to decorate the beginning and end of fine manuscripts, particularly copies of the Quran. One small manuscript of the Quran, for example, has five sets of double pages, three at the beginning of the manuscript and two at the end. Some manuscripts contain tables with writing added on top of the geometric and floral ornament; others are purely geometric and vegetal. The designs are elaborately drawn in brown ink and enhanced with gold, blue, white, green, and red. The circles on the vertical axis are self-contained, but those on the horizontal axis can be extended infinitely; the design thus achieves an equilibrium between static and dynamic.

The new style of geometricized vegetal designs was widely popular. Here, in the ruins of a small mosque erected at Balkh, Afghanistan, in the ninth century, artists carved these motifs into the wet plaster covering the piers and arches.

Arabesques, in which vegetal forms grow infinitely in all directions according to the laws of geometry, appeared in many media. In this detail of a carved marble panel, probably added to the Great Mosque of Córdoba in 965, the arabesque ornament betrays its early stage of development because it is still restrained by a frame.

These pages are the work of a master hand, and according to the colophon, this manuscript was completed by the scribe Ali ibn Hilal in Baghdad in 1000–1001. He can be identified as the famous calligrapher commonly known as Ibn al-Bawwab, who refined the "proportioned script"—developed a century earlier by the Arab calligrapher Ibn Muqla—in which letters were measured in terms of dots, circles, and semicircles. The script used in this manuscript confirms Ibn al-Bawwab's talents; the 280 folios are transcribed in a bold rounded hand of the type called *naskh*. The script is remarkable for its clarity and regularity, all the more impressive because there are no traces of blind-tooled lines of the kind used by later calligraphers to guide their hands. The manuscript also represents a technical innovation because it is one of the first surviving copies of the Quran transcribed on paper.

Arabesques were a major element used in decorating books, particularly manuscripts of the Quran. This page of illumination from the copy of the Quran transcribed by the noted calligrapher Ibn al-Bawwab in Baghdad in 1000–1001 is one of the earliest examples to survive.

The double pages of illumination with geometric designs, often known as carpet pages, became increasingly splendid over the years. Some of the finest were produced under the Mamluks, the sequence of sultans who controlled Egypt and Syria from 1249 to 1517. These rulers and their intimates commissioned elaborate copies of the Quran as furnishings for the large charitable foundations that they ordered in Cairo and elsewhere to preserve their names and fortunes after their death. According to Islamic law, property endowed to institutions founded for charitable purposes was safe from seizure by the state. This type of charitable endowment is known as *waqf* (pl. *awqaf*) or, in North Africa, as *habus*. In unsettled times, when rulers fell like dominoes, such charitable foundations allowed families to pass on their fortunes safely, as the deed of endowment could specify that the founder or his descendants be appointed as trustee.

Egyptian woodcarvers transformed the abstract curved forms of the beveled style into birds and other animals, as on this ninth- or tenth-century panel of Aleppan pine.

To furnish these charitable foundations, the Mamluks often ordered large manuscripts of the Quran, typically embellished with elaborate frontispieces decorated with designs of star polygons. The most famous is a manuscript commissioned by an amir of Sultan Shaban, Arghun Shah al-Ashrafi, who was put to death in 1376. Its rectangular frontispiece is divided into a square central field bordered by rectangular panels with a stylized kufic script. The central square contains is a sixteen-pointed star set within a geometric trellis. This composition, which is often likened to a sun, seems to explode from the center but is actually closed and cannot be extended beyond the frame. The various frames are decorated with arabesque and floral arrangements, including many Chinese-inspired elements such as peonies and lotus flowers.

Complex geometric effects were also achieved in other media, including woodwork. Wood was often used for fine mosque furniture, such as Quran stands, lecterns, and bookcases, but the largest pieces were minbars or pulpits. The minbar was the place in the congregational mosque from which the weekly sermon was given during the Friday bidding prayer, so it became a potent symbol of political authority. Patrons who ordered new minbars wished to make them as splendid as possible, but with the deforestation of the Mediterranean lands due to overharvesting in medieval times, wood was increasingly scarce. To make the most of this expensive material, new techniques of woodworking were exploited. One technique common from the eleventh century was marquetry, in which large panels were formed of angular interlacing strapwork radiating from central stars. To make these large and important pieces even fancier, artisans used different colors of exotic woods, which were sometimes inlaid with other precious materials, such as ivory and mother-of-pearl.

Aleppo (located in modern-day Syria) became a center for woodworking in the marquetry technique, and the finest and most famous piece produced there was the exquisite minbar that the Zangid ruler Nur al-Din ordered in 1168–69 for the Aqsa Mosque in Jerusalem. The city was then in the hands of the Crusaders, and Nur al-Din ordered the minbar in anticipation of taking the city. It was installed in its intended place two decades later after his nephew, the Ayyubid sultan Salah al-Din (also known as Saladin), successfully conquered the city, in 1187. This minbar, which was the most famous example of this prolific school of woodworking and signed by no less than four craftsmen, was destroyed by arson in 1969.

Nur al-Din's minbar followed the typical triangular form. Along the hypotenuse was a narrow flight of steps leading to a platform at the top; both the steps and the platform were enclosed by railings, and the platform, evident in many other examples, was surmounted by a cupola. The major fields of decoration were the large triangular sides. On Nur al-Din's minbar they were decorated with eight-pointed stars, and the extensions of their sides were traced in a net of joinery. The polygonal interstices were filled with minutely detailed arabesques. The intricacy of the design was matched by the expense of the materials, for the minbar showed an extensive use of inlaid ivory, both for the outlines of the polygonal figures and for some of the smaller interstitial stars. The marquetry technique made the most of expensive materials, but the geometric design, in which the arabesques varied from polygon to polygon, added to the aesthetic effect by inviting contemplation of the design from near and far.

Geometric designs were also popular methods of decorating buildings in the Islamic lands. In Iran and much of the eastern Islamic lands there was no suitable stone for construction, so the typical building material was brick. Mud brick had the advantage of being cheap and remarkably serviceable in areas with little rain, and its fragile surface could be protected by plaster or stucco revetments, which could be carved or painted to enliven the inherent drabness of the material. In the ninth century when the Abbasids needed to decorate the enormous palaces and other mud brick structures in their sprawling new capital of Samarra, they used molded panels with geometric designs that could be quickly executed in stucco.

Baked brick was more expensive because it required scarce supplies of fuel for firing. It had the advantage that it was much more durable, however, and where affordable, its durability was preferred, particularly in regions with greater precipitation and a more extreme climate, such as the Iranian plateau. Although baked brick could also be covered with plaster, particularly on interiors, it was usually left exposed on exteriors. With the adoption of fine quality baked brick, builders in Iran and adjacent areas quickly turned the material of construction into the material of decoration. By setting the bricks in patterns, they could

Builders in the Seljuk period exploited the decorative possibilities of light and shade on brick, particularly for the tall cylindrical towers known as minarets. Horizontal bands with different brick designs decorate the shaft of the Kalyan ("tall") minaret finished in 1127 in Bukhara, Uzbekistan.

enliven the wall surface. These patterns were particularly effective in a climate in which bright sun often rakes over the brick walls, and projecting and receding bricks could create patterns of light and shade.

One of the earliest examples of this decorative use of brickwork is the tomb of the Samanids in Bukhara. Constructed and decorated with baked brick, the tomb is a small cube with sloped walls supporting a central dome and little cupolas at the corners. Despite the simple forms, the interior and exterior are elaborately decorated with patterns worked in the cream-colored brick. The quality and harmony of construction and decoration show that this building, although the first of its type to have survived, could not have been the first to have been built. By the early tenth century there must have been a long tradition of building ornate brick structures in the greater Iranian world.

This so-called naked style of brickwork became a hallmark of medieval architecture in the region. Builders exploited the decorative possibilities of brick patterning, particularly for the tall cylindrical towers known as minarets. These towers, often attached to mosques and used as the place from which the muezzin gives the call to prayer (adhan), are often considered to be hallmarks of Islamic architecture. Although a common feature of Islamic religious architecture, the minaret is neither a necessary or ubiquitous one. Minarets were apparently not used under the Umayyads, and only under the Abbasids was the idea of a single massive tower located in or beyond the middle of the wall opposite the mihrab disseminated throughout the Islamic lands, perhaps as a sign of caliphal authority.

By the end of the twelfth century the minaret, in the form of a slender freestanding shaft, had become the universal symbol of Islam from the Atlantic to the Indian Oceans. Minarets were often added to earlier mosques. They were less expensive than building a new mosque and were gratifyingly visible both from afar, where they indicated the presence of a town—or from nearby, where they indicated the location of the mosque. They served to advertise the presence of Islam at the same time that they demonstrated the piety of the founder.

More than sixty towers dating from the medieval period still stand in Iran, Central Asia, and Afghanistan, either attached to mosques or isolated and freestanding. This large number attests to the explosion in popularity of this form, and the assurance of their decoration attests to the skill of their builders and the esteem in which these tall towers were held. Their shafts are typically decorated in broad bands of geometric brick decoration, often separated by guard bands and inscriptions. Builders exploited the decorative possibilities of the geometric patterns, deliberately widening the bands or setting the bricks in deeper relief along the height of the tall shaft.

Muqarnas, tiers of superimposed niche-like elements, is a unique contribution of Islamic architects to the decoration of their buildings. Muqarnas half-vaults were often above important doorways, as on the entrance to the hospital Nur al-Din, founded in Damascus in 1145.

Another form of architectural decoration that developed at this time is known as *muqarnas*. Sometimes likened to stalactites, muqarnas consists of tiers of niche-like elements that project out from the row below. Apparently developed in the late tenth century, muqarnas was first applied to supporting elements inside domes, such as squinches or arches over the corners, and to dividing elements between different parts of buildings, such as cornices on tombs or minarets. By the eleventh century muqarnas elements were used to cover the entire inner surface of vaults. Although the earliest muqarnas may have had a structural role, they increasingly became a purely decorative element. In Iran and the eastern Islamic lands decorative muqarnas vaults were made of plaster and suspended by wooden beams from the brick vault above. In the Mediterranean region, where stone is the prevalent medium of construction, muqarnas vaults, set over the portals of important buildings, were often laboriously carved in stone. Like writing, muqarnas was adopted by builders from Spain to Central Asia and beyond, so that it became the most distinctive decorative feature of Islamic architecture. Unlike other decorative motifs, muqarnas was never applied to any medium other than architecture and such architectural fittings as minbars.

The repeated module typical of brick construction made geometric ornament appropriate decoration; such ornament was equally appropriate to textiles, where the crossing of warp and weft threads also generates a geometric grid. Nowhere is this more apparent than in knotted carpets, where a weaver could easily create geometric designs by tying knots of different colors onto the warp threads. Throughout history, weavers worked to combine more-or-less stylized floral and animal motifs with the geometric grids. Knotted carpets have been produced for millennia in the Near East and Central Asia. The oldest surviving example, perhaps dating to the fifth century B.C.E., is the carpet that was discovered in a frozen tomb at Pazyryk in Siberia. Other fragments perhaps dating from the ninth or tenth century have been discovered in Egypt. The oldest carpets to have survived in significant quantities, however, were made in Anatolia in the early fourteenth century, using a fairly limited range of strong colors, such as red, yellow, blue, brown, and white. Some of the carpets have designs of repeated geometric motifs, others have extremely stylized representations of animals, but all have borders of geometrical motifs or stylized letter forms.

The Exuberant Use of Color

The epigraphic and geometric designs commonly used in Islamic art were often enhanced by color, and the exuberant use of color is another hallmark of Islamic art. The Arabic language itself has a particularly rich chromatic vocabulary, and in it concepts can easily be associated through similarities in morphology. The Arabic root kh-d-r, for example, gives rise to *khudra* (greenness), *akhdar* (green), *khudara* (greens or herbs), and *al-khadra* (the verdant, or the heavens). Blue, the color of the sky in the western tradition, is often conflated with green in the Islamic lands, where the spectrum is traditionally divided into yellow, red, and green. Tonality was less important than luminosity and saturation, probably

Geometric designs were especially easy to execute in the traditional techniques of woven textiles and knotted carpets. One of the earliest carpets to survive, probably from the fourteenth century, shows four stylized quadrupeds.

because of the sun-drenched environment in much of the region.

In the early Islamic period various philosophical schools elaborated the Aristotelian theory of color, and this interest in color was taken up by mystics, who saw parallels between the phenomenon of colors and the inner vision of the divine. The symbolic use of color runs throughout much Islamic literature. The great Persian poet Nezami (ca. 1141–1203 or 1217), for example, structured his classic poem, *Haft paykar* (Seven portraits) around the seven colors (*haft rang*) traditional in Persian thought (red, yellow, green, and blue complemented by black, white, and sandalwood). In this poem the ideal ruler, exemplified by the Sasanian king Bahram Gur, visits seven princesses, each housed in a pavilion of a different color; the princesses recount seven stories, which can be interpreted as the seven stations of human life, the seven aspects of human destiny, or the seven stages along the mystical way. The seven colored pavilions of the *Haft paykar* became favorite subjects for book illustration in fifteenth- and sixteenth-century Iran.

One of the most famous manuscripts of Nezami's poem has an unusually long and witty colophon that recounts the manuscript's peregrinations and shows how important these illustrated manuscripts were to rulers of the time. The Timurid prince Abul-Qasim Babur, ruler of Herat (in northwestern Afghanistan) from 1449 to 1457, commissioned the calligrapher Azhar to transcribe the manuscript, but it was unfinished at the prince's death. After Jahan Shah (r. 1438-67), the Qaraqoyunlu ruler of Azerbaijan, sacked Herat a year later, the manuscript passed to Jahan Shah's son Pir Budak. It then went to the Aqqoyunlu ruler Khalil Sultan (r. 1478), who commissioned the calligrapher Abd al-Rahman al-Khwarazmi (known as Anisi) to finish copying the text and two artists, Shaykhi and Darvish Muhammad, to illustrate it. Still unfinished at Khalil Sultan's death in 1478, the manuscript passed to his brother Yaqub (r. 1478–90). He also died before the book was finished, and the manuscript ultimately passed to the Safavid shah Ismail I (r. 1501–24), founder of the Safavid dynasty, under whose patronage the last of the nineteen illustrations were completed.

The painting *Bahram Gur in the Green Pavilion* exemplifies the lush style of manuscript illustration practiced at the Aqqoyunlu court. It was probably added by the artist Shaykhi when the manuscript was in the possession of the sultan Yaqub. It shows the Sasanian monarch reclining with his writing table and books beside him, listening to one of his ladies read a poem while another massages his feet. The reclining figure may actually represent the young Aqqoyunlu prince, who would have been less than twenty years old at the time. The nominal subject, the prince in the pavilion, however, is engulfed in a riot of fantastic vegetation. Nature bursts from the constraint of the frame, as lollipop trees with imbricated leaves sprout among rocks concealing human and animal faces. The colors are particularly vivid, with acid greens set against rosy reds and brilliant blues.

This flamboyant color typical of the Aqqoyunlu court style can be contrasted with the carefully modulated style that is associated with contemporary Herat and exemplified in the work of Bihzad (ca. 1450–1535) the most famous Persian painter, and the one whose name is attached (rightly or wrongly) to more paintings than any other artist. Bihzad's masterpiece is generally acknowledged to be

(Right) Color was used symbolically and extravagantly in much of Islamic art and culture. The Persian poet Nezami structured his classic poem, *Haft paykar*, around the seven colors traditional in Persian thought. In a fine manuscript of the poem prepared for several fifteenth-century princes, the painter Shaykhi used brilliant color to depict *Bahram Gur in the Green Pavilion*.

Medieval potters revolutionized the industry by developing a technique to paint on the surface of a ceramic with designs that did not run into the glaze. A black heron struts across the turquoise-glazed surface of this twelfth-century Syrian bowl.

The Seduction of Yusuf. The painting illustrates a manuscript of the Persian poet Sadi (ca. 1213–92) entitled *Bustan* (Orchard), transcribed in 1488 for the library of the Timurid ruler Sultan Husayn Mirza by the most renowned calligrapher of the age, Sultan Ali Mashhadi. Sadi's text, written on uncolored paper in cloud bands at the top, middle, and bottom of the illustration, mentions the seduction of Yusuf, the biblical Joseph, by Potiphar's wife, known in Islamic tradition as Zulaykha, but nothing in the text requires Bihzad's elaborate architectural setting. Instead, this setting is described in the mystical poem, *Yusuf and Zulaykha,* written by the Timurid poet Jami (1414–92) five years before the Sadi manuscript was transcribed. Four lines from Jami's poem are inscribed in white on blue around the arch in the center of the painting.

According to Jami, Zulaykha built a palace with seven splendid rooms that were decorated with erotic paintings of herself with Yusuf. She led the unwary Yusuf from one room to the next, locking the doors behind her until they reached the innermost chamber. There, she threw herself at Yusuf, but he fled from her grasp through the seven locked doors, which miraculously opened before him.

Just as Jami's text is an allegory of the soul's search for divine love and beauty, Bihzad's image invites mystical contemplation. The splendid palace stands for the material world, the seven rooms represent the seven climes, and Yusuf's beauty is a metaphor for God's. As there was no witness, Yusuf could have yielded to Zulaykha's passion, but he realized that God was all-seeing and all-knowing. The seven locked doors, which form the matrix of the composition, can be opened only by God. This brilliant image transcends the literal requirements of the text and evokes the mystical themes that were prominent in contemporary literature and society. Bihzad was obviously proud of his creation, because he signed it on the architectural panel over the window in the room on the upper left and dated it 893 (corresponding to 1488) in the final blue-and-white cartouche on the arch following the verses from Jami's poem.

Metalworkers exploited the chromatic possibilities of metals by inlaying copper, silver, gold, and a black bituminous substance into brass and bronze. The master metalworker Muhammad ibn al-Zayn inlaid this large basin with an extraordinary range of figural scenes, many depicting life in the Mamluk lands around 1300.

Bihzad's masterpiece shows a sophisticated but subdued use of color, in which blues and greens predominate but are tempered by complementary warm colors, especially a bright orange. The carefully modulated use of color leads the eye through the complex architectural setting to focus on Zulaykha, striking in her flamboyant orange robe, a stark contrast to Yusuf, who is dressed in cool green. The colors are jewel-like; the fine quality pigments were made from such expensive minerals as lapis lazuli and gold, which were carefully ground, mixed with binder, and applied with fine brushes. The colors appear all the more brilliant in the dream-like world of Persian book painting, as they were unmodulated by cast shadows or atmospheric perspective, two pictorial techniques that were only introduced into Persian painting from European art in the seventeenth century.

The use of brilliant color was not limited to fancy books made in the Persian world in the later centuries. The spirited use of color is found in most Islamic art from an early date. Potters in the Islamic world hid drab earthenwares under cloaks of brightly colored slips and glazes. The most significant invention for the future history of ceramics in the Islamic lands, as well as in China and Europe, was underglaze decoration, in which a fine and white ceramic body provided an ideal surface for painting in colored metallic oxides. This painted surface was

then covered by a transparent alkaline glaze, which protected the painted surface but, unlike lead glazes, did not cause the pigments to run together during firing.

Similarly, one of the most important contributions of medieval Islamic metalworkers was the development of the inlay technique, in which the monochrome object, usually made from brass or bronze, was enlivened with inlays in gold, silver, and copper, as on the Bobrinski Bucket. Other objects, such as magnificent basins to be used for handwashing before and after eating, were inlaid with inscriptions and figural scenes worked in silver and a black bituminous substance.

Color is also one of the most distinctive features of Islamic architecture, for glittering azure domes and dazzling expanses of multicolored tile decorate many of the best known buildings. The first great monument of Islamic architecture, the Dome of the Rock, originally had polychrome and gold glass mosaic covering both inside and outside. The coloristic effects of the interior mosaics were enhanced by a brilliantly painted and gilded ceiling and a lavish use of marble. The dadoes (lower walls) were decorated with panels of quartered marble, sliced and arranged so that the natural grain would form symmetrical patterns. In some cases vegetal motifs were inlaid in black mastic to contrast against the white marble. The same color combination was extended to the arches, which were constructed of alternating black and white voussoirs (the wedge-shaped pieces forming the arch).

This brightly colored style typical of Umayyad architecture set a precedent that was often repeated by later patrons. But just as the fragile mosaics on the exterior of the Dome of the Rock suffered from weathering, the coloristic effects on many other buildings, much like those on Greek temples and Romanesque churches, have often faded under a haze of dust and smog to uniform earth tones, giving an erroneous impression that only later buildings were brightly colored. In other cases, as under the puritanical Almohad dynasty, which ruled in Spain and Morocco in the twelfth and thirteenth centuries, rather plain exteriors and whitewashed interiors were preferred for mosques.

But many buildings were brightly colored. In the tenth century, for example, when one of the Umayyad caliphs of Spain decided to enlarge the congregational mosque at his capital of Córdoba, his builders attempted to imitate many of the coloristic effects of Umayyad architecture in Syria, although they knew these only at great remove. The original Córdoba mosque, completed in 786–87, had used an inventive system of double-tiered columns and arches to support the wooden roof, probably because only short, stubby columns were available from abandoned Visigothic buildings in the region. By stacking two short columns on top of each other, the mosque's designers could achieve the necessary height, although they needed to add intermediate arches to stiffen the inherently unstable construction. They unified this motley collection of columns and capitals

(Left) The coloristic effects of the mosaics decorating the interior of the Dome of the Rock in Jerusalem were enhanced by a brilliantly painted and gilded ceiling and lavish use of marble paneling.

with a striking design for the voussoirs of the arches, which were alternately of white stone and courses of red brick.

The striped effect of the two-tiered arches was maintained by later builders, who enlarged the mosque in the ninth and tenth centuries. These renovations culminated when the Umayyad caliph al-Hakam II (r. 961–76) expanded the prayer hall and added a dome over the center entrance to the addition and domes in front and on either side of the new mihrab. The screened area, which was connected to the palace by a passageway in the wall of the mosque facing Mecca, was a *maqsura*, an enclosure for the ruler, meant not to protect the caliph from harm (as the early maqsuras were said to function) but to emphasize the great pomp and ceremony with which the Umayyad caliph surrounded himself. These areas were distinguished by elaborate screens of intersecting arches and richly colored revetments in glass mosaic; the glass mosaics were clearly meant to evoke the great mosaics that decorated the Umayyad buildings of Syria. According to local Arabic histories, there were no laborers in Spain capable of executing these mosaics, so the caliph sent an ambassador to the Byzantine emperor in Constantinople, requesting him to send a workman to decorate the mosque. The

The area immediately in front of the mihrab added to the Great Mosque of Córdoba in 965 was elaborately decorated with intersecting arches supporting mosaic-covered vaults, clearly meant to recall the mosaic-covered buildings of Umayyad Syria.

emperor complied, and the ambassador returned with a master craftsman and sufficient mosaic cubes to complete the job.

Although the difficult technique of glass mosaic was infrequently repeated in later centuries and usually with some reference to the Umayyads of Syria, multicolor revetment in glazed ceramic tile became a hallmark of later Islamic architecture from Spain and North Africa to the borders of India. By the late eleventh century builders in the eastern Islamic lands had reached the ultimate exploitation of carved- and patterned-brick decoration and were ready to experiment with glazed revetment. They began by incorporating small pieces of cut tile, mainly colored a light (turquoise) blue, which was easy to make from the readily available copper deposits in Iran. Soon they expanded the surfaces covered, and by the fourteenth century the palette was extended to include dark blue (colored with cobalt), black (manganese), and white as well as green and ocher. Including the buff natural color of the brick surface, this brought the total number of colors to seven, the number of colors in the traditional Persian palette. With the expanded range of color came the elaboration of design, and geometric patterns gave way to naturalistic and floral designs, made by cutting small pieces from monochrome tiles and fitting the irregular pieces together.

The technique reached its apogee in the late fourteenth and fifteenth centuries, alongside the development of Persian book painting. Some of the finest tile panels were prepared for the gargantuan palace that the Turkic conqueror Timur erected in his hometown of Shahr-i Sabz, but only fragments remain to attest to its original spendor. More can be seen at the Blue Mosque, built by the Qaraqoyunlu in their capital at Tabriz (in northwestern Iran) around 1465. The mosque takes its name from its superb tile revetment, which was never surpassed in later monuments.

Although in ruins, the Blue Mosque displays an unusual variety of tile decoration of magnificent quality. Seven-color tile mosaic covers the exterior and much of the interior walls above a marble dado. Particularly striking are the fluid arabesque motifs and the inscriptions, often set out in white or gold against a deep blue or green background. The building is a virtual catalog of tile techniques. Hexagonal dark blue glazed tiles covered the upper surfaces and vaults of the main chamber, and purple tiles overpainted in gold were set in the sanctuary. Luster tiles were set at the base of the cable molding on the entrance portal, one of the very rare instances of this technique in the fifteenth century. Highly embossed molded fragments of underglaze-painted tile remain on the corner buttresses.

Tile mosaic is a laborious and expensive technique because it is time-consuming to cut and fit the tiny pieces together. In the fifteenth century it was gradually replaced by a cheaper technique in which large tiles of uniform shape were painted with patterns worked in different colors of glaze. To prevent the glazes from running together during firing, they were separated by a greasy substance mixed with manganese, which left a matte black line between the colors after firing. The technique, known in Spanish as *cuerda seca*, is much faster than tile mosaic, but the colors are not as brilliant because they are all fired at one temperature.

Tile mosaic was also popular at the other end of the Islamic lands in the Maghreb or Islamic west, where it is known locally as *zallij*. The technique may have developed even earlier there, but it flowered during the fourteenth century under the Marinids in Morocco. In the eastern Islamic lands the predominant color was blue, whereas in the west the main colors were green and tan, usually on a white background. Lower walls were covered by tiled dadoes, which were normally surmounted by epigraphic friezes with the black letters formed by scraping through the glaze to the clay body. Upper walls were covered with elaborately carved stucco decoration and capped by wooden friezes, consoles, and cornices. Floors, unlike those in the east, often had glazed highlights or were completely covered in tiles. Even the piers and columns in courtyards were revetted in tile. The overall effect of such interiors is glistening, and the tripartite com-

Builders enveloped their structures with glittering webs of glazed ceramic tile. Perhaps the finest example is the ruined Blue Mosque in Tabriz (ca. 1465), decorated with exquisite tile mosaic in seven colors.

Builders in the western Islamic lands decorated interiors with tilework combined with carved plaster and wood, as in the courtyard of the Attarin Madrasa (1325) in Fez, Morocco.

bination of tiled dado, stucco wall, and wooden superstructure remained standard in the region for centuries.

Perhaps the most refined coloristic effects were achieved in the buildings erected under the Mughals in the Indian subcontinent. Polished white marble that reflected light was played off against matte red sandstone that absorbed it. The effect was heightened by the use of *pietra dura*, multicolored inlay in such hard and rare stones as lapis, onyx, jasper, topaz, carnelian, and agate, which emphasized the jewel-like qualities of the building. The small tomb of Itimad al-Dawla, the minister of finance to the emperor of India, Jahangir (r. 1605–27), is like a jewelbox. Constructed by Nur Jahan, who was Itimad al-Dawla's daughter (and Jahangir's wife) after her father's death in 1622, the small tomb is decorated with traditional geometric designs and arabesques, combined with representational motifs of wine cups, vases with flowers, and cypress trees, visual allusions to the Quran's descriptions of Paradise. The intricate inlay in yellow, brown, gray, and black contrasting with the smooth white marble prefigures the later phase of Mughal decoration in which white marble was garnished with gold and precious stones. Elsewhere, particularly in more public settings, the repertory of designs and colors was somewhat narrower. For example, at the Taj Mahal, the tomb constructed by Jahangir's son, Shah Jahan, this decoration is restrained and used only for slender arabesques and extensive inscriptions done in black that constrast with the polished white marble.

The Taj Mahal, the enormous tomb built by the Mughal emperor Shah Jahan for his wife, shows a sophisticated sense of color. The polished white marble used for the tomb reflects light and contrasts with the red sandstone used for the outlying buildings and with the black inlaid decoration of arabesques and inscriptions.

Perhaps the most sumptuous of the Mughal private quarters were at the Red Fort in Delhi. They were part of Shahjahanabad, the quarter of the city laid out under the emperor Shah Jahan's auspices from 1639 to 1648. These palaces, now called the Rang Mahal (Painted Palace) and the Divan-i Khass (Private Audience Hall), are set behind the main audience hall and overlook the river. They are decorated with lavishly carved marble, paintings, and pietra dura inlay in gold and precious stones.

The extravagant use of color in Islamic art and architecture has been explained in several ways. It is often thought to be a reaction to the dull and monochromatic landscape in much of the traditional heartland of Islam, but this explanation is simplistic. Colors also had a wide range of symbolic associations in the Islamic lands, but these were often

Mughal architects achieved some of the most refined coloristic effects by inlaying white marble with semiprecious colored stones, as on a panel from the Red Fort in Delhi, built by Shah Jahan (r. 1628–57).

contradictory and meaningful only in specific geographical or chronological contexts. Thus, black was often associated with the mysterious Black Stone embedded in the Kaaba at Mecca toward which all Muslims pray, but black was also associated with vengeance and revolt, as in the black flag that became the standard of the Abbasid dynasty. In the Maghreb black could be the accursed color of hell, and in order to avoid pronouncing the name, the opposite color (white) was substituted. Thus, to this day coal is sometimes known in North Africa as *al-abyad* ("the white [thing]").

White generally conveyed a sense of brightness, loyalty, royalty, and death, much the same values as in many other cultures. Two seamless white lengths of cloth made up the garment worn by all male pilgrims to Mecca, and these were often saved for use as a burial shroud. White was also the color associated with the Fatimid caliphs, the opponents of the Abbasids. Blue had prophylactic connotations, and many people wore blue, particularly beads, to ward off the evil eye. The magical power of blue made it the dispenser of evil fortune and at the same time a defense against it. Green, the color of plants, was thought to bring equilibrium, good luck, fertility, and youth. Green was the color of the Prophet Muhammad's flag and the cloak of his son-in-law and successor Ali. In later times green turbans were worn by descendants of the Prophet, and the heavenly throne is said to have been carved from a green jewel. Tiled domes and roofs were most often green or blue, but the auspicious or heavenly associations may have been outweighed by practical considerations, because copper oxide, a ubiquitous coloring agent, produces a green color in a lead glaze and a turquoise or blue color in an alkaline one.

The Notion of Willful Ambiguity

The changing and variable interpretations given to any particular color at any particular time or place exemplify a final characteristic of much Islamic art: its willful ambiguity. Because there is no clergy in Islam to prescribe or maintain any given meaning for any particular symbol or theme, there was much more latitude for the viewer to interpret it at will. One example is found on a luster-ware dish discovered in the course of the 1911–13 German excavations at the Abbasid capital of Samarra. The design is caught somewhere between abstraction and representation. At first glance the design seems to be abstract, but on closer observation it can be interpreted as a plant or a bird. A circle in the middle of the dish is transformed into the body of a bird by adding palmettes at the sides to form wings and at the top to form the bird's head holding another sprig in its mouth.

Similar ambiguity marks much of the stucco decoration of the contemporary Abbasid palaces at Samarra. Scholars have distinguished three styles of stucco carving there. The first style is a carved technique derived from the geometricized vegetal decoration used in the Umayyad period. The second style is characterized by the use of crosshatching for details. Subjects are somewhat simplified but are still distinguished from the background. The third style, known also as the beveled style, is a molded technique suitable for covering large wall surfaces. It uses a distinctive slanted cut which allows the plaster to be released easily from the mold. Decoration in the beveled style is distinguished by rhythmic and symmetrical repetitions of curved lines ending in spirals that form abstract patterns in which the traditional distinction between subject and background has been dissolved. The beveled style was undoubtedly developed for stucco, but was soon applied to wood and other carved media such as rock crystal, not only in the major cities of Iraq but also in provincial centers.

The transfer of techniques and designs from one medium to another is another hallmark of Islamic art. By contrast, in pre-Islamic times specific designs had been used for different materials—one design was appropriate for textiles, another for metalwares, still others for architectural decoration or for glassware. This division does not hold in Islamic art, where a textile design might reappear on metalware or ceramics and an architectural motif on glassware, despite the enormous differences in scale. For example, the same design of roundels with pearl borders enclosing mythical lion-headed birds, called *simurghs*, is known on textiles, metalwares, and wall paintings made in early Islamic times over a wide region from Central Asia to the Mediterranean.

The beveled style clearly derived from plant motifs, but contemporary viewers, like modern ones, must have seen that these repeated motifs could also be interpreted as human faces or other animate motifs. A wooden panel from Egypt, for example, is carved in a pure abstract beveled style, but the vegetal motifs have been arranged in such a way that they can also be seen as representing

Ambiguity characterizes many of the designs decorating works of Islamic art. The figure on this ninth-century luster-painted dish might be interpreted as as an abstract design, a plant, or a bird.

a bird. Although it clearly is not a bird, it is more than some abstract leaves. This willed sense of ambiguity is an essential part of the object's artistic content.

Writing, too, could deliberately be made ambiguous, as on the Bobrinski Bucket. The body of the bucket is decorated with five horizontal bands. The top, middle, and bottom bands contain Arabic inscriptions bestowing good wishes on an (anonymous) owner. The two bands in between contain figural scenes. The second band from the top shows scenes of entertainment, includ-

The interior walls of many residences at the Abbasid capital at Samarra were decorated with molded decoration, characterized by a distinctive slanted cut that allowed the panels to be released easily from the mold.

The design of a simurgh on an octagonal silver dish attributed to ninth- or tenth-century Iran probably derives from a textile pattern.

ing drinking, music making, and game playing such as backgammon, which was known in the medieval Islamic lands as *nard*. The second band from the bottom contains scenes of horsemen hunting and fighting. Unlike the dedicatory inscription written clearly around the rim and handle in Persian, the Arabic inscriptions on the body of the bucket are extremely difficult to read. In the top and bottom bands, the upper parts of the letters are formed from human figures and some of the lower parts are formed from animals. In the middle band the stems of the letters are elaborately knotted. The text in the anthropomorphic and knotted scripts is so banal—"glory and prosperity and power and tranquility and happiness . . . to its owner"— that any viewer could immediately guess its content. These inscriptions were probably not meant to be deciphered and read literally but rather taken metaphorically as representing the same good life depicted in the accompanying figural scenes.

Even architecture could be made ambiguous. Designers and builders juxtaposed and played with the concepts of interior and exterior. This is seen readily in the Alhambra, the medieval palace complex built on the hills overlooking the city of Granada in southern Spain. One of its most distinctive and attractive features is the commingling of the outside and the inside. A courtyard is open to the sky but is inside a building; a porch is covered on three sides but opens to the courtyard. This ambiguity was enhanced by the use of water to connect the exterior with the interior. Water, carried by aqueducts from the surrounding hills, was piped into buildings, where it flowed from fountains through an elaborate system of channels in the floor. The ubiquitous sound of flowing water further blurred the distinction between inside and outside. Vistas also brought outside and inside together. Many rooms had windows or loggias (roofed open galleries) designed to command an extensive outlook and from which one could gaze on gardens or the city below.

Similar ambiguity can be seen in muqarnas, the distinctive stalactite-like motif used in Islamic buildings from Spain to Central Asia. The playful ambiguity inherent in the form often makes it difficult to determine its load-bearing capability in individual cases. Just as its visual and structural roles were often ambiguous, so were its symbolic implications, and it may well have had different implications at different times. Some scholars have suggested, for example, that the fragmentation and ephemerality inherent in muqarnas were suitable metaphors for the atomistic theology of Abbasid apologists. In Iran and neighboring areas muqarnas vaults were often used over the tombs of saints and mystics, probably to enhance the sanctity of the specific site. At the shrine of Ahmad Yasavi, for example, stunning muqarnas vaults cover the tomb room and the mosque.

The muqarnas motif was also exploited as a metaphor for the dome of heaven. This is clear at the Alhambra palace, where writing drives home the message suggested by the form. Two magnificent muqarnas vaults are suspended over the rooms in the center of the long sides of the Court of the Lions. To the north is the so-called Hall of the Two Sisters, a romantic name applied in memory of two captive sisters who are

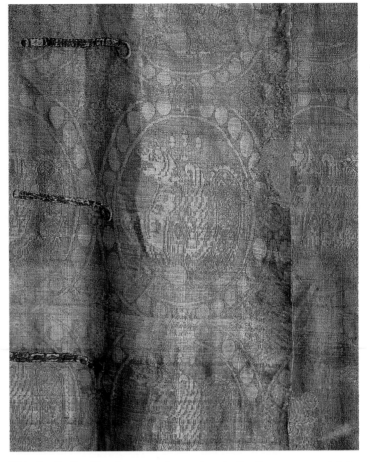

This detail of a silk caftan worn by a prince in the Caucasus mountains in the eighth century shows the same design of a simurgh as seen on the octagonal silver plate.

said to have perished from love at the sight of the amorous happenings they could witness in the gardens below but in which they could not participate. The muqarnas vault is set over an octagonal drum with eight paired windows, itself supported by muqarnas squinches over the square room. On the opposite side of the court is the so-called Hall of the Abencerrajes, whose apocryphal name derives from the famous family brutally murdered at the end of Muslim rule in Spain. In this case the muqarnas vault is set over an eight-pointed star. The walls of both rooms are inscribed with verses taken from a longer poem by the fourteenth-century court poet Ibn Zamrak. The verses describe the movement of the celestial bodies through their orbits in the heavens and reinforce the metaphor of the rotating dome of heaven. As sunlight passed from window to window in the drum of

Writing could be ambiguous. The Bobrinski Bucket, for example, is decorated with an inscription band in which the letters end in human heads. They contrast with the figural scene of a game of backgammon below.

the muqarnas vaults in these two rooms, the movement of shadows would create the effect of a rotating starry sky.

Paradoxically, the ambiguity inherent in many forms and motifs used in Islamic buildings may have contributed to their survival, as they were reinterpreted to suit the needs and aspirations of later users. This hypothesis of variable meaning and changing interpretation may in part explain why the Dome of the

Muqarnas vaults were often used to sanctify the space underneath, as at the late fourteenth-century shrine of Ahmad Yasavi at Turkestan City.

Rock in Jerusalem, especially its interior mosaics, has survived so well. Scholars are still at somewhat of a loss to explain why the caliph Abd al-Malik ordered its construction, although several different and even contradictory explanations were put forward for its presence. One early explanation, known since the eighth century, was that Abd al-Malik had the Dome of the Rock erected as a substitute focus of pilgrimage to replace the Kaaba in Mecca, which at that time was in the hands of his rival Abdallah ibn al-Zubayr. This heretical idea is discounted by many today, but it certainly carried currency for a long time. A second interpretation, still held by many today, connects the Dome of the Rock to Muhammad's miraculous night journey (isra) from Mecca to Jerusalem and his ascension (miraj) into heaven. This event is mentioned in the Quran (17:1). According to the text, Muhammad traveled from the sacred mosque (masjid al-haram) to the farthest mosque (masjid al-aqsa). The sacred mosque is commonly taken to refer to the mosque in Mecca, and by the mid-eighth century the farthest mosque was taken to refer to some location in Jerusalem. Gradually, each of the events in the journey was related to a specific site in the city, but only from the twelfth or thirteenth century can a direct association between the Dome of the Rock and the

Muqarnas vaults could also be exploited as a metaphor for the dome of heaven. This one soars over the fourteenth-century Hall of the Two Sisters at the Alhambra, the palace-city of the Nasrid rulers of Granada.

Prophet's journey be documented. Regardless of the ultimate truth of either explanation, what is important is that variable explanations could be and were accepted by different audiences.

The same is true of the mosaic program in the interior of the Dome of the Rock. Some scholars have related the iconographical program of trees and other vegetation to medieval stories about Solomon's temple, particularly his palace, and associated the mosaic decoration with the garden paradise that is promised to believers. Similar eschatalogical explanations have been proposed for the contemporary mosaics in the Great Mosque of Damascus, and such an explanation fits Jerusalem, the third holiest city in Islam. A second interpretation focuses on the jewelry depicted in the mosaics, particularly the crowns and other regalia. These are interpreted as trophies from conquered enemies that were arranged as offerings in a sanctuary or memorial monument. However, none of these explanations—pilgrimage, night journey, ascension, paradise, or victory—are mentioned in the contemporary inscriptions, which speak about Islam and Christianity.

Patrons, artists, and consumers in the Islamic lands seem to have delighted in such ambiguity. Just as the Arabic language encourages plays on words, so too was Islamic art open to multiple and even contradictory interpretations. Writing could impart information, but it was also decorative. Geometry formed the architectural module of construction, but it was also used as a major theme of decoration not only for buldings but also on objects. Color was attractive and enlivening to the eye, but it also had symbolic overtones. The multiple meanings and willed ambiguities are part of the appeal of Islamic art, which can be both unchanging and variable to the modern eye.

الجزو الثاني من كتاب

الشيخ الامام حجة الاسلام الامام ابو حامد محمد بن محمد الغزالي رضي الله عنه

احياء علوم الدين

وقف مولانا المقام الشريف الملكي الاشرف ابو النصر قايتباي نصره الله
هذا الجزو والذي قبله وقف بعد على طلبة العلم الشريف لينتفعوا به وجعل مقره بمدرسته
التي انشأها بالصحراء والشرط الا يخرج منها الا برهن لمن توجه تاريخ سادس عشر ذي القعدة الحرام

شهد عند فلان بن ...
شهد على مولانا المقام
المنيع بن ...
محمد خير الدين الط...

شهد على مولانا المقام الشريف
عبد الرزاق بن احمد البقلي

التي انشأها بالصحراء وشرط الواقف المذكور ضاعف الله تعالى له الاجور ان لا يخرج
من المدرسة المذكورة الابرهن يوضع ومحله وشهد بذلك تاريخ سادس عشر ذي القعدة الحرام
...الله ...

CHAPTER SIX

Philosophy and Theology

FROM THE EIGHTH CENTURY C.E.
TO THE PRESENT

Majid Fakhry

Islamic theology (*kalam*) was to a large extent a by-product of Islamic philosophy. To place Islamic philosophy in its proper historical context, one must first review the various stages through which its predecessor, Greek-Hellenistic philosophy, passed, to the eventual capture of Alexandria by Arabs in 641 C.E. Founded by Alexander the Great in 330 B.C.E., Alexandria had become during the Ptolemaic period (323–30 B.C.E.) the heir to Athens as the cultural center of the ancient world. By the beginning of the common era, Alexandria had become the major hub of philosophical, scientific, and medical studies, as well as the center of the interaction of Greek thought with Near Eastern religions: Egyptian, Phoenician, Chaldean, Jewish, and Christian. By the third century C.E. a new brand of philosophy known as Neoplatonism attempted to fuse the purely Greek legacy with those of the ancient nations of the Near East. What characterized the new amalgam was the profound religious and mystical spirit that animated it and the urge to transcend the intellectual categories that Greek philosophy in its greatest moments had consecrated as the chief channels for truth seeking. Identified with Aristotle, known in Arabic sources as the Master of Logic and the First Teacher, this ancient brand of philosophy was now challenged by a new variety that claimed Plato as its master and fully exploited the religious-mystical tendencies inherited from Pythagoreanism.

The Egyptian-Greek philosopher Plotinus (205–70) is the accredited founder of Neoplatonism, but he made no claims to originality. Plotinus contends in his

(Left) Abu Hamid al-Ghazali (d. 1111) was the greatest theologian of Islam, and his treatise *Ihya ulum al-din* enjoyed wide circulation. The Mamluk sultan Qaitbay donated this fine copy to his *madrasa* at Sahra in 1495.

work the *Enneads*, that his sole aim was to comment on or interpret the works of the "Divine Plato." Plotinus' disciple and editor, Porphyry of Tyre (ca. 234–305), a Syrian, carried on his teacher's legacy and pushed it one step further in the direction of mysticism. Porphyry argued that the ultimate goal of philosophy is self-purification, or cleansing of the soul from worldly passions and turning toward the intelligible world. One of the most influential figures in the history of Islamic logic and ethics, Porphyry was a great critic of Christianity. He found support for this thesis in Plato's *Theaetetus*, which describes philosophy as an attempt to rise above the material world and to seek "likeness unto God" (*homoiosis Theo*). Porphyry's successor was another Syrian, Jamblichus (d. 330), a shining star in the Neoplatonic firmament. Jamblichus' disciple Syrianus (d. ca. 430) was the teacher of Proclus of Athens (ca. 410–485), who wrote *Elements of Theology*. This work was partially translated into Arabic in the tenth century as the *Pure Good* and later into Latin as *Liber de causis* (Book of Causes), and it forms a major link in the development of Islamic and Latin Neoplatonism.

The Eclipse of Philosophy during the Byzantine Period

The school of Athens, which had been philosophy's home for almost a thousand years, was the last bastion of Greek paganism. In 529 the Byzantine emperor Justinian, as defender of the Orthodox faith, ordered that school to be closed, because its teachings constituted a threat to Christianity. After the school's closing, seven of its teachers, headed by Simplicius and Damascius, crossed the border into Persia, lured by reports of the philhellenic sympathies of the Persian emperor Khosrow I, known in Arabic and Persian sources as Anushirvan (the

The Sasanian academy at Gundishapur, founded in southwest Iran around 555 by Anushirwan, continued in the early centuries of Islam to be a major center for the transmission of Greek science and medicine. Nothing is left at the site, but the nearby ruins of the Sasanian dam and bridge over the Juhayl River at Shushtar testify its importance.

Just). Around 555, Anushirvan founded the school of Gundishapur, which became a staging station in the transmission of Greek medicine and science to the Muslim world. When Baghdad became the capital of the Abbasid Empire in 762, Gundishapur provided the caliphs with a long list of court physicians, such as the members of the famous Nestorian family of Bakhtishu. These physicians served the caliphs well and were instrumental in setting up the first hospital and observatory in Baghdad, modeled on those in Gundishapur during the reign of the caliphs Harun al-Rashid (r. 786–809) and his second son, al-Mamun (r. 813–33). Medicine, astronomy, and philosophy flourished in Gundishapur, primarily because of Yahya al-Barmaki (d. 805), Harun's vizier and mentor, whose zeal for Hellenic studies was instrumental in promoting the translation of Greek philosophical works into Arabic.

The primary channel through which Greek philosophy was transmitted to the Muslim world was Alexandria, where the study of Greek philosophy and science was flourishing when the Arabs conquered it in 641. In Syria and Iraq the study of Greek was pursued by Nestorians and Jacobites, Syriac-speaking scholars in the cities of Antioch, Edessa, and Nusaybin, who read or translated theological writings from Alexandria. These writings included Eusebius' *Ecclesiastical History*, St. Clement's *Recognitiones*, the *Discourses* of Titus of Bostra against the Manicheans, and the works of Theodore of Mopsuestia and Diodore of Tarsus.

The translations of Greek logical texts often accompanied the translations of these theological texts, to serve as preparatory instruction. Accordingly, Porphyry's *Isagoge* and Aristotle's *Categories*, *Hermeneutica*, and the first part of *Prior Analytics* were translated into Syriac, laying the groundwork for their eventual translation into Arabic. There is no evidence that Syriac scholars were interested in the other parts of Aristotle's *Organon*—including the *Posterior Analytics*, which dealt with demonstrative syllogisms, and *Sophistica*, which dealt with sophistical arguments or fallacious modes of discourse—perhaps because it was feared that these parts constituted a threat to the Christian faith. It was left to Baghdad's Muslim logicians some centuries later, with the philosopher Abu Nasr al-Farabi (ca. 878–950) leading the way, to break this tradition. These logicians eventually commented on or paraphrased the range of Aristotle's logical treatises, as well as his *Rhetoric* and *Poetics*, which were regarded as an integral part of the *Organon* in the Syriac and Arabic traditions.

The Arabic Translation of Greek Philosophical Texts

It is significant that the first accredited Arabic translations of Greek philosophical texts correspond to the same Syriac tradition of logical scholarship, as attested by the logical translations from Pahlevi by the eighth-century Arab translator Abdullah ibn al-Muqaffa or his son Muhammad. These translations were confined to the first three parts of Aristotle's *Organon*: *Categories*, *Hermeneutica*, and *Prior Analytics*. They were made during the reign of the Abbasid caliph al-Mansur (r. 754–75), who is commended in Arabic sources for his frugality and love of learning. Also translated into Arabic during al-Mansur's reign was Ptolemy's *Almagest*, Euclid's *Elements*, and several of Aristotle's treatises. This was followed, during the caliph Harun's reign, by the translation of a variety of astronomical and medical works, including Ptolemy's *Quadripartius* and the Indian treatise *Sidhanta*, known in Arabic as *Sindhind*, by Brahmagupta.

The earliest translations from Greek or Syriac of philosophical texts (as a distinct from logical and astronomical texts), however, appear to have started toward the end of the eighth century. A number of Platonic *Dialogues* in the synopses of the great Alexandrian physician-philosopher Galen (129–ca. 199), including *Republic*, *Timaeus*, and *Laws*, were translated by Yahya ibn al-Bitriq (d. 820) and revised shortly thereafter by Hunayn ibn Ishaq al-Ibadi (808–73) and his associates. This translation process was at first haphazard, but with the accession of the Abbasid caliph al-Mamun in 813, the picture changed dramatically. A poet and scholar in his own right, al-Mamum appears to have had a passion for "foreign learning," especially Greek philosophy and science. As a concrete expression of this passion, in 830 he founded the House of Wisdom in Baghdad to serve as an institute for translation and research; accordingly, the translation movement accelerated during his reign. Aristotle's *Metaphysics* and the apocryphal *Theology of Aristotle*, a paraphrase of Plotinus' last three *Enneads*, were translated during this period. Before long, the entire Aristotelian corpus was translated into Arabic, with the exception of *Politics*, for which a fabrication by ibn al-Bitriq called *Secret of Secrets* was substituted and falsely attributed to Aristotle.

In addition, a large number of Galen's ethical and logical treatises were translated along with his vast medical corpus in sixteen books, which formed the basis of medical instruction for centuries. A number of Porphyry's logical, ethical, and metaphysical treatises were also translated into Arabic. Porphyry's works included his famous *Isagoge*, or introduction to Aristotle's logic; a lost twelve-book commentary on Aristotle's *Nicomachean Ethics*, known only from the Arabic source; as well as the already-mentioned paraphrase of Plotinus' last three *Enneads*, attributed to Aristotle and translated by Ibn Naimah al-Himsi (d. 835) during the reign of al-Mamun. The unknown Greek author of the *Enneads* could very well have been Porphyry himself.

The Beginning of Systematic Philosophical Writings

Also during al-Mamun's reign, in addition to these translations (which formed the groundwork of Arabic-Islamic philosophy), the first genuine philosopher of

Islam, Yaqub ibn Ishaq al-Sabah al-Kindi (795–866), started his literary activity. A prolific encyclopedic author to whom some three hundred works are attributed, al-Kindi was the first champion of Greek philosophy, which was approached with some suspicion in traditional and popular circles as a foreign and pagan import. Al-Kindi believed that the study of philosophy, regardless of its foreign extraction, should not be feared by the true believer, because philosophy's chief subject of inquiry is the True One, source of all being and unity. Rather than conflicting with religious or Islamic truth, al-Kindi held, philosophy actually reinforces that truth. More explicitly than any other Muslim philosopher before or since, Al-Kindi proclaimed his adherence to the principal Muslim articles of faith, including the existence of God, the creation of the world out of nothing and in time, the resurrection of the body, and the truth of prophetic revelation. According to al-Kindi, these articles, embodied in the Quran, could be demonstrated philosophically and their truth dialectically reinforced. They belong to that body of divine wisdom, which surpasses human wisdom but is perfectly compatible with it. As a pioneering writer on philosophical subjects— which covered the entire range of classical learning, from logic to astronomy, ethics and metaphysics—al-Kindi was responsible for developing an adequate philosophical and scientific vocabulary that influenced his successors although it was later replaced by a more precise vocabulary.

The next outstanding writer on philosophical subjects was the great Persian physician-philosopher Abu Bakr al-Razi (ca. 865–between 923 and 935), who took a diametrically opposite stand to al-Kindi on the relationship between philosophy and revelation, generally referred to in Arabic sources as "prophethood." Like al-Kindi, al-Razi was a great admirer of Greek philosophy. In Platonic-Socratic fashion, al-Razi saw in the study of philosophy the only means of liberating the soul from the bondage of the body and its ultimate release from the wheel of birth and rebirth. Accordingly, his chief ethical treatise is entitled *Spiritual Physic* (therapy), to serve as a counterpart of the bodily physic (conventional medicine). The greatest nonconformist in Muslim religious history, al-Razi repudiated the entire concept of revelation or prophethood as superfluous, because for him reason was perfectly competent on its own to lead to the discovery of truth and the cultivation of morals. More radical, perhaps, was his concept of the five eternal principles from which the world was originally fashioned: the Creator, the soul, matter, space, and time. Because most of these principles can be shown to have a basis in Plato's *Timaeus*, al-Razi should be regarded as Islam's greatest Platonist. He refers to Plato in his *Spiritual Physic* as the "master and leader of the philosophers," whose theories of the soul, creation in time, and the ultimate liberation of the soul from the bondage of the body he incorporated into his own system through the study of philosophy. Al-Razi even defended in the strongest terms the Platonic theory of the transmigration of the soul, which was never in vogue in philosophical or the-ological circles. The only part of Plato's philosophy that al-Razi overlooked is pol-itics. Later philosophers, such as Abu Nasr al-Farabi in the tenth century and Ibn Rushd in the twelfth century, inspired by Plato's *Republic*, either commented on or used it as a model in their political writings. For reasons unknown, al-Razi also seems to have overlooked in his some two hundred works another favorite Platonic discipline: mathematics.

Islamic Neoplatonism and Neopythagoreanism

Neither the eclecticism of al-Kindi nor the Platonism of al-Razi was destined to determine the shape or direction of Islamic philosophy and give it its character-istic stamp; rather, an Islamic brand of Neoplatonism and Neopythagoreanism, whose foundations were laid in the tenth century, played this role. Abu Nasr al-Farabi (ca. 878–950), from northern Persia and of Turcoman origin, was the first truly systematic philosopher of Islam and the founder of Islamic Neoplatonism. In his best-known work, the *Opinions of the Inhabitants of the Virtuous City*, he devel-oped a cosmological and metaphysical system at the head of which stood the First Principle or the One of Plotinus, from which a series of ten intellectual ema-nations arose, and generating in progressive fashion the series of heavenly spheres, beneath which lay the world of the elements. In this system, humankind, who marks the apex of the terrestrial order of generation and cor-ruption, is the highest by-product of the combination of the elements and for that reason is described as the microcosm. Unlike inanimate objects or lower ani-mals, however, humankind possesses, in addition to the nutritive, sensitive, and appetitive faculties, the faculty of reason with its four subdivisions: the theoret-ical, the practical, the deliberative, and the productive.

The ultimate goal of human activity is the "acquisition of happiness," which al-Farabi discussed in a number of treatises. This happiness consists in the soul's total dissociation from everything material or bodily and as a result joining the hosts of "separate intelligences" in the intelligible world, which, like Plato, al-Farabi believed to be the ultimate abode of the soul. Like Aristotle, however, al-Farabi believed humankind to be a *zoon politikon*, or political animal, who cannot achieve the human goals of happiness outside society. Al-Farabi rejected the soli-tary life advocated by the Sufis, and postulated human association as humankind's natural condition in this life. Of the three forms of human asso-ciation—the large, or inhabited world; the intermediate, or nation (*ummah*), and the small, or city-state—the last form is the appropriate vehicle for achieving humankind's goal of happiness or virtue, which when properly ordered may be called "the virtuous city." This virtuous city corresponds to Plato's ideal state; all other forms of association are corruptions thereof. Because of this profound preoccupation with political association and the virtuous or ideal mode of such association, to which al-Farabi returned in a number of treatises, he is regarded as the founder of political philosophy in Islam. He was the first major logician of Islam to comment on all parts of Aristotle's *Organon* as well as his *Rhetoric* and *Poetics*. Furthermore, better than any medieval logician, al-Farabi devoted a series of treatises to the analysis of logical terms in a manner that was unequaled until modern times.

Al-Farabi's emanationist scheme was further developed and refined by the best-known Neoplatonist of Islam, Ibn Sina (known in the West as Avicenna, 980–1037). Although Ibn Sina acknowledged his debt to al-Farabi, his style of writing was more fluid and lucid than that of his predecessor, which ensured a wider diffusion in medieval learned circles, both in the East and the West. His greatest work, *Book of Healing*, covered the entire range of learning known in his day—from logic to physics, psychology, metaphysics, and astronomy. The work consists of some twenty volumes of which he wrote an abridgment entitled *al-Najat* (Salvation). In these two books and elsewhere, Ibn Sina fully developed al-Farabi's notion of "conjunction" of humankind's material intellect with the active intellect, or tenth emanation from the One or Necessary Being. When the soul has attained that stage, he wrote in *al-Najat*, it would become "an intelligible world of its own, in which are inscribed the form of the whole, the rational order of that whole, and the good pervading it." In other words, the soul would become a replica of the intelligible world, from which the whole order of intellectual, celestial, and terrestrial entities originally emerged by way of emanation.

Ibn Sina, who was born in Afshaneh in northern Persia, mentioned in his autobiography that he was drawn to the study of philosophy as a result of discussions in which his father and brother, who were addicted to reading *Epistles of the Brethren of Purity*, apparently engaged. His brother had been won over to the Egyptian (Ismaili) cause that the *Epistles* advocated. Written by a secret society called the Brethren of Purity, these *Epistles* (totalling fifty-two) embodied a popular version of Neopythagorean doctrine. According to the Brethren, this doctrine derived from the teaching of Pythagoras, "who was a monotheistic sage who hailed from Harran," and his first-century disciple, Nicomachus of Gerasa, who is sometimes confused with Aristotle's son in Arabic sources.

The key to understanding the world, according to the Brethren, is the study of "number," which possesses certain physical and metaphysical properties. When properly understood, this study will lead the diligent searcher to the knowledge of the soul, the spiritual world, and ultimately God. For the Brethren, number had more than a numerical or arithmetical connotation; it had a metaphysical and ethical connotation as well, because it reflected the very nature of reality. Number

رسائل اخوان الصفاء وخلان الوفا

The Epistles of the Brethren of Purity embodies a popular version of Neopythagorean doctrine. This fine illustrated copy made in Baghdad in 1287 has a double-page frontispiece showing the author and his attendants.

four, for instance, was intended by God to reflect the quadruple reality of the spiritual world, which consists of the Creator, the universal intellect, the universal soul, and prime matter. Similarly, God caused the elements to consist of a total of four or quadruples thereof: the basic natures or properties, the humors of the body, the seasons, the corners of the earth, and so on. Even justice, according to the Brethren, corresponds to this primordial number.

The chief advantage of the study of number, according to the Brethren, is twofold: it leads to the knowledge of the soul and this knowledge leads in turn to the knowledge of God, as stated in the prophetic tradition (*hadith*): "He who knows his soul will know his Lord." This refers to the refinement of character and the sharpening of the mind. This double knowledge will lead one who is born under an auspicious sign of the zodiac to discover the true nature of the soul as a spiritual substance. Furthermore, one will then strive to assist the soul to regain its original abode in the intelligible world, "through the profession of spiritual, religious creeds and the discourse on noble philosophical matters according to the Socratic path, while practicing mysticism, asceticism, and monasticism, according to the Christian path, and clinging to the Hanafi religion (i.e., Islam)." The chief merit of philosophy, then, is that it enables its adepts to probe the hidden (*batin*) meaning of revealed texts and teaches them not to stop at their external (*zahir*) meaning in the manner of the ignorant and the vulgar.

Ismailism, the extreme variety of Shiite Islam, achieved political ascendancy in the tenth and eleventh centuries, when it was proclaimed the official creed of the Fatimid caliphate of Cairo, which entered into violent confrontation with the Sunni Abbasid caliphate of Baghdad. In this confrontation, the Brethren formed the philosophical arm of Ismailism and the Assassins of Alamut formed its militant arm. Those Assassins targeted the Crusaders, who gave them their infamous name in the European languages, as well as important Abbasid statesmen such as the famous vizier of the Seljuks, Nizam al-Mulk, who in 1092 fell victim to the dagger of an Ismaili Assassin.

Interactions of Philosophy and Dogma

The chief merit of the Brethren's teachings is that it recognized no serious conflict between philosophical and religious truth. The other philosophers discussed until now concurred in principle in the harmony of the two forms of truth, but they developed elaborate cosmological and metaphysical systems inspired by the legacy of the great Neoplatonic philosopher Plotinus and his master Plato. Aristotle figured prominently only in those more discursive areas, such as logic, ethics, physics, and cosmology. A parallel development in learned circles gaining ground in the ninth century was systematic theology, generally referred to as the science of dialectic (*ilm al-Kalam*). Kalam began to take shape toward the end of the seventh century or the beginning of the eighth, at the hands of such scholars as al-Hasan al-Basri (d. 728) and his disciple Wasil ibn Ata (ca. 700–748), Amr ibn Ubayd (d. 762), and others, who belonged to a religious group known as the Qadaris, advocates of free will or "human *qadar*." Originally the leader of that group, al-Basri was a paragon of piety and asceticism. In his extant *Epistle on Free Will*, he argued in response to the query of the Umayyad caliph Abd al-Malik ibn Marwan (r. 685–705) that both the Quran and sound opinion affirm that God, who is supremely just, cannot hold people accountable for actions over which they have no control. When asked what he thought of "those kings [the Umayyad caliphs] who spill the blood of Muslims, appropriate their possessions, do what they please and say: 'Our actions are part of God's decree [*qada wa qadar*],'" al-Basri answered: "The enemies of God are liars." The controversy over free will and predestination had serious political implications. The early Qadaris, whose position al-Basri clearly championed, had challenged the authority of the Umayyads, who justified their most heinous crimes on the grounds that their actions were part of the divine decree. Two leaders of the Qadari movement, Ghaylan al-Dimashqi and Mabad al-Juhani, challenged those Umayyad claims and were put to death by order of Umayyad caliphs in 743 and 699, respectively. It is possible that al-Basri, known for his Qadari leanings, may have recanted out of fear for his own life, as some sources mention.

Wasil ibn Ata, continuing al-Basri's libertarian or the Qadari line, is generally regarded as the founder of the greatest theological movement in Islam: Mutazilism. This movement reached its zenith in the first half of the ninth century, when it enjoyed the patronage of the great Abbasid caliph al-Mamun, whose passion for Greek philosophy and the "ancient sciences" was great, as well as his two immediate successors on the caliphal throne. In token of his Mutazilite sympathies, in 827 and 833 al-Mamun instituted the notorious *mihna* or inquisition, which stipulated that any religious judge (*qadi*) who refused to profess the Mutazilite thesis of the "created" Quran would be dismissed or jailed. The most famous opponent of this thesis was the renowned scholar and Traditionist, Ahmad ibn Hanbal (780–855), who was uncompromising in his conviction that the Quran, as the word of God, was both "uncreated" and eternal. Thrown into jail and publicly scourged, he refused to relent but was eventually released and restored to favor by the Abbasid caliph al-Mutawakkil, who ascended the throne in 847 and reversed in a decisive way the religious policies of his three predecessors.

During the first half of the ninth century the leading Mutazilite theologians flourished. They included Abul-Hudhayl al-Allaf (d. 836/845), Ibrahim al-Nazzam (ca. 775–ca. 845), Amr ibn Bahr al-Jahiz (ca. 766–868 or 869), who belonged to the Basra branch of Mutazilism, Bishr ibn al-Mutamir (d. 825), Abu Musa al-Mirdar (d. 841), Jafar ibn Harb (d. 851), and Ahmad ibn Abi Duad (d. 855), who belonged to the rival Baghdad branch. Despite their divergences on certain peripheral points, these theologians were in agreement on five fundamental principles, as reported by the ninth-century scholar Abu Husayn al-Khayyat in his *Book of Vindication*, one of the earliest Mutazilite treatises. These five principles consisted of God's justice, God's unity, the "intermediate position," God's irreversible threats and promises, and God's commanding the right and prohibiting the wrong. These principles can best be understood as Mutazilite responses to their rivals: the Literalists, (literal interpreters of Quranic texts), the Determinists (believers in unqualified predestination), and the Traditionists (specialists in the study of the hadith). These principles further illustrate the unconditional commitment to the rationalist and humanist perspective of the philosophers and their new methodology, as developed by al-Kindi, whose Mutazilite sympathies are well documented.

The chief aim of Mutazilite moral theology was the vindication of God's justice, which Determinists like Jahn ibn Safwan (d. 745) threatened, and which the Quran affirmed in numerous verses. By reducing human actions to natural or mechanical occurrences, the Determinists (*Jabriyah*) made a mockery of the entire concept of divine justice and religious obligation (taklif). To be worthy of God's promises in the hereafter—which like His threats are both true and irreversible, according to the Mutazilah—humans must be able to discriminate rationally between right and wrong, even before revelation (sam), and must be able to freely choose their actions. That discrimination is connected to the fact that right and wrong are intrinsic qualities of human actions that are known intuitively to be either commendable or reprehensible, susceptible of reward and punishment. God, being entirely wise and just, can only command the former and prohibit the latter. This is contrary to the claims of the Determinists and Traditionists that as the Lord of Lords, God is not subject to compulsion of any kind; so that what God commands is by definition right and what God prohibits is wrong.

The Mutazilites disagreed with those religious groups that like the Kharijites (the secessionists who broke away from the ranks of Ali, the fourth caliph) contended that a believer who commits a grave sin (kabirah) ceases to be a Muslim and becomes thereupon an infidel (kafir) deserving of death. For the Mutazilah, such a person is really in an intermediate position between sound belief and infidelity and is in fact simply a sinner (fasiq) to whom the sanctions against apostates or infidels do not apply. Regarding the second grand thesis of God's unity, the Mutazilite theologians vehemently protested the Attributists and Anthropomorphists, who held that God possesses a series of attributes, usually seven in number: knowledge, power, life, will, speech, hearing, and sight. These attributes were regarded by both groups as distinct from God's essence (dhat) and co-eternal with God, so that He was compared by some Anthropomorphists (also called Corporealists in some Arabic sources) to an "eternal man," as the philosopher Ibn Rushd later wrote. For the Mutazilah, apart from its gross character, this view entailed a plurality of "eternal entities" and accordingly threatened belief in God's unity. Their own view was that in God essence and attribute are identical, a view that corresponded to Aristotle's and Plotinus', as well as to those of tenth- and eleventh-century Muslim philosophers, including al-Farabi and Ibn Sina.

The two attributes of will and speech presented the Mutazilah with a cluster of problems, however. First, insofar as divine will bears on created accidents, it was difficult to safeguard its eternity. Accordingly, some Mutazilites, like Abul-Hudhayl, argued that the divine will is a contingent accident that does not inhere in any substratum and is in fact reducible to God's command (amr), whereby God has created the world. Other Mutazilites, like Bishr ibn al-Mutamir, argued that it is necessary to distinguish between two aspects of the divine will: essential and active. Essential will includes God's essence, whereas active will is simply the act of creating the willed objects. Still other Mutazilites, like al-Nazzam, found the concept of will so baffling that they decided that it is not predicable of God at all. They maintained instead that the statement that God has willed an inanimate object means that He has created it, and the statement that He has willed the actions of human agents means that He has commanded them. For al-Nazzam and his followers, the question of divine will was a purely a semantic question.

The problem of divine speech raised the same cluster of difficulties. The Mutazilah argued that divine speech, manifested in divine utterances in the Quran and elsewhere, was a created accident and for that reason could not be joined as eternal (qadim). When the caliph al-Mamun proclaimed the Mutazilite thesis of the "created" Quran as the official doctrine of the state, the theological battle was sparked in a most violent way. The Hanbalites (followers of the renowned Traditionist Ahmad ibn Hanbal) and the masses at large could not reconcile themselves to the notion that the Quran, as God's word (kalam), could be described as a created accident, because it has existed since the beginning of time in the Mother of the Book or the Preserved Tablet, as stated in the Quran in a variety of places, such as 13:39, and 85:22.

The star of the Mutazilites began to set when the caliph al-Mutawakkil ascended the throne in 847 and reversed state policy on the question of the created Quran and other Mutazilite propositions. Throughout the second half of the ninth century, however, Mutazilite theologians, such as al-Jubai (d. 915) and his son Abu Hashim (d. 933), Abul-Husayn al-Khayyat (d. 902), and Abul-Qasim al-Balkhi (d. 931), continued to bear the Mutazilite torch. Before long, however, a successor theological movement appeared on the horizon: Asharism. Its founder, Abu al-Hasan al-Ashari (873–935), had been a Mutazilah up to his fortieth year, when the Prophet appeared to him in a dream, urging him to "take charge of my community [ummah]." After this, al-Ashari mounted the pulpit at the mosque at Basra and proclaimed his recantation of the "follies and scandals of the Mutazilah."

The teachings of the new theological movement that al-Ashari launched was eventually identified with orthodox Sunni Islam. It differed radically from the teachings of earlier scholars or Traditionists, such as Malik ibn Anas (ca. 715–795) of Medina and Ahmad ibn Hanbal of Baghdad. Unlike those two scholars, who founded two conservative Muslim schools, the Maliki and the Hanbali, al-Ashari was not willing to foreclose the use of Kalam's dialectical methods and tended to tread a middle course between theology's conservative and liberal wings. Thus in methodology, he agreed with the Mutazilites that it was the duty of every "reasonable Muslim," as he wrote in his *Vindication of the Use of the Science of Kalam*, to defer in those matters that are the subject of controversy "to the body of principles consecrated by reason, sense-experience or common sense" as well as to the explicit pronouncements of the Quran and the hadith. On all substantive issues, however, al-Ashari diverged from his Mutazilite masters and embraced the traditionist or Hanbali perspective. Thus, he rejected the Mutazilite view that a person is the "creator" of his or her deeds on the ground that this amounts to polytheism (ishrak) or dualism, charging the Mutazilah for that reason as being the Magians or Manicheans of Islam. For al-Ashari, God's power is unlimited and His decrees irreversible, therefore "all good or evil is the result of God's decree and fore-ordination," which no human can escape or alter. Nevertheless, al-Ashari, as much as he rejected the libertarianism (*qadariyah*) of the Mutazilah, was not willing to endorse the strict predestinationism (*jabriyah*) of their opponents, the Traditionists and Hanbalites. He opted instead for a theory of acquisition (*kasb*), for which he found a basis in the Quran, according to which God creates the actions of humankind, but humankind acquires them and becomes accordingly liable to punishment or reward.

Al-Ashari was not willing to concede, however, that God's attributes are identical with God's essence or distinct from it, because the mode of predicating them of God is unknown. His chief objection to the Mutazilites and the philosophers' view that God's attributes are identical with God's essence was that it rendered those attributes identical with God, so that humankind could address prayers or petitions to God's power, God's knowledge, or God's life, instead of God Himself. God's unity was unquestioned, however, because His essence was unknown and must be believed without asking how (*bila kayfa*). As for God's justice, it is not an object of rational discourse either, because whatever God does or commands is by definition just; whatever God prohibits is by definition unjust.

To rationalize the way God operates in the world, the Asharite theologians, starting with Abu Bakr al-Baqillani (d. 1013), developed an elaborate theory of atoms and accidents. According to this theory, everything in the world consists of atoms (sg. *juz*), in which a series of accidents, whether positive or negative, inhere. The nature of these accidents, however, is such that they cannot endure for two successive moments. Thus, God has to constantly create or recreate them for as long as God wishes the body in which they inhere to endure. Otherwise, that body would cease to exist. Some Asharite theologians argued that the destruction of the body in question, however, requires that God create in it the accident of cessation or extinction (*fana*), whereupon the body ceases to exist. The triumph of Asharism in subsequent generations was ensured by a long list of outstanding scholars, the best known of whom were al-Baghdadi (d. 1037), al-Juwayni (d. 1086), Abu Hamid al-Ghazali (1058–1111), al-Shahrastani (d. 1153), and Fakhr al-Razi (d. 1209). These theologians laid the foundation for all subsequent theological discussion, and their writings continue to be studied today in such major Sunni institutions as al-Azhar University in Egypt.

The Assault on Islamic Neoplatonism

The flowering of Asharism in the tenth and eleventh centuries signaled the renewal of the struggle between the Neoplatonic philosophers, represented primarily by al-Farabi and Ibn Sina, and the Asharite theologians. To begin with, the Asharite theologians, as well as the grammarians and legal scholars, looked with suspicion on the deductive methods of the logicians and the philosophers and were content to apply the linguistic and explanatory methods of interpretation to the sacred texts or juridical problems. Metaphysics, whether in its Neoplatonic or Aristotelian forms, was deemed inimical to the Islamic worldview and the teachings of the Quran because it rested on the twin principles of causal efficacy and the uniformity of nature, which are irreconcilable with the Quranic concept of God's unlimited power and inscrutable ways.

Abu Hamid al-Ghazali, the greatest theologian of Islam and one of its most fascinating figures, was the Asharite theologian who was the standard bearer of the assault on philosophy in the eleventh century. Born in Tus, Persia, in 1058, al-Ghazali started his studies of logic, philosophy, mysticism, and theology with a series of outstanding scholars, the most important of whom was al-Juwayni. In 1091 al-Ghazali was appointed by the vizier of Persia, Nizam al-Mulk, as head of the Nizamiyah school in Baghdad, where he remained until 1095. The assassination of Nizam al-Mulk in 1092 by an Ismaili commando and the death of the Seljuk sultan Malik-Shah shortly thereafter probably impelled al-Ghazali to leave Baghdad and travel throughout the Muslim world disguised as a Sufi. Al-Ghazali eventually returned to Nishapur, Persia, where he resumed his teaching until his

The Seljuk vizier Nizam al-Mulk (d. 1092) founded theological schools known as Nizamiyah in the major cities of the realm. The ruins of the one at Khargird in northeastern Iran are silent testimony to the way it once flourished as a center of scholarship and teaching.

death in 1111. Al-Ghazali was particularly well equipped to mount the onslaught on Neoplatonism in the name of Asharism and Sufism, because he was fully conversant with the philosophers' teachings, evident in his *Intentions of the Philosophers*, a succinct summary of Neoplatonic physics and metaphysics, which he wrote as a prelude to that onslaught in the *Incoherence of the Philosophers*. His epitome of logic, the *Criterion of Knowledge*, which is a very lucid summary of Aristotelian logic, should be added to this summary as well as his ethical treatise, *The Balance of Action*, which has an Aristotelian base and a Sufi capping.

Al-Ghazali began *Incoherence of the Philosophers* by defining his strategy as clearly as possible, distinguishing three parts of the philosophical sciences: (1) a part that includes logic and mathematics and has no direct "bearing on religion" and should therefore not be questioned, except by "an ignorant friend, who is worse than a learned foe"; (2) a part that deals with political and ethical maxims ultimately derived from the teachings of the prophets and the Sufi masters, which should not be questioned either but should be approached with caution; and (3) a part that contains the bulk of the philosophers' errors, namely physics and metaphysics. Al-Ghazali then listed the three most pernicious questions on which the philosophers deserve to be declared infidels (*takfir*); namely, the eternity of the world, God's knowledge of universals but not of particulars, and the denial of bodily resurrection. On all other issues, which he reduced to seventeen, the philosophers should be declared heretical (*tabdi*).

The philosophers' thesis of the eternity of the world opens the list of the twenty "pernicious" questions of *Incoherence*, because according to al-Ghazali this thesis entails that the world is uncreated and therefore the existence of its Creator is indemonstrable. Al-Kindi and the Asharite theologians had in fact predicated the existence of God on the existence of a created (*hadith, muhdath*) world; because it is created, the world necessarily requires a Creator (*muhdith*), as al-Kindi put it. In time, this became the favorite argument of the *mutakallimun* (Muslim theologians), both Mutazilite and Asharite, for the existence of God.

As for God's knowledge of universals but not of particulars, al-Ghazali leveled his attack on Ibn Sina in particular, because Ibn Sina had contended that the knowledge of changing particulars entails change in the essence of the "knower"; so that the only knowledge God can have of the world is universal, bearing on species and genera and not individuals. For al-Ghazali, however, not only reason but the Quran itself affirmed that "not a single atom's weight in the heavens or on earth is hidden from Him" (34:3). To deny God's knowledge of particulars, then, reduces God to the status of the ignorant or the dead.

Regarding bodily resurrection, al-Ghazali accused the philosophers of having failed to prove demonstratively the immorality of the soul, let alone the resurrection of the body. Because of this failure, the only recourse open to the believer, he argued, is to defer to the authority of scripture, wherein both the Quran and the hadith are explicit that on the Day of Judgment, souls shall be united to the appropriate bodies, made up of the same matter as the original body or one of a different nature. Once the soul has thus "repossessed the instrument," or the material body to which it was originally united or its analog, the individual will not only revive, but he or she will immediately regain the ability to experience those bodily pleasures and pains of which the Quran has spoken so graphically.

A fourth major issue, assigned to the physical part of *Incoherence*, is that of the Aristotelian concept of necessary connection between causes and effects. Neither experience nor reason, argued al-Ghazali, justifies the assertion of necessary causal connection. Experience (*mushahadah*) simply proves that the alleged effect occurs simultaneously with the cause, not through it (*ma ahu la bihi*). The association between the two creates in the mind the belief that the former is indeed the effect and the latter the cause. Individuals should believe instead, he wrote, that effects in the world are caused directly by God, who is the sole agent in the universe, or through the agency of those angels "charged with the affairs of this world." To assert that effects follow necessarily from their antecedent causes, as Aristotelian physical theory stipulates, concluded al-Ghazali, is in the end incompatible with the universal Muslim belief in God's power for miracle making.

The Resurgence of Peripateticism in Muslim Spain

Partly as a consequence of the reverses it received in the East at the hands of the Asharites, the Hanbalites, and others, and partly as a deliberate attempt to rival the Abbasid caliphate of Baghdad, philosophy in Muslim Spain (Andalusia) received a new lease of life under the aegis of the Umayyad caliphs of Córdoba in the tenth century. The Umayyad caliph Hakam II, known as al-Mustansir (r. 961-76), ordered the import of scientific and philosophical books from the East, so that with its university and library Córdoba during his reign rivaled Baghdad. The three outstanding scholars during this period were Ibn Masarrah (d. 931), al-Majriti (d. 1008), and al-Kirmani (d. 1068), whose interests were not confined to philosophy and included geometry, occult sciences, and mysticism.

The first truly eminent philosopher of Muslim Spain was Abu Bakr ibn Yahya ibn al-Sayigh (ca. 1095–1138 or 1139), better known in Arabic sources as Ibn Bajjah and in Latin as Avempace. He was born in Saragossa, in northeastern Spain, lived in Seville and Granada, and died in Fez, Morocco, probably by poison. Ibn Bajjah was a versatile philosopher and physician who wrote significant commentaries on Aristotle's works, including *Physics*, *De Anima*, and *Meteorologica*. Although these extant commentaries reveal a sound philosophical acumen, they are not fully developed. Ibn Bajjah also wrote extensive interpretations of all the parts of al-Farabi's logic. Perhaps because of al-Farabi's ethical and political interests, Ibn Bajjah singled him out as his chief master. He exhibits a certain measure of dependence on al-Farabi in his best-known work, *Conduct of the Solitary*. In that book—which, like al-Farabi's *Virtuous City*, exhibits definite Platonic influences—Ibn Bajjah's chief problem was not to delineate the type of ideal city or mode of association, which al-Farabi tried to do in his utopia. Rather, as the title of this treatise implies, he examined the mode of life suited to the solitary or true philosopher, who is destined to live in a "corrupt" city-state that has fallen short of al-Farabi's ideal of the "virtuous" city. In this connection Ibn Bajjah did not question Aristotle's (or al-Farabi's) maxim that humankind is a political animal by nature (a *zoon politikon*); rather, he observed that humankind may nevertheless be forced in certain circumstances to shun this ideal and to seek fulfillment in a life of solitude. For him, this life is intellectual and is achieved ultimately through conjunction or contact (*ittisal*) with the active intellect. Although Ibn Bajjah vacillates at this point between the mystical ideal of the Sufis and the Aristotelian ideal of the contemplative life, his basic sympathies remain Aristotelian and Neoplatonic. In his *Farewell Message*, he stated categorically that "reason is God's dearest creation to Him . . . and to the extent man is close to reason, he is close to God. This is possible only through rational knowledge, which brings man close to God, just as ignorance cuts him off from Him."

The Neoplatonic tradition in Muslim Spain was revived in even more dramatic fashion by another physician-philosopher of the Almohad period, Abu Bakr ibn Tufayl, who died in 1184. Unlike most of his predecessors, Ibn Tufayl chose an original literary form, the philosophical novel, to express his ideas. The title of his famous novel is *Risalat Hayy ibn Yaqzan*, which depicts the life and growth of a fictitious figure, born on a desert island in the Indian Ocean. This figure is able

Córdoba, under the Umayyad caliphs in the tenth century, became a center of philosophy equal to Baghdad. The library of the caliph al-Hakam (r. 961–76) is reputed to have housed over four hundred thousand volumes. The city, with the Great Mosque at its center, grew around a bridge crossing the Guadalquivir River.

to rise by degrees to the highest level of philosophical insight or discovery. Through observation and reflection, he is able, without any contact with other human beings, to discover the truth about God, the physical world, and the ultimate "conjunction" with the active intellect. Unlike his predecessor Ibn Bajjah, Ibn Tufayl argued that the contemplative or intellectual ideal of the Neoplatonists is not enough, because in that ideal the soul is not able to overcome the consciousness of its separate identity in relation to the Necessary Being. In Sufi fashion, Ibn Tufayl argued instead that to achieve the condition of perfect union with its source, the soul must rise to that level of ecstasy that the Sufis have called extinction (*fana*) in unity. This represents the total annihilation of selfhood and the recognition that in reality nothing exists other than the True One; everything else, spiritual or corporeal, considered in itself is nothing, as the Sufi masters, including al-Ghazali, had always contended.

These Sufi overtones did not make much headway in Muslim-Spanish philosophical circles, as illustrated by the case of the greatest Aristotelian of Islam: Ibn Rushd, known in the West as Averroës. Born in Córdoba in 1126, he was introduced at the age of forty to the caliph Abu Yusuf Yaqub by Ibn Tufayl, the caliph's court physician and minister. As a result of this introduction, the caliph ordered Ibn Rushd to expound for him the works of Aristotle, which the caliph had found "intractable." In addition to this commission, Ibn Rushd was appointed *qadi* (religious judge) of Seville in 1169 and two years later as chief judge of Córdoba. In 1182 he was appointed physician-royal at the Almohad court in Marrakesh. In 1195, probably in response to public pressure incited by religious conservatives and critics, the caliph Abu Yusuf Yaqub ordered Ibn Rushd to be exiled to Lucena to the southeast of Córdoba, his books to be burned in public, and the teaching of philosophy and the "ancient sciences" with the exception of astronomy and medicine, to be proscribed. Ibn Rushd's disgrace did not last long, however, because two years later he was restored to favor. He died shortly thereafter in 1198.

Ibn Rushd's contributions in philosophy, theology, medicine, and jurisprudence were voluminous and match in scope and thoroughness those of al-Farabi and Ibn Sina, his only equals in the East. He outstrips them both, however, in his thoroughness in commenting on Aristotle's works and his serious attempt to grapple with the perennial problem of reason and faith in two of his most important theological works: *Decisive Treatise* and *Exposition of the Methods of Proof Concerning Religious Beliefs*. Another important work is his response to al-Ghazali's *Incoherence of the Philosophers*. Known in the Middle Ages as "the commentator," or as the Italian poet Dante called him *che'l gran commento feo*, Ibn Rushd wrote three types of commentaries on Aristotle's works: large, intermediate, and small. Rather than commenting on Aristotle's *Politics*, which for an unknown reason was not translated into Arabic until modern times, Ibn Rushd wrote a unique commentary on Plato's *Republic*. Almost all his commentaries have survived in Hebrew or Latin translations and a fair number of them in the original Arabic. The Latin commentaries were reprinted in 1967 as part of the edition of *Omnia Opera Aristotelis Cum Commentariis Averrois*.

Ibn Rushd stands out as the greatest advocate since the ninth-century philosopher al-Kindi of the harmony of philosophy and religion, or more specifically of Aristotle and the Quran. According to Ibn Rushd, the issues that had pitted the Muslim theologians against the philosophers of Islam were often matters of semantics. Properly interpreted, he believed, the statements of the Quran are readily reconcilable with philosophy. The Quran itself recognized this fact: in 3:5–6, the Quran distinguishes between those verses that are "sound" and those that are ambiguous. The former constitute the core of the Quran or the Mother of the Book, the latter are open to various interpretations. Only God and those "well-grounded in knowledge," Ibn Rushd argued on the basis of his own readings of these verses, know its interpretation. By those "well-grounded in knowledge," Ibn Rushd was emphatic that the philosophers or "people of

Ibn Rushd (1126–98), known in the West as Averroës, was the most important medieval commentator on the works of Aristotle. Ibn Rushd attempted to harmonize Aristotelian philosophy with the teachings of the Quran. Raphael portrayed Ibn Rushd wearing a green robe and white turban and standing behind Aristotle in his painting *The School of Athens* in the Stanza della Signatura in the Vatican.

demonstration" should be understood. The others—including the theologians or "people of dialectic" and the masses at large or "rhetorical" group—are not competent to engage in this interpretation and are thus prohibited from disclosing this interpretation, which can only lead to dissension and strife among Muslims.

To demonstrate this point, Ibn Rushd proceeded in his *Incoherence of the Incoherence* and *Exposition* to rebut al-Ghazali's arguments against the philosophers. On the first issue of the eternity of the world, he argued that contrary to al-Ghazali's contention, the philosophers do not believe the world to be really eternal or really temporal. According to Ibn Rushd, the former thesis entails that like God, the world is uncreated; the latter that it is corruptible. The genuine teaching of the philosophers, he explained, is that the world is generated *ab aeterno* (from eternity). This is so because the claim that it was generated in time (*muhdath*) simply derogates from God's power or perfection, because it would entail that God could not have brought the world into being before the specific time He created it and would raise the question why He chose to create it at that specific time and no other. On the second issue, that the philosophers deny God's knowledge of particulars, Ibn Rushd reported that what the philosophers in fact deny is that God's knowledge is analogous to that of humans and thus divisible into particular and universal. The two are radically different: human knowledge is an *effect* of the thing known, whereas God's knowledge is the *cause* of the thing known and accordingly is neither universal nor particular but is of its own kind. Moreover, its mode is unknown to us, because, like God's will, it is part of the mystery of God's creative power. On the third issue of resurrection, Ibn Rushd explained, the philosophers and the religious creeds of his day are in accord regarding the fact of resurrection, but they differ on its mode. The philosophers, he held, subscribe to spiritual resurrection or immortality (*maad*) and regard the Quranic references to corporeal resurrection and the pleasures and pains of heaven and hell as so many pictorial or sensuous representations of spiritual truths, intended to sway or deter the masses, who are unable to understand the subtle, spiritual language of revelation.

Ibn Rushd further impugned al-Ghazali's sincerity in denying the necessary correlation between cause and effect, on the ground that this denial is a sophistical gambit in which "one denies verbally what is in his heart," that is, without serious conviction or simply out of malice. He then proceeded to ridicule al-Ghazali's notion that the alleged correlation between cause and effect is a matter of *habit*, born of humankind's observation of the recurrence of cause-effect sequences. By *habit*, al-Ghazali could only mean God's habit, which the Quran (35: 45) denies on the ground that God's ways are immutable; that of inanimate objects, which is absurd; or finally, humankind's own habit of judging the correlation of events in the world. This is synonymous with the activity of reason, which is nothing other than the knowledge of the cause underlying any given effect or series of effects. Thus, "he who repudiates causality," Ibn Rushd wrote, "actually repudiates reason." This repudiation logically entails the repudiation of that divine wisdom that presides over creation and has ordered it according to a fixed causal pattern from which the mind is able to rise to the discovery of its Maker or First Cause.

In the context of European medieval thought, Ibn Rushd's standing was unrivaled. When his commentaries on Aristotle were translated into Latin in the first half of the thirteenth century at the hands of a galaxy of European scholars—Michael the Scot, Herman the German, Gundissalinus, and many others—they caused a genuine stir in intellectual circles. By the mid-thirteenth century a large contingent of Latin Averroists, led by the French philosopher Siger of Brabant and the theologian Boethius of Dacia, were battling in Paris against the Augustinian-Avicennian party, championed by the Franciscans. Eventually, in 1270 a condemnation of thirteen Aristotelian-Averroist theses was issued, at the insistence of the Bishop of Paris, Etienne Tempier, and was followed in 1277 by a more sweeping condemnation of 219 theses, many of which were of Averroist inspiration. They included the eternity of the world, the double truth, the denial of divine providence, the unity of the intellect, the impossibility of individual resurrection, the superiority of philosophical over religious truth, and the impossibility of miracles. Although Ibn Rushd was innocent of some of these charges, especially that of the double truth, it is a measure of his intellectual impact that European philosophers and theologians during the thirteenth century, including Thomas Aquinas (1225–74), were actually battling under the strange banner of pro-Averroists and anti-Averroists.

The Recrudescence of Literalism and Theological Reaction

Al-Ghazali's assault on philosophy in the tenth century was devastating, but it allowed for the right of reason to arbitrate in theological conflicts. Even the founder of the Asharite school himself, Abu al-Hasan al-Ashari, had lauded "the merits of engaging in theological discourse [kalam]." Before long, the antirationalist tide began to swell, however, as illustrated by the cases of Ibn Hazm, the Zahirite (or literalist) (994–1064), Ibn Taymiyah (1263–1328), and Ibn Qayyim al-Jawziyah (1292–1350) in the eleventh through the fourteenth centuries.

Ibn Hazm was a leading figure in the history of Islamic literature, ethics, and historiography. His learning was vast, as shown by his *Discriminations of Fancies and Religious Creeds*, his *Ethical Traits and Modes of Conduct*, and his *Book of Rebuttal*. In the *Book of Rebuttal*, he rejected, out of hand, all forms of deduction, analogy, opinion, or imitation of authoritative masters (taqlid), which the various schools of theology and jurisprudence had applied over the centuries in some form or other. He then proceeded to denounce all methods of theological discourse, whether Mutazilite or Asharite, and conceded only the testimony of sense experience, intuition, or the explicit statements of the Quran and the hadith, literally interpreted.

Ibn Hazm was outstripped in his advocacy of empiricism and literalism by a thirteenth- and fourteenth-century scholar: Ibn Taymiyah. Like Ibn Hazm, Ibn Taymiyah denounced all theological and philosophical methods of proof and called for a return to the ways of the "pious ancestors" (al-salaf al-salih). This call was destined to become the slogan of modernists in the nineteenth century and is still a potent religious slogan today. According to Ibn Taymiyah, the only genuine sources of religious truth are the Quran and the hadith, as interpreted by the Companions of the Prophet or their immediate successors. The authority of those interpreters, confirmed by the consensus (ijma) of the community, is infallible. All subsequent interpretations or theological, philosophical, and mystical developments since that time are deviations or heresies (bida). In his *Harmony of Reason and Tradition*, Ibn Taymiyah attacked Ibn Rushd for limiting the number of theological groups to four: the esoteric, the Literalist, the Mutazilite, and the Asharite. This excluded the creed of the "pious ancestors," which is the "best creed of this (Muslim) community till the Day of Resurrection."

Ibn Taymiyah also attacked the philosophers, but unlike al-Ghazali, he did not spare any of the philosophical sciences, including logic, which al-Ghazali had regarded as an "instrument of thought" and as such religiously neutral or innocuous. The Aristotelian theory of definition, which is one of the cornerstones of logic, is untenable according to Ibn Taymiyah because of the difficulty of determining the infinite number of species and the essential distinguishing traits upon which definition actually depends. The theory of the syllogism is equally unten-

Damascus was a center of theology in medieval times. Sunni rulers of the Ayyubid and Mamluk dynasties built theological colleges around the Great Mosque, founded by the Umayyads in the early eighth century. Al-Ghazali, the major figure in the assault against Neoplatonism, spent several years in meditation there, and Ibn Taymiyya (d. 1328), great champion of empiricism and literalism, spent most of his life in the city.

able because the ultimate validity of the syllogism depends on self-evident propositions intuitively apprehended. Considering the diversity of human aptitudes, such apprehension will always remain dubious or questionable. Even demonstration (*burhan*), regarded by the philosophers as the highest form of reasoning, is vacuous because it bears on universals that exist in the mind and are far removed for that reason from particulars that constitute the very fabric of reality. Ibn Taymiyah's best-known disciple was Ibn Qayyim al-Jawziyah, another key figure in the history of the reaction against philosophy and theology that was initiated in the ninth century by Ahmad ibn Hanbal. This reaction culminated in the eighteenth century in the rise of the Wahhabi movement, founded by Muhammad ibn Abd al-Wahhab (1703–92), which in time became the official creed of the Saudi dynasty in Arabia. The Wahhabis share with Ibn Taymiyah and his school, in addition to literalism, strict observance of the Muslim rituals and the condemnation of the cult of saints and what they consider to be "similar excesses" of the Sufi orders.

The fourteenth century is dominated by the Arab philosopher, historian, and sociologist Ibn Khaldun, who was born in Tunis in 1332 and died in Cairo in 1406. A versatile and encyclopedic genius, Ibn Khaldun developed the only coherent philosophy of history in Islam that was based on the dialectic of transition from nomadic life to sedentary or urban life and in which geographic, ecological, and economic factors were the potent forces determining the cyclical pattern of social and political change in the world. An empiricist by nature, Ibn Khaldun agreed with al-Ghazali and Ibn Taymiyah in their repudiation of the philosophical methods of discourse, because their

Tunis, located near the ancient site of Carthage, was the birthplace of Ibn Khaldun (1332–1406), the encyclopedic genius who developed the only coherent philosophy of history in Islam. Religious learning there centered around the Zitouna Mosque, founded in the ninth century, particularly when Tunis became home to many scholars fleeing the Marinid invasion of Morocco in the mid-fourteenth century.

arguments turn on universals or conceptual matters, whose correspondence with reality cannot be conclusively demonstrated. In fact, the "spiritual entities" that form the subject matter of metaphysics can never be known rationally; thus the philosophers' conclusions regarding those entities are, at best, matters of opinion (*doxa*), as Plato himself acknowledges. As for their physical speculations, they are entirely futile, "because questions of physics do not concern us, either in our religion or our livelihood, and therefore we should abandon them," as Ibn Khaldun wrote in his discussion of the philosophical sciences in his famous

Ibn Khaldun spent the last years of his life in Cairo, where he served in several capacities under the Mamluk sultans. In 1387, for example, he was appointed to the newly built Zahiriyya madrasa.

Prolegomena. Ibn Khaldun, who was mystically inclined, also rejected the Neoplatonist concept of happiness as lying in "conjunction" with the active intellect. This conjunction, he believed, is purely intellectual and rests on rational deductions rooted in "bodily cognitions." Genuine happiness is attainable only through the practice of the Sufi way and the mortification of the self.

To return to theological developments, the most important figure during the twelfth century was Fakhr al-Din al-Razi, who was born in Rayy in 1149 and died in Herat in 1209. Unlike al-Ghazali and Ibn Taymiyah, al-Razi recognized no serious conflict between philosophy and theology and deferred constantly in his discussion of philosophical and theological questions to the authority of Ibn Sina, whose influence on al-Razi's thought was profound. During the thirteenth and fourteenth centuries theology began to decline and the contributions of scholars during that period and beyond was limited to commentaries or supercommentaries on the writings of the classical masters. The noteworthy theologians of this period include al-Nasafi (d. 1310), al-Iji (d. 1355), al-Taftazani (d. 1390), and al-Jurjani (1339–1413). The most important theologians of the fifteenth and sixteenth centuries are al-Birgili (d. 1570), al-Laqani (d. 1621), and al-Sialkuti (d. 1657). In the nineteenth century al-Bajuri (d. 1860) heralded the modern period, of which the Egyptian scholar Muhammad Abduh (1849–1905), considered the founder of Islamic modernism, was the chief representative.

The Ishraqi Movement in Persia

A partial reaction against Aristotelianism, known as the "wisdom of illumination" (*ishraq*), took in the twelfth century the form of a revised version of Avicennian Neoplatonism, which succeeded in reconciling philosophy to Sufism. Ibn Sina himself had expressed in some of his later works a certain dissatisfaction with the purely discursive methods of the Peripatetics and proposed to lay the groundwork of an "Oriental wisdom" into which certain "oriental" (Eastern) elements were incorporated. He did not work out the full implications of this philosophy, however. It was left to another Persian philosopher-mystic to draw these implications. Shihab al-Din al-Suhrawardi was born in Aleppo, Syria, in 1154 and was killed by order of the sultan Saladin in 1191 on an undefined charge of blasphemy. Like Ibn Sina, al-Suhrawardi expressed his dissatisfaction with the discursive method of the Peripatetics of his day, who misunderstood the intent of Aristotle, the First Teacher and Master of Wisdom, as he called him. Aristotle appeared to al-Suhrawardi in a dream and engaged him in a discussion of the nature of knowledge, conjunction, and union, as well as the status of the philosophers of Islam and the Sufis, who had attained the level of "concrete knowledge" and visual contact and were accordingly the true philosophers and sages of Islam. What distinguishes those sages, al-Suhrawardi believed, is that they have partaken of an ancient wisdom that goes back to Plato, and beyond him to Hermes and the other ancient Greek sages such as Empedocles and Pythagoras. In addition, this wisdom has an Eastern source and rests on the dualism of light and darkness that was preached by such ancient Persian sages as Jamasp, Frashustra, Buzurgimhr, and their predecessors. The chief representatives of this wisdom in the West were Plato, Agathadaimon, and Ascelepius, and it culminated in the work of al-Bistami (d. 876), the mystic al-Hallaj (ca. 855–922), and al-Suhrawardi himself.

The Syrian philosopher Shihab al-Din al-Suhrawardi (1154–99) developed a revised version of Avicennian Neoplatonism, called the "Wisdom of Illumination" (*ishraq*), which succeeded in reconciling philosophy to Sufism. The walls of the Firdaws madrasa, built in his native city of Aleppo in 1236, are inscribed with texts that suggest Suhrawardi's philosophy was studied there.

The core of the "wisdom of illumination" al-Suhrawardi proposed is the science of light, which he defined as a substance diffused throughout the universe that gives everything its reality and its capacity for self-manifestation. At the top of the scale of being stands the Light of Lights, identified with Ibn Sina's Necessary Being. It is the source of all being and luminosity in the world. The first emanation from the Light of Lights is the first light, corresponding to Ibn Sina's first intellect, followed by the secondary lights that differ from the Light of Lights only in the degree of their purity or perfection. Then come the heavenly bodies, physical objects and material compounds or simple elements, which together constitute the physical world. A combination of light and darkness, this

world may be described as the shadow or penumbra of the world of light. Like its original source, this world is eternal.

This Ishraqi wisdom became Persia's distinctive philosophy, in response to al-Ghazali's onslaught on Neoplatonism and the enthusiastic patronage of the Safawid dynasty, inaugurated by Shah Usmail (r. 1500–1524), who claimed descent from a Sufi family. A number of Shiite scholars distinguished themselves during this period, of which Mir Damad (d. 1631) and al-Amili (ca. 1546–ca. 1622) are worth mention. They were teachers of Sadr al-Din al-Shirazi, who is generally regarded as the greatest philosopher of modern Persia. Al-Shirazi, better known in Persia as Mulla Sadra, was born in Shiraz around 1571 and died in Basra in 1640 on his way back from the seventh pilgrimage to Mecca. Al-Shirazi's philosophical contributions were voluminous, but his most important work is *Transcendental Wisdom*, intended as a counterpart to al-Suhrawardi's *Wisdom of Illumination* and better known as *Four Journeys*. These four journeys are (1) from creation to the true reality, (2) through the true reality to the true reality, (3) from the true reality to creation, and (4) in creation through the true reality.

According to al-Shirazi, the Necessary Being or Light of Lights creates the world in time "by ordering it to be and it becomes," as the Quran 3:42 and 16:42 state. Accordingly, it is far from being eternal, as al-Suhrawardi, Ibn Sina, and the Neoplatonists generally held. Being a combination of light and darkness, the soul serves as a link between the intelligible world or "world of command," as the Sufis

Mulla Sadr-al-Din (1571–1640), regarded as the greatest philosopher of post-medieval Persia, left his native Shiraz for the new Safavid capital of Isfahan, where he studied for several years with leading scholars attracted there by Shah Abbas' patronage. The great square with its new congregational mosque dates from this period.

called it, and the material world or "world of creation." The world of creation begins with the universal sphere, which separates the world of intelligible forms or souls from the material world of sensible entities. Al-Shirazi is categorical that both soul and body will rise from the dead on the Day of Resurrection. Once resurrected, the body will assume an ethereal form and thereupon become identified with the soul, because "in the Hereafter, everything is alive and its life is identical with its essence," as he wrote in his treatise, *Mustering and Resurrection*.

A noteworthy feature of al-Shirazi's metaphysical and historical doctrine is the application of philosophical categories to Shiism. He argued that world history's prophetic stage came to an end following the death of Muhammad, the Seal of the Prophets, and thereupon started the Imamite stage, which is represented by the chain of twelve Shiite imams. This stage continued until the return of the twelfth imam, who was in temporary concealment, according to Shiite doctrine. Since the seventeenth century Al-Shirazi's influence has continued to dominate Persian thought.

Modern Philosophical and Theological Developments

As already mentioned, the Ishraqi tradition, which culminated in al-Shirazi's transcendental wisdom during the Safavid period, continued well into modern times. Al-Shirazi's disciples and successors include his two sons, Ibrahim and Ahmad, and others: Fayaz al-Lahiji (d. 1662), Muhsin Fayd Kashani (d. 1680), Muhammad Baqir Majlisi (d. 1700), and Nimatulla Shustari (d. 1691). In the nineteenth century, al-Shirazi's most important successor was the Persian philosopher Haji Hadi Sabzevari (1797 or 1798–1878), who commented on al-Shirazi's works. Other commentators include such eminent philosophers and scholars as Mirza Abul Hasam Jilwah, Mirzah Mahdi Ashtiyani, and Mirza Tahir Tunikabuni.

In more recent years, the Ishraqi tradition has continued to flourish in Persia (modern Iran), as illustrated by the contributions of Muhammad Qasim Assar, Sayyid Abul-Hasan Qazwini, and Muhammad Husayn Tabatabaii. Although these scholars have aligned themselves with the Ishraqi tradition as represented by al-Shirazi, some have contended that al-Shirazi was far more dependent on Ibn Sina's Peripatetic philosophy than most of his disciples or successors have been willing to admit. Other contemporary Persian philosophers who have commented on the works of Ibn Sina and al-Shirazi include Mahmud Shahabi, Muhammad Mishkat, the Persian Lady, Yak Banu-yi Irani, and Sayyid Jalal Ashtiyani. Other philosophers, such as Murtada Mutahhari, Akkamah Shaiati, and the Ayatollahs Khomeini, Muntaziri, and Taliqani, have concentrated on political subjects and the problems facing Islam today. Their thought, however, continues to reflect the influence of the Ishraqi-Shiite tradition. Sayyed Hossain Nasr is often mentioned as the leading Persian philosopher to write in English and to address the question of the encounter of Islam with modern Western thought.

In what is now India and Pakistan, Islamic philosophy was introduced by the Ismaili propagandists (*dais*) as early as the late ninth century. The Ismailis, who succeeded in founding an Ismaili state in Sind (part of the Indus River valley) in 977, were overthrown by the Ghaznavid dynasty. During the Ghaznavid period, the most noteworthy scholar was Abul-Hasan al-Hujwiri (d. 1072), author of a famous mystical treatise entitled *Uncovering the Hidden*. During the rule of the successor dynasty, the Ghurids, the two most eminent scholars were Fakhr al-Din al-Razi and Adud al-Din al-Iji (d. 1355), who were succeeded during the Mongol period by such scholars and theologians as Sadr al-Din al-Taftazani (d. 1390), al-Sharif al-Jurjani (1339–1413), Jalal al-Din al-Dawwani (d. 1501), Shaykh Ahmad Sirhindi (1593–1624), and Abd al-Hakim Siyalkuti (d. 1657). The most famous Indian scholar of the eighteenth century was Shah Walliullah (d. 1762), who wrote in both Arabic and Persian. He attempted to reconcile the four schools of Islamic law and to bring together the Sunni and Shiite branches of Islam.

As Islam came into contact with Western thought in the nineteenth and twentieth centuries, some Indian scholars, such as the educator and jurist Sayyid Ahmad Khan of Bahador (1817–98), spearheaded a modernist movement that saw no genuine conflict between Islam and Christianity because of their common moral message. Ahmad Khan's disciple, Sayyid Amir Ali (1849–1928), believed the spirit of Islam is ultimately reducible to that cluster of moral ideas or principles that are at the basis of modern Western liberalism and humanism. The poet-philosopher Muhammad Iqbal (1877–1938) continued essentially the same line of speculation and attempted, more seriously than his predecessors, to interpret Islam in contemporary philosophical terms. In his famous *Reconstruction of Religious Thought in Islam*, Iqbal rejected the antirationalism of al-Ghazali and Ibn Taymiyah and argued that religion is not in opposition to philosophy but is rather the core of that total experience upon which philosophy must reflect, as born out by the Quranic exhortation to reflect upon God's creation and to pursue knowledge for its own sake. For Iqbal the Quranic worldview is that of a dynamic reality in which the ideal and the real coalesce. It is not a "block universe" or finished product; rather, it is in process of constant actualization, at the hands of humankind, the principal co-worker with God. In some respects, Iqbal's ideas appear to be an adaptation of the "creative evolution" of the French philosopher Henri-Louis Bergson, the "process philosophy" of Alfred North Whitehead, and the "absolute idealism" of the German philosopher Georg Wilhelm Friedrich Hegel.

In Southeast Asia, which came under Islam's influence as early as the thirteenth century, a profusion of writings on jurisprudence, theology, and Sufism appeared during the sixteenth and seventeenth centuries in Malay. Of these writings, the works of Hamzah al-Fanzuri (d. ca. 1600), Nur al-Din al-Raniri (d. 1666), Shams al-Din al-Sumatrani (d. 1630), and Abd al-Rauf al-Singkeli (d. 1693) are particularly noteworthy. These writings reflected the profound impact of Sufism on the Malaysian mind, which tended to be less philosophical or discursive than the Indian or Persian.

Interest in Sufism began to decline during the eighteenth and nineteenth centuries, but the situation changed somewhat during the twentieth century, as the works of Muhammad Naguib al-Attas and others show. Of al-Attas' many writings in English, *The Mysticism of Hamzah al-Fanzuri*, *Meaning and Experience of Happiness in Islam*, and *Islam, Secularism, and the Philosophy of the Future* are noteworthy. In *Islam, Secularism, and the Philosophy of the Future*, al-Attas vehemently criticized Western Christianity, which he said is not a revealed religion but a "sophisticated form of culture religion." Like other fundamentalists, al-Attas dwelled on Islam's superiority, as the only religion that is truly global because it encompasses every aspect of human life, private or public, spiritual and temporal, in contradistinction to Christianity, which he claimed only stresses the spiritual aspects of life.

Philosophy in the Arab World Today

When the political activist and journalist Jamal al-Din al-Afghani (1838–97) visited Egypt for the first time, he was struck by the fact that although the study of philosophy had continued in Persia, it was completely forgotten in Syria and Egypt. His disciple, the Islamic modernist Muhammad Abduh (1849–1905), was actually the first Muslim scholar to lecture on philosophy at al-Azhar University, which he sought to reform. Significantly, Abduh chose as his theme the philosophy of Ibn Khaldun, the last great writer on the history of ideas and the original author of Islam's only philosophy of history. Around the same time, Farah Antun (1874–1922) wrote on philosophical questions in his Arabic magazine *al-Jamiah*, and in 1903 he published the *Philosophy of Ibn Rushd*, one of the first impressive treatises on the subject in Arabic. Serious work on the history of Islamic philosophy flourished during the first decades of the twentieth century at the hands of such eminent scholars as Jamil Saliba, Ibrahim Madkour, Yusuf Karam, and Father George Anawati, who laid the foundation of historical scholarship in Arabic. Their pioneering work was continued by such leading scholars as Abd al-Rahman Badawi and Zaki Najib Mahmud. In the 1970s, Badawi made a valuable contribution to philosophical scholarship with his critical editions of a vast number of Arabic philosophical texts and his French *Histoire de la Philosophie Musulmane*. Mahmud contributed to the critical reinterpretation of the Islamic philosophical heritage with his 1971 publication of *Renewal of Arabic Thought*. His Egyptian disciple, Fuad Zakariyah, carried the discussion and evaluation of the

Arabic philosophical heritage (*al-turath*) one step further, calling for total commitment to rationalism, positivism, and modern scientific culture.

Modernism, Secularism, and Fundamentalism

Today the major religious currents, with their divergent theological presuppositions, take a variety of rival forms. Modernism (which calls for a modern interpretation of Islam), secularism (which calls for the separation of religion and politics), and fundamentalism (which is unwavering in its commitment to traditional Islam and its anti-Western bias) are the major contending currents. The modernist (or reformist) movement was launched by Sayyid Ahmad Khan and Sayyid Amir Ali in the second half of the nineteenth century. Both of these religious thinkers conceived of modernism as a mode of isolating the moral and spiritual core of Islam, which Ahmad Khan believed to be analogous to Christianity and Amir Ali believed to be timeless and universal. The philosopher Muhammad Iqbal conceived of Islam in dynamic terms best understood in light of modern Western philosophical developments.

In Egypt the two chief protagonists of modernism were Jamal al-Din al-Afghani and his disciple, Muhammad Abduh, who spearheaded a religious movement known as the Salafi movement. This movement aimed to modernize Islam, demonstrate its viability for all times, and promote social and political change within the confines of the Shariah. In their defense of Islam against its European detractors, such as the French politician Gabriel Hanotaux and the English Lord Cromer, these Islamic modernists proclaimed, like their Indian counterparts, Islam's global character and its complete compatibility with rational canons of argument or debate. According to Abduh, although Christianity calls for giving to Caesar what is Caesar's and to God what is God's, Islam calls for the subordination of *everything* to God and thus rejects the separation of the spiritual and the temporal. In addition, unlike Christianity and other supernatural religions, Islam is fully committed to rationality and rejects any preternatural or supernatural explanations, such as miracles or mysteries.

More radical, and in some cases more violent, post-midcentury fundamentalists, such as Sayyid Qutb (1906–66) in Egypt and Mawlana Abul Ala Mawdudi (1903–79) in Pakistan, have tended to target Christianity and the West as the causes of the decadence of the Muslim people on the one hand and the spread of secularism and irreligion on the other. Because of its exclusive spiritual character, they have argued, Christianity has abandoned humankind to its egotistic and materialistic resources and has violated the supreme principle of divine unity (*tawhid*), which stipulates that God's sovereignty and lordship is not confined to the spiritual aspects of human life; rather, it dominates and regulates every aspect of that life. In his critique of Western civilization, Abul Ala Mawdudi inveighed against Western nationalism, democracy, and secularism. According to Abul Ala Mawdudi, nationalism culminates ultimately in the cult of the nation, democracy in the tyranny of the majority, and secularism in the repudiation of God's universal lordship and ultimately in irreligion or atheism. To the extent that Muslims are willing to adopt Western democracy, nationalism, or secularism, he proclaimed, they are in fact abandoning their religion, betraying their Prophet, and rebelling against God Himself. Based on these sentiments, the Islamic Movement was founded in 1941 in Pakistan; Abul Ala Mawdudi was its first president, and it was dedicated to leading the Muslim people back to God, to fighting Western ideologies, and to renouncing corrupt leadership. These aims could not be achieved without recourse to *jihad*, which Abul Ala Mawdudi defined in his *Moral Foundation of the Islamic Movement* (1976) as "the attempt to establish the divine order," by wresting leadership from the corrupt and unbelieving men who are in power. Islam demands from its followers total submission to God and shuns every form of polytheism and materialism. It thus "purifies the soul from self-seeking, egotism, tyranny, and wantonness," he wrote, "It induces feelings of moral responsibility and fosters the capacity for self-control."

Sayyid Qutb in Egypt was as vehement as Abul Ala Mawdudi in his critique of Western civilization, which he said has led humanity down the road of corruption and irreligion, from which only Islam can save it. As he wrote in his *Islam and the Problems of Civilization* (1962), Islam, unlike Christianity, recognizes no conflict between reason and faith, science and religion, and it conceives of religion "as the crucible of the whole of life in which all its forms and hues are fused." As the "global religion," Islam was thus at peace with science from the earliest times and has paved the way for the rise of the inductive method and the scientific progress of modern times.

As one would expect, secular intellectuals have been at loggerheads with the fundamentalists on a variety of issues. To begin with, they challenge the concept of theocracy upon which the medieval caliphate rested and call for the separation of the political and spiritual. In that respect, they are unquestionably inspired by Christian theology and Western political thought. The most thoughtful Muslim secularists have gone beyond this somewhat negative stand and have taken the line, championed in the first half of the twentieth century by a learned Azharite scholar, Ali Abd al-Raziq. In his classic work, *Islam and the Principles of Government* (1925), Abd al-Raziq argued that Islam is essentially a religious call to the whole of humankind and as such a purely spiritual religion. The Quran, the hadith, and *ijma* (consensus of the Muslim community)—the three principal sources of Islamic law and doctrine—all concur in affirming the spiritual character of Islam and the consequent separation of religion and politics. During the early decades of Islamic history, the Prophet acted as the political head of the nascent Muslim community in Medina, not in his capacity as Prophet or religious teacher but rather as the acknowledged leader of that community. He was compelled by circumstances to attend to legislative, judicial, and military matters peripheral to his prophetic office, which was purely spiritual. In support of these claims, Abd al-Raziq quoted a number of prophetic traditions purporting to stress the duty of Muslims to rely on reason and common sense in the management of their worldly affairs, rather than on divine revelation, which legislates exclusively for spiritual matters and is addressed to the whole of humankind. In that respect, the separation between the spiritual and temporal is clearly recognized by Islam.

In the mid-twentieth century, Khalid Muhammad Khalid, a fellow-graduate of al-Azhar University in Cairo, pursued and defended this secularist thesis more radically in his *From Here We Begin* (1950). In this work, he highlighted, like Abd al-Raziq, the sharp distinction in Islam between the truly spiritual, which is universal and timeless, and the temporal, which is susceptible to constant change or modification. Unlike his predecessor, Khalid sounded an anticlerical and socialist note, which has marked the thought of many contemporary secularists. Some secularists, like the Egyptian Zaki Nagib Mahmud, aligned themselves with logical positivism; others, like the Moroccan Abd al-Aziz Larawi and the Syrian Sadiq al-Azm, aligned themselves with Marxism. Still others, like Hasan Sab and Hisham Sharabi, took a liberal, pro-Western stand on current political and religious issues. The list of such liberal and secular intellectuals and scholars can of course be expanded, but they continue today to be outnumbered by the much larger contingent of traditional fundamentalist Muslim apologists. These apologists have achieved great notoriety throughout the world, chiefly because of their radicalism, anti-Westernism, and open espousal of violence.

The Interactive Relationship of Philosophy and Theology

Philosophy, which found its way into the Muslim world as early as the eighth century, was in constant interaction with theology. Although as early as the first decade of the eighth century, theology (*kalam*) grew out of moral and political disputes, closely linked to the interpretation of the Quran and the hadith in Damascus and Basra, in its more sophisticated form, theology in the Muslim world was dependent to a large extent on Greek philosophy. By the beginning of the ninth century, a vast number of Greek and Syriac philosophical texts had become available to scholars in Baghdad and elsewhere. This was shown by the lively discussion in both Mutazilite and post-Mutazilite circles of such questions as atoms and accidents, the "natures" or primary qualities (*tabai*), being and nothingness, causes and effects, and similar physical or metaphysical questions.

During the tenth and eleventh centuries, however, the most violent controversies between Asharite theologians, such as al-Baghdadi and al-Ghazali, and the Muslim Neoplatonists, represented chiefly by al-Farabi and Ibn Sina, began to rock the Muslim community. The upshot of these controversies was the gradual eclipse of philosophical activity and the virtual triumph of Asharite theology. Attempts by such philosophers as Ibn Rushd (Averroës) or such theologians as Fakhr al-Din al-Razi to moderate the conflict between philosophy and theology were not entirely successful. Those attempts proved the vitality of Arabic-Muslim philosophy, however, which received a new lease of life in Muslim Spain to the West and Persia to the East.

The chief historical significance of the Muslim-Spanish phase in the rise and development of Muslim philosophy is that it served as a major link in the transmission of Greek philosophy to western Europe. The Muslims had been the chief custodians of that philosophy, which had been almost completely forgotten in western Europe since the sixth century, when the Roman consul Boethius (d. 525) was chiefly responsible for the Latin translation of Aristotelian logic. By the end of the twelfth century the translation of Arabic philosophical and medical works into Hebrew or Latin, at the hands of such eminent scholars as Gerard of Cremona, Michael the Scot, and Herman the German, wrought a genuine intellectual revolution in learned circles. The most influential Muslim philosopher to leave a lasting impression on Western thought was Ibn Rushd, the great commentator on Aristotle. During the thirteenth century philosophers and theologians split into two rival groups: the Latin Averroists with Siger of Brabant and Boethius of Dacia at their head, and the anti-Averroist group with Albertus Magnus and Thomas Aquinas at their head. The confrontation between the two groups became so violent that by the second half of the thirteenth century the

The Persian or Ishraqi tradition of philosophy that began in the twelfth century has continued into modern times. It is still taught in theological centers such as Qum, the city in central Iran that grew up around the tomb of Fatima, sister of the eighth Shiite imam, which stands under the golden dome.

Bishop of Paris, Etienne Tempier, had to intervene, and in 1270 and 1277 he issued an ecclesiastical condemnation of a total of 219 propositions that were of Aristotelian or Averroist inspiration. Thanks to the Latin translations of Averroes' commentaries, the rediscovery of Aristotle in western Europe and the concurrent emergence of Latin Scholasticism, one of the glories of late medieval thought, were made possible.

The other phase of the revival of Islamic philosophy and theology was the Persian or Ishraqi tradition, which has continued well into modern times. Inaugurated by al-Suhrawardi, this phase culminated in the rise of the "transcendental wisdom" of al-Shirazi, a blend of Neoplatonism and Sufism. A characteristic feature of the Ishraqi tradition, which continues to be taught in the theological centers of Qom, Meshhed, and Tehran in northwestern Iran and Najaf in Iraq, is that it recognizes no conflict or hostility between philosophy and theology of the type that became the hallmark of Asharite (Sunni) theology. In fact, the Ishraqi tradition dwells on the analogies between philosophical categories and Shiite (Imamite) theology.

In the Arab world of today, controversy at the theological level has taken the form of modernism, secularism, or fundamentalism. At the philosophical level, throughout the second half of the twentieth century, the output of Arabic-speaking scholars has turned on historical and textual research and publication, although a small number of Western-oriented authors have grappled with contemporary philosophical and theological issues, either from a logical-positivist, existentialist, or Marxist perspective. Although proscribed in some parts of the Arab world, such as Saudi Arabia, philosophy continues to be taught in most educational institutions, secondary or collegiate, throughout most of the Arab countries. As the handmaid of philosophy, theology tends to follow in its footsteps: Where philosophical activity proliferates, theology tends to proliferate; where philosophy is proscribed, theology (kalam) tends to be proscribed too.

CHAPTER SEVEN

Islam and Christendom

HISTORICAL, CULTURAL, AND RELIGIOUS INTERACTION FROM THE SEVENTH TO THE FIFTEENTH CENTURIES

Jane I. Smith

The Christian world into which Islam so unexpectedly burst in the seventh century C.E. had undergone a succession of divisions, controversies, and power struggles such that east and west were at serious odds, and each contained within its regions deep tensions and disagreements. It is little wonder that the new religion of Islam, arising out of the heart of Arabia, appeared to those who knew of its existence as another Christian heresy, not unlike the many other heresies that had wrinkled the face of Christendom since its inception. The fact that within a century of the death of the Prophet Muhammad in 632 Islam had spread across much of the known world was for many Christians inexplicable, frightening, and theologically incomprehensible.

Muslims, for their part, on the basis of the Quranic revelations, found it impossible to understand why Christians insisted on impugning the oneness of God by their affirmation of the divinity of Jesus and use of Trinitarian formulas. In the beginning of his career, Muhammad seems to have understood his role as the final prophet of a monotheistic faith of which Jews and Christians, before their perversion of the original revelations given to them by God, were the earlier members. It was only when Muhammad encountered unexpected resistance from these communities and their refusal to recognize his status as the final prophet of true monotheism that his community came to understand itself as the bearers of a faith that was related to, but different from, the extant

(Left) After the Christians reconquered Spain from Muslim rule, many mosques were changed into churches. In Seville, for example, the top of the fifty-meter-high minaret of the Almohed mosque, built from 1184 to 1198, was remodeled and transformed into a cathedral belltower.

religions of the Jews and Christians. This faith became known as Islam, sub-mission to the one God.

The Effect of Early Islam on Christians and Christianity

Arabia was the home of significant Jewish and Christian communities, particu-larly in the south. During the Prophet's lifetime, Christians were living in Medina, Mecca, Khyber, Yemen, and Najran, although their numbers were small in the areas in which Muhammad carried on his preaching mission. Although Muslim doctrine attests to the fact that the Prophet could not read or write, thus ensuring that he did not "copy" from the scriptures or writings of Christians and Jews, there is also a record of his interaction with Christians throughout his life. One popular tradition records a meeting in Syria between a young Muhammad and a Christian monk named Bahira. The monk recognized the seal of prophet-hood between the boy's shoulders as attested to by scripture. The use of Christian scripture to confirm Muhammad's prophethood was also evidenced when a Christian cousin of his first wife Khadijah, Waraqa ibn Nawfal, acknowledged Muhammad's recitation of the revelation to be identical with that sent down to Moses. During the early prophetic period in Mecca, Muhammad's small com-munity was often persecuted by the Quraysh tribe, which was concerned for the maintenance of its hold over the city's ancient and lucrative holy places. At one point the Prophet sent a number of his followers to Abyssinia (what is how Ethiopia) to find shelter. The Abyssinians are reported to have listened to the preaching Prophet with great respect and awe, especially the description of Mary, mother of Jesus, leading them to affirm that this indeed was God's revelation.

These and other incidents confirm for Muslims their belief that Islam is not a derivative of Christianity but a divine revelation, a fact that at least some of the Christians of Muhammad's lifetime recognized. The Quran itself identifies Jews and Christians as the recipients of earlier revealed books or scriptures, namely the Torah, the Psalms, and the Gospel. These scriptures are believed to have been cor-rupted by the communities to which they were sent and are thus abrogated and in some senses superseded by the Quran. They are nonetheless held in esteem insofar as they were originally God's revelation, and the peoples to whom they were given are thus considered in a special category, namely the People of the Book. All prophets are said to have taught the identical message that came from God to Muhammad.

Perhaps because of their greater resistance to the presence of the Muslim com-munity in Medina, Jews are treated more harshly in the Quran than are Christians. The primary offense of the Christians is that they hold to a Trinitarian doctrine of God and the divinity of Jesus. Jesus is referred to in ninety-three verses of the Quran, affirming that he was born of Mary the Virgin, that he was a righteous prophet, that he was given clear signs from God, that he had disciples (helpers), that he performed such miracles as healing the blind and the lepers and raising the dead by the power of God, and that he will be a sign of the coming of the hour of judgment. The Quran also says very specifically that those who refer to Jesus as God are blasphemers, and that Christians saying that Christ is the son of God is an imitation of Jews, who earlier had said that Ezra is the son of God. According to the Quran Jesus was only a servant; Jesus the son of Mary was no more than an apostle of God. Quranic verses dealing with Jesus' death have been interpreted differently by commentators, but generally they have been taken to mean that Jesus did not die by crucifixion. For Christians the Quran has thus served as a denial of Jesus' incarnation and death on the cross and of the reality of the Trinity.

About Christians themselves the Quran is quite charitable. Apart from accusations of heresy for their stand on the Trinity and some chiding for their conviction that theirs is the true religion, the Quran declares that Christians are people of compassion and mercy, that they will be able to enter paradise, and even that they are nearest in love to the (Muslim) believers. One Quranic verse is interpreted to mean that Jesus himself foretold the coming of a prophet called Ahmad (from the same root as Muhammad). In 632, only months before he died, Muhammad apparently met for the first time with a Christian community as such. An official delegation of Christians, probably led by a bishop, came to Mecca from Najran in Yemen. After engaging the Christians in discussion, the Prophet is said to have realized that Christian teachings are indeed incompatible with Islam, after which the revelation followed that only Islam is acceptable to God as a religion.

The early community of Muslims in Medina established its presence and extended its domain primarily through carrying out a series of *razzias* or marauding expeditions against hostile tribes. These led to more serious encounters, during which Muslims were not always the aggressors. In any case, it was only the pagans to whom the choice of becoming Muslim or suffering serious consequences was given. As the so-called People of the Book, Christians and Jews, along with Magians, Samaritans, Sabians, and later Zoroastrians and others, were treated as minorities under the protection of Islam (*dhimmis*), believers in God despite their refusal to accept the prophethood of Muhammad. Adult male Christians were thus not required to convert (although that option was always open to them), but they were required to pay a poll tax as the price for this protection. Because of the income accrued from this tax, Muslims in general preferred that Christians (and Jews) not convert to Islam but maintain their status as protected minorities. Dhimmis were granted the right to practice their religion in private, to defend themselves against external aggression, and to govern their own communities. Later they were exempted from military service, although some Christians fought on the side of Muslims in the early expansion of Islam. In fact, Christian subjects were often allowed a good deal of latitude in paying their poll and other taxes.

The specifics of the requirements for Christians who enjoyed dhimmi status were spelled out in what has come to be referred to as "the covenant of Umar," which exists in several versions and most likely was attributed to rather than designed by the second caliph, Umar ibn al-Khattab (r. 634–44). The covenant stipulated prohibition of the building of new churches or repair of those in towns inhabited by Muslims, although in some cases when financing was available Christians did construct new places of worship. Beating the wooden clapper that Christians used to call people to prayer was forbidden, as was loud chanting or carrying the cross or the Bible in processions. Dhimmis were allowed to keep their own communal laws, although they could apply to a Muslim judge if they wished. They were not, however, allowed to give testimony concerning a Muslim in a court of law. The recruiting of new Christians was forbidden, as was any insult about Islam or its Prophet. As a means of identification, particular dress, such as a special girdle, was required for Christians. Over the first several centuries of Islam, dress stipulations grew increasingly stringent for Christian men and women. A Muslim woman was not allowed to marry a Christian man, although the Quran does allow marriage of a Muslim man to a Christian woman. Nevertheless, Islamic law from early on stipulated a great range of conditions under which such a marriage might take place. The children of a mixed marriage were always considered Muslim. A Muslim could own a dhimmi slave, but never the opposite.

Some of the judges and lawyers of Islam were strict in the interpretation of dhimmi status, especially in reaction against Christians and Jews occupying high administrative positions, while others showed more flexibility. The different legal schools were not in complete agreement as to what privileges should be allowed to dhimmis, and customs differed from one place to another. The strictest interpretations were applied in Baghdad and other major Islamic cities, while enforcement of regulations in small towns and rural areas was often more lenient. Dhimmis were allowed to live anywhere except in Mecca and Medina. In actual practice, Christians and Muslims often had very friendly relations. Muslims, for example, are said to have especially enjoyed the hospitality of monks in Christian monasteries. Christians occupied high positions in the caliphal courts as physicians, engineers, architects, and translators, and sometimes they were treated as having virtually equal rights with Muslims. Muslim writers and poets sometimes gave great tribute to Christians in their literature.

The dhimmi status seems to have been a changing one, in that laws were made and either broken or forgotten, and relations between Christians and Muslims obviously were dependent on individual whim and personal advantage as well as on what was stipulated by the law. Although Christians and Jews were often in positions of public service in Muslim communities, and sometimes were among the ranks of the very wealthy, they were never free from the whims of individual rulers who might choose to enforce strict regulations, or from the caprice of mobs expressing their passions in prejudicial and harmful ways. In general, the first Arab Muslim dynasty, that of the Umayyads, was fairly flexible in terms of its Christian citizens, but in Islam's second century the laws became more stringent. Under the reign of the caliph al-Mutawakkil (r. 847–61), laws against dhimmis were most severe, sometimes resulting in persecution of Christians as well as of Mutazilis, Shiites, and others considered opponents of the state. Through the Middle Ages there was a hardening of attitudes against dhimmis, due more to political than to religious reasons, especially after the period of the Crusades.

The Expansion of Islam into Christian Territories

The Christian world into which Islam moved with such rapidity was one that was far from united. The church was divided into five apostolic sects, located in Rome, Antioch, Constantinople, Jerusalem, and Alexandria. A series of controversies over the nature of Jesus' relationship to God had failed to bring all Christians under one umbrella of belief. The resulting sectarian divisions, pitting Christian against Christian, had significant consequences for the spread of Islam. To no small degree, these controversies served to exacerbate the already existing divisions between Greek-speaking and Syrian-, Armenian-, or Coptic-speaking Arab Christians.

Christianity flourished in Syria in the centuries before the rise of Islam. A magnificent and extensive monastery, for example, grew up around the site near Antioch where St. Simeon Stylites (d. 459) spent twenty-seven years in a small cell atop a pillar.

The creed resulting from the Council of Nicaea in 325 affirmed that Christ was one substance with God, a perspective that dominated ensuing theological discussions. This was reaffirmed in succeeding sessions at Constantinople, Ephesus, and finally at Chalcedon in 451, and was held by both Latin-speaking Roman Catholic and Orthodox Christians. This creed was opposed by dissenting groups such as the Arians, the Monophysites, and the followers of the Antiocene theologian Nestorius, each with their own subtle but distinctive theological interpretations. The Council of Ephesus branded Nestorianism a heresy, but Nestorian missionary activity continued to move eastward through inner Asia.

The church of Alexandria split between the Copts, who held to the Monophysite doctrine condemned at Chalcedon, and the Melchites, who affirmed the orthodoxy of Chalcedon. In Syria the Monophysites organized into an independent Jacobite church, following one of its leaders, Jacobus Baradaeus. A fifth church council in 556, held in Constantinople, basically reaffirmed the Chalcedonian understanding, a position held by both the Roman Catholic and the Greek Orthodox communions. Arab Christians who affirmed this doctrine, mainly from Syria, were also referred to as Melchites. In the second half of the sixth century, the Maronite church came into being, later to become the first eastern church to accept the supremacy of the Pope.

This was the complex background of the Christian church that the forces of Islam encountered. The Roman church of the West was in an uneasy compromise with the Byzantines; Oriental communions fragmented over long-standing

Damascus was an important center of Christianity before the Muslims took the city in 635, but many Christians soon converted to Islam. The Umayyad mosque, founded by the caliph al-Walid in 705, was built on the site of the Byzantine church dedicated to St. John.

Christological controversies and were generally considered heretical by both Romans and Greeks. The Byzantine state ruled its eastern subjects with an authority that was often experienced as ruthless and oppressive. Thus it was that many Oriental Christians welcomed Muslim political authority as a relief from Byzantine oversight and cooperated with their new Muslim rulers. This was one of the most important factors in the remarkable ease with which Islam was able to spread across Christian lands. Within twenty years of the Prophet's death, the Byzantine Empire lost the provinces of Palestine, Egypt, and Syria.

For many Christians the arrival of Islam was actually seen as a liberation from the tyranny of fellow Christians rather than as a menace or even a challenge to their own faith. Such acquiescence, of course, was encouraged by the fact that under Islam they were guaranteed the right to continue as independent communities. The dhimmi status, despite the obligations and lower status attached to it, was for many a preferable option to Byzantine oppression. The grandfather of John of Damascus, for example, was instrumental in the capitulation of Damascus to the forces of the Muslim commander Khalid ibn al-Walid in 635, signaling the end of Byzantine rule in Syria. Tensions between Syria and Constantinople had been high because of theological disagreements between the Monophysites and the Chalcedonians as well as for reasons of taxation and heavy-handed Byzantine rule. The arrival of the Muslims in Damascus was welcomed by a significant portion of the population, many of whom were only vaguely

Jerusalem is holy to the three great monotheistic religions. This nineteenth-century lithograph by David Roberts, seen from the Mount of Olives, shows sites venerated by Jews, Christians, and Muslims.

aware that their new rulers represented another religious faith. The Muslims, for their part, had little interest in Christian theological disputes, and although they forbade Christians from building new edifices, their rule was considerably more benign than that of the Byzantines. Significant numbers of the members of these eastern communions eventually converted to Islam, significantly reducing the size of the Nestorian and Jacobite communities.

It was because of a combination of factors, then, that Islam spread so rapidly after the Prophet's death; Christian accommodation for both political and religious reasons was only one of those reasons. The two major empires in the Middle East—the Persian Sasanian and the Greek Byzantine—were exhausted after many years of struggle, and Islam was able to occupy what amounted to a power vacuum in many of the areas to which it spread. The raiding tactics that had worked so well, as one after another Arabian tribe capitulated to the new faith, continued to function in expanded ways, with the plunder rendered in goods and taxes. Military expeditions were political in nature and not undertaken for the purpose of forcing conversion to Islam as an alternative to the sword. Dhimmi status was too profitable for this to have been the case. Conversion was accepted, of course, but not encouraged, and for a number of centuries Christians remained the majority in much of what was nominally Muslim territory.

Of the many victories enjoyed by Muslims in Christian territories soon after the Prophet's death none was to have more significance for the relationship of Islam and Christendom than the taking of Jerusalem shortly after the defeat of the Byzantine troops at the Battle of Yarmuk in 636. Always considered the Holy City by Christians, Jerusalem from Islam's beginning was also a place greatly venerated by Muslims. Originally it was the place toward which the Prophet Muhammad asked his followers to turn in prayer. Although he later changed the prayer direction to Mecca, the city continued to be a site of pilgrimage and prayer. For Christians, Jerusalem is the place of the death and resurrection of Jesus. For Muslims it is venerated as the location from which Muhammad is said to have ascended on his miraculous "night journey" through the heavens. The conquest of the city was one of the most peaceful of its long and painful history. Shortly after its capture, the caliph Umar himself is said to have traveled to the Holy City to establish a treaty with the patriarch Sophronius, by which Christians living there were allowed freedom of life, property, and worship in return for paying the poll-tax and helping to fight off Byzantine raiders. Umar ordered the

Christians venerate Jerusalem as the place where Jesus died and was resurrected. The Church of the Holy Sepulchre, erected by the Byzantine emperor Constantine in the early fourth century and repeatedly restored and rebuilt, marks the site of Christ's tomb. Its prominent dome is visible on the skyline of Jerusalem's Old City as seen from the platform on which the Dome of the Rock stands.

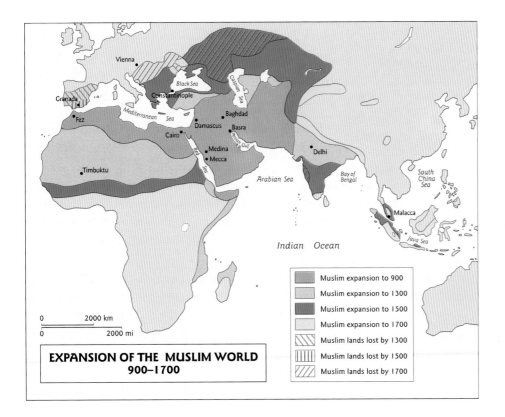

Vienna

Black Sea

Granada

Constantinople

Mediterranean   Sea

Fez

Baghdad

Damascus

Cairo

Basra

Medina

Mecca

Delhi

Timbuktu

Arabian Sea

Bay of
Bengal

South
China
Sea

Red Sea

Persian Gulf

Caspian Sea

Malacca

Java Sea

Indian   Ocean

0   2000 km

0   2000 mi

EXPANSION OF THE MUSLIM WORLD
900–1700

Muslim expansion to 900

Muslim expansion to 1300

Muslim expansion to 1500

Muslim expansion to 1700

Muslim lands lost by 1300

Muslim lands lost by 1500

Muslim lands lost by 1700

Temple Mount to be cleansed of the piles of garbage that had accumulated on it, and he had a temporary mosque built on the site. Christians remained the majority population in Jerusalem for many years; the city thus consisted mainly of dhimmis. In 661 Muawiyah (r. 661–80) was proclaimed caliph in Jerusalem, first ruler of the near century-long Umayyad dynasty. Muawiyah is said to have done the initial planning for the construction of the Dome of the Rock on the site of Umar's mosque; the edifice was completed by his successor Abd al-Malik ibn Marwan in 691. The oldest Islamic monument still existing, the Dome has held a place of enormous importance in the religious life of Islam and was the scene of great rejoicing when it was returned to Muslim hands after the defeat of the Franks at the time of the Crusades. The adjacent mosque of al-Aqsa, in Islamic tradition the second and holiest sanctuary on the Temple Mount, was built either by Abd al-Malik or his son al-Walid I, and it has served through the centuries as a preeminent place of worship and prayer.

As Muslims pushed the boundaries further in virtually all directions, military advances were made by both land and sea. From the middle of the seventh century Muslim naval strength grew in the Mediterranean, where the Byzantines had ruled supreme. Occupying Cyprus and Rhodes, Muslims besieged Constantinople until finally retiring in 667. On the northern coast of Africa they moved again to consolidate power, gaining control of the major Mediterranean base of Tunis at the turn of the eighth century. Resistance originally put up by the Berbers of North Africa was overcome with their (at least nominal) conversion to Islam, which was to prove key to the Muslim advance into Spain and France. In 711 an army of Berber converts crossed the Straits of Gibraltar and soon took control of southern Iberia. Two years later the governor of North Africa claimed Toledo to be under the sovereignty of the caliph of Damascus. The final advance of the Muslim east into the Christian west came when Muslim armies crossed over the Pyrenees into the south of France in 718. They took Bordeaux, destroyed the army of the defending Duke Eudes of Aquitaine, and pillaged Poitiers. Eudes then fled north to seek assistance from the Frankish ruler Charles Martel, while the Muslim armies sacked and pillaged cities and abbeys. In 732 the Muslim troops were met by Eudes and Charles Martel near Poitiers, where Islam's advance into western Christendom was finally checked. Muslims continued to foray into Frankish lands, maintaining their hold on the coast of Provence until 759, when Charles Martel's son Pépin was able to secure the city of Narbonne in southern France, eliminating the last outpost of Muslim strength north of the Pyrenees.

The picture of Christian-Muslim interaction during this period is far from clear, as is the reality of who the adversaries actually were. Accounts of the events are sketchy from both western and Arab sources. What is now France was divided among the northern Franks, the southern Franks, and the Visigoths, who ruled parts of Languedoc and Provence. The drawing of lines of allegiance was often complicated by the fact that rulers were generally not strong, court intrigues were commonplace, and the population consisted of many conflicting elements.

Jews venerate Jerusalem as the site of Solomon's Temple, which was repeatedly destroyed and rebuilt. In 70 C.E. the Romans destroyed the temple built by Herod the Great, and the site remained largely vacant until Muslims conquered the city in 638. They built the first mosque in the city, later known as the al-Aqsa, over the huge stone blocks remaining from the walls of the Herodian platform.

Alliances were in constant flux. Christian rulers, concerned with maintaining their own power, are known to have invited Muslim forces to garrison their cities for protection. Duke Eudes himself, for example, gave his daughter in marriage to the Muslim ruler of Cerdaña (in the eastern Pyrenees), thereby forging an alliance to secure his southern borders.

North of Spain the Muslims were never again serious opponents of the Carolingian Christians, who under the reign of the emperor Charlemagne, crowned in 800, consolidated power down to the Pyrenees. Muslim incursions into the area in the early part of the ninth century were little more than annoying. More

Muslims from North Africa conquered Sicily from the Byzantines in the ninth century. After the Normans reconquered the island in the late eleventh century, a cosmopolitan culture developed that merged Byzantine, Islamic, and Latin Christian elements. The twelfth-century palace chapel of the Norman rulers in Palermo, for example, is decorated with a typically Islamic *muqarnas* ceiling.

troublesome were the raids of Muslim pirates along the eastern coasts of the Mediterranean. Attacks on monasteries were sometimes devastating, with the result that many monks abandoned them to move further inland. Monastic revival that had been going on in Provence was stopped, and there are records of existing abbeys simply disappearing. In the tenth century Muslim raids continued in the interior of Provence, causing considerable damage in areas around Aix and Marseille. Ports and cities in the western Mediterranean were virtually deserted because of the raiding Muslim pirates.

At the same time that Muslims were advancing through Spain into France, Muslims were also moving into the Christian territories of Switzerland, northern and southern Italy, and Sicily. In the early part of the ninth century, Muslims advanced well into Italy, moving to the walls of Rome before being pushed back by Christian forces. By this time Christians had virtually lost control of the Mediterranean. As the medieval Muslim historian Ibn Khaldun (1332–1406) remarked, the Christians could no longer float a plank upon the sea. Christians only navigated the ports of the east, where the Byzantines effectively prevented Muslims from complete domination. What had formerly been the most active part of the empire had become the most threatened and attacked, and thus the most economically devastated. On land the Muslims were stopped at the northern border of Spain in the west and on the boundaries of Byzantium in the east. In the meantime they had taken much of what had formerly been Byzantine territory, including Syria, Egypt, and the African provinces.

While Hispano-Romans in Spain capitulated with relatively little resistance, such relative ease of conquest was never the case in southern Europe. Several centuries of repeated invasion of the island of Sicily, for example, were needed before it finally became a Muslim territory. Beginning in 652 Muslim forces raided Sicily, first from Syria and then from the coast of North Africa. In 831 the citizens of Palermo finally surrendered and accepted dhimmi status. Muslims quickly occupied nearly half of the island, though it was not until 966 that the Byzantines finally signed a peace treaty acknowledging complete Muslim sovereignty. Events turned around completely when a group of Norman Crusaders returning from Palestine began to reconquer the island. In 1072 the last small rebel states in the interior had been subdued, Palermo yielded to the Normans, and a new Christian Sicilian kingdom was established. Muslim culture flourished in Sicily in the tenth and eleventh centuries, and was allowed to continue even under Norman rule. By the end of the Crusades, however, most of the oriental ethos of the island had been destroyed.

Despite the continuing raids and pirate attacks, in the early centuries of Islam the Frankish Carolingian rulers were much more focused on the possible expansion of territories to the north, namely into Saxon lands, than they were concerned about Arab advances. There was even some diplomatic exchange as relations began to develop between Baghdad and the French court. These began under the Carolingian House of Pépin, who in his zeal to be seen as a cosmopolitan ruler is said to have received embassies from many Mediterranean nations including the Saracens (Arabs). The emperor Charlemagne, whose coronation was not recognized by the Byzantines, is said to have sought his allies further to the east. In 797 an ambassador was sent from the court of Charlemagne to the caliph Harun al-Rashid, from whom it is reported that Charlemagne obtained precious gifts, including an elephant for the royal menagerie and a marvelous clock. Popular belief, based on Frankish chroniclers, was that after a series of missions back and forth between the east and the west by Harun al-Rashid and Charlemagne, somewhere in the period from 797 to 802, the emperor traveled to the east to gain from the caliph protective rights for Christian pilgrims in Jerusalem. This supposed journey of the Frankish king was recorded in one of the twelfth-century *Chansons de Geste* (literally "songs of heroic deeds," a genre of literature filled with warfare and chivalry) entitled "The Pilgrimage of Charlemagne." Although recent scholarship has disproved most of this, it does affirm the fact that Charlemagne and the caliph were on friendly terms and corresponded with each other, and that through this an important church in Jerusalem was secured for the Latin clergy.

Christians and Muslims in Andalusia

In the Iberian peninsula the establishment of a Muslim presence did not take place without serious difficulties. The ruling group was composed of Arabs, Syrians, and Egyptians with Berber troops, all uncertain of the trustworthiness of the other. Aside from the Berbers, the actual number of invaders from the east was very small. Nonetheless, in the forty years it took to set up a stable administration in Spain, it was clear that the Islamic presence was a reality and that their successes were not to be seriously reversed for a long time. In 756, six years after the overthrow of the Umayyads by the Abbasids in the eastern Islamic territories, an Umayyad prince named Abd al-Rahman fled west to escape Abbasid persecution. He established the emirate of Córdoba, forming an administration that would last for two and a half centuries.

The time during which Muslims and Christians, along with Jews, lived in proximity in the Iberian peninsula has often been cited as a kind of ideal era of interfaith harmony. To some extent that claim may be justified, but if so the era was fairly short and was soon supplanted by the tensions, prejudices, and treatment of minorities by both Muslims and Christians that more often has characterized relationships between the communities. By the tenth century the chaos of earlier invasions had settled, and the Iberian peninsula was pretty well split between the Christian Kingdom of Leon in the north and the considerably larger Muslim al-Andalus (known as Andalusia) in the south, with a thin frontier zone in between. During the rule of Abd al-Rahman III in Córdoba (912–61, the first Andalusian caliphate officially beginning in 929), the Spanish Islamic state reached the height of power and fame. It was a time of great opulence and achievement, in which intellectual circles of Muslims, Jews, and Christians under Abd al-Rahman's patronage contributed to a flourishing of the arts, literature, astronomy, medicine, and other cultural and scientific disciplines. Muslim tolerance of the so-called People of the Book was high, and social intercourse at the upper levels was easy and constant. It was also a period during which a significant number of Christians chose to convert to Islam, although Christians continued to outnumber Muslims in Andalusia until the second half of the tenth century.

Christians living in Andalusia gradually became Arabized, adopting certain elements of the speech and dress of their rulers, often including Arabic names. They were thus known by the designation of *Mozarabs*. This was not always received well by the jurists of Islam, who saw in this a danger of contamination and a threat to the faith of Muslim societies. Arabs, whether for reasons of pride

Córdoba was the capital of the Umayyad caliphate in Spain. Although Christians and Jews occupied high positions at court in the tenth century, many converted to Islam. The center of the Muslim community was the Great Mosque, founded in the eighth century and repeatedly enlarged and restored, as shown by this tenth-century portal.

or disdain, refused to learn the language of the populations they conquered, forcing the westerners to learn their language. Arabic words began to infuse the vocabulary such that some Arabic words still remain in Spanish today and many have found their way into the English language. Learned Christians, who had once written in Latin, increasingly composed their works in Arabic. Eulogius, Bishop of Toledo (martyred in 859), is said to have complained that his co-religionists of Córdoba knew the rules of Arabic grammar better than the infidels, and that many among them were ignorant of Latin.

Jewish culture flourished under Islamic rule in Spain. The lavish carved plaster decoration of the thirteenth-century synagogue of Toledo, later converted into the church of Santa Maria la Blanca, attests to the intermingling of faith and culture in this period.

Arabization did not stop with the language. Mozarab women of a certain social status became accustomed to going out with their faces veiled. Many Christians living in Muslim Spain gave up the practice of eating pork and often refused even to raise pigs. They found themselves increasingly appreciating and appropriating Arabic music, poetry, and other forms of culture. Popular pre-Islamic melodies were conserved in Spain over the centuries. Records even tell of Christians and Muslims joining together in merrymaking and sexual indulgences. Christian moralists denounced as corruption what they saw to be the libertine nature of the conquerors' manners, whereas in fact both Muslim clerics and Christian theologians were worried that sensuality was taking over the culture. One important means of rapproachment between the elites of the two populations was the marriage of an Arabic-speaking Christian of high rank with a Muslim. Nevertheless, records indicate that actual contacts between Muslims and Christians were relatively limited.

Mozarabs of the Iberian peninsula, who were living comfortably in the Muslim state, seemingly did not attach much importance to the difference in religion. Nonetheless, Arabization had its limits. As assimilated as he or she might be, the dhimmi always remained an infidel in the eyes of the Muslim. No matter how integrated Christians were in the Arabo-Islamic culture, by virtue of their Christian identity ultimately they remained strangers in their own society. This became more evident as the centuries of Muslim rule in Spain passed. In the days of the high Córdoban caliphate under Abd al-Rahman III, Christians generally were tolerated, protected, and treated with charity. This began to change with the rule of Abu Amir al-Mansur (Almanzor) in the late tenth century, who began a series of ruthless campaigns against Christians, including the plundering of churches and other Christian sites. Almanzor was regarded by Christian writers as a kind of satanic scourge.

With the decline of the prestige of the Córdoban caliphate, official policies became reflected in social intercourse. The most pious Muslims refrained from speaking to the infidels except at a distance. If a Muslim and Christian met on a public road, the Christian always had to give way to the Muslim. Houses of Christians had to be lower than those of Muslims. An "infidel" Christian could never employ a Muslim in service. It was forbidden for Christians to learn the Quran or to speak about it to their children, as it was forbidden for them to speak about Christ with Muslims. Christians could not build new churches or monasteries or repair old ones if they deteriorated, although they could provide minimal maintenance. Churches and chapels had to be kept open day and night should a Muslim traveler wish to find lodging. Church bells could only be sounded softly, voices could not be raised in prayer, and no cross could be placed outside of any building. A priest could not carry a cross or gospel in a visible manner in case he should pass a Muslim. Christians were buried in their own cemeteries, far from Muslims, and funeral processions could not pass through Muslim areas. A Muslim who converted to Christianity was immediately sentenced to death, even if he had formerly been a Christian who converted to Islam. Islamic authorities, concerned that Muslim society not be contaminated and in the attempt to contain rebellions, forced Mozarabs to live in special quarters. By 1250 most of Iberia was ruled by the kings of Aragon, Castile, and Portugal, with only the Muslim principality of the Nasrid emirate of Granada surviving. Schools of Latin and Arabic were established in Seville, especially to train missionaries to Muslims. Rebellions of *mudejars* (Muslims who submitted to Christian rule) in Castile and Aragon led to severe persecutions and expulsions.

Thus the era of harmonious interaction between Muslims and Christians in Spain came to an end, replaced by intolerance, prejudice, and mutual suspicion. Muslim Almoravids and Almohads from North Africa, coming to power in the eleventh century, represented a much more aggressive Islamic fervor, and relations with Christians became increasingly hostile. Christian attitudes hardened against Islam, influenced by the revival and spread of the Catholic monastic houses of Cluny. In the meantime Christian forces from the north were moving gradually but steadily to recapture Andalusian territories. By 1212 the Almohads were defeated by major Christian powers who then reconquered Córdoba, Valencia, and Seville. By the middle of the thirteenth century Muslim control in Spain was greatly reduced, and Christian fervor, kindled also by the temporary

ISLAM AND CHRISTENDOM   321

successes of the Crusades in the Holy Land, led to persecutions, emigrations, and the expulsion of Muslims from newly regained Christian territories. Those Muslims who remained were forbidden from giving the call to prayer from minarets, from going on pilgrimage, and from publicly practicing their faith. High taxes led to an increasingly low standard of living for Muslims. The ground was laid for the final expulsion of Islam from the land of Andalusia at the end of the fifteenth century.

Medieval Christian Views of Islam and Its Prophet

It is clear that from the earliest encounters of the West with Islam, the Arab (Saracen) invaders were not seen as essentially different from any other marauders or predators. For most of those whose territories were threatened by Muslims, there was very little reference to the fact that the intruders represented a new religion. Clerics and those who were interested in religion identified Islam as a Christian heresy, but few others took account of its religious significance. The names by which Christians knew and referred to Muslims changed over the centuries. During the early period they were often referred to as *Agarenes*, a rough identification for Arab descendants of Hagar. Later the Greek word *Saracen* became more popular. This was a term that had been used from the early centuries of Christianity for all nomadic people but came to be applied specifically to Arabs. From the twelfth century, when with the Crusades the "enemy" became better known to the Franks, the term *Saracen* was an umbrella term for any Muslim and it no longer applied to other Arabs. The term *Moor* was used both generally for Muslims and specifically to refer to those who came directly from Africa. Later, with the advances of the Turkish armies, *Turk* was the general term applied to the followers of "Mahomet" or Muhammad. At times when anger at Muslim aggression was the highest, as in western Europe, the term used to identify the aggressors was not *Saracen* but *Barbari*, meaning both barbarian and enemy.

During the Middle Ages the West in general found it very difficult to formulate a coherent vision of Islam, constrained by its own narrow horizons as well as by a lack of sufficient and accurate information. For the most part Christians knew virtually nothing about the religion of Islam, but saw the Saracens only as the enemy. It was only in Spain, where the two communities were in close though often hostile interaction, that a clearer picture of the religion as such emerged. Two quite different populations in the West expressed a vision of Islam. One was that of the common people, fostered primarily by the propaganda that led up to and supported the Crusades and fed by the largely inaccurate information from the Chansons de Geste (the body of literature filled with adventure and romance, warfare and chivalry). The other was that of the scholastics, emerging primarily in the context of Spain. Although sometimes it was reactionary, seeing Islam as violent and fanatic, in general the scholastics' vision of Islam was reasonably balanced and attempted to portray Islam more realistically than was the case through the stereotypes that intrigued Christian society at large.

Although the factual information conveyed by these two segments of society differed considerably, westerners in general shared an underlying attitude toward those described as Saracens, Moors, and Turks. Governed by a "we" and "they" mentality, most Christians saw the lands of Islam, despite their scientific and cultural advances, by definition to be outside the civilized world as they knew it. The way in which Islam was condemned was not unlike the way many in the western church condemned Oriental churches as heresies, as beyond the bounds of orthodoxy. Considered as alien peoples, Muslims were natural candidates for the objects of crusade at the time when that was called for.

One of the earliest Christians to undertake a serious study of Islam was John of Damascus, a government official during the reign of the Umayyad caliph Abd al-Malik (r. 685–705), who left his public post to take up a life of contemplation at a Greek Orthodox monastery. Knowledgeable in Arabic, he was well versed in the main doctrines of Islam, especially those relating to Jesus and Christianity. His major theological work contains a section dealing with the so-called heresy of the Ismailites (Muslims) and his designation of Muhammad as the Antichrist. In another more moderate work he presents a series of supposed debates between a Christian and a Muslim, in which the Christian (not surprisingly) wins. Although not overly appreciative of Islam, he nonetheless expressed a desire for both sides to reason together in their debate. For his pains, despite his standing as a church theologian, John was condemned at the iconoclastic synod of 754 for being "Saracen-minded" and inclined toward the religion of Islam.

Scholastic writings coming out of the eastern part of the empire in the ninth and tenth centuries, especially from Byzantium, tended to be contemptuous and even abusive of the Prophet. In general this polemic was apocalyptic (prophesying the end of the Arabs) and highly uncharitable. The work produced in Spain, such as the writing of Isadore of Seville in the mid 800s, provided the first attempt at a comprehensive view of the religion of the Saracens, despite its predilection to see Islam as a preparation for the final appearance of the Antichrist. Spanish Christian apologetic quickly took on more of the character of philosophical argumentation, even using Islamic methods based on Aristotelian logic. Notable among several significant attempts in the twelfth century to present Islam in a somewhat more tolerant, or at least realistic, way was that of the French monk Peter the Venerable, Abbot of Cluny (ca. 1092–1156). After having visited the Cluniac monasteries in Spain, Peter began a movement to better understand Islam, to be able to combat it more intelligently. As part of this effort he engaged the English scholar Robert of Ketton to translate the Quran, which he completed in 1143. This first full translation, despite its errors and omissions, provided the Latin West its first tool for significant study of the religion of the Saracens, an opportunity that unfortunately few chose to pursue. Despite the importance of his pioneering efforts, Peter continued like such earlier writers as John of Damascus to view Islam as a Christian heresy that must be combated, reflected in the title of his Latin polemic, *Against the Loathsome Heresy of the Sect of the Saracens*.

The reality of the Crusades in the twelfth and thirteenth centuries and the anti-Muslim feelings encouraged in the efforts to support the wars did little to foster interfaith understanding. The fact is that Islam was never really believed to be any kind of alternative to Christian truth, and for the most part it was not treated seriously by the scholastics. In the late 1200s, for example, the great Italian scholastic Thomas Aquinas (1225–74) in his *Summa Contra Gentiles* included some polemic against Muhammad, yet on the whole it paid little attention to Islam as a religion. The Andalusian philosopher and theologian Ramon Llull (ca. 1235–1316), writing at the same time, again resorted to the familiar tactic of positing dialogical argumentation between Christians and Muslims, in which Muslims never fared well. One of the few westerners opposed to the Crusades as evil, Llull urged other means of bringing the Saracens to "the truth." He was prophetic in his concern that the Tartars, then on the move in the eastern lands, should become attracted to the law of Muhammad, warning that it would be a great danger to Christendom. By the end of the thirteenth century Ricoldo da Montecroce of Florence, a Dominican scholar and missionary in Baghdad, was one of the first to report the fall of Acre to the Mongols and the reality that they were turning to Islam and not to Christianity. Ricoldo, unlike many other Europeans, knew Arabic well and drew creatively on the similarities he saw in the Quran and the Bible. Nevertheless, like others he could not resist lumping together all the heresies to which he saw Christianity opposed, including Nestorianism and Islam, with little critical distinction drawn between them.

One of the few medieval Christians to take both Islam and religious pluralism seriously was the German philosopher Nicholas of Cusa (1401–64) in the middle of the fifteenth century. At a time when absurd stories were being spread about Islam and its founder, Nicholas tried to understand the faith of the Saracens. He undertook a thorough historical and literary study of the Quran, even though it was for purposes of refutation. Such efforts at better understanding were not reflected in the work of the giants of the Protestant Reformation in the early 1500s. The German religious reformer Martin Luther (1483–1546) saw the Turks, as they were then called, as God's rods of chastisement, whose god was equal to the devil and whose so-called holy book was both foul and shameful. The French theologian and reformer John Calvin (1509-64), for his part, likened the Turks to his more immediate enemies the Papists, attributing to both the evils of gross deception.

Despite the fact that in the understanding of medieval Christian clergy Islam was a Christian heresy (although technically a heretic is one who has been baptized in the faith), in the popular literature of this time Muslims were clearly considered to be pagans. This tension between the necessity of seeing Islam both as "other" and at the same time of understanding it as a deviation from, a salacious heresy within, the body of Christianity itself remained throughout the Middle Ages. Christians enjoyed feelings of both repulsion for and fascination with the Prophet and his religion. Muhammad was almost universally thought of among Christians as a man of depravity, dishonor, falsehood, and illicit power. In addition, he was seen as a sexual libertine, demonstrated most specifically by the well-known facts of his own multiple marriages and the details of his (that is, the Quran's) description of the pleasures of the gardens of paradise, which was seen by the west as both material and carnal. Such rewards promised to the faithful were convincing proof to the Christians that Islam was a religion utterly devoid of spirituality. The ill regard with which Christians held the Prophet of Islam did nothing to prevent them from a fascination with what they deemed to be the more sordid aspects of his life and teachings. They saw him as having presented throughout his life a prime example of sensuality, violence, and immorality, an example that guaranteed that his followers would demonstrate those same unfortunate qualities. Christians' opinions about the Prophet and his religion had as their starting point the conviction of the depravity of Muhammad, but this never stopped them from analyzing whatever elements of the faith were familiar to them and pronouncing them to be further proof of the absolute inadequacy of Islam as a religion.

In western eyes, the other primary offense of the Prophet Muhammad and his followers was the advocacy of force and violence. This moved from the realm of simple analysis of the life and teachings of the founder of Islam to the actual experiences that Christians had, or sometimes believed that they had, of Muslims invading their lands and profaning their churches. Such violence was seen as a natural outgrowth of the Saracen terror that was associated with Arab lands as a legacy from the warring tribes of the Old Testament. It was at once projected upon Islam and expected of it, fostered in the awareness that Muslims understood the world to be divided into what they termed "the abode of Islam" and that which is not Muslim, namely "the abode of war." (One school of Islamic law, the Shafi, added a third category, "the abode of truce," for those territories with which a Muslim government has concluded a treaty.) This was especially true in

Europe's southern regions, where the skirmishes continued at such a pace that it was difficult not to impute to the Muslims marauders qualities of violent behavior. The hardening of this mind-set in the European consciousness is at least part of the explanation of the apparent lack of conscience displayed in the acts of aggression and violence perpetrated by the Franks at the time of the Crusades. Although in reality a great deal of reliable information was available about Islam and its Prophet, it was fashionable and served the appropriate polemical purpose to circulate popular tales that ranged from gross exaggeration to complete and baseless fiction.

Much of the information of the medieval western writers and poets came from the Byzantines, whose hatred for the Prophet of Islam had always been intense. It fueled the propaganda efforts of those generating enthusiasm for the Crusades, both in the Chansons de Geste and in the notably inaccurate histories of such medieval writers as Hildebert of Tours, Walter of Compiegne, and Vincent of Beauvais. Hildebert was the author of the eleventh-century Latin poem *Historia de Muhamete*, probably the most widely read medieval poetic work dealing with Islam. It includes scurrilous narratives about the Prophet of Islam, such as his having returned home in a drunken stupor, fallen into a dunghill, and been eaten by pigs. In some versions of the poem, it includes the mention of Muhammad having prophesied his own resurrection three days after he was to have died, an obvious slander of Islam based on a Christian theme. After three days, the poem reads, Muhammad's followers left, disgusted by the lack of a miracle and nauseated by the stench of putrefaction, and the body was devoured by dogs. This is reported as the reason Muslims do not eat pork. Hildebert's *Historia* also contains the tale, repeated throughout the Middle Ages, of Muhammad's remains being buried in a temple of marble and gold, with his coffin suspended by magnets to trick his followers into believing he had miraculous powers.

One of the most influential narratives about the Prophet of Islam was the French *Roman de Mahomet*, written by Alexandre du Pont in 1258. This is a rhymed story based on a Latin poem of the same theme by a monk named Walterius (Gautier), which pretends to be the recitation of a converted Saracen. In Gautier's work Muhammad is portrayed as an imposter who founded his religion with the help of childish trickeries. Although Hildebert and Gautier were clerics, du Pont wrote from a lay perspective and turned his work into a novel reflecting the ideals of chivalrous life. His narrative is a kind of compendium of the various stories that were current about the Prophet, nearly all of it repeated in the popular poetry of the time. Included are Muhammad's marriage to a wealthy widow out of greed and ambition, such false "miracles" to dupe his followers as a trained calf appearing with pages of the Quran fastened on its horns, his licentious relationships with women, and the magnet-suspended coffin. This version of Muhammad's life omits the popular tale of a dove trained to pick corn out of his ear, which he pretends is the holy spirit giving him revelations, and of his body having been devoured by swine. Included in du Pont's "biography" is the often-repeated story that Muhammad was actually a Christian cardinal who had been promised the pontifical throne if he converted the Saracens to Christianity. Having fulfilled that task, he was subsequently betrayed and as a result started the heretical sect of the "Mahometans."

Much of this apocryphal narrative about the Prophet Muhammad was available through the Chansons de Geste. For the most part, lay people were neither knowledgeable about nor much interested in Islam, but they found the tales related in the Chansons entertaining and reflective of many of the societal ideals that they most valued. The songs were written from the eleventh to the fourteenth centuries, many at the height of crusading fervor, but they purported to be set in the time of the emperor Charlemagne and his son Louis. There are three principle cycles of the Chansons in which the Saracens appear, of which the "Song of Roland" is considered to be the oldest. In the first two cycles the action takes place mainly in Europe. The third cycle is situated entirely in the east, written after the Crusaders first took Jerusalem in 1099. These songs became the vehicles for a kind of revenge for the defeats suffered earlier at the hands of the Muslims, and it is not surprising that in them the Saracens are mightily conquered. This literature was extremely popular in the west, simple in style and intended for a wide audience, reflecting sentiments and beliefs that were commonly accepted. The context was one in which Christians and Saracens both shared in a single chivalrous culture. The songs illustrate the religious faith of the knights as well as their desire for conquest, the spoils of war, personal glory, romance, and victory over their enemies.

Descriptions of Islam in the Chansons are wildly inaccurate, not reflective of what was certainly known in the west at that time but rather designed for popular appeal and crusading fervor. Some descriptions relate that Muslims worshiped a great number of gods, of whom the most important and powerful was "Mahomet" or "Mahon." Occasionally there was reference to his claim that he was a prophet sent by God who would become a god himself when he died. Other poets imagined that Islam supported a trinity of deities composed of Mahomet (Mahon), Tervagent (Tervagan), and Apollin. None of these notions is found in literature outside the Chansons. The "Song of Roland" knew only the three idols, but the list of accompanying gods, to whom the Christian writers assigned the names of various devilish creatures, grew longer with the other cycles. In the songs the name of God is never cited. In fact, they put the expression "By Mahon [Muhammad]!" in the mouth of the Saracens, suggesting that it is he who is in fact their god. The places of worship of the Saracens often are referred to as "sinagogues," revealing a tendency to attribute to Islam some of what was known about Judaism, or as "mahomeries." Images of Mahomet were said to be huge, carved in marble or crystal, with brilliant colors, sometimes studded with jewels, gold, and silver. As a god, Mahomet could be carried around by his people on their expeditions or in battle and could be consulted for advice. There are even references to Mahomet having made an idol of himself while he was still alive and filling it with a legion of devils. Saracens could approach the idol safely, but should a Christian come near it, the Christian would perish. A number of the songs note the anger with which the Saracens treat the idols when they have suffered losses on the battlefield. According to the "Song of Roland," they rush on Apollin in his shrine, striking and cruelly shattering him, and throw Muhammad into a ditch where hogs and dogs devour and trample him. This renunciation of the idols is said to be in contrast to the Christians, who never renounce their God upon defeat.

On the whole the songs are far less interested in Muhammad either as a man or as a god than they are in portraying his followers. The Saracens themselves are often described in grotesque terms, having huge noses and ears, blacker than ink with only their teeth showing white, eyes like burning coals, teeth that can bite like a serpent, some with horns like the antlers of stags. Typically they are said to be enormous in size, no doubt to make Christian victories over them more impressive. Despite the fact that there are various instances of the poets referring to the Saracens as creatures of Satan, it is clear that Muslims were not regarded as truly diabolical beings. They were recognized as having souls, although they could not go to paradise because they were pagans, and a few were even presented as having pure hearts, inviting admiration as well as pity for the fact that they were not Christian. Underlying all the songs is the theme that if the Saracens could be defeated on the battlefield, they could be persuaded to accept the religion of the vanquisher, namely Christianity. The goal was not the extermination of the enemy, but the conversion of as many as possible.

The Saracen soldiers themselves are often portrayed as brave and noble, worthy enemies of the Christian knights, whose primary fault is that they follow such a depraved religion as Islam. The false references to bizarre Islamic practices were only a small part of this body of literature that was, in fact, reflective also of a deep respect for the military skills and even the chivalry of the Arab warriors. This is especially true in the cycle that represents the writing of the second crusade, notably in the poem entitled "Saladin" after the great twelfth-century Muslim leader and hero Salah al-Din. Despite the extremity with which Muhammad and his religion are portrayed, there was an understanding that Franks and Arabs shared a world and even a culture in which certain ideals such

In the popular mind, medieval Christians saw Muslim warriors as brave and noble, worthy enemies of Christian knights. This marginal illustration to a psalter made before 1340 for Sir Geoffrey Luttrell (1276–1345) shows King Richard I of England on the left tilting at the great Muslim leader Salah al-Din, known as Saladin in the west.

as chivalry, loyalty, and bravery were reflected. Such qualities were thus appreciated in both the Christian heroes and the Muslim warriors. The theme of romance also runs through many of the songs, often with Saracen women falling in love with Christian knights. The romance generally begins when the French knight is a prisoner of the Saracens, and he eventually regains his liberty, thanks to the efforts of the Muslim princess. The romantic conclusion was all the more delicious for having been set in the context of battle and intercultural prejudices. The Saracen women who were wooed by the knights were portrayed as beautiful, intelligent, devoted, virtuous, humble, and courageous, well worthy of the love of their Christian consorts. The inevitable conclusion is the conversion of the Saracen women to Christianity, only after which is any sexual relationship allowed.

Thus although the Chansons de Geste and other forms of romance literature served as vehicles for Crusade propaganda, they also reflect attitudes that are more generous toward Muslims. Often the stories were based on real interactions and relationships with those whom official dogma proclaimed to the ultimate enemies of Christendom. The more charitable expressions were based on the experience of Frank to Arab, however, and not Christian to Muslim. Those who were most knowledgeable about Islam—that is, those writing for religious purposes—were generally the least charitable. The greatest falsehoods were contained in the literature of those who were least knowledgeable about the faith, but who also expressed the greatest appreciation for the Saracens as worthy participants in a common feudal and chivalrous culture.

Medieval Muslim Views of Europe, Christians, and Christianity

The vast majority of Muslims in the eastern part of the empire had little if any knowledge of the western regions of Christendom, as well as little interest in discovering anything about lands they considered bleak and remote, inhabited by peoples they thought to be little more than barbarians. They considered the Europeans' manners and habits to be loathsome, their level of culture exceedingly low, and their religion superseded by Islam. The fact that Europeans spoke many different languages was regarded as a serious liability, allowing none to understand the other. The earliest available records of any Muslim notation of western Europe were in the ninth century, taken primarily from Greek sources. A century later the great Muslim geographer al-Masudi reported in his *Fields of Gold* on the peoples of the north, listing sixteen Frankish kings, of whom at least ten are authentic. In his *Book of Instruction* he talked about the translation of the Septuagint, the ecumenical councils of the church, Christian sects and heresies, and a number of details of Christian theology. Al-Masudi was one of the few Muslims who had any interest in the west, however, and it was really the only time that a medieval Muslim historian dealt with any kind of history of the lands of Christendom. To the extent that Muslims knew anything of the papal city of Rome at all, it was often confused with Byzantium, because both were referred to as *Rum*. A few venturesome easterner travelers managed to visit the city, which served as the center of Roman Christianity, but their records are meager. Most Muslims preferred to go east, to areas that they considered more civilized, than to venture into the cold and inhospitable areas of Europe. In the middle of the tenth century Ibrahim ibn Yaqub al-Israili provided an interesting and at that point unprecedented account of France, Germany, and the lands of the Slavs, one of the few personal descriptions given by a named Muslim visitor to Europe until reports of the Ottoman embassy centuries later.

Even by the twelfth to the fourteenth centuries Muslims had little interest in, and thus generally little knowledge of, the west. What few reports are available come from geographers from the far western reaches of the Islamic empire, namely Andalusia or North Africa. The eleventh century saw the production of the *Book of the Categories of Nations* by the Andalusian Qadi Said ibn Ahmad, in which he discusses the Greeks, Romans, Franks, and a number of groups from eastern Europe, categorizing Frankish Europeans along with Negro Africans as white and black barbarians of the regions beyond the civilized world. In 1154 a geography by the Arab geographer and cartographer al-Idirisi, written in Sicily, gave some descriptions of Italy and other parts of western Europe, which was the basis for much of what Muslims knew about the Franks. Muslim chronicles from this period treat the activities of the Christian Crusaders in some detail, but they contain little information on what motivated the invading armies or what the differences were in their national constituencies. With very little exception, Muslims were quite unaware of, and clearly disinterested in, the possibility of any kind of cultural developments in the west in the areas of religion, philosophy, science, or the arts. Even the great historian and philosopher Ibn Khaldun did not give much attention to areas north of Spain except to note that some Slavs, other Europeans, and Turkish nations adopted Christianity; the qualities of those living to the north, he noted, are akin to what one finds in animals living in savage isolation who have no community and even eat each other. In discussing Christianity itself, Ibn Khaldun displayed his knowledge of the Bible and church organization. Virtually no works in Latin or any other western language were translated into Arabic.

By the fourteenth century, when the conversion of many of the Mongol tribes was greatly changing the face of eastern Islam, the Persian physician and scholar Rashid al-Din (1247–1318) wrote his history of the Franks (1305–06), part of the second volume of a larger world history. This work deals with ancient Rome and its monuments, miracles of the saints, and some pagan traditions. It contains information about the birth and youth of Jesus, the conversion of the emperor Constantine, some of the better-known popes, and a good deal of legendary material concerning Christians in the Middle Ages. It was through Rashid al-Din's history that the eastern Islamic world learned for the first time much of this Christian history and lore. On the whole, it was viewed as somewhat of a curiosity, however, without significant importance or influence.

This general lack of interest on the part of medieval Muslims in the lands of western Christianity did not mean, however, that the Christian religion itself was not a matter of concern for many Islamic theologians and scholars. Along with the development of the schools of law and exegesis of the Quran there developed a body of literature dealing with Christian doctrine for reasons of polemic and refutation. As was true with Christian polemic against Islam, Muslims sought to support their refutation by looking to their own scripture. For both sides of the argument such retreat into internal resources was doomed to failure. Christians could not be persuaded by the Quran, a scripture that they believed to be false, as Muslims could not be persuaded by the Gospel, a scripture they believed to be distorted from its original form.

The Bible itself, in the form held sacrosanct by Christians, received little attention from Muslim polemicists. A few used portions of the Biblical text to buttress their arguments, relying on traditional Muslim exegetical style to do so. Their primary interest in the Bible was as a proof-text for predicting the coming of the Prophet Muhammad, finding occasional references through the text that could be employed for that purpose. In rare instances portions of the Gospel were translated into Arabic and modified to make the text more congenial to the tenets of

Islam. This was justified by the Muslim conviction that the Christian scripture had been changed and distorted and was thus fair game for revision to bring it closer to the original revelation. After Islam had spread to Syria and Mesopotamia, Persia, North Africa, and Spain, the polemical debate between Muslims and Christians was sparked by the different forms of contact between members of the two faiths. The Arabic language was adopted by growing numbers of Christian dhimmis, especially those living in urban centers, allowing people to read the Quran for themselves and providing for the translation of the Bible into Arabic. Even when both sides were able to quote not only their own scripture but that of the other, however, it was still difficult to move beyond attacking the texts held sacred by their opponents on the basis of their own texts.

As early as the ninth century there were a number of Muslim efforts at refutation of the doctrines of Christianity, particularly as they were known through Christians living in Arab lands. Ali al-Tabari (d. 855), a Nestorian Christian who converted late in life to Islam, wrote a rebuttal of Christianity that sounds like a version of Nestorian polemics against other Christian sects. In the 860s Abu Isa al-Warraq provided the most comprehensive of the early anti-Christian polemical works, entitled *Reply to the Three Sects of the Christians*. Aimed especially at the Nestorians, Jacobites, and Melchites, it deals particularly with the "inconsistencies" of the doctrines of the Trinity and the incarnation. Shortly after that Amr ibn Bahr al-Jahiz wrote a refutation of the Christians for the caliph al-Mutawakkil, who was waging an offensive against the Christians. It is an especially biting attack on the Trinity and on Christianity as a false religion, which, said al-Jahiz, is a sore and a social evil in the midst of the body politic.

When the Abbasid caliph al-Mamun (r. 813–33) established the institute of philosophy or "House of Wisdom" in Baghdad in 830, Greek and Syriac texts on a range of issues, from philosophy to medicine to astrology and mathematics, were translated into Arabic. Muslim scholars soon became as well versed in these materials as their Christian counterparts, often more so, changing the playing field from scriptural argumentation to the more commonly agreed-on basis of the authority of Aristotelian logic and philosophy. In some cases, such as that of the ninth-century Arab philosopher Abu Yusuf Yuqub al-Kindi (795–866) in his *Refutation of the Christians*, Aristotelian logic was used to combat the Christian idea of the Trinity. (It is an interesting illustration of the way in which refutation was used to promote one's own interpretation that al-Kindi's work, not itself extant, is known through the countering arguments of the Jacobite Christian scholar Yahya ibn Adi, who refuted these Muslim arguments in making his own case for the Trinity.) The numbers of scholars on either side who were able to engage in this kind of intellectual debate were limited, however, which is why both Muslims and Christians for the most part carried out their polemic from within their own theological and scriptural frames of reference. In Islam most jurists and theologians were suspicious of such philosophical methodology as somehow running counter to the explicit revelations contained in the Quran. Most of the surviving Islamic writing that has made up the body of anti-Christian polemics, then, is Quranically based apologetic not intended to debate any issues but simply to affirm what Muslims already believed to be true.

Some Muslim speculative theologians made use of forms of Aristotelian logic in shaping their doctrinal arguments, however, still keeping within the bounds of what was acceptable to the main schools of Islamic theology. They used these arguments to the extent to which they were engaged in combating the ideas of Christian writers, especially regarding the doctrine of the incarnation. The Maliki jurist Abu Bakr al-Baqillani (d. 1013), for example, writing in Baghdad in the eleventh century, is said to have effectively silenced the arguments of Christians by means of sophisticated philosophical arguments, especially in relation to claims of Jesus' divinity. Such a conclusion, of course, was made by his fellow Muslims, and for either side of the debate the result was predetermined by their unshakable faith in the truth of their own dogmas. The eleventh century also gave birth to the work of the Andalusian philosopher-theologian Ibn Hazm (994–1064), who attacked the Christian scriptures harshly on the basis of a very thorough knowledge of the Bible. His well-known and erudite *Book of Sects*, purported to be the first Muslim work on comparative religion, is really a defense of Islam against the error of other faiths, particularly Christianity.

The most famous of the late Middle Ages critics of Christianity was the fourteenth-century Hanbali jurist, theologian, and religious reformer Taqi al-Din ibn Taymiyah (1263–1329). He was an independent thinker who was well grounded in a wide range of religious and nonreligious sciences. His enormous work, more than one thousand pages long, entitled *The Correct Answer to Those Who Have Changed the Religion of Christ*, is a refutation in particular of the work of a Transjordanian Melchite bishop named Peter who wrote at the end of the ninth century. Ibn Taymiyah argued against the possibility of the incarnation of God in Christ, which he refuted by using Peter's own arguments against him. A deeply scholarly and incisive work, *The Correct Answer* provides a good example of the way in which challenges between Christianity and Islam were much more often made by the process of textual refutation than through actual face-to-face exchange.

The Influence of Islam on Medieval Europe

It has long been recognized that one of the most significant and lasting contributions of the medieval Muslim world to Christendom was to provide access for western scholars to the great classics of Greece and Rome by their translation into Arabic, from which they were rendered into European languages. Most of the works of Plato and Aristotle were known to Arab Muslims. Among the earliest of the translators was the Nestorian Hunayn ibn Ishaq al-Ibadi (808–73), who was active in the court of the Abassid caliphs in Baghdad. Hunayn ibn Ishaq and those working with him in this important school of translators rendered more than one hundred of Galen's medical and philosophical treatises into Arabic. The use of Greek did not cease in provinces that came under Muslim rule; rather, it continued at least until the middle of the ninth century, allowing Hunayn ibn Ishaq to further his translation work in the early part of that century with manuscripts from Egypt, Palestine, Syria, and Mesopotamia. Although in the Latin-speaking west there had been little if any interaction with the Greek world from the second century, there was an unbroken continuity in the eastern Mediterranean in terms of philosophical and medical teaching to which the Arab Muslims were heir. There was also, of course, no lack of struggle within Islam itself between the basic Islamic formulations of faith and the traditions of Hellenism, and the issues contained in Greek philosophy were hotly debated among the scholars of Islam. One of the primary tasks of those who translated Greek texts into Arabic was to make available the body of materials necessary for the proper understanding of the issues and the resolution of conflicts.

Transmission of knowledge from Arabic to Latin came close on the heels of the Christian reconquest of Sicily and of large areas of Muslim Spain. When Toledo was taken in 1085, a major step in the Christian reconquest of Spain, a large number of Arabic manuscripts were made available to Christian scholars. By the twelfth century Toledo had become a center of study as scholars from all over Europe came to work with native speakers of Arabic. This served as an initial foray into the study of Arabic and Arabic texts that flourished in later centuries. Missionary activities of Dominican and Franciscan friars, based on their hope of the conversion of Muslims, encouraged more serious study of Islam and Arabic. Before the sixteenth century, however, it was very rare for

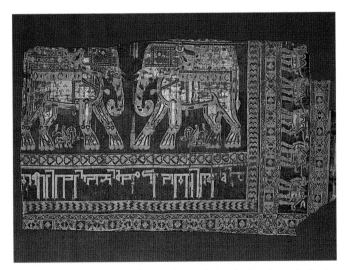

Crusaders and other travelers to the Holy Land often brought back luxury objects and souvenirs, which became treasured in ecclesiastical and princely collections. This silk textile, made for a Samanid commander in eastern Iran in the mid-tenth century, was used in 1134 to wrap relics in the abbey of St. Josse-sur-Mer in northern France. The cloth was probably brought back by Étienne de Blois, patron of the abbey and a commander of the First Crusade.

European scholars to have acquired, or have had much interest in, Arabic manuscripts. Some exceptions were found at Cluny in France, in the episcopal library at York, in England, and in the Vatican library.

By the tenth century most Arabic translators had lost the use of Greek and worked exclusively from Syriac translations. It is remarkable that the outstanding Muslim philosophers of the Middle Ages—notably al-Kindi, al-Razi, al-Farabi, Ibn Sina, and Ibn Rushd—all were ignorant of Greek and relied completely on translations rendered for the most part by Jacobite or Nestorian Christians. Thus the survival of Greek philosophy in the world of Islam came through the medium of the Syriac language. Naturally enough, those doing the translating used their own judgment as to what was worthy of transmission, most often turning to those works that appealed to their own philosophy and theology. Thus the writings of Plato and Aristotle, as well as the works of Hellenistic scientific medicine, were preserved, with the resulting achievements of Arabs in these sciences far surpassing those of the Christian inheritors of Greek civilization.

By the beginning of the twelfth century Aristotle's writings were being translated in the west, both from the Arabic and directly from the original Greek. It is not entirely true, therefore, that western scholars were wholly dependent on Arabic versions of these works. Some scholars have argued that it was chiefly for the sake of their commentaries that the Arabic works were considered so important, especially those of Ibn Sina and Ibn Rushd. It is clear that the medieval Catholic world of the west was willing, even eager, to take what it could through the mediation of the Islamic east in the areas of science and technology, materials reasonably neutral in content. For the most part the subject matters that it absorbed and took into its own culture were those that reinforced its own culture rather than threatened it. Europe was clear about what it wanted and needed and was free to leave the rest. As was the case earlier with Muslim translators, little was taken that was in conflict with what European scholars and theologians believed and held dear.

In the western mind there was never an association between Arab science and the religion of Islam. Those who advocated the use of scientific principles gleaned from the Arabic texts were never suspected of being crypto-Muslims. Robert of Ketton, known for his employment by Peter the Venerable as a translator of the Quran in the twelfth century, worked tirelessly in the effort to translate from Arabic into Latin out of the conviction that the knowledge of the Latin west was greatly inadequate in the scientific fields. By the thirteenth century Arabic thought was really more of an influence than a direct source of western intellectual speculation, as writers were better able to control and make use of the material than in the earlier centuries. Europe was no longer dependent in the same way on the Arabs for knowledge of the Hellenic world, and translation directly from the Greek was more common than translation through the medium of the Arabic, although Arabic remained a very strong influence on Europe at that time. Europe had by then recovered what it wanted in terms of philosophy and science, received initially in a form that had been modified by many centuries of Arab reflection on it.

Christian Visitors to the Holy Land

One of the ways in which Christians came to learn more about the Muslims who inhabited and ruled the Holy Land of Palestine was through centuries of visitations by explorers and pilgrims. Beginning as early as the fourth century, after the triumph of Christianity in the Roman Empire, pilgrimage to the east was fashionable among Europeans, encouraged by the church as a kind of private penance. The arrangements made between the emperor Charlemagne and the caliph Harun al-Rashid for establishing a hostel in Jerusalem gives evidence that there were significant numbers of pilgrims coming to the city. Most of these visitors, whose numbers increased during the following centuries, were motivated by a sincere desire to visit the holy places of Jerusalem and its environs, for which they felt that they received special religious merit. In many cases an important person would make such a pilgrimage, accompanied by numbers of followers who would take advantage of the security provided by such group travel. The great abbey at Cluny in France, established in the early tenth century, sponsored significant numbers of pilgrims both to Christian shrines in Muslim Andalusia and to Jerusalem. The Cluny abbey was responsible for building hostels along the eastern route to provide shelter for pilgrims. In some instances pilgrims came by sea, but most pilgrims normally followed a route through the lands of western Christendom, through eastern Europe and the Byzantine Empire.

By the beginning of the eleventh century the numbers of pilgrims to the Holy Land increased considerably. This was due to a number of reasons, including the more conciliatory attitude of Muslims toward Christians after the destruction of the Holy Sepulchre by the Fatimid caliph al-Hakim (r. 996–ca. 1021) in 1009 (for which act he was designated by some western Christians as the Antichrist spoken of in the Apocalypse), and the opening of the overland route to Jerusalem through the conversion of Hungary to Christianity and the retrieval of Antioch into Byzantine Christian hands. Most of the pilgrims, although significant in number, actually came from a few provinces of France and the Rhineland. The dukes of Normandy were only fairly new Christians by the eleventh century and were devoted to sending alms to the Holy Land. Their subjects were known as the most enthusiastic of pilgrims, some of whom became the leaders of the early crusading movements. During the time when the Crusades were taking place it was dif-

Medieval Christian rulers appreciated the luxury goods made by the Muslims. Hugh IV of Lusignan, King of Cyprus and Jerusalem (r. 1324-59), for example, ordered this splendid inlaid bronze basin from metalworkers in the Mamluk domains.

ficult to distinguish the pilgrims from the crusader crowds, although Christian pilgrims were generally motivated not by political but by votive purposes. Such visitors were primarily not interested in the contemporary conditions of the area but were attracted to the historical and religious significance of the holy places of the Old and New Testaments. The importance of pilgrims in the Christian Kingdom of Jerusalem is attested to by the treaties concluded with the Muslims during the thirteenth century to assure Christians free access to the sacred places when those were reoccupied by Islam. Special roles were played by Christian saints who visited the Holy Land, most notably Francis of Assisi, who in 1219–20 was one of the first to attempt to convert the Muslims to Christianity. It is reported that Francis was impressed by the piety and reverence of those he came to missionize.

For the most part the pilgrims were from the lower classes of European society, obscure men and women encouraged for reasons of personal piety and hope for absolution of sins to undertake the arduous journey east. Some represented more educated and elite strata of society, including distinguished churchmen and lay princes. No matter what their educational level, however, these explorers and pilgrims did not leave behind many records of their observations. From the available information it is clear that western Christians had no more expectation of finding anything of religious or philosophical value in Islam than did their Muslim counterparts in reflecting on the barren lands of northern Europe and its misguided Christianity. Up to the thirteenth century these travelers remained strangers to the lands they visited, recording only the vaguest impressions of the indigenous populations. Knowing only that Muslims were outside the circle of Christianity, and therefore generally to be despised, they exhibited little interest in Islamic religion and culture. This began to change significantly by the thirteenth century, when as a result of the Crusades, as well as a rising interest in Islam among the learned in western Europe, visitors to the Middle East began to take more notice of the cultures to which they had traveled, and they thus provided better written records.

By the fifteenth century and later, missionaries, pilgrims, businessmen, explorers, and others were giving voluminous reports of their own journeys and of the customs, habits, and religious practices of Muslim populations. Such a visitor was Ghillebert de Lannoy, knight of the court of Bourgogne in the early fifteenth century, who traveled to Andalusia, Egypt, and Syria and provided unusually detailed commentary on Muslim dress, habits, and customs. Rarely until the latter centuries of the second millennium, however, were Christian travelers able to break free from their own deep preconceptions about Islam. Pilgrims and scholars outdid one another in presenting Islam as an erroneous and idolatrous religion that must be condemned in any way possible. Those who actually stayed for some period of time in Muslim lands, however, found themselves observing and even admiring what they saw of Muslim piety and moral conduct. Proceeding initially from preconceived ideas about Islam as idolatrous, impious, licentious, and immoral, by the end of the medieval period they often came to see the religion of the Saracens as at least providing a code of behavior deserving of praise.

The Crusades and Their Aftermath

Many complex factors went into the call of Pope Urban II for a crusade against the Muslims, who since 638 had occupied Jerusalem. For more than four centuries Christians had been allowed to practice their religion freely in that city. In 1076, however, Jerusalem was taken by the Seljuk Turks, who were said to have desecrated the holy places of Christianity and treated the Christian population with brutality. Pilgrims returning from Jerusalem brought sad news of their fellow Christians there. Although the notion of avenging these wrongs and regaining the holy city for Christianity had been seeping into western consciousness for some time, it was not until the preaching of such monks as Peter the Hermit of Amiens that popular opinion began to rise in support of such an effort. Encouraged by an appeal for assistance from the emperor Alexis I in Constantinople, Pope Urban II promised his help and sent out the call for the first crusade.

At the Council of Clermont in 1095 the Pope was greeted with great enthusiasm when he called for an international crusade to recapture Jerusalem from the infidels. Europe at that time was generally ignorant of the lands of the east, whether Christian or Muslim, and was intolerant and xenophobic. Narrowness of mind met with religious zeal for the liberation of the Holy Land, driving the Franks to a near frenzy of enthusiasm and excitement. Virtually for the first time since the early spread of Islam, except for some movement against Muslim-held territories in the Iberian peninsula, Christians were in a position of reacting offensively and not just defensively to Islam. It was a heady venture, combining centuries of pent-up resentment against the Saracens with the hope for spiritual regeneration both of the individuals who dedicated themselves to the venture and for a morally lax Christendom itself. It was supported eagerly by the medieval papacy and by the feudal knights and commoners alike. Many of the crusading efforts were grossly misguided, however, and like the ill-fated "Children's Crusade" in which numbers of youth were sold into slave markets, they ended in disaster. But in the beginning, however, at least in the eyes of the west, there were crucial victories and the temporary attainment of the prize of Jerusalem.

The first significant group of crusaders to arrive in Palestine, consisting primarily of knights and others from France and Italy, set out in 1096. They moved through the lands of the Byzantines, who despite the emperor's plea for help greeted them with extremely mixed feelings and offered support and aid out of self-interest rather than enthusiastic approval. In March of 1098 the crusaders captured Antioch in Syria, and by July 1099 they were finally able to claim Jerusalem. The victory, unfortunately, was accompanied by a vicious and cruel slaughter of Jews and Muslims in the city, chronicled by both Christian and Muslim writers. Many Muslim writers referred to the arrival of the Christians not as a crusade but as a Frankish invasion, and they described the carnage of the Christian massacre of Muslims, including many religious leaders and Sufi mystics, as the acts of savage and cruel western barbarians. The sack of Jerusalem is often said to be the effective beginning of many centuries of an active mutual hostility between east and west that was rarely known in earlier days.

During the tenth century the Byzantines, taking advantage of political disorder in the Muslim lands, had declared war against Islam and gained back much of northern Syria with the hope of recovering Jerusalem. When the Fatimid

In 1095, Pope Urban II called for a crusade to liberate the Holy Land, especially the city of Jerusalem, from the Muslims. One of the leaders of the First Crusade was Godfrey of Bouillon (ca. 1060–1100), who was elected first ruler of Jerusalem. He became the hero of two French Chansons de Geste dealing with the Crusades. This fourteenth-century illustration shows Muslims defending their city against the Christian invaders.

caliphate was established in 983, however, the tide began to turn and much of the territory taken by the Byzantines was returned to Muslim hands. The violent attack from the west in the form of the crusading armies took the world of Islam by surprise. In a general state of political disunity, it was to be almost half a century before the Muslims gathered their forces to move against the Christian invaders in a call for jihad or holy war. The Latin Kingdom of Jerusalem, a monarchy established under the leadership of Baldwin of Edessa, was established partly because of the prevailing disunity of the Muslim world under the Seljuks, the Fatimids, and the waning Abbasid caliphate. The Muslims attempted to restrain the invaders, but the crusaders were able to spread and consolidate their power in the principalities of Edessa and Antioch and finally the Kingdom of Jerusalem. This conquered territory was referred to in the west as "Outremer" (over the sea). The principality succeeded well for some time, but when the Turks moved into Edessa in 1144, an appeal was made for a second crusade. An army consisting of the rulers of Germany and France set out in 1147, but after an unsuccessful attempt to capture Damascus they were forced to return home.

By this time the Muslim Turks were gaining in strength, while the Christians were starting to lose ground. Crusader zeal was giving way to luxury and waste and territorial squabbling on the part of the Christian rulers. The death of Amalric I, king of Jerusalem, to whom no successor seemed worthy, came at the time of the rise to power of the

In 1168–69 the Zangid prince Nur al-Din ordered woodworkers in Aleppo to make a splendid minbar for the al-Aqsa mosque at Jerusalem in anticipation of his reconquest of the city from the Crusaders. His successor, the Ayyubid ruler Salah al-Din, installed the minbar in the mosque after his conquest of the city in 1187. The minbar, one of the finest examples of medieval woodwork, was destroyed by arson in 1969.

Ayyubid general Saladin. In 1187 the Christian hold on the Holy Land was effectively ended when Saladin defeated them at Hattin, although they continued for some time to maintain a small portion of the area. The Muslim leader moved swiftly to gain control of most of the other territories held by Christians, and finally he regained Jerusalem for Islam nearly a century after the first Christian invasion. Records of the time indicate that Saladin's treatment of the Christian population was humane and reasonable, in notable contrast to the way in which Christians had earlier dealt with Muslims and Jews upon their arrival in Jerusalem. Although he returned the Church of the Holy Sepulchre to Greek

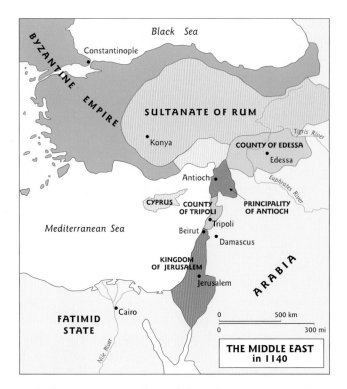

Orthodox custody, however, a number of churches were turned into mosques, and Jerusalem clearly was once again a Muslim city.

The loss of the holy city prompted a third crusade from the west in 1189. Accompanied by much dissension within and slaughter without, these crusaders gained little except for Christian possession of coastal towns in Palestine and free access to Jerusalem for Christian pilgrims. Further struggles represented in the fourth, fifth, and final sixth crusades continued until the Mamluks, who had taken over control of Egypt from the weakened Ayyubids, finally drove the crusading Christians from all of Palestine. Throughout the two centuries of active conflict, members of the eastern church, Byzantines and Arab Christians, were caught in a terrible middle position. Although part of the crusader rhetoric in the west had to do with freeing the eastern Christians from the yoke of Islam, actual encounters with the Byzantines led to increased political and cultural hostility between the co-religionists. When the Franks moving through eastern Christian lands from Hungary through Greece to Syria and Palestine were not met with aid and support, they had no compunctions about looting and plundering. Christian Arabs were never any more sympathetic with, or loyal to, the Frankish kingdom in Palestine than they had been to the Byzantines. All parties to the years of conflict—Romans and Byzantines, eastern and western Christians, Christians and Muslims—too often thought of each other as barbarians and frequently had those prejudices confirmed in the reality of hostile interaction.

The Latin Kingdom of Jerusalem itself during the near century of its greatest flourishing saw most of Syria, Lebanon, and Palestine in Christian hands. The Muslim population was divided among the farmers, the city dwellers, and the slaves. It was now the turn of the Christians to exact on the Muslims a poll tax as well as rental of farming properties. Those Muslims who tried to resist were treated harshly, and there were numerous attempts at rebellion. In fact, treatment of the subjugated Muslim population differed among the various Frankish lords. Baldwin, king of the Latin Kingdom, was known for his humane administration, and for many Muslims life under the Franks was no worse and perhaps better than they had known previously. The earliest of the crusaders, who then became the long-standing inhabitants of the Latin Kingdom, were generally more tolerant of the native population than the newer arrivals and tried to maintain more supportive relationships. Those more recently arrived were intent on expanding Christian territory and thus on seeing the Muslims as the Saracen enemy. Often the new arrivals forced their co-religionists who had become "native" to revoke existing treaties made with the Muslims in order to aid their aims of expansion.

Nevertheless, as in Spain, the two communities of Christians and Muslims attempted to cooperate and coexist, although they constituted two separate societies with their own laws and administration. Battles were pitched, but those who were not engaged in fighting continued to live normal lives. Muslims and Christians traded with each other, rented properties from each other, and generally carried out their commercial activities uninterrupted. Christians controlled the eastern coast of the Mediterranean, but they allowed Muslims to sail their ships with the appropriate passes. Piracy and pillaging continued as ever, of course, with all parties participating to some degree in looting and taking prisoners to sell on the slave markets.

During the two centuries in which the Christians occupied Palestine, there was a constant pattern of shifting alliances. Muslim rulers were played off against each other, and Franks were sometimes in treaty with one, sometimes with another. This gradually changed as the disarray in which the first crusaders found the Muslims was replaced by a more united front. Many prisoners from among both Muslims and Christians were taken, and elaborate negotiations often were made for their release. Trading in prisoners was an active industry, with many never returned to their original homes. Women prisoners in particular were victimized, often being taken into domestic service upon release, taken as wives or concubines, or sold into slavery.

The End of the Middle Ages

The last several centuries of the near millennium of interaction between Islam and Christendom saw a number of events that served as a kind of transition from the Middle Ages to a new era of international engagement. Two events in particular, the fall of Constantinople in the middle of the fifteenth century and the final expulsion of Muslims from Andalusia at the end of that century, illustrate this transition.

Beginning in the eleventh century the Turks, both armies and tribesmen, had taken over a significant part of Anatolia from the Byzantines. The frontier between Islam and Christendom, defined for centuries by the Greek Christian hold on the eastern borders of Byzantium, began a process of redefinition. The Turkish Empire, first under the Seljuks and then the Ottomans, grew into one of the three great empires in the history of Islam. Much of that growth was at Christian expense. In the mid-1300s a Byzantine contender to the throne brought over a Turkish army as an ally, giving the Turks a hold on the European side of the Dardanelles. They occupied the ancient city of Gallipoli as a garrison and moved quickly over other parts of what was then known as Thrace. Soon they had gained control of all of the Balkan peninsula, and in 1430 the Turks conquered the Byzantine city of Thessalonica. Less than a quarter century later, under the leadership of the sultan Mehmed II, they were able to mount their successful siege of Constantinople.

For some eleven hundred years of its more than two thousand years of existence, Constantinople had stood as the capital of the Byzantine Empire, an international city of fame, beauty, and repute, and the seat of eastern Christianity. It had been besieged many times in its long history, but during the rule of the Byzantines, Constantinople had been captured only by western Christians in the ill-fated Fourth Crusade. In 1261, a half century later, it was recaptured by the Byzantines. By the middle of the fifteenth century the Byzantine Empire had long been in decline, caught in the middle of struggles between east and west. Suffering from internal political strife, the population of Constantinople had shrunk drastically over the centuries. Nonetheless, it remained a tempting plum for Muslim military objectives. Its fall to the invading Turks in 1453 signaled a dramatic change in the power relationships between Islam and Christendom. Mehmed II, as ruler of Constantinople, became the titular heir of the Roman Empire, and the specter of a Muslim takeover of all of Europe was raised anew.

This Anatolian base gave the Ottoman sultans the opportunity to lay siege on Vienna in 1529, and by 1542 they were in control of Hungary. They were perceived by western Christians to be a more potent threat to the integrity of Europe than the Muslims who had been confined to the lower part of the Iberian peninsula were. In the fifteenth and succeeding centuries Muslim naval forces roamed the Mediterranean, attacking European ships as well as coastal towns. By the beginning of the seventeenth century, Algerian and Moroccan sailors under Ottoman control raided as far as the southern coasts of England and Ireland.

Muslim fortunes went otherwise in Spain, where after the glory of ninth- and tenth-century Córdoba, and the succeeding rule of the Almoravids and Almohads from North Africa, they suffered a steady loss of territories under the Christian

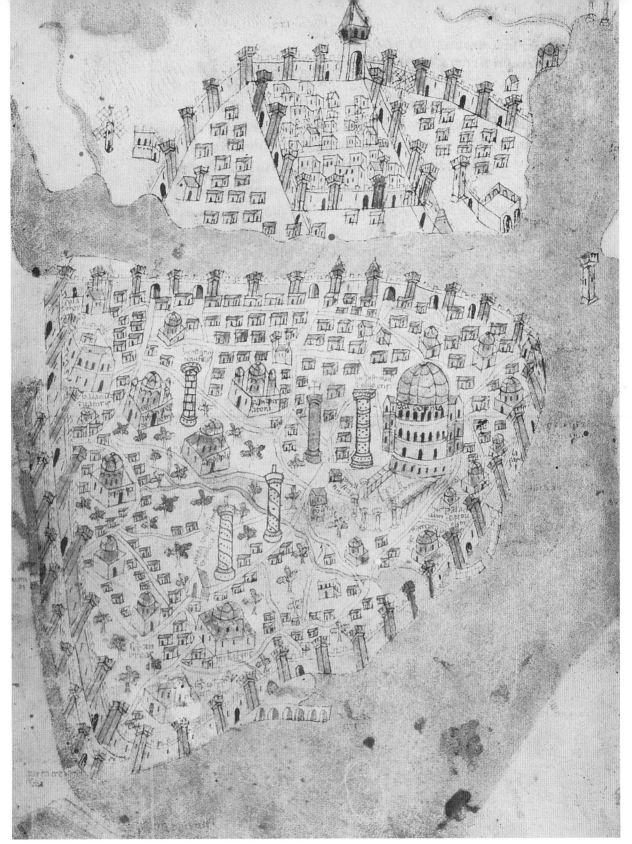

The conquest of the great Byzantine city of Constantinople had been the goal of Muslims since the seventh century. The city had been beseiged repeatedly but unsuccessfully, and it remained a tempting plum for Muslim military commanders. Several decades after this drawing was made in 1422, the city was successfully conquered by the Ottoman sultan Mehmet II.

reconquering forces. Initially Muslims under Christian rule, called *mudejars*, were the recipients of a policy of toleration for the so-called People of the Book. They were permitted freedom of worship and the right to be governed under their own laws. Gradually, however, this gave way to increased forms of intolerance and persecution. Muslims in Christian territories were forbidden from making the call to prayer, perform public sacrifice during their feast days, or going on pilgrimage, and many mosques were converted into churches. Muslims were forced to wear special kinds of dress, as they had previously required their Christian citizens to do, and they had to prostrate themselves before the cross as it was carried in procession. The two communities became completely segregated, and the death penalty was meted out to Christians who tried to convert to Islam. A rising tide of anti-Semitism had serious consequences for both Muslim and Jewish communities in Spain.

In 1474 Ferdinand II of Aragon and Isabella of Castile, husband and wife, succeeded to conjoint but separate thrones. For the first time in nearly eight centuries the Iberian peninsula was governed by one united authority, the Christian kingdoms of Castile and Aragon. The king and queen were to be remembered as "the Catholic monarchs," a measure of their dedication to the reuniting of all of Spain under Christendom. By 1492 they had recovered Granada, the last stronghold of Muslim occupation. With that conquest the struggle for control of Andalusia, which had continued between Muslims and Christians for some eight centuries, ended with a victory for Christianity and control of the Iberian peninsula. The takeover was followed by intense efforts at conversion, accompanied by translation of the Christian scripture and liturgy into Arabic. Soon baptisms were no longer optional but forced, and by the turn of the fifteenth century not only in Granada but throughout Castile Muslims had to choose between conversion, emigration, or death. Because the emigrants had to leave their children behind, most chose to stay and "convert." Of course many continued to practice their Islamic faith in secret (thereby known as Moriscos), remaining for generations to come an unpersuaded, unassimilated, and unaccepted segment of Spanish society. After a rebellion in the next century they were finally expelled from the land that earlier had seen, at least for awhile, one of the few examples of Christian and Muslim cultural harmony.

Despite the fact that the spread of Islam was often peaceful and sometimes even received favorably by Christians into whose territories it moved, and despite the protected status afforded by Islam to its fellow "People of the Book," the centuries of Christian and Muslim interaction were marked as much by strife and warfare as by harmonious relations. Yet official tensions or hostilities at the political level often were balanced by local cooperation and even friendships between members of the two faiths. Trade and commerce between east and west continued in the same areas in which parties were technically at war with each other. Both communities illustrated in their respective leadership examples of tolerance and of prejudice, sometimes with protection offered to their subject minorities and other times subjection to the extremes of persecution. By the close of the Middle Ages, hostilities between Islam and western Christendom once again were intense, with active warfare to continue on a number of fronts for several centuries.

Many factors contributed to this layered history of Christian and Muslim interaction. Territorial ambitions cut both ways, as armies vied over territories held by the other and the spoils of war attracted mercenaries as well as faithful to the attack. Cultural interactions sometimes fostered mutual respect and even camaraderie, as in Andalusia at the time of the Córdoban caliphate or among certain strata of society in Palestine under the Latin Kingdom. But deep-seated prejudices seldom fully abated, as Muslim historians, jurists, and clerics viewed with disdain the barbarous and theologically misguided Christian population of the west, and Christian theologians judged the warlike

Following the Christian reconquest of the Iberian peninsula, many mosques were converted into churches. Around 1187, for example, the small brick mosque of Bab Mardum, built in Toledo in 999–1000, became the Church of Cristo de la Luz, and a voluminous apse was added to its east side.

and deluded followers of "Mahomet" by doctrine and deed alike. Yet although the seeds of mistrust and antipathy so often sown from the rise of Islam to the fall of Constantinople continued to grow in the following centuries, new developments came to bear, such as the forging of significant changes in the relationship of Islam and Christendom. The rise of rationalism, a fascination on the part of the west with the cultural trappings of the east, and the necessities of international political and economic exchange were soon to move the worlds of Islam and Christendom inevitably closer.

CHAPTER EIGHT

Sultanates and Gunpowder Empires

THE MIDDLE EAST

Ira M. Lapidus

The era of gunpowder empires represents a new phase in the development of Middle Eastern and Islamic societies. The term *gunpowder empires* imputes a great importance to the innovative military technology of infantry armed with muskets, operating in conjunction with siege and battlefield artillery, that allowed the new empires to sweep away their rivals and to establish a dominion that would last until the eve of the modern era. Yet the achievements of the Ottoman and Safavid empires were not merely technological or tactical. Their endurance and their success in deploying new technologies was based on a deeper structure of political institutions. In turn the political regimes must be understood as the embodiment of a comprehensive civilization. The Ottoman and Safavid empires were the umbrellas, the holding companies, for complex societies. They represented novel military tactics, the consolidation of political institutions, and the restoration of imperial political controls over vast territories after centuries of near anarchy. They also fostered important economic and urbanistic developments, new forms of religious organization, and a fresh phase in the history of Middle Eastern and Islamic cultures. Illustrated manuscripts and mosques from the Ottoman and Safavid empires remain to the present day treasures of world civilization. Less well-known but equally brilliant are the achievements in poetry, philosophy, and religious studies in these empires. As comprehensive systems of government, society, economy, and culture, the Ottoman and the Safavid empires represent a culminating phase in the history of Middle Eastern civilization—the high

(Left) The Ottoman sultans built great mosque and school complexes to adorn their cities and express their authority. The crowning achievement of Ottoman architecture is the immense domed Selimiye mosque at Edirne designed by the architect Sinan for sultan Selim in 1574.

imperial phase, which precedes the nineteenth-century transformations and the advent of the modern era.

The Fundamental Structures of Middle Eastern Societies and the Early Islamic Era

The basic features of these empires derive from the historical past. From ancient times, and even into the modern era, the small community has remained the focus of the deepest loyalties, the basis for widespread, communal cooperation, and the wellspring of common identity. Those who formed a family, a lineage, a clan, or a clientele group loyal to a master—the people of a hamlet, a village, a nomadic camp, a town quarter, living in close proximity to each other—constituted the community for reproduction, for nurturing and educating the young, for earning a living, and for defense and mutual aid. Their story will not be told in this history of the Ottoman and Safavid eras, but nonetheless they were the fundamental entities in the empire systems. Such groups sustained the more encompassing domains of the economy, the religious institutions, and the state, and in turn their well-being was the ultimate measure of the success and the value of the empire systems.

Small communities were the building blocks of larger formations. Three such formations were of particular historical importance: tribal organizations; religious communities; and political regimes, states, and empires. Tribal organizations consisted of various groups—families, lineages, clienteles, and political gangs—that coalesced under the leadership of a patriarch or other political or religious chieftain. Although tribes have commonly been thought of as extended families, in reality they were alliances of families, clientele groups, and bands of warriors who promoted common interests.

The second large-scale communal institutions were religious communities. Since ancient times, family, lineage, and tribal units had been affiliated in common worship and in the shared construction, maintenance, and veneration of shrines and temples. With the emergence of the monotheistic religions, Judaism, Zoroastrianism, and Christianity, certain beliefs became virtually universal: belief in the transhuman world of spiritual forces, in the sacred quality of all being, and in a supreme divine being, universal, transcendent, and unknowable; belief in the ethical responsibility of all human beings; and belief in a life in the world to come. These religions also taught the brotherhood of mankind and promoted the organization of congregations for worship and parishes for the administration of their educational, legal, and charitable affairs. Jews and Christians in particular, in synagogues and churches, formed strong communal bodies and had a strong sense of shared identity.

The third agglomerating institution—political regimes, states, and empires—was the umbrella organization that ruled over the families, client groups, tribes, and religious bodies within its territorial reach. The ruler was considered to represent the divine plan for order in society. Rulers had a quasi-religious function, in that their good behavior was supposed to ensure the favor of the gods. Empires were supposed to defend the realm of civilization, primarily agricultural and urban, against the barbarians, who were usually nomadic peoples. Internally, the rulers were supposed to protect their subjects against injustice and to secure order in society. In practice, empires represented the domination of the ruler—the ruler's household, courtiers, armies, and bureaucrats—over the rest of the population. Rulers policed, taxed, punished, and subdued their own peoples. At the same time, the apparatus of rule depended on the resources it could draw from the subordinated political, religious, and communal units—revenues and supporting labor from families, legitimation from churches and religious groups, and military support from tribes. Rulers' relations with tribal and religious bodies, however, were always contested. The struggle for power in these societies turned on the state's relations to these partly independent bodies.

Middle Eastern peoples also shared linguistic, cultural, or regional identities, but these identities did not necessarily have political meanings. Thus there were Arabs, Armenians, Greeks, Kurds, Persians, Turks, and so on and such cultural identities as those of the Hellenistic, Iranian, and Semitic literary cultures, but in premodern times the most important units were tribes, religious groups, and empires. Only in the modern era have ethnicity and nationality become the basis of modern states.

Many technologies (such as those for producing food: agriculture and herding; the techniques for preparing clothing: spinning, weaving, and tanning; and methods of construction) and institutions (such as the institutions of money, markets, and commercial law) also derived from ancient times. These were older and more widespread than either the Ottoman or Safavid empires.

The Arab-Islamic conquests and the early Islamic empires perpetuated the basic constellation of earlier institutions but redefined them in Islamic terms. From the seventh to the tenth centuries the Arab empires created the first Middle Eastern–wide political regime, bringing an overarching unity into the region from the Aral Sea to the Atlantic Ocean. Regions that had been part of the Byzantine and the Sasanian empires as well as regions in the far east (in Central Asia) and in the far west (in North Africa and Europe) that had never been part of a Middle Eastern empire were brought under the reign of Islam. The new unified Middle Eastern empire allowed for an expanded international trade and a larger arena for the cooperation of local elites, their integration into the imperial system, and the creation of new elite identities on the basis of Islam and the Middle Eastern high-literary cultures in Arabic and Persian.

Although the new empires inherited the institutional framework of the past, they gave it a distinctly Islamic character. The Arab-Islamic empires built on the administrative mechanics of their predecessors—the ruler's court, which was the empire's command center; the military, which was constituted in part by a central army and in part by tribal auxiliaries; and the bureaucracies developed for tax collection and communication—but at the same time they redefined their political identities. The new rulers were called caliphs, heirs and executors of the teachings of the Prophet Muhammad, as well as heirs to the Byzantine and Sasanian empires. Through patronage of architecture and the visual arts, philosophy, science, and new literatures in Arabic and Persian, they assimilated the heritage of antiquity into their Islamic identity, creating a new form of Middle Eastern courtly, aristocratic high culture.

In the early Islamic era the new religion was established not only in court and ruling circles but throughout the Middle East. Islam, which espoused religious beliefs analogous to those of Judaism and Christianity, was at first the religion of the imperial elite and of the Arab conquering forces settled in garrison towns and cities throughout the empire. Gradually it became the religion of converts who joined the Arab rulers in their garrison centers. As late as the tenth century, however, Islam was still the religion of urban elites and of only some peasant and bedouin elements. The great masses of the Middle Eastern population had yet to be converted.

From these Muslim populations emerged a new Islamic culture. Muslims generated studies of the Quran and the *hadith* (verified accounts of a statement or action of the Prophet Muhammad) as well as legal, theological, and mystical studies; they opened up the study of philology, grammar, and history as auxiliary subjects. Muslim holy men, readers of Quran, teachers of hadith, scholars of law, and mystics gathered adherents and followers, and they created a plethora of small communities, sometimes sectarian, dedicated to the study and living out of one or another variant version of Muslim beliefs and practices. By the tenth century a Muslim literary-religious culture and many committed communities were in full bloom. Islam was established in parallel to the previously existing Christian, Zoroastrian, and Jewish populations.

Although the early Islamic era did not complete the process of the Islamization of the Middle East, it provided the critical concepts and social models. The legacies of this early era included the concept of the caliphate and the Islamic state as a unified expression of moral and political interests; the system of beliefs that constituted the Islamic religion; such social organizations as schools of law, Sufi coteries, and Shiite communities; the institutional forms of mosques and colleges; and the authority of *ulama* (religious scholars) and Sufis, scholars, and holy men as leaders of their people.

The Sultanate Era, 950–1500:
Between the Abbasid Caliphate and the Gunpowder Empires

The collapse of the Abbasid empire in the tenth century opened the way for the further transformation of Middle Eastern regimes, societies, and cultures and for a new and creative, albeit tumultuous era in the history of the region. On the surface the political changes were anarchic. With the breakup of the Abbasid empire, provinces and even small districts came under the rule of new military elites. Nomadic peoples broke through the frontier defenses, invaded, and migrated en masse into the Middle East. Agricultural and trading economies were badly damaged, and the standard of living declined. Yet on a deeper level this period of upheaval was also an era of reconstruction. New forms of state and communal organizations were created and innovative variants of culture and identity were expressed, setting the foundations for the later Ottoman and Safavid empires.

The period 950–1500 fell into four phases. In the first phase (950–1050), local elites took control of the empire's former provinces. In Egypt and Syria, the Fatimids, a Shii, rival of the Abbasids, came to power with their own claims to the caliphate. In Mesopotamia tribal forces, including the Hamdanid dynasty, seized control. Military adventurers from Daylam seized control of western Iran, much of Iraq, and Baghdad, which were the heartlands of the former caliphate. Eastern Iran and Transoxiana were ruled by the Samanids, a local landowning elite. They were partly supplanted by the Ghaznavids, a regime based on slave military forces, who for the first time selected their own sultan.

The second phase lasted from about 1040 to 1200, when the collapse of a unified central authority and the many regional power struggles allowed for the breakdown of the eastern Iranian frontiers against nomadic invasions. Already in the seventh century the T'ang rulers of China had closed their frontiers to Central Asian nomads, thus setting in motion a westward movement that would in the tenth, eleventh, and later centuries spill over into the Middle East. Inner Asian nomads searching for pasturage moved into the regions north of the Aral Sea and into Transoxiana and Afghanistan. From contact with settled peoples, trade, and the activity of missionaries, Turkish peoples began to convert to Islam, and their chieftains became tutored in the ways of agriculture, city administration, and trade, and knowledgeable about the imperial conception of rule and order. By the end of the tenth century the Qarakhanids, leaders of the Qarluq peoples, established their regime in Transoxiana, while the Oghuz peoples under the leadership of the Seljuk family went on to conquer much of the former Abbasid empire. The Seljuks took control of Khurasan in 1040; by 1055 they ruled over Baghdad. The migrations led to the formation of Seljuk offshoot states in Mesopotamia, Syria, and eventually Egypt. Turkish peoples also moved into lands that had not been under caliphal control, which brought Islamic dominion to parts of Armenia, Georgia, and Anatolia at the expense of the Byzantine Empire. An important Seljuk offshoot state established in Anatolia, the sultanate of Rum, was the direct ancestor of the Ottoman Empire. The Seljuk conquests lent but a temporary and superficial political unity to the Middle East. The conflicts of nomadic peoples seeking independence and ruling families wishing to subordinate the tribal forces, the rivalries among the members of ruling families for fiefdoms and independent territories, and the widespread distribution of iqtas (lands instead of salaries) led to an ever greater decentralization, fragmentation, and dispersal of political power. Seljuk-related regimes broke up into numerous independent states and tiny territorial fragments.

The period after the collapse of the Abbasid caliphate in the tenth century led to the rise of new military elites, often of nomad origin. The Turco-Mongolian conqueror known as Timur or Tamerlane (d. 1405) created a vast but ephemeral empire centered on his capital at Samarqand. The Gur-i Mir, his majestic blue-domed tomb there, epitomizes the splendor of Timurid architecture.

The Seljuk decline opened the way to a third phase in the history of the region, from about 1150 to 1350. This was a period of further nomadic invasion from inner Asia, culminating in the Mongol invasions and the establishment of Mongol regimes over much of the Middle East. In 1153 Ghuzz peoples destroyed the Seljuk regime in eastern Iran. They were followed by the Naymans and then the devastating Mongol invasions. The Ilkhanid Mongol regime in Iran (1256–1336), however, brought renewed stability and ushered in a brilliant period in Iran's art and culture. To the west, the slave military forces in Egypt and Syria, the only holdouts against Mongol rule, consolidated the Mamluk regime (1250–1517).

The final phase of this interregnum was the Timurid period in Transoxiana and Iran (1400–500). Mongol rule was succeeded by a new time of troubles

and the extraordinary conquest of the Turkic conqueror Timur (known in English as Tamerlane, 1336–1405). Although Timurid rule left a number of unstable succession regimes, like Mongol rule it also promoted greatness in architecture, the arts, and the sciences. This era of repeated nomadic invasions brought profound demographic changes in the ethnic and religious identity of populations. A new Turkic-speaking population migrated into Transoxiana, the Hindu Kush mountain range, eastern and northwestern Iran, the Caucasus, Anatolia, and Mesopotamia. Large portions of this northern tier became Turkic-speaking. Turkish settlement led to the Islamization of parts of north-eastern Iran, Armenia, and Anatolia, both from the settlement of newcomers and by the conversion of existing populations. Islam was also carried into Transoxiana and further parts of inner Asia and the northern steppes. Turkish migrations meant an expansion of the boundaries of Islamdom.

Ethnic changes also led to important ecological changes. In some regions the newcomers displaced former nomadic populations, as in Transoxiana and Mesopotamia. In other areas the Turkish migrations increased pastoralism at the expense of agriculture. Turkish tribal formations also became a lasting part of the political process. Under the leadership of warrior chieftains and holy men, the migrations shifted the balance of power in favor of tribes at the expense of central-ized states. These conquests are interesting to compare with the Arab invasions of earlier centuries. Although in many ways the conquest process and the formation of new empires was much the same, there is one striking difference. The Arab con-quests brought a new linguistic and religious identity to the Middle East that became the predominant identity of later Middle Eastern civilization, while the Turkish con-querors accepted Islam. While maintaining their Turkic language and identity, they became patrons of Arabo-Persian civilization.

The New Political and Social Order

The basic political facts make it hard to grasp that beneath the surface of events, this was also a period of reconstruction and the creation of new governmental and soci-etal institutions. Everywhere the legacy of the Islamic caliphate and the heritage of Persian concepts of imperial monarchy were blended with Turkish concepts of political chieftaincy, law, and world conquest. While regimes came and went, while conquerors succeeded each other, the system of governing came to be fixed in sim-ilar modes. The Seljuk period (1040–1200) was particularly important in this regard. Seljuk institutions, first formed in Khurasan and western Iran and Iraq, were carried westward to Syria, Egypt, and Anatolia. Later Mongol and post-Mongol period governments added additional elements from their historical heritage to the synthesis of new institutions.

During the period when nomadic chieftans ruled, authority often passed to *atabegs*, guardians for princes who had not yet reached the age of majority. The Armenian-born convert Badr al-Din Lulu, for example, served as vizier to the last Zangid prince of Mosul in 1222 and then became regent of the city from 1234 until his death in 1259. Badr al-Din is depicted on a frontispiece from a multivolume copy of *Kitab al-Aghani* (The Book of Songs), al-Isfahani's collection of early Islamic poetry, made in 1219.

The caliphate, although deprived of administrative and military power, retained its symbolic importance as the emblem of a Muslim world order and as the bearer of ultimate guarantees for religious belief, justice, and political order. For centuries all provincial governors and warlords looked to the caliphs for recognition of their right to rule. Even after the extinction of the Abbasid line in 1258, regional substitutes emerged. The Mamluks in Egypt crowned a survivor of the Abbasid family as their caliph. Great warlords claimed implicitly and explicitly to embody the caliphate in their own persons. The Ottoman sultans considered themselves caliphs, and the Safavids regarded themselves as descendants and embodiments of the Shiite imams.

At the same time, the conquerors and warlords cultivated a parallel non-Muslim concept of authority. They gave themselves such titles as shah, malik, and sultan, all supreme rulers. They recalled historical tribal genealogies to guarantee their descent from famous rulers of the past; they patronized court cultures replete with poets, scientists, philosophers, theologians, artists, and architects. They built magnificent mosques, tombs, colleges, minarets, caravanserais, and palaces in the fashion of past Middle Eastern rulers, to say by their patronage of culture that they were the protectors and overlords of the domain of human civilization. They sponsored religious activities, schools, worship, and charities, and gave gifts and pensions to scholars and holy men. In practice, they made themselves patrons of religion and necessary to the success of Islam.

The governments established after the fall of the Abbasid empire were of two principal types. The most common, represented by the Qarakhanids, Seljuks, and Mongols, were nomadic chieftaincies transformed into monarchies. The nomadic chief ruled by virtue of his conquests or descent from conquerors. He was supported by a coalition of aristocratic lineages that was entitled to share in the spoils of victory. Nomadic states commonly divided their territories into domains for the leading members of the ruling family. Family chieftains and the guardians of chieftains who were still underage (known as *atabegs*) became the provincial governors and tributaries of the reigning sultans. The nomadic populations constituted a military elite that was commonly moved toward the frontiers, both to further the conquest of new lands and to prevent further harm to the agricultural and urbanized societies that had become part of the chieftain's domains. The post-Abbasid states were typically built on the support of tribal populations that extended the reach of the ruling circle beyond that of the governing family coalition.

Although the empires were conquered by nomadic peoples, they were ruled from the center by quite different elites. Turkish chieftains commonly built up a governing apparatus that made them independent of their own nomadic supporters. Adopting historic mechanisms of rule, they created court complexes of family retainers, servants, noble companions, military officers, and high-ranking administrators that constituted the political elite of their regimes. The sultans built up slave military corps to serve as praetorian guards and to serve in battle against both foreign enemies and their own nomadic supporters. These slaves were the best trained, best equipped, and were thought to be the most loyal subjects of the ruler.

The court and the slave military apparatus were supported by a tax-collecting administration. Post-Abbasid rulers continued to use the bureaucratic techniques of their predecessors, maintaining scribal staffs for recordkeeping, tax collection, correspondence, and payment of salaries and pensions, but bureaucratic administration greatly shrunk in the post-Abbasid era. Economic regression cut into the cash flows that were essential for a centralized administration and forced post-

Abbasid governments to rely more and more heavily on decentralized forms of administration. The most common method came to be the direct assignment of *iqtas*—tax revenues from specific territories paid as salaries to military officers and often collected directly from the peasants. The iqta system bypassed the cumbersome process of tax collection, sale of produce, and redistribution of the revenues in the form of cash salaries, but it also gave direct access to and control of the land to the warlords. This was a quasi-feudal system of government, but one in which the central government retained authority over the land and the right to grant and withdraw grants of land made in return for military service. It was not feudal in the European sense because in principle assignment of a benefice did not imply ownership of the land, or judicial, administrative, or personal control of the peasants. In practice, it often meant just that.

The second type of regime was the purely military slave elite. In the case of the Ghaznavids in Afghanistan or the Mamluks in Egypt, the slave officers themselves overthrew dynastic rulers and built governments solely of slaves, from ordinary soldiers to the heads of states. The slave regimes, however, functioned in much the same manner as the nomadic chieftaincies in terms of court, military, and bureaucratic structures.

These regimes faced two political problems. The first problem was the tendency toward progressive decentralization of power. Control of the provinces had to be delegated to family members and nomadic chieftains. Iqtas had to be assigned to the military leaders. The weakness of the bureaucratic apparatus prevented close control over these assignments. The result was usurpation of power at both provincial and local levels and the establishment of independent microregimes, sometimes even hereditary regimes, within the nominal territories of the state. The second problem was the paradoxical relationship of the sultans and the central government to the nomadic forces. The nomads conquered the new territories, but they soon came into conflict with their own chieftains. The royal and would-be royal families wanted to centralize power, protect the conquered and settled populations from damage, and tax the productive economies, while the nomadic interest lay in obtaining booty, lands for pasturage, and freedom from government control. In the early phases of a conquest, sultans channeled the nomadic migrations toward the frontiers; but as each wave of conquerors settled, nomadic populations and their royal chieftains commonly came into conflict over territory, privileges, and taxation. Rulers tried to reduce the once conquering peoples into docile subjects. The success, power, and longevity of their regimes depended in good measure on the balance of central and nomadic powers.

In many respects the critical achievement of the ephemeral post-Abbasid regimes was cultural. Each ruler maintained a court as the center of literary, artistic, and religious production, as an indispensable sign of his legitimacy and his claims to equal status with other rulers. In the post-Abbasid period not only Baghdad but also Samarqand, Bukhara, Ghazna, Nishapur, Isfahan, Mosul, Damascus, Cairo, Fez, Córdoba, and many other cities became important centers of Muslim learning, art, and literature. Political fragmentation fueled an extraordinary outburst of cultural creativity. Many local courts became patrons of architectural construction and producers of books and illustrated manuscripts as well as patrons of such luxury objects as fine pottery, metalware, rugs, glass, and other finely crafted materials. Courts were also often patrons of scientific research, philosophical speculation, literature, poetry, history, and religious subjects.

Moreover, the courts commonly patronized very similar, often the same, versions of culture. Poets, writers, and philosophers made their livings by moving from court to court, creating the same achievements in different places. Skilled craftsmen, seeking refuge from the Mongols, fled Mesopotamia for Cairo in the middle of the thirteenth century, reviving the old regional arts in a new location. Sometimes conquerors forcibly transferred skilled artists to their new capitals, as did the Turkic conqueror Timur when he tried to build the glory of Samarqand. Also, rulers demanded similar products. Copies of the *History of Alexander the Great* or the tales of the *Kalila wa Dimna* were translated and illustrated for numerous courts, such as Samanid Bukhara, Timurid Samarqand, and Mamluk Cairo. By these processes a common culture of kings emerged, and with it the concept of the family of kings and the brotherhood of rulers who had the same responsibilities, the same status, and a common lifestyle.

Thus, out of the conquest and fragmentation there developed broad zones of common culture. In the courts of the Samanids and Ghaznavids a new Irano-Islamic language and Persian culture developed. It was characterized by the preservation of the literary legacy of ancient, pre-Islamic Iran, and it was deeply influenced by caliphal Arabic poetry and by the translation of literary and religious classics from Arabic into Persian. The new language had its own standard metrical forms for odes and the common Sufi love and wine poems. A standard architectural form for mosques and madrasas also developed—a building arranged symmetrically around a central dome, constructed of brick and decorated with tiles and *muqarnas* (a decorative element that resembles a stalactite).

The new Persian language, literature, and artistic style quickly became the common cultural idiom of all the former eastern lands of the caliphate, including Iran, Transoxiana, and inner Asia, and they eventually reached into newly conquered Islamic lands in India and the East Indies. This Irano-Islamic culture in turn fostered the creation of a new Turko-Persian culture. The Qarakhanid rulers of Transoxiana, followed by the Mongols and the Timurids, sponsored the translation of Persian classics into Turkic languages. Variants spread throughout inner Asia under Mongol and Chagatay rule and later became the basis of

Ottoman culture. Meanwhile, Arabic literature derived from the caliphal era and from Islamic religious studies became the common language and literary medium of the former western territories of the Arab-Islamic empire, from Iraq to the Atlantic Ocean. Just as certain political institutions had become by imitation and diffusion the common forms of state organization among the numerous regimes of the interregnum era, so too a common high culture had emerged in Arabic, Persian, and Turkic versions, despite intense decentralization in all the domains of Middle Eastern Islam.

The political upheavals of the intermediate era were also the impetus for a correspondingly profound transformation of the social organization of Middle Eastern populations. Throughout the region, the subject population was exposed to extraordinary danger from marauding armies, economic hardship, rapid changes of political overlords, the decline of older landowning and bureaucratic elites, and the imposition of new foreign rulers. In response, people throughout the region drew together in defensive movements and created a new communal structure. This new order was based on Islam.

Paradoxically, the Abbasid empire in many ways delayed the diffusion of Islam to the mass

The Persian language became the cultural idiom both of all the former lands of the eastern caliphate and of the newly conquered regions of the Indian subcontinent. Arabic texts, such as Ibn Bakhtishu's bestiary, *Manafi al-Hayawan* (The advantages of animals), were translated into Persian, as in this illustrated copy made at Maragha in northwest Iran in the 1290s.

of Middle Eastern populations. Although the empire was the official sponsor and protector of Islam and promoted Islamic law and worship, the new religion remained nonetheless the religion of a minority. The Abbasid empire accepted the existing Christian, Jewish, and Zoroastrian communities, accepted the authority of church elites, and cooperated with non-Muslim administrators, landowners, and bankers in the management of the empire. The political system had thus removed the worldly incentives for conversion to Islam.

With the breakup of the Abbasid empire, however, the old social elites were swept away. Churches could no longer protect their peoples, landowning families were dispossessed, and the administration crumbled. The result was a vacuum of leadership into which was drawn the only surviving elite element—Muslim scholars (*ulama*), teachers, preachers, and holy men. The

Karramiya (a religious movement that combined theological principles, Sufi practices, and a social mission) established networks of *khanaqas* or Sufi residences, which eventually became the basis of community organization and conversion in eastern Iran. Sufis in western Iran, for example, under the leadership of the Sufi preacher Shaykh Abu Ishaq al-Kazeruni (963–1033), began to convert Zoroastrian villagers to Islam. Town quarters became organized under the aegis of Islamic schools of law, Shii communities, or Sufi and other religious leadership. By the twelfth century the majority of Middle Eastern populations was identified with Islam; its communal leaders were Muslim ulama and Sufis; Christians, Jews, and Zoroastrians had become demographic as well as political minorities everywhere.

The newly Islamized populations were provided with new forms of communal organization. These forms had their origins in the earlier Islamic period. As early as 660, Muslims had begun to divide into two camps: the Sunnis, supporters of the existing Umayyad and later Abbasid caliphates, and the Shiites, who opposed the established regimes and held that only the descendants of Ali had the right to the leadership of the Muslims. In the tenth century the Shiites, by then deprived of the living imams, codified their tradition in books of hadith, law, and theology, and elaborated a ritual calendar focused on the veneration of the tombs of Ali at An-Najaf (in southern-central Iraq) and Husayn (who was massacred by Umayyad troops at Karbala in 680) at Karbala (in central Iraq).

Among the Sunnis a variety of small religious communities took form as people gathered around readers of the Quran, reciters of the hadith, scholars of law, and theologians and mystics, to whom they looked for religious inspiration and guidance. The legal schools evolved from informal discussion groups of scholars, students, and judges into quasi-administrative bodies producing codes of law under state patronage, staffing the judiciary, carrying on legal instruction, administering communal and intestate properties, and providing informal leadership and instruction for the common people. By the ninth century the Hanbali school (founded by the theologian and jurist Ahmad ibn Hanbal) was already an organized pressure group trying to impose its concept of Islam on the caliphate.

With the breakup of the Abbasid empire, the legal schools were modified to become the basis of a mass Islamic society. Provided with endowments, the schools created permanent institutions known as *madrasas* (teaching colleges and residences) as the basis of their activities. The colleges provided buildings, residences, libraries, kitchens, and stipends for both teachers and students. The ulama also assumed a larger role in their communities. They often married into local landowning and administrative families and organized gangs, quarters, and sectarian associations under their leadership. The ulama also represented the urban populations to the conquerors, providing local administration and justice, arranging for local security, public works, taxation, charities, and other services.

At the same time, a new form of Islamic communal organization under Sufi auspices came into being. Sufis had for centuries coalesced around charismatic holy men, sometimes taking up residence in khanaqas provided to shelter them and facilitate their meetings, worship, and instruction. In the twelfth century Sufi organizations, partly under the influence of the legal schools and of state support, became more formal still. The authority of shaykhs over disciples became absolute; the rituals of devotion and transmission of authority were more elaborate, as Sufis adapted the *khirqa* (the transmission of the robes of the master) and the *silsila* (the chain of masters and disciples going back to the Prophet himself) as the badges of their affiliation. Soon Sufis became organized in *tariqat* (brotherhoods), as disciples and lieutenants created new branches to whom they transmitted their particular forms of worship. The transmission of *dhikr* (the meditational method of concentrating the soul on the veneration of God) was the defining quality of each brotherhood. As Sufi brotherhoods became more formally organized, they took on more important social roles. In towns and villages throughout the Middle East lay Muslims came to the Sufis for supplementary worship, for spiritual consolation, healing, and charity, and for political mediation of problems between the people and the governments or between factional and tribal rivals. Alongside the legal schools, Sufi communities emerged as a basic organizing social force among Muslims.

Sufism also provided the rationale for a looser type of communal organization. The tombs of famous ancestors and Sufi masters came to be venerated as the providers of miraculous help, and shrines emerged as a focus of Muslim wor-

Sufism, or Islamic mysticism, emerged as a basic socializing force during this period. The authority of shaykhs became absolute, and they passed their authority to their disciples, who were organized into brotherhoods. The shrine of Shaykh Nimatullah Vali (d. 1431) at Mahan, for example, became a major Sufi center for southeastern Iran and India.

ship. Descendants of sainted Sufis, and their lineages and brotherhoods, became custodians of the holy places to which thousands of people would come, seeking the intercession of the buried holy men and the transmission of *baraka* (God's power through the Sufi to his needy clients). Shrines became the focus of pilgrimages and fairs. In many parts of Iran, Sufi brotherhoods organized military defense and resistance to predatory nomadic clans and governing chieftains. Often espousing a mix of Shii and Sunni views—or from the perspective of the governments and the urban ulama, heretical teachings—Sufi movements became the expression of religio-political protest against abusive elites.

The consolidation of Shiite sectarian communities, Sunni schools of law, and Sufi lineages, brotherhoods, and shrine communities thus provided a communal structure for Muslims throughout the Middle East. In this period of upheaval, Islamic authority and Islamic religious bodies provided the basis for community order and solidarity. A new mass Middle Eastern society based on Islam had come into being.

The State and Religion

The emergence of new political and religious bodies raised again the problem of the division of authority between the state and religious institutions. In Middle Eastern societies this issue goes back to the ancient temple communities of Mesopotamia and the emergence of the first empires. Ever after, the boundaries of authority and functions between rulers and priests would be an open question. The Islamic era began with its own position on this issue. For Muslims the Prophet himself embodied both religious and political authority. He revealed God's will and God's law for his people; he was the ruler of the community, who also collected taxes, waged wars, and arbitrated disputes. The early caliphs also claimed religious authority to make pronouncements on religious law and beliefs as well as the prerogatives of emperors. In the evolution of the caliphate, however, the tendency to separate political and religious authority seemed unavoidable. As conquerors and emperors, the caliphs increasingly became political leaders with only a symbolic form of religious authority; the authority to promulgate or discover law, to make judgments on matters of belief, and to instruct ordinary Muslims devolved on the ulama and the holy men. By the time of the Abbasid empire's collapse, political and religious authority thus belonged in practice to different people, although this was not yet recognized in theory.

The Turkish invasions and the establishment of nomadic or slave military regimes made acute the question of religious or state authority and functions. Nomads and slaves were foreigners in origin and culture, warriors imposed on the civilian populations, while the town and village elites of the post-Abbasid era were Muslim religious leaders. The division of personnel and realms of authority was patent. What would be the relation between the two elites: state military and administrative on the one hand or local, communal, and religious on the other? This problem was solved in the interregnum period by the creation of two autonomous but cooperating elites. Turkish nomadic and slave military authorities were eager to establish internal order, to facilitate taxation, and to minimize resistance from their subject populations. They needed the help of educated functionaries and scribes. They needed the legitimation and recognition that only the holders of religious purity could supply. They wanted the presence of cultivated scholars and holy men, poets, philosophers, historians, teachers, intellectuals, and artists to adorn and glorify their courts. They craved to enter into the fraternities of cultured Middle Eastern peoples.

The military elites thus sought the support of the religious elites by underwriting their activities. They lent their forces to the suppression of Shiism; they provided endowments for mosques and khanaqas and stipends for teachers, holy men, and students. Seljuk rulers constructed and endowed madrasas in every major city of their empires. They endowed Sufi khanaqas to foster the holy men who served as missionaries for Islam. Although Seljuk rulers at first patronized particular schools or factions, by the twelfth and thirteenth centuries, Middle Eastern rulers had worked their way to a pan-Sunni policy, supporting all the major schools of law, hadith, and theology. In return, the religious leaders accepted the Seljuk states, recognized their legitimacy, justified them to the subjects, and taught the necessity of obedience. They cooperated in routine administrative matters, occupying an intermediary position representing the regime to the people and the interests of the people to the regime. By the twelfth century the two elites of state and religion had worked out a policy of cooperation. A Muslim society became in practice a society governed by state elites, who protected and patronized Islam, and religious leaders, who legitimized alien states. This condominium of elites and cooperative relations between institutions would be for many centuries the Middle Eastern Muslim solution to the problem of state and religion.

Not all Middle Eastern peoples accepted this arrangement, however. Mountain, nomadic, and tribal peoples sought to maintain political independence, avoid economic subordination, and cultivate cultural autonomy. To unite disparate small communities, to organize and justify resistance to state control, many harked back to the image of the Prophet, embodying both political and religious authority, making political interests a holy cause and holy aspirations a worldly endeavor. Such groups often looked to Sufi holy men to provide them with unified religio-political leadership, sometimes in opposition to established states, sometimes in conquering ventures of their own. The Safavid empire had its origins in this alternative concept of Islamic religious leadership.

The Safavid Empire

The Safavid empire was strongly shaped by the political and religious institutions and the cultural accomplishments of the previous era. The Turkish and Mongol migrations had profoundly changed the character of northern Iran. A large Turkish population had settled in eastern Iran, in the region of the Oxus River, and in northwestern Iran and eastern Anatolia. Turkish peoples constituted about 25 percent of the total population, and the Turkish presence radically changed both the economy and the society. Large districts were converted from agriculture to pasturage, and a new political system was introduced. Turkish territories were parceled out among tribal chieftains, who gathered their families, clients, bands of individual freebooters, and others into a single political unity. These units, commonly called tribes or *uymaq*, used their power to bring lesser chieftains into line and to subdue and govern local towns and villages. They became the de facto government in much of northern Iran.

In reaction, religious leaders emerged to shelter the local populations. Sufi preachers promised to invoke occult and mysterious powers that would protect their followers. Other leaders taught the doctrine of the *qutb* (saintly pillar of the world) who would protect oppressed peoples. Still others taught that a savior would come to redeem the good people from the traumatic upheavals of the time. In these turbulent regions a number of Sufi-led religio-political opposition movements emerged to contest the power of Turkish and Mongol chieftains. One of these Sufi leaders was the Persian mystic Shaykh Safi al-Din (1252–1334), based in Ardabil in northwestern Iran, who founded the Safavid Sufi brotherhood, provided schools and residences, and cultivated a hierarchy of students, disciples, lieutenants, and missionaries. The heads of the brotherhood brought uprooted individuals and small-lineage chieftains into the order, and they occasionally married into local tribal princely families. The Safavid followers, whatever their political origins, considered themselves devotees (*murshids*). By the fifteenth century they had come to believe that the head of the order was their Sufi master, their shah or king, the reincarnation of Ali, and the hidden imam whom they awaited as God's messiah. In the turbulent fifteenth century, after the breakup of the Timurid empire, the Safavids turned to more militant political activities, attacking Christian populations in Georgia and eastern Anatolia in the name of *jihad* (religiously sanctioned warfare against non-Muslims). Bound together by religious belief, the Safavids waged war against other Turkish principalities and conquered Iran in a rapid set of victories between 1500 and 1510. Out of the conflict of Turkish tribal and religious movements came the first stable empire to rule Iran since the Abbasid dynasty.

This stability, however, was not based on a direct continuation of the movement's own religious culture and organization. Rather, in the very first Safavid postconquest reign, Shah Ismail (r. 1500–1524) began to replace his Sufi enthu-

To support their legitimacy, the Safavid dynasty of Iran (1501–1732) developed a cultural policy to establish their regime as the reconstruction of the historic Iranian monarchy. To that end, they commissioned elaborate copies of the *Shahnameh*, the Iranian national epic, such as this one made for Shah Tahmasp in the 1520s and 30s and illustrated with more than 250 exquisite paintings.

siasts with the apparatus of a centralized state. For more than a century, from the reign of Shah Ismail through the reign of Shah Abbas I (r. 1588–1629), the successive leaders of the dynasty built up loyal slave cadres apart from their tribal and religious supporters and tried to establish a centralized bureaucratic apparatus to make possible direct taxation and administration of the area.

The leaders also attempted to develop a cultural policy that would support the legitimacy of the new regime, not just as a Sufi religious movement but as the reconstruction of the historic Iranian monarchy. The shahs became the patrons of those imperial arts that for centuries had been understood to be the hallmark of kings. Shah Ismail transferred the Timurid school of painting from Herat to the Safavid capital of Tabriz. Safavid rulers endowed workshops to produce illustrated manuscripts and a royal library to house them. Their patronage led to the production of the *Shahnameh* (Book of Kings), which contains paintings of battles, hunting scenes, and royal ceremonies that are adorned with exquisite animal images, real and mythical, and depictions of gardens. There are some 250 paintings in all; this work is one of the masterpieces of Iranian and Islamic art. It is a celebration of the glory of Iranian monarchy and of the Safavids as the heirs of that tradition. In the seventeenth century, however, a more mature regime preferred realistic depictions of daily life, paintings that bore emotional expression and secular scenes of beauty and love. The first period expressed the need for political legitimation, while the second era expressed the taste of aristocratic soldiers, officials, and courtiers for the good life. Safavid rulers also maintained workshops that produced famous carpets, silk cloth and hangings, and metalworks and ceramics to adorn the imperial court, mosques, and shrines as a reminder of the glory of the monarchy.

Perhaps the supreme artistic creation of the Safavid regime and the ultimate symbol of the restoration of Iranian monarchy was the city of Isfahan. Built as a great new capital, Isfahan was the geographic base for administrative centralization. It was also the locus of a vibrant urban economy whose products and rev-

Fearing the proximity of the Ottoman frontier, in the late sixteenth century the Safavids moved their capital from northwestern Iran to Isfahan in the center of the country. The Safavids extended the city with a new royal square surrounded by two stories of shops that symbolized the key role of trade in the centralized state.

Safavid rulers maintained state workshops that produced fine carpets made of silk and metallic threads. Many of the finest carpets were made for export to Europe. This example, which retains its vivid colors, is one of a pair once owned by the Doria family in Italy.

enues were essential to imperial finances. Isfahan's bazaars concentrated the production and marketing of goods, competing with the resources of tribal chieftains; they were an essential river of tax revenues to support the central state and the basis of Iranian international trade. Built with unparalleled grandeur and beauty, Isfahan embodied Safavid legitimacy. The new city was built around a single great central square, the Maydan-i Shah, which measured more than 500 by 1600 feet and served as a market, polo grounds, and carnival arena. The square was surrounded by two-storied rows of shops and by great archways on each of the cardinal sides. Monumental buildings adorned the square. The Mosque of Shaykh Lutfallah rose on the east side (constructed from 1603 to 1615); the royal mosque stood to the south (constructed from 1611 to 1629). On the west stood the Ali Qapu or the royal palace, the Sublime Port of the Safavids. To the north a monumental arch marked the entrance to the mile-long covered bazaar of Isfahan, itself a glorious achievement of Middle Eastern urban design, with its innumerable shops, caravanserais, baths, mosques, and schools. From the central square the Chahar Bagh Avenue, bordered by gardens and the residences of courtiers and foreign ambassadors, ran two and a half miles to the summer palaces of the shahs.

Shiism in Early Iran

The most astonishing chapter in the Safavid consolidation of power was the decision to promote Shiism as Iran's official religion. Until the Safavid era, Iran was largely Sunni, although there was a minority Shiite presence in Qum and Isfahan. Although the Safavid shaykhs claimed descent from the seventh imam and integrated Shiism into their religious identity and authority, the original Shiism of the Safavids was a minority orientation. The murshids and loyalists understood Shiism as a claim to embody divinity. They worshiped the master of the order as the bearer of the living spirit of God. The new official religion of the shahs, however, was Twelver or ithna ashari Shiism, a much more institutionalized and mainstream version of Islam, but one that was neither grounded in Iranian culture and history nor even acceptable to their most devout followers. It was a way of elevating the shahs above both their supporters and their subjects.

The new Shiite establishment was built up over the course of a century. The process began with the importation of Shiite scholars from Syria, Iraq, Arabia, and Bahrain. The new cadres were organized into an administration controlled by the state. An official called the *sadr* was appointed to be the intermediary between the shahs and the ulama, and eventually this functionary was given responsibility for the appointment of judges and teachers and for the administration of endowments. A supreme religious court was created. The Safavids further extended their control over religion by endowing the principal Shiite shrines, founding the teaching colleges, and providing grants of income from landed estates for the leading ulama families. An ulama landed aristocracy was created as a buttress of the regime.

The creation of this apparatus was in some respects an extension of earlier Iranian Islamic practices and in other respects extremely innovative. The Seljuks had originated the policy of patronage for religious activists, who were all Sunni, as a way of gaining influence over the religious elites. The Safavids adopted this policy as well, but went much further in centralizing control of the ulama in the hands of the shahs. They brought the ulama from the position of clients to that of servants of the state. The Safavids also suppressed all rival forms of religion in Iran. The Seljuks had waged war with minority Shiite communities; the Safavids destroyed Iranian religious pluralism by the persecution of Sunni, alternative Shiite, and Sufi rivals. Sufi shrines were destroyed; Sufi brotherhoods were banned. For example, tombs of the Naqshabandi Sufi order were desecrated; khanaqas of the Nimatullahi Sufi order were seized and turned over to Shiite organizations. The pilgrimage to Mecca was deemphasized and replaced by the visitation of Shiite shrines.

Isfahan's royal square is dominated by entrances to four great buildings. On the west is the Ali Qapu, or "Sublime Port," the entrance to a vast palace precinct. From its verandah overlooking the great square, the ruler and his court could view the ever-changing pageantry below.

The success of Twelver Shiism in Iran, however, was not just a question of state power. Under Safavid sponsorship, Shiism entered a period of extraordinary religious, literary, and philosophical creativity and genuinely became the religious culture of Iranians. Although the original Sufi–Shiite concepts of the Safavids and the Sufi movement were proscribed, the veneration of Ali and Husayn became an integral part of Iranian Islam. The great shrines of Mashad and Qum were rebuilt during the reign of the shah Abbas I (r. 1588-1629), generously endowed, and made an essential part of the practice of Shiism in Iran. Shrines called *imamzadehs* were founded in memory of the imams or associates of the imams; *imambaras* (shines devoted to Husayn and Hasan) replaced villages shrines. The pilgrimage to Karbala became for Iranian Muslims even more important than the pilgrimage to Mecca.

The commemoration of the death of Husayn in the month of Muharram (the first month in the Islamic year) became the emotional core of Iranian Shiism. In the first ten days of Muharram, Iranians gathered to hear the heartrending stories of the martyrdom of Husayn at the hands of the Umayyads in 680 C.E. Sermons, recitations of elegies in memory of Husayn, passion plays, and the processional movement of shrines accompanied by columns of mourners and flagellants anchored Shiism in popular feeling. Neighborhood groups, youth gangs, and religious sects competed to outdo each other in the veneration of Husayn. Shiism was not just a state-sponsored bureaucratic religion; it had seized hold of popular feeling to become the deeply felt religious identity of the Iranian masses.

At the same time, high-culture gnosticism and philosophy also flourished. The Iranian philosopher and teacher Mir Damad (d. 1630) and his disciple Mulla Sadra (1571–1640) sought to integrate neo-Platonic ideas with the mystical vision of the Persian theologian and philosopher al-Suhrawardi, the sayings of Ali, and the philosophy of the Islamic mystic Ibn al-Arabi (1165–1240). Thus Shiism emerged as one of the great philosophical religions of the Islamic era. As a form of state religion, intellectual culture, and mass passion, Shiism had become a comprehensive alternative version of Islam. Despite this singular institutional creation, however, relations between the state and the religious establishment eventually became strained. Already in the seventeenth century there were subtle shifts in the position of the religious elites. Although Shiism had been institutionalized by the power of the state, deeply held religious values encouraged an attitude of withdrawal from worldly affairs and disdain for political engagement. As religious leaders withdrew

Under the Safavids, Twelver Shiism became the state religion of Iran. The great shrines at Qum and Mashhad were enlarged, and *imamzadehs*, smaller shrines in memory of other descendants or associates of the imams, became the focus of local piety and veneration.

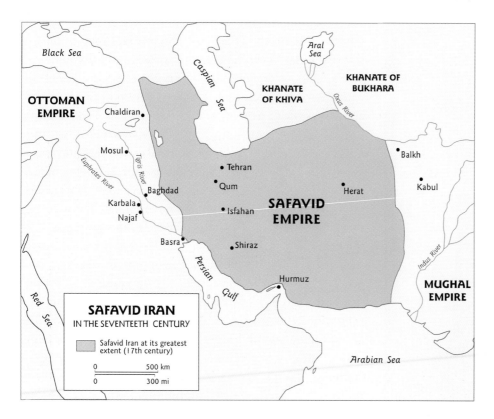

from politics, they were no longer willing to passively accept the authority of the state. Shiite scholars began to contest the notion that the Safavid shahs were the representatives of the hidden imam. They claimed instead that the scholars themselves were the highest religious authority and the true representatives of the imam on earth.

As the religious establishment separated itself from political control, the scholars began to debate the basis of their own authority. The *usuli* school claimed that religious scholars knowledgeable in the teachings of the Quran, the sayings of Ali, and the historical consensus of the community (*ijma*) were *mujtahids* (scholars-jurists) entitled to independent religious judgment (*ijtihad*). Their opponents, the *akhbaris*, restricted the authority of individual scholars and insisted on literal adherence to the letter of the tradition passed on by the Prophet and the imams. By the eighteenth century the debate had shifted from the role of the monarch to the limits of ulama authority. The religious establishment, although born as the creature of the state, had effectively become independent, with consequences that echo in Iran to the present day. This transformation of the religious establishment from a servant of the state to an independent institution was actually the consequence of

Safavid society was a court-centered regime, and people flocked to the capital to work for royal patrons. The painter Reza (d. 1635), for example, earned his epithet "Abbasi" from his major patron, Shah Abbas, and earned his living painting portraits of Abbas' courtiers, such as this turbaned man in a blue coat.

a second aspect of Safavid history—the relation of the state to the tribes. As much as the Safavid regime was able to build up slave forces and a central tax administration, as much as it created a religious organization, it was not able to fully subordinate the tribal forces. In northeastern and northwestern Iran, and to the south in what is now Afghanistan, Turkish *uymaqs* (bands of tribal chieftans, their clients, and individual free-booters organized into a single political entity) remained powerful. In many places they were able to rule independently; in other areas they were tributaries, but never were they crushed or eliminated. In most parts of Iran the monarchy had to rely on quasi-independent intermediaries for the government of the country. Apart from the reign of Shah Abbas I, the Safavid state remained a court-centered regime with relatively little power in the countryside.

For reasons that are still unclear, the late seventeenth century was a time of decay for the Safavid central state. The Safavid army was no longer a competent military machine, and central administration fell apart. The uymaqs—Afghans, Afshars, Qajars, Zands, and others—rose up and partitioned the country among them. In 1722 Ghalzai Afghans seized Isfahan, and in 1726 they eliminated the dynasty that had ruled Iran for more than two hundred years. In some respects the Safavids were the direct continuation of the political system of the Mongols and the Timurids. Although they raised the concept of Iranian imperium to new level of legitimacy and cultural brilliance and adapted the same institutional mechanisms to centralize state power, like their predecessors they could not fully succeed in taming the Turkish tribes. The Safavid state remained a court regime in a fluid society in which power was widely dispersed among competing tribal forces. These forces would in the end overthrow the dynasty.

The Safavids differed profoundly from their predecessors in their relation to Islam. While earlier states had been patrons of Islamic activity, the Safavids took this further. Initially they claimed to be the living representatives of the divine command. In a later phase, however, they created a highly centralized and controlled religious elite as the backbone of their administration of Iran and their claim to legitimacy as the defenders and patrons of Islam. The Safavid state thus left as its legacy to modern Iran a Persian tradition of glorified monarchy, a society partitioned among tribal principalities, and a monolithic but liberated and autonomous religious establishment.

The Ottoman Empire: Its Origins and World Conquests

The Ottoman empire also had its origins in the two great trends of earlier centuries: the Turkish migrations and the post-Abbasid reconstruction of state and society, which provided the institutional and cultural precedents for later Ottoman society. The legacy of Persian monarchical, Byzantine and Roman, Seljuk Anatolian, and Mongol and Timurid precedents interacting with Turkish cultures and transformed by the Ottoman synthesis led to the Ottoman version of high imperial, late Middle Eastern civilization.

At the time of the Ottoman conquest, the people of western Anatolia were slowly converting to Islam. The small mosque of Haci Ozbek, built at Iznik in 1333, two years after the Ottoman sultan Orhan took the city from the Byzantines, exemplifies the combination of Muslim needs and Byzantine building techniques.

The Seljuk invasions had brought Oghuz peoples into Georgia, Armenia, and Byzantine Anatolia in frontier conditions similar to those that existed in northern Iran. In the vanguard of the conquering forces were small bands of nomadic peoples under the leadership of *beys* (warrior chieftains) and Sufi holy men (*babas*). Like the tribes of northern Iran, these small bands were likely to have been groups of allied families and clients of an admired or venerated chieftain. The Sufi babas not only provided military leadership, they helped to organize a viable community life in the new territories. These holy men established residences, brought lands into cultivation, built hospices, mills, and schools, mediated disputes, and created the infrastructure of a settled life among migrant warriors. In the wake of the conquering bands came the Seljuk nobility, which set about to construct a centralized state on the model of those that had been created by Seljuk family elites in Iran and Iraq. The Seljuks built up slave forces, administrative cadres, and an Islamic religious infrastructure. Scholars were invited from Iran; *qadis* (judges) were put into office, colleges were built, and professorships were endowed.

A consequence of the activities of both the state and the migratory Sufi influences was the eventual transformation of Anatolia into a Muslim society. Under Seljuk rule (1071–1243), much of the Greek, Armenian, Georgian, and Syrian population was progressively converted to Islam. The weakening of the

The Ottomans ruled the greatest of Muslim empires, which extended into Europe, North Africa, Egypt, Arabia, Mesopotamia, Iran, and Anatolia. In 1529 Ottoman forces unsuccessfully besieged Vienna, and Ottoman-Hapsburg wars continued for more than 150 years without major territorial change. In the summer of 1683, an Ottoman army of 150,000 unsuccessfully attacked the city, marking the beginning of the end of Ottoman domination in eastern Europe.

Byzantine state, the decline of the orthodox church, and the breakdown of Anatolian society in the face of conquest facilitated the ultimate conversion of the region. The socially constructive measures taken by the conquerors, their tolerance of non-Muslim peoples, and the many common points of popular Islam and popular Christianity—Christians and Muslims revered the same saints and holy places and shared magical and superstitious beliefs as well as common monotheistic and ethical principles and Biblical lore—worked over the centuries to create a Muslim majority.

Sufis played an important role in these conversions. They were generally more accepting of a great variety of religious practices and beliefs, whether Muslim or not, as possible routes to God. Sufis also organized residences as centers of social service and assistance to ordinary people. The Bektashi Sufi order in the rural areas, Mevlevi Sufis in the cities, and in the smaller towns *akhis* (young men providing charity to the poor and to travelers) created the devotional, charitable, educational, and communal environment that led to the Islamic conversion of

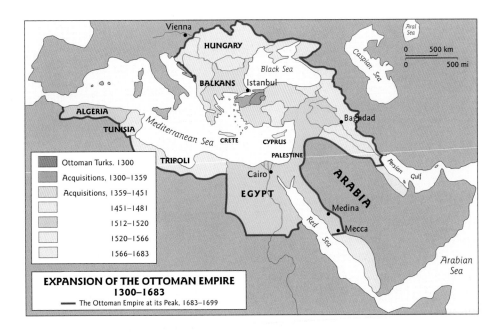

EXPANSION OF THE OTTOMAN EMPIRE
1300–1683
—— The Ottoman Empire at its Peak, 1683–1699

Anatolia. Although there would later be substantial conversions in the Balkans too, there the majority remained Christian, largely because of the smaller Turkish population and because of the Ottoman policy of supporting and using the Balkan churches as an administrative convenience.

Although effective in its domains, the Seljuk Turkish system of expansion and occupation generated chronic tension between the central state and a host of peripheral nomadic principalities and warrior bands. Although the state tried to consolidate its power, the outlying peoples sought to maintain their autonomy. This impelled many of them to further expansion in western Anatolia at Byzantine expense, as the local chieftains sought to enhance their power, win glory for Islam, and maintain their distance and independence from the Seljuk state.

The Ottoman empire had its origins in just such a band of frontier warriors operating in late thirteenth-century western Anatolia. Ertugrul, who may have died around 1280, was the founder of a dynasty that over two centuries, not swiftly but ineluctably, first conquered Bursa in western Anatolia in 1326, crossed the straits of Gallipoli in 1345, conquered what is now Bulgaria, Macedonia, and much of Greece, and defeated the Serbian empire at the Battle of Kosovo in 1389.

On the basis of their Balkan conquests, the Ottomans turned eastward and absorbed Muslim-ruled Anatolia as well. In 1453 the Ottomans seized Constantinople, bringing to an end the eleven-hundred-year tenure of the Byzantine Empire and establishing themselves as successors to the Roman Empire.

The conquest of Constantinople was both the capstone of previous Ottoman achievements in war and the opening of a new phase in Ottoman ambitions. Mehmed the Conqueror (r. 1444–46, 1451–81) saw himself as successor to Roman emperors and Arab caliphs. His victories realized age-old Turkish ideas of a destiny of world domination, the imperial ambitions of the Roman empire, and Muslim jihad and expansion of the domain of Islam. With the conquest of Constantinople, the Ottomans redoubled their ambitions. The conquest of the Balkans opened the way for a two-century-long struggle against the powers of Europe. The Ottomans were opposed by the Habsburg emperors of Spain, by the Netherlands, by Austria and Hungary, and by the czars of Russia. The wars unfolded along three principal fronts. In central Europe the Ottomans pushed beyond the Danube River and absorbed Romania by 1504. Belgrade was taken in 1520 and Hungary came under Ottoman rule in 1529, and in the same year the Ottomans besieged but failed to take Vienna. Without major territorial changes, Ottoman-Habsburg wars continued for another century and a half until the second Ottoman siege of Vienna in 1683.

In the Mediterranean the Ottomans waged an equally vast struggle. They seized Algiers in 1529 and Tunis in 1574. In 1580 they negotiated an historic truce with Philip II of Spain that confirmed the boundaries of their domains. This was a fateful agreement because it still marks the boundaries between the Christian and Muslim parts of the Mediterranean. In the north the Ottomans and Russia struggled for control of the steppes beyond the Black Sea and the regions between the Black and the Caspian seas. While the Ottomans held Romania and the Crimea, the Russians dominated the lower Volga region. The struggle continued until 1676, when for a short time the Ottomans consolidated their control of the Black Sea, the steppes, and part of the Ukraine. This was the apogee of their expansion in northern Europe.

Mehmed and his successors brought the Ottoman domains eastward to the borders of Iran, absorbed the Arab provinces and North Africa and the holy places of Arabia, and they carried their ambitions into the Indian Ocean, fighting the Portuguese for control of the spice trade. Ottoman expansion, beginning in western Anatolia, continued for three centuries until the Ottomans had brought southern and eastern Europe as far as Vienna; the northern steppes of the Black Sea as far as the Ukraine; Anatolia to the borders of Safavid Iran; and the Arab countries, Egypt, Yemen, and North Africa as far as the borders of Morocco, under their control. This was the greatest of the Muslim empires. Much of Ottoman history was shaped by their extraordinary commitment to conquest in the name of Islam. The Ottoman wars gave them a reputation among Muslims as the greatest of Muslim states devoted to the jihad. In Europe they left the reputation of the scourge of God and a terror for centuries. The image of the ferocious Turk lives on today.

The Ottoman success can be attributed to a number of considerations. The first was the tactical advantage of their frontier location and the skill with which they seized locations that were important to administration, communications, and trade. Also the Ottomans kept their territories intact under a single heir as opposed to the practice of most of the rival principalities, which divided territories among the descendants of the ruler. Their political flexibility in creating alliances across religious, ethnic, and tribal lines and among nomadic and settled communities was another factor in their favor. So too was the ghazi (frontier warrior) ideology, which motivated them to wage jihad in the name of Islam and self-interest, and justified a flexible policy in dealing with allies and enemies.

Yet in the last analysis the Ottomans owed their success to the policy of strengthening the hand of the dynasty and the central state as opposed to that of the Turkish warrior leaders. The Ottomans were the greatest of Middle Eastern conquerors, in part because they ran the most highly centralized imperial state in the region's history. They eliminated the frontier warriors and warlords, babas, and tribal chieftains. They suppressed independent local dynasties and replaced the pre-Ottoman elites with Ottoman functionaries. With the conquest of Constantinople, the centralist tendency won out completely. A nomadic conquest was transformed into an Islamic monarchy. The ruler was reconceptualized from patriarch and elder to monarch and emperor. The *levee en masse* of tribal peoples was replaced by slave and client forces; the boon companions and warrior cohort of early days by professional administrators.

The Ottoman State Apparatus and Religion

The Ottoman state was built on the very same institutional base as its Middle Eastern predecessors. At the center was the court or palace apparatus, the household of the ruler, comprising his family, his harem, his boon companions, and his highest ranking officers, administrators, and religious functionaries. The court served as an extended family and the government's nerve center, a training institute for Ottoman cadres, and a theater of cultural display. Centered at the Topkapi Serai, overlooking the Golden Horn of Istanbul, the court was divided into two sections. The inner section was made up of the residences of the sultan and his harem, the treasury, and the school for pages and officers. In Ottoman society and politics the women of the royal family were particularly important. In the historic Turkish understanding, powers were vested not only in the reigning prince but also collectively in his fam-

The nerve center of the Ottoman capital at Istanbul was the palace known as Topkapi Saray. Unlike European palaces, it comprised a series of four concentric courtyards of ever-increasing privacy. In this depiction from the official history of Suleyman's reign, the sultan receives the admiral Barbarossa in the third court.

ily. Women were therefore important in the ceremonials of the regimes, in its charitable activities, and by their role in negotiations and intrigue at court. They were important in the selection of officers and policies. The outer section of the court was the administrative zone proper, including state offices and palace functionaries.

The city of Istanbul could be considered an extension of the royal palace. After the conquest, the sultan Mehmed found Constantinople rich in history but virtually abandoned by its population. The Ottomans resettled the city and built up its population not only with servants of the state but with useful communities of Muslims and minorities, who could do the commercial, craft, and other work essential to an expanding society. Successive sultans built great mosque and school complexes, provided with such facilities as hospitals, libraries, bazaars, bakeries, inns, residences, and soup kitchens. Such great complexes as the Selimiye and the Suleymaniye, named after the sultans who founded them, became neighborhood community centers for Istanbul's population. Just as the Safavids built Isfahan, so too did the Ottomans rebuild Istanbul as an essential base of operations and adornment for their empire. At its apogee, Istanbul had a population of about seven hundred thousand, an enormous number for a sixteenth- and seventeenth-century city.

The military was essential to Ottoman power, and as early as the reign of the sultan Murad I (r. 1360–89) they had begun to build up slave forces to supplement, subdue, and replace free Turkish warriors. The Ottomans went further than any previous Middle Eastern regime to ensure the supply of slave soldiers. In the past, slave soldiers originally came from the Caucasus or from Central Asia, outside the areas in which they would serve. The Ottomans changed this by instituting the *devshirme*, a tax in manpower on the Christian population of the Balkans. This was both the first systematic recruitment of slaves and the first recruitment from within the domains of the state itself.

The Ottomans created a further innovation in slave armies. Whereas most Middle Eastern slave forces were trained to be elite cavalry, with a keen sense for military and tactical innovation the Ottomans trained their most important units as infantry, provided them with firearms, and used phalanx tactics to combine massed musket firepower with artillery. Thus were born the famous janissaries and the tactics that made them for centuries the most advanced of European and Middle Eastern armies. In part a result of this innovation, the appellation Gunpowder Empire applies above all to the Ottomans. The Ottomans organized cavalry as well as infantry forces, but the cavalry forces were completely different in character from the janissaries. The cavalry were recruited among Turkish warriors. They were not garrisoned as a central army; rather, they were provided with incomes from land grants throughout the Ottoman domains. From their *timars* (the equivalent of the Arab *iqtas*) the timar holders provided local security and served in Ottoman campaigns. They were an old-fashioned quasi-feudal rather than a centralized army. The slave system was also used to build up a powerful bureaucratic apparatus. The Ottomans converted their young slaves to Islam and educated them in the palace schools to be pages in the royal household, officers in the army, or government officials. Whatever their origin, the slaves were united by devotion to the sultan and by their upbringing in the "Ottoman way."

The fourth and most private of Topkapi courtyards contained freestanding garden pavilions in which the sultan and his intimates lived. The Baghdad Kiosk, built in 1638–9 to commemorate the victory of Murad IV at Baghdad, overlooks a garden and the Golden Horn.

Thus the regime was built not on ethnic homogeneity but on the slaves and clients of the rulers, coming from a variety of backgrounds, who by training and education were qualified as a ruling caste.

Until the seventeenth century, when the Ottoman system began to break down, the political class was organized to prevent the accumulation of private power and its transmission to later generations. The slave system was the key to this concept, because only newly recruited slaves could be inducted into positions of power. Children of slaves could not be. Although middling administrators, sons of governors, and rich timar holders were sometimes able to pass estates to their children, Ottoman policies were inimical to the accumulation of private property. Large private fortunes could be and were readily confiscated. Unlike the Safavids, who failed to suppress tribal resistance to the state, the Ottomans progressively eliminated all rival organized political bodies and imposed a salaried bureaucracy in most of their provinces. Most tributaries were annexed and subjected to centralized rule. Eastern tribal populations were subordinated. Independent rural landowners and Sufi leaders were incorporated into the Ottoman state. Only a few remote provinces, such as Romania, the Crimea, and parts of eastern Anatolia, remained in the control of quasi-independent Greek, Turkish, and Kurdish tributaries. More than any other Middle Eastern state, the Ottomans succeeded in centralizing political power and overcoming tribal autonomy. They brought to an end

The domed mosque with pencil-thin minarets came to symbolize Ottoman domination throughout their realm. This detailed 1559 drawing of the Istanbul skyline by the German artist Melchior Lorichs shows the mosque complex Mehmet the Conqueror built immediately after he took the city in 1453.

in their region the historical struggle of tribes and states.

The Ottoman drive toward centralization was particularly marked in the domain of religion. Like the Seljuks before them, the Ottomans continued the practice of patronizing the ulama and the Sufis. They built mosques and madrasas. They endowed teachers and students; they organized judicial administration and employed religious scholars as judges and professors. They employed religious functionaries, such as notaries, registrars, and administrators of orphans' and intestate properties. The Ottomans went further than their Seljuk predecessors, however, in that they not only patronized the religious elites, they incorporated them into a hierarchically ordered bureaucracy and made them functionaries of the state as well.

The position of shaykh al-Islam or chief mufti (a mufti was an expert in Islamic law and a member of the ulama establishment) dates to 1433. Originally, the man holding this position was the personal religious adviser to the sultan, and his office may have been created to increase the religious legitimacy of the state—perhaps to parallel the ancient caliphate and to respond to criticism about the regime's secularization. The earliest muftis had no administrative functions; only late in the reign of Mehmed II was the chief mufti recognized as the head of the ulama. The power of appointing other ulama seems to have been given to the chief mufti in the middle of the sixteenth century.

The teaching system was also transformed into state offices. Whereas previous regimes had endowed madrasas in the important cities, the Ottomans gave them a hierarchical rank: those of the reigning sultan at the top, followed by foundations of earlier sultans, followed by madrasas founded by government officials and religious functionaries. By the middle of the sixteenth century the principle that a scholar had to serve in a graded series of colleges was firmly established. Professors were no longer merely appointed to teaching positions for life; now they could be promoted from one position to another. The schools were also organized by functions. The lowest-level madrasas

The sultans commissioned elaborate furnishings for their mosque complexes. This magnificent walnut box, designed to hold a manuscript of the Quran in thirty volumes, was ordered by Bayezit in 1505–6, probably for his mosque complex in Istanbul completed in the same year.

were assigned to teach Arabic language and linguistic studies, astronomy, mathematics, theology, and rhetoric; the middle-level colleges taught literature and rhetoric; and the highest-level subjects were law and theology.

The judiciary was organized in a similar way. The original judicial positions were located in Istanbul, Edirne, and Bursa, but many positions were added in other cities in the late sixteenth century, probably to create new jobs for an ever larger cadre of position seekers. The positions in Istanbul, Bursa, and Edirne ranked at the top of the hierarchy, followed by those in Damascus, Cairo, Baghdad, Medina, Izmir, and Konya. The shaykh al-Islam was the head of the judicial administration as a whole; the *qadi-askars* (chief judges of the military) of the Balkans and Anatolia ranked next. Judges were seasoned by appointment up the ladder of positions. The judicial hierarchy and the teaching hierarchy were linked in that an appropriate level in the teaching system was a prerequisite to appointment to a judicial position. Qadis had considerable administrative importance; their duties not only included the judging of petitions but also inspection of the military, oversight of tax collection, supervision of the urban economy, and the application of government regulations in all domains of state interest. To get

The Ottomans transformed the teaching system into a state bureaucracy. *Madrasas* were organized hierarchically, with those founded by the reigning sultan at the top of the system. The Suleymaniye complex (1557) at Istanbul was the largest in the empire, with four theological colleges, a medical school, and another school for prophetic traditions, as well as other charitable institutions.

a job in this system, the student had to be sponsored by someone who held a high-ranking post. The student's first position would as a repeater in a college. He would teach at a number of graded colleges, and eventually he could reach the level of a judgeship. The position of a mufti was not reached through a hierarchical gradation of "mufti-ships"; rather it was approached through the college professorships and judgeships.

The Ottomans thus gained control over the ulama and made them functionaries of the state, and they also co-opted the leading Sufi brotherhoods. Sufi-led tribal rebellions were crushed during the fourteenth to the sixteenth centuries. The Bektashis became the patrons of the janissaries. Urban Sufis were provided in the time-honored manner with gifts, endowments, and a place in Ottoman court ceremony. The Mevlevi leaders had the ceremonial function of girding a new sultan upon his accession with a holy sword. The representatives of spiritual otherworldly power thus became the protectors of the state. In comparison with other Muslim societies this was an extraordinary organizational achievement, but it came at a high price. Insofar as the ulama and leading Sufis became functionaries of the state, they ceased to represent the mass of Muslim believers and could no longer protect the people from abuses of political power. To the extent that they were the servants of the state and the defenders of Ottoman legitimacy, they could not effectively resist corruption in the government. As much as they became a class of functionaries dependent on government offices and on offices for their children and students, they became a self-interested and powerful interest group within the state itself. By the eighteenth century a closed aristocracy of Ottoman ulama was in existence. The ulama were particularly favored because they had considerable opportunities to acquire properties through *waqfs* (endowments), and they were not threatened with confiscation of property after death. Ulama families lasted longer in power than any other element of the government elite, and a small group of families dominated the religious establishment. From 1703 to 1839, eleven Istanbul families accounted for twenty-nine of the fifty-eight shaykh al-Islams.

But as the bureaucracy became ossified, the protest movement of Kadizadeli developed. Named after Kadizade Mehmed (d. 1635; he was a preacher at the mosque of Aya Sofia), it was a puritanical movement to reform both the ulama and the general society. The movement was opposed to the consumption of coffee, tobacco, and opium; to singing, music, and dancing in Sufi ceremonies; and to pilgrimages to saints' tombs; they denounced the writings of the thirteenth-century philosopher Ibn al-Arabi and called on good Muslims not only to lead moral lives but to force others to follow "the straight path." The movement in many ways was implicitly anti-Ottoman, because the Ottomans had long tolerated religious variation in their empire and historically had parlayed religious spectacles into Ottoman legitimacy. The movement was only partially successful, however, because the dominant Istanbul families fought to keep control of the bureaucracy. Their reaction led to more conservative religious teaching and to the further consolidation of a small religious elite. Imperial support was always forthcoming because it seemed that this was essential to the stability of the empire. The religious elites, once recruited to sustain the regime, had thus become a self-perpetuating body.

Ottoman Culture and the Concept of Empire: Rulers and Subjects

The authority of the Ottoman sultans was derived from several layers of Middle Eastern cultural tradition. The Ottomans primarily derived their legitimacy from Turko-Mongol concepts of royal family supremacy, warrior sovereignty, and what they considered to be a divinely given mission to conquer the world. This patrimonial conception, which based the right to rule on aristocratic noble lineage combined with victories in battle, had its origin in the Ottoman Turkish and Central Asian past. In the early centuries of Ottoman rule, this conception was dramatized by the open struggle for power among the sons of a deceased ruler. The winner of that struggle was considered to have been selected by God for his reign. Furthermore, the whole of the conquered domain was considered in patrimonial terms to be the personal property of the sultan. The state was his household; the soldiers, courtiers, and administrators were his slaves, personally devoted to him; the subjects were his flocks. The territory of the empire was his to distribute among his family and retainers.

From the Islamic tradition came the claim to be the protector and defender of Islam and therefore successor to the caliphate. Suleyman I (r. 1520–66) took the title *Halife-i Ru-i Zemin* (caliph of the world). The sultan was viewed in Islamic terms as the defender of Islam, the protector of Muslim peoples; a ghazi, a warrior who waged jihad to expand the domains of Islam. The sultan thus protected Muslims against Christian enemies without and maintained their supremacy over Christians within the empire. The Ottomans were the defenders of the two holy sanctuaries of Mecca and Medina. Muslims outside Ottoman domains appealed to them for help against infidel enemies. From Spain, from Acheh, on the island of Sumatra, and from Central Asia came appeals for aid against non-Muslim enemies. As the greatest conquering state in Islamic history, the Ottoman empire acquired an absolute legitimacy in Muslim terms.

Moreover, the Ottoman sultans were considered to be tantamount to caliphs, because they were the executors of Islamic law. The rulers provided justice and protection for the common people against the depredations of government officials. They patronized, sponsored, and organized Muslim judicial and educational affairs. Their duty to implement the Shariah gave them the right to issue supplementary regulations (firmans) that were later gathered into legal codes (kanuns). The sultans issued decrees defining the status, duties, and dress codes for all of their functionaries; laws to implement the landholding and tax systems, economic regulations, military and administrative matters, criminal justice, the discipline of officials, and the organization of religious affairs. The sultans' activities as lawgivers supplementing the Shariah derived from both Muslim and Byzantine traditions. This function was itself a source of legitimacy. It was an historical part of the emperor's prerogative.

Ottoman authority was further based on a cosmopolitan culture, comprising Arab, Persian, Turkish, Byzantine, and European elements. From Middle Eastern monarchical concepts came the conception of universal glory. From eastern Roman tradition came the notion of the Ottoman ruler as emperor and heir to the Roman empire, causing Ottoman rulers to take the title Padishah (supreme shah). Sultan Mehmed II generously patronized Persian poetry and European painting. Arab and Persian writers, Italian artists, and Greek and Serbian poets were part of his entourage. Many of the sponsored arts had themes that

Like the Safavids, the Ottomans were great patrons of the arts. Under their patronage, the tribal craft of carpet-weaving was transformed into a state industry. Some of the finest pieces, such as this small prayer rug knotted in wool and silk on a cotton ground, were made for the court.

SVLIMAN·OTOMAN·REX

The Ottomans manipulated ceremony to legitimize their authority. They staged processions and pageants in the capital and received foreign ambassadors with elaborate ceremony. Although Muslim rulers traditionally wore turbans, Suleyman commissioned an extraordinary crown from Venetian goldsmiths whose four tiers were meant to outdo the crowns of the pope and the Hapsburg emperor.

embellished royal claims. For example, illustrated manuscripts produced in the sultans' own workshops, like those of the Safavids and other rulers, depicted the greatness of the monarchy. Histories of the conquests of Alexander the Great and of past Persian emperors, mystical poetry, love stories, fables, and other works long part of the repertoire of royal patronage were produced to demonstrate the sophistication, cultivation, and grandeur of the Ottomans. In the sixteenth century, Ottoman workshops turned from classic works to the illustration of contemporary history with depictions of court ceremonies, receptions of ambassadors, conquests of famous fortresses, festivals, and processions. In these manuscripts the sultans appear in realistic fashion, directing their armies, presiding over the court, surrounded by their janissaries, viziers, scholars, holy men, merchants, craftspeople, and their subjects. These illustrated histories are a particular Ottoman contribution to the many varieties of Muslim world artistic culture, self-consciously celebrating the Ottoman sultans and the Ottoman elite as rulers of the world.

The patronage of philosophy, science, and other universal subjects was also a way of asserting the Ottoman claim to universal authority. Ottoman architecture, while devoted to mosques and colleges, nonetheless borrowed the stylistic motifs of Aya Sofia and Greek ecclesiastical structures to symbolize the Ottoman triumph over and the appropriation of the genius of Christianity and the Byzantine empire. The Ottoman palace itself was organized in a way that symbolized the cosmic nature of the ruler's power. Both public ceremonies in which the sultan spoke and his known private pleasures (hunting, drinking, and dancing girls) were crafted to symbolize that he stood above ordinary mortals. In the seventeenth century the increasing importance of pleasure in the daily life of sultans probably reflected the rising power of an institutionalized bureaucracy that intensified the symbolic roles of the sultanate.

The Ottomans also sought to present their claims in symbols derived from Europe. Mehmed II had invited important Italian artists to Istanbul, and in the 1530s Suleyman the Magnificent renewed this orientation. In 1532 he acquired an extraordinary Venetian-made gold and jeweled helmet or crown. Built with four crowns superimposed, it rivaled the papal tiara. Other regalia, such as scepters, orbs, and ceremonial canopies intended to rival those of Western enemies, were also acquired in this period (1532-36), even though the possession of such emblems was until this point outside the Ottoman tradition. This Western orientation symbolized the ambition to be recognized as a dominant figure among European rulers and was connected to Ottoman claims to be heirs to the Roman Empire, the rulers of Italy and indeed the whole of the Mediterranean basin.

Ottoman power was further legitimized by ceremonial demonstrations. Istanbul, the capital, was used as the stage for demonstrations of Ottoman authority. Imperial constructions and public works undertakings, parades of guilds and the military and of foreign ambassadors and their gifts, celebrations of campaign victories and feasts celebrating life events for the ruling family were all demonstrations of Ottoman authority. Public festivals, especially at an Ottoman prince's circumcision, a princess's marriage, or a sultan's ascension, were a form of theater that renewed the population's attachment to the ruler. Finally, the Ottoman rulers were thought of in mystical terms as the viceroys of God on earth, who were meant to bring order into human affairs. The language of divine selection and personal charisma was thus invoked to glorify each sultan as a quasi-divine being. This was the ultimate expression of the sultans' almighty supremacy.

The Ottoman elite was a heterogeneous, cosmopolitan class recruited from diverse origins, but it did not mirror the empire's populations. The elites were a caste apart, elevated above the common people by their education, aristocratic manners, court and political functions, and personal devotion to the ruler. This elite group was mainly Turkish, Arab, and Balkan Muslim, but the Ottoman Empire was not, strictly speaking, a regime of Muslims over non-Muslims. The elite also included Jewish bankers, Phanariot Istanbul Greek merchants, and European renegades.

The subject population belonged in all respects to another and lesser order of existence. The Ottomans were the rulers of an extremely heterogeneous, multiethnic, multilinguistic, multireligious, and multitribal population. All commoners, Muslim and non-Muslim, were considered the *reava* (the flocks), taxpayers to be shorn in the interests of the political elite. Both Muslim and non-Muslim commoners were organized into small religious communities, which were permitted a considerable internal autonomy regulated by religious laws and values. For the Muslims these included the schools of law and the Sufi fraternities. Most of the non-Muslims were considered eastern Orthodox, which included Greek, Romanian, Slavic, Bulgarian, and Arab churches. The Armenian church was the administrative body for Armenians, Monophysites in Syria and Egypt, Assyrians, Bogomils, and Gypsies. Maronites, Uniate Armenians, and Latin Catholics in Hungary, Croatia, and Albania were considered separate churches with doctrinal affiliations to Rome and administrative organization under Ottoman authority.

The Ottoman Empire proved a haven for the Jews of Mediterranean Europe and the Middle East. Ashkenazis from Germany, France, and Hungary; Italian Jews from Sicily; and Sephardic Jews from Spain and Portugal settled in Ottoman domains. Mehmed the Conqueror invited Jews from Anatolia, Salonica, and Edirne to move to Istanbul, and he gave them special privileges not given to Christians, such as permitting them to build new synagogues. Jews generally lived in their own quarters, each of which operated as a separate municipality responsible for tax collection, expenditure for community activities, maintaining schools, synagogues, settling internal disputes, and so on. Ottoman Jews did not form a single organized body, but rather numerous quasi-dependent *kahila* or local community congregations with many different religious practices and beliefs.

All subjects, Muslim and non-Muslim, were thus organized into small communities that served to administer their educational, judicial, familial, and charitable affairs and to assist the state by collecting taxes and enforcing social discipline. All were headed by religious, clerical, or priestly leaders (and sometimes by lay representatives), and they enjoyed a degree of internal autonomy, although they were responsible to the sultan and the Ottoman authorities. This organization of the populace into quasi-autonomous religious bodies is commonly referred to as the "millet system." Although there was never an empire-wide administration of the non-Muslim populations, the Ottomans made high religious functionaries responsible for their communities under Ottoman authority and intervened even in the appointment of patriarchs, bishops, and other non-Muslim religious officials. The non-Muslims were considered *dhimmis* or protected peoples, subject to a special tax and some discriminatory measures.

The Economy of the Ottoman Empire: Land, Urban Markets, and International Trade

The Ottoman empire was unusual among Middle Eastern empires in the degree to which it was able to bring the subject population under state control. Critical to this control was the regulation of the economy. The Ottomans operated on the principle that the subjects should serve the interests of the state, and the economy was organized to ensure the flow of tax revenues, goods in kind, and services needed by the government and the elites. The populace was systematically taxed; the Ottomans were the best recordkeepers in Middle Eastern history. The tax base was exhaustively described in cadastral surveys that took stock of the population, households, property, and other resources. Ottoman economic policy on trade was based on a fiscal-

ism that was aimed at accumulating as much bullion as possible in the state treasury, but at the same time balancing this with a concern for the general well-being
of the Muslim population. The Ottomans did not see trade policy or scientific and
technological development as a means of creating wealth. Rather, they still thought
in terms of wealth derived from conquered and annexed territories.

Peasant lands were organized into family farm units; villages were not usually collectivities in possession of lands but rather agglomerations of independent peasant households, although there were common interests, such as
village meadows, threshing floors, water, and pasturage. For the Ottomans the
productivity and the taxation of the land was the primary concern. In theory
all lands were owned by the state (*miri*), but there were two subclassifications:
tapulu, lands that were on perpetual lease to peasants who had the right to the
usufruct and to assign that right to their male descendants, and *mukatalu*, lands
that were leased to a tax collector in return for the payment of a fixed lease.
Incomes from state lands were also distributed in the form of *timars* and other
stipends. The peasants were taxed by measuring the surface of the land, the size
of the household, and the oxen available for labor, which was in effect a rough
measure of productivity. This system of taxation (called the *cifthane* system) was
appropriate to semiarid, dry farming devoted largely to wheat and barley, and
it was derived from Roman and Byzantine precedents.

A study of north-central Anatolia in the fifteenth and sixteenth centuries provides a deeper understanding of the workings of the land and tax systems. When
the Ottomans obtained control of these regions in the mid-fifteenth century, they
had to concede Turkish military rulers and Muslim religious leaders ownership
rights to the land. In the course of the next century and a half the state struggled
to dispossess the local notables and to reassign the tax rights to timar holders
appointed by the central government. Still, much property remained *mulk* (private property) or *waqfs* (endowments), but these tended to be fragmented small
holdings often in the possession of allies of the central government.

In the sixteenth century general population growth was stimulated by
increased security and by the settlement of nomads. The regional economy grew
enormously, with an expansion of peasant production of perhaps one hundred
percent accompanied by considerable population growth. As surplus population
moved to the towns, increased demand provided new markets for agricultural
produce. Truck gardening, fruit growing, and viticulture expanded. Peasants
produced ever more fruits, vegetables, and sheep, for which they had a cash market, though grain production for taxes and subsistence still dominated the rural
economy.

The economy's expansion took place by an increase of output from small peasant plots. Although the surplus was largely taken by officials and revenue collec-

tors, this did not result in the dispossession or enserfment of peasants or their conversion to wage laborers on large holdings. Limited commercialization favored revenue holders but did not go so far as to disrupt the peasant economy. State protection of peasant interests also played a large role. The state protected the rights of peasants to the usufruct of the land, controlled the amounts of produce that could be taken in taxes, and set the rules for the marketing of the produce. The state thus protected the peasants against the rise of feudal authorities and kept a smallholding peasantry on the land.

The provisioning of Istanbul was a principle concern of Ottoman economic policy. The Ottomans did not use market mechanisms so much as requisitions to supply the court, the army, the administration, and the populace of Istanbul. Provincial merchants and officials were required to provide a steady stream of goods—grain, sheep, food products, leather, wood, metal, and other products—for direct imperial use or for sale on the Istanbul market. Ottoman workshops produced luxury products such as silk garments directly for the court. Ottoman regulations forbade the export of numerous products until the needs of the capital had been met. The Ottomans also regulated production through an extensive guild system that organized workers under the control of guild functionaries, market officials, and military authorities to ensure the production of goods of standard quality, at reasonable prices, for distribution to the state elites and to the population of the capital. The enormous size of Istanbul and its economic demands had a tremendous impact on the surrounding territories. Istanbul's demand for grain turned the region from the Dnieper River to Varna (in modern-day east Bulgaria) into a commercial agriculture and livestock region. Along the Sea of Marmara (in northwest Turkey), villages produced wine, olives, and fruit for the Istanbul market. From Anatolia came sheep, hides, grain, and many other products.

Although the Ottoman economy was based primarily on agricultural and craft output and Ottoman policy was oriented toward the conquest and control of territory as the basic source of wealth, international trade was nevertheless of considerable importance. The Ottomans held a central place in world trade linking the Middle East and East Asia to Europe, and in the north-south trade from India and Arabia to central and eastern Europe. A great deal of Ottoman foreign policy, including its interventions in the Mediterranean, Central Asia, Yemen, Iraq, and the Indian Ocean, can be seen in terms of the importance of international trade. After the conquest of Constantinople, the first political task for the Ottomans was to wrest control of the Black Sea, the Aegean, and the eastern Mediterranean from the Venetians and the Genoese. The conquest of the Arab provinces and Egypt in 1517 gave the Ottomans control of the trade routes and the flow of resources through the Levant (the eastern shores of the Mediterranean between western Greece and Western Egypt), and positioned them to take over Mecca and Medina, Yemen, and southern Iraq and to fight the Portuguese for control of the Indian Ocean trade.

With these territories in Ottoman control, Bursa emerged as the principle entrepôt of the empire. Indian spices coming to Jidda (a port on the Red Sea) were caravanned to Mecca and then to Damascus, Aleppo, Konya, and Bursa. The sea route from Alexandria to Antalya (in southwestern Turkey) was also in use. Eastern goods from the Sudan, Egypt, Syria, and Arabia passed through Bursa on their way to Istanbul and to further destinations in eastern and central Europe. Edirne, Sarajevo, and Dubrovnik became important centers for the trade of the Balkans, the Adriatic, the Mediterranean, and Europe. On these routes the Ottomans exported silk, rhubarb, wax, pepper, drugs, fine cotton cloth, hides and furs, imported woolen cloth, metals, and money. Another route from Bursa to Istanbul to Akkerman (in southwestern Ukraine; renamed Belgorod-Dnestrovski in 1944) brought Ottoman and eastern goods into Poland and central Europe. This trade consisted of such local products as wheat, fish, and hides, and such oriental luxuries as paper, silk, and English, Florentine, and other fine woolen cloths. An alternative route from Bursa brought goods into Romania and Hungary. The Black Sea trade was equally lively. Important routes ran from Caffa to Kiev and to Moscow. Caffa gathered goods from the whole of the Black Sea region but also from Istanbul, the Aegean Sea region, and Europe. Slaves, including Slavs captured in war, sub-Saharan Africans, and captives taken from the steppes of inner Asia, were an important product in the international trade.

The Portuguese incursions into the Indian Ocean in the sixteenth century led to a major reorientation of world trade. Now eastern goods could be shipped around Africa to Lisbon, avoiding the Ottoman-controlled Middle East and the Venetian hold on luxury trade in the Mediterranean. Nonetheless, the Portuguese did not cut off the spice trade through Ottoman territories. The Ottomans maintained forces in both Yemen and Basra; they inaugurated cooperative ties with Gujarat (in Western India) and Acheh in Sumatra to keep alive both political resistance to the Portuguese and commercial contacts. Even Venice's Levantine trade recovered in midcentury. By the late sixteenth century goods caravanned to Damascus or to Cairo were being picked up at Alexandria and Tripoli by Venetian ships. Trade through the Ottoman empire was reinforced by the ever-growing popularity of coffee from Yemen.

Despite this restoration of the international transit trade through Ottoman territories, a more dramatic menace made itself felt by the end of the sixteenth century. The British and the Dutch entered the struggle for control of the international spice trade and seized colonies in India and the East Indies as bases for an effort to monopolize the trade. By 1625 the north Atlantic sea powers finally cut off the spice trade to the Mediterranean. The Ottomans could still compensate by a lively trade in silk and coffee and in Indian cotton goods and dyes, but the most lucrative part of the trade was lost to the cape routes to western Europe. Moreover, from their controlling position in the Indian Ocean the British and the Dutch began to compete directly with Ottoman trade in the Mediterranean. In 1580 the British made their first trade treaty with the Ottomans and began to buy silk and sell cotton goods and metals to the Ottomans. Even spices began to come into the Mediterranean from Europe rather than directly from the Indian Ocean.

At the end of the sixteenth century, Izmir became the leading Ottoman port, gradually eclipsing both Bursa and Aleppo. As the Ottomans lost their grip on the Izmir region, French, Dutch, English, and Venetian merchants flocked to the area. Izmir became a cosmopolitan town, home to Arab camel caravaners and Armenian, Greek, Jewish, and Turkish merchants. The Europeans promoted a lively trade in cotton, wool, dried fruit, and grain, and built up a strong internal supply system. Ottoman janissaries, customs collectors, and other officials began to act as free agents and to evade the authority of Istanbul. Izmir's links to Istanbul were cut as it was partially integrated into the European economy. The Ottomans were losing control of the Mediterranean trade to European merchants.

In other respects, too, the Ottoman empire was falling behind in international trade competition. The Atlantic economy and the growth of trade in such western staples as sugar, coffee, tobacco, and cotton had come to greatly overshadow the silk trade. Now the most lucrative trade was shifting from rare luxuries to goods for mass consumption, to the advantage of the Atlantic trading states. Europeans were gaining relative advantages in banking, insurance, and shipping profits, and with the beginnings of the industrial revolution they were in a position to sell high value-added manufactured goods and skilled services in return for raw or semi-processed raw materials.

Until the end of the sixteenth century the Ottoman empire was a self-contained trading system not dependent on the world economy. In the seventeenth century the Ottoman empire still retained a degree of commercial autonomy. Ottoman merchants were still able to build their own trading networks, accumulate capital, and dominate the trade in locally produced products, but by the mid- to late eighteenth century European economic supremacy was assured, and the Ottoman empire became a dependent part of a European-dominated world trading economy.

Crisis and Change in the Ottoman System: The Seventeenth and Eighteenth Centuries

For centuries the Ottoman ruling system was built up on the basis of the systematic rationalization of regional political, cultural, and historical precedents. Ottoman state power was grounded in a refinement of the Byzantine, Muslim,

Seljuk, and Mongol precedents for regional power. By the seventeenth and eighteenth centuries the era of construction was over and the Ottoman society was evolving in ways that were detrimental to the continuation of a dominant centralized state.

One critical factor in the deformation of Ottoman power was the decline of the central state. As the slave elites gained full control of the government and as religious functionaries were entrenched in a bureaucratic regime, they began to serve their own interests rather than the long-term interests of the sultan and the state. Janissaries demanded and received exemptions from the strict requirements of the slave system and were allowed to establish families, to work in the civilian economy, and eventually to remain on the state payroll without providing military service. Provincial officials squirmed out of central control and began to usurp local resources, competing with the capital for control of local economies, diverting the flow of requisitioned goods to Istanbul, converting tax farms into various types of quasi-private property, and building up local military support. As patronage relationships became ever more important throughout the seventeenth century, Ottoman officials at all levels created large households resembling the sultan's household, households that served as a basis for patronage networks and the employment of large numbers of men. Prominent chieftains in pastoral regions rose in importance. Tax farmers had an opportunity to make themselves independent and to build political bases in the countryside. Though peasant landowning continued to be the most important form of tenure, large estates were being formed in the Black Sea region, Macedonia, Thessaly, and some parts of Anatolia, as it became increasingly lucrative to supply Istanbul and the European markets. Throughout the empire local notables—*beys*, *pashas*, and *ayans*—were taking power into their own hands.

Economic changes beyond Ottoman control helped to undermine the centralized state. The discovery of the new world and the tremendous supplies of silver brought back to Europe from American mines undermined the price stability of the whole Mediterranean and unleashed an intense competition in the Ottoman empire for control of resources. European economic competition was winning away control of international trade. The competition from India and Italy, and later from Britain, was undermining Ottoman craft production. Raw materials grew more costly, but selling prices declined. Moreover, there were deep disturbances in the economy of the Anatolian heartlands. Ottoman security and prosperity was undermined at the end of the sixteenth century and in the seventeenth century by rising population, large increases in the number of unemployed, demobilized, and unsalaried soldiers, and vagabond students and bands of armed peasants roaming and ravaging the countryside. Provincial administrators and irregular soldiers fought against the government forces.

Istanbul janissaries and local militias struggled for power in the provinces.

The Ottoman response was counterproductive. The treasury tried to reduce the expenditure on armed forces, which led to the further displacement of provincial soldiers, who then turned to brigandage. To reinforce central authority, the government had to station permanent garrisons, which then became identified with local economic interest groups that exploited their positions for their own benefit. These upheavals, collectively known as the *celali* rebellions, appear chaotic, but they had a deep political significance. As the central state weakened and as provincial officials and notables struggled to aggrandize their power, Anatolian Muslim subjects also fought to acquire the privileges reserved for the political elite. The celali rebellions then were not criminal or peasant protest movements; rather, they represented a political struggle of upwardly mobile peasants and small-town populations attempting to gain a share of the prerogatives of power.

From the Ottoman perspective, these changes were particularly ominous in the Balkans, where the tendencies toward decentralization of power and usurpation of lands, tax revenues, and supplies were exaggerated by the trade with Europe. The ready availability of export markets increased local incentives to evade Ottoman regulations and to develop local power by trading with Europe. Merchants who refused to ship fruits and grains directly to Istanbul but instead sold them to European merchants also imported muskets to defend their interests. As the de facto autonomy of the Balkan provinces increased, a new political philosophy began to take hold among Balkan intellectuals, merchants, landowners, traders, and others. Mainly Christians, less closely identified with the Ottomans than were the Muslims, Greeks, Serbs, Romanians, and others began to speak of their national identity and heritage and their right to independence from the Ottoman empire. The seeds that would undo the multireligious, multiethnic Ottoman society in favor of modern national states were already sown.

The declining power of the central state was part and parcel of a disastrous series of military setbacks. The empire, which was still expanding in the sixteenth century and stable in the seventeenth, began to lose ground to its Russian and Habsburg opponents. The Habsburgs defeated the Ottoman attack on Vienna in 1683 and invaded Hungary and Serbia, and in 1696 the Russians took Azov and gained a foothold on the Black Sea. Although the Ottomans were able to counterattack in the early decades of the eighteenth century, by the later decades of that century they suffered staggering losses. In 1774 the Russians established their supremacy in the Crimea and Romania; by the Treaty of Jassy in 1792 they were in control of the Black Sea and in a position to threaten Istanbul. In 1798 the French emperor Napoleon invaded Egypt. These defeats were clear warnings that the Ottoman empire had fallen militarily as well as commercially behind its European competitors and that its territorial integrity, even its survival, had come into question.

In this crisis the empire was swept by proposals for reform and rejuvenation. Conservative critics called for a return to the policies of the great sultan Suleyman the Lawgiver; more radical critics called for the adoption of European technology, military organization, and administrative arrangements. Ottoman society was awash in a wave of European cultural fascination. European painting, rococo decoration, and tulip gardens were the rage. A celebration of personal sensibility and expressiveness overcame the Ottoman elites. Out of this cultural ferment, the Ottoman Empire would renew itself again in the nineteenth century.

CHAPTER NINE

The Eastward Journey of Muslim Kingship

ISLAM IN SOUTH AND SOUTHEAST ASIA

Bruce B. Lawrence

Islam is above all a pan-Asian religion. It shapes the beliefs and practices of millions of Asians, from Central to South to Southeast Asia. There are other pan-Asian religions—Hinduism to the far south, Buddhism to the far east—but none that spans the southern rim of the Asian continent to the extent that Islam does.

But how did Islam become not only a religious marking but also a civilizational force from the Arabian Sea to the shores of the Pacific? That question cannot easily be answered. The emergence of distinctive social patterns in South Asia have parallels, though not equivalents, in Southeast Asia. Muslim invaders from the northeast brought with them (or developed after their arrival) traits that have since characterized the Islamic experience in South Asia for much of its known history. Centuries later, Muslim traders, coming from Arabia and India, began to settle in significant numbers in the archipelago known today as Southeast Asia. They also professed and pursued Islamic loyalty, but in different circumstances, with disparate outcomes.

Despite their conjunction in this chapter, the Muslim communities of South and Southeast Asia remain discrete and separate, both in the ideal norms they profess and in the day-to-day practices they pursue. Although it is difficult to link together two distant regions of Asia that have never known a fully shared history, the one symbolic marking that they share, Islam, justifies such an effort, especially in book that takes as its subject the entire spectrum of Islamic history.

(Left) The Mughal emperor Shah Jahan (r. 1628–66) considered himself the apogee of the dynasty that the great steppe conquerer Timur had founded 250 years earlier. Shah Jahan is depicted in this painting as the just emporer standing on a globe, and the roundels in the umbrella over his head give his genealogy back to Timur.

The Prehistory of Islamic South Asia

Certain patterns of social mobility and civic organization typify South Asia from the Indo-Aryan period (1000 B.C.E.) on: a militarized society, with a standing army that requires regular use, often to invade and conquer adjacent regions; the autocratic rule of a military leader who is invested with instrumental power but who often claims divine authority and patronizes scholars to further that claim; and the existence of monuments that commemorate religious heroes and rulers of the past, built by military leaders to strike awe in their subjects. In this sense the prehistory of Islamic South Asia is not located in the life of Muslim societies further to the west; rather, this history is located in the reigns, or the imagined reigns and legacies, of the most illustrious kings of earlier dynasties. Two such figures stand out: Alexander the Great (356–323 B.C.E.) and Asoka the Munificent (r. 272–236 B.C.E). Together they projected Greek and Buddhist legacies into South Asia. Alexander was a brilliant soldier who wanted to be remembered as a wise king. Among the scholars he patronized was Aristotle. He represented the Achaemenid style of governance linked to the Persian emperors Cyrus and Darius. Asoka founded the Mauryan dynasty. He had no courtier to rival Aristotle, but through the monumental building inspired by his dramatic conversion to Buddhism he continued the style of royal patronage familiar from his Persian-Greek predecessors. Even though no literary texts survived, Asoka's monuments did, and they were used and reused by successive dynasties, including the later Muslim monarchs of Central Asia.

Persian is the crucial element, and the thesis thus presented about Islam in South Asia accents Persian influence. Although Arabic and Turkish elements can be identified, they matter less than the Persian. Despite the fact that Islam is often identified with Arabic language and Arab norms, these merely provided the patina for Muslim expansion into the subcontinent. Although the Turks comprised the main source for Muslim armies, neither the Turkic language nor its cultural forms characterized the outlook of these newcomers to Hindustan (South Asia). Beyond the Arabic patina and the Turkic frame was the central image of this newly emerging social formation. The picture had its own design: Persianate.

Persianate is a new term, first coined by the world historian Marshall Hodgson. It depicts a cultural force that is linked to the Persian language and to self-identified Persians. But the term applies to more than either a language or a people; it highlights elements that Persians share with the Indo-Aryan rulers who preceded Muslims to the subcontinent. Two elements are paramount: hierarchy, which consists of top-down status markings that link all groups to each other in a clear order of rank that pervades all major social interactions; and deference, which requires rules of comportment toward those at the top of the status scale, especially the reigning monarch or emperor. The office of emperor first depended on military prowess, with defense of the realm, provision of public works, cultivation of land, collection of taxes, and dispensation of justice among his major administrative tasks. Equivalent to these functional aspects of his office, however, were the adornments of that office: magnificent palaces, expansive gardens, a lofty throne, and garments of unimagined splendor. In short, the emperor was the focal point of a court culture that included a range of specialists: architects and artists, craftsmen, musicians, poets, and scholars.

If this profile describes the totalitarian ideal of a hermetically sealed hierarchical system of governance, it omits several crucial elements that came to describe the kind of imperial rule exercised by the new Aryan elites—the Persianate Turks, who came to dominate North India from the tenth century on. Chief among these, as noted by Robert L. Canfield, were the use of the Persian language itself in a wide range of functions, administrative as well as literary, and the development of an expanding cultural elite that saw itself as expressing Persianate values, even when they were not fully allied with Islamic norms. This expansion and rearticulation of Indo-Aryan social values may be called either *Persianate*, to stress the importance of Persian as a linguistic component, or *Islamicate*, to acknowledge the way in which Islam was invoked even when the connection between cultural observance and religious loyalty was very slim. The two terms are so close that sometimes they can be used interchangeably. Crucial in each case is the expansion of connotative meaning to include more than linguistic usage (Persian) or religious commitment (Islamic).

The Great Indo-Muslim Rulers in South Asia

Four Indo-Muslim rulers stand out as embodiments of this new Turko-Persian Islamicate culture that prevailed in South Asia from the eleventh century on: Mahmud of Ghazna (r. 997–1030), Iltutmish (r. 1211–36), Muhammad ibn Tughluq (r. 1325–51), and Akbar (r. 1555–1604).

Because the reign of Sultan Mahmud of Ghazna (what is now Ghazni in eastern Afghanistan) set the tone for much of what followed, his legacy has been marked by controversy. Mahmud was a dogged campaigner who conducted no less than seventeen military forays into India, and he delighted in chronicling his own military feats. Like other Persian and Turko-Persian rulers, Mahmud commissioned the official histories that he wanted to stand as the record of his reign for posterity. Was he a religious zealot or a cosmopolitan pragmatist? Historians remain divided, but Mahmud's repeated military campaigns provided the basis for his successful rule. He not only pillaged and destroyed; he also built and rebuilt cities within his reign. As a patron, he was particularly adroit. In the 1020s the celebrated poet Firdowsi

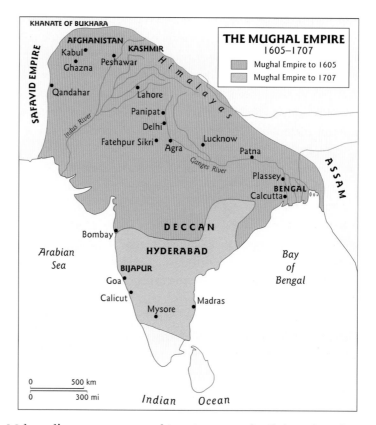

came to Mahmud's court to present his epic poem, the *Shahnameh*. Other courtiers included historians, lingists, and mathematicians, and even a polymath who was all three: the incomparable comparativist, Abu al-Rayan Ahmad al-Biruni.

Mahmud lured al-Biruni to join his royal entourage in 1018, but because the sultan was often campaigning, the scholar had to accompany him. Al-Biruni crisscrossed northwestern India with the Ghaznavid army during several forays before Mahmud and al-Biruni settled in Ghazna in the mid-1020s, where they remained until Mahmud's death in 1030. Al-Biruni resented the imposition of royal demands, but his forced travels allowed him to expand his mathematical achievements to include a comprehensive cultural and historical survey of India that still remains a classic. His *Kitab al-Hind* (Book of India) surveys the range of Hindu culture, distinguishing among history, social customs, and doctrines with a rare ethnographic sensitivity. It was completed just before Mahmud's death. Despite his prolific output, with more than 146 writings to his credit, al-Biruni is renowned chiefly for this survey and a handful of roughly twenty-one other extant works, a mere 15 percent of his entire corpus.

Mahmud's legacy fared better than al-Biruni's, at least for awhile. Because Ghazna was a city on the edge of a powerful Iranian empire, the Samanid,

Mahmud built it up to be a capital city to rival Baghdad in its cultural refinement. The warriors, who were the mainstay of Mahmud's conquests and his administration, were actually Turkic slaves who had served under Persian rulers. In the eleventh century they asserted their independence, so much so that this initial period of Turko-Persian-Islamicate expansion is often known as "the Slave Dynasties." The new Muslim elites of South Asia were Turks who favored Persianate culture and who governed in the name of Islam. They still favored their westward flank, and in addition to seeking caliphal recognition, they tried but failed to conquer Khurasan (in northeastern Iran). Instead, they expanded to the east and south, not limiting their patronage to Ghazna but extending it to another city, Lahore. The wealth of India drew them further into the subcontinent, leading them to develop Lahore as another center of Islamicate culture.

The Ghurids displaced the Ghaznavids in 1192, and pushed the leading edge of Turko-Islamicate culture further into the Aryan heartland to Delhi. Invading from the Hindu Kush mountain range, the Ghurids razed Ghazna and captured Lahore before winning Delhi. The Ghurids then made Delhi their capital and established a composite architectural style that became a pattern for other parts of Hindustan. The Ghurids' successors became known as the Mamluks, or "slave kings," of North India (not to be confused with the Mamluks of North Africa, another slave dynasty of premodern Islamic history). The Mamluks and their successors—the Khaljis, the

The immense congregational mosque in Delhi known as Quwwat al-Islam ("Might of Islam") was one of the first built in India. Begun in 1191, the mosque stands on the site of a pre-Islamic temple whose ruins were incorporated in the structure. The tall iron pillar in the courtyard, originally dedicated to the Indian god Vishnu around 400, was re-erected as a trophy to symbolize Islam's triumph over Hinduism.

The towering Qutb Minar (1199–1368), the minaret attached to the Quwwat al-Islam mosque in Delhi, combines foreign and indigenous elements. Like earlier minarets in Afghanistan, it was built in flanged stages separated by balconies, but it uses a local material, sandstone.

Tughluqs, the Sayyids, and the Lodis—were collectively known as the Delhi Sultanate. From the thirteenth to the early sixteenth centuries (1206–1526), they dominated North India. In the aftermath of Mongol incursions to the north and west, they welcomed refugees, including architects and artists, musicians, poets, and religious scholars, most of them specialists in high Persianate culture. What these specialists had learned in Central Asia, in regions such as Transoxiana and Khurasan, they in turn transmitted (and further refined) in the new cosmopolitan centers of South Asia that were now ruled by former Turkic slaves.

Among the many monuments that come from the Mamluk period, few rival the Quwwat al-Islam mosque ("The Might of Islam") located in Delhi. Although the actual name of the mosque is still debated, its central location in the new capital underscores its symbolic importance to Muslim rulers. Construction of the mosque began in 1191. It featured an enormous open quadrangle courtyard set on an earlier Hindu temple site. Hindu craftsmen used material from the demolished temples to construct a culturally hybrid place of worship, combining Hindu tastes and art in an Islamic structure. Included in the central courtyard of the mosque is a huge iron pillar of particular interest. The pillar predates Muslim rule by at least six hundred years. It is an imposing structure made of pure malleable iron, impervious to rust, and an inscription, still preserved, dedicates it to the god Vishnu in memory of a Hindu king. That same hybrid is confirmed in another edifice that separates the Quwwat al-Islam mosque from others: the dominant minaret known as the Qutb Minar that stands next to the mosque. Five stories in gradually diminishing height, it shows a perfection of calligraphic symmetry and floral ornamentation. Depending on the perspective of the viewer, it can seem to be a markedly Islamic building, with Arabic words clearly etched in each band, or a distinctive blend of Islamic and Hindu motifs can be noted, because the floral patterns that frame and interlace the Arabic words are reminiscent of both Hindu and Buddhist structures from South Asia.

Also part of the same mosque complex is a tomb that is among the earliest that Muslim rulers in India had built for themselves. Its construction was ordered by the powerful Mamluk ruler, Sultan Shams al-Din Iltutmish (r. 1211–36), six years before his death. Iltutmish did what no ruler before had done: He consolidated the disparate regions of North India into an independent polity, a kingdom bearing an Islamic stamp but allowing Hindus first safety then inclusion within the ruling strata of the Delhi Sultanate. He also held off, as

much by diplomacy as by armed force, the feared
Mongols, whose zeal for conquest had brought them to
the borders of Hindustan. He further cultivated Sufi
masters, acknowledging them as spiritual lodestones,
not only for his subjects but also for himself and his
court. It is fitting that Iltutmish would choose to have
his own tomb set within the premier mosque of thirteenth-century Delhi, because he himself had extended
the scope of the Quwwat al-Islam mosque and completed the Qutb Minar. Although never completed, his
tomb became the benchmark for royal mausoleums in
Muslim South Asia. It boasts a marble cenotaph beautifully centered within receding red sandstone arches. Its
decorative inscriptions and geometrical designs exhibit
a high level of workmanship, reflecting both Islamic
and Hindu aesthetic motifs.

If Iltutmish set the tone for inspired rule in the thirteenth century, the most important of the Turkic slave
rulers in the next century was the sultan Muhammad
ibn Tughluq (r. 1325–51). His father, Ghiyas ud-Din
Tughluq, had earlier militarily defended the sultanate
against Mongol threats. The levels of fear and revulsion
of the nascent Indo-Muslim Turks at the Mongol legions
would be difficult to exaggerate. In the words of the premier mid-fourteenth-century Deccani historian, Isami,
the Mongols were "a wretched people, with narrow
eyes, flat noses, and mouths as wide as the gates of a
palace. From their depressed noses flows a paste-like
yellowish fluid, day and night."

Ghiyas ud-Din not only coped with the Mongols,
he also annexed a major region in the south and put down a rebellion in
Bengal. Upon his death in 1325, he left his son and successor a vast, though
far from integrated, territory. It was the singular mark of Muhammad ibn
Tughluq's reign that he tried to subdue and consolidate several rebellious
rulers—Muslim as well as Hindu—in the south to forge an expanded
Islamicate realm. He picked a bold means to effect this goal: he shifted many
Turko-Persian elites from the northwest to the central south, from Delhi to
Devagiri in Deccan (the Indian peninsula south of the Narmada River). This
was not an easy move. It involved the forced transfer of approximately 10 per-
cent of Delhi's Muslim population. It wrought havoc upon the Muslim elites

In carving the decoration of
the Qutb Minar, Indian
stonemasons replaced the
traditional representational
motifs of Indian architecture
with Arabic inscriptions and
vegetal ornament.

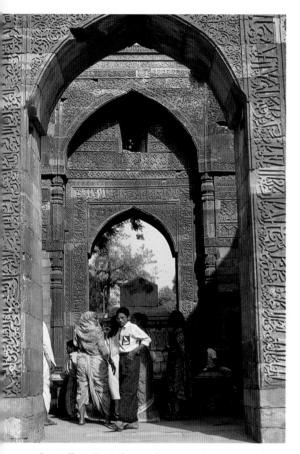

The Delhi sultan Shams al-Din Iltutmish (r. 1211–6) exemplifies the Turko-Persian-Islamicate culture that dominated South Asia from the eleventh century. His tomb in Delhi, made of red sandstone that contrasts with the white marble cenotaph, set a standard for royal mausoleaums in the region.

who were "chosen" to realize the imperial project. Many died from the rigor of the long journey from northern to southern India.

One can document the suffering and resentment felt by the unfortunate migrants, and several contemporary and later historians have taken this approach, but one may also see in this move Muhammad ibn Tughluq's pragmatic genius. He was faced with a daunting challenge in the northwestern part of his kingdom. From the mid-thirteenth century on the Mongol threat loomed large, preempting other imperial strategies. Although his predecessors plundered the south in order to reinforce the north, Muhammad ibn Tughluq sought to integrate the south (the Deccan region) into the northwest (the Indo-Gangetic plain). His goal was to safeguard and protect Islamicate society from the feared Mongol infidels. The resulting migration lasted ten years (1313–23), and it made possible what otherwise would have been unimaginable: the annexation of the formerly independendent kingdoms of Deccan into the Delhi Sultanate. To seal the symbolic significance of this large shift, Muhammad ibn Tughluq had the former capital city of Devagiri renamed Dawlatabad and made it a co-capital of the Sultanate, on a par with Delhi.

The success of the sultan's managerial boldness depended on spiritual as well as material resources. But which had priority? Even for those who opposed the move from Delhi to Dawlatabad, as did the historian Isami, its outcome was seen as dependent on a spiritual resource whose mediators were shaykhs rather than sultans. In a bold reversal of hierarchical loyalty, Isami attributed the ultimate source of power not to the Muhammad ibn Tughluq but to the spiritual slave or faqir. The "true" masters of the realm were the Sufi masters, those whom Iltutmish had earlier acknowledged as superior beings. Later rulers also identified faqirs with the core values of Turko-Persian-Islamicate culture, and among their major representatives in Hindustan were the Chishti saints of North and South India.

This logic of hierarchic reversal presents a new reading of history. What had saved North India from the Mongols, according to Isami, was was not Muhammad ibn Tughluq's army but his respect for the shrine of Shaykh Muin ad-Din Chishti (d. 1236) in Ajmer. The evidence was the sultan himself, who had journeyed to Ajmer as a pilgrim after a successful engagement

The burgeoning Muslim population of the Indian subcontinent in the thirteenth and fourteenth centuries led to the construction of mosques and the copying of the Quran. This manuscript of the Quran, transcribed at Bijapur in Deccan in 1483, uses the rough paper and
swooping bihari script typical of the region.

with the Mongols. The sultan could not control saintly power, however, and
the decline of Delhi as an imperial city from 1327 on was considered a
result, above all, of the loss of its saintly patron, in this case, Muin ad-Din's
principal successor in Delhi, Nizam ad-Din Awliya (d. 1325), but also to the
sultan's subsequent rudeness toward Nizam ad-Din's successor, Nasir ad-Din
Chiragh-i Dihli (d. 1356).

By the same logic, Isami explained the prosperity of Dawlatabad after
the great migration ending in 1323. The city's prosperity was not due to
military, political, social, or economic factors but rather to the spiritual
influence of the Chishtiya. Again, the link was to Shaykh Nizam ad-Din, for
the Chishti patron of Delhi had commissioned one of his own successors
to migrate to Deccan. It was the lineage of this man—Burhan ad-Din (d.
1337), then succeeded by Zain ad-Din Din Shirazi (d. 1369)—that made
Deccan prosper. In the words of a poem by Isami:

It was the grace of Zain ad-Din that made
This stormy world like the garden of heaven.

From his aroma the Chishti garden became fragrant;
Under his protection the whole of Deogir was saved.
Because the Tughluq governor sought his shelter,
The Tughluq star rose to the height of Saturn.
Wherever you see a fortunate amir
It's due to the blessing of a lowly faqir.

Discerning the relationship between *amir* and *faqir* is complicated, however, by the natural tension between their respective roles. Often that tension is concealed in the historical sources that project the only existing record, apart from archeological artifacts, of premodern South Asia. As previously indicated, nearly all the sources result from imperial patronage: the story is thus told by the ruler's appointed historian; they are versions doublechecked, then approved by the subjects being recorded. In every sense, these records are official biographies or chronicles. In the case of Muhammad ibn Tughluq, for example, it is not his own historian but the historian of a political rival, the Bahmanid empire of Deccan, who gives him both a backhanded compliment, to have been blessed by Muin ad-Din, and a direct rebuke, to have neglected Nizam ad-Din's successor, Nasir ad-Din (d. 1356).

At the same time, the Sufi sources are often reluctant to acknowledge links between notable saints and non-Sufi rulers. For example, Muhammad ibn Tughluq is usually classed as a non-Sufi ruler, yet it is known from an Arabic source, the travelogue of the famous traveler Ibn Battutah (1304–68 or 1369), that Muhammad ibn Tughluq, even before he became the sultan, had consulted Shaykh Nizam ad-Din. The shaykh allegedly exclaimed: "We have given him the kingdom." It would seem natural then that Muhammad ibn Tughluq was one of the privileged few to bear the bier of the shaykh to his final resting place in 1325, yet no Chishti source records that fact. The key is to see the relationship, always fraught with tension, between the autocratic temporal ruler and his ally, who was also his rival, the all-powerful eternal ruler, the Sufi saint. The most frequent outcome was cooperation between the shaykhs and the sultans. That tradition continued throughout the Delhi Sultanate as well as in other parts of India, but it did not supplant or erase the implicit rivalry between these two repositories of public authority.

The Influence of Saints

Indeed, one can trace the influence of saints, and their rivalry with rulers, from Muhammad ibn Tughluq to the next giant of Indo-Muslim culture, the Mughal emperor Akbar (r. 1555–1604). If saints had become the major custodians and transmitters of Turko-Persian-Islamicate values by the mid-fourteenth century, by the mid-sixteenth century they were even more important. A revealing barometer of this development is Akbar's checkered relationship to Chishti saints in general, and to Shaykh Salim Chishti (d. 1571) at Fatehpur Sikri (in northern India) in particular.

The Mughals were not Mongols, as their name implies, but Indo-Timurids; they were the Indian legatees of the Turkic conqueror Timur (1336–1405), who, though not a Mongol, claimed lineage traceable to Genghis Khan. Timur (or Tamerlane) was also heir to Mongol military and ruling ideals. He was both a great military conqueror and a supreme spiritual leader. His function was similar to that of the familiar Turko-Persian kings, but his extensive conquests lent even more credibility to his claim of divine inspiration and support. Characteristic of Mughal veneration for their esteemed ancestor is the miniature in a Mughal chronicle embellishing his death. From the ornate dome at the top to the humble servants at the bottom, all seem to be frozen in the moment of loss that is represented by the deceased hero in the center. Although the focus of the miniature is Timur, its patron is Akbar. The exquisite execution is characteristic of the numerous album folios that date from the period of Akbar. It indicates Akbar's interest in, and patronage of, the whole spectrum of art from the portable to the monumental. Akbar identified with Timur, and at the same time he raised the Indo-Timurid legacy to new heights.

Akbar began, as did all his most illustrious ancestors, with a stunning record of military success. He assumed rule when he was merely thirteen years old. A brief glance at the extent of the Mughal empire in the mid-sixteenth century reveals the challenge Akbar faced. He ruled a realm that represented more closely the Ghurid than the Tughluq map of Hindustan. His father Humayun, after succeeding Babur as the second Mughal ruler, had spent more than fifteen years in exile in Safavid Iran and the reconquest of India was left to Babur's grandson, Akbar. Akbar spent almost all the early years of his reign engaged in military campaigning. The results of his tactical skill and extraordinary presence as a military leader are evident. He won

To emphasize his dynasty's descent from Timur, the Mughal emperor Akbar often commissioned lavishly illustrated manuscripts about Timurid history. This scene showing the death of Timur is one of 132 large illustrations from a manuscript made in the late sixteenth century.

The Mughal emperor Akbar commissioned a magnificent tomb for his father, Humayun. The octagonal tomb is built of red sandstone enhanced with white marble, a combination that had been introduced several centuries earlier. Unlike earlier tombs, Humayun's is located in a large garden crossed by water channels and pathways.

major battles that consolidated Mughal rule over northern, central, and western India. Akbar combined military success with economic reform. Among his major economic achievements was uniting the maritime, commercial province of Gujarat with the agricultural heartlands of the Punjab and Gangetic basins, making possible an enormous expansion of trade and production. But it was his ability to conquer militarily and then to assuage his former enemies diplomatically that earned him the most revered place in Mughal annals.

Akbar also succeeded in attracting able men, both Hindu and Muslim, to serve him as courtiers. His chief tax officer was Todar Mal, a Hindu whom Akbar recruited over objections from Muslim notables. Through Todar Mal, Akbar experimented with tax reforms until he developed a system of administration and

extraction that optimized his resources. This system remained in place until modern times. Akbar had more trouble achieving control and accountability in the religious establishment, including his management of Sufi shaykhs as an alternative source of authority, not only to the *ulama* (guardians of everyday ritual and law) but also to the Mughal court. None of the official Mughal accounts explain either the nature of the Sufi brotherhoods or the attitude of their legatees and devotees toward the emperor. The *Akbarnameh*, the official history of Akbar's reign, written by Abul-Fazl under Akbar's direction, tells only the perspective of Akbar's royal patron and reduces the emperor's attitude toward Sufi masters to a single central frame narrative that highlights the blessings Akbar received from Shaykh Salim Chishti. In the story the reclusive, ascetic saint from a village near Agra solves the major problem facing the young emperor: how to produce a male heir. At age twenty-eight Akbar had produced only daughters, but in a visit to Shaykh Salim en route to Ajmer, Akbar was told by the saint that his favorite wife would produce a male heir and that he would be blessed with no fewer than three male heirs. Both predictions proved true, and in witness to the saint's power and its sequel, the future emperor of India, Jahangir (r. 1605–27), was named Prince Salim at birth.

The account of Shaykh Salim, Emperor Akbar, and Prince Salim looms large in the *Akbarnameh* because it provided the pretext for Akbar's later decision to move his imperial capital from Agra to Sikri, renamed Fatehpur Sikri. What the imperial version omitted, however, is what later readers must deduce: a series of suppressed motives that bound the emperor to the shaykh while still allowing the emperor to be the final repository of truth and authority. Without denying the spiritual motives that Abul Fazl attributed to the emperor in the official account, also evident is another pragmatic motive: Akbar identified with an illustrious India-specific order, enhancing his own legitimation as a South Asian Muslim monarch. For all the retrospective stress on the solidity of Akbar's claim to rule, it is unlikely that he quickly forgot the exile of his father Humayun from India, an exile prompted in part by Humayun's inability to counter the ideological claims and military prowess of the Afghan emperor Sher Shah of Sur (r. 1540–45), who defeated Humayun at the Battle of Chansa in 1539 and again at Kananj in 1540.

Alternatively, Akbar might have linked himself to the then-dominant tomb complex of North India, the *mazar* (tomb) of Shaykh Nizam ad-Din in Delhi. Why didn't he? His decision to build a tomb honoring his father, Humayun, was in part dictated by the proximity of its site to the tomb of Nizam ad-Din. The tomb complex of Humayun remains today a magnificent example of Akbar's attention to memorials for the dead. Although the tomb's actual designer may have been Humayun's widow, its patron and guiding force was the young emperor. Its central structure combines indigenous building traditions with familiar Persianate emphases. As white marble inlaid in red sand-stone lightened the octagonal formality of Humayun's tomb, its setting in a four-cornered garden on a vast plane augured a new tradition of tomb gardens known as the Mughal style.

Although his predecessors favored Delhi, the young Akbar was suspicious of its past. Delhi was, after all, the stronghold of Turko-Afghan elites with mini-mal loyalty to the fledgling Mughal dynasty. For more than three hundred years, Delhi had been the capital of Muslim dynasties in North India, and it was only the Afghan king Sikander Lodi (r. 1489–1517) who had opted to make Agra his new capital. Agra continued to serve as the capital for his successor, the last Lodi sultan, Ibrahim (r. 1517–26). It remained the imperial center for the brief period of Babur's reign (r. 1526–30), but Humayun, both before and after his exile in Iran, preferred Delhi. In securing his own rule at Agra (1556–70), Akbar had to be aware of the tension between Agra and Delhi as rival imperial centers. In part because of their asymmetry (Delhi had the longer history, Agra the more imme-diate strategic advantage), Akbar sought still another base from which to pro-ject his distinctive version of imperial authority. But another site could not simply be chosen; the choice had to have symbolic and legitimating power such that others would be led to accept the rightness of the emperor's decision. By linking the location of Sikri to the saint who predicted the birth of Akbar's heirs and successors, Akbar made its selection as a new imperial center seem logical, even compelling.

There were also other advantages that appealed to the spiritual dimension of Akbar's multifaceted personality. Having chosen Fatehpur Sikri, he was able to confirm and continue his affiliation with the tomb of Shaykh Muin ad-Din in Ajmer while also drawing on the power of a living saint, Shaykh Salim, and

Akbar founded a red sand-stone capital twenty-five miles west of Agra at Sikri, site of the hermitage of Sufi Shaykh Salim Chisti (1479–1571). The emperor hoped to tap the Sufi's *baraka* or "spiritual power" and promote his claims to legiti-macy. The saint's grave was marked by a splendid white marble tomb.

through him on the spiritual *baraka* (blessing) that derived from his ascetic patron, Shaykh Farid ad-Din Ganj-i Shakar (d. 1265) in Punjab. Through a two-fold, redoubled Chishti loyalty, Akbar could spiritually anchor his imperial legitimacy in provinces adjacent to Uttar Pradesh: Punjab and Rajasthan. Both regions were crucial to the politicol-military ambitions of his reign.

The Monumental Art of the Mughal Emperors

Akbar had begun to sponsor monumental art on a new and expansive scale even before the foundation the new capital at Fatehpur Sikri. As important as Akbar's affiliation with Chishti saints was for the Fatehpur Sikri phase of his life, it became irrelevant during the final twenty years of his reign, as he moved from one temporary capital to another. This abrupt shift in loyalty had an impact on institutional Sufism that reverberated throughout the Mughal period. As neither Shaykh Salim nor Shaykh Muin ad-Din remained a constant focus of Akbar's allegiance, Fatehpur Sikri was sited as a temporary rather than a permanent capital city. For Akbar it was the emperor, not a place or a saint, who lauded as the apogee of spiritual and temporal authority in the Mughal polity. To the extent that his person became the metaphor for his realm, spiritual luminaries could only function by being linked to or subordinated within the aura of his ultimate, imperial authority. The absolutist claims that were raised by Akbar, or by Abul-Fazl in Akbar's name, forced a redefinition of both sainthood and dynastic succession.

In 1577 Abul-Fazl's father, Shaykh Mubarak, drafted the *mahzar* (decree). Its intention was to affirm the emperor's spiritual supremacy; at this time the emperor officially became superior to all religious functionaries and institutions. By this time the Chishtiya had already lost whatever benefit its partisans—whether shrine custodians, living saints, or Hindu-Muslim devotees—may have gained by the favor that Akbar had showered on them. Such courtiers as the chief religious officer, Abd an-Nabi, and Shaykh Mubarak were removed from active advocacy of either their own Sufi legacy or the active mystical interests of others. Nor did the construction of Shaykh Salim's tomb within the walled courtyard of the central mosque at Fatehpur Sikri promote the spiritual agenda of the Chishti lineage that he represented. Instead, the founding of the capital at Fatehpur Sikri affirmed Akbar—his brand of Islamic observance and his legitimate claim to rule as Timur's offspring.

Akbar's visits to saints' tombs after 1577 reveal his changed mood. He visited Delhi only once, and spent most of his time at Humayun's tomb. When he did visit a couple of provincial saintly shrines, he used these visits to draw attention to his own superior claims to spiritual favor. The Sufi exemplars who shaped the first phase of Akbar's rule were eclipsed and then gradually forgotten toward the final years of his life.

Like Humayun's tomb at Delhi, Akbar's own tomb at Sikandara, five miles northwest of Agra, was set in a vast garden complex crossed by water channels. A soaring gateway crowned by four white marble minarets gave access to the complex.

One of Akbar's most solemn acts of remembrance concerned his own burial site. Like the powerful Mamluk ruler Iltutmish, Akbar planned his own tomb. The site—named Sikandara, suggesting the link between Akbar and another legendary military genius, Alexander the Great—was located on the outskirts of Agra in a sumptuous garden complex. The actual construction, and perhaps even the elements of the design, were left to Akbar's son and successor, Jahangir. Its major feature, dwarfing the tomb itself, is the tomb's enormous gate, which was not finished until 1614. Red sandstone forms the backdrop for intricate geometric patterns, including the reverse swastika, as well as delicate floral designs, all etched in black and white marble. Floating atop the entire edifice, almost suspended by their light surface, are four white marble minarets. The elderly Akbar may not have anticipated the full beauty of his final resting place, but the depiction of him commissioned by his grandson, Shah Jahan, shows a figure so engaged by nature (in this case, by a tiny sparrow) that the ethereal quality of his tomb seems entirely fitting.

If the glorification of the emperor lay at the heart of Mughal art and architecture for Akbar, it was an emphasis that he transmitted to his successors. The Great Mughal—whether Akbar, Jahangir, Shah Jahan, or Aurangzeb—was more concerned with his own office and image than with loyalty to another spiritual or temporal authority. Sufi saints fit the emperor's clothes, not the reverse. Jahangir (1569–1627) is often portrayed as similar to his father, devoted to brotherhoods in general but to the Chishtiya in particular. But after 1618 Jahangir also turned from Chishti devotionalism to a more diffuse spirituality, one that also encompassed the rival Naqshbandi Sufi order. In a miniature thought to have been painted in 1616, toward the end of a three-year period when Jahangir resided in Ajmer, Jahangir is portrayed as handing a book to a saintly figure, Shaykh Husain, who was the primary custodian of the Ajmer shrine. A Persian quatrain on the border suggests that the emperor, although courted by kings (including James I of England), looks to dervishes instead for guidance. But the miniature communicates another message that may contradict lyrical truth: angelic figures above and below an hourglass throne attend to the emperor, and the emperor alone, as the figure of destiny. The ones above register both awe at his halo and distress at their broken arrows, while the ones below are writing a band that reads: "O king, may the span of your life be a thousand years." In the register of eternity, both the saint and other kings are but witnesses to the axis of Divine Favor, the Indo-Timurid emperor.

What is hinted at in this miniature becomes more compellingly clear in the architectural achievements of Jahangir's reign. Many are monuments to the dead. While Jahangir's father's tomb at Sikandara registers Akbar's own genius, other mausoleums of lasting influence are at least in part due to the impact of Jahangir's favorite wife, Nur Jahan, whom he married in 1611. Nur Jahan, together with her brother, Asaf Khan, and her father, Itimad al-Dawla, formed a family clique that increasingly came to control the affairs of the Mughal empire, especially as Jahangir began to suffer ill health in the 1620s. When her father and mother both died in 1621, Nur Jahan, as an act of filial devotion, oversaw the financing and construction of a garden tomb for them that is at once lovely and lavish. It builds on the concept of nine bays, which characterized Humayun's tomb, but subordinates each bay to a central vault. Each interior room is painted with flowers, vases, and wine vessels, while the exterior surface of white marble is suffused both with precious stone inlays of paradisiacal images and with marble screens not unlike those found at the tomb of Shaykh Salim Chishti at Fatehpur Sikri.

What is perhaps most intriguing about the tomb of Itimad al-Dawla, however, is its anticipation of the crowning achievement of Mughal funerary architecture, the Taj Mahal. It is no accident that the tomb, which was not completed until 1628 and only after the outlay of vast sums, was the first major monument of Mughal India to be fully executed by a woman. Although Humayun's tomb and Akbar's plan for his own mausoleum signaled the honor accorded emperors, the mausoleum for Itimad al-Dawla indeed honored a first minister and his wife, but also the woman who made its construction possible, his daughter, who was also the emperor's wife, Nur Jahan. More than proximity in Agra link the tomb of Nur Jahan's parents, known as Itimad al-Dawla, and the Taj Mahal. It was soon after her own marriage to Jahangir in 1611 that Nur Jahan arranged to have her niece, the daughter of her brother, Asaf Khan, himself a courtier at the Mughal court, married to the heir apparent, Prince Khurram, who later became Shah Jahan. Nur Jahan's niece, Arjumand Banu, later became known as Mumtaz Mahal. It is she, of course, who occasioned the still more extravagant outpouring of funds from the imperial treasury, the result of which was the monument known as the Taj Mahal.

It is not possible to understand the vagaries of history that produced such an extraordinary architectural legacy without realizing that its planning and execu-

The red sandstone gateway to Akbar's tomb is decorated in white, gray, and black marble. In addition to Arabic inscriptions, the panels contain geometric designs and large-scale floral arabesques derived from the patterns on contemporary textiles.

Like other Mughal emperors, Akbar glorified his lineage, and paintings made for him emphasize his kingly role. In this portrait commissioned by his grandson Shah Jahan around 1650, the emperor holds a small turban ornament. The small vignettes in the margins of the page show Mughal interest in the natural world, daily life, and European prints.

Like his father, Akbar, Jahangir was devoted to the Sufis. This image, made for an album now in St. Petersburg, shows the emperor presenting a book to the aged Shaykh Husayn, descendant of Muin al-Din Chishti and superintendent of his shrine at Ajmer, where Jahangir lived from 1613 to 1616.

tion depended on the absolute supremacy of the reigning monarch. The notion of divine kingship, stretching back to the Turkic conqueror Timur but strengthened by Akbar, was continued by Jahangir but even more by his son, the emperor Shah Jahan (r. 1628–58). During his reign, he guided the affairs of state as a military officer, an administrator, a patron, and a conciliator, with the firm hand that his grandfather, Akbar, had earlier displayed. The result was extraordinary material wealth but also the recirculation of that wealth through patronage, in portable arts but even more so in monumental architecture.

Illustrated in one miniature is the extent to which Shah Jahan, whose name means "world ruler," conceived himself as the apogee of the Timurid lineage. Not only are the angels more riveted on him than those on the earlier miniature of Jahangir, but an angel in the middle holds an umbrella on the border of which is inscribed Shah Jahan's geneaology going back to Timur. Like the lion and the sheep, natural rivalries among humans are eliminated; all are cowed by the imperial presence. So too are the holy men depicted on the miniature: in two rows they stream toward the center. They face two scales, representing the balance of justice maintained in the world by the emperor, who combined power

The tomb at Agra built for Itimad al-Dawla (1622–28), Jahangir's father-in-law and minister of finance, and for his wife, was the first major Mughal monument commissioned by a woman. Like other imperial tombs, it is set in a quadripartite garden, but the tomb itself is the first structure in India in which white marble is inlaid with multicolored semiprecious stones.

(the angel with the sword) and patronage (the angel with the crown). Although the artistic technique of this miniature might be criticized as less than perfect (imperial trousers should never be fully exposed!), its message is clear: Shah Jahan ruled as *Shahanshah-i Adil*, the Just Emperor.

The Taj Mahal, even more than the actual seat of Mughal emperors, the Peacock Throne, or the massive monuments of Delhi, became the major achievement marking Shah Jahan's thirty-year reign of justice. It commemorates Nur Jahan's niece, Mumtaz Mahal, who died in childbirth in 1631. It was her death that spurred the grief-stricken emperor to construct a monument of staggering proportions. Situated on the bank of the Yamuna River in a garden complex covering forty-two acres, it is flanked by two perfectly proportioned mosque structures (only one of which is an actual mosque) that serve as a backdrop to the transcendent perfection of the central tomb complex, the Taj itself. Begun one year after Mumtaz Mahal's death, it was nearly completed by 1643 when Shah Jahan lavishly celebrated the anniversary, or *urs*, of his wife's death. The whole complex is essentially Persianate in tone and Timurid in structure. Its basic structure resembles Humayun's tomb, yet its fluid character, its graceful inclusion of inlaid motifs with marble screens, harks back to the tomb of Itimad al-Dawla. Because of the extensive and haunting Quranic verses that lace its borders from every side, the Taj Mahal may be a vast allegorical anticipation of the Day of Resurrection as imagined in Muslim cosmology and graphically depicted in the writings of the major Andalusian shaykh, Ibn al-Arabi (1165–1240), well known both to

The Taj Mahal (1631–47), the tomb that Shah Jahan built in memory of his wife Mumtaz Mahal, is the crowning achievement of the emperor's reign and one of the landmarks of world architecture. The octagonal shape and tall dome hark back to Timurid prototypes, but the vast scale and perfect proportions attest to Mughal mastery of materials and forms.

Set in a garden complex on the banks of the Yamuna River in Agra, the Taj Mahal stands opposite the tomb of Itimad al-Dawla. Like its predecessor, the Taj Mahal is made of white marble inlaid with multicolored semiprecious stones. The cenotaphs of the emperor and his wife are decorated with Arabic inscriptions and exquisite floral arabesques.

Shah Jahan and to his courtiers. It is possible to relate every feature of the Taj to the allegory of the Final Judgment. Its vast gardens become the gardens of paradise, the main entrance its gateway, the fountains heavenly streams, while the marble tomb looms as the base of the throne of God, supported by the four minarets.

Even in a less-exalted interpretation of the Taj Mahal, it remains an architectural wonder, the apotheosis of Shah Jahan's attempt to harmonize his vision of Islamic loyalty and Timurid glory. His vision of perpetual justice, divinely ordained and artistically etched, was channeled to his oldest son and successor, Dara Shikoh (1615–59). He was a mercurial figure, trained in the military and diplomatic arts, without which no ruler could succeed, but at the same time he was genuinely com-

mitted to mystic pursuits. Unlike his father, grandfather, and great-grandfather, Dara Shikoh seemed not only to engage saints in his service but also to submit himself to their guidance. While still a youth, he is said to have visited a famous Qadiri saint in Lahore when in the throes of a debilitating illness. He recovered and credited his recovery to that saint, Miyan Mir. Later, in 1640, he became the disciple of one of Miyan Mir's major successors, Mullah Shah Badakhsi. A miniature completed in 1635, just before Miyan Mir's death, shows Dara Shikoh at the feet of the two saints. The contrast with the earlier miniatures of Jahangir and Shah Jahan could not be more complete.

It was not Dara Shikoh, however, but his younger brother, Aurangzeb (1618–1707), who succeeded Shah Jahan and became the last, longest ruling, and possibly most controversial of the great Mughal emperors. After defeating his brothers in a bitter war

Although primarily known for their monumental tombs, the Mughal emperors also founded congregational mosques. Shah Jahan, for example, included a large one in his new walled city of Shahjahanabad in Delhi. Built between 1650 and 1656, the mosque, like the Red Fort opposite, is faced with red sandstone.

Dara Shikoh, eldest son and successor of Shah Jahan, was interested in mysticism like his forefathers, but his devotion seemed more sincere. In this painting, made around 1635, Dara Shikoh (wearing an orange robe) is seated before two Sufi saints, his teacher Miyan Mir (wearing white), the great Sufi mystic from Lahore, and his successor, Mulla Shah (wearing black). The halos distinguishing these three figures are allegorical elements assimilated from European paintings.

of succession, he also imprisoned his aged father, Shah Jahan, in Agra Fort. From 1658 to 1707 Aurangzeb (also known as Alamgir) maintained at least the outer unity of the far-flung Mughal domain. During the first half of his reign (1658–81), he conducted protracted military operations against the insurgent Marathas from Delhi. He moved his capital to a town in Deccan, which he expanded, fortified, and renamed Aurangabad. Although he was not successful in defeating the Marathas, Aurangzeb perpetuated the Turko-Persian-Islamicate tradition. More than his Indo-Timurid predecessors, he stressed Islamic juridical norms as the heart of his own life quest. He lived a simple life, keeping dress, food, and diversions to a minimum. He earned income from writing copies of the Quran, which he then distributed to the poor. His own modesty is reflected in his tomb, originally a stone cenotaph near the Chishti tomb complex known as Khuldabad. It was covered with a plain marble slab inside a marble-screened terrace by the Nizam of Hyderabad in the early twentieth century.

Aurangzeb was not only personally pious, he extended his own preferences to the administration of the empire. He either curtailed or altogether eliminated official patronage of music, poetry, history, and even painting. Although his efforts to repair and maintain mosques won him the gratitude of the Muslim religious classes, less popular was his creation of a moral policeman (*muhtasib*) for all major towns and cities in the empire. The muhtasib could enforce juridical limits on wine consumption, gambling, and other "objectionable" forms of behavior. Even less popular was his decision in 1679 to reimpose the *jizya*, which obliged his Hindu subjects to pay a property tax levied on all non-Muslims.

Not all aspects of Aurangzeb's personality were consistent. He is said to have criticized the extravagance involved in the construction of the Taj Mahal, even though its occupants were his own mother (and after 1666 his father as well). Yet he clearly loved gardens and could not suppress the urge to have his own favorite wife, Rabia Daurani, who died in 1657, buried in a monumental white tomb that he had modeled after the Taj Mahal. The resulting edifice is a gaunt structure. Completed in four years by the son of the architect of the Taj Mahal, it captures the marvelous central dome of the Taj but the structure is only half the size of its model, and it seems to have its minarets so sharply positioned near the tomb that its verticality, not its

Aurangzeb, the last and most controversial of the Mughal emperors, was buried near the tombs of Chisti saints at Khuldabad in western India. His grave was originally marked by a simple stone cenotaph, reflecting his piety and modesty, but in the early twentieth century, the Nizam of Hyderabad added a white marble facing and screened terrace.

harmony, is accented. Furthermore, there is no inlaid work in the tomb itself and the exterior panels are covered with less intricate or gracious panels than the Taj Mahal. Yet the Bibi ka Maqbara (Tomb of the Wife), as it is popularly known, is the last imperial Mughal tomb built in a four-cornered garden complex. Like its patron Aurangzeb, it represents the fading of an aesthetic tradition that dominated for more than a century from the accession of Akbar in 1556 to the imprisonment of Shah Jahan in 1658.

Although it is impossible to bring out the full legacy of Mughal rule, and by extension Muslim rule, in South Asia, this is evident in the tombs and books that stand out as royal emblems. They remain marks of a Turkish then Timurid imperial will to stamp the future with the actions of the past. From Iltutmish to Akbar to Shah Jahan, one can glean a consistency of intent, if not of style, and Aurangzeb, even though he tended to stress the sacred word, still made room for the visual, expressive element of Persianate culture. In every case, it is kings and kingships that perpetuate, even as they redefine, a tradition of absolute rule in the name of Islam.

The Emergence of Islam in Southeast Asia

The emergence of Islam in Southeast Asia is both an extension of Muslim history in the Asian subcontinent and an independent expression of Islamic civilization unrelated to any history except its own. The major feature of Southeast Asia is topographical: it provides access to major trading routes, allowing it to connect two main land masses, India and China, by sea. The strait of Malacca (Melaka) was the strategic link in the trade between India and China. It connected the Bay of Bengal with the South China Sea. Like the Malabar coast, the strait was a hinge in the monsoonal sailing system. Vessels crossing the Bay of Bengal eastbound on the summer monsoon could normally reach China before

The presence of Islam in Southeast Asia should be understood through the series of harbor cities that served as places for the exchange and transshipment of goods between China and the West. Melaka, founded around 1400, was the major entrepôt on the northern side of the strait of Malacca, and the city's power and culture expanded to include other neighboring regions, such as Kuala Kangsar, 200 miles to the northwest.

the opposing northeast wind set in. They would then winter in a port along the strait before continuing around the Malay peninsula and across the South China Sea in April or May. The easiest option for India-based merchants was to sell their goods in the strait towns and then return directly to Malabar on the winter wind. Chinese shippers would follow the same seasonal pattern of travel and trade, only in reverse. So important was trade and travel to Southeast Asia that one might expect to find pictures of the vessels in which merchants and migrants voyaged to the archipelago. Yet such pictures are rare. The closest existing replica may be a figure taken from a Mughal manuscript, which describes a sixteenth-century Indian ship doing service as "Noah's ark," although it may in fact resemble the kind of vessels that brought Indian traders to parts east, including the archipelago.

Because trade impelled Indian Muslims to make the long, often perilous trips to Southeast Asia, it is not surprising that the Muslim traveler Ibn Battutah provided the first written record of Muslim settlements in the archipelago. A fourteenth-century exemplar of wanderlust, Ibn Battutah journeyed from the west to the east, sailing from Andalusia to northern Africa, then across the Mediterranean, the Red Sea, and the Indian Ocean until he reached the Malay archipelago en route to China. In 1345 Ibn Battutah was on board an Indian vessel that stopped in Pase, a port city in present-day Sumatra. He noted the presence of a flourishing Muslim community there, yet Ibn Battutah tells little else about the history of either Pase or the surrounding communities. His tantalizing record mirrors the rest of the Malay archipelago: it has a vibrant past but little contemporary data, either archeological or historical, on which to reconstruct the emergence of Muslim polities.

The first task for serious inquiry into Southeast Asia's past is to go behind the names of such modern nation-states as Indonesia and Malaysia. Even the term Southeast Asia must be abandoned, and the simple geographic facts of the region must be considered. There is a string of islands, most of which are incapable of sustaining large populations. Above all, there is severe internal fragmentation, with the primary focal points being the harbor cities, which become places for the exchange and transshipment of goods between China and the West. In other words, there is not a history, a heritage, or a tradition that could identify and stand for the region as a whole in the way that the Turko-Persianate tradition came to dominate Islamic South Asia in the premodern period. Instead, in Southeast Asia there is a mosaic of starts, stops, and piecemeal development. One must never lose sight of the discrete, idiosyncratic, and diverse character of the port cities of the region, which were the focus of Islamic settlements.

The most significant feature of Islam in Southeast Asia before 1700 therefore is the absence of main narratives. In vain, scholars have looked for official or unofficial records that might have been preserved in the multiple manuscripts now available for public scrutiny. Unlike the Delhi Sultanate or the Mughal empire, which shaped the Turko-Persianate tradition of the Indian subcontinent, the Malay archipelago does not provide signposts to use to identify and discern the patterns of Southeast Asian Islamicate civilization. Instead, there are discrete areas, of which five will be discussed: Acheh, Samudra, Melaka, Moluccas and Sulawesi, and Java.

The Early Muslim Kingdoms of Acheh

Acheh was the first region of modern-day Indonesia in which Muslim kingdoms were founded. Marco Polo observed a Muslim king on the north coast of Sumatra in 1292, more than a half century before the oceanic voyage of Ibn Battutah landed him further to the south on the same island. The Portuguese voyager Tome Pires, writing in the early sixteenth century, provided the earliest ethnographic record of Acheh. His account reinforces the notion of fragmentation: the center is held together by a strong ruler, but the surrounding villages both protect and challenge the harbor cities. There are no city walls, no forts, no mountain castles but instead a system of constant exchange and negotiation. The rulers of Acheh are identified as orthodox Muslims holding sway over a splendid court. Their wealth depended on the tribute that they levied from neighboring regions and also from ships that used the harbor at Acheh.

Later the rulers of Acheh were able to benefit from overseas ties to powerful Muslim allies, both in India (the Mughals) and Turkey (the Ottomans). Yet they never subdued the interior of the island. Even when the Achinese empire was at its height, during the second half of the sixteenth and first half of the seventeenth centuries, the sultan's authority was confined to the immediate vicinity of the capital. Acheh itself was divided into many smaller districts, each governed by hereditary chiefs who constantly feuded with one another. It was the prince of the port of Acheh who served as the common overlord and carried the title of sultan.

It is tempting to see parallels with the Mughals, because the seal of the sultan of Acheh was based on a ninefold pattern, as was that of the Mughal emperors. A mid-nineteenth century coin, which traces the Achinese royal lineage back to the early thirteenth century, further suggested continuity with South Asian Muslim monarchs, but this continuity is limited by two immediate, overriding differences: first, the meaning of the seals was not the same, because the shadow of God on earth, a key epithet of the ruler in both polities, projected the great Mughal as the semidivine lord of a vast realm, while it is doubtful that more than

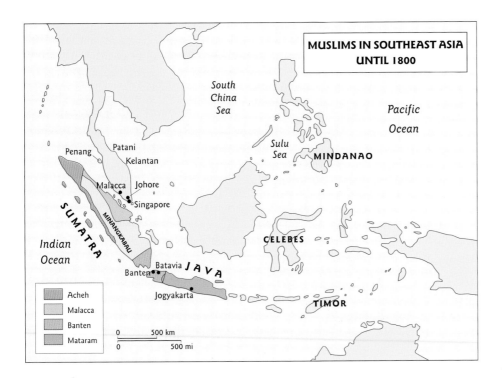

a handful of Achinese courtiers ever attributed suprahuman qualities to the sultan of Acheh; and second, the ninefold seal was not itself the most important seal of the Achinese court. For the hereditary chiefs of Acheh, James Siegel has argued, the paramount seal was the fivefold seal, which signified the hand as a symbol of power and meant the chief's ability not only to project power over others but also to protect his own possessions and territory.

From a religious perspective, what became evident is the development of a form of Islamic devotion that is linked to the mediating power of Muslim saints. Scholars imagine that there may have been intricate relationships between temporal and spiritual power in Southeast Asia that resembled those in South Asia, but that remains a conjecture. Despite occasional literary giants, such as the Sufi poet Hamzah al-Fansuri, who wrote in the mid-sixteenth to the early seventeenth centuries, there is no contemporary history of major saints or their tombs. Yet saint's tombs were built and their mere existence is itself important. Even though the tombs are less grand than those of Mughal India, in Acheh as elsewhere the tradition of visiting saintly tombs still exists. The purpose of these visits resembles what was observed in South Asia: whatever their background or status, pilgrims came with gifts and vows seeking the spiritual favor of saints for material or medical relief.

More open to question is the relation of formal religious authorities to representatives of indigenous traditions. The oft-repeated dyad pits preconversionary disbelief (*jahliya*) against divinely revealed faith (*iman* or *islam*). This is an attractive dyad because it suggests a radical experiential break between the old and the new, the impure and the pure, the false and the true. In Southeast Asian Islam the dyad is framed as *adat*, referring to all that stands outside juridical Islam, and *hukum*, meaning "laws" or the announced guidelines of an Islamic code that governs collective life. Yet the distinction is more projected than observed; it remains an ideal type, not a lived experience. In Achinese history the two polar extremes of social identity can, and often do, merge. Instead of outright hostility, one finds at least tacit politeness, and frequently mutual respect, between the so-called representatives of adat, the hereditary chiefs, and the champions of hukum, the *ulama* (religious scholars).

The greatest source of tension in Achinese history, and Malay history in general, lies outside religious worldviews and their exponents. It is the unending struggle between marginal and central groups. Before the Dutch ascendancy in the archipelago from the early seventeenth century and in Acheh from the mid-nineteenth century, the harbor sultan tried to keep Acheh integrally cohesive by subsuming hereditary chiefs under his authority. But the Dutch declared war against the Achinese, and that war lasted more than thirty-five years, continuing into the twentieth century. It reduced the prominence of Acheh and shifted the reins of political power to Java. Not until 1956, and only after a bloody guerilla campaign against Indonesian forces, did Acheh become again what it had been in the premodern period: an autonomous province, characterized by independent practices, both political and religious, from the dominant center.

The Pivotal Role of Samudra in the Expansion of Islam

Although the history of Samudra is linked to that of Acheh, it is nonetheless discrete and independent in many respects. The first recorded Muslim king of Samudra, Merah Silu (d. 1297), assumed the Islamic title of *al-Malik as-Salih* (the Righteous King). There are no chronicles, either official or unofficial, to trace the subsequent history of his dynasty. Samudra, along with Melaka, seems to have played a pivotal role in the expansion of Islam throughout the archipelago. All conjectures depend on decoding opaque references in tombstones and coins as well as a handful of chronicles, mostly foreign. Dynastic power and influence were linked to the port cities. From the port of Samudra, also known as Pasai, Islamic loyalty radiated to other parts of the Malay archipelago. Its internal vehicle of transmission remained linked to courts, which were also located in or near the major port cities. Rather than extracting wealth from interior sources, whether through commerce or agriculture, the rulers of Samudra and other harbor sultans depended on the wealth that was generated through trade. From the fourteenth century on, foreign trade remained in Muslim hands, and so the ethos of port cities reflected Islamic cultural norms. Indigenous norms were incorporated but never eliminated. Retrospectively, then, the historian is perpetually faced with the question of what should be stressed, the Islamic difference (epitomized as *hukum*) or the persistence of indigenous norms (*adat*).

Again, the precious details from Ibn Battutah's account allow scholars to imagine a Muslim court in Samudra-Pasai. The Andalusian adventurer attended the central mosque for the Friday prayer service. He also frequented the court with foreign scholars in attendance, speaking Arabic or Persian to a small group of like-minded people. (Modern scholars presume that the conversations were then summarized in Malay for the ruler's benefit.) In every other respect, however, the palace of Samudra followed custom and ritual that differed little from the Hindu-Buddhist states of the Malay archipelago. What most concerned the Muslim rulers of Samudra-Pasai was not the propagation of Islam to the hinterland but relations with their regional rivals. The traditional enemy of Pasai was another Sumatran regional power, Pedir, but Pasai also rivaled Acheh for overseas trade. When the Portuguese captured Melaka in 1511, Acheh was temporarily weakened to Pasai's benefit, but by the end of the sixteenth century Pasai was already in the throes of an economic and political decline from which it never recovered.

The Muslim Port State of Melaka

Because Melaka (also known as Malacca) was founded in about 1400, it has claims to be almost as early a Muslim port state as either Acheh or Pasai, yet this kernel of historical truth is elusive. In the case of Melaka, the historical account derives both from the Portuguese records of Tome Pires, written after the conquest of Melaka in 1511, and from an indigenous source, the *Sejarah Melayu*, which can only be corroborated as a written record in the early seventeenth century. Both accounts agree that an extraordinary entrepôt emerged on the northern side of the Strait of Malacca. It can be traced back to the pre-Muslim kingdom of Srivijaya, and it was no doubt the power and wealth of mercantile culture in the Malay peninsula that produced both Srivijaya and its successor state, the Melaka state. The Melaka state, like its archipelago rivals, boasted a Muslim royal lineage that began with its founder and ruler, the Malay prince Paramesvara (r. 1403–24), who converted to Islam in 1413, and extended to the sultan Mahmud Shah (r.

1488–1511). Though it never conquered either Pasai or Acheh, Melaka rivaled them for regional influence.

Because Melaka was also a conquering state and expanded territorially to include other regions to the north and vassal states to the south, it might even be said that Melaka provided the catalyst for a common cultural idiom that over time came to characterize much of the archipelago. In literature, governance, music, dance, dress, and food, Melaka set a standard that other port city sultanates emulated. Startling even to the Portuguese conquerors was the extent to which most of Sumatra's east coast had been influenced by its northern neighbor; almost all urban elites spoke Melakan Malay, and they also acknowledged not only correct speech but also good manners and appropriate behavior as Malay custom. Islam also came to be measured by its practice in Melaka. Although both Acheh and Samudra-Pasai had a major role in promoting Islamic identity among their own vassals, the Malay society of Melaka set its stamp on the newly emergent forms of Islamic loyalty and identity, so much so that to become Muslim was in effect to *masuk Melayu*, that is, "to enter the realm of the Melayu" or Malays.

In the late fifteenth century the Portuguese became committed to monopolizing the Asian spice trade, and they viewed Melaka as a crucial target of future conquest. Because of superior firepower, aided by internal dissent among Melaka's ruling elites, the Portuguese warrior extraordinaire, Afonsode Albuquerque, was able to capture the capital city in 1511 and to expand Portugese influence progressively further to the east. Eventually Portugese commercial and military ambitions were thwarted, although not by indigenous resistance but rather by the arrival of a superior European naval force, the Dutch, in the early seventeenth century.

The Spice-Rich Islands of the Moluccas and Sulawesi

The prize for both the Portugese and the Dutch were the spice-rich islands known as the Moluccas and Sulawesi. Although the Moluccas are so small as to merit almost no attention in studies of Southeast Asia, they are significant as the furthest edge of the Malay cultural zone, which begins in Acheh but had its center of diffusion to the north, in Melaka (Malacca). If *Molucca* sounds like *Malacca*, it is because the two extremes of the Malay archipelago are related by common linguistic and cultural patterns as well as by commercial and social exchange. Despite the earlier caveat that there is too much internal fragmentation in Southeast Asia to speak of a common civilization in the premodern period, the history of the Moluccas suggests that at least the elements of a core Southeast Asian Islamicate world can be derived from the Malay cultural complex and then traced eastward through much of the archipelago.

The Moluccas bring out what is only hinted at in most sources but needs to be stressed repeatedly: Adat and hukum can and do coexist, without existential angst or psychic breakdown, in the same groups who identify themselves as Muslims. In parts of the central Moluccas participation in the more iconic practices of Islam—such as abstaining from eating pork, attending communal prayer, and observing Ramadan—coexist with an open invocation of the ancestors, magic, and sorcery. In some places pilgrimage to sacred places is regarded as an acceptable substitute for the *hajj*, with it being seen as an Arab custom not required of "true" Muslims. In practice, the seeming contradictions between adat and hukum are often minimized; they remain latent and potential rather than actual, especially because they can often be resolved through skillful resort to the *Shariah* (eternal Islamic law).

Next door to the Moluccas, in Sulawesi, it is equally difficult to demarcate too sharply the particular from the universal. Hereditary kingship, however spottily documented, seems to be the linchpin to understanding the emergence of new Islamic communities. Islam was introduced to Sulawesi through the connection with Melaka and Acheh. As the Malay language increasingly became a lingua franca for the entire archipelago through the fifteenth and sixteenth centuries, the rulers of southern Sulawesi were drawn to imitate the Muslim model of success. Impressed by the example of the sultanate of Acheh, they embraced Islam in 1605. There are no coins celebrating kingship, as noted in Samudra, but because commerce between India and the archipelago was constant, the legend of Mughal dynastic success must have been at least as impressive in Makassar, the capital of south Sulawesi, as it was in Rome or London. It is also likely that the sultan of Sulawesi knew that the power of Acheh, especially after the fall of Melaka, had been buttressed by help from the Ottoman king of kings, Suleyman the Magnificent (r. 1520–66).

Despite the anti-Arab bias in many circles, pilgrims returning from the Hejaz (the seat of the holy cities of Mecca and Medina) would have reinforced the mystique of Muslim kings, whether Ottoman or Mughal. Each Sulawesi ruler, like his Achinese counterpart, was thus able to project himself through court chroniclers and Sufi poets as the true king, just and wise, the shadow of God on earth, the axial point of a new and expanding Muslim community. The problem of fragmentation remained, however. In Sulawesi, as in Acheh and Melaka, the number of those receptive to such a lofty notion of Islamic kingship was limited to the port cities and the regions that supported them through tax levies.

What is evident to even the casual observer is that Islam itself became an idiom for symbolic and administrative control: the sultan who claimed divine lineage could be supreme arbiter and absolute monarch without challenge to his dual exercise of authority. Yet the hereditary chieftains of the archipelago in Melaka, Samudra, and Sulawesi continued to claim their rights on the basis of ancient customary law. In effect, the struggle—and it was a protracted struggle from the fifteenth century on—was between two very different kinds of leaders: centripetal rulers, who converted to Islam and invoked Islam to retain all rights within their own courtly purview, and traditional rulers, who also became Muslim but continued to embody and protect the customary practices of the community, often described as magic, superstition, or soothsaying.

The multiple invocation of Islam can be seen in the portrayal of spiritual contests, which are often depicted in folklore as pitting Muslim kings against their opponents. The common theme is the mandate of Islamic kingship to overcome and eradicate local pre-Islamic beliefs. Muslims kings do not always win; what is perhaps even more interesting, at least from a narrative perspective, is the identical structure of the tales. There are always two combatants who represent the opposing communities. The loser always goes first, doing a seemingly impossible task that is then topped by his opponent, the eventual winner. For instance, in a spiritual contest waged in northern Sumatra, in the region of Acheh, it is the Muslim sultan who outduels an Indian yogi. Yet in southern Sulawesi the contest takes a different turn: it involves a kind of tag-team contest in which a cadre of Muslim religious officals (ulama) are locked in duel with a cadre of local soothsayers (botos). A religious official goes first: he sits on top of a banana leaf to say his prayers, after which a soothsayer proceeds to recite his prayers standing on his head on the same banana leaf! A second religious official then piles up thousands of eggs without breaking one, and of course, the second soothsayer then takes out rows of eggs from different parts of the pile . . . without breaking a single one. And so it goes until the ulama are vanquished and the soothsayers emerge victorious.

The details of the narrative are finally less important, despite their intrinsic appeal as displays of mind-numbing virtuosity, than the limits that they place on official, centrist rule: although wrapped in a seamless Islamic ideology of autocratic control, Muslim officials are not able to vanquish adroit local practitioners, who also define themselves as Muslim. Contest stories, for example, do not explain which prayers the religious official and the soothsayer recited, but presumably both performed Muslim ritual prayer (salat).

The Islamic Conquest of the Javanese Kingdom

Although Java is very important to contemporary Southeast Asia, providing both the demographic and the bureaucratic center of modern-day Indonesia, scholars find that importance receding as they move back toward the precolonial period. Again, there is a paucity of historical data that would allow scholars to trace plausible connections between the Indic past and the Islamic present of Javanese cities or their hinterland. Most scholarship has tried to find historical clues in extant Islamic literature, yet too little is known about the major manuscript collections, which were only assembled in the nineteenth century, and there is almost no background information available on their provenance.

Some contemporary monuments do exist, however, that reflect structures originally built to commemorate the arrival of Muslim rule in Java. Among them are two mosques: the Yogyakarta and Cirebon mosques. The community mosque of Yogyakarta is said to have been built by the foremost Muslim ruler of the second Mataram dynasty, Sultan Agung (r. 1613–45), although it was not completed until the late eighteenth century. The mosque is an impressive structure, although it has been renovated often since its original foundation. It is dwarfed by the central palace complex known as the Kraton, built in the late eighteenth century to reflect a Javanese-Indic worldview that highlights the ruler as the center of the universe in a manner reminiscent of the Turko-Persianate model discussed earlier.

The pattern of juxtaposing royal structures with religious sites occurs elsewhere in Java, notably in Cirebon on the north coast. The community mosque of Cirebon is among the oldest landmarks of the Muslim presence in Java; its construction is said to go back to the early sixteenth century. Its elaborate wooden scaffolding and expansive outer courtyard reveal a refined aesthetic tradition, yet it too has been much renovated in subsequent centuries. At the same time, the Cirebon central mosque is architecturally dwarfed by the royal complexes on either side of it, both of which bear witness to a style of ornamentation that is too diffuse to be neatly classified but that accents furnishings from Europe and China within an overall Javanese structure.

Overall, the locus of spiritual power for Java was not dissimilar from its locus in the neighboring islands of Sumatra and Sulawesi. It was rural rather than urban; even when it embraced an Islamic idiom, it continued to reflect the distinction between court and countryside, with priority given to those landscapes of villages, rice fields, forests, and mountains, which, according to A. Day, could extend into seascapes, islands, and mythical places across the seas, forming a continuum of literary space outside and moving away from the palace.

Although the actual Islamic conquest of the Javanese kingdom of Majapahit took

Mosques were built on the island of Java to commemorate the arrival of Muslims there. The congregational mosque at Yogyakarta in central Java, for example, was founded by the foremost ruler of the Mataram line, Sultan Agung (r. 1613–45), but it was not completed until the late eighteenth century.

place in 1478, regional courts and rural customs persisted, underscoring the emergence of a unique pattern of Muslim loyalty. On the one hand, Southeast Asian Islam could be linked to the patterns of Turko-Persianate Islamic culture examined in South Asia, but that would be to adopt the viewpoint of sultans and the courts that were constructed to reflect and perpetuate their vision of a "perfect" Islamic society. On the other hand, it is impossible to ignore the durability of a broad spectrum of local traditions: customary law had its custodians and its exemplars, most of whom were attracted to aspects of the Islamic worldview but who adapted it to their needs rather than replacing the local with the universal, the indigenous with the foreign.

It is wise to refrain from too dichotomous a reading of Islam in Southeast Asia. To compartmentalize and then philosophize is to indulge in an excess of present-mindedness; that is, to try to read all history through the most recent developments without according sufficient difference to premodern, earlier epochs and their distinctive features. Present-mindedness undergirds the familiar dyadic reading of Malay and then Indonesian religious history: it provides a main narrative to explain modern-day events. Consider the complexity of modern Achinese history. In 1945, following the Japanese occupation, Acheh witnessed internal turmoil on a massive scale. Not only hereditary chiefs but also their families were the principal victims. Was that atrocity the final settling of a centuries-old struggle between customary law and Islam, as some have suggested, or was it rather the use of religion as an ideology, in this case, Islamic "orthodoxy" serv-

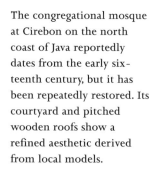

The congregational mosque at Cirebon on the north coast of Java reportedly dates from the early sixteenth century, but it has been repeatedly restored. Its courtyard and pitched wooden roofs show a refined aesthetic derived from local models.

ing as the instrument of drastic socioeconomic change? Customary law and Islam do not represent cultural oppositions so much as temporary political alliances, and the invocation of Islam by the "victorious" group in 1945 had as much to do with efforts to centralize and homogenize all parts of the newly independent island-nation of Indonesia as it did with doctrinal or ritual differences among the Achinese.

One caveat remains for Southeast Asia as for South Asia: Islam should be examined as more than either its exponents or detractors wish to make it. Civilizations draw on the symbolic and institutional power of all available religions, yet they do not exhaust the availability of any one religion to oppositional groups. In the case of Acheh and the neighboring Malay polities, scholars find groups who resist a Muslim ruler in the name of the same God, the same Prophet, and the same community of believers. The contest is over political authority even when it is framed as a contest over religious truth. The lesson from both South and Southeast Asia is to recognize Islamic norms and values as transferable and persistent in many contexts, whomever the rulers and whatever the stake in local or regional contests for power.

CHAPTER TEN

Central Asia and China

TRANSNATIONALIZATION, ISLAMIZATION, AND ETHNICIZATION

Dru C. Gladney

During his 1994 visit to each of the newly established Central Asian states (except Tajikistan), Li Peng, then premier of China, indicated that China intends to build a "new Silk Road" in the region, through investments estimated to surpass all other foreign investments by the end of the twentieth century. This prediction began to ring true when Premier Li traveled to Kazakhstan in 1996 to sign an exclusive agreement for Chinese rights to the Ozen oil field, the largest oil field in Kazakhstan, and perhaps in Central Asia. This indicates the growing importance of Central Asian trade to China's international economy. In short, China hopes to downplay its political role in the region by emphasizing its historical and economic roles, attempting to "buy" stability on its new Central Asian borders.

The history of this policy extends back to the Han and Tang dynasties, when strong, centralizing Chinese empires sought to establish tributary states on its borders and to employ nomadic khanates as buffer zones between more established Eurasian kingdoms. China's desire for influence in Central Asia today is reminiscent of the Great Game of the late nineteenth century, when China competed with Russia and Britain for dominance over the strategic region of Central Asia. A new Great Game is currently being played out in the region for critical access to its important mineral and energy resources. But today the players include not only China, Russia, and to a lesser extent Britain but also multinational corporations, the United States, Japan, South Korea, Iran, Saudi Arabia,

(Left) There are nearly twenty million Muslims in China, more than in all of Saudi Arabia. Seagoing merchants brought Islam to coastal China, while overland traders brought it across the mountains of Central Asia to western China. Here, Muslims in a cemetery at Kashgar in the western province of Xinjiang recite prayers at a funeral.

and Turkey. Caught in the midst of this "game" are the local peoples and cultures, mostly Muslim and Turkic, with a large variety of different cultural and historical traditions.

This chapter examines current Sino-Central Asian relations in light of the long history of exchanges across the Eurasian continent through the rise of the southern and northern Silk Roads. Three aspects of the Sino-Central Asian historical and contemporary relations endure until this day: transnationalization (both because of the rise of the Silk Road and unification under the Mongols), Islamization (leading to social and economic transformations affecting both Chinese and Central Asian sides of the region), and the ethnicization of local identities (because of imperial, Soviet, and Chinese socialist policies). These issues pervade China's historical and contemporary relationship with Central Asia and go beyond traditional analyses of the region, which have been primarily concerned with trade and state-to-state relations, generally taking for granted the identities of the people concerned and the ability of the economic development model to integrate them.

Each of these processes significantly transformed the vast region of Eurasia into what it is today. Transnationalization was thus a gradual process that linked disparate tribes and kingdoms through the interlinks of the ancient Silk Road, the unification of the Mongols, and the gradual transformation of ancient satrapies and kingdoms into modern nation-states. Islamization molded the plethora of multireligious and pluralistic cultural traditions (including Manichaeanism, Buddhism, and widespread shamanism) into a fairly widespread acceptance of the basic tenets of one major world religion: Islam. Finally, ethnicization is an ongoing process in which formerly

Inner Asia is distinguished by a rugged terrain, with soaring peaks and harsh deserts. The Tien Shan mountains divide the region into two sections, an eastern part comprising the Chinese province of Xinjiang, and a western section now divided between the central Asian republics of Tajikistan, Kazakhstan, and Uzbekistan.

tribal and religious communal groups have gradually come to think of themselves as ethnic groups with rights and aspirations for nationhood. Perhaps the best example of this process is the Uighur people, once a tribal confederation, then a kingdom, and finally a Muslim nationality of the People's Republic of China, with many Uighurs seeking to establish their own separate nation, Uighuristan.

China has recently awakened to the fact that it is a nation with a significant Muslim and Central Asian population; the expansion of Islam through Central Asia into China is an important issue throughout this chapter. With nearly twenty million Muslims, China ranks as one of the world's most populous Muslim nations. Although its Muslim population is minuscule when compared with China's total population (about 2 percent of 1.1 billion), the Muslims of China play a crucial role disproportionate to their numbers in influencing China's domestic and international relations with Central Asia. This is particularly true in the border regions of Xinjiang, Gansu, and Ningxia where Muslims are in concentrated populations and where recent Muslim-led unrest and independence movements have influenced China's domestic and international relations.

The opening of the Pakistan-China Karakoram highway in 1986, the establishment of the direct air route from Urumqi to Istanbul in 1988, to Almaty (in southeastern Kazakhstan) in 1992, and to Islamabad in 1994, and the completion of the Sino-Soviet Trans-Eurasian Railway through Central Asia in 1991 have led to dramatic increases in the trade of goods and hard currencies. This heralded the first real reopening of the ancient Silk Route since its decline nearly a thousand years ago. For the first

As far back as the Han and Tang dynasties of pre-Islamic times, strong centralizing Chinese empires tried to establish tributary states on their borders and use nomadic khanates as buffer zones. The nomadic Kazakhs, who still herd sheep in the Heavenly Mountains, were one of these groups.

New communication links, such the Karakoram Highway linking China with Pakistan, opened in 1986, and the Sino-Soviet Trans-Eurasian Railway, completed in 1991, have led to dramatic increases in trade in the region.

In addition to the special sections where Russian bulk goods such as cloth, cotton, and steel are sold, the bazaars in Urumqi and Kashgar also stock local produce.

time, the markets in the Chinese cities of Kashgar and Urumqi have special sections for "Russian Goods" that sell such bulk goods as cloth, cotton, steel, fencing, and so on, trucked in and sold to private entrepreneurs, who then sell the goods to small industries in the region or throughout China. At the same time, Chinese shops with manufactured goods from China line the market streets of Almaty, Bishkek (in Kyrgyzstan), and Tashkent (in Uzbekistan). However, discussions that regard the peoples of the region as "60 percent Muslim" often fail to take into account each state's role in the "ethnicization" of these identities, their cross-border interactions, interethnic rivalries, religious factionalisms, and regional diversities within the groups themselves. Not only must the progress of Russian-Turkic and Muslim relations in the new Central Asian states be watched, but Han Chinese majority and (mainly Muslim) minority relations in the region, as well as improving Sino-Russian ties, must also be examined.

Rather than taking for granted national identities in the new Central Asian states as a resurfacing of pre-Soviet "tribal" identities, this chapter argues that Marxist policies have directly contributed to the ethnicization of local identities in the region. This chapter not only examines the economic, political, and transnational connections that link China to Central Asia, but it also discusses how the legacy of Stalinist-Leninist nationality policies continues to affect the specific peoples involved in the region, particularly the Dungan (Hui Muslim Chinese), Han, Kazakh, Kyrgyz, Russian, Uighur, and Uzbek populations. Although most recent analyses of China's relations with Central Asia have stressed economic ties, state-to-state exchanges, and government policies, this chapter suggests that larger forces, such as state-sponsored Islamization, transnationalism, and ethnicization, are the lines by which these interactions should be measured. These fault lines of interaction have become more salient in the post–Cold War era, when security issues have become more localized and territory has become increasingly associated with national identity. After examining the history and development of such issues as Islamization, transnationalism, and ethnicization, and their influence on the region's peoples, the chapter concludes with a discussion of how the reassertion of national identities in the region will become increasingly significant for interregional trade and economic development, involving a new Great Game in the post–Cold War era.

Transnational Connections on the Old Silk Road

Although scholars once believed that the early civilizations of the Eurasian continent were fairly isolated from each other, recent archaeological, textual, and historical evidence suggests that the civilizations of Europe and China were linked transnationally since the dawn of time. Not only have several Neolithic sites been linked to early African migrations and DNA evidence used to suggest descent from a common "Eve," but scholars such as William Watson have traced the origin of the bronze-socketed ax that arrived in Europe from China in the Late Bronze Age, and Victor Mair has recently reported that the "mummies of Xinjiang" found naturally preserved as desiccated corpses in the Taklimakan Desert, are possibly more than four thousand years old and originated in the Caucasus. The extensive trade in silks and other precious commodities that flourished between the Roman and Han empires from the second century B.C.E. to the second cen-

The ethnic groups of Central Asia and China were linked by trade, and nomadic civilizations were important in fostering cultural continuities between sedentary populations. The traditional means of transport has always been the Bactrian (two-humped) camel, which is able to carry large burdens across the harsh terrain.

Some Chinese blue-and-white porcelains were specifically made for export to Muslims, for Arabic inscriptions form part of their decoration. This large bowl, made in the early sixteenth century at the famous kilns in Jingdezhen in eastern China, is inscribed with good wishes in Persian.

tury C.E. followed well-worn tracks that only became labeled as the *Silk Road* in the late nineteenth-century heyday of European orientalism by the German scholar Baron Ferdinand von Richthofen. Indeed, the term could not be more misleading because the roads and caravan tracks that crisscrossed the region were legion, and they carried much more than just silk. They were also complemented by the southern maritime route that linked Africa and South Asia with China through southeast Asia, a route that rose in importance as the overland trade declined.

Furthermore, the term *central Asia*, which presumes an "outer" Asia and a large gap between Europe and Asia, between East and West, is also a product of orientalist scholarship, a tradition that Edward Said says is as misleading as it is informative about different cultural practices and is often politically motivated. China, as the late Joseph Fletcher said, was never as closed off from the outside world as Western scholarship portrayed. This is demonstrated by the importance of the central Asian and European trade to the various empires of China and its being subject to the same flows of ideas and commodities that influenced much of the history of the region, including its transformation by such world religious traditions as Buddhism and Islam. Indeed, even the Greek historian Herodotus did not speak in terms of the migrations of isolated "ethnic" groups (although the Greek term *ethnos* was certainly known to him) but rather of a "cultural continuum" that flowed across the Pontic steppes to the far east. This chapter suggests that current thinking about isolated "ethnic" and "national" groups is a product of the rise of the nation-state and the writing of nationalist histories. Indeed, the region now known as central Asia is perhaps the best example there is of intermingled and interconnected peoples, places, and political processes.

Herodotus himself wondered why the old world in his day was already divided into three places, Asia, Europe, and Africa: "Why three names . . . should ever have been give to a tract of land which is in reality one?" In his masterful introduction to the concept of central Asia in *The Cambridge History of Early Inner Asia*

(1990), Denis Sinor has suggested that a more appropriate term for the region would be *central Eurasia*. The region developed not on the so-called periphery but at the core intersections of civilizations that included Europe, the Middle East, India, Southeast and East Asia. Because all of the great civilizations of central Asia flourished before the middle of the first millennium, and no single civilization occupied all and only that particular region (the Mongols controlled nearly the entire continent, from Europe to east and southeast Asia), the term *central* or *inner* Asia was always relational and never stable. It was known as inner Asia to include Pannonia (a province including territory now mostly in Hungary), and the Greek territories in Asia Minor (Anatoha) by the Romans, then by the Huns (fifth century) and the Seljuk Turks (eleventh century). Northern China was considered to be inner Asia once it was occupied by the Khitan, the Jürchen, the Mongols, and the Manchus. Except for the periphery of the Eurasian continent, the surface features of the land prevented dense populations with agrarian empires. At the core of inner Asia, one finds "agricultural alternatives" that involved pastoralist and other highly adaptive technologies, none of which supported large populations. Cultural continuities developed between the sedentary civilizations, and transitory or nomadic civilizations often became the mediators and brokers for much more than just material commodities. To mention perhaps the greatest examples, Buddhism and Islam thus became dramatically transformed in their migration eastward from the south and west. One might suggest that globalization had its beginnings in the region now known as central Asia. Certainly, transnationalism and the flow of goods and ideas between innumerable peoples was never new to the area. The horse and perhaps the cart were the only material commodities that linked the entire region with its peripheral kingdoms.

Other Chinese blue-and-white porcelains bear owners' marks showing that they were exported through Central Asia to the Islamic lands. This large dish with a landscape scene, made in the early fifteenth century, was probably imported into Persia under the Timurids. Inscribed on the back with the owner's name—Qarachaghay, chief page at the court of the Safavid shah Abbas—it was part of the imperial collection of Chinese porcelains endowed to the shrine of Ardabil in northwestern Iran by the Safavid shah in 1611.

China's direct relations with central Asia date to one century before the common era, when the Han dynasty general Zhang Qian returned to the capital of Changan (modern Xian) from a mission in 138 B.C.E. to form an alliance against the Huns. This was one among many military missions to central Asian capitals

The Silk Route, a term coined in the nineteenth century by the German orientalist Baron Ferdinand von Richthofen, existed since pre-Islamic times as the major route for goods and ideas between China, India, and the West. Buddhism was carried along it from India to China, and monasteries were established along the way. Here, at Bezelik, on the fringe of the Taklimakan Desert, Buddhist monasteries were carved into the cliffs.

as far as Samarqand, Bukhara, Andkhui, Herat, Shiraz, and Isfahan. These missions solicited alliances and "tribute" (*gong*), which Joseph Fletcher said only indicated an exchange of gifts and never clearly established political submission. There were times when Chinese military control extended into central Asia, such as in the Han (206 B.C.E.-220 C.E.) and Tang (618-9097) dynasties, but it was just as frequently controlled by inner Asian empires, such as the Jin, Liao, Yuan, and Qing dynasties. The region today known as Xinjiang (meaning "new dominion") received that label in 1759, when the region was finally brought under the control of the Qing, a dynasty established by the inner Asian Manchus to rid the region of continued Mongolian (Zungharian) control. Even Manchu control was short-lived in the region, disrupted by Taiping and Uighur rebellions, Russian influence, and finally its own collapse in 1911.

The so-called Silk Road was one of several routes that Zhang Qian traveled again in 126 B.C.E. in search, not of silk, but of the famous Ferghana horses that "sweated blood," which the Han emperor had hoped to use against the nomadic Huns. In addition to silk and horses, there were innumerable commodities traded along the way, and rarely did one person or group travel the entire route. Chinese merchants were never sighted in Rome, and Romans were not found in Changan. Even later, Europeans rarely traveled overland to China, and scholarly doubt regarding the great Marco Polo expedition has been popularized. China-bound caravans carried gold and other precious metals, wool and linen, ivory, amber, coral, jade and other rare stones, asbestos, and glass, which was not produced in China until the fifth century. Outbound caravans carried a wide variety of bronze weapons and tools, iron, furs, pottery, ceramics, cinnamon, and rhubarb. From the China side the famous collection of tracks across the Eurasian steppe started from Changan, passing the famous Hexi corridor in Gansu in the northwest, to Dunhuang on the fringe of the Gobi Desert. From Dunhuang the route passed through the famous Jade Gate (*Yumen guan*, where the Chinese collected taxes on jade, among other things, entering China from Central Asia) and then divided into a northerly and southerly route, skirting the impassable Taklimakan Desert,

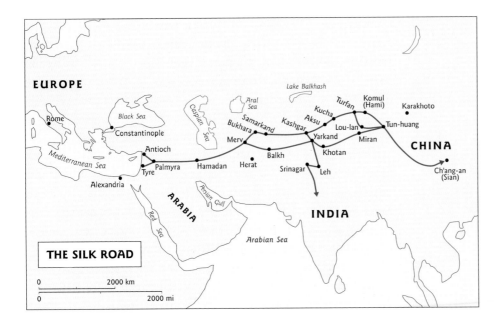

following glacial-fed oases at the base of the Tian Shan mountains in the north and the Himalayan escarpments and great Pamirs in the south. Once reconnecting in Kashgar, the main route continued westward through Kokhand, Samarqand, Bukhara, Merv, Persia, and Iraq to the Mediterranean, while southern and northern routes wound their way to India and Russia. Lesser spurs intersected these routes and formed a network of intermittent communications, although travel between the nodes was lengthy and was hampered by political and economic ruptures.

Along these routes Buddhism and then Islam found their ways into China. In central Asia and the oasis cities around the Taklimakan Buddhism was transformed into its current "Serindian" form, which in the ancient city of Gandhara gave the image of the Buddha his physical and Greco-Indian and even Chinese features. These features included a physical body with Hellenic features (a chiseled nose and forehead, wavy hair, and classical lips), adorned in a toga-like robe. Buddhist art as found in the cave library at Dunhuang and the Chinese capitals of Changan and Loyang took on decidedly east Asian features, as well as absorbing Chinese and even Taoist notions of the afterlife and the way of suffering, con-

With the advent of Islam, Muslims added their distinctive religious buildings to Buddhist sites. At Turfan, for example, a tall tower known as the Imin Minaret marks the presence of the nearby congregational mosque.

tributing to the rise of the new Pure Land and Chan (or Zen) schools of Buddhism. Nestorianism and Manichaeanism also found their ways into China along these transnational tracks, transforming Christian and Persian teachings into new hybrid forms, as the Nestorian monument in the Xian provincial museum indicates. The religion is remembered in China by this stele, which depicts a Nestorian cross on a lotus flower base, dating to the mid-seventh century when a Nestorian church was officially established in Changan. Indeed, during the heyday of the Tang dynasty, its capital was a truly transnational city, with an official population of five thousand foreigners, including Hindus, Jews, Manichaeans, Nestorians, and Zoroastrians, and peoples described as Arabs, Armenians, Indians, Iranians, Japanese, Koreans, Malays, Mongolians, Sogdians, and Turks. Dwarfs from all over Europe were particularly sought out as entertainers, accompanied by exotic animals from throughout the world.

With the decline of the Tang dynasty, the Silk Road also declined. This process was heralded by the gradual retreat of the glaciers at the end of the Ice Age, and the drying up of the glacier-fed streams that made life on the fringe of the Taklimakan possible for several smaller oasis cities, including such prominent cultural centers as Lou Lan, Lop Nor, Niya, and Yotkan, now known only as sand-buried cities. More important, the arrival of Islam signaled the beginning of a new transnationalization of central Asia, with its roots not in Europe, China, or south Asia but in the Middle East. The rapid Islamization of central Asia, beginning as early as the mid-seventh century and reaching Balkh (in northern Afghanistan), across the Pamirs from Kashgar by 699, led to the cultural, political, and social transformation of the entire region, superseding its earlier transnationalization but certainly not displacing it. Interestingly enough, although Islam reached the Pamir borders of China by the end of the seventh century, not unlike Alexander the Great, it was almost prevented from going any further. Islamization did not take place in Kashgar until the eleventh century, and it took nearly four hundred years to travel across the Taklimakan to the eastern oases of Turpan and Hami, where people who called themselves Uighurs continued to practice Buddhism until the sixteenth century. As Islam penetrated China by land across the Taklimakan and by sea along the southeastern coast, the people known as the Hui emerged, and the Uighurs disappeared, only to reappear again in the early twentieth century.

Islamization and China

Though Denis Sinor, in emphasizing the early multicultural and multireligious roots of central Asia, has suggested that "in Inner Asia no one faith has ever commanded the allegiance of more than a fraction of its population," this certainly cannot be said to be true of Islam. Scholars estimate that today nearly 60 percent of the entire region bows toward Mecca in religious allegiance, although political allegiance may bend to various national capitals, including Moscow, Beijing, Tehran, Istanbul, Almaty, and Tashkent. In China the largest Muslim group today call themselves the Hui people, and they are recognized by the state as the third largest minority nationality. They represent perhaps more than any other Muslim group in China today, a fascinating blend of Chinese, Middle Eastern, and central Asian cultural, religious, and historical traditions.

The Hui are the most numerous of ten Muslim nationalities recognized by the state in China. Numbering more than half of China's nearly twenty million Muslims, the Hui are classified by the state as the one Muslim minority that does not have a specific language shared by all of its members. The other Muslim nationalities include eight Turkic-Altaic Muslim language groups in China (Uighur, Kazakh, Kyrgyz, Uzbek, Tatar, Salar, Bonan, Dongxiang) and one Indo-European Tadjik group). Unlike these other groups, who are concentrated primarily in northwest China near the Sino-Soviet frontier, the Hui have communities in 97 percent of China's counties, with concentrations in the northwest (Xinjiang, Gansu, Qinghai, and the Ningxia Hui Autonomous Region), the southwest (Yunnan, Guizhou), and the north China plain (Hebei, Henan, Shandong). They are the largest urban ethnic minority in most of China's cities (200,000 in Beijing, 150,000 in Tianjin, and 50,000 in Shanghai), and they traditionally dominated certain trades throughout China (noodle, beef, and lamb restaurants, leather making, jewelry making, and wool trading).

Although the Hui have been labeled as the "Chinese-speaking Muslims" or "Chinese Muslims," this is misleading because many Hui speak only the non-Chinese dialects of the place where they live, such as the Tibetan, Mongolian, Thai, and Hainan Muslims, who are also classified by the state as Hui. Yet most Hui are closer to

The Memorial Mosque to the Prophet, the Huai Sheng Si, also known as the Beacon Tower Mosque, at Guangzhou (Canton) in Guandong province, is reportedly the oldest mosque in China. It is said to have been founded in the Tang period by the Arab missionary Abu Waqqas.

The largest Muslim group in China calls itself the Hui people. They represent a blend of Chinese, Middle Eastern, and central Asian cultural, religious, and historical traditions. Here Muslims in Gansu province gather together for prayer in the house of a recently deceased saint.

the Han Chinese than the other Muslim nationalities in terms of demographic proximity and cultural accommodation, adapting many of their Islamic practices to Han ways of life, which often became the source for many of the criticisms of the Muslim reformers. In the past this was not as great a problem for the Turkic and Indo-European Muslim groups, as they were traditionally more isolated from the Han and their identities not as threatened, although this has begun to change in the last forty years. Cultural proximity of the Hui and Han may account for some of the dynamics and urgency of Islamic reforms among Hui Muslim communities. Because they have no single language of their own and are so widely dispersed, the Hui did not originally conceive of themselves as one nationality. As a result of state-sponsored nationality identification campaigns over the course of the last thirty years, they have begun to think of themselves as a national ethnic group, something more than just "Muslims," which is what the term Hui originally meant. Islam in China was known as the "religion of the Hui" (Hui jiao) until the nationalist campaigns of the 1940s and 1950s classified the Hui as one among several nationalities who believed in Islam. The Hui became the residual Muslim group that contained anyone who did not fit the more stringent linguistic categories, many of which had been previously established in the Soviet Union (Uzbek, Kazakh, Kyrgyz, Tatar, Uighur, and so on). The Hui are also unique among the fifty-five identified nationalities in China in that they are the only nationality for whom religion is the only unifying category of identity. Through a process of state-influenced ethnogenesis and transnational association, the Hui, like such other nationalities as the Uighurs, began to think of themselves as one nationality category officially recognized by the state and eventually as one ethnic group. Today it is possible to travel throughout China and meet people who identify themselves solely as Hui—only later do tremendous linguistic, cultural, and religious differences become apparent.

Resulting from a succession of Islamic reform movements that swept across China over the last six hundred years, there exists a wide spectrum of Islamic belief among the Hui today. The variety of religious orders within Hui Islam represents a history of reforms and Islamic movements that derived from both interaction with and isolation from the Islamic world. Joseph Fletcher was the first to suggest that the nature of China's present-day Islamic communities and orders can be traced to successive "tides" of influence and individuals who entered China during critical periods of exchange

Chinese Muslims follow a wide spectrum of beliefs. Followers of traditional Islam are called Gedimu, from the Arabic *qadim*, meaning "old." They usually live in small communities clustered around a central mosque. Here in Beijing, Muslim men meet for communal prayer in the congregational mosque.

with the outside world. Like a swelling and ebbing tide, Fletcher argued, the influence of these movements grew or diminished with the interaction of China's Muslims and the Islamic world. This influence was not based on population movements so much as the gradual and profound exchanges of ideas between the two regions. Fletcher's argument had a profound influence on the history of Islam in China, but reflection on the Salafiyya (the early twentieth-century Islam reform movement that called for a return to the principles followed by the venerable ancestors) has led some scholars to reject his metaphor of "tides" of Islam, because it suggests not only unidirectional movement (from the Middle East to China) but also the notion that there was one moment, individual, or movement that touched all of China's Muslims and transformed them in one wave of religious reformation. In reality, among China's Muslims there is enormous complexity, discontinuity, and continued coexistence of a wide variety of religious orders. Each new "tide" or religious movement did not replace the former movements; rather, they debated each other, sometimes violently, and generally established uneasy coexistences. They were also not only one way. Rather, China's Muslims and Chinese culture exerted as much if not more influence on the movements that came into China from the Middle East and central Asia as the other way around. Moreover, each "tide" is not easily isolated to one narrow period of time, but hundreds of Islamic movements spread throughout China over the course of a millennium, and many of them are just as vibrant today as they were from the beginning.

These "tides" are better understood as "modes" of Islamic reform in conjunction with other Islamic movements that spread throughout the Islamic world, reaching China when it became more open politically, economically, or philosophically to the outside world. Newer movements did not replace earlier modes of belief in China; rather, they helped to define them. For example, the association known today as the Gedimu in China are not one "tide" (Fletcher's first) of Islam in China; they represent a wide variety of Islamic practices and organizational orientations that are similar only in their rejection of later Sufi- and Wahhabi-inspired reform movements. Followers of traditional Islam in China only began to define themselves as Gedimu or "old teachings" when "new teachings" an reform movements rose in their midst and criticized the "old teachings." Although these newer modes of Islamic practice and belief drew their converts from the earlier Muslim communities, they did not replace the older communities entirely. Instead, they provided a wide spectrum of religious alternatives from which Muslims in China could choose. For it is often ritual practice that distinguishes Islamic affiliation in China and elsewhere, but this practice is only an icon indicating the appeal of one movement over another for Muslim believers in the northwest enmeshed in the Chinese state and society.

Although this chapter does not begin to address Islam's complex history in China, an introduction to the context of Islamic reforms is necessary for an understanding of the rise of Islamic reform movements in China. Each of these "modes" can be characterized by certain kinds of related and successive reform movements seeking to reform Islam in China by reference to discursive and moral standards encountered in the Middle East by Muslims from China on the *hajj* (pilgrimage), or preached by peripatetic Middle Eastern representatives of these movements in China, often arriving in China overland from central Asia. The somewhat quixotic quest of these Muslims at the distant edge of Islamic expansion for the fundamentals of their faith, and the dialectic interaction between periphery and center, society and state, engendered the rise of a series of reformist tides that washed across the Chinese Islamic hinterland.

The First Mode: Traditional Chinese Islam

The earliest Muslim communities in China were descended from the Arab, Persian, Central Asian, and Mongolian Muslim merchants, militia, and officials who settled along China's southeast coast and in the northwest in large and small numbers from the seventh to the fourteenth centuries. Generally residing in independent small communities clustered around a central mosque, only later did they become known as the Gedimu (from the Arabic *qadim*, "old"), when later Islamic movements criticized them as old and antiquated. The mode for these communities was characterized by what Jonathan Lipman has termed a patchwork of relatively isolated, independent Islamic villages and urban enclaves that related with each other through trading networks and recognition of belonging to the wider Islamic *ummah* (community). For these communities Sunni Hanafi Islam became so standard that few modern-day Hui in the northwest had even heard of Shiism even during the Iran-Iraq war.

From the beginning, the earliest Islamic communities established a consistent pattern of zealously preserving and protecting their identity as enclaves ensconced in the dominant Han society. Each village was centered on a single mosque headed by an *ahong* (from the Persian *akhun*[d]) who was invited to teach on a more or less temporary basis. These ahong generally moved from one mosque to another on an average of every three years. A council of senior local elders and ahong were responsible for the affairs of each village and the inviting of the itinerant imam. Late nineteenth-century and early twentieth-century travelers noted the maintenance of these isolated communities: "I know of no strictly farming village where there is an equal mixture of the two groups [Han and Hui]," Robert Ekvall once observed in *Cultural Relations on the Kansu-Tibetan Border* (1939), "in every case the village is predominantly one or the other. In some instances, the population is composed almost entirely of one group, with only a few hangers-on of the other." He goes on to suggest that because of different cultural, ritual, and dietary preferences that sometimes led to open conflict, the communities preferred physical separation.

This isolation was mitigated somewhat during the collectivization campaigns in the 1950s, when Han and Hui villages were often administered as clusters by a single commune. They have also been brought closer together through national telecommunications and transportation networks established by the state, including such umbrella organizations as the China Islamic Association, established in 1955, which seeks to coordinate religious affairs among all Muslim groups. With the dismantling of the commune system in the early 1980s in many areas, however, these homogeneous Hui communities are once again becoming more segregated. Although these disparate communities among the Gedimu were generally linked only by trade and a sense of a common religious heritage—an attachment to the basic Islamic beliefs as handed down to them by their ancestors—it was the entry of the Sufi brotherhoods into China that eventually began to link many of these isolated communities together through extensive socioreligious networks.

The Second Mode: Sufi Communities and National Networks

Sufism did not begin to make a substantial impact in China until the late seventeenth century, during the second mode of Islam's entrance into China. Like Sufi centers that proliferated after the thirteenth century in other countries, many of these Sufi movements in China developed socioeconomic and religio-political institutions built around the schools established by descendants of early Sufi saintly leaders. The institutions became known in Chinese as the *menhuan*, the "leading" or "saintly" descent groups. The important contribution that Sufism made to religious organization in China was that the leaders of mosques throughout their order owed their allegiance to their shaykh, the founder of the order who appointed them. These designated followers were loyal to the leader of their order and remained in their prayer communities for long periods of time, unlike the Gedimu ahong, who were generally itinerant, not well-con-

Sufism, or Islamic mysticism, made a substantial impact in China from the late seventeenth century. Four major orders, locally called *menhuan*, became important. The Naqshbandiyya emphasized popular practices, which often revolved around the veneration of saints. Believers often sought inspiration and blessing by visiting and meditating at saints' tombs, as in Hezhou, in Gansu province.

nected to the community, and less imbued with appointed authority. Gedimu mosque elders were loyal to their congregation first and connected only by trade to other communities.

Many Sufi reforms spread throughout northwest China during the early decades of the Qing dynasty (mid-seventeenth to the early eighteenth centuries). Increased travel and communication between Muslims, in both east and west, during what Joseph Fletcher called the "general orthodox revival" of the eighteenth century and A. H. Johns refers to as the "second expansion," had great influence on Muslims from west Africa to Indonesia, not least of all on China's Hui Muslims. Exposure to these new ideas led to a reformulation of traditional Islamic concepts that rendered them more salient, posing a challenge to both traditional clerical and state authorities.

Although a mystical interpretation and social organization were perhaps Sufism's most lasting contributions to Islam in China, the public conflict between Sufis and non-Sufis was over the contested turf of Islamic practice. Sufis criticized traditional Hui Muslims for being too Chinese: materialistic, bound to their mosques, incense, and Chinese texts, and refusing to fully experience the presence of Allah in their worship. They condemned the non-Sufis for their use of Chinese in worship, adorning their mosques with Chinese Quranic quotations and hadith. They condemned the Muslims for wearing traditional Chinese white funeral dress and sullying Islam with many other Chinese cultural practices, calling for a purified return to the ascetic ideals of the Prophet and his early followers. They also offered a more immediate experience of Islam through the rituals of remembrance and meditation, and the efficacy of the saints, instead of the daunting memorization and recitation of Quranic texts. Although theirs was a reformist movement, it was less textual than experiential, revealing the power of Allah and his saints to transform lives through miracles, healings, and other transformative acts.

Sufi orders were gradually institutionalized into sociopolitical organizations known as the menhuan. Only four orders maintain significant influence among the Hui today, what Claude Pickens as a Protestant missionary in northwest China first discovered as the four menhuan of China: the Qadariyyas, Khufiyyas, Jahriyyas, and Kubrawiyyas. Although these are the four main groups, they are subdivided into a myriad of smaller branch solidarities, divided along ideological, political, geographical, and historical lines. These divisions and alliances reveal the disparities encountered between the indigenous practice of Islam in China and new Islamic ideals as represented by returned *Hajji* or itinerant, often Central Asian, preachers who maintained, in their eyes, more "orthodox" interpretations of Islam.

It is unfortunate that Western scholarship has prolonged the confusion of early Chinese writers over the rise of Sufism and later Islamic orders in China. As each

Islamic reformer established a new following in China, often in conflict with other older Islamic orders, these "new" arrivals challenged or converted the "old" traditional Islamic communities. Chinese officials and even less knowledgeable Muslims from the beginning naturally referred to these communities with their new teachings as *xin jiao* (literally, "new religion" or "teaching," not "new sect," as it has been erroneously translated). As each new arrival replaced the older Islamic communities, they became known as the "new" or even "new new teachings" (*xin xin jiao*), as in the case of the arrival of the Ikhwan in China, which will be described below. Traditional Islam among the Hui generally was referred to as *lao jiao* ("the old teachings"), and even some orders that were new at one time when others arrived were gradually classed as lao jiao. This was the case with the Khufiyyas, an early Naqshbandiyya Sufi order, which itself is now classified as an "old teaching" even though when it first flowered in China as a Sufi reform movement it was known as a "new teaching."

It was often the case that those who regarded themselves as maintaining the established traditional beliefs of Islam in China represented the reformers, who were their critics, as "new" and thus suspect, while they portrayed themselves as "old" or more true to their traditions. The reformers generally thought of themselves as the more orthodox, based on a more informed, sometimes esoteric interpretation of Islam due to more recent contact with movements in the Muslim heartlands. They thus resented the title of "new teachings" or the even more derisive "new new teachings," calling themselves by the more exact names of their orders: Qadariyya, Naqshbandiyya, Wahhabi, Yihewani, and so forth. The stigmas "new teachings" or "new sects" stuck, as they were applied not only by their critics but often by the state as well. Even the name Gedimu for the "older" Islamic communities in China is a not-so-subtle jibe at the other Islamic orders as being newer and thus removed from the traditional fundamentals of Islam in China. Thus, in China there is a continued debate over orthodox discourse, with each Islamic movement seeking to portray itself as loyal to the original ideals, the spirit as well as the texts of Islam. As each movement sought to exert taxonomic control over the labeling of itself and its rivals, the state was often called in to adjudicate, leading to further debates over legitimacy according to the categories of the state. No longer Islamic, these criteria were often Confucian or legalistic in content, seeking to judge a movement's compatibility with the Chinese order.

The designations of the movements thus became important politically as well as theologically. For example, during the mid-nineteenth-century rebellions in the northwest, some of which were led by Sufi leaders, the Chinese state proscribed all of those movements that became known as "new teachings" in order to root out what they saw as the more rebellious Hui communities. The state became convinced by opponents to the largely Sufi-led uprisings that they were all similarly "new" and thus suspect. This is precisely the rationale whereby a wide variety of Buddhist sectarian movements were proscribed under the general rubric of the "White Lotus" rebellion in China, whereas recent scholarship has revealed that only a few Buddhist movements fell under the shadow of that term. Unfortunately, Chinese and Western scholars perpetuated the designations of "new" and "old" teachings, and until recently there were no accurate representations of the Hui's own history of their Islamic orders in China. The opening of China to the West after 1979 has allowed the appearance of Chinese publications on these groups as well as Western fieldwork for the first time, giving a better, albeit still quite limited, glimpse into their origins and socioreligious complexity. These depictions by outsiders continue to plague Muslim reform movements and their quest for legitimacy.

Although there is some dispute among the Sufis themselves about which order was the earliest to enter China proper, because there had been regular contact on an individual basis with the Sufi orders of Central Asia that had already begun to proliferate in Xinjiang in the early part of the fifteenth century, it is generally agreed that one of the earliest to be established firmly on Chinese soil was the Qadari *tariqah* (Sufi order or brotherhood, literally "path"). The founder of the Qadariyya group in China was Qi Jingyi, Hilal al-Din (1656–1719). Known among the Hui as Qi *Daozu* (Grand Master Qi), he was buried in Linxia's "great tomb" (*da gongbei*) shrine complex, which became the center of Qadariyya Sufism in China. One of the reasons that Grand Master Qi continues to be greatly revered among all Sufis in China is that the tradition suggests that he received his early training under two of the most famous Central Asian Sufi teachers, Khoja Afaq and Khoja Abd Alla. Qi Jingyi supposedly met with the revered Naqshbandi leader Khoja Afaq in Xining in 1672, where according to Qadariyya records, the master sent the sixteen-year-old acolyte home, saying "I am not your teacher, my ancient teaching is not to be passed on to you, your teacher has already crossed the Eastern Sea and arrived in the Eastern land. You must therefore return home quickly, and you will become a famous teacher in the land." Qadariyya followers today feel that their saint received the blessing of the great Naqshbandi Khoja Afaq, while their order was formally founded by his second teacher, Khoja Abd Alla, a twenty-ninth-generation descendant of Muhammad. Chinese Sufi records state that Khoja Abd Alla entered China in 1674 and preached in Guangdong, Guangxi, Yunnan, Guizhou and Linxia, and Gansu, before his eventual death in Guizhou in 1689. While Abd al-Kadir al-Jilani is the reputed founder of the Qadari order, it is not surprising to find that Khoja Abd Alla perhaps studied in Medina under the renowned Kurdish mystic Ibrahim ibn Hasan al-Kurani (1616–90), who was initiated into both the Naqshbandi and Qadari tariqahs, as well as several other Sufi orders.

The appeal of Qadariyya Sufism as a renewal movement among the Hui is related to its combining ascetic mysticism with a noninstitutionalized form of worship that centers around the tomb complex of deceased saints rather than the mosque. The early Qadariyyas advocated long-term isolated meditation, poverty, and vows of celibacy. The head of the order did not marry and eschewed family life, a radical departure from other Islamic traditions in China. Qadariyya Sufis continue to attend the Gedimu mosques in the local communities in which they live, gathering at the tombs for holidays and individual worship. The founder Qi Jingyi was known for his emphasis on poverty, self-cultivation, and ascetic withdrawal from society. Formalized Islamic ritual as represented by the Five Pillars of Islam (fasting, pilgrimage, prayer, almsgiving, and recitation of the *shahadah*, the obligatory Muslim profession of faith) was de-emphasized by Qi Jingyi in favor of private meditation. The Qadariyya maintain that "those who know themselves clearly will know Allah" and "the Saints help us to know ourselves first before knowing Allah." Union with the divine, then, is accomplished through meditation and self-cultivation, rather than formalized public ritual. "The moment of thinking about Allah," they maintain, "is superior to worshipping him for a thousand years." Although the Qadariyya menhuan has always been less influential than other Sufi orders in China because of its rejection of "worldly" political involvement, it set the stage for many Sufi orders to follow. By stressing the intimate experience of Allah through the power of his appointed shaykh, Sufism in China became a force for renewal and transformation: a return to the pure ascetic ideals of Islam, as well as initiating a new sociopolitical Islamic order. At once fundamentalistic and transformative, it initiated a new tide of reform that swept across China.

The Naqshbandi order became most rooted in Chinese soil through the establishment of two groups: the Khufiyyas and Jahriyyas. Both groups exercised tremendous influence on the history of Islam in China, specifically in the northwest. As Joseph Fletcher argued, the reform movement emphasized a shar'ist orthoproxy, political activism, propagation of the religion, and a strong Sunni orientation that came to mark the Naqshbandiyyas in a way that proved definitive in the mystical path's subsequent history. Two other general characteristics of popular mysticism—namely the veneration of saints (misleadingly called "saint worship" by non-Muslim writers) and the seeking of inspiration by visiting and meditating at the saints' tombs (misleadingly referred to as "tomb worship") were also prominent features of the Naqshbandiyyas in southern Xinjiang and later in northwest China.

Founded by Bahaad-Din Naqshband (1318–89), who lived in Mawarannahr (a Central Asian region west of the Pamirs), the Naqshbandiyya order gradually spread east across the trade routes and by the middle of the fifteenth century gained ascendance over other Central Asian Sufi orders in the oasis cities of Altishahr, surrounding the Tarim river basin in what is now southern Xinjiang. The Naqshbandi order that gained the most prominence in the Tarim basin and played an important role in later eighteenth- and nineteenth-century politics in Xinjiang was the Makhdumzada, established by Makhdum-i Azam (also known as Ahmad Kasani, 1461-1542). It was his great grandson, Khoja Afaq (d. 1694), known in the Chinese sources as Hidayat Allah, who was the saint most responsible for establishing the Naqshbandiyyas among the Hui in northwest China. Khoja Afaq (Khwaja-yi Afaq, "the Master of the Horizons"), founded the Afaqiyyas in Xinjiang, and from 1671 to 1672 he visited Gansu, where his father, Muhammad Yusuf, had previously preached, reportedly converting a few Hui and a substantial number of the Salars to Naqshbandi Sufism. During this influential tour, Khoja Afaq visited the northwest cities of Xining, Lintao, and Hezhou (now Linxia, China's "little Mecca"), preaching to Hui, Salar, and northeastern Tibetan Muslims. Two of these early Hui Gansu Muslims became his disciples and went to Central Asia and the pilgrimage cities to become further trained in the order. When they returned to China, they established the two most important Naqshbandi brotherhoods among the Hui in the Northwest: the Khufiyyas and the Jahriyyas.

As AnneMarie Schimmel has eloquently documented, throughout its history the Naqshbandiyyas have stressed an active participation in worldly affairs. Their shaykhs worked wonders, chanted the powerful Mathanawi texts of the Turkish mystic Jalal ad-Din al-Rumi al-Balkhi, Mawlana Jalluddin (ca. 1207–73), and advocated scriptural reforms. They emphasized both self-cultivation and formal ritual, withdrawal from and involvement in society. Unlike the Qadariyyas, their leaders enjoyed families and the material wealth accrued from the donations of their followers. They also became committed to political involvement and social change based on the principles of Islam. Some of the Naqshbandiyya orders in China advocated more of a "transformationist" perspective, in which they sought to change the social order in accord with their own visions of propriety and morality. This inevitably led to conflicts with Chinese rule and local governments, causing some Naqshbandiyya orders, especially the Jahriyyas, to be singled out for suppression and persecution. "Due to the arduous way it has traversed," one Hui scholar Yang Huaizhong (himself raised in a Jahriyya home) wrote "the branch [Jahriyya] has always advocated the militant spirit of the Muslims, organizing uprisings to resist the oppression of the Qing and KMT [Nationalist, or Kuomintang] governments against the ethnic Hui minority and their religious belief." By contrast, the Khufiyyas tended to seek more conformist solutions to local conflicts, stressing personal internal reform over political change. The different stance that the Naqshbandiyya orders took in China with regard to the state and Chinese culture reflects their dialectical interaction with local interpretations of identity and changing sociopolitical realities in the Northwest. A brief introduction of these two movements is necessary for understanding the later challenges to the movements by the Yihewanis and the Salafiyyas.

During his 1672 visit to Hezhou, Khoja Afaq played an important role in the life of Ma Laichi (1673–1753), a Hezhou Hui of extraordinary talent who went on to found one of the earliest and most influential Naqshbandiyya orders in China: the Khufiyyas. According to Sufi tradition, Ma Laichi was born to a childless couple after they received Khoja Afaq's blessing. He was later raised and trained by one of Khoja Afaq's disciples, Ma Tai Baba ("Great Father"), who later gave Ma Laichi his daughter in marriage and passed on to him the leadership of the mystical path that Ma Tai Baba had received from Khoja Afaq. From 1728 to 1781 Ma Laichi went on the pilgrimage to Mecca, Yemen, and Bukhara, where he studied several Sufi orders and became particularly influenced by Mawlana Makhdum, a man of uncertain origin whom John Fletcher hypothesized may have been Indian. When he returned from his pilgrimage, Ma Laichi established the most powerful of the Khufiyya groups: the Huasi ("flowery mosque") branch. He propagated the order for thirty-two years among the Hui and Salar in Gansu and Qinghai before his death in 1766 at the age of 86. The group is still quite active and centered in Linxia Hui Autonomous Region, Gansu, at the tomb of Ma Laichi, which was restored in 1986.

Originating in an earlier Central Asian and Yemeni Naqshbandi Sufism, the Khufiyya order was permeated with an emphasis on a more passive participation in society, the veneration of saints, the seeking of inspiration at tombs and the silent dhikr ("remembrance"; properly, "Khafiyya" means "the silent ones"). There are now more than twenty subbranches throughout China, with mosques in Beijing, Xinjiang, and Yunnan. Most Khufiyya orders are concentrated in Gansu, Ningxia, Qinghai, and Xinjiang, with several of the original Khufiyya practices in such outlying areas as northern Ningxia beginning to lose their distinctiveness over time.

The second Naqshbandi order, the Jahriyyas, was founded in China under the dynamic leadership of Ma Mingxin (1719–81). One of the most fascinating detective stories in historical discovery is the tracing of Ma Mingxin's spiritual lineage to Mizjaja, a village on the outskirts of Zabid in northern Yemen, by Joseph Fletcher. Although Chinese Sufis have known for generations that their saint Ma Mingxin studied in the Middle East, it was never clear whom he received his "new teaching" from or where he studied. Middle Eastern Sufi accounts recorded the presence of Chinese Muslims studying in certain Sufi areas, but only Joseph Fletcher was able to put the two together. This was an important discovery, as Ma Mingxin's Sufi practice was thought to be novel, even heterodox, and the subject of many conflicts in Northwest China. This controversy is mainly over Ma Mingxin's use of the *jahr* in remembrance (vocal *dhikr*, from whence comes the name Jahriyya, "the vocal ones"), which he openly advocated in opposition to the Khufiyya's silent remembrance, the more standard Naqshbandi practice. After an extensive search through arcane Sufi documents in Arabic, Persian, Turk, and Chinese, and a final personal trip to Yemen, Fletcher discovered that the name of the Sufi saint under whom Chinese Muslim records indicated Ma Mingxin studied but whose identity was unknown was a Naqshbandi Sufi named az-Zayn ibn Muhammad Abd al-Baqi al-Mizjaji (1643 or 1644–1725), whose family home was in Mizjaja, the Zabid. Chinese Sufi records only indicate that Ma Mingxin studied in Yemen in a Sufi order known as the Shazilinye, whose shaykh was Muhammad Bulu Seni, but the records do not contain the full ancestry and origins of the order. Most Jahriyyas only say: "The root of our order is Arabia, the branches and leaves are in China."

It is known that az-Zayn had studied in Medina under the famous Kurdish mystic Ibrahim ibn Hasan al-Kurani (1616–90), who also advocated the use of vocal formulas in the remembrance of Allah (*al-jahr bi-dh-dhikr*). Al-Kurani's students were at the forefront of Islamic reform and fundamentalist movements throughout the Islamic world. Under al-Kurani's student's direction, it is not surprising that Ma Mingxin returned after sixteen years of study in Yemen and the Arabian peninsula in 1744 with more activist and radical reforms on his mind. While advocating the use of the vocal remembrance, he generally opposed the heavy emphasis on the veneration of Islamic saints that had become popular in China. These disputes led to bloody conflicts well into the early twentieth century. As the disputes grew worse and conflicts erupted, Qing troops, fresh from the conquest of Xinjiang in 1759, did not wish to have any more trouble among the Muslims in Gansu. They arrested Ma Mingxin in 1781 and executed him as his followers attempted to free him. Three years later they crushed another uprising led by a Jahriyya Sufi, Tian Wu. From this point on, the Qing sought to limit the spread of the movements, outlawing many of the so-called new teachings, primarily the Jahriyyas.

The great Northwest Hui rebellion (1862–76) was led by Ma Hualong, another Jahriyya Sufi leader fifth-generation descendant of Ma Mingxin. His rebellion was responsible for cutting the Qing state off from the Northwest, making way for the great 1864–1877 Uighur-led rebellion in Xinjiang under Yakub Beg. In 1871 Ma Hualong was captured and executed, supposedly with his entire family. His body is entombed in Dongta Township, Jinji, just east of the Yellow River in Ningxia, although his head is reported to have been buried in Xuanhuagang, a Jahriyya center, north of Zhangjiachuan in south Gansu. There is also evidence that suggests Du Wenxiu, the Panthay Hui Muslim rebellion in Yunnan (1855-73), was also

Sufis in China often wear distinctive dress. Most Chinese Muslims wear round white hats.

influenced by Jahriyya ideas. Following the failure of these uprisings, the Jahriyyas became much more secretive and dispersed, leading to the establishment of five main Jahriyya branch orders, all named after their ritual and historical centers: Banqiao, Beishan, Nanchuan, Shagou, and Xindianzi.

The importance and extensiveness of these Sufi orders for uniting disparate Hui communities across China must not be underestimated. Unlike the isolated "patchwork" Gedimu communities that had been the norm until that time, Sufi orders provided the leadership and organization that could help the Hui survive politically and economically. During the fragmented Republican period (1911–49), extensive Sufi networks proved helpful to some Hui warlords in the Northwest and disruptive to others. Even today, membership in various Islamic orders and their concomitant Islamic practices often significantly influence social interaction, especially among the Sufi orders who often distinguish themselves by dress. Unlike the rounded white hat worn by most Hui men, Sufi followers often wear a six-cornered hat, sometimes black. Many Jahriyya Hui shave the sides of their beards to commemorate their founder, Ma Mingxin, whose beard is said to have been shorn by Qing soldiers before his execution in 1781. Although these markers are almost universally unnoticed by the Han majority— for whom a Hui is a Hui—the Northwest Hui can easily identify in the marketplace members of the various orders that divide them internally. The exclusivity of Sufi orders in China illustrates the cruciality of identity and authority for Sufi Hui. The Hui can enter these orders through ritual vow or by birth but seldom maintain allegiance to two orders at once. This is unlike Sufi traditional orders, which tend to be less exclusive and allow simultaneous membership in several orders. In China membership in these orders is exclusive; changing to a new order is tantamount to an "internal" conversion experience for Muslims in China, perhaps the only one they will ever have, because most Muslims in China entered Islam by birth.

Despite the tremendous variety found among Sufis in China today, from the traditionalist and fairly apolitical Khufiyyas to the politically active Jahriyyas and the mystically esoteric Qadariyyas, Sufism may still be generally characterized as a modality that has influenced much of Islam in China. It is distinguished from other Islamic modalities in its hierarchical organization, its veneration of saints and tombs, and its emphasis on meditation and self-transformation. Given its often tightly organized networks and capability to form secretive oppositional movements, it is not surprising that it is one modality that the state in China has most often sought to either eradicate or co-opt. To the extent that various Sufi orders and their shaykhs have been able to maintain their legitimacy through either secret resistance to the state or public compliance, they have maintained their appeal among Muslims not only in the Northwest, where Sufism is most popular, but in the eastern urban centers and northern plains as well.

The Third Mode: Scripturalist Concerns and Modernist Reforms

A third mode identifiable in Chinese Islam began at the end of the Qing dynasty, a period of increased interaction between China and the outside world, when many Muslims began traveling to and from the Middle East. In the early decades of the twentieth century, China was exposed to many new foreign ideas and in the face of Japanese and Western imperialist encroachment sought a Chinese approach to governance. Intellectual and organizational activity by Chinese Muslims during this period was intense. Increased contact with the Middle East led Chinese Muslims to reevaluate their traditional notions of Islam. The missionary Claude Pickens recorded that from 1923 to 1934 there were 834 known Hui Muslims who made the hajj to Mecca. In 1937, according to one observer, more than 170 Hui pilgrims boarded a steamer in Shanghai bound for Mecca. By 1939 at least thirty-three Hui Muslims had studied at Cairo's prestigious al-Azhar University. Although these numbers are not significant when compared with pilgrims on the hajj from other Asian Muslim areas, the influence and prestige attached to these returning Hui hajji was profound, particularly in isolated communities. "In this respect," Joseph Fletcher once observed, "the more secluded and remote a Muslim community was from the main centers of Islamic cultural life in the Middle East, the more susceptible it was to those centers' most recent trends."

As a result of political events and the influence of foreign Muslim ideas, many new Hui organizations emerged. In 1912, one year after Sun Yat-sen was inaugurated provisional president of the Chinese Republic in Nanjing, the Chinese Muslim Federation was also formed in that city. This was followed by the establishment of other Hui Muslim associations: the Chinese Muslim Mutual Progress Association in Beijing in 1912, the Chinese Muslim Educational Association in Shanghai in 1925, the Chinese Muslim Association in 1925, the Chinese Muslim Young Students Association in Nanjing in 1931, the Society for the Promotion of Education Among Muslims in Nanjing in 1931, and the Chinese Muslim General Association in Jinan in 1934.

Islamic reformist movements emerged in China in the late nineteenth and early twentieth centuries. Pilgrims returning from Arabia, where the conservative Wahhabis were in power, introduced the Yihewani movement, Chinese for the Ikhwan al-Muslimin (Muslim Brotherhood). Stressing orthodox practice, they proscribed such cultural accretions as the decoration of mosques with Arabic and Chinese calligraphy, the most striking feature of traditional Chinese mosques.

The Muslim periodical press flourished as never before. Although it was reported that circulation was low, there were more than one hundred known Muslim periodicals produced before the outbreak of the Sino-Japanese War in 1937. Thirty journals were published between 1911 and 1937 in Beijing alone, prompting one author to suggest that although Chinese Islam's traditional religious center was still Linxia (Hezhou), its cultural center had shifted to Beijing. This took place when many Hui intellectuals traveled to Japan, the Middle East, and the West. Caught up in the nationalist fervor of the first half of the twentieth century, they published magazines and founded organizations, questioning their identity as never before in a process that Hui historian Ma Shouqian has termed "the New Awakening of the Hui" at the end of the nineteenth and the beginning of the twentieth centuries. As many of these Hui hajji returned from their pilgrimages to the Middle East, they initiated several reforms, engaging themselves once again in the contested space between Islamic ideals and Chinese culture.

Influenced by Wahhabi ideals in the Arabian peninsula, returning Hui reformers introduced the Yihewanis (Chinese for the *Ikhwan al-Muslimin*) to China—a religio-political movement that supported, in some cases, China's nationalist concerns, and in others, its warlord politics. Although the Ikhwan Muslim Brotherhood elsewhere in the Islamic world has been depicted as antimodernist and recidivist, this is not true of the movement in China. In fact, the Yihewanis in China eventually diverged so far from their Ikhwan Muslim Brotherhood beginnings, that it is misleading to even refer to the Yihewanis in China as "Ikhwan" or as a single movement or order. It has now become merely an another "mode" of Islamic practice, an alternative to Gedimu (traditional Islam) and Sufism in China.

The beginnings of the Yihewani movement in China can be traced to Ma Wanfu (1849–1934), who returned from the hajj in 1892 to teach in the Hezhou area. The initial reformers were primarily concerned with religious scripturalist orthodoxy—so much so that they are still known as the "venerate-the-scriptures faction" (*zunjing pai*). Although the reformers were concerned with larger goals than merely "correcting" what they regarded as unorthodox practice, like previous reforms in China, it is at the practical and ritual level that they initiated their critique. Seeking perhaps to replace "Islamic theater" with scripture, they proscribed the veneration of saints, their tombs, and their shrines, and sought to stem the growing influence of well-known individual ahong and Sufi menhuan leaders. Stressing orthodox practice through advocating a purified "non-Chinese" Islam, they criticized such cultural accretions as the wearing of white mourning dress (*dai xiao*) and the decoration of mosques with Chinese or Arabic texts. At one point, Ma Wanfu even proposed the exclusive use of Arabic and Persian in all education instead of Chinese. Due to Ma Wanfu's contacts with the Wahhabi during his sojourn, the Yihewani follow strict Wahhabi practice. Their mosques are distinguished by their almost complete lack of adornment on the inside, with white walls and no inscriptions, as well as a preference for Arabian-style mosque architecture. This contrasts sharply with other more Chinese-style mosques in China, typical of the "old" Gedimu, whose architecture resembles Confucian temples in their sweeping roofs and symmetrical courtyards (with the Xi'an Huajue Great Mosque as the best example). The Yihewanis also proscribed the adornment of their mosques with Arabic and especially Chinese Quranic texts and banners. This is the most striking iconographic marker of Sufi mosques and worship centers in the Northwest, whose walls and tombs are often layered with Arabic and Chinese texts on silk and

Traditional Chinese-style mosques often resembled Confucian temples, with sweeping roofs and symmetrical courtyards, as at the mosque in Yunnan shown here. The Yihewanis rejected this style, preferring plain white mosques.

cloth banners in the distinctive Hui-style art that fluidly combines Arabic and Chinese calligraphy.

The Yihewanis flourished in Northwest China under the patronage of several Muslim warlords during the Nationalist period, most notably Ma Bufang. In a modernist discourse, arguing that the Yihewanis supported education, a rationalized, less-mystical religious expression, and a strong Chinese nation, Ma Bufang supported the expansion of the Yihewanis throughout Northwest China. He must have also been aware that wherever the Yihewanis went, the hierarchical authority of the Sufi shaykhs and the solidarity of their menhuan were contested, thus protecting Ma Bufang from other organized religious organizations that might orchestrate an effective resistance to his expansion. This could not have been lost on the early Communists either, who traveled through Ma Bufang's territory and the Northwest on their Long March, which ended in Yenan, near Ningxia, a heavily populated Muslim area dominated at that time by Ma Hongkui, a cousin of Ma Bufang's, who also supported the Yihewanis. After the founding of the People's Republic in 1949, the state quickly suppressed all Sufi menhuan as feudalistic and gave tacit support to the Yihewanis. Although Ma Bufang and Ma Hongkui both fled with the Nationalists to Taiwan, their policy of opposing Sufi organizations was left behind with the Communists. The China Islamic Association, established in 1955, was heavily dominated by the Yihewanis and was supportive of the 1957–58 public criticisms and show trials of the Naqshbandi Shaykh Ma Zhenwu specifically and Sufism generally as feudalist and exploitative of the masses. After the purges of the Cultural Revolution (1966–76), in which all Islamic orders eventually were affected, the Yihewanis were the first to receive renewed state patronage. Most of the large mosques that were rebuilt with state funds throughout China as compensation for damages and destruction caused by the Red Guards during the now repudiated Cultural Revolution happened to be Yihewani mosques, although all orders were equally criticized during the radical period.

Although no Chinese official will admit that the Yihewanis receive special treatment, this is cause for some resentment among Muslims in China. The great South Gate Mosque in Yinchuan, the capital of the Ningxia Hui Autonomous Region, was one of the first mosques rebuilt in Ningxia with state funds—it just happened to be staffed by Yihewani imams, although the state said it was a nonsectarian mosque. After the state spent more than fifty thousand yuan to rebuild the mosque in 1982, the local Muslims, most of whom were Gedimu and Khufiyya, refused to attend. The building sat almost empty for the first few years and the state attempted to recoup its losses from the large Arab-style architectural structure by turning it into a tourist attraction and selling tickets at the entrance. This, of course, only confirmed its lack of religious legitimacy among many local Hui Muslims, especially the Gedimu and Sufis. In 1985 a visiting Kuwaiti delegation to the mosque became aware of the situation and instead of donating money to the South Gate Mosque as originally planned, they gave $10,000 (about thirty thousand yuan) for refurbishing the much smaller traditional Central Mosque, a Gedimu mosque popular among the locals.

The Yihewanis continue to be a powerful Islamic group throughout China. Like the Gedimu, the Yihewanis emphasize leadership through training and education rather than inheritance and succession. The Yihewanis differ from the

Much to the resentment of other Chinese Muslims, the reformist Yihewani movement receives special treatment from the Chinese government. The great South Gate Mosque in Yinchuan city was rebuilt with state funds in 1982. It is staffed by Yihewani imams.

Gedimu primarily in ritual matters and their stress on reform through Chinese education and modernism. Unlike the Gedimu, they do not collectively chant the scriptures, visit tombs, celebrate the death days of their ancestors, or gather for Islamic festivals in remembrance of saints. Because of their emphasis on nationalist concerns, education, modernization, and decentralized leadership, the movement has attracted more urban intellectual Muslims. This is why the Yihewanis in China cannot be regarded as a tightly founded "order" as the Muslim Brotherhood is often portrayed in the Middle East; it is instead a mode of Islamic reform and orientation in China. The Yihewanis' nationalistic ideals, and their co-optation by the earlier Republic Nationalists and the Communist Party led many of the more religious Yihewanis to become disillusioned with the order. It was seen by many to be no longer a fundamentalistic agent of reform, but an institutionalized organ of the state for systematizing and monitoring Islamic practice. Though still influential politically, it has lost its dynamic appeal to many of the most conservative Muslims in China. For the vast majority of urban Hui Muslims, and even many rural Muslims in the small towns of the northern plains, however, it is merely the mosque that they belong to by virtue of birth or marriage, and few Hui Muslims can tell the difference between the Yihewanis and the Gedimu, let alone between the myriad orders of Sufis. A Hui worker in Hangzhou once said that the basic difference between the Gedimu (he used the term *lao jiao*, "old teachings") and in this case the Yihewani (*xin jiao*, "new teachings") was that the Yihewanis did not eat crab and the Gedimu did; the Yihewanis did not because "crabs walked sideways."

Although the total population of the various Islamic associations in China has not been published, one Muslim Chinese scholar, Yang Huaizhong, estimates that of the 2,132 mosques in Ningxia Hui Autonomous Region, 560 belong to the Yihewanis, 560 to the Khufiyyas, 464 to the Jahriyyas, 415 to the traditional Gedimu, and 133 to Qadariyya religious worship sites (some of which include mosques). The most comprehensive estimate given so far for Hui membership in Islamic orders throughout China is by Ma Tong. Of an estimated total at that time of 6,781,500 Hui Muslims in the late 1980s, Ma Tong recorded that there were 58.2 percent Gedimu, 21 percent Yihewani, 10.9 percent Jahriyya, 7.2 percent Khufiyya, 1.4 percent Qadariyya, and 0.7 percent Kubrawiyya.

Ethnicization of the Silk Road Peoples: The Case of the Uighur

In 1997 bombs exploded in a city park in Beijing on May 13 (killing one) and on two buses on March 7 (killing two), as well as in the northwestern border city of Urumqi, the capital of Xinjiang Uighur Autonomous Region, on February 25 (killing nine), with more than thirty other bombings in 1997 and six in Tibet alone. Most of these bombings are thought to have been related to demands by Muslim and Tibetan separatists. Eight members of the Uighur Muslim minority were executed on May 29 for alleged bombings in northwest China, with hundreds arrested for suspicion of taking part in ethnic riots and engaging in separatist activities. At a time when China celebrates its recovery of Hong Kong, which took place on July 1, 1997, many wonder if it can hold on to rebellious parts of its restive west.

Most analysts agree that China is not vulnerable to the same ethnic separatism that split the former Soviet Union. But few doubt that should China fall apart, it would divide, like the Soviet Union, along centuries-old ethnic, linguistic, regional, and cultural fault lines. These divisions showed themselves at the end of China's last empire, when it was divided for more than twenty years by regional warlords with local

Modern-day China has to confront many ethnic problems. For example, the Uighur people were first a tribal confederation, then a kingdom, and finally a Muslim nationality of the People's Republic. The main Uighur town is Urumqi, capital of the Xinjiang Autonomous Region, and the main mosque there is known as the Grand Islam Mosque.

and ethnic bases in the north and the south, and by Muslim warlords in the west. Ethnicization has meant that the current cultural fault lines of China and Central Asia increasingly follow official designations of identity. For Central Asia the breakup of the Soviet Union thus did not lead to the creation of a greater "Turkestan" or a pan-Islamic collection of states, despite the predominantly Turkic and Muslim populations of the region. Rather, the breakup fell along ethnic and national lines. China clearly is not about to fall apart, not yet anyway. But it also has ethnic problems, and it must solve them for more pressing reasons. This section examines recent events in Xinjiang in light of a nearly century-long process of ethnicization that has taken place among the Uighurs and many other peoples of Central Asia and China as a result of Sino-Soviet policies and the rise of the nation-state in the region. Although it was noted earlier that Islamization was an important force in forming the contemporary consciousness of the people known as the Hui, this section discusses the role of ethnicization in the region.

Chinese histories notwithstanding, every Uighur firmly believes that his or her ancestors were the indigenous people of the Tarim basin, which did not become known in Chinese as Xinjiang ("new dominion") until the eighteenth century. Nevertheless, the identity of the present people known as Uighurs is a rather recent phenomenon related to Great Game rivalries, Sino-Soviet geopolitical maneuverings, and Chinese nation building. Although a collection of nomadic steppe peoples known as the Uighurs have existed since before the eighth century, this identity was lost from the fifteenth to the twentieth centuries. It was not until the fall of the Turkish khanate (552–744 C.E.) to a people reported by the Chinese historians as Hui-he or Hui-hu that the beginnings of the Uighur empire are found. At this time the Uighurs were but a collection of nine nomadic tribes, who initially, in confederation with other Basmil and Karlukh nomads, defeated the second Turkish khanate and then dominated the federation under the leadership of Koli Beile in 742.

The Uighurs defeated the Turkish khanate and settled down as agriculturalists just as trade with the unified Tang state became especially lucrative. Sedentarization and interaction with the Chinese state was accompanied by socioreligious change: the traditional shamanistic Turkic-speaking Uighurs came increasingly under the influence of Persian Manichaeanism, Buddhism, and eventually Nestorian Christianity. Extensive trade and military alliances along the old Silk Road with the Chinese state developed to the extent that the Uighurs gradually adopted cultural, dress, and even agricultural practices of the Chinese. Conquest of the Uighur capital of Karabalghasun in Mongolia by the nomadic Kyrgyz in 840, without rescue from the Tang, who may have become by then intimidated by the wealthy Uighur empire, led to further sedentarization and crystallization of Uighur identity. One branch that ended up in what is now Turpan, took advantage of the unique socioecology of the glacier-fed oases surrounding the Taklimakan Desert and were able to preserve their merchant and limited agrarian practices, gradually establishing Khocho or Gaochang, the great Uighur city-state based in Turpan for four centuries (850–1250).

The Islamization of the Uighurs from the tenth century to as late as the seventeenth century, while displacing their Buddhist religion, did little to bridge these oases-based loyalties. From that time on the people of "Uighuristan" centered in Turpan, who resisted Islamic conversion until the seventeenth century, were the last to be known as Uighurs. The others were known only by their oasis or by the generic term of Turki. With the arrival of Islam, the ethnonym Uighur fades from the historical record. According to Morris Rossabi, it was not until 1760 that the Manchu Qing dynasty exerted full and formal control over the region, establishing it as their "new dominions." (*Xinjiang*), an administration that lasted barely one hundred years, when it fell to the Yakub Beg rebellion (1864–77) and expanding Russian influence. The end of the Qing dynasty and the rise of Great Game rivalries between China, Russia, and Britain saw the region torn by competing loyalties and marked by two short-lived and drastically different attempts at an independence: the short-lived proclamations of an "East Turkestan Republic" in Kashgar in 1933 and another in Yining (Gulja) in 1944. As Andrew D. W. Forbes has noted in *Warlords and Muslims in Chinese Central Asia* (1986), these rebellions and attempts at self-rule did little to bridge competing political, religious, and regional differences within the Turkic people, who became officially known as the Uighurs in 1934 under successive Chinese Kuomintang warlord administrations. This designation was achieved under Soviet sponsorship in a meeting of regional delegates in Tashkent in 1921, who voted to revive the ancient ethnonym *Uighur* and apply it to the sedentarized Turkic people of the Tarim basin. Today, despite continued regional differences along three and perhaps four macroregions—including the northwestern Zungaria plateau, the southern Tarim basin, the southwest Pamir region, and the eastern Kumul-Turpan-Hami corridor—there are nearly nine million people spread throughout this vast region who regard themselves as Uighurs. Many of them dream of, and some militate for, an independent "Uighuristan." The recognition of the Uighurs as an official Chinese "nationality" (*minzu*) in the 1930s in Xinjiang under a Soviet-influenced policy of nationality recognition contributed to a widespread acceptance today of continuity with the ancient Uighur kingdom and their eventual ethnogenesis as a bona fide nationality. The so-called nationality policy under the Kuomintang identified five nationalities of China, with the Han in the majority. This policy was continued under the Communists, eventually recognizing fifty-six nationalities, with the Han occupying a 91 percent majority in 1990.

The "peaceful liberation" by the Chinese Communists of Xinjiang in 1949, and its subsequent establishment of the Xinjiang Uighur Autonomous Region on October 1, 1955, perpetuated the Nationalist policy of recognizing the Uighurs as a minority nationality under Chinese rule. This nationality designation not only masks tremendous regional and linguistic diversity, it also includes such groups as the Loplyk and Dolans that had very little to do with the oasis-based Turkic Muslims that became known as the Uighurs. At the same time, contemporary Uighur separatists look back to the brief periods of independent self-rule under Yakub Beg (1820–77) and the eastern Turkestan republics, in addition to the earlier glories of the Uighur kingdoms in Turpan and Karabalghasan, as evidence of their rightful claims to the region. Contemporary Uighur separatist organizations based in Istanbul, Ankara, Almaty, Munich, Amsterdam, Melbourne, and Washington, D.C., may differ on their political goals and strategies for the region, but they all share a common vision of a unilineal Uighur claim on the region, disrupted by Chinese and Soviet intervention. The independence of the former Soviet Central Asian republics in 1991 has done much to encourage these Uighur organizations in their hopes for an independent "Uighuristan," despite the fact the new mainly Muslim Central Asian governments all signed protocols with China in early 1996 to the effect that they would not harbor or support separatist groups.

Within the region, although many portray the Uighurs as united around separatist or Islamist causes, the Uighurs continue to be divided from within by religious conflicts, in this case competing Sufi and non-Sufi factions, territorial loyalties (whether they be oases or places of origin), linguistic discrepancies, commoner-elite alienation, and competing political loyalties. These divided loyalties were evidenced by the attack in May of 1996 on the imam of the Idgah Mosque in Kashgar by other Uighurs, as well as the assassination of at least six Uighur officials in September of 1997. It is also important to note that Islam was only one of several unifying markers for Uighur identity, depending on those with whom they were in cooperation at the time. For example, to the Hui Muslim Chinese discussed earlier, the Uighurs distinguish themselves as the legitimate indigenous minority, because both share a belief in Sunni Islam. In contrast to the nomadic Muslim peoples (Kazakh or Kyrgyz), Uighurs might stress their attachment to the land and oasis of origin. In opposition to the Han Chinese, the Uighurs will generally emphasize their long history in the region. This suggests that Islamic fundamentalist groups, such as the Taliban in Afghanistan, will have only limited appeal among the Uighurs. This contested understanding of history continues to influence much of the current debate over separatist and Chinese claims to the region.

Another pressing issue for the Uighurs is economic. Since 1991 China has been a net oil importer. It also has twenty million Muslims. Mishandling of its Muslim problems will alienate trading partners in the Middle East, who are primarily Muslims. After an ethnic riot in February of 1997 in the northwestern Xinjiang city of Yining, which left at least nine Uighur Muslims dead and several hundred arrested, the Saudi Arabian official newspaper *al-Bilad* warned China about the "suffering of [its] Muslims whose human rights are violated." Turkey's defense minister, Turhan Tayan, officially condemned China's handling of the issue, and China responded by telling Turkey not to interfere in China's internal affairs. Muslim nations on China's borders, including the new Central Asian states, Pakistan, and Afghanistan, although officially unsupportive of Uighur separatists, may be increasingly critical of harsh treatment extended to fellow Turkic or Muslim co-religionists in China.

Unrest in the Xinjiang Uighur Autonomous Region may lead to a decline in outside oil investment and revenues, which are already operating at a loss. Exxon recently reported that its two wells came up dry in China's supposedly oil-rich Tarim basin of southern Xinjiang, with the entire region yielding only 3.15 million metric tons of crude oil, much less than China's overall output of 156 million tons. The World Bank loans more than $3 billion a year to China, investing more than $780.5 million in fifteen projects in the Xinjiang region alone, with some of that money allegedly going to the Xinjiang Production and Construction Corps (XPCC), which human rights activist Harry Wu has claimed employs prison (*laogai*) labor. Senate hearings in the United States on World Bank investment in Xinjiang have led Assistant U.S. Treasury Secretary David A. Lipton to declare that the treasury department would no longer support World Bank projects associated with the XPCC. International companies and organizations, from the World Bank to Exxon, may not wish to subject its employees and investors to social and political upheavals. It is clear that ethnic separatism or Muslim complaints regarding Chinese policy will have important consequences for China's economic development of the region. Tourists and foreign businesspeople will certainly avoid areas with ethnic strife and terrorist activities. China will continue to use its economic leverage with its Central Asian neighbors and Russia to prevent such disruptions.

China's international relations with its bordering nations and internal regions such as Xinjiang and Tibet have become increasingly important not only for the economic reasons discussed earlier, but also for China's desire to participate in such international organizations as the World Trade Organization and the Asia-Pacific Economic Council. Although Tibet is no longer of any real strategic or substantial economic value to China, it is politically important to China's current leadership to indicate that they will not submit to foreign pressure and withdraw its iron hand from Tibet. Uighurs have begun to work closely with Tibetans internationally to put political pressure on China in international forums. In an April 1997 interview in Istanbul that this author held with Ahmet Türköz, vice-director of the Eastern Turkestan Foundation, which works for an independent Uighur homeland, Türköz noted that since 1981 meetings had been taking place between the Dalai Lama and Uighur leaders, initiated by the late Uighur nationalist Isa Yusup Alptekin. The elected leader of the Unrepresented Nations and People's Organization, based in The Hague, an organization originally built on Tibetan issues, is Erkin Alptekin, the son of Isa Alptekin. These international forums cannot force China to change its policy any more than can the annual debate in the United States over the renewal of

China's Most Favored Nation status. Nevertheless, they continue to influence China's ability to cooperate internationally. As a result, China has sought to respond rapidly and often militarily to domestic ethnic affairs that might have international implications.

In addition to the official minorities, China possesses tremendous ethnic, linguistic, and regional diversity. The ethnicization of the Uighurs has important implications for other cultural groups across China. Intolerance toward difference in Xinjiang might be extended to limiting cultural pluralism in Guangdong, where at least fifteen dialects of Cantonese are spoken and folk religious practice is rampant. Memories are strong of the repressions of the Cultural Revolution, when all forms of diversity, political or cultural, were severely curtailed. If rising Chinese nationalism entails reducing ethnic and cultural difference, then anyone who is regarded as "other" in China will suffer, not just the Uighurs.

China and Central Asian Relations: Contemporary Connections and Contradictions

Since the breakup of the Soviet Union in 1991, China has become an important competitor for influence in Central Asia and is expected to serve as a counterweight to Russia. Calling for a new interregional Silk Route, China is already constructing such a link with rails and pipelines. As noted earlier, the ethnicization of several Central Asian peoples and their rise to prominence as the leading members of the new Central Asian states means that economic development and cross-border ties will be strongly influenced by ancient ethnic relations and geopolitical ties.

A 1997 study by James P. Dorian, Brett H. Wigdortz, and Dru C. Gladney discussed the growing interdependence of the region. Trade between Xinjiang and the Central Asian republics has grown rapidly, reaching $775 million in 1996, and the number of Chinese-Kazakh joint ventures continues to rise, now approaching two hundred. Xinjiang exports a variety of products to Kazakhstan as well as to Uzbekistan, Kyrgyzstan, Russia, and Ukraine. Increased economic cooperation with China provides Central Asia with additional options for markets, trade routes, and technical assistance.

As noted in the discussion of the Uighurs, whose modern identity depended on a conference in Tashkent in 1921 that revived their long-extinct ethnonym, cross-border ethnic ties and interethnic relations within Xinjiang continue to have tremendous consequences for development in the region. Muslims comprise nearly 60 percent of Xinjiang's population, and most of them are Uighurs. Being Turkic, the Uighurs share a common Islamic, linguistic, and pastoralist heritage with the peoples of the Central Asian states. Turkic nationalists proclaimed an "East

Turkestan Republic" in Kashgar in 1933, and another one in Yining in 1944. As Linda Benson has documented, both republics were short-lived.

The Uighurs and other Turkic groups in the region are also closer culturally and linguistically to their Central Asian neighbors than they are to the Han Chinese. The Han (the official majority nationality of China) are also relatively recent immigrants to Xinjiang. The beginning of the twentieth century marked an enormous movement of Russian and Han Chinese settlers to outlying Central Asian regions. From 1949 to 1979 China sent Han professionals to Xinjiang to help "open the Northwest." In 1990 estimates put the Han Chinese at 38 percent of Xinjiang's population, up from 5 percent in 1949. Although Russian populations have begun to decline in parts of the former Soviet Union since independence, the Han migration to Xinjiang continues to escalate.

Opportunities in Xinjiang's energy sector attract many migrants. China's rapidly growing economy has the country anxiously developing domestic energy sources and looking abroad for new sources. In 1993, with domestic oil consumption rising faster than production, China abandoned its energy self-sufficiency goal and became a net importer of oil for the first time. During 1996 China's crude oil production reached a record high of 156.5 million tons, while imports of crude were up 37.5 percent over 1995, to 22 million tons. China is expected to import as much as 30 percent of its oil by the year 2000. As China develops into a modern economy, it should see a rise in demand comparable to that experienced in Japan, where demand for natural gas and other energy needs has quadrupled in the past thirty years. This is particularly why China has begun to look elsewhere for meeting its energy needs; in September 1997 Li Peng signed a contract for exclusive rights to Kazakhstan's second largest oil field. It also indicates declining expectations for China's own energy resources in the Tarim basin. Once estimated to contain 482 billion barrels, even the president of China National Petroleum Corporation admits that today there are known reserves of only 1.5 billion barrels.

China hopes to make up for its dependence on Kazakhstan oil by increasing trade. China's two-way trade with central Asia has increased dramatically since the Chinese government opened Xinjiang to the region following the collapse of the Soviet Union in 1991. By the end of 1992 formal trade had jumped by 130 percent; total border trade, including barter, is estimated to have tripled. Ethnic ties have facilitated this trading surge: those with family relations benefit from relaxed visa and travel restrictions. Large numbers of "tourists" from Kazakhstan, Tajikistan, and Kyrgyzstan make frequent shopping trips into Xinjiang and return home to sell their goods at small village markets. Xinjiang has already become dependent on central Asian business, with the five republics accounting for more than half of its international trade in 1993.

Most China-Central Asia trade is between Xinjiang and Kazakhstan (Xinjiang's largest trading partner by far). From 1990 to 1992 Kazakhstan's imports from China rose from just less than 4 percent to 44 percent of its total. About half of China-Kazakh trade is on a barter basis. Through 1995 China was Kazakhstan's fifth largest trade partner, behind Russia, Holland, Germany, and Switzerland. China's trade with Kyrgyzstan has increased rapidly. Through 1995 Kyrgyzstan was Xinjiang's third largest trading partner, after Kazakhstan and Hong Kong. As early as 1992, China ranked as Uzbekistan's leading non-former Soviet republic trading partner. Since then, bilateral trade has increased by as much as 127 percent a year, making Uzbekistan China's second largest central Asian trading partner. This may be one of the most promising economic relationships developing in central Asia. The large and relatively affluent Uzbek population will eagerly purchase Chinese goods when the remaining border restrictions are relaxed and better transportation is built. Bilateral trade with Tajikistan increased nearly ninefold from 1992 to 1995. With much of Tajikistan recently in turmoil and the country suffering from a deteriorating standard of living, however, trade dropped by half in 1996. Trade between China and Turkmenistan has also risen rapidly. China is expected to eventually import Turkmen gas to satisfy the growing energy requirements in the northwest corner of the country. The sale of natural gas accounts for 60.3 percent of the total volume of Turkmen exports.

Although the increasing trade between central Asia and China is noteworthy, it reflects China's rapidly growing trade with the entire world: trade with central Asia increased 25 percent from 1992 to 1994; during the same period total Chinese trade increased almost twice as fast. In fact, during 1995 only 0.28 percent of China's $280.8 billion in overseas trade involved the five central Asian republics, about the same as with Austria or Denmark. Despite the small trade values, China is clearly a giant in the region and will play a major role in central Asia's foreign economic relations. For example, China's two-way trade with Kazakhstan is greater than Turkey's trade with all five central Asian republics. This is so even though predominantly Muslim central Asia is of a much higher priority for Turkey than for China.

Multinational corporations are beginning to play a larger role in the region's development. In Kazakhstan, for instance, foreign firms are estimated to control more than 60 percent of electric power output. A proposed Turkmenistan-China-Japan natural gas pipeline, part of the envisaged "energy Silk Route," which would connect Central Asia's rich gas fields with northeast Asian users, demonstrates the potential for cooperation among countries. But it also highlights the growing importance of international companies—in this case Mitsubishi and Exxon—in financing and influencing the course of oil and gas development in the region. With a potential price tag of $22.6 billion, this pipeline—as well as many smaller and less costly ones—would not be possible without foreign participation. The new Great Game between China and central Asia thus involves many more players than the largely three-way Great Game of the nineteenth century. Yet these new international corporate forces do not supersede local ethnic ties and connections that extend back for centuries.

Landlocked Central Asia and Xinjiang lack the road, rail, and pipeline infrastructure needed to increase economic cooperation and foreign investment in the region. Oil and gas pipelines still pass through Russia, and road and rail links to other points are inadequate. A new highway is planned between Kashgar in Xinjiang, China, to Osh, Kyrgyzstan, to facilitate trade in the area. China is also planning a new rail link between Urumqi and Kashgar. New links from central Asia could follow several routes west through Iran and Turkey, or Georgia and Azerbaijan, to the Black Sea or the Mediterranean; south through Iran to the Persian Gulf or through Afghanistan and Pakistan to the Arabian Sea; or east through China to the Pacific. All the routes pass through vast, remote, and perhaps politically unstable regions, and those involving Iran face difficulties in gaining Western financing.

Following the breakup of the Soviet Union, the Chinese government feared that the new independence of the neighboring Central Asian republics might inspire separatist goals in Xinjiang. It also worried that promoting regional economic development could fuel ethnic separatism by resurrecting old alliances. China, however, was reassured by an April 1996 agreement with Russia, Kazakhstan, Kyrgyzstan, and Tajikistan to avoid military conflict on common borders. It is also resting easier after assertions from Muslim states that they would not become involved in China's internal affairs. China's policy of encouraging economic development while keeping a tight lid on political activism thus seems to have the support of neighboring governments, despite not satisfying many demands of local and cross-border ethnic groups. Despite increasing investment and the creation of many new jobs in Xinjiang, the Uighurs and other ethnic groups complain that they are not benefiting as much as are recent Han immigrants to the region. This is a major contributing factor to recent Uighur Muslim activism. The Uighurs insist that the growing number of Han Chinese not only take the jobs (and eventually the profits) back home with them, but that they also dilute the natives' traditional way of the life, and leave them with little voice in their own affairs.

More than one hundred ethnic groups live in central Asia: Muslim peoples (Kazakhs, Kyrgyz, Uzbeks, Tajiks, Turkmens, Karakalpaks, and Dungans), Russians (and other European settlers), and peoples who were brought to the area by Soviet authorities during the Stalinist period (Germans, Crimeans, Tatars,

Koreans, Armenians, Chechens, and Meskhetian Turks). Deteriorating living standards are increasing tensions among many of them. The densely populated Fergana valley, home to many of the region's ethnic groups, has been the site of clashes over jobs, land, and natural resources, especially water. In June 1989 Meskhetian Turks, who had been exiled to the area by Stalin, were attacked by Uzbeks and Tajiks. Another skirmish followed a year later between Uzbeks and Kyrgyz in Osh. There is particular concern about the Tajik-Uzbek conflict, given serious tensions between the two groups and their proximity. One million Tajiks live in Uzbekistan, while both Tajikistan and Kyrgyzstan have sizable Uzbek populations in their parts of the Fergana valley. In Kazakhstan, Russian-Kazakh tensions remain high; 60 percent of Kazakhstani Slavs and Germans still consider their homeland to be the former Soviet Union, not Kazakhstan. Throughout the region, Russians, mostly technicians and other professionals who came after the 1917 revolution, make up roughly one-fifth of the population. Their fears that growing nationalism in countries of the region may become increasingly anti-Russian has prompted many of them to return to their homelands. Efforts to build a Kazakhstani identity have failed to bridge Slavic-Turkic and Orthodox-Muslim differences.

The New Great Game and the Old Silk Route

China and central Asia will continue to be shaped by historical forces, policies, and economic development that have brought them closer together in the last few years than in the past thirty, when the breakdown in Sino-Soviet relations in the early 1960s virtually cut off almost all direct contact except between Moscow and Beijing. Historically, however, central Asia has always been an important crossroads and meeting place in the heart of Eurasia; it is now reassuming this role in the international marketplace. The post-Deng Xiaoping leadership of China must seek new solutions to the old ethnic problems in the region. Deng's many crackdowns on separatist movements in the borderlands (he led the 1959 invading army to Tibet) no longer make sense in a country trying to open itself to world markets and global expectations. China must go beyond its former two-pronged policy in the border areas: political repression coupled with economic reinvestment. Not only has erecting a "steel Great Wall," to use Regional Party Secretary Wang Lequan's terms, failed to keep out separatists in Xinjiang, but it can no longer hide China's problems from the world.

China's Muslims are the last Muslims who live under communism. With the independence of the largely Muslim nations of former Soviet central Asia, the end of the war in Bosnia, the Israeli-PLO rapprochement, and the recent peace accords with Muslim separatists in Chechnya and the Philippines, world Muslims have begun to focus their attention on the Uighur situation in China. China cannot ignore the fact that support for the Bosnian Muslims was the only issue on which Iranian, Saudi, and Turkish governments could agree. Turhan Tayan, Turkish minister of defense, recently told China "that many living [in Xinjiang] are our relatives and that we will always be interested in those people's welfare. Our government is and will continue to be sensitive over the plight of our Turkic and Moslem brothers throughout the world." Through a modern process of transnationalization and ethnicization, Turks see themselves as directly linked to their "brothers" in China and central Asia. Muslims, through the global community of Muslims (ummah) and Islamization, also see themselves linked to the region. These international connections and ethnoreligious ties will continue to shape and influence China and central Asian relations.

Interethnic cooperation and political stability are critical if plans to develop the region are to succeed. Faced with newly independent Muslim nations on its border and interethnic conflicts within Xinjiang, China is stressing economic development and national unity. These are crucial issues in this time of post-Deng transition and reunification with Hong Kong. These issues also signal a new beginning for the ancient Silk Road linking China and central Asia.

CHAPTER ELEVEN

Islam in Africa to 1800

MERCHANTS, CHIEFS, AND SAINTS

Nehemia Levtzion

Islam moved into Africa from three directions. It came from North Africa across the Sahara to *Bilad al-Sudan* (The Lands of the Black People), which is between the Atlantic Ocean and Lake Chad. Despite six centuries of resistance from Nubian Christians, Islam expanded from Egypt southward, up the Nile valley, and west to Darfur and Wadai. Islam also moved from the Arabian peninsula across the Red Sea to the Horn of Africa, and from there further south to the coast of East Africa. This chapter will analyze the diverse patterns of the Islamization of Africa and the variety of religious experiences encountered by African Muslims until the beginning of the nineteenth century. During the eighteenth century, several factors contributed to the change from accommodation with local cultures to Islamic militancy, which brought about the jihad movements of the nineteenth century.

Ghana and Mali

The earliest Arab expeditions in North Africa in the seventh and eighth centuries penetrated the Sahara in two directions, from Tripoli toward Fezzan in southwestern Libya and from the Sus in southern Morocco. These Arab expeditions made their way on beaten routes along which trade had been carried for some time. Trade across the Sahara was carried by nomadic Berbers, who occupied both ends of the Sahara. By the tenth century Muslim traders from North Africa had their base

(Left) Islam was carried to Sub-Saharan Africa from the Maghreb, where most mosques had square minarets. Builders in Sub-Saharan Africa adopted this form to their local architectural traditions, as at this mosque at Agagdes in Niger.

Arab expeditions penetrated the Sahara Desert along trade routes from the north. Sijilmasa, located in an oasis in southern Morocco, was one of the great trans-Saharan entrepôts of the Middle Ages. Archaeologists are just beginning to penetrate the mounds that remain at the site.

in the commercial centers of Awdaghust and Tadmekka in the southern Sahara. From these towns they traded with the capitals of the kingdoms of Bilad al-Sudan, Ghana and Gao (in eastern Mali). Each capital city was composed of a Muslim town and a royal town. This residential separation allowed each group to practice its own religious rites without offending the other.

Writing in 1068, the Andalusian geographer al-Bakri (d. 1054) was able to gather precious information about Islam in three contemporary African kingdoms: Gao, Ghana, and Takrur (in lower Senegal). The king of Gao was Muslim, but the common people adhered to their ancestral religion, and pre-Islamic customs persisted at the court. The partial acceptance of Islam in Gao is contrasted with the zealous adherence to Islam of the king of Takrur, who compelled his subjects to observe Islamic law and carried out a jihad against his neighbors. The Islamic militancy of Takrur was exceptional, whereas Gao's symbiotic relationship between Islam and the traditional religion was more typical of Islam in West Africa.

In Ghana, Muslims lived under the auspices of a non-Muslim king, who invited Muslim traders to the capital and employed literate Muslims in his court. According to the geographer Abu Abdallah Muhammad ibn Abi Bakr al-Zuhri (fl. 1137–54) writing in 1137, the people of Ghana converted to Islam in 1076. This must have happened under the influence of the Almoravids, a militant Islamic movement in the southwestern Sahara. According to the geographer al-Sharif al-Idrisi (1100–65), Ghana was a Muslim state in 1154 and was still among the most powerful in western Sudan. By the middle of the thirteenth century, however, Ghana's power had declined and the political center of gravity shifted southward, where Mali, on the upper reaches of the Niger River, emerged as the dominant power. Al-Bakri's writings imply that there were also local Muslims in Ghana, traders who were part of a commercial network that extended from the towns of the Sahel to the sources of gold in the south. Muslims established trading centers that by the end of the fifteenth century

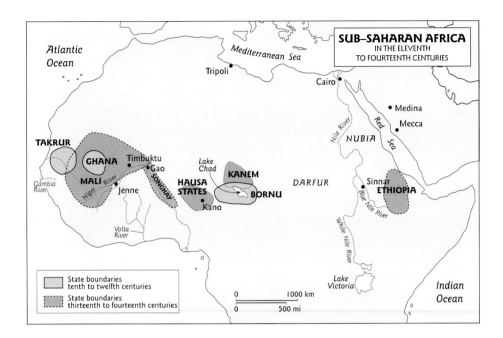

reached the fringes of the forest. They created a commercial diaspora with a common religion, language, and legal system, the *Shariah*, a personal and extraterritorial divinely ordained law, which added to the mutual trust among merchants. Conversion to Islam thus became necessary for those who wished to join the commercial network.

The next phase in the process of Islamization began when Muslim religious leaders established communication with host kings. Al-Bakri presents an account of such an encounter that brought about the Islamization of the king of Malal, a small principality that two centuries later developed into the empire of Mali. The Muslim religious leader, according to this account, succeeded in winning over the king by demonstrating Allah's omnipotence. In this instance, praying to Allah saved the kingdom, whereas the sacrifices performed by local priests had failed. Al-Bakri's accounts, like other traditions, emphasize the role of the rulers as early recipients of Islamic influence and therefore the importance of kingdoms in the process of Islamization. Indeed, Islam did not penetrate into segmentary societies even when and where Muslim traders and religious leaders were present, because there were no rulers to mediate Islamic influence.

In the principality of Malal, as in Gao, only the king, his family, and his entourage accepted Islam. In this respect, Islam could have become a divisive factor between the Islamized kings and the non-Muslim commoners. Situated between their subjects and an influential Muslim minority, kings adopted a middle position between Islam and the local traditional religion. Kings behaved as Muslims in some situations but followed traditional customs on other occasions. They patronized Muslim religious experts but also referred to traditional priests. From this middle position, dynasties and individual kings could develop greater commitment to Islam or fall back on ancestral religion.

The Malinke (literally, "the people of Mali") were the Mande-speaking people associated with the empire of Mali. Malinke chiefs had come under Islamic influence before the time of Sundiata, the founder and ruler of Mali. Sundiata, a great hunter and magician, led his people in a war of liberation against another powerful magician, Sumanguru, the king of Soso, in the Battle of Kirina. Though a nominal Muslim, Sundiata turned to the traditional religion for support. Two centuries later, Sonni Ali, who made the small kingdom of Songhay into a large empire, behaved in a similar way. Kings such as Sundiata and Sonni Ali, founders of empires, are the heroes of the national traditions, whereas the exploits of their Muslim successors—Mansa Musa of Mali and Askiya Muhammad of Songhay—were recorded only by the Arabic sources. From its center on the upper Niger River, Mali expanded into the Sahel in the direction of the Sahara. Muslim towns became part of the empire, and Muslim traders traveled over routes that traversed the empire. Through the control of the Saharan trade and the pilgrimage to Mecca, Mali came closer to the larger Muslim world. As the small Malinke kingdom evolved into a vast multiethnic empire, with influential Muslim elements inside and extensive Islamic relations outside the empire, its kings moved along an imaginary continuum, from attachment to the traditional heritage toward greater commitment to Islam. The emperor Mansa Musa (1312–37) made his empire part of the land of Islam. He built mosques with minarets, instituted public prayer, and attracted Maliki scholars. Mansa Musa visited Cairo on his way to Mecca in 1324, where he was described by an Egyptian official as a pious man, who "strictly observed the prayer, the recitation of the Quran, and the mention of Allah's name." The same informant told Mansa Musa that his treatment of free women as if they were slave concubines was forbidden by Islamic law. "Not even to kings?" Mansa Musa asked. "Not even to kings," replied the official, "Ask the learned scholars." Mansa Musa responded, "By Allah. I did not know that. Now I will renounce it completely." Shortcomings in the application of Muslim law were most apparent in marriage customs and sexual behavior.

In 1352-53, during the reign of Mansa Sulayman, Mansa Musa's brother, the great traveler and author Ibn Battutah (1304–68) visited the king's court. He was impressed by the way Muslims in Mali observed public prayer on Fridays and by their concern for the study of the Quran. He described the celebration of the two great Islamic festivals: the "sacrificial feast" on the tenth day of the month of the pilgrimage and the festival of the "breaking of the fast" at the end of Ramadan. The presence of the king made public prayer an official occasion to which non-Muslims were also drawn. In return, the prestige of the new religion was mobilized to exhort loyalty to the ruler. The alliance between kingship and Islam made Islam into an imperial cult. As national feasts the Islamic festivals accommodated such traditional ceremonies as the recitation of songs praising the king and the appearance of masks. Ibn Battutah crtiticized these and other pre-Islamic customs. Ibn Battutah was also critical of the practice of sprinkling dust and ashes on the head as a sign of respect before the king. In eleventh-century Ghana, under a non-Muslim king, only those who followed the king's religion knelt down and sprinkled themselves with dust; Muslims were exempted from this practice and they greeted the king by clapping hands. In the Islamized empire of Mali all subjects, Muslims and non-Muslims, had to follow the custom. In other words, under a non-Muslim ruler Muslims were not obliged to perform some traditional ceremonial acts, but under Islamized kings, who themselves combined Islamic and traditional elements, pre-Islamic customs had to be accommodated.

In the fifteenth century Mali lost its control over the Sahel and was cut off from direct contact with the trans-Saharan routes and the larger Muslim world.

In much of West Africa a vernacular style of architecture is used for mosques and other large Muslim buildings. They are generally constructed of mud-brick, with wooden posts used to hold scaffolding when the surface needs repair, as at the mosque in Telli in the Dogon area of Mali.

The Tuareg, a Saharan tribe of Berber origin, conquered Timbuktu in 1433 and became rulers of the area. More than a million Tuareg still live in Niger, Mali, Morocco, Algeria, and Libya. Tuareg men wear large turbans and wrap the ends across their faces to protect them from blowing sand.

The capital declined and was eventually deserted by the foreign Muslim community. As more ethnic groups escaped Mali's domination, the kingdom gradually contracted back to its Malinke nucleus, and the traditional particularistic spirit of the Malinke nation triumphed over the universal supratribal appeal of Islam. Muslim religious leaders, remained attached to the courts of the successor states of Mali and continued to render religious services to those Islamized chiefs, but they lost the Islamic zeal encouraged by the fourteenth-century kings of Mali. The chiefs returned to the middle position between Islam and the traditional religion, with a greater inclination toward the latter. Muslims in the capital and in provincial centers of government became integrated into the state's social and political systems. They were pious and observant believers themselves, but they often had to tolerate the more diluted forms of Islam as practiced by their kings and to take part in ceremonies in which pre-Islamic rites were performed. The situation of these Muslims was different from that of Muslims in commercial towns, which were often autonomous. For example, the king of Mali did not enter Diaba, a town of the fuqaha (those who are experts on Islamic jurisprudence), where the qadi (a judge administering religious law) was the sole authority. Anyone who entered Diaba was safe from the king's oppression and outrage; it was thus called "the town of Allah."

Merchants were carriers of Islam rather than agents of Islamization. They opened routes and exposed isolated societies to external influences, but they were not themselves engaged in the propagation of Islam, which was the work of religious leaders. The leaders became integrated into African societies by playing religious, social, and political roles similar to those of traditional priests. Like traditional priests, Muslim men of religion were peacemakers, who pleaded for those who broke the king's laws. Mosques, like traditional shrines, were considered sanctuaries. Immunity of life and property was extended to men of religion only as long as they kept out of politics and posed no threat to the existing sociopolitical order.

Songhay and Timbuktu

In the fourteenth century, Walata—which served as the southern terminus of the Saharan trade—was still more important as a commercial town than was Timbuktu. The emperor Mansa Musa sought to encourage intellectual life in Timbuktu and Malian scholars to study in Fez. By the first half of the fifteenth century the level of scholarship in Timbuktu was such that a student who came from the Hejaz realized that the scholars of Timbuktu surpassed him in the knowledge of Islamic jurisprudence (fiqh).

Under Malian rule the imams of the Friday mosque were Sudanese. (A Friday mosque is the large mosque where a town's entire population could gather for Friday prayer. A town could have many regular mosques but would most likely have only one Friday mosque.) After the Tuareg conquest of Timbuktu in 1433, scholars from the oases of the northern Sahara replaced Sudanese scholars as the imams of the Friday mosque. It was about the same time that the Sankore scholars, members of three Sanhaja families who had migrated from Walata, became prominent in Timbuktu. Those three Sanhaja families became very closely associated with Akillu, the Tuareg chief. When Sonni Ali, founder of the Songhay kingdom, conquered Timbuktu, Akillu brought a thousand camels to carry the fuqaha of Sankore to Walata. Those people of Sankore who had remained behind in Timbuktu were persecuted, killed, and humiliated by Sonni Ali because, he claimed, "they were close friends of the Tuareg." Even a source as hostile to Sonni Ali as Tarikh al-Sudan (The history of the Sudan) admits that Sonni Ali's persecution of the scholars of Timbuktu notwithstanding, "he acknowledged their eminence, saying: 'without the ulama the world would be no good.' He did favors to other ulama and respected them." The ulama favored by Sonni Ali were the descendants of scholars who had come from the northern Sahara and beyond, who unlike the Sanhaja of the southern Sahara had no relations with the Tuareg, Sonni Ali's enemies.

Sonni Ali combined elements of Islam with beliefs and practices of the Songhay traditional religion and was greatly respected as a magician-king. He observed the fast of Ramadan and gave abundant gifts to mosques, but he also worshiped idols and sought the advice and help of traditional diviners and sorcerers. He pronounced the shahadah (declaration of faith), without understanding its meaning. He prayed but was careless in observing the correct time of the prayers. Sonni Ali therefore was no different than most West African kings who maintained a middle position between Islam and the traditional religion, but he encountered unique historical circumstances. His successful military exploits brought him to rule over regions that had previously been under stronger Islamic influence. The political confrontation with the representatives of Islam, not the deficiency in the practice of Islam, brought about the declaration of Sonni Ali as an infidel. The legal and doctrinal justification of the *takfir* (charge of belief) against Sonni Ali, against the general consensus, was provided by the North African militant Muhammad ibn Abd al-Karim al-Maghili (d. 1503).

Shortly after Sonni Ali's death his son was overthrown by Askiya Muhammad, a senior commander in Sonni Ali's army, who entered into an alliance with the scholars of Timbuktu and with chiefs and governors of the more Islamized western provinces. A new balance was achieved between those provinces west of the Niger bend and Songhay proper, down the river, which remained strongly traditional and had hardly been affected by Islam. Askiya Muhammad made Islam one of the central pillars of the state. He made the pilgrimage to Mecca and visited Egypt on the way. There he met the Egyptian writer and Sufi teacher Jalal al-Din al-Suyuti (1445–1505), who introduced him to the Abbasid caliph. According to al-Ifrani, Askiya Muhammad "took from him [al-Suyuti] his theological teachings and learned from him what is lawful and what is forbidden. He [Askiya Muhammad] also heard his [al-Suyuti's] lessons on the precepts and prescriptions of the Shariah and benefited from his advice and admonitions." He came back with the title of caliph, which was granted him by the Abbasid caliph in Egypt.

From what is known about Songhay under the *Askiyas* (the royal title of the dynasty established by Askiya Muhammad), little was done in practice to reform the empire in line with Islamic political theory. The Askiyas sought the advice of the scholars of Timbuktu on religious issues rather than on matters of state policy, in which army commanders and other senior officials at the court were more influential. In 1498 Askiya Muhammad appointed Mahmud ibn Umar Aqit as qadi. He was succeeded by his three sons, who held office until the end of the sixteenth century. The transfer of the office of qadi to the Aqit family marked the growing influence of the Sankore Sanhaja scholars. As qadi Mahmud ibn Umar Aqit asserted his independence in Timbuktu to the extent that he sent away Askiya Muhammad's messengers, preventing them from carrying out the askiya's orders. There were also tensions in the next generation between Askiya Dawud, son of Askiya Muhammad, and the qadi al-Aqib, son of the qadi Mahmud. Once, following an exchange of hostile words, the qadi refused to see the Askiya, who was made to wait before the qadi's home for a long time before he was given permission to enter. The Askiya humiliated himself before the qadi until reconciliation. There were other ulama in Songhay, who played the traditional role of Muslim divines in Sudanic states as intimate advisers whose relations with the rulers were devoid of the tensions between the Askiyas and the qadis. These ulama prayed for the ruler and recruited supernatural aid to protect him and his kingdom, receiving in return grants of land and charters of privilege. Such documents were known as *hurma* in Songhay and *mahram* in Bornu, meaning "sanctity," "immunity," or "inviolability."

Askiya Muhammad was deposed in 1528 by his son Musa, who defied the intercession in the dispute with his brothers. This was a departure from the accepted norms of political conduct, a sign of the unmitigated rule of violence. The period of illegitimate despotism came to an end with the accession of Askiya Ismail in 1537. He set free his father, Askiya Muhammad, who in return ceremonially invested Askiya Ismail with the insignia that he had received in Cairo from the Abbasid caliph: a green gown, green cape, white turban, and an Arabian sword. Askiya Dawud, the last ruler in the line of Askiya Muhammad's sons, ruled for thirty-three years (1549–82). As a prince he received a good Islamic education, and as king he continued to study with a shaykh who came to the palace every morning. He exceeded his father in generosity toward Muslim scholars. He gave his daughters in marriage to scholars and merchants. When one of the scholars of Timbuktu visited Askiya Dawud in his palace, he was shocked by the persistence of pre-Islamic practices at the court. "I was amazed when I came in," the scholar said, "and I thought you were mad, despicable, and a fool, when I saw the people carry dust on their heads." The askiya laughed and replied, "No, I was not mad myself, and I am reasonable, but I am the head of sinful and haughty madmen, and I therefore made myself mad to frighten them so that they would not act unjustly towards the Muslims." Even a devoted Muslim like Askiya Dawud was therefore unable to relieve the monarchy of its pre-Islamic heritage.

There were between 150 and 180 Quranic schools in Timbuktu in the middle of the sixteenth century, which formed a broad basis for higher levels of learning in all the branches of the Islamic sciences. Students studied a subject with the scholar best known for his authority in that field. By the end of the sixteenth century scholarship in Timbuktu matched that of Morocco. During the time that the most prominent Muslim scholar in Timbuktu, Ahmad Baba (1556–1627), was exiled to Marrakesh (1594–1607), the leading scholars of the Maghreb, including the qadis of Fez and Meknes and the mufti of Marrakesh, came to hear his lessons. At that time intellectual life in Timbuktu was influenced by Egyptian scholars, with whom scholars from Timbuktu studied when they visited Cairo on their way to Mecca. Most of those scholars were from the Shafii school of law, with whom the Maliki scholars of Timbuktu studied subjects other than law, such as the hadith and mysticism. Scholarship in Timbuktu thus had wider exposure than the parochial Maliki scholars of Morocco. Indeed, the scholars of Timbuktu preferred the view of the more sophisticated Egyptian al-Suyuti to the zealous Maghrebi reformer Muhammad ibn Abd al-Karim al-Maghili on issues that were central to West African Muslims. Al-Suyuti saw no harm in the manufacture of amulets, provided there was nothing reprehensible in them, but al-Maghili was against any trade in amulets. Al-Suyuti gave license to some forms of association with non-Muslims, but al-Maghili insisted that between Muslims and infidels there was only jihad.

Sufism was brought to Timbuktu from the Maghreb and the northern Sahara in the fifteenth century. In the sixteenth century the leading scholars of Timbuktu were Sufis. Like contemporary Egyptian Sufis, they were not affiliated to any Sufi brotherhood (*tariqah*). Commerce seems to have been problematic for mystics; a mystic who engaged in commerce was gradually deprived of his nightly visionary encounters with the Prophet. Still, some of the scholars famous as saints and ascetics were quite wealthy, mainly from gifts by the city's merchants, and more so through the generosity of the Askiyas. Members of scholars' families were sometimes important merchants. Individuals might have spent the first part of their lives as merchants before they retired to pursue advanced studies. The scholars of Timbuktu were also spokesmen for the city's trading community. Even legal opinions were influenced by commercial interests, such as Ahmad Baba's ruling on the lawfulness of tobacco, because Timbuktu became an important center for the tobacco trade.

Songhay and Timbuktu in the Seventeenth and Eighteenth Centuries

Following the Moroccan conquest in 1591, under the qadis' leadership the people of Timbuktu adopted a policy of passive submission and noncooperation with the conquering army. Timbuktu, which had been autonomous under the

Students traditionally learned the Quran by memorizing verses copied onto an oblong wooden tablet. With the increased availability of paper this tradition has been abandoned in many regions, but it is still practiced in West Africa, where these two young students display their tablets.

Songhay rule, became the seat of a military government. The presence of an occupying force disturbed life in this city of commerce and scholarship and led to a conflict between the military and the civilian populations. The pasha (highest-ranking official) and his troops resorted to harsh disciplinary measures when all conventions were broken. The pasha ordered the arrest of the leading fuqaha, and their houses were pillaged. Seventy prominent fuqaha were deported in chains to Marrakesh, among them the qadi Umar ibn Mahmud Aqit and Ahmad Baba. The fuqaha were under arrest in Marrakesh for two years, and Umar died in prison. Even after their release they were not allowed to return to Timbuktu. Only Ahmad Baba returned, after almost twenty years in exile.

After the exile of the fuqaha, according to the seventeenth-century author of *Tarikh al-Sudan*, Timbuktu "became a body without a soul." The suffering of the people of Timbuktu increased as the struggle for power among the Moroccan military commanders intensified. The supply of food from the inner delta was cut off, as the routes were intercepted by the Fulbe and the Tuareg. During the seventeenth century the elite of Timbuktu was made up of the *arma*, descendants of the Moroccan conquerors, who held military and political power, the merchants, and the scholars. The political influence of the merchants increased because the pashas needed their financial support, and the merchants no longer needed the scholars as intermediaries. By the end of the seventeenth century, Timbuktu's impoverished mercantile community was no longer able to support a large specialized community of scholars. Lesser scholars, known as *alfas*, earned their livings as traders and artisans, mainly weavers and tailors. By the middle of the eighteenth century the pashalik of Timbuktu was in total eclipse. In about 1770 the Tuareg took possession of Gao, and in 1787 they entered Timbuktu and abolished the office of the pasha. The harshness of the nomads was mitigated by the scholars, whose religious prestige also carried political influence, reaching its peak with the revivalist movement led by Sidi al-Mukhtar al-Kunti (1729–1811).

Linked by the Niger waterway to Timbuktu, the town of

Sufism came to Timbuktu from the Maghreb in the fifteenth century. The Moroccan mystic al-Jazuli (d. 1465), for example, became the center of a popular religious brotherhood that revolved around the recitation of his celebrated book of prayers, and many copies of this work circulated in the region.

Djenné (in south-central Mali) developed as a distribution center for trade to the south. Merchants from the Sahara and North Africa extended their business from Timbuktu to Djenné. Their agents were the Dyula, who carried the trade to the sources of gold and kola in the Akan forest. In Djenné, deep in world of the Mandingue, Islam slowly gained ground, and pre-Islamic customs persisted there until the end of the fifteenth century, when a pious Dyula came from the south and destroyed the "idols' house," where people had continued to worship. The ulama in Djenné were all Soninke and Mandingue and were highly respected by the rulers of Djenné, who sought their blessings.

The Bambara state of Ségou (in southern Mali on the Niger River) was founded in the middle of the eighteenth century by Biton Kulibali, who forced greater centralization to overcome older egalitarian patterns of Bambara communal life. He was supported by Muslim merchants and the ulama but was careful to maintain the balance between traditional and Islamic elements. It was customary for chiefs to send their sons to study with a Muslim cleric as part of their princely education. Although they were not meant to become Muslims, some did; some even became scholars. A qadi of Djenné in the second half of the sixteenth century was "from among the sons of the chiefs of Kala. He withdrew from authority and became a scholar." In this way Biton Kulibali's son, Bakary, became a Muslim. As the ruler of the young Bambara state, Bakary failed to maintain the balance between Islam and tradition and was therefore deposed and killed. At that point N'golo Diara, a former slave of Biton Kulibali, seized power and established a new dynasty in Ségou. He also communicated on several occasions with the ulama in Djenné and Timbuktu, but he skillfully maintained the balance between traditionalism and Islam. While observing some Islamic rites, N'golo also remained the "great priest of the protecting idols."

Through chiefly courts, where Islamic rituals were held, Islamic elements penetrated the culture of the Bambara, including the celebration of Islamic festivals as national feasts. The Scottish explorer Mungo Park (1771–1806), who visited Ségou in 1796 during the reign of Mansong, N'golo's son, was impressed by the influence of the Muslims at the court of Ségou. In the rival Bambara state of Kaarta, Park observed that "the disciples of Mahomet composed nearly one-half of the army," and therefore "the mosques were very crowded" when the entire army gathered into the capital. But Park also recognized the persistence of pre-Islamic beliefs and practices: "Those Negroes, together with the ceremonial part of the Mahomedan religion, retain all their ancient superstitions and even drink strong liquors."

In the eighteenth century there was an abundant supply of slaves in West Africa. Muslims owned more slaves for farming than did their non-Muslim neighbors. Whereas Bambara peasants owned a few slaves, who worked in the fields alongside members of the household, the Muslim Marka owned many slaves, who worked in the fields under the supervision of a foreman, who was himself a slave. The Marka master was then able to follow his commercial or clerical pursuits. Using slaves for farming gave Muslims the leisure to pursue learning and to teach. This was elaborated by the Jakhanke, who contributed to the growth of a rural tradition of Islamic scholarship.

By the fifteenth century Muslims developed a commercial network covering the area from the fringes of the Sahara in the north to the fringes of the forest in the south, and from the Atlantic coast of the Senegambia in the west to Hausaland and Bornu (in northeastern Nigeria) to the east. Most of the traders over this network were extensions of the Wangara, the Mandingue traders who carried on trade and Islam from at least the eleventh century. Those who traded to the west on the Gambia were the Jakhanke. Those Wangara who opened routes to Hausaland merged with the Hausa-speaking traders. Those traders of the middle Niger who entered the Akan forest, where the gold was, in the fifteenth century became known as the Dyula. These traders and the ulama, whether Dyula or Jakhanke, operated in the lands of the unbelievers, and for long periods they had to live in symbiotic relations with non-Muslims. They developed an ideology and a worldview that helped them to survive under these conditions, which Ivor Wilks has associated with al-Hajj Salim Suwari, who lived probably in the late fifteenth century. Suwari is regarded by the Dyula and

Dyula traders made the town of Djenné, two hundred miles downstream from Timbuktu, an entrepôt in the fifteenth century. The congregational mosque, built in traditional style on the foundations of an earlier mosque, still provides the backdrop for a large market.

the Jakhanke as the architect of their ways of life, having formulated precepts for the conduct of Muslims living among unbelievers. Under this ideology, Muslims may accept the authority of non-Muslim rulers, and even support them through the provision if religious services, so far as the Muslims are allowed to strictly observe Islam. Because they were aware of the danger of spiritual back-sliding, as they lived in close proximity to unbelievers, the Muslims were also dedicated to Islamic learning. Because of their relative isolation, they were urged to travel to central places of learning in search of knowledge.

In their southern dispersion, west of the Black Volta River where most of the Dyula operated, the Dyula settled among "stateless" peoples, with whom they interacted socially and culturally but over whom they had little religious influence. Sometimes warriors who shared with the Dyula a common cultural Mandingue background moved along the trade routes, perhaps even as armed guards, and imposed their authority over these stateless people, as was the case of the Kong and the Gonja peoples. In the process of the state formation of Gonja, the warriors accepted Islam from the hands of a Dyula cleric who helped them to win a battle. The Gonja rulers were probably the first in the Volta basin to accept Islam. Shortly thereafter, at the beginning of the eighteenth century, Islam was introduced to Dagomba, where the king encouraged trade and the migration of Muslims. A study of Islam in Dagomba reveals it to be a model for the cultural, social, and political integration of Islam into a state structure in ways that were typical of Mali and Songhay further north four or five centuries earlier.

The Senegambia

The first chapter in the history of Islam in present-day Senegal began with Takrur, whose Islamic militancy was described earlier by al-Bakri. Except for a few references in the Arabic sources of the twelfth and thirteenth centuries, and some oral traditions that are difficult to interpret, little is known about the history of Islam in this region until the end of the fifteenth century. At that time Portuguese sources and the chronicles of Timbuktu converge to shed light on a process of state building led by a Fulbe warrior named Tengella. He first created a Fulbe state in Futa Jallon (the mountainous district in western Guinea), and then moved further north to Futa Toro. In 1512 Tengella was defeated and killed by a Songhay army, and the conquest of Futa Toro was accomplished by Tengella's son, Koli Tengella, who created the Deniankobe dynasty of Futa Toro.

According to *Tarikh al-Sudan*, the descendants of Koli Tengella were considered as good Muslims as the rulers of Mali. But contemporary Tokolor scholars of Futa Toro viewed the Deniankobe as warrior chiefs. At the intersection of the Sahara and the Senegal valley, scholars were in confrontation with warriors. The Tokolor scholars of Futa Toro were known as *Torodbe*, a term that covered people of diverse social status and ethnic origins. They spoke Fulfulde and embraced customs of the pastoral Fuble, but unlike the Fulbe they were sedentary, and they were not necessarily of Fulbe origin. The maxim "Torodo is a beggar" associated them with the mendicant activities of Muslim scholars and students, who lived on charity. The openness of the Torodbe society is expressed in another maxim: "If a fisherman pursues learning, he becomes a Torodo." In Futa Toro, however, learning among the Torodbe was at a lower level compared with the scholarship of their Toronkawa brethren of Hausaland. The Torodbe of Futa Toro were an integral part of the peasant society, unlike the Toronkawa of Hausaland, who separated themselves from both the Fulbe pastoralists and the Hausa-speaking peasants. Although the Toronkawa lived in rural enclaves, they cultivated an urban tradition of learning.

The symbiotic relations between the Deniankobe and the Torodbe had first been disturbed in 1673, when the Torodbe joined the militant movement of Nasir al-Din that spilled over the from the southern Sahara to Futa Toro. This movement was defeated by a coalition of the Deniankobe and Arab warrior tribes. The nomads of the Sahara, north of the Senegal River, continued during the eighteenth century to disturb life in Futa Toro. The Torodbe rose again in the 1770s against the Deniankobe, who had failed to stop the nomads' raids. This uprising developed in a jihad movement that overthrew the Deniankobe and created an Islamic imamate in Futa Toro.

Oral traditions connected the history of the Wolof to the Almoravids through the founding king of Jolof, who is said to have been a descendant of Abu Bakr ibn Umar. Though little known compared with Mali, Jolof, in the west, was nevertheless one of the great Muslim states in medieval West Africa. Its origins go back to the thirteenth century. For some time it was a tributary of Mali, but because of its marginal position, and with its own direct commercial relations with the Sahara, Jolof was culturally and economically autonomous. The kingdom of Jolof disintegrated in the sixteenth century, however, under the impact of the Atlantic trade. Kayor emerged as the most powerful state of the Wolof, both because of its favorable position on the coast and the benefits it derived from European trade. Intensive commercial activities and a process of political centralization enhanced the position of Muslims in Kayor. Since the middle of the fifteenth century European visitors were impressed by the role of Muslims in the courts of the Wolof chiefs as secretaries, counselors, and religious leaders. They considered the Wolof chiefs themselves as Muslims. It is significant, however, that neither in the European sources nor in the oral traditions is there any account of a viable traditional African religion among the Wolof. Oral traditions know no other religion than Islam from the dawn of Wolof history. It seems that most vestiges of organized traditional religion were eliminated under Islam's influence. Muslim religious leaders took over functions of the traditional priests, and even magic and religion were the prerogative of Muslim religious leaders.

The political and military elite were a warrior class, for whom drinking alcohol became a symbol of belonging, which only contributed to the tensions and confrontation between the ulama and the warriors. The growing influence of the Muslims in the court was counterbalanced by the *tyeddo*, the military core of Kayor. For the military and political elite, conversion to Islam implied joining the clerical community, a change of vocation and lifestyle. The Wolof chiefs therefore rejected demands by Muslim militants to convert. Tensions in the Wolof states grew when militant Islamic movements erupted in neighboring countries, mainly in Futa Toro. When Wolof clerics collaborated with the militants, they were severely punished and even sold into slavery, which was a violation of cler-

The foundation of the Fulbe (or Fulani) state in the early sixteenth century marked a major turning point in the history of the Senegambia, the region comprising modern Senegal, Gambia, and Sierra Leone. The recent Great Mosque at Touba, 90 miles east of Dakar, Senegal, shows the internationalization of Islamic culture there, where Islam remains the dominant religion.

ical immunity. Confrontation with militant Islamic movements changed political perceptions toward Islam. Whereas earlier European accounts referred to the Wolof as Muslims, later European travelers (since the end of the eighteenth century and throughout the nineteenth century), said that the Wolof were Muslims but their rulers were "pagans." It was only since the end of the nineteenth century that the entire Wolof society converted to Islam.

Kanem and Bornu

An early trans-Saharan route connected Tripoli on the Mediterranean with Lake Chad. Kanem (now part of Chad) emerged as one of the earliest African kingdoms on the northeastern corner of Lake Chad.

According to *Kitab al-Istibsar*, an anonymous work written in 1191, and Ibn Said (1217–86), writing some time after 1269, the people of Kanem converted to Islam at the beginning of the twelfth century. More than in any other early African state in which Islam remained restricted to the court, in Kanem Islam spread throughout the land to the entire population shortly after the king's conversion. According to the fifteenth-century Egyptian historian al-Maqrizi, the king of Kanem went on a pilgrimage to Mecca and built a madrasa in Cairo for students from Kanem in the first half of the thirteenth century. At the same time a devout Muslim king broke with tradition by opening "a certain thing wrapped up and hidden away, whereon depended their victory in war, called Mune, which no one dared to open." Traditions suggest that this act brought about the hostilities between the Saifawa ruling dynasty and the rival Bulala clan, of more traditionalist disposition. The Saifawa were forced to abandon Kanem and to resettle in Bornu, on the southwestern corner of Lake Chad. This was in the middle of the fourteenth century, but the Saifawa consolidated their hold over the new country only toward the end of the fifteenth century, with the establishment of the capital at N'Gazargamu.

This took place during the reign of Ali Ghaji ibn Dunama (r. 1476–1503), who is remembered as an exemplary Muslim, always surrounded by ulama, who were his confidants. He was a contemporary of other reformist rulers, such as Rumfa of Kano and Askiya Muhammad of Songhay. He was also the first ruler of Bornu to assume the title of caliph. The claim to the caliphate might have been in response to a similar claim by the Songhay ruler Askiya Muhammad. Ali Ghaji visited Cairo on his way to Mecca in 1484 and met the Egyptian writer and Sufi teacher Jalal al-Din al-Suyuti. It is likely that al-Suyuti obtained the title of caliph from the Abbasid caliph of Cairo for Mai Ali Ghaji, as he had earlier for Askiya Muhammad. The Bornu caliphate reached its peak under Mai Idris Alawma (r. 1570–1603), when all the state dignitaries were Muslim and the capital at N'Gazargamu was an important center for Islamic learning. Qadis, imams, and

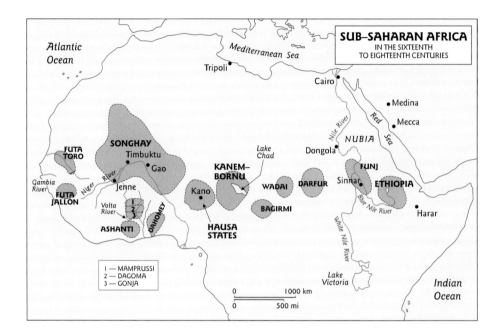

teachers were granted privileges and were exempted from taxation. The shariah became the law of the state, which was imposed on the entire population. Mai Idris had diplomatic relations with the Ottomans, who conquered Tripoli in 1551 and annexed Fezzan (in southwestern Libya) in 1577. Fearing the growing power of the Ottomans, in 1582 Mai Idris sent a delegation to the Moroccan sultan al-Mansur (1578–1603) who also had ambitions toward Sudan.

In western Sudan the opening of new sources of gold extended trade routes further south, which encouraged the development of chiefdoms and the spread of Islam. But around Lake Chad the provision of slaves by raids created a hostile boundary. Until the sixteenth century Kanem and Bornu expanded only northward to the Sahara. The countries south of Lake Chad, a hunting ground for slaves, were left outside the boundaries of Bornu. The southward expansion of Bornu was also hindered by natural barriers: the Mandara mountains, the dense vegetation, and marshes created by the seasonal flooding of Lake Chad and the Logone and Shari Rivers. The southern boundaries of Kanem and Bornu were also the southern frontier for the expansion of Islam. After the Ottomans conquered Fezzan, Bornu could not expand to the north and thus turned to the south. Mai Idris occupied the northern parts of the land of the Kotoko as well as Mandara and the region of Lake Fitri. People in the conquered lands became Muslim. About the same time, in the sixteenth century, the state of Bagirmi emerged on the right bank of the Shari River, in a region that had formerly been raided for slaves. Shortly thereafter, the rulers of Bagirmi became Islamized.

The rulers of Bornu in the seventeenth and eighteenth centuries were pious and learned. Scholars held disputations before the mai concerning doubtful points of law and dogma. Scholars and venerated saints received *mahrams* (charters), which removed all obstacles from their worldly existence, on condition that they seek divine favors for their royal benefactors. The mai generously supported scholars and attracted students from far and wide. Distinguished scholars were persuaded to live there, they were given houses, and great honor was bestowed upon them. The greatest scholars of the eighteenth century in central Sudan spent time in N'Gazargamu as a necessary part of their education and enjoyed the mai's patronage. Scholars from Bornu studied at al-Azhar University in Cairo, where the madrasa that had been established in the thirteenth century was still in existence in the eighteenth century. But even when most of the scholars collaborated with the Bornu ruler and recognized him as caliph, there were scholars who criticized their colleagues for holding institutional offices of the state. These radical scholars withdrew from the centers of political power and established autonomous religious communities. But even they received mahrams, to encourage and sustain the development of Islamic learning. These enclaves of rural scholarship, known as *mallamati*, were considered among the most important centers of learning in central Sudan. Succession to leadership in the mallamati was hereditary because of the belief that the *baraka* (divine blessing) is transmitted in the family and because the mahram was granted to the ulama and his descendants. These communities jealously guarded their autonomy and maintained minimal communications with the larger society and with the state. They criticized existing religious practices and provoked the hostility of the established scholars. The scholars sensed the threat of such communities that refused to be integrated into the existing sociopolitical order. The mallamati were in fact Sufi communities in rural enclaves that performed mystical exercises, including retreats in the bush. Like their contemporary Sufis in Timbuktu, they claimed no affiliation with a *tariquah* or Sufi brotherhood.

By the end of the eighteenth century Islam was deeply rooted in the everyday life of the ordinary people, affecting them from the naming ceremony to their funerals. This was admitted by Muhammad Bello in *Infaq al-Maysur* (1951): "Islam was widespread not only among the rulers and ministers, but also among the local people. Indeed there are not to be found in these countries ordinary people more scrupulous than they in reciting the Quran and reading it and memorizing it and writing it out." But even in Bornu, perhaps the most Islamized of all African states, pre-Islamic elements persisted. There was much dissatisfaction in the eighteenth century. Many of the scholars who criticized Kanuri society were Fulbe. But the most damaging criticism of the contemporary scene was made by a Kanuri scholar, Muhammad ibn al-Hajj Abd al-Rahman al-Barnawi (d. 1755), known as Hajirmai, who called the rulers of Bornu tyrants, accusing them of being corrupt and for imposing illegal taxation; the rich for hoarding food at times of famine in the hope of profit; and judges and governors for accepting gifts. There were allegations of human sacrifices at the time of the annual flood in the river Komadugu Yobe, and of libations of milk from a black cow before the annual repairs to the city wall. These accusations were echoed by Muhammad Bello as a pretext to the jihad against Bornu: "Their rulers and chiefs have places to which they ride, and where they offer sacrifices and then pour the blood on the gates of their towns. . . . They also perform rites to the river. . . ."

Hausaland before the Jihad

In the entire corpus of Arabic sources for West African history there is no reference to the Hausa states, with one exception. When in Takedda in the Aïr (the mountainous region in north-central Niger), Ibn Battutah referred to Gobir as one of the destinations for the export of Takedda copper. Because the information of the Arab geographers came through commercial routes, Hausaland was not directly connected to North Africa by trade routes across the Sahara.

The *Kano Chronicle*, which is the principal source for the development of Islam in Hausaland, had first been written in the middle of the seventeenth century. The reigns of leaders and the events since 1650 were recorded as contemporary or eyewitness accounts. Records of the century before 1650 were based on living memory. But accounts of earlier periods were basically oral traditions, reflecting seventeenth-century interests and realities. The *Kano Chronicle* provides a chronological framework for the opening of trade routes to Hausaland. In the middle of the fourteenth century Mandingue traders, the Wangara, came from Mali in the west. A century later salt came from Aïr (called Asben until conquered by Berbers) in the north and kola nuts from Gonja in the south. Bornu traders came from the northeast.

Traders from Mali brought Islam to the central African region of Hausaland in the fourteenth century. Pre-Islamic traditions remained strong and were often integrated into traditional Islamic practices. This small copy of the Quran, made in the late seventeenth or early eighteenth century, combines a distinctive African type of Arabic script with bold graphic designs.

The Wangara ulama that accompanied the traders from Mali in the fourteenth century are credited in the traditions of Kano as being the first to bring Islam to Kano. Under their influence, the chief of

Kano began to pray, and a mosque was built beneath the sacred tree. The leading ulama were given official appointments to serve the king and the Muslim community. Opposition to the Muslims came from the local priests, but they were unable to stand the magical power of the Muslim prayers. The custodians of the traditional religion were defeated on their own ground by a superior magical power. But the real test to the efficacy of the new religion was when the Muslims brought victory to the king of Kano over his most forceful enemy. During the first crisis, when the king of Kano failed to win a war, disappointed by the Muslims, he turned back to the traditional priest, who promised his help if the king restored the rites that his father had destroyed. The chief of Kano complied and the traditional priest secured victory over the enemies. Islam temporarily lost ground.

The second generation reverted to traditional religion, but the third generation turned over completely to Islam. In Kano, as in other African states, kings' sons received elementary Quranic instruction. A few went beyond what was expected of princes, became attached to their masters, and turned sincere Muslims. There was, however, the built-in contradiction between being a warrior chief and being a Muslim. This was explained to Umar, the king of Kano, by his Muslim friend, after which Umar remained faithful to Islam and abdicated as king. The coming of Islam to Kano coincided with the shift of the Saifawa dynasty from Kanem to Bornu, closer to Hausaland. Although the first Muslim ulama came from Mali in the west, it seems that Islamic influence from Bornu was at least as important.

In the middle of the fifteenth century the Toronkawa, settled Fulbe scholars, brought a higher level of Islamic learning compared with that of the earlier Wangara ulama. The Islamic tradition of learning among the Toronkawa was similar to that in Timbuktu in the fifteenth and sixteenth centuries. The Toronkawa lived in rural enclaves, did not render religious services to the local rulers, and were not involved in non-Islamic ceremonies. They communicated with the rulers but did not become integrated into the political system. The tensions generated by that mental and physical distance later led to confrontation and to a jihad. The Toronkawa did not seem to have been softened physically by their clerical habits, and unlike urban scholars, they were not strangers to horsemanship and warfare. Islam became integrated into Hausa religious, social, and cultural life without breaking with the past, which was symbolized by the cutting of the sacred tree under which the original mosque had been built. This reform is associated with the king of Kano, Muhammad Rumfa, a contemporary of the reformist kings Askiya Muhammad in Songhay and Ali Ghaji in Bornu. The reformist ideology was articulated by Abd al-Karim al-Maghili, the North African militant scholar, who visited Kano in 1491 before his visit to Songhay.

In the sixteenth century the level and sophistication of scholarship was heightened, with the growth of the repertoire of books taught in Kano. Piety and scholarship among the kings of Kano seem to have reached their peak in the second half of the sixteenth century, a period parallel to that of Mai Idris in Bornu. Scholars from Timbuktu visited both Kano and Katsina, the most important market town in Hausaland until the end of the eighteenth century, on their way to the pilgrimage to Mecca, taught there for some time, and contributed to the growth of local Hausa scholarship. Non-Muslims who were absorbed in the Hausa states and culture became known as Maguzawa, from the Arabic *majus*, "the Magi." They were of diverse ethnic origins but shared a common Hausa language and culture. For the majority of the peasants, Islam was no more than one cult among many. The cult of *bori* spirits was the most widespread pre-Islamic prac-

As everywhere in the Islamic lands, Muslims celebrate the end of Ramadan, the month of fasting, with a festival. Here, a group of mounted notables rides through the streets of Kano, Nigeria, celebrating the Id al-Fitr with drums and tambourines.

tice that survived in Hausaland, mainly among women. Bori spirits were given Muslim names, and Muslim jinns (genies, whose existence are completely accepted in official Islam) became identified with the bori spirits. The fact that the bori spirits became Islamized made it more difficult to eradicate them.

During the seventeenth and eighteenth centuries Kano was repeatedly attacked by the Jukun, called Kwararafa in the *Kano Chronicle*, from the south. The kings of Kano sought relief in rituals and magic from both "non-Muslim" Maguzawa priests and from local Muslim divines who employed similar practices. Each of the Hausa city-states had its own experience with Islam. Katsina also had the largest Wangara commercial community, which influenced politics there. By the end of the eighteenth century the rulers and the population of Katsina were largely Islamized. But the legitimacy of the dynasty was still based on the traditional belief system. Even those rulers more committed to Islam were genuinely torn between two systems of religious beliefs. The slaves of the palace opposed attempts to revive the Sunna and to impose the shariah.

The ulama, who were alienated from the rulers, preferred to live in the periphery of Katsina, in towns within a radius of fifteen kilometers from Katsina, where they enjoyed greater autonomy. The mosques of these towns attracted more people to pray than mosques in the capital. The rulers ignored them because of their small numbers and their peripheral location, but it was from these small towns that the supporters of the jihad of Uthman dan Fodio (1755–1817) came. Yandoto had been created by the Wangara merchants for the trade in kola nuts from the Akan forest, southwest of Hausaland. Yandoto prospered in the second half of the eighteenth century when the kola trade was at its peak, which made its merchants and scholars supporters of the status quo and opponents of the jihad of Uthman dan Fodio. He enumerated the sins of the Hausa rulers that justified the jihad: the veneration of trees and rocks by making sacrifices and pouring libations; divination by sand, stars, spirits, and by the sound of the movements of birds; consultation with soothsayers; use of magic; and writing of the names of Allah or extracts of the Quran on polluted things, such as the bones of the dead, and drinking the solution when it is washed off and mixed with snake skin. All these "sins" may be counted in many Muslim societies in Africa, representing the surviving pre-Islamic traditions. Most scholars did not challenge this ambiguous situation. The dramatic point of no return in the development of Islamic militancy was when militants reintroduced the concept of takfir by declaring as infidels those who had previously been considered Muslims.

Eastern Sudan

The defeat of the Arabs in 652 before the walls of the Nubian capital was the worst that they suffered during their conquests. The Nubians were able to resist the Muslim expansion to the south for almost six centuries. Arab and Muslim

For more than two centuries the sultans of the Funj dynasty (1553–1762) of Sinnar (modern Sennar) on the Blue Nile dominated the eastern Sudan. The court of Sinnar attracted many holy men, and dervishes still play an important role in Sudanese life, as shown by these dancing dervishes in Omdurman.

penetration into the country south of Egypt was not by means of military conquest but through gradual infiltration. Slave raiding and gold mining brought Arabs to the land of Béja, between the Nile and the Red Sea. Immigrant Arabs who became absorbed among the northern Béja developed bilingual communities of mixed descent, which during the tenth century were the first Béja Muslims. By the tenth century Muslims represented a quarter of the merchants in the capital of the Christian kingdom of Nubia. In the tenth and eleventh centuries the Fatimid rulers of Egypt were anxious to push the Arab nomads of the Banu Hilal and related tribes away from the cultivated lands of Egypt. Most of the Banu Hilal moved west toward North Africa, while others penetrated the northern parts of the Christian kingdom of Nubia. By 1174 this zone had a majority of Muslims and was recognized officially as an Islamic province under an Arab dignitary known as Kanz al-Dawla.

As the Christian kingdom was disintegrating, the Mamluk sultan of Egypt and Syria, Baybars (r. 1260–77), sent a force in 1276 that conquered Makuria (in the Sudan). As "protected people," the Nubians were allowed to keep their Christian religion. The Egyptians appointed a member of the old royal family to rule in their name. Repeated attempts by the Nubians to shake off foreign rule were defeated and caused the reinforcement of Muslim garrisons. In 1324 Kanz al-Dawla seized the throne from the old dynasty and the country disintegrated into warring factions. During the time between the eclipse of the Christian kingdom around 1300 and the rise of the first Muslim states around 1500, the pastoral communities who inhabited the extensive lands beyond the irrigated banks of the Nile were free of any political authority. The central lands of eastern Sudan were dominated for more than two centuries by the sultans of the Funj dynasty of Sinnar. It is said that the Ottoman sultan Selim (r. 1512–20), who conquered Egypt in 1517, did not advance further south to conquer Sinnar because of the Islamic credentials of the first Funj sultan. Whatever the historicity of this tradition, it clearly indicates that from the beginning, Islam played an important role in the sultanate of Sinnar.

Militant puritanical movements, sometimes with millenarian elements, transformed central African Islam from the late eighteenth century. Observance of the rules of Islam became the criterion to evaluate a person's status as a Muslim. These prayer beads from el-Fasher in the western Sudan were a pilgrim's souvenir of his pilgrimage to Mecca, one of the Five Pillars of Islam.

The court of Sinnar attracted immigrant holy men, who received generous royal patronage through royal grants of landed estates or through appointments to privileged positions. Holy men enjoyed various exemptions from taxation and rights of geographical mobility and personal security. The formal status of Muslim holy men in Sinnar was in between that of noblemen and that of commoners. An immigrant holy man held a higher status than a native-born cleric. Holy men who used their power to defend the interests of the common people enjoyed greater popularity than those who held official positions as courtiers and judges. Adherence to Islam in the sultanate of Sinnar was not individual; rather, it was corporate and communal, because all subjects of a Muslim ruler were assumed to be Muslims by definition, even without a formal act of conversion, and regardless of lifestyle. Disobedience to the king, however, implied rejection of Islam and therefore the community, and penalties were appropriate to apostasy and unbelief.

The next significant stage in Sinnar began in the third quarter of the seventeenth century, when the sultan of Sinnar established a fixed capital and built an impressive royal mosque. He also encouraged trade by sending caravans to Egypt and to the Red Sea port of Sawakin, which was controlled by the Ottomans. Before that, commerce had been a royal monopoly, and contacts with visiting merchants were only through royal agencies, at designated places near the capital. As trade became free of royal monopoly, an indigenous urban-based middle class developed, and new towns appeared at the beginning of the eighteenth century. Social and economic changes undermined the existing political system in Sinnar. The old matrilineal dynasty was overthrown in 1718. The Funj system, which had united the elite and enforced hierarchy among its members, gave way to the sale of titles and offices to competing warlords. In the second half of the eighteenth century these warlords engaged in internal civil wars.

In the new towns, people made wealth and achieved status through economic gains. For the new urban population, legally oriented interpretations of Islam offered authoritative paradigms of lifestyles. Islamic instruction, public prayers, and conformist dress gave the new urban-based middle class an entirely new cultural and ethnic identity as Arabs. Observance of the rules of Islam became the criterion to evaluate a person's status as a Muslim. Following the conquest of eastern Sudan by the Egyptian ruler Muhammad Ali Pasha in 1821, this emergent middle class of Sinnar allied itself with the Turko-Egyptian regime. In Sinnar as well as in Darfur and Wadai, the two western states that emerged in the seventeenth century, the southern communities—known as Nuba in Sinnar, Fertit in Darfur, and Kirdi in Wadai—were compelled to pay taxes in the form of ivory, gold, or slaves. If they failed, they were liable to punitive raids and selective or mass enslavement.

The Horn of Africa

In the seventh century, when Islam began its expansion into Africa, Christianity was the dominant religion in the lands that extended along the Mediterranean, from

Morocco to Egypt, in the hinterland of Egypt and of the Red Sea, in Nubia and Ethiopia. By the twelfth century the last indigenous Christians disappeared from North Africa west of Egypt. In Egypt the Christians, who still formed about half of the population in the tenth century, were later reduced to a minority of no more than fifteen percent. In eastern Sudan Christianity began to loose ground in the twelfth century and was eliminated by the fourteenth century. It was therefore only in the highlands of Ethiopia that Christianity survived centuries of confrontation with Islam. Ethiopia is Arabia's closest neighbor, separated only by the Red Sea. In the pre-Islamic periods the Ethiopians crossed the Red Sea to invade Arabia, but the narrow stretch of water was enough of a barrier to the Arab bedouins. But what deterred these Arab warriors was not a problem for Arab traders, who from the ports of the Red Sea and the gulf developed a maritime trade that brought Islam to the islands and the shores of the Red Sea and the Indian Ocean.

As early as the eighth century the island of Dahlak Kebir was the outlet for Arab trade and a point of departure for the diffusion of Islam to the Ethiopian hinterland. Mogadishu (a seaport of Somalia), which had been founded sometime between the eighth and tenth centuries, developed into a sultanate in the twelfth century. By the thirteenth century there were Muslim communities in the Ethiopian highlands that traded under the protection of the Christian state. There were also a number of Muslim principalities along trade routes from the coast to the Christian highlands and to the Rift Valley Lakes to the south. By that time many of the nomads of the Horn, such as the Afar and the Somali, had become Muslims. As the Solominid dynasty of Ethiopia began its expansion to the south, it clashed with the Muslim principalities over the control of the long-distance trade routes. In 1332 an alliance of the Muslim principalities was defeated and the principalities became tributary to Ethiopia. The sultanate of Adal, which emerged as the major Muslim principality from 1420 to 1560, seems to have recruited its military force mainly from among the Somalis. In its protracted wars with the Christian state of Ethiopia, Adal sought the support of the Mamluk sultanate of Egypt.

Ethiopia's continuous military campaigns encouraged the development of Islamic militancy, which in 1529 took the form of a jihad led by Ahmad Ibrahim al-Ghazi of Harar, known as Ahmad Gran (ca. 1506–43). Ahmad Gran conquered most of the Ethiopian state. The strife between Muslims and Christians in the first half of the sixteenth century in Ethiopia and the Horn became part of a larger Muslim-Christian confrontation in the Red Sea between the Portuguese, who had penetrated the Indian Ocean, and the Ottomans, who had conquered Egypt in 1517 and Yemen in 1525. Ahmad Gran was killed in 1543 in an engagement with a small contingent of Portuguese soldiers that came to the aid of their Christian

In 1322–23 Abu Bakr ibn Muhammad, ruler of the city of Mogadishu in what is now Somalia, struck coins made mostly of base metal and inscribed with his name (above). In the twelfth century, Sultan Hasan ibn Sulayman of the island of Kilwan, off the coast of modern Tanzania, minted this copper coin (below).

Ethiopian allies. Because Ahmad Gran had not consolidated his conquests, the entire Islamic imamate that he was about to create collapsed. By 1555 the Ethiopian state regained all the territories it had held before the jihad, where they found a significant number of Muslims. In about 1630 a Portuguese missionary estimated that Muslims constituted one-third of Ethiopia's population. The emperor of Ethiopia, Yohannes I (r. 1667–82), who sensed the threat of the expansion of Islam, took measures to isolate the Muslims. He ordered that Muslims live in separate villages and town quarters, and that Christians must not eat with Muslims or drink from cups used by Muslims. They greeted Muslims with the left hand, as a sign of contempt.

More important still, the weakening of both the Christian state and the Muslim principalities left the land open to the mass migrations of the pastoral Oromo people into the fertile highlands. The Oromo, who inserted themselves between the Muslims and the Christians, brought about the suspension of hostilities between the two contending religions. By the eighteenth century the Oromo gradually became Muslim and played an active role in the expansion of Islam in the region. Their chiefly families embraced Islam, gave patronage to Muslim scholars, and appointed qadis to make Islam increasingly an integral part of their subject's lives.

The East African Coast

The story of Islam on the East African coast is told by a mosque at Shanga in the Lamu archipelago (off the eastern coast of Kenya). Its original construction is dated between 780 and 850, and it survived until the early fifteen century. The con-

tinual reconstruction of this mosque was aimed at accommodating a constantly growing Muslim community. The accelerated expansion of Islam on Africa's east coast occurred in the thirteenth century, as suggested by the remains of medieval towns in excavations at Kilwa (in southeastern Tanzania) and elsewhere. By the fourteenth century there were more than thirty Muslim communities with mosques along the coast and in the Comoro Islands and in Madagascar. From Arabia the Shafii school of law spread to East Africa and elsewhere along the shores of the Indian Ocean.

The reconstruction of the history of Islam on the East African coast, according to the archaeological evidence, is confirmed by the Arabic sources. In the tenth century the Arab historian and traveler al-Masudi recorded the presence of Muslims in the land of the Zanj, as the East African coast was known to the Arabs. Muslims gradually became the majority in settlements that enjoyed the prosperity of an ever-growing trade. Islamic influences came to East Africa from several directions, but the most important influence was from Yemen and the Hadramawt

Islam came to East Africa primarily from Yemen and the Hadramawt on the south coast of Arabia. Muslim sailors crossed the Indian Ocean in special lateen-rigged ships called dhows, similar to the ones still seen in the harbor of Lamu on the Kenyan coast.

(a region in the southern Arabian peninsula), from where shurafa families reached the East African coast, particularly since the thirteenth century. One of these families provided the Abul-Mawahib dynasty of Kilwa. Ibn Battutah visited Kilwa in 1331, where the ruler's court was frequented by holy men and shurafa. Ibn Battutah reported about the experts on Islamic jurisprudence also in Mogadishu.

Conversion in the early centuries proceeded slowly and unevenly, but by the time the first Europeans arrived Islam had already achieved majority status in dozens of coastal towns. In the seventeenth century Pate (in Kenya) became an important entrepôt of the slave trade. The Muslim traders of Pate had connections with Arabia, with India, and even with Java. Knowledge of spoken and written Arabic was restricted to first-generation migrants from the Arabian peninsula and to those few who studied abroad. Swahili became a written language only in the eighteenth century, and the Swahili-speaking Muslims were therefore practically illiterate. The limited interaction of Arabic and Swahili explains why there was no significant borrowing of Arabic words into the Swahili language before the seventeenth century. The Hadrami immigrants contributed to the development of a written coastal literature. They began by writing works in their native Arabic, but as they became integrated into the local Swahili-speaking society, coastal scholars of Hadrami background began writing in Swahili. Consequently, the earliest written poetry from the coast dates from the middle of the seventeenth century.

The Lamu archipelago became the religious and cultural heartland of the East African coast between 1550 and 1800. Many mosques were built there, including this one, at Shela on Lamu Island.

The Lamu archipelago became the religious and cultural heartland of the coast between 1550 and 1800. From Pate shurafa families moved further south, bringing with them their spiritual charisma and scholarly traditions. The Swahili dialect of the Pate-Lamu region had a large preponderance on the southern coastal dialects at that time, thus indicating a southward migration of a large and prestigious group of northern immigrants from the Pate region. The shurafa, scholars and holy men of Pate, known for their learning and piety, might have contributed to infusing a certain militancy to East African Islam. They fueled Islamic resistance to the Portuguese, which spread from Pate to other parts of the East African coast. The final expulsion of the Portuguese from the coast north of Mozambique in 1728 opened a new era in the history of Islam in East Africa. This new period is connected with the arrival of the Omanis in the eighteenth century and the establishment of the Zanzibar sultanate in the 1820s. One aspect of the change was the institutionalization of the administration of the shariah through appointed qadis, whereas before the relocation of the sultanate from Oman to Zanzibar, the administration of the shariah had been informal and irregular in most coastal centers. Local scholars served in advisory capacities to local rulers, who reserved for themselves the actual rights of adjudication.

Muslims arrived to the Cape colony in South Africa as early as 1652. They were political exiles from Indonesia, whom the Dutch defeated in their homelands.

Many Muslims came to East Africa from India in the nineteenth and twentieth centuries, when both regions were part of the British Empire. Muslims comprise only a small portion of the population of modern-day Kenya, but they play an important role in life there. The main mosque in Nairobi is modeled on Indian prototypes.

Muslims were therefore referred to in the Cape as "Malays." The Dutch also brought convicts from all over the Indian Ocean to work in gangs on the fortification and harbor of Cape Town. The convict population remained a source of Muslims, provided the early ulama, and became leaders of an alternative Cape community. There were many Muslims among the sixty-three thousand slaves who came ashore in South Africa between 1652 and 1807 from the Indian Ocean. By the 1790s free Muslims were numerous enough to form a small but self-assured mercantile community in Cape Town. Some of them made the pilgrimage to Mecca by way of Mauritius.

The Islamization of Africa

The process of Islamization began when Muslims' prayers and amulets succeeded where the local priests failed. Rulers were the early recipients of Islamic influence, and the royal courts mediated Islamic influence to the common people. Pre-Islamic customs persisted even at the courts of rulers who were fully committed to Islam, however. In about 1500 the rulers of Songhay, Kano, and Bornu attempted to reform Islam, with limited results. Most scholars collaborated with the rulers, but the more radical scholars withdrew from the centers of political power and established autonomous religious communities, enclaves of rural scholarship based on slave farming, where the spirit of Islamic militancy was cultivated. Pre-Islamic customs that had persisted for centuries and been accepted as part of the accommodation of Islam became unforgivable in the view of militant Muslims. Rulers who had previously been considered Muslims were declared infidels, and became the target for jihad.

In Sudan, three major states developed in the grasslands south of Nubia since 1500—Funj, Darfur, and Wadai—where Islam was corporate and communal. All obedient subjects were considered Muslims, whatever their way of life, while disobedience implied rejection of the corporate Islam of the community, and therefore apostasy. Toward the end of the seventeenth century a new urban-based middle class emerged that assumed an entirely new cultural and ethnic identity as Arabs. Observance of the rules of Islam became the criterion to evaluate a person's status as a Muslim. The popular Islam of the holy men and the more conformist Islam of the urban population were brought together by reformed brotherhoods that developed in Sudan since the last quarter of the eighteenth century.

It was only in the highlands of Ethiopia that Christianity survived centuries of confrontation with Islam. Ethiopia's continuous military campaigns encouraged the development of Islamic militancy, which in 1529 took the form of a jihad led by Ahmad Gran. The weakening of both the Christian state and the Muslim principalities laid the land open to the mass migrations of the pastoral Oromo people into the fertile highlands. By the eighteenth century, the Oromo gradually became Muslim and played an active role in the expansion of Islam in the region.

The accelerated expansion of Islam on the coast of East Africa occurred in the thirteenth century. Muslims gradually became the majority in settlements that enjoyed the prosperity of an ever-growing trade. By the sixteenth century, when the first Europeans arrived, Islam had already achieved majority status in the coastal towns. The arrival of the Omanis in the eighteenth century, and the establishment of the Zanzibar sultanate in the 1820s, brought about the creation of more formal Islamic institutions on the East African coast.

CHAPTER TWELVE

Foundations for Renewal and Reform

ISLAMIC MOVEMENTS IN THE EIGHTEENTH AND NINETEENTH CENTURIES

John Obert Voll

The Muslim world experienced many different movements of activism, revival, and reform during the eighteenth and nineteenth centuries. Although some of these movements were responses to the declining effectiveness of military and political institutions, many of them show the continuing expansion of the Islamic community of believers. The period following the sixteenth-century era of the greatness of the major sultanates and gunpowder empires was a time of transition in terms of social and political institutions. Throughout the Muslim world intellectuals and rulers were actively engaged in interpreting the Islamic heritage in ways that would provide effective foundations for the emerging sociopolitical structures. In Islamic terms this involved long-standing traditions of invoking and using individual informed judgment in interpreting the fundamental principles of Islam (called *ijtihad*) and engaging in renewal of faith and society.

The eighteenth and nineteenth centuries were times of transformation of societies and states throughout the eastern hemisphere, and movements of Islamic renewal and reform were also part of that broader context. In Europe the new institutions and ideologies associated with the emergence of the early modern nation-states were developing, and by the early nineteenth century the industrial revolution was creating bases of increased economic and military power for western European states. The imperial expansion of these states brought much

(Left) Following the political chaos of eighteenth-century Iran, the town of Karbala in Iraq, site of the martyrdom of Muhammad's grandson Husayn ibn Ali in 680, became the major center of Shiite scholarship. The mosques near the graves of Husayn and his half-brother Abbas have golden domes, signifying their importance as shrines for the many Shiite pilgrims from Iran, where Shiism has been the dominant sect since the Safavid period.

of the Muslim world under either direct or indirect European control by the beginning of the twentieth century.

The European imperial expansion of the eighteenth and nineteenth centuries became an increasingly important factor in Muslim movements of renewal and reform. Although the older dynamics of Islamic renewal continued to operate, the internal evolution of Muslim societies within the older historical modes of renewal and reform was preempted in many ways by the success of European military and economic expansion. During the eighteenth century most reform efforts were within the more Islamic framework, but in the nineteenth century Islamic activist movements were increasingly involved in resistance to European imperial expansion and in intellectual adaptation to the challenges of European ideas and technologies.

The early modern era was a time of important transitions and transformations in the Muslim world. The great imperial states of the sixteenth century began to lose wars and lost their characteristic openness to new technologies and techniques. For many observers, and later historians, this is identified as an era of decline because of this reduction in military power and regional political domination. The long-term trends of the Islamization of societies in Sub-Saharan Africa and in South, Central, and Southeast Asia continued, however, and sometimes accelerated as movements of renewal and reform emerged in response both to weakness and to new opportunities for nonmilitary expansion. This expansion was at times aided rather than hindered by European imperial expansion.

Reform and Renewal in the Large Central States

During the seventeenth and eighteenth centuries the three largest states in the central parts of the Muslim world—the Ottoman, Mughal, and Safavid empires—faced both internal and external challenges. There were administrative and institutional reform efforts that were sometimes not specifically Islamic in the way they were defined. In the eighteenth century, however, movements that were explicitly Islamic in their advocacy of renewal and reform became important elements in the responses of Muslim societies to the changing historical conditions.

The military expansion of the Ottoman Empire ceased by the end of the seventeenth century. The failure of the last great effort by the Ottomans to capture Vienna in 1683 was a sign of Ottoman weakness, which was confirmed by the defeats of the Ottomans in wars at the end of the century. The Treaty of Karlowitz in 1699 ratified the loss of significant territories to European powers and set the stage for a new era of Ottoman history. Ottoman governmental and official reform efforts were not distinctively Islamic, either in style or in the way the need for change was presented. During the late seventeenth century members of the

Koprulu family served as grand viziers and succeeded for a time in imposing reforms that increased administrative efficiency and reduced official corruption. Although these reforms were presented as a necessary part of the preservation of the sultanate, they were not programs of explicitly Islamic renewal.

A different style of official reform efforts developed in the eighteenth century. Ottoman officials had previously been aware of problems, but they had largely used past successful experiences and domestic sources of inspiration as the basis for their reform programs. Governmental reform, especially in military developments, gradually came to be based on efforts to adopt European methods and technologies, however. European advisers, such as Comte de Bonneval in the 1730s and Baron de Tott later in the century, were recruited to introduce new military techniques. Such fads as the "tulip craze" during the reign of Sultan Ahmed III (r. 1703–30) reflected the greater interest in European culture among some of the ruling elite. The climax of this type of reform effort came with the attempt to implement a relatively comprehensive governmental reform program called the Nizam-i Jedid or "New System" by Sultan Selim III (r. 1789–1807). This program called for the creation of a Western-style army and significant changes in administrative structures. Although Selim was deposed by a coalition of conservative forces, a significant foundation for the identification of official governmental reform with westernization had been laid. Although such reform programs were not anti-Islamic, they were not primarily programs of Islamic renewal.

Movements of Islamic renewal developed within the Ottoman Empire during the eighteenth century, but they did not have governmental reform as their goal.

The 1718 Treaty of Passarovitz with the Austrians and the Venetians opened Ottoman society to European methods and technologies. In the trail of European advisers came European artists, such as Antoine Ignace Melling, court artist of the French emperor Louis XVIII. Melling's *Voyage pittoresque de Constantinople*, published in Paris in 1819, contained engravings showing scenes of daily life in the Ottoman capital.

They worked for a sociomoral reconstruction of society in a broader sense. Some movements built on long-standing traditions of encouragement of a strict adherence to the specifics of Islamic law in the traditions of such scholars as the fourteenth-century teacher Ahmad ibn Taymiyyah, while others worked within the framework of some of the great Sufi orders to encourage a more active life of individual and group piety. In the central Ottoman lands, revivalist movements were less likely to take overtly political forms than those that were in territories that were on the fringes of Ottoman control.

The great Sufi brotherhoods and devotional traditions (tariqahs) had become an important part of societal structure throughout the Muslim world by the eighteenth century. In the Ottoman Empire many of the scholars among the ruling elite were identified with orders that combined a relatively strict adherence to Islamic law with an active participation in Sufi brotherhoods as a way of emphasizing the importance of Islamic piety within society. Scholarly and especially Sufi networks were cosmopolitan in nature and not tied to the boundaries of the Ottoman state. The developments of the Naqshbandiyyah and Khalwatiyyah tariqahs in Ottoman lands illustrate some of the most important aspects of this style of Islamic revivalism. The Naqshbandiyyah originated in Central Asia and came relatively late to Ottoman territories. By the late seventeenth century it was well established in a number of areas, and some of its leaders were supported directly by Ottoman sultans. One major center was in Damascus, where Murad al-Bukhari settled as a scholar and a transmitter of the Naqshbandiyyah traditions after coming from Central Asia. He had traveled extensively and developed close contacts with Sultan Mustafa II (r. 1695–1703), who granted him properties in Damascus. The descendants of Murad, the Muradi family, were prominent leaders in Syria, serving as teachers and muftis (legal consultants) as well as working within the order. The Naqshbandiyyah, as presented by people like the Muradis, was not a militant or activist reformist order, but it did represent a commitment to traditions of Islamic piety by people who were also actively involved in the political processes of the day. The order provided a cosmopolitan reminder of the broader community of believers and the importance of combining personal piety with a sense of an authentically Islamic sociolegal order of society.

Another Naqshbandiyyah center in the broader eighteenth-century Ottoman world was in the coastal cities of Yemen, especially the city of Zabid. Students and scholars coming from many different parts of the Muslim world gathered in Zabid and engaged in the study of the traditions (hadith) of the Prophet and of Sufism. Naqshbandiyyah teachers in such scholarly families as the Mizjaji attracted and trained scholars from many different places, including Muhammad Murtada al-Zabidi, a scholar who came from India and went on to become one of the leading intellectuals of eighteenth-century Cairo, and Ma Ming-hsin, a stu-

dent from western China who returned to his homeland and organized a
Naqshbandiyyah movement that opposed older-style Muslim practices and
Chinese imperial rule, leading a rebellion in 1781.

The Khalwatiyyah order was important in the eastern Mediterranean and
North Africa. By the eighteenth century it had become an important part of the
lives of scholars in Egypt, who again combined piety with an emphasis on a
more universalist and cosmopolitan mode of Islam as opposed to local styles of
shrine cults and what some observers speak of as "saint worship." Mustafa al-
Bakri (1688–1749), a Syrian scholar who spent considerable time teaching in
Egypt, gave greater visibility to the Khalwatiyyah. Some of his students, especially
Muhammad ibn Abd al-Karim al-Samman (1718–75) and Muhammad ibn Salim
al-Hifnawi (1688–1767), established their own orders, which had significant
influence in many different parts of the Muslim world, from West Africa to
Southeast Asia. Sometimes orders such as the Sammaniyyah provided the organizational framework and inspiration for more militant movements of Islamic
renewal. In other contexts, they were more a factor in giving vitality to devotional life in times of rapid change.

The experiences of the Mughal Empire were different in many important ways
from that of the Ottoman. Although there had been some loss of power and effectiveness during the seventeenth century, as a result of internal factional conflict as
well as external threat, the European imperial and military challenge was still lim-

Following the British victory at the Battle of Plassey in Bengal in 1757, the British East India
Company expanded its interests in the Mughal domains. British artists and architects flocked
to India, and views such as Thomas Daniell's 1789 aquatint of the Taj Mahal provoked an
interest in orientalism back in Europe.

ited. Greater problems were raised by the fact that the vast majority of the subjects were non-Muslim, and the Muslim rulers always had to balance the demands of the Muslim teachers with those of the Hindu majority. An exclusivist position demanding allegiance to Islamic law and rejecting some of the policies and customs that represented a blending of Islamic and Hindu elements had been articulated by Ahmad Sirhindi (1564–1624), who claimed to be the renewer (*mujaddid*) of the second Islamic millennium (which began during his lifetime). Sirhindi was identified with the Naqshbandiyyah, and his branch of the order came to be called the Mujaddidi. Sirhindi's style of a more activist reformism that opposed conciliation with Hindus became the characteristic tone of Mughal policy during the reign of the emperor Aurangzeb (r. 1658–1707). His reign was followed by a long period of civil wars among South Asian powers and the gradual expansion of the activities of the British East India Company. Mughal leadership did not undertake any significant reforms involving adoption of new European technologies.

During the eighteenth century Islamic renewal was advocated by Shah Wali Allah (1703–62), an intellectual who developed important approaches to the study of the traditions of the Prophet and advocated the sociomoral reconstruction of Muslim society. He worked to define an approach to Islamic law that could combine the different schools of law in a broad-based legal synthesis while recognizing the legitimacy of some diversity of views among the scholars. His teachings were important in providing a foundation for subsequent Muslim thought in South Asia, but he himself did not create a formal reformist organization or lead an activist movement. The cosmopolitan nature of the networks of renewalist scholars in the eighteenth century is reflected in the fact that Muhammad Murtada al-Zabidi, who had studied with the scholars of Zabid in Yemen and became a major figure in Cairo's intellectual life in the eighteenth century, was initially a student of Shah Wali Allah in India before he began his travels.

The Safavid state came to an end early in the eighteenth century. After the reign of Shah Abbas (r. 1588–1629), the effectiveness of Safavid central administration and military capacity declined significantly. Local revolts and invasions by regional rivals created a crisis for the dynasty, which came to an end when a military commander, Nadir, deposed the Safavid incumbent and named himself shah in 1736. Nadir Shah was successful militarily, but he was not able to establish the basis for a central state that could survive his death in 1747. Iran entered a time of political and military anarchy until the conquests of the Qajar family in the 1790s reestablished the basis for a centralized monarchy and the Qajar dynasty, which ruled until 1924.

Nadir Shah attempted a major religious reorientation by promoting a reconciliation of Sunni and Shiite Islamic traditions. The Safavid state had confirmed Shiite Islam as the religion of the dynastic state in Iran, and the majority of the population had become strongly Shiite during the Safavid era. At the same time the Sunni identification of the Ottoman state had been emphasized, so a Sunni-Shiite synthesis might have provided a basis for better relations between Nadir's state and the Ottomans. Nadir proposed the recognition of the Shiite school of law associated with the sixth Shiite imam, Jafar al-Sadiq (ca. 700–765) as an equal to the four Sunni schools of law. Both the Ottoman *ulama* (religions scholars) and the leading Shiite ayatollahs rejected this effort.

The political chaos in Iran during the eighteenth century increased the importance of the great schools and shrines under the control of the Shii ulama. These institutions developed an autonomy and capacity for action independent of the political and military institutions of the day, which continued throughout the modern era in many different forms, ultimately providing the basis for the establishment of the Islamic Republic in 1979, which was based on the principle of the "rule of the legal scholars." Safavid patronage for scholarship had strengthened schools and shrines in Iran. The end of Safavid rule opened the way for a restoration of the importance of the older major shrines in Iraq around the tomb of Ali in Najaf and especially around the shrine of Husayn in Karbala. During the eighteenth century Karbala emerged as the premier center of Shii scholarship.

The Peacock Throne was one of the imperial trappings that the Afsharid military prince Nadir brought home to Iran after he sacked the Mughal capital at Delhi in 1739. It came to symbolize the Iranian monarchy. Although Nadir had declared himself shah in 1736, he could not establish the basis for a central state, and his line was replaced by the Qajars. Nasir al-Din Qajar is shown seated in front of the Peacock Throne in this official photograph, taken around 1895.

The major reform movement within Shiism in the eighteenth century was the victory of the Usuli school of legal thought over the Akhbari school. The Usuli school (from the term *usual al-fiqh* or "principles of jurisprudence") emphasized the importance of rational informed analysis (*ijtihad*) as the basis for legal rulings and implementation of Islamic law. This school had been dominant in the early Safavid era. Beginning in the late seventeenth century, however, the Akhbari school came to dominate the Shiite legal scholarship, especially in the chief centers of Shiite scholarship in Iraq following the collapse of the Safavid state. The Akhbari position was a radically restrictive one, demanding that rulings be based solely on *akhbar*, the reports of the sayings of the Twelve Imams of Shiism, who were believed to be infallible. Rational analysis was thus rejected. By the late eighteenth century debates between the two schools raged, particularly in the great shrine schools. The final victory came to the Usulis under the leadership of Aga Muhammad Baqir Bihbahani (1704–93), whose triumph reached a point at which he was able to declare that the Akhbaris were "unbelievers."

The victory of the Usuli school had great long-term significance. The role of those scholars who were recognized as being capable of exercising ijtihad because of the breadth of their learning and the excellence of their scholarship became central to Shiite life. It became widely accepted that every believer who did not have the capacity for ijtihad should select a scholar who would serve as a "source of imitation." Obedience to such a capable legal scholar became a requirement of the faith, and this gave the leading ulama tremendous influence and power. Although the faithful could choose any appropriate scholar as a guide, by the middle of the nineteenth century recognition in the main Shiite community of one scholar as the supreme authority in matters of law became established. The first such scholar was Shaykh Murtada Ansari (1800–1864), a scholar in Najaf. In the later twentieth century more than one scholar was sometimes recognized as such authoritative "sources of imitation." In the great central states movements of reform and renewal had great impact, not only in the context of the times but also in shaping societies in the nineteenth and twentieth centuries. In Safavid and Mughal domains most reform efforts continued to be shaped by the dynamics of internal and Muslim history. In the Ottoman Empire, however, in addition to such renewal movements, a new type of reform emerged that was primarily based on adapting Ottoman institutions to ideas and techniques that were developing in western Europe.

Renewal on the Muslim Frontiers and Peripheries

Movements of Islamic renewal developed throughout the Muslim world in the eighteenth century. Outside of the major central states, there was a great diversity of format and style in a wide variety of contexts and circumstances. Such movements could draw from a broad repertoire of experiences within Islam. Some were more legal or puritanical in tone, while others took more charismatic and messianic forms. In some areas reform was a response to the declining effectiveness of existing institutions, while in other areas, movements that were conceived of as movements of "renewal" were in fact more a part of the ongoing processes of Islamization of societies on the frontiers of the Islamic world. They were, in effect, part of the "formation" of Islamic societies rather than the "reformation" of existing ones. In other cases the movements arose in response to particular crises, such as early European imperial expansion.

The Wahhabi movement, which developed on the peripheries of the Ottoman Empire, is possibly the best known of the eighteenth-century movements of Islamic revival. It is called "Wahhabi" after the name of the scholar who was its initiator, Muhammad ibn Abd al-Wahhab (1703–91). Born in the Nejd region of central Arabia, he was raised in a family of strict Hanbali scholars. He was educated by these scholars and also in the schools of Mecca and Medina. He soon became convinced that most Muslims were not living in accord with the rules of the Quran and the traditions of the Prophet, and he was especially disturbed by the popular religious practices that were common in central Arabia. These included visitation of tombs and apparent veneration of natural sites. He began a campaign against this idolatry in the name of the special theme of his renewalism: the absolute one-ness and sovereignty of God (*tawhid*). Although this affirmation of monotheism is at the heart of the faith of all Muslims, Ibn Abd al-Wahhab expanded its meaning to include opposition to anything that appeared to be claiming authority separate from God. This brought him into opposition to the Sufi orders, whose shaykhs were respected as being especially close to God and able to give particular spiritual guidance to their followers, who submitted to the shaykhs' authority.

Muhammad ibn Abd al-Wahhab began his campaign of renewal in the smaller city-states of central Arabia, and his zeal aroused the opposition of established authorities who feared that he might cause unrest. In 1745 he established a relationship with Muhammad ibn Saud, the ruler of Ad Diriyah (in modern central Saudi Arabia). The alliance between the warrior and the teacher was successful and a militant renewalist state was established. The new Wahhabi-Saudi state expanded relatively rapidly, gaining control of much of central Arabia and establishing its capital in Riyadh after it was conquered in 1773. Although Ibn Abd al-Wahhab died in 1791, the movement and the state continued to expand, with the successors capturing Mecca and Medina in 1805–06. The military success of the Saudi state threatened Ottoman authority, and the sultan sent the governor of Egypt, Muhammad Ali, with a newly reorganized Egyptian army to Arabia to restore control. Mecca and Medina were retaken in 1812, and the last areas of the first Saudi state were conquered by 1818.

Although the movement was defeated militarily, the Wahhabi experience was highly visible in the Muslim world. It represents the most legally oriented and literalist of the major eighteenth-century renewalist movements, in contrast to movements associated with Sufi orders, such as the Naqshbandiyyah. Because of

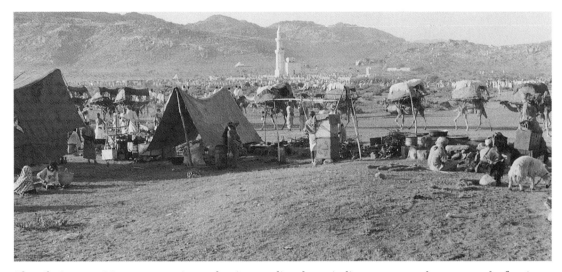

The pilgrimage to Mecca was a major catalyst in spreading the revivalist movements that came to the fore in the eighteenth century. Pilgrims to Arabia, like the ones shown in this photograph taken in 1936–37 near Muzdalifa, became familiar with the revivalist interpretations of Islam and the activities of renewalist movements in many areas. Upon returning home, the pilgrims often worked to renew the Islamic authenticity of faith and practice in their homelands.

its geographic location at almost the center of the Islamic world, later observers tended to see the Wahhabis as the inspiration for the many movements of renewal that had developed in the eighteenth century. This was not the case, however, as Muhammad ibn Abd al-Wahhab was not the teacher of any of the other major revivalist leaders. He and his movement were a part of the broader spectrum of movements of renewal, however, and it is worth noting that both Muhammad ibn Abd al-Wahhab and Shah Wali Allah studied under some of the same teachers as students in Mecca and Medina.

The Wahhabi movement arose within the context of a society that had been part of the Muslim world from the very earliest times. It was a movement that opposed what its leaders thought was a regression into unbelief. On the frontiers of the Muslim world, however, there were many "renewalist" movements whose efforts to establish greater adherence to Islamic rules and norms were part of the longer historical dynamic of the Islamization of society. In many societies in which Muslim merchants and itinerant teachers had been active, a new phase in the processes of Islamization would be reached when a significant proportion of the population would become more directly familiar with Islam's more universal and cosmopolitan articulations. Earlier combinations of Islamic and indigenous elements came to be viewed as idolatrous innovations by scholars who were familiar with Islam's more standard versions. The catalyst in this awareness was often a pilgrimage to Mecca, following which a local scholar would return home and begin work to "renew" the Islamic authenticity of faith and practice in his homeland. At times this could create tensions and conflict with those rulers and establishment scholars whose prestige was built on the syncretism of the early stages of the Islamization of society. Sometimes, as in the movement led by the scholar Ma Ming-hsin in western China, this would be expressed as a conflict between the "old teachings" and the "new." In the frontier areas such movements of renewal were more likely to result in major political conflict and the creation of new states and state systems than was the case in the central Muslim lands.

In west Africa a major tradition of renewalist holy war (jihad) developed, with the result being the creation of a number of explicitly Islamic states. Jihads were proclaimed and jihad states were established in the Senegambia region during the eighteenth century. In the Futa Jallon region a teacher known as Karamoko Alfa (d. 1751) declared a jihad in 1726 against non-Muslim elites and established a state ruled by a combination of warriors and scholars, which lasted until the French conquests of the region in the late nineteenth century. A similar jihad state was established in the Futa Toro region under the leadership of Sulayman Bal (d. 1776). Muslim teachers who were part of a broader network of scholarship played an important role in the development of the ideology and the subsequent state structures. This tradition of militant reformism reached a climax with the jihad of the scholar and reformist Uthman dan Fodio (1755–1817) in the area of modern Nigeria and beyond at the end of the eighteenth century.

Other scholars avoided the extreme of a jihad, while working for closer adherence to more standard Islamic norms. There were important families of scholars that often combined legal scholarship with leadership in a Sufi order. The Qadiriyyah order was the most widespread in West Africa in the eighteenth century, and its leaders played an important role in Islamization. One of the best-known families identified with the Qadiriyyah was the Kunta family, whose influence was felt in Mauritania, Senegambia, and elsewhere in West Africa. Sidi al-Mukhtar al-Kunti (1728–1811) strengthened the importance of the Maliki school of law and established schools and Qadiriyyah centers in many areas. Other Qadiriyyah leaders, such as Jibril ibn Umar (fl. late eighteenth century) in the central Sudan region, were more active advocates of reformist jihad. Jibril was a teacher who provided training in the study of hadith and law as well as Sufism for Uthman dan Fodio, the leader of the major jihad in Nigeria.

A similar interaction of reformism with Islamization of the broader society is visible on Islam's "eastern frontier" in Southeast Asia. By the eighteenth century many of the states in the region had become officially Islamic, with a broad-based synthesis of earlier traditions with Muslim ideas of social structure and political authority. Some areas emerged as particularly identified with Islam. In Acheh on northern Sumatra the sultanate became one of the major Muslim states and a major center of scholarship. As in West Africa, scholars were also frequently associated with Sufi orders and traditions, and a distinctive Southeast Asian Islamic literature developed that combined Sufi mysticism with studies of law and hadith and recognition of important local customs and traditions. A leading figure in the development of this early synthesis was the Sufi poet Hamzah al-Fansuri (died around 1600), who established the Qadiriyyah order in the Southeast Asian islands. During the seventeenth century debates over Islamic legitimacy were vigorous, as the communities became more directly involved in the world of cosmopolitan Islamic scholarship. Nur al-Din al-Raniri was a scholar from India who came to Acheh in the midcentury. He was a strong critic of the local synthesis, and his writings provided an effective basis for more standard-style scholarship in the region. Later in the century Abd al-Rahman Singkeli returned to Acheh following a pilgrimage to Mecca and gave further strength to this "renewalist" tendency and established the Shattariyyah order in the region.

By the eighteenth century the tensions between more localized and more standard, cosmopolitan constructions of Islamic life were a major part of Southeast Asian Islamic history. In Minangkabau in western Sumatra the older social order faced a movement calling for a more strict adherence to the rules of Islamic law and celebration of Islamic rather than more purely local religious festivals. A key figure in this movement was Tuanku Nan Tua, an eighteenth-century leader of the Shattariyyah order. By the end of the century the renewalist challenge had reached the point at which the next step was the jihad, led by people who have come to be called the Padris.

On the northern frontiers of the Muslim world in Central Asia similar developments took place, although by the eighteenth century the broader lines of Islamization were made more complex by the expansions of the Russian and Chinese empires. Some Central Asian societies had long been parts of the Muslim world, while others were still in relatively early stages of Islamization. Significant conversion of Kazakhs to Islam, for example, only began in the eighteenth century. In the case of the Kazakhs, conversion was accelerated by Russian conquest; Catherine the Great gave official support to Sunni scholars in hopes that conversion to Islam would bring stability to the newly conquered nomadic Kazakhs.

Some of the major cities, like Samarqand and Bukhara, had been important centers of trade and Muslim learning in the days of the early caliphates. Changing economic and political conditions, however, left these areas out of the mainstream of trade and intellectual developments. This was the region within which the Naqshbandiyyah order had originated and where it developed its distinguishing characteristics—giving emphasis to the strict observance of Islamic law, active missionary work, and a rejection of quietism, which meant that the order was actively involved in the region's political systems. By the seventeenth century in many of the principalities Naqshbandi leaders dominated the rulers or became part of the ruling families themselves. The Juybari shaykhs of the order played an important role in the politics of Bukhara and the Uzbek state, while further north and east two lines of descendants in the branch of the Naqshbandiyyah order established by Ahmad Kasani (1461–1542), known as Makhdum-i Azam ("the Supreme Teacher"), ruled in Altishar and Uighuristan in the eighteenth century.

The Manchu (Qing) dynasty, which came to power in China in the mid-seventeenth century, began active expansion into Central Asia. This created a context in which a movement of Islamic renewal also became a movement of opposition to foreign imperial rule. Ma Ming-hsin (1719–81) studied at many of the Naqshbandiyyah centers while he went on a pilgrimage to Mecca as a young man. He was apparently especially influenced by the teachers in Zabid in Yemen, and on his return to western China he established a branch of the Naqshbandiyyah order called the "new teaching," which criticized many of the existing practices among Muslims, even among the established Naqshbandi groups. The followers of the "old teachings" had accommodated themselves to the new imperial rulers, and when Qing officials arrested Ma Ming-hsin, his followers rebelled. When Ma Ming-hsin was executed in 1781, the new teachings became identified with opposition to Chinese imperial rule as well as a more renewalist form of Islam.

In East Africa the response to foreign imperial rule was more successful but less clearly involved in movements of Islamic renewal. The Portuguese had defeated the established Muslim merchant city-states on Africa's east coast during the sixteenth century. The Portuguese position in the western parts of the Indian Ocean weakened relatively quickly, however. They were driven out of the Persian Gulf by 1650, and they faced increasingly strong competition in East Africa from the emerging maritime power of the sultanate of Oman. In 1696 the Portuguese were driven from their strong point of Fort Jesus in Mombasa (an island off the southern coast of Kenya), and by the end of the eighteenth century they had been driven from all of their positions on the East

Bukhara and Samarqand, major centers of learning in the early period, were left out of the mainstream of trade and intellectual development in the eighteenth and nineteenth centuries. Traditional centers of learning such as the Kalyan complex of mosque, madrasa, and minaret, founded in Bukhara in the twelfth century as one of the largest teaching establishments in Central Asia, attracted fewer and fewer students.

African coast north of Mozambique. The mercantile Swahili city-states revived and ultimately became a part of an extended Omani maritime empire with a capital in Zanzibar. Even in Mozambique, Islam continued to expand so that in the modern independent state of Mozambique, possibly as many as 15 percent of the population is Muslim. The later reestablishment of European imperial control in East Africa did not stop the continuing processes of Islamization.

With the vast variety of forms and content, it is clear that the advocates of Islamic renewal and reform in the eighteenth century were not part of a single grand movement. Yet, at the same time, it is also clear that the eighteenth century was a time of major change and transition in societies throughout the Muslim world. Some of the most effective responses to the changes and crises, at least in terms of ability to inspire and sometimes mobilize large numbers of Muslims, were those that represented a continuation of the long tradition of renewal in its many forms in Islamic history. In this, networks of scholars interacted to help develop the language of renewal, which could then provide the repertoire of ideas, concepts, and organizations for the movements in their different forms. In these networks the Sufi brotherhoods often provided a framework within which the revivalists could work, both in terms of institutional organization and of personal interactions within the organizations. Similarly, the pilgrimage provided a context for communication and interaction, and the sanctuary cities of Mecca and Medina were vital centers for renewalist scholarship, just as within the Shiite world the sanctuaries in Najaf and Karbala were central places in important redefinitions of the Shiite traditions.

One dimension of the transformations taking place in the Islamic world in the eighteenth century was the changing role of European states and societies and their relationships with Muslims. The changing patterns of trade and the beginnings of the industrial revolution had an impact on Muslim societies, creating new markets for products and changing the terms of trade for Muslims in their economic relations with the West. In the Indian Ocean basin the emergence of the British and Dutch East India Companies represented the beginnings of the rise of the British and Dutch empires in the region. In the eighteenth century, however, this was balanced by the decline of Portuguese power. Western European imperialism was at this time only one of many factors involved in the dynamics of the histories of Muslim societies. Much of the history of Muslim movements of renewal and reform was still shaped more by Islamic than by external factors.

Renewal in Transition: The Early Nineteenth Century

At the end of the eighteenth century a number of major movements of renewal in different parts of the Muslim world represented both a culmination of the

developments of the preceding century and a prologue to the dynamics of the era of European imperial domination. These movements reflect the critical transitions that were taking place throughout the Muslim world. Starting with the older-style emphases on rejection of synthesis of local popular religions with Islam and the affirmation of the more cosmopolitan, standard Islamic faith and practice of such reformers as Muhammad ibn Abd al-Wahhab and Shah Wali Allah, these movements engaged in more activist reform and sometimes jihads. In the process their activism would contact and frequently come into conflict with expanding European imperial powers, so that jihads in the nineteenth century developed more in response to external threats and foreign rule than to the older stimulus of syncretism and compromise.

In the major states in the central Islamic lands the most important aspects of the transitions at the beginning of the nineteenth century were political and military. New rulers and new approaches to state structures were the keynotes in terms of change and reform. At the center of the Ottoman Empire, the sultans continued the reform efforts in the style set by the efforts of Sultan Selim III. Reform meant the effort to change techniques and administrative structures using western European experience as the model. The programs of Sultan Mahmud II (r. 1808–39) represented the beginning of comprehensive westernizing reform. Although this activity was an attempt to preserve a major Muslim state, *Islamic* reform or renewal was not its primary goal. Explicitly Islamic endeavors did not become a highly visible part of government policy until later in the century, and the major movements of Islamic renewal in Ottoman lands were not part of the political system. Even in this arena of more secular reform,

Dolmabace, the palace built in 1853 on the shores of the Bosporus near Istanbul, epitomizes the Ottomans' efforts to continue the reforms begun in the previous century. Modeled on European-style palaces with imposing facades, terraces, a grand staircase, and a clock tower, it was designed to replace Topkapi Palace, which was identified with the past.

The Nusretiye Mosque (1826) was designed by Krikor Balyan, the first Ottoman architect to study in Europe. He was one of the many artists and architects whom Ottoman rulers sent to study in Europe as part of their reform effort, and his buildings combine traditional Ottoman forms such as slender minarets and hemispheric domes with Baroque curves and sinuous moldings popular in European architecture.

however, the transition character is important, with the reforms of Selim III representing in many ways the culmination of the developments of the preceding century and the work of Mahmud II being the prologue and foundation-creating stage of reforms in the era of explicit westernization and growing European imperial domination.

Iran was reunified as a result of the conquests of the Qajars in the 1790s. The Qajar dynasty led a tribal confederation that was able to reestablish the central monarchical state. However, the Qajar shahs faced the increasing and independent strength of the Shiite ulama, whose influence was increased by the new importance given them and their leadership as a result of the victory of Usuli doctrines at the end of the eighteenth century. The Qajar state also faced the growing power of Russia, which conquered territories in the Caucasus. Westernizing reforms were attempted but on a much more limited scale than in the Ottoman Empire, leaving Iran open to increasing European political, economic, and military influence. The establishment of the Qajar state and dynasty was an important transition in bringing an end to the last era of political decentralization and anarchy in the area and in establishing the central state as the core of the political system in modern Iran. In contrast to the Safavids, the Qajars were not a religious brotherhood seeking to establish a state. Their conquests did not represent a conscious effort of Islamic revival. Movements of Islamic renewal and reform took place but not within the political networks of the Qajar state itself.

The eighteenth-century decline of the third major central state, the Mughal Empire in India, continued and intensified in the early nineteenth century. The areas under British control grew and the nature of that control changed. Although the East India Company was still the agent for this growing British domination, it had become more and more of a local government rather than a trading company. The India Act of 1784 made company officials responsible to the British parliament, and India was gradually transformed into a crown colony in a process that was completed in 1857–58, when both the East India Company's administrative roles and the Mughal sultanate were brought to an end. Already in 1803 the Mughal sultan had accepted the formal protection of the East India Company, much to the distress of Shah Abd al-Aziz, the son of the eighteenth-century renewalist Shah Wali Allah. In response, Shah Abd al-Aziz wrote a legal ruling (fatwa) declaring that India was no longer part of the formally recognized Islamic world, "Dar al-Islam."

In the three central Muslim states, there were major movements of Islamic renewal and revival, but they were outside the formal structures of those states. Throughout the world this was still an era of experimentation and even the nation-state format in western Europe was still being defined. While the rulers in the Ottoman Empire and Iran were increasingly inspired by developing

Western models for state and society and the Mughals were forced to adapt to British modes of rule, many Muslims were still engaged in efforts of sociomoral and political reconstruction that were primarily Islamic in their inspiration. The movements of renewal were not simply doctrinal reformations, they were efforts to establish new societies that would be in conformity with the norms of Islam. Almost inevitably, this spirit of renewal came into conflict with the established authorities and the result was some form of jihad.

In the central Ottoman lands Sufi orders provided the most important framework for explicitly Islamic renewalism. One of the most significant leaders in this type of effort was Shaykh Khalid al-Baghdadi (1776–1827). Khalid was born in southern Kurdistan (in modern Iraq) and as a student went to India, where he studied with a leading teacher in the Mujaddidi tradition of the Naqshbandiyyah order. He returned to the Middle East in 1811, where he worked to establish a clearly centralized order. His goals were to establish Islamic law as the basis for society and to oppose European expansion. This was a program of political reconstruction of society, and Khalid was successful in recruiting important members of the Ottoman elite, including the Shaykh al-Islam, the head of the Islamic administration within the imperial structure.

The Khalidi movement was not a movement of governmental administrative reform, however, in contrast to the contemporary efforts of more secular-oriented reformers in the capital. Instead, Khalid's attention was focused more broadly on societal goals, with the community of believers rather than the state being the basic unit. This broader vision is reflected in the fact that Khalid's followers had significant effects in many areas, ranging from providing organizational and inspirational bases for emerging Kurdish nationalism and for Muslim

The early nineteenth-century gate at Simnan is typical of buildings erected under the Qajars, rulers of Iran from 1779 to 1925. The multicolor tile decoration, with pictures of the rulers juxtaposed to scenes from Persian epics, was meant to underscore the role of the shah as the mainstay of the political system.

opposition to Russian expansion in the Caucasus to strengthening renewalist movements in Southeast Asia. Within the Ottoman Empire the followers and successors of Shaykh Khalid helped to give strength to pan-Islamic policies that developed during the reign of Sultan Abd al-Hamid II (r. 1876–1909) at the end of the century.

Shaykh Khalid and his followers illustrate the transitional character of the renewalist movements in the early nineteenth century. In many ways Khalid is similar to previous renewers, explicitly identifying himself with the tradition of the Mujaddid ("the renewer"), Ahmad Sirhindi. The Khalidi branch of the Naqshbandiyyah order is a culmination of that renewalist tradition, and the writings of his followers can be seen as a final florescence of scholarly Sufi writing in the Ottoman Empire. At the same time the Khalidiyyah order faced different challenges, providing ways of responding to the new threats of European imperial expansion and also opening the way for setting an Islamic dimension for developing national ethnic identities like the Kurds. Anti-imperialism and coping with modernity could be done within the older framework of the Naqshbandiyyah order as renewed by Shaykh Khalid.

In India, Muslim revivalism was solidly rooted in the framework set by Shah Wali Allah in the eighteenth century but shaped by the changing context of the increasing ineffectiveness of the Mughal state. Islamic reformism moved in the direction of creating alternatives to the old Mughal traditions of state-based political Islam. Shah Abd al-Aziz (1746–1824), Shah Wali Allah's son, continued

The Kurds, seen here in a photograph taken by Major K. Mason at Serdka in Iraq around 1915–19, have been fighting to establish a nation for centuries. Followers of the Sufi Shaykh Khalid (d. 1827) often provided organizational and inspirational support to the Kurds, who achieved a measure of autonomy by playing up the rivalry between the Ottomans and Persians. Following World War I and the demise of the Ottoman Empire, however, Kurdish lands were divided among Syria, Iraq, and Turkey.

his father's work as a scholar and teacher, compiling large collections of legal rulings (*fatwas*) that could serve as a comprehensive resource for Muslims engaged in the sociomoral reconstruction of society. One of his major concerns was the rise to prominence in India of Shiite Muslims, and he worked actively to refute Shiite positions as a part of his efforts to reestablish a reformed and renewed Muslim society. This work of refutation of Shiism is a long-standing concern among Sunni movements of renewal and was an important part of the writings of Muhammad ibn Abd al-Wahhab at this same time in Arabia. Shah Abd al-Aziz also took note of the new conditions that were developing in South Asia, and some of his rulings related directly to the issues that were raised by the growing British power and social influence. Some rulings dealt with specific issues relating to social and economic interactions with British officials and wearing Western-style clothing. Of broader concern was his position on the impact of British rule on India's place in the Muslim world: he believed that a British-ruled India could not be considered a part of the world of the community of believers. Such a position laid the legal and theological foundations for jihads.

A student of Abd al-Aziz, Sayyid Ahmad Barelwi (1786–1831), developed the theme of jihad more fully and ultimately led a holy war to establish a new, strictly Islamic state and society in India. Sayyid Ahmad was born in a family known for its scholarship and piety and studied as a young man in Delhi with members of Shah Wali Allah's family. He soon left for a more active life and spent seven years as a warrior in the armed forces of a Pathan chief, Amir Khan, during which time he gained important military experience. He returned to the scholarly community of Delhi in 1811 and soon distinguished himself by the severity and strictness of his opposition to popular religious practices and local customs. A group of followers gathered and first followed him on an extensive preaching tour of northern India and then, in 1821, on a pilgrimage to Mecca. Sayyid Ahmad's pilgrimage experience further confirmed his conviction of the need for activist renewal of Muslim society, and on his return to India he began to prepare for a jihad. He began work to establish his new Islamic state in the North-West Frontier areas and assumed the title of imam and "commander of the faithful." The new state was an alternative to existing political structures and independent of the old Mughal political system. He came into conflict with a number of local rulers and was killed in a battle with a large Sikh army in 1831. Although his example and ideas helped to encourage later militant reformers, his state and movement collapsed as an effective force with his death. Sayyid Ahmad's career takes the sociomoral reconstruction effort one step further than the work of Shah Abd al-Aziz by trying to create an alternative sociopolitical order. This new order was neither "traditional" nor modern in its format but shows the diversity that was still possible for reformism in the first half of the twentieth century.

The transitional reform in the third major central state in the Muslim world, Qajar Iran, took a different form, shaped to some extent by the Shiite context. However, in Iran there was also a major renewalist movement, which represented both a culmination of the trends of the previous century and a prologue to the dynamics of the modern world. This was the movement of Sayyid Ali Muhammad Shirazi (1819–50), known as the Bab. In the competition between the Usuli and Akhbari positions during the eighteenth century, the Usuli victory did not mean the disappearance of followers of the Akhbari position. The emphasis on the traditions of the imams, which was characteristic of the Akhbari position, was expanded by Shaykh Ahmad al-Ahsai (1753–1826), whose position came to be identified as the Shaykhiyyah. He argued that the Imam of the Shiite tradition, who was now considered to be hidden, had an agent or deputy in each age who would act as the gate (al-bab) to the presence of the "Hidden Imam." Al-Ahsai's student, Sayyid Kazim Rashti, continued this teaching in Karbala and developed this into a relatively formal school with a number of followers. One of his students was a young merchant from a prosperous family in Shiraz, Muhammad Ali. Although this student did not have the extensive training of one of the ulama, he came to be recognized as possessing special spiritual qualities. When Rashti died in 1844, a number of younger ulama who were Rashti's students recognized Muhammad Ali as Rashti's successor and as the Bab, or "the Gateway of the Age to the Hidden Imam." The Bab gained growing ulama and popular support for his claims, which he expanded to include the claims of receiving special divine inspiration for the definition of prophetic revelation for the new age.

The Bab gained a relatively large popular following in a time when many people were expecting dramatic events of a cosmological character. His vision was not a modernizing vision but a traditional messianic message proclaiming a new society of the rule of God's designated agent on earth, but it appealed to many in a time of great change in Iranian society. He was arrested and executed in 1850, and with his death the medieval messianic phase of the movement came to an end. One of his followers, Mirza Hussein Ali Nuri, who later became known as Baha Allah (1817–92), redefined the message of the new age in more cosmopolitan and universalistic terms, however, and by the end of the nineteenth century the Shiite messianic revolt of the Bab had become the modern Bahai faith, with followers in many different parts of the world.

In the large states in the central parts of the Muslim world there were new-style reform efforts, which began the process of the modernizing reforms of the state systems. Parallel to these more secular reform efforts, however, there were major movements of Islamic renewal that also aimed at the creation of new styles of institutions for state and society. These movements were both culminations of developments that had been important in the eighteenth century and also the beginnings of important Islamic initiatives in the new contexts of growing European-controlled modernity.

Frontier Revivalism in Transition

In the frontier regions of the Muslim world, the issues of Islamic renewal were also those of transition. The movements of the eighteenth century that worked to create more clearly Islamic societies that were free from syncretism and compromise reached a culminating phase of activism and sometimes jihads. These movements also became involved in the interactions with growing European domination in many areas, however, and provided foundations for responses to Western expansion. It is clear from the experiences of movements from West Africa to Southeast Asia that Islamic renewalism was not simply a response to European imperialism but was an already established dynamic of Islamic history that became involved in the process of confronting the new conditions of the nineteenth-century modern world.

One of the major figures in the development of movements that shaped Islamic life in many different regions was Ahmad ibn Idris (1749 or 1750–1837). He was a scholar who was born in Morocco, where he received his early education. This included training in the standard Islamic disciplines in the great mosque school of Qarawiyyin. It was the era of Mawlay Muhammad (r. 1757–90) and Mawlay Sulayman (r. 1792–1822), rulers committed to supporting active reforms that encouraged study of basic works rather than secondary commentaries (with special emphasis on the study of the hadith) and that opposed the more extreme versions of popular veneration of "holy men" or *marabouts*. Ibn Idris began his life as an active Sufi with affiliation to the Shadhiliyyah, a tariqah of major importance in North Africa.

Ibn Idris left Morocco around 1798 and spent the rest of his life in the eastern Arab world. For much of that time he was a teacher in Mecca and Medina, although he traveled briefly to upper Egypt. In 1828 he was forced to leave Mecca, possibly as a result of disputes with the ulama in the sanctuary cities, and settled in Yemen, where he died. He was a well-known spiritual guide within the framework of Sufism but was also a prominent and controversial scholar of the hadith. In his teaching he emphasized the importance of individual piety and fear of God and the responsibility of the individual believer to strive to understand the Quran and the Sunna. Ibn Idris strongly opposed strong adherence to individual schools of Islamic law and worked to create a more unified foundation for faith and action based on fear of God rather than legal rules.

As a teacher in Mecca, ibn Idris came into contact with students from many different parts of the Muslim world. He did not establish his own independent and separate tariqah, but he taught a more general Sufi path that was a synthesis of his devotional guidance and other existing orders. It was only later that one of his sons, Abd al-Al, formally established the Ahmadiyyah-Idrisyyah as the tariqah of Ahmad ibn Idris. However, many of his students established orders that were to play important roles in different parts of the Muslim world. Among the most important of these orders is the Sanusiyyah in Libya and North Africa, the Khatmiyyah in Sudan, and other orders in East Africa. By the end of the nineteenth century his prayers were translated into local languages and were well known in places as far apart as Bosnia, India, and Southeast Asia.

Ibn Idris lived in a time when European influence was growing in the central Muslim lands, and he traveled in Egypt in the days of the reforms of Muhammad Ali. There is little trace in any of his works or activist piety of an explicit response to the West, however. His life and thought were well within the long-established traditions of renewal and reform. His students, though, were actively involved in the politics of faith in the mid-nineteenth century and faced the choice of opposing or working with westernizing reformers and European powers. Like Khalid al-Baghdadi and others in this era of transition, ibn Idris represents both a culmination and a prologue in the development of movements of renewal and reform in the Muslim world.

The zawiya of Sayyid Ahmad al-Tijani in Fez is the center for propagating the teachings of the Tijaniyya order, a Sufi brotherhood with many adherents in the Maghreb and West Africa. Its founder Ahmad al-Tijani (1737-1815) was instrumental in bringing revivalist Sufism to the region, and the order became an effective vehicle for organizing efforts to reform society and enforce a stricter adherence to Islamic law and practice.

Other Sufi orders were also important parts of the movements of renewal and reform in the era of transition. Ahmad al-Tijani (1737–1815) was another North African scholar who established an important tradition of activist Sufism. He was born in southern Algeria and studied in Fez before he went on pilgrimage to Mecca. While on pilgrimage, he became affiliated with some of the important revivalist teachers of the time, especially those associated with the Khalwatiyyah order, such as Mahmud al-Kurdi in Cairo and Abd al-Karim al-Samman in Medina. When al-Tijani returned to Algeria, he began to have distinctive visionary experiences that gave special character to the devotional practices that he formulated as the basis for a new order, the Tijaniyyah. The litanies of the order are believed to have been taught to al-Tijani directly by the Prophet Muhammad in al-Tijani's visions. In these visions al-Tijani was also instructed to break ties with other orders, and followers of the Tijaniyyah path were restricted to affiliation with only the Tijaniyyah. At the time such exclusivity was rare among tariqahs. In devotional practice the Tijaniyyah was a simplified path that did away with many of the complex prayer requirements and chains of authority and authorization. It opposed many of the practices associated with tomb visitations and the veneration of holy men that were common in North Africa. The order became an effective vehicle for organizing efforts to reform society and to enforce a more strict adherence to Islamic law and practice.

As al-Tijani's following grew, Ottoman authorities in Algeria compelled him to leave and he settled in Fez. Morocco at that time was under the rule of a renewal-minded sultan, Mawlay Sulayman, who welcomed al-Tijani and provided him and his order with support and patronage. The Tijaniyyah in return provided an important source of support for the sultan in his campaigns to limit the power of the marabouts and the sharifs (descendants of the Prophet). Mawlay Sulayman was himself an important representative of the renewalist tradition, committing the state to a more activist role. Although he is often identified as sympathetic to the Wahhabis, and is quoted as saying that he was "Maliki in law but Hanbali [sometimes quoted as "wahhabi"] in doctrine," he was not as extreme as Muhammad ibn Abd al-Wahhab in his opposition to Sufi concepts and practices. As a result, the Tijaniyyah provided an important expression of this style of renewalism. Although the Tijaniyyah order was closely identified with governmental structures and was sometimes an important force for social stability, it also provided the means for organizing effective opposition. Al-Tijani's work was an important transition. His tariqah was presented and conceived within older traditions of piety and renewal, but during the nineteenth century it became a vehicle both for jihad opposition to European imperial expansion in Africa and for working with the new imperial rulers.

Sufi orders were also laying the foundations at this time for later jihad opposition to imperial expansions. Followers of Shaykh Khalid al-Baghdadi spread the Khalidiyyah-Naqshbandiyyah orders into such regions of the Caucasus as Dagestan and Chechnya, where Islam itself was expanding at the same time as Russian imperial conquest was intensifying. In the early years of the nineteenth century these activities did not create open militant opposition but rather laid the organizational foundations for midcentury jihads. Shaykh Ismail al-Kurdumiri, a follower of

Khalid, was active in Shirvan (which now forms a part of northeastern Azerbaijan) in the 1810s but was forced to leave when the Russians took control of the khanate in 1820. In Dagestan, Russian punitive expeditions and economic policies created problems and disruptions for the general populace, while in Chechnya programs of settling Cossacks on Chechen lands and military sanctions created additional hardships. Many of the local rulers submitted to Russian rule as a way of preserving some of their own positions, so that the political establishment was increasingly discredited. In

Iman Shamil, who led the Muslims of Dagestan and Chechnya in their resistance to Russian rule, posed for this fiercely formal portrait around 1850.

this context the message of the renewalist Naqshbandiyyah order had strong popular appeal, and the movement grew under the leadership of Muhammad al-Yaraghi, a student of Shaykh Ismail. Although there were many uprisings against Russian rule, which the Russians attributed to al-Yaraghi's followers, there were few organized jihad efforts at first. Al-Yaraghi's first concern was to establish respect for and adherence to Islamic law and to reform local practice. In this context the message was that it was permitted to submit to Russian rule until the conditions were appropriate for a victorious jihad. The Russian victory in 1829 over the Ottomans changed the situation, however, as many local rulers prepared to surrender to the Russians. In 1829 a gathering of tariqah leaders under the leadership of the imam of Dagestan met to organize what was to become thirty years of militant resistance to Russian expansion under a series of imams, including the most famous, imam Shamil (1798–1871).

More militant movements developed in this era of transition in a number of areas. In Southeast Asia the renewalism of such eighteenth-century teachers as Tuanku Nan Tua in Sumatra laid the foundations for more activist revivalism at the beginning of the nineteenth century. Among the most important of the resulting groups was the Padri movement. In 1803 a small group including a former student of Tuanku Nan Tua, Hajji Miskin, returned from a pilgrimage to

In nineteenth-century Sumatra, leaders of the local monarchy joined the Dutch in opposing the revivalist Padri movement based in coffee-growing villages. Following the Padri War of 1821–38, the Dutch retained administrative control, and the Great Mosque in the capital Kota Raja on the north coast was built under their auspices.

Mecca. Their pilgrimage experience had confirmed their conviction of the need for more explicit adherence to the fundamentals of Islam. The results of their first efforts at reform were limited, and soon Padri leaders established control over certain villages, which were reorganized as special separate communities in which popular religious customs were forbidden, the inhabitants wore distinctive clothing, and Islamic practice was enforced. The Padri villages engaged in jihads against nonadherent villages and the local monarchy, and by 1819 they seemed poised to gain full control over the Minangkabau region. At that time, however, the Dutch had returned to Southeast Asia following Napoleon's defeat and worked to establish control in Sumatra and other major islands. The remaining leaders of the local monarchy and anti-Padri village leaders quickly accepted Dutch sovereignty and joined the Dutch in fighting Padri control.

The relationship between the rise of the Padri movement and the expansion of European states is complex. In many ways the Padri movement can be viewed as a continuation of long-established renewalist traditions. However, the socioeconomic context of village life in Sumatra was being changed significantly already in the eighteenth century. Later that century the demand for coffee in the world market expanded rapidly and provided new wealth for the coffee-growing areas of Sumatra. The more formal Islamic school-centers had provided important regulation for the developing trade networks. When the Padri movement developed, some of its important centers were coffee villages, and this may have provided the economic resources necessary for the establishment of the independent renewalist village communities. In this way, although the early goals were within the older renewalist traditions, the context was new. Soon, however, the early renewalist jihad became the Padri War of 1821–1838, a war of anti-imperialist resistance as well as a jihad.

In Java the restoration of Dutch rule following the hiatus of the Napoleonic era was a time for a similar combination of Islamic revivalism and anti-imperialism. During the eighteenth century some of the old princely states, built on a combination of local traditions of divine rule and Islamic concepts, had been supported by the Dutch East India Company in their rivalry with the ulama, whose ideas were more in accord with the cosmopolitan, more standard articulation of Islam. By the beginning of the nineteenth century, some Dutch officials had begun to establish a more centralized control, and these trends were emphasized when the British took control of Java in 1811 and further strengthened when the Dutch returned to Java in 1816. As the Dutch imposed increasing taxes and controls on court elites and the peasantry alike, discontent grew and reached a breaking point in 1825. Dipo Negoro (ca. 1785–1855), a prince with a reputation for piety and mystic vision, came into conflict with a Dutch official and a major conflict broke out. Among his early and strongest supporters were the leading ulama, who led him to assume the role of head of the community of faith, and the conflict rapidly took on the character of a jihad. In this conflict, often called the Java War of 1825–1830, the Dutch tended to identify Islam as the basis for opposition to them, and the war took on the tone of being an anti-imperialist jihad. Dutch military superiority, and eventually divisions among the resistance, brought an end to the war after much loss of life and property. One important consequence of the war was that renewalist, ulama-defined Islam became identified with opposition to foreign rule. The Dutch, in response, worked to associate the old court elites with their rule, leaving cosmopolitan Islam as the ideology of revolt and giving added strength to the processes of Islamization of social life among the peasantry.

Militant movements of renewal also were an important part of this era of transition in West Africa, where the well-established tradition of reformist jihad reached a culmination in the movement of Uthman dan Fodio (1755–1817). Throughout Hausaland, as was common elsewhere in West Africa, Islam was an increasingly important part of society, and the political systems reflected the efforts to combine Muslim and local traditions. As the number and importance of Muslim scholars in these societies grew, their ability to challenge the validity of the syncretistic systems strengthened. Dan Fodio was born into a Fulani family of Muslim scholars in the Hausa kingdom of Gobir, in the northern region of modern Nigeria. He received a standard education and became associated with the renewal-minded teacher Jibril ibn Umar and with the Qadiriyyah order. He began a career as an itinerant scholar in 1774 and taught for a while in the court of Gobir. He insisted on a more explicit adherence to Islamic practices and was strongly critical of compromises with local cultural traditions and practices. He combined a knowledge of Muslim law (and clear loyalty to the Maliki legal school) with a strong sense of mystical experience within the framework of Sufism. Dan Fodio was a talented writer of both scholarly literature and popular poetry, and he soon gained a substantial following.

When the ruler of Gobir attempted to place restrictions on dan Fodio and his followers, an open conflict resulted. The teacher left Gobir territory and established a separate communal society in which dan Fodio was recognized as the imam and head of the Muslim community. He also became the commander of the believers in a jihad declared against the Hausa states in 1804. Much of the actual leadership of the military campaigns and administration was in the hands of dan Fodio's brother, Shaykh Abdallah, and dan Fodio's son, Muhammad Bello, who succeeded his father as commander of the believers in 1817. By 1808 the jihad had defeated most of the major Hausa states and continued to expand into the Lake Chad region and other areas.

The state established by dan Fodio is known as the Caliphate of Sokoto, which he led as "caliph," with his brother controlling the western territories and his son the eastern lands. In many ways the Sokoto state was still a synthesis of Islamic and Hausa monarchical traditions, but Islamic law had a substantial and highly visible role in defining policy and the legal system. The jihad state represented a significant phase in the Islamization of society in West Africa in which Muslim scholars and teachers gained a primary role in the articulation of the public dimensions of civil society, and the state system was changed from a basically Sudanic monarchy that tolerated Islam to a formally Islamic state that continued to use some of the forms and customs of the earlier Sudanic-Hausa monarchies. This laid the basis for much of state and society in modern West Africa.

In both the large central states of the Muslim world and the societies on the frontiers, significant changes were taking place in terms of adaptations of basic institutions and perspectives to new conditions. Such changes can be viewed as being a normal part of the dynamics of the history and development of great societies. Movements of Islamic renewal had long been a part of Muslim historical experiences. These changes can also be seen within a more global framework, however. Throughout the major societies of the world, there were significant transformations taking place. In all major urban societies the basic structure of the sociopolitical order was in a process of transformation involving both local and global factors.

The victory of Western industrial-imperial societies in global military and political terms focused attention on the influence and impact of the Western models on the rest of the world. However, the movements of Islamic renewal in the era of transition at the beginning of the nineteenth century show that there was still a strong development of institutional alternatives that were emerging without direct influence of Western models or attack. There were many efforts to reformulate the way state and society should operate, ranging from the efforts of Uthman dan Fodio and Sayyid Ahmad Barelwi to create new Islamic societies to the more reformist and less radical Sufi affiliations developed by Ahmad al-Tijani and Ahmad ibn Idris. The European expansion efforts tended to overwhelm and preempt these efforts, so that the context of Muslim renewalism was transformed during the nineteenth century, but the traditions of Islamic renewal did not disappear.

The Warrior-Defenders of the Faith

The Muslim world faced the military powers of European imperial expansion in many different areas. In the late eighteenth and early nineteenth century an important part of the Muslim response took the form of jihads organized by more traditional movements of Islamic renewal. Many of these early movements had begun as efforts of reform within society and were only later drawn into conflict with European forces. By midcentury, however, new movements of Islamic revival developed in direct response to European attack, although the older type of evolution from movements of local renewal to jihads defending against imperial expansion continued to be important. Some of the most effective efforts of military opposition to European expansion were these movements, while the newly modernized armies of the larger Muslim states proved to be much less of an obstacle to the European forces.

The emerging warrior-defenders of the Muslim world were not Luddite opponents of new technologies or methodologies. When modern weapons were available, they were used by the renewalists. The strength of these movements, however, came from their abilities to mobilize large numbers of people in organizations whose formats were familiar. Most frequently, the new defense groups were Sufi tariqahs in structure, in their self-definition, and in their leadership. An additional source of strength for these movements was that they were able to use the tactics of guerrilla warfare of a modern style long before these had been more formally defined by Mao Zedong.

Militant jihad movements were not as important a factor in the large central Muslim states as they were in other parts of the Muslim world during the nineteenth century. Significant movements of explicitly Islamic reform did develop in the central Ottoman lands. However, they were not actively advocating jihads, nor were they within more traditional organizational formats that provided a basis for militant renewal movements in other parts of the Muslim world. Instead, this reformism that developed in the second half of the nineteenth century would later be called "Islamic modernism." Major governmental reform programs in the central lands of the Ottoman Empire were primarily efforts in modernization using Western models and inspiration rather than being actions of Islamic renewal and were part of the rulers' ongoing activities to strengthen the empire.

Movements that sought to affirm a historical identity or tradition often developed in nationalist rather than religious forms. Nationalism among the non-Muslim peoples within the Ottoman Empire developed as an early and powerful force of opposition. Later in the century nationalist sentiments also were manifested among Muslims in the empire who advocated significant change, either demanding recognition of their rights as citizens within the empire or independence. In this way assertions of identity and demands for political reform among Arabs in the Ottoman Empire began to be articulated in nationalist terms by the end of the century. During World War I, when there was a significant revolt against Ottoman rule in Arab lands, even though it was led by the Grand Sharif of Mecca, the movement was known as the "Arab Revolt" and made no claims of offering a program of Islamic renewal. Although the Grand Sharif suggested that he might be named caliph, this was a political proposal rather than a statement of advocacy for a program of Muslim revival. In Egypt the dynasty established by Muhammad Ali achieved a high degree of autonomy within the Ottoman Empire and was actively reformist in policy, but its program was based on westernization rather than Islamic renewal. Late in the century, similarly, the emergence of a movement of Egyptian nationalism sometimes made appeals for popular support in Islamic terms, but it was primarily a nationalist movement in more secular and Western terms than an Islamic movement.

In Qajar domains, governmental reform was also in the framework of attempting to modernize in the Western mode. Outside of the movement of the Bab, there was little popular mobilization for explicitly Islamic motivations of reform or societal transformation. By the end of the century new Iranian nationalism was beginning to emerge as a synthesis of more traditional groups with those created by the economic and cultural changes of the modern era. The opposition to the Tobacco Concession of 1890 and the Constitutional Revolution of 1905–06 were crucial parts of the transformation of Iranian politics but in many ways were not basically movements of Islamic renewal.

Militant movements did develop in the third major central Muslim state, the Mughal sultanate of India, and this reflected the militancy and renewalism of the transitional era, which in many ways were parallel to the movement of Sayyid Ahmad Barelwi. A student of Barelwi, Titu Mir (1782–1831), returned to his home of western Bengal and gathered a group of followers, who formed a separate community distinguished by dress and dietary restrictions. Titu Mir emphasized strict adherence to Islamic law and soon came into conflict both with the Sufi orders and the local landlords, who feared his ability to arouse and organize their peasant tenants. After he declared a jihad, he was killed in 1831 by the military forces sent to suppress his uprising. Similar to some other movements of the time, Titu Mir attempted to create an alternative society.

A more significant and broad-based militant movement developed in eastern Bengal under the leadership of Hajji Shariat Allah (1781–1840), who was born in Bengal and had lived and studied for an extended period of time in Mecca. When he returned to Bengal, he organized an effort to impose a stricter observance of the *faraid* (religious duties), and his movement became known as the Faraidi. He gained a large number of followers, especially among the peasants and workers, who were increasingly oppressed by British plantation owners and Hindu landlords. Following his death in 1838, his son, Dudu Mian (1819–62) gave the movement a more explicitly communal organization with a hierarchical administrative organization. The Faraidi clashed with authorities, and Dudu Mian was jailed a number of times.

The more explicitly Islamic movements that resulted in militant opposition to existing conditions and the declarations of jihads were not primarily aimed at combatting the expansion of British control in India. They did involve conflict with British authorities, however. The largest uprising to be specifically directed against the British in the nineteenth century was the great revolt in 1857, sometimes called the Sepoy Mutiny. The cumulative pressures of British policies helped to create conditions within which growing Indian frustration expressed itself in a widespread revolt against British authorities in which Muslims and Hindus joined together. The British crushed opposition severely and formally abolished the Mughal sultanate, as well as bringing an end to the administration of the British East India Company. A wide spectrum of Muslim leaders participated, but the uprising did not assume the character of a unified jihad. Despite the fact that many British officials continued to believe that there was a major threat to British rule

The Qajar palace in Tehran, seen here in a photograph taken by W. L. Schnaider around 1913, symbolized the old regime in Iran. In the late nineteenth century reformers attempted to modernize the country following Western models. During the reign of Muzaffar al-Din Shah (r. 1896–1907), they demanded political reforms, including a new constitution.

from Muslim militants, the events of 1857 marked the end of the era of potentially effective jihad movements in South Asia until well into the twentieth century.

Warrior-defenders of the faith were more active in a number of the Muslim world's frontier areas. Although the movements continued to be inspired by renewalist traditions, many came to be increasingly involved in efforts of opposition to expanding European control and less concerned with the purification of local practices. Some movements were direct continuations of earlier renewal movements, while others represented new organizations or traditions.

In a number of areas, Sufi orders provided a framework for some of the most effective resistance to European imperial expansion. In the Caucasus region the foundations laid by Naqshbandi shaykhs earlier in the century opened the way for leaders to organize jihad opposition to Russian imperial rule as the Russians attempted to consolidate control in the region. A series of active imams inspired the peasants in the region, especially in Chechnya and Dagestan, to rise in jihad against the Russians. These imams continued the dual emphasis of fighting the foreigners and insisting on rejection of local religious customs, replacing them by a more strict adherence to Islam. In this way the Naqshbandi holy wars were an important part of the Islamization process of the societies as well as a significant deterrent to imperialist expansion. The jihads began in the 1820s and reached their peak of effectiveness under the leadership of Imam Shamil, who led the war effort from 1834 until 1859. Although the movement was defeated and its leaders killed or in exile, the Naqshbandiyyah and activist Islam remained a force in the region. There was another uprising in 1877, and in the interim period between the collapse of the czarist state and the establishment of Communist rule at the end of World War I, the Naqshbandiyyah established a short-lived imamate. The long-term impact is reflected in the fact that a portrait of Imam Shamil continues to have a place of honor in offices of officials in post-Soviet Dagestan.

The Qadiriyyah tariqah developed along parallel lines in the Caucasus and was at times in alliance with the Naqshbandiyyah order; at at other times they were competitors for influence and support. The Qadiriyyah was brought to the region by Kunta Haji Kishiev, who was born in Dagestan and lived in Chechnya. He joined the order while on pilgrimage, and on his return in 1861, after the defeat of Imam Shamil, he advocated acceptance of Russian rule and was less puritanical in his devotional path. He gained a large following in a region that was exhausted by decades of fighting, and Qadiri teachers successfully continued the process of the conversion of the Ingushetians (people who lived in a region north of the Caucasus Mountains and west of Chechnya), whose conversion was completed by the 1870s. The Russian rulers feared the rapidly growing tariqah, however, and arrested Kunta Haji, who died in prison in 1867. The members of the Qadiriyyah took an active role in the major revolt of 1877, joining with the Naqshbandiyyah. Although advocacy of a jihad was abandoned, both orders were major forces, with Qadiri influence strongest in Chechnya and the Naqshbandiyyah strongest in Dagestan.

French imperial expansion in North Africa in the first half of the nineteenth century found its most effective opponent in a leader of the Qadiriyyah tariqah, the amir Abd al-Qadir (1808–83). The French invaded Algeria in 1830 and rapidly conquered the coastal cities, bringing an end to Ottoman rule in the country. Abd al-Qadir's father, Sidi Muhyi al-Din al-Hasani, was the head of the Qadiriyyah in the region, and he declared a jihad against the European invasion. Abd al-Qadir assumed leadership of the resistance and soon worked to establish a Muslim state in which he took the title of the commander of the believers. The new community was to be a state organized in the traditions of renewalism as well as an army engaged in jihad. The combination of the state organization and the Sufi foundations for loyalty created an effective vehicle for mobilizing tribal opposition to the French as well as creating a new military force.

Abd al-Qadir and the French alternated between open war and negotiations. At one point in the conflict in 1837, there was a treaty that provided mutual recognition for the French rule in the urban areas and Abd al-Qadir's authority in some interior areas. Hostilities resumed, however, and the French finally defeated Abd al-Qadir's forces in 1847. Abd al-Qadir went into exile, finally settling in Damascus, where he died.

Most effective resistance to the French ended with the defeat of Abd al-Qadir, but there were some significant opposition movements after 1847. There were a number of movements led by people claiming messianic authority, which were rapidly suppressed. In this turmoil a recently established tariqah, the Rahmaniyyah, played an important role. In 1870–71 the various movements of local discontent were brought together in a major uprising when a local administrator, Muhammad al-Muqrani, worked with leaders of the Rahmaniyyah order in eastern Algeria to oppose French rule. After the defeat of the opposition forces, the French confiscated large amounts of land and worked to complete the process of the destruction of Algerian Muslim society.

The combination of renewalist reform of Muslim society with a jihad against foreign control within the organizational framework of Sufi orders continued to be one of the most visible modes of Islamic reform in many areas of the Muslim world in the nineteenth century. The long tradition of such reform movements in West Africa continued with great strength throughout most of the century. The successors to Uthman dan Fodio in the jihad states maintained an advocacy of renewalism but now within the framework of an established state structure. This meant that when Great Britain established control in Nigeria, the leaders of the dan Fodio tradition represented states that came to an agreement with the British rather than creating a new jihad movement.

In the Senegambia region, the Tijaniyyah order was a vehicle for a major renewalist jihad. Al-Hajj Umar Tal (1794–1864) combined many important lines of renewalism. He was born in Futa Toro, the heartland of the old jihad tradition, and went on a pilgrimage in 1826 to Mecca, where he was initiated into the Tijaniyyah. On his return to West Africa he stayed in Sokoto, where he married a granddaughter of Uthman dan Fodio. When Umar arrived back in his homeland, he began an major effort to oppose compromises with local religious customs and to create an authentically Islamic community. He created an army that used French weapons and gained a large following. He declared a jihad in 1852, conquered Futo Toro, and established a new jihad state of which he was the commander of the believers. Umar used the hierarchical organizational principles as well as many of the theological concepts of the Tijaniyyah order in creating his movement. Umar's new state soon came into direct conflict with the French in the Senegal River valley. He was defeated in 1860 and signed a treaty with the French. In his reform activities he came into conflict with Muslim groups along the Niger valley, especially facing the Qadiriyyah order led by the Kunta family, who had emerged as a major force by this time. A coalition of forces opposed to Umar defeated and killed him in 1864. However, he had established a strong enough political system so that his son succeeded him as ruler of a smaller state centered around Hamdallahi in the Niger bend region, which lasted until the French conquest of the area in 1893.

The vitality and appeal of the renewalist message, as well as its viability in the context of nineteenth-century West Africa, are shown by the number of other jihad movements that were relatively successful. Each movement built on a base of reformist mission and worked to establish a separate and authentic alternative community. For example, Ma Ba (1809–67), a teacher in Gambia, declared a jihad against the political leaders of his area to establish an Islamic state. He was aided by Lat Dior, a local ruler who had been deposed by the French and who continued the efforts to expand the Islamic state after Ma Ba's death in 1867. These and other smaller jihad efforts resulted in the effective conversion of the Wolof people to Islam and hastened the Islamization of society.

In many ways the final phase of the older jihad tradition in West Africa came with the career of Samory Ture (ca. 1830–1900), who was born in Guinea and spent his early life as a merchant working in the area's trade networks. He then became a soldier and a student in a small jihad state established by a local commander, More-Ule Sise, and in 1845 he succeeded Sise as the state's leader. Samory transformed the state into a major conquest empire in the 1870s and 1880s. He created as modern an army as was possible at the time and established Muslim teachers as officials in his conquered territories to ensure compliance with Islamic law. He actively destroyed non-Islamic religious sites and cult symbols. He came into conflict with the French and came to an agreement with them that caused him to shift his state to the east in the upper Volta region. In the 1890s, however, Samory fought with both the French and the British, was defeated in 1898, and died in exile in 1900.

In the 1890s British and French military expansion brought European control to all of the areas of western and central Africa. The existence of an independent African-ruled state in any form was no longer possible. The long tradition of the jihad states came to an end as Samory was defeated, the last of the followers of al-Hajj Umar Tal were conquered, and the territories of the Sokoto caliphate were occupied by the British. For two centuries, however, the combination of a renewal mission, opposition to local non-Islamic customs, and defense against foreign rule provided a highly successful format for the efforts to create alternative, authentically Islamic communities and states. For a time these jihad states were more effective than virtually all other alternatives in resisting European expansion.

In Southeast Asia much of the region had already come under European control by the midcentury, and even the early nineteenth-century warrior-defenders had been engaged in major anti-imperialist jihads. During the second half of the century, in broad terms, there was a significant development of greater involvement in activities of Muslim piety. Much of this was related to the impact of European expansion. The opening of new transportation facilities meant that many more people went on the pilgrimage to Mecca, and the expansion of modern means of communication meant that many more Muslims in Southeast Asia had access to the world of Islamic learning. A significant community of scholars from Southeast Asia developed in Mecca, and pilgrims studied with these scholars and became affiliated with major tariqahs. On their return home, the orders provided structure for renewalist activities. These developments created a larger audience of support for Muslim renewalism, although this did not inevitably involve jihad.

The Dutch did face significant revolts representing the opposition of the Muslim scholar class and peasants, however, which was expressed in terms of renewalist Islamic opposition to both the Dutch and those local elites who worked with the imperial rulers. In western Java there was a major uprising against the Dutch in 1888 in which the Qadiriyyah tariqah played a major role. One of the longest jihads was the wars in Acheh, in northern Sumatra, which lasted from 1871 to 1908. By the end of the nineteenth century the Dutch began to implement policies that sought to work with less militant ulama rather than viewing all Muslim movements as threats to Dutch rule. This helped to bring an end to the era of jihads of the old renewalist style. By the early twentieth century opposition to the Dutch began to take on a more nationalist and less religious tone.

One of the last traditionally conceived jihads organized by Sufi leaders against the European imperial powers was in Somalia. In the late nineteenth century the

Somalis faced a number of challenges. The Ethiopian empire was expanding, but more important, in the "scramble for Africa" in the late nineteenth century Italy, France, and Great Britain all hoped to gain control of Somali territories. Territories of various Somali clans were being conquered by these forces, but the Somalis had no centralized organization to develop effective opposition. Somali society was held together by a shared language and poetic traditions and structures of clan relationships rather than by a more unitary state. The major ties that transcended clan loyalties were affiliations to Sufi orders, the largest of which was the Qadiriyyah. It was Sufi organization that provided the basis for the Somali battle against imperial expansion at the end of the nineteenth century.

The leader of the jihad in Somalia was Muhammad Abdallah Hasan (1864–1920), a scholar who combined knowledge of Islamic law and activist Sufism with a great poetic talent that made his message readily accessible to all Somalis. He was born in north-central Somalia into a family with some reputation for Islamic learning and piety. He received a standard Muslim education, traveling as a young man to such regional centers of Islamic learning as Harer and Mogadishu. In 1893–94 he went on a pilgrimage and studied for a time in Mecca and Medina. While there he came into contact with Shaykh Muhammad ibn Salih al-Rashidi, who initiated him into his newly established order, the Salihiyyah. This order was part of the broader cluster of tariqahs following the tradition of Ahmad ibn Idris and helped to confirm in Muhammad Abdallah Hasan a sense of renewalist mission. Muhammad Abdallah Hasan returned to Somalia in the late 1890s and began a campaign of opposition to local practices of veneration of holy men and other activities, such as the use of tobacco, coffee, and qat (whose leaves are chewed as a stimulant), which were not in accord with a strict interpretation of Islamic fundamentals. He worked to promote a life of strict piety and began the process of establishing a separate communal association that was tied together within the format of the Salihiyyah order. This brought him into conflict with another important, newly established tariqah in Somalia, the Uwaysiyyah, a branch of the Qadiriyyah organized by Shaykh Uways al-Barawi (1847–1909).

Uways had left his homeland of southern Somalia for a pilgrimage and study and received extended instruction in the Qadiriyyah at the center of that order in Baghdad. The Uwaysiyyah believed in the importance and efficacy of the mediation of holy men, and the traditional practices of tomb visitation were an important part of the devotional life of the Uwaysiyyah. Uways was also willing to work with the rulers of the day, especially the sultans of Zanzibar, but he also made some accommodation with Italians. By the 1890s the Uwaysiyyah was a large and influential order along the East African coast. The Uwaysiyyah clashed with the Salihiyyah in many different ways, and some of this was reflected in exchanges of hostile poetry, because Uways was also a talented poet. The rivalry reached a climax when a group of members of the Salihiyyah attacked an agricultural settlement that Uways had established and murdered the shaykh in 1909.

By the time of the killing of Shaykh Uways, the primary war in which Muhammad Abdallah Hasan was engaged was a jihad against European imperialism. In 1899 he had declared a jihad against the British, Italians, and Ethiopians. For a short period of truce, his control was recognized in 1905 by the British and the Italians, but fighting soon resumed. The community that was given recognition by the truce arrangement emphasizes the similarity of the Salihiyyah's efforts with other jihad groups in working to create alternative societies in which the message of Islam was comprehensively applied. The jihad soon resumed and continued throughout World War I, although the shaykh was unable to benefit from potential German and Turkish support. After the war in 1920 the British mounted a major military campaign that crushed the movement, and Muhammad Abdallah Hasan died in the same year in a hiding place to which he had fled. His jihad had succeeded in slowing European expansion in the Horn of Africa for almost two decades.

The Spectrum of Renewal in the Nineteenth Century

There were significant movements of renewal and reform in the nineteenth century that were not in the format of the tariqah-oriented movements of jihad. There was a broad spectrum, which ranged from messianic movements and continuations of earlier reform to expressions of Islamic reform within the new contexts of the modern era. There was virtually no part of the Muslim world that did not experience some major renewal and reform effort. The continuation of the Wahhabi tradition of absolutist renewalism was the strongest link to earlier movements. Although many of the nineteenth-century movements, like that of Sayyid Ahmad Barelwi in India, were identified as Wahhabi, the only movement that was a direct continuation of the work of Muhammad ibn Abd al-Wahhabi was the reestablishment of the Wahhabi-Saudi state in central Arabia. Following the destruction in 1818 of the state established by ibn Abd al-Wahhab and ibn Saud, there were still many people in central Arabia who remained loyal to the Wahhabi cause. In the middle of the century descendants of ibn Saud reestablished a Saudi state as a small principality in Nejd for a time, but the family was driven into exile by the end of the century. The foundation remained, however, to enable Abd al-Aziz ibn Saud to return in 1902 and restore the Wahhabi-Saudi political system as the modern kingdom of Saudi Arabia. Within this framework, the concept of an absolute renewalism that rejected most Sufi practice, demanded strict adherence to a literal interpretation of Islamic law, and rejected much of the culture of modern Western society continued to be called the "Wahhabi" mode of renewal and had continuing influence.

The messianic mode of renewal is usually associated with the concept of the *mahdi*, the divinely designated leader who will come and fill the world with justice at a time ordained by God. The coming of the mahdi in the "Last Days" is most frequently identified with Shiite eschatology, but throughout Islamic history there have been been Sunni mahdist movements as well. The best-known modern mahdist movement began in the 1880s and was led by Muhammad Ahmad (1844–85), the Sudanese mahdi. The Sudanese mahdist movement had many of the characteristics of other activist Sunni renewalist movements. The mahdi began his career as an active member of a Sufi order and began to preach against the excesses and non-Islamic practices of many of the people in his society. At that time Egypt ruled Sudan as a result of Muhammad Ali's conquests. The mahdi opposed the oppressive Egyptian rule and soon came into direct conflict with Egyptian forces. By 1885 the mahdi's army conquered Khartoum, and a new mahdist state was established in which there was a demand for strict adherence to Islamic law as interpreted by the mahdi and then by his successor, Khalifah Abdallahi, who ruled Sudan from 1885 until the country was reconquered by an Anglo-Egyptian army in 1898.

Although most other explicitly mahdist movements were relatively small in the nineteenth century, many jihad movements included some significant elements of mahdist expectations. There were strong mahdist themes, for example, in the movements and teachings of Uthman dan Fodio and al-Hajj Umar Tal in West Africa. The success of the Sudanese mahdi was widely known in the Muslim world and helped to give strength to the belief that the late nineteenth century, which was the end of the thirteenth Islamic century, was a time of messianic importance. Mahdist messianism remained an important part of the perspective of renewal even after the era of the Sufi-based jihad movements had passed.

In some areas Islamic renewal efforts and concepts were only part of the motivation for movements of Muslim activism during the nineteenth century. In China a number of movements resulted in the establishment of Muslim states. In Yunnan a Muslim state was proclaimed and maintained from 1856 to 1873, while a Muslim revivalist movement in the tradition of the Naqshbandi "new teaching" provided the basis for a state in Shaanxi and Ili, which received recognition from Great Britain and Russia during the 1870s. It was suppressed by Chinese imperial forces, and in the 1880s diplomatic agreements between the Russian and Chinese empires completed the division of Muslim Central Asian lands.

In the nineteenth century Islam provided a basis for organizing revolts against oppressive social conditions in places as distant as Brazil. During the first half of the century large numbers of slaves were brought directly from West Africa to work in mines and plantations in northeastern Brazil. Muslim slaves were directly involved in at least twenty revolts in Bahia province, where most of the Muslim slaves had been sent. The most serious of these was in 1835 and was explicitly led by Muslim teachers.

Although the older traditions of Muslim reform and renewal had been remarkably successful in providing a basis for activist efforts to hasten the Islamization of society and for jihads against corrupt and foreign rulers, the era of the old-style tariqah-jihad and other older formats for renewal and revolt had passed. Such movements had flourished in the eighteenth and nineteenth centuries, but general historical conditions were being transformed by the end of the nineteenth century. In region after region the ability to organize movements in the old formats disappeared as European imperial control was firmly established and also as the socioeconomic conditions within the Muslim communities themselves changed. New types of associations were needed to provide effective vehicles for mass mobilization or for persuasion of the intellectual elites.

The long-standing heritage of renewal and reform was not disappearing, however. It was, instead, beginning to find new formats and modes of expression that could be effective in the conditions of the modern world. Similar transformations had taken place in earlier eras of great societal change. Older concepts of community and communal identity were being challenged by the new ideas of "nation," "nationalism," and other ideals. Similarly, the older understandings of reason and religion, of science and faith, appeared to require new forms of articulation while affirming the fundamental truth of the Islamic heritage.

The older traditions of renewal and reform provided important resources for the many new movements and ideologies that were being developed by Muslims in many parts of the Muslim world by the nineteenth century. The active affirmation of pan-Islamic ideals by Jamal al-Din al-Afghani (1839–97) and the development of Islamic modernism in many different forms by Muhammad Abduh (1849–1905) in Egypt, Sir Sayyid Ahmad Khan (1817–98) in India, and Ismail Gasprinskii (1851–1914) in Russia reflect the vitality of the aspiration for Islamic renewal at the beginning of the twentieth century. Even in more secular nationalist movements that developed within the Muslim world, there was a strong element of Islamic renewalist inspiration. Such movements represent a new era and new ways of expressing the aspirations of Islamic renewal.

The eighteenth and nineteenth centuries were an important era of major movements of Islamic renewal and reform. These movements had distinctive characteristics, which made them effective in the conditions of the time. By the end of the nineteenth century, however, both local and global conditions had been transformed. The desire for renewal in Muslim societies did not end, but the effective ways of manifesting that aspiration changed. The beginning of the twentieth century marked the end of one great era in the history of movements of renewal and reform and the beginning of another.

CHAPTER THIRTEEN

European Colonialism and the Emergence of Modern Muslim States

S. V. R. Nasr

There are today more than fifty Muslim states, extending from the Atlas Mountains in the West to the Malay Archipelago in the East, and from Sub-Saharan Africa to the steppes of Central Asia. They include some of the most populous countries in the world, such as Indonesia, Nigeria, Bangladesh, and Pakistan, as well as some of the smallest, such as the Maldives and the Comoros. Some are strong states with effective government institutions; others, like Bosnia-Herzegovina, enjoy only a precarious existence. Some, like Mali and Bangladesh, are poor; others, like Libya, Brunei, Turkmenistan, and Saudi Arabia, are endowed with great natural wealth; still others, like Malaysia—the world's seventh most exporting country in 1997—owe their wealth to successful industrialization. Some Muslim states are ethnically uniform; others include sizable ethnic, linguistic, or religious minorities. Nearly the entire spectrum of social, economic, ideological, institutional, and political expressions are represented in these states. From the Islamic Republic of Iran to secular republics in the Arab world or Indonesia, from monarchies in the Arab world, Malaysia, Nigeria (where monarchies rule over provinces), and Brunei, to democracies in Turkey, Pakistan, Bangladesh, and Malaysia, Muslim states include great diversity in politics and the workings of governments.

Despite this diversity, a common thread also exists in the politics of Muslim states. The most obvious is Islam, not only as a faith but also as a source of identity and an important factor in social relations and politics. Islam has long been

(Left) Islam is a common thread in the politics of Muslim states and is often crucial in overcoming the ethnic nationalism that is a legacy of the colonial era. Although ethnic rivalries continue, they can be overshadowed by a sense of Islamic community, as in the celebration of Id by rival factions during the Afghan civil war, following the expulsion of the Soviet army in 1989.

important to Muslim politics. It has played a role in the struggles for liberation from colonialism in Sub-Saharan Africa, South and Southeast Asia, and the Middle East. In various stages of the colonial era, Islamic forces, thinkers, and political leaders have played an important part in shaping Muslim politics. Liberation from colonialism was elaborated as an Islamic movement, from Sayyid Ahmad Shahid's (1786–1831) uprising in India in 1826 to the anti-imperialist undertakings of Iran's Mirza Hasan Shirazi (1815–94) and Shaykh Fadlullah Nuri (1843–1909) or Central Asia's Imam Shamil (1796–1871), Algeria's Amir Abd al-Qadir (1808–83), Somaliland's Muhammad ibn Abdille Hasan (1864–1920), Sudan's Mahdi (d. 1885), Iran's Jamal al-Din al-Afghani (1838–87), or the Tijani *jihads* (holy wars) in West Africa between the 1780s and the 1880s (the Sokoto caliphate of Uthman dan Fodio [c. 1754–1817] and the revolt of al-Hajj Umar Tal of Futa Toro [c. 1794–1864]). Other "Islamic" movements have included Malaya's Hizbul Islam (Islamic Party), India's Jamiat-i Ulama-i Hind (Party of Ulama), Iran's Shiite ulama in the 1920s, Libya's Sanusiyyah (led by Umar Mukhtar, 1858–1931), or Egypt's Muslim Brotherhood. The Muslim leaders of various intellectual endeavors during the colonial period have included Muhammad Iqbal (1877–1938), Abul-Kalam Azad (1888–1958), and India's Mawlana Husain Ahmad Madani (1879–1957) and Mawlana Abul-Ala Mawdudi (1903–79), later of Pakistan. These movements and thinkers were among the first to organize an indiginous anticolonial movement. They articulated anticolonialism in the language of the jihad, relating struggles for liberation to Islam—a powerful paradigm that continues today to be relevant to Muslim struggles against imperialism, most lately in the Afghan jihad against the Soviet Union in the 1980s

Anticolonialists in the Muslim lands have often invoked Islam in their struggle for liberation from imperialism. Chechnya's war of liberation against Russia in 1996 is one of the most recent examples. It left much of Grozny, the capital, in ruins.

and Chechnya's war of liberation against Russia in 1996. In this the Islamic movements were the precursors to the later nationalist uprisings. In Indonesia the efforts of Masjumi (Majlis Sjuro Muslimin Indonesia, the consultative council of Indonesian Muslims) would play an important role in nationalist anticolonialism efforts and early state formation in Indonesia.

Later, Islam influenced the values and the goals of politics, and in recent years Islamist movements have redefined the nature of politics and laid claim to control of the state. The continued political importance of Islam, its relevance to the struggle against colonialism in particular, has prevented secular nationalism from completely dominating politics in the Muslim world. This has in turn made state formation, and its relation to precolonial and colonial eras, complex and at times problematic. Another feature that Muslim states share is the fact that without exception, they are developing states; namely, for the most part they have emerged during the course of the twentieth century and have been closely tied to the efforts of their societies to advance and industrialize. In so doing, they share in the historical legacy, cultural milieu, and often the political and social problems that confront development in the Third World. Muslim states have responded to the challenges before them differently, just as size, geographic location, and economic endowment have also meant different patterns of development.

The French ruled vast territories in Africa and Asia. This engraving from the February 1894 edition of *Le Petit Journal* shows a French view of their flag being raised in Timbuktu in Mali.

The legacy of colonialism is key in explaining both the diversity and the unity of different experiments with state formation in the Muslim world. Just as Islam, ethnic identity, social characteristics, and other indigenous religious and cultural factors can explain the commonalities between Muslim states—and conversely, economics, ideology, and leadership can explain divergences—colonialism too can explain the points of convergence and divergence in experiences with state formation across the Muslim world. Muslim have lived with nearly all the colonial powers. In much of Africa, Asia, and the Arab world, the British and the French ruled over vast Muslim territories. The Dutch ruled over territories that later became Indonesia, and the Germans, Spanish, Portuguese, and Russians held Muslim territories in East Africa, the Philippines, Malaya (what is now known as Malaysia), the Caucasus, and Central Asia. Israel's control of the West Bank and Gaza Strip may be seen as the last and only ongoing colonial relationship in Muslim lands. Although the defining characteristics of colonialism were at work in all of these locales, there were differences in how colonial powers approached their colonial mandates, even differences in how the same colonial powers exerted power and influence in different territories. There are thus fundamental similarities between various Muslim polities as there are particularities, which have their roots in history, and more important, with the experience of each colonial territory.

This chapter identifies colonialism's legacy for the development of the Muslim states in the twentieth century. It discusses the common legacy that Muslim states share as a result of their experiences with colonialism and explains how colonization also accounts for differing patterns of development by looking at individual experiences with colonialism. The colonial era lasted less than a century, but it forever changed all aspects of geography, the economy, social relations, and politics in the areas that it ruled.

Shaping the Modern Muslim World: Colonialism and State Boundaries

The colonization of Muslim territories began with the rise of European empires, the conquest of India, and the scramble for Africa in the nineteenth century. Its last phase included the division of the Arab territories of the Ottoman Empire after World War I. The colonial era ended after World War II, when Britain and then France withdrew from the majority of their colonial territories. Muslim states began to emerge in earnest from 1947 on—although some, such as Iran or Afghanistan, had always remained independent, albeit nominally. The emergence of Muslim states involved negotiated withdrawals of colonial powers, as was the case in Malaya, India, and the Persian Gulf emirates, as well as brutal and bloody wars of independence, as in Algeria. The decolonization also occurred in spurts, as European powers sought to protect their economic interests following their political and military withdrawals in a changing global environment. Iran in 1953 and Egypt in 1956 were examples of the reassertion of colonialism, which nevertheless marked the gradual yet effective end of direct European rule over Muslims.

By the mid-1970s most Muslim territories, from Sub-Saharan Africa to Southeast Asia, had gained independence from colonialism and constituted either independent Muslim states or parts of independent non-Muslim states. Still, the legacy of colonialism continued to shape and reshape their polities, economies, and societies. The impact of colonialism went far beyond the relationships of economic and political imperialism that theorists of the Left have amply elaborated upon. Colonialism also survived in the forms that state ideologies, political visions, and institutions of the new states took. The impact of colonialism was circumspect, but it was nevertheless pervasive. It was a manifestation of the historical continuity between a past from

"SAVE ME FROM MY FRIENDS!"

"IF AT THIS MOMENT IT HAS BEEN DECIDED TO INVADE THE AMEER'S TERRITORY, WE ARE ACTING IN PURSUANCE OF A POLICY WHICH IN ITS INTENTION HAS BEEN UNIFORMLY *FRIENDLY* TO AFGHANISTAN."—*Times, Nov. 21.*

Afghanistan was created as a buffer state between the British Indian and Czarist Russian empires, both of which sought to control Central Asia's access to the Indian Ocean in the south. Colonial intervention left a powerful legacy in the region, including the dependence of Afghan governments on colonial powers, as depicted in a *Punch* cartoon of 1878.

which the new states sought to distance themselves and their independent existences.

The Muslim world today is a collection of nation-states. Although Islamic unity continues to animate politics across the Muslim world and has been a central demand of Islamic movements, the unity of Muslim states does not extend beyond the limited mandate of the Organization of Islamic Conference, an international organization of Muslim states that is modeled after the United Nations. The concept of a territorial state is of relatively recent origin in the Muslim world. In the premodern era Muslims were conscious of ethnic, linguistic, and regional differences among them, but politically they were united under first the caliphate and later empires and sultanates, whose shifting boundaries represented not the borders of nation-states as the term is understood today, but the writ of rulers who ruled in the name of Islam. The idea of a Muslim territorial state, much like the idea of nationalism, is thus an import from the West. The

The Organization of the Islamic Conference (OIC) is the major force for unity among the diverse collection of nation-states in the modern Muslim world. Modeled after the United Nations, it has 55 members, whose heads of state meet every three years in different countries to review conditions in the Muslim world and consider international political developments.

inclusion of the concept of the territorial state into Muslim politics and the actual boundaries of Muslim states are both products of colonialism.

This is not to say that ethnic affiliations and national identities were absent in the Muslim world before the advent of colonialism. Such sentiments were always strong. For instance, Iranians from early on viewed themselves as distinct from Arabs and Turks, and Shiism in Iran in many ways became a mark of its national identity, separating Iranians from the Sunni Turks, Arabs, and Türkmen around it. Similar distinctions between Arabs and Berbers, Arabs and Turks, or Malays and Javanese have also been prominent. Ethnic nationalism and its association with a nation-state, however, is new to the Muslim world and has its origins in the colonial era. It was then that nationalism as a primary form of political identity—one that is not subservient to Islamic identity but supersedes it absolutely and is associated with a territorial state modeled after those in the West—grew roots and became a part of Muslim political consciousness.

For this reason tensions have existed across the Muslim world between conceptions of the nation-state—associated with the relatively more recent nationalist political ideal—and the Islamic ideal of the *ummah* (holy community), which continues to undergird the Muslim political ideal. The concept of the ummah calls Muslims not only to unite across national boundaries but to place Islam above all other political allegiances in their everyday lives. The scope of tensions between the state and its citizens over this issue has depended on the extent to which the state has been willing to accommodate Islamic consciousness. Whereas Saudi Arabia, Pakistan, Bangladesh, and Malaysia have sought to bring about harmony between nationhood and the ideal of the ummah, Turkey, Pahlavi Iran, Tunisia, Algeria, and Indonesia have consciously sought to assert the primacy of the nation-state over the ummah. Also important in this regard is how strong the notion of nationalism is. In states with strong national identities, such as Turkey, Iran, and Egypt, the state has asserted its prerogatives more forcefully, as is also the case where large non-Muslim minorities reside, such as Malaysia or Nigeria. Conversely, in places such as Pakistan, where national identity is weak, the ideal of the ummah holds greater sway.

Muslim states gained independence in territories that were delineated by the colonial powers. They largely accepted the shapes in which they were born as well as the fact that states would be bound by international borders into distinct sovereign entities. Expansionism did occur, however: Morocco's claim to Western Sahara, Indonesia's to East Timor, Turkey's to northern Cyprus, Iran's to Bahrain until the mid-1970s, Syria's to Lebanon, and Iraq's to Kuwait. These claims were put forward in the name of nationalism and on behalf of a nation-state, as defined and legitimated by international norms. Muslim states, by and large, have not challenged the division of the territories of the Islamic empires, and by implication, the Islamic world by colonial powers or the criteria used by those powers in determining new borders. Muslim states have not sought to reconstruct the ummah but only to expand the boundaries of nation-states. The reality of those borders have been accepted, although where they lie has on occasion been contested.

The only exceptions to this general rule have been the ideologies of Arab nationalism and Islamism. Arab nationalism, which was a widely popular political ideal in the 1960s and has been a general political and cultural thrust since then, has in principle questioned the division of the Arab world into twenty-two states. Even in this case, though, the rhetoric of unity, beyond yielding a number of symbolic unification pacts—most notably the United Arab Republic, consisting of Egypt and Syria between 1958 and 1961 and the Arab League—never effectively undermined the division of Arab lands by colonialism. Only North and South Yemen successfully united and then not in the name of Islam or Arab nationalism but of Yemeni nationalism. Even Jordan, a state that was created arbitrarily by England when Amir Abdullah, its first king, was given a fixed stipend and six months to see if the idea worked, has stood the test of time. Furthermore, Arab nationalism was not an

Islamic ideology, and in that sense it did not seek to reverse the division of Muslim lands so much as it did the division of Arab ones. Islamist movements too have argued for the unity of all Muslims above and beyond their national identities and to accept the reality of the ummah in lieu of nation-states. In practice, however, Islamist movements have conducted their politics in accordance with the territorial reality of the Muslim world. The Islamic Party (Jamaat-i Islami) organizations of Pakistan, India, Bangladesh, and Sri Lanka are thus independent of one another, as are the Muslim Brotherhood organizations from Nigeria and Senegal to Sudan, Egypt, Syria, Jordan, and Palestine.

If and when state boundaries have given way, it has not been because of lack of resolve in statehood, but rather because of the ability of a larger expansionist state to overwhelm a smaller neighbor. Kuwait has remained independent owing to outside assistance; others have not been as fortunate. For example, Western

The region of Kuwait has been governed since the early eighteenth century by shaykhs of the al-Sabah clan. The modern nation was one of the Gulf states created by British oil interests in the region. The first well in Kuwait was drilled at Bahrah in 1936.

Sahara was forcibly united with Morocco, as was East Timor with Indonesia. Iran annexed some small islands in the Persian Gulf that it took from the United Arab Emirates in the 1970s. The emirates continue to demand the return of the islands, and the struggle for independence from Morocco, led by the Polisario movement, has been waged unabated; the chapter on an independent Western Sahara is far from closed.

Consequently, the colonial division of Muslim territories, in principle as well as along the lines that were initially introduced, have been largely accepted by the successor Muslim states and have been instituted into the international system. The legacy of colonialism here has not been free of tensions, however. First, many of the divisions were problematic. Some were carried out arbitrarily to accommodate local colonial officials without regard to their impact on peoples and resources. Other divisions reflected the needs of colonial powers to resolve diplomatic tensions among themselves. In many cases colonies were thus created to satisfy disgruntled European allies or to serve as buffers against expansionist ones. The post-World War I plans for the division of the Ottoman Empire were made to appease France, Italy, and Greece. The need to protect India from Russia meanwhile led to the creation of Afghanistan, as similar concerns about France after 1798 led to British occupation of Egypt, which in turn warranted British control of Palestine after World War I. Strategic decisions and economic interests finally led to the creation of new colonial territories, which more often than not became the bases for future states. British interests in Persian Gulf oil led to the creation of Kuwait and a similar attempt at creating "Arabistan" out of Iran's Khuzestan province in the early twentieth century. Decades later, similar economic considerations led Britain to encourage Brunei not to join Malaysia. Local political considerations led to further divisions. France created Lebanon out of Syria to fulfill its desire to create a Christian-Arab state; and Britain created Jordan to accommodate Amir Abdullah, who had fought on the side of the British in World War I and whose family felt betrayed by the division of the Arab lands of the Ottoman Empire between European powers.

How colonialism actually worked and what its imprints were have shaped Muslims' perception of their identities and politics and separated the path that various Muslim states have taken since independence. Early on, through the aspiring new elite that the colonial rulers trained in European languages and ways to create a machinery of government, the division of Muslim territories took shape. As perceptions of whom the elite would control and what the possibilities and limits before them were became entrenched, commitments to borders took form. These commitments built on existing ethnic identities, articulating visions of nationalism that would give greater meaning to those boundaries. A bureaucrat in Kuala Lumpur or Damascus eventually developed a vested interest in "Malaysianness" or "Syrianness," for example, lest his power remain limited as that of a provincial functionary in a larger Malay or Arab entity. It was such feelings that in later years doomed the Egyptian-Syrian unity pact of 1958–61. Iraqi and Syrian bureaucrats, who under the Ottomans would operate in the same ambient political, social, and literary culture, now developed ties to different European traditions and languages and helped to finalize their "separateness." The varied administrative and political experiences thus helped to consolidate parochial nationalisms at the cost of more universal ones. The colonial experience, and the arenas of operation that it presented the new elite, ultimately laid the foundations of states where none had existed before.

In the Malay world the same process forced a separation between Malaysian and Indonesian identities and between Muslim Malay and non-Muslim Malay identities as well. Bureaucrats and politicians in British Malay and the Dutch Indies came to view the diverse cultural, linguistic, and religious arena of respective British and Dutch territories as their political and administrative arena, whereas the possibility of a Malay arena including the Malay parts of Indonesia and Malaysia, or a Muslim-Pattani region in Thailand and Mindanao in the Philippines, and excluding the non-Muslim and non-Malay parts of both became an unworkable idea. Boundaries of colonialism and the differences in cultural and historical experiences and developments that it engendered determined the shape of future states and polities. A united Islamic Malaya would not emerge because its peoples were ruled by different colonial authorities. Conversely, Borneo, and briefly Singapore, would become part of Malaysia because all were ruled by the same British colonial administration. Colonialism thus helped to define the borders of states and their realities in contradistinction to other conceptions of independence and statehood.

New states often appropriated existing ethnic identities or semblances thereof, such as "Iraqiness" or "Syrianness," and at other times contrived nationhood, as in the cases of Jordan or Malaysia, to produce nationalist ideologies that could sustain state formation. The process also entailed sublimating competing ethnic identities and preventing them from developing into nationalisms. Iran, Iraq, and Turkey have sought to prevent Kurdish identity from asserting itself as a nationalism. Iran sought to integrate Kurds into an Iranian nationalist identity, and Turkey depicted them as "Mountain Turks." The success of experiments with state formation often depended on how successful the development of national consciousness was. That, in turn, depended on the strength of the ethnic identity that formed the basis of nationalism. Over time, ethnic and territorial definitions became the boundaries for national identity formations; they grew roots and developed as a secular and dominant form of political identity in lieu of memories of a united Islamic world in history. Colonial powers had perhaps never meant for the territorial demarcations to have the lasting effects that they had, but in reality these boundaries became embedded in the future states.

Territorial divisions have also been a source of tension between various Muslim states that claim mutually exclusive rights to the same territories. Jordan and Syria, for example, early after independence both set their eyes on reconstituting larger Syria, while Jordan also maintained a claim to Palestine and Morocco to Mauritania and parts of Algeria; Syria and Turkey have contested sovereignty over Alexandretta (Iskenderun); Iran and Iraq over the Shatt al Arab channel; Egypt and Sudan over waters of the Nile; Pakistan and Afghanistan over the Durrand line; Pakistan and India over Kashmir; Saudi Arabia and Qatar, and Saudi Arabia and the United Arab Emirates, over borderline oases and oil fields; Libya and Chad over their border regions; and Iran and the United Arab Emirates over the Tunbs and Abu Musa islands. In some cases the very existence of some Muslim states have been challenged by neighbors that view the Muslim states as artificial constructions of colonialism. Syria's claims to Lebanon, Malaysia's to Brunei (until recently), Iraq's to Kuwait, and Morocco's to Western Sahara are examples. Borders produced the shape of the states but did not guarantee their viability. Colonial authorities drew boundaries but did little to unify the peoples that fell within those boundaries into a national culture. At times they did exactly the opposite; namely, the colonial powers sought to maintain control by encouraging competition between ethnic, linguistic, religious, or tribal groupings. The territorial division of Muslim lands thus remained unchallenged, but it went hand in hand with national confusion and the fracturing of the future national society.

Unresolved tensions between peoples and regions that were included within the same state, but never consolidated into one nation, have resulted in challenges to state boundaries. Confessional tensions in Lebanon; ethnic and religious clashes in Nigeria, Pakistan, and Malaysia; and the Kurdish plight in Iran, Iraq, and Turkey are examples of the many problems inherent in state formation on the basis of colonial territorial demarcation. Still, none of these problems has been a result of attempts to reconstitute "Islamdom." In fact, the preponderance of nationalism in Muslim political consciousness is so pervasive that Pakistan, which was created in the name of Islam, divided along ethnic lines in 1971 into Pakistan and Bangladesh. Although fraught with problems, the territorial conception and reality of Muslim states continues today in the colonial mold.

The Modern Muslim State and the Ideological Legacy of Colonialism

Many Muslim states today view the transformation of society, its development and modernization, to be their principal aim. As a result, they have been concerned

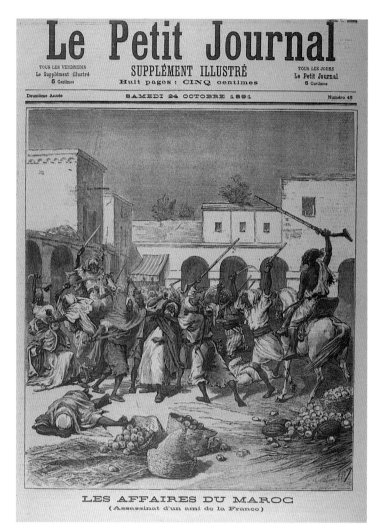

Le Petit Journal

TOUS LES VENDREDIS
Le Supplément illustré
5 Centimes

SUPPLÉMENT ILLUSTRÉ
Huit pages : CINQ centimes

TOUS LES JOURS
Le Petit Journal
5 Centimes

Deuxième Année   SAMEDI 24 OCTOBRE 1891   Numéro 48

LES AFFAIRES DU MAROC
(Assassinat d'un ami de la France)

European colonialists often believed that they had a paternal responsibility for their subjects. The British spoke of the "white man's burden" and the French "la mission civilatrice," as shown in this cover from the October 1891 edition of *Le Petit Journal*. A "friend of France" was assassinated by Moroccan chieftans who thought he had made a secret deal with the colonial rulers.

with such ideals as social change, economic advancement, and industrialization. What distinguishes the Muslim state from the modern West, however, is its preoccupation with the central role of Islamic culture in the discussions over modernization and development. The attention to cultural dimensions of change—molding the individual as a prelude to carrying out successful social transformation—has been at the heart of the state's development agenda and is a legacy of the colonial state, which unlike its parent state in Europe was overtly concerned with its subjects' cultural life. Controlling popular culture as a prerequisite for socioeconomic change has been the avowed policy of secular nationalist states from Turkey to pre-revolution Iran, from socialist Indonesia to the revolutionary Arab states. To a lesser extent, this has also been the case in Malaysia, Pakistan, Bangladesh, and the Arab emirates and monarchies. The state's concerns with music, dress, popular beliefs, and the cultural outlook of Muslims has perforce made the issue of cultural change, and its implications for development, and the extent of state control of society central to politics. This is a legacy of the colonial state, not the consequence of emulating the Western model of the state.

The ideology of colonialism was rooted at some level in the belief that European powers had a paternal responsibility for their subjects. This meant that not only were they obliged to protect and manage them but also to strive to better them. Evelyn Cromer, a British colonial administrator, saw colonialism as an exact process of management of colonial subjects, who were incapable of ruling over themselves. Colonialism provided a "government of subject races," which managed their affairs and as such also changed them "for the better." Notions of the "white man's burden" or *la mission civilatrice* clearly captured the essence of this belief. French colonialism was more attached to such goals than was British colonialism. French colonial administrations sought to change their vassal populations more aggressively, viewing the introduction of the superior French culture to the locals as a noble and necessary objective. But the British accepted cultural diversity more easily and thus operated through local cultural institutions and beliefs, rather than seeking to simply supplant them. Still, to varying degrees all colonial administrations pursued cultural change and charged their policy makers and institutions with the duty to realize this change. These efforts were tied to colonialism's claim to be doing good for the people, as the colonial order tied development and advancement to westernizing cultural change. The postcolonial state, often ruled by those who served in the colonial administrations, remained true to the colonial ethos and its views on cultural change.

The postcolonial Muslim state has therefore modeled itself after the colonial one and thus seeks to change society according to blueprint that leads to its claim to unlimited authority. The Muslim state has been ruled by a westernized elite that has internalized the vision of the colonial state, which is dissociated from local social institutions and values, at least in its public policy choices. The blueprint that is propagated as the state's agenda for progress is thus deeply rooted in colonialism's ideologies, from the *volksraad* in the Dutch Indies to the *Raj* in British India and the *Bula Matari* (literally, "crusher of stones," a term used to refer to the colonial state in Africa) in Sub-Saharan Africa.

The continuity between the colonial and postcolonial eras has created a disjuncture between what the states have viewed as the proper course of development and the values that Muslim society holds near and dear; between how the state envisions the society and how Muslims view themselves and their goals. Whereas the state followed a secular vision of development, the society has been deeply rooted in Islam. The disjuncture between the secular nationalism of Kemalism in Turkey, Pahlavi rule in Iran, or the National Liberation Front (Front de Liberation Nationale, FLN) in Algeria and popular perceptions of politics attests to this fact. State policies have therefore created social tensions and ultimately political crises. In Iran and Algeria these tensions translated into serious challenges to state authority. In Turkey, Egypt, Tunisia, and Indonesia they have produced significant Islamic opposition to the state.

The ideology and political programs of contemporary Islamist movements across the Muslim world have been shaped in response to this disjuncture.

Islamists have questioned the state's agenda and put forth alternative visions of sociopolitical change, which they claim both include Islam and promote development, while anchoring state policy in society's Islamic values. This line of argument is reflected in the programs of diverse Islamic movements from Malaysia's Islamic party (Partai Islam Se-Malaysia, PAS), to the Jamaat-i Islami in Bangladesh and Pakistan, Afghanistan's Hizb-i Islami, Turkey's Welfare (Refah) Party, Tajikistan's Islamic Renaissance Party (Hizb-i Nahzat Islami), the Muslim Brotherhood in Sub-Saharan and North Africa and the Arab Near East, Indonesia's Muhammadiyyah movement or its ulama movement (Nahdat al-Ulama), Tunisia's Islamic Tendency Movement (Mouvement de la Tendance Islamique, also known as the Renaissance or Ennahda Party, later known as Hizb al-Nahda), Morocco's Justice and Benevolence party (al-Adl wal-Ihsan), to Algeria's Islamic Salvation Front (Front Islamique de Salut, FIS). The Islamic Republic of Iran has followed such a policy since 1979, and the state in Pakistan, Bangladesh, Malaysia, Sudan, and even Saudi Arabia have incorporated some of the Islamists' demands into their policy making. In this sense Islamism has emerged not as a rejection of development but as a consequence of the disjuncture between the state's vision of society and how it should be developed and the society's perception of itself and its goals.

Similar tensions between state policy and national aspirations have also existed. Colonial administrators generally viewed themselves as the most capable representatives of the aspirations and hopes of the local populations and the most efficient vehicle for the advancement and progress of their subjects. In fact, nationalist liberation struggles often began with challenges to this claim; local elites from Muhammad Ali Jinnah of Pakistan, Sad Zaghlul of Egypt, Abu al-Kalam Azad of India, and Onn Jafar and Tunku Abdul-Rahman of Malaysia, or activists from Gamal Abdel Nasser of Egypt, Ahmad Ben Bella of Algeria, and Sukarno of Indonesia began to question whether colonialism could possibly manifest local aspirations and if indigenous leaders were not clearly better suited to do so. These nationalist figures formed parties from the Istiqlal (Freedom) party in Morocco to the Neo-Destur (Constitution) party in Tunisia, the Wafd (Delegation) in Egypt, the All-India Muslim League in India, and the United Malays National Organization (UMNO) in Malaysia. Many of these parties continued after independence, forming the basis for politics in the new states.

Still, that the colonial administrations viewed themselves as representing local interests vested colonialism with a mission—however dubious—of serving the development of the local populations. That the nationalist elite challenged this claim of colonialism, and the nationalist struggle was animated by the competition for the right to represent local aspirations, made the task of development central to the mission of the Muslim states that succeeded colonialism. The postcolonial Muslim state thus became even more openly tied to the goals of development, which has since independence become the measure of the state's success or failure and the most important determinant of its legitimacy. As a result, undermining colonialism's legitimacy, from Java to Algeria, meant rejecting its claim to serving local interests and proposing a superior agenda for progress. Nationalism and development efforts were therefore joined and became the bedrock of the struggle independence under Sukarno, Nasser, and the Algerian FLN, among others.

Beyond anchoring state function and legitimacy in the goals of development, colonialism affected the state's view of the development process and its concomitant processes of social change. Colonialism was disdainful of local cultural beliefs and practices. It viewed local religions as inferior to Christianity—a belief that undergirded its support of missionary activities—and local customs as archaic and harmful to progress. Although colonial administrations tolerated many local beliefs and practices

LES TROUBLES A LA FRONTIÈRE ALGÉRO-MAROCAINE
Un agitateur musulman prêchant la guerre sainte

Colonialists often looked down on local practices. Muslims were seen as prone to violence, and Muslim doctrines such as jihad were used as evidence of Islam's hostility to progress. This French magazine cover from 1906 illustrated the French view of an Algerian urging his followers to wage holy war against the oppressors.

and did not always seek to change them, there was never any doubt that they were not held in high esteem. Whereas the earliest officers of the British East India Company adopted Indian ways in Bengal, with the consolidation of British rule over India all such practices were eventually abandoned, and instead the local recruits into the bureaucracy were made to adopt British ways, at least in the public sphere. At the height of the empire figures such as Thomas Babington Macaulay in India or Evelyn Baring Cromer in Egypt—known for their patronizing attitudes toward the local cultures—set the tone for evaluating and characterizing local customs and mores. Macaulay once said of the cultural worth of the East, "[A] single shelf of European books [is] worth the whole literature of India and Arabia"; and Cromer opined, "The European is a close reasoner . . . he is a natural logician. . . . The mind of the oriental [Arab], on the other hand, like his picturesque streets, is eminently wanting in symmetry. His reasoning is of the most slipshod description . . . [they] are singularly deficient in the logical faculty."

Islam received particularly harsh criticism from colonial rulers. Muslims resisted colonialism in Africa and South and Southeast Asia. For this they were seen as prone to violence and less likely to be controlled, changed, or converted. Islam was therefore viewed as a challenge to both colonial control and efforts to transform the local population's life and thought. Such Islamic doctrines as jihad, polygamy, strict obedience to religious law (shariah), and the tendency to introduce Islamic values to public life were seen as evidence of Islam's hostility to progress. These criticisms shaped colonial attitudes from Morocco to Malaya; they also shaped the broader intellectual and academic interest in Islam through the works of early scholars of Islam who were tied to colonial administrations,

Some European colonialists were interested in local culture. Major Gayer-Anderson, an Englishman who lived in Cairo from 1935 to 1942, for example, joined together two medieval houses that he restored and furnished in traditional style. Known as the Bayt al-Kritliya, the house is now maintained as the Gayer-Anderson Museum by the Islamic section of the Egyptian Antiquities Organization.

such as W. W. Hunter in India or Snouck Hurgronje in the Dutch Indies. In time, their scholarship would become entrenched in Western attitudes toward Islam and in turn would condition Muslim attitudes toward the West and therefore what the West has in store for Islam.

The impact of all this was to instill a sense of inferiority among many local elites and rising bureaucrats. Even those who rejected colonialism were deeply influenced by the persistent denigration of their cultural, religious, and social values. Although reactions varied from accommodation to rejection of the colonial culture, all reactions showed the mark of colonialism's successful assertion of its claim to civilizational superiority. In India, for instance, Sayyid Ahmad Khan's reform movement—which would produce many of Muslim South Asia's future leaders—sought to uplift the Muslims by accepting many precepts of Western thought and social values. Other movements of revival and reform showed to varying degrees, explicitly as well as implicitly, the impact of grappling with colonialism's assertion of its cultural superiority. Most expressions of Islamic thought in the postcolonial period, from Islamic modernism to Islamism, thus in some form were (and still are) concerned with addressing what is seen as the problem of Western cultural superiority.

Various proponents of Islamic modernism—from its earliest exponents of Egypt's Muhammad Abduh to the Young Ottomans in Turkey, the Jadidis in Central Asia, the Aligarh movement in India, to its more recent advocates, the Muhammadiyyah movement in Indonesia, Malaysia's Sisters-in-Islam, Pakistan's Tulu-i Islam (Dawn of Islam), Iran's Ali Shariati or Abdul-Karim Surush, Egypt's Hasan Hanafi, Algeria's Muhammad Arkoun, Pakistan's Fazlur Rahman, Syria's Muhammad Shahrur, Malaysia's Kassim Ahmad, or India's Asghar Ali Engineer—have all sought to grapple with the problem of Islam's decline on the one hand and Islam's accommodation in modern society on the other hand. The two issues are interconnected, and for the modernists these issues involve interpreting Islam in terms of dominant Western values.

Islamists from Mawlana Sayyid Abul Ala Mawdudi to Sayyid Qutb (1906–66) to the Ayatollah Khomeini (1902–88) have also been animated by the same concerns. Unlike the modernists, the Islamists have not sought to interpret Islam in terms of dominant Western values—at least not explicitly. Rather, they have sought to assert Islam's domination, to interpret modernity according to Islamic values. Discussions of the Islamic state, Islamic economics, or the Islamization of knowledge all have this goal in mind. Both the modernist and Islamist interpretations as intellectual endeavors have failed. Islamism, however, has proved politically potent, whereas modernism has failed on that account as well.

In the political arena those who inherited the colonial state were even more directly influenced by colonialism's ideological vision. The bureaucratic, military, and political elite who constituted the ruling order in Muslim states at the end of the colonial era were often educated in colonial educational institutions, worked for the colonial order, and were deeply influenced by the ideology and vision of the colonial administration. Consequently, this elite core believed that the task of development, to which it was utterly committed, was only possible if those aspects of the local culture that were deemed to be regressive were discarded and replaced with progressive Western ones. Thus, new states—and interestingly also Iran and Turkey, which were not direct colonies but subject to similar ideological pressures—initiated changes in script, dress, and customs and sought to secularize society and culture and to adopt Western mores, laws, and practices. They targeted Islam, its values, institutions, and role in public life, blaming it for the ills of society and promising that secularization would pave the way for modernization. In these efforts they were supported by those segments of the population that had already been affected by colonialism and had to varying degrees adopted Western ways, as well as by those who accepted the state's promise—for the time being at least—that secularization and westernizing cultural change will bring about development. As a result, secularization and westernization became embedded in the developmental ethos of the new states.

The postcolonial Muslim state therefore emerged in the mold of the colonial one—development-oriented in aim, hostile to Islam, and modernizing and westernizing in practice. The ideology that guided the evolution of the postcolonial state, however, was not uniform across the Muslim world. Some Muslim states remained allied with the west and followed capitalist economic policies; others gravitated toward the Soviet Union and the Non-Aligned Movement and adopted socialist practices. Although these ideological positions produced different historical experiences and levels of industrialization and political change, the developmental goal and westernizing direction of state formation was largely the same across the Muslim world. In short, although in foreign and economic policy making, states may have been distinguished according to their commitments to capitalism or socialism, to the West or the Soviet bloc, in domestic politics the fundamental issue was the same: secular development at the cost of Islamic identity of society.

Patterns of Development

Muslim states are also distinguished by the pace with which they pursued development. Some arrived at their independence more developed than others. For example, Turkey was more advanced economically and politically than the Arab territories of the Ottoman Empire. Some Arab states, such as Egypt and Syria, were more developed than others, such as Yemen or Oman. Some Muslim states developed more quickly, because of greater international aid, natural resources, or their size and the possibilities of trade. After the oil price hike in the 1970s, the Arab monarchies thus outpaced the Levant states (Syria, Jordan, and Lebanon) and Egypt in development. But, Iran and Egypt were better able to use international aid and assistance in their development programs in the 1960s and the 1980s, respectively. Larger states were better able to mobilize resources to push ahead with development. Smaller states proved more versatile in responding to changes in the international economic trends, however. Whereas Indonesia initially advanced faster in industrialization than Malaysia, since 1980 Malaysia has outpaced Indonesia in that regard.

The centrality of the western model to the evolution of the Muslim states has been important to their politics. Given the legacy of the struggle against colonialism, any development model that looked to the west and purported to westernize ran the risk of mobilizing political opposition and cultural resistance. Such reactions tended to escalate when and if the promises of development failed to materialize, as in Nasser's Egypt, or were deemed as too costly in terms of cultural sacrifices, as was the case in Pahlavi Iran. In the 1960s and the 1970s resistance to, and the critique of, state-led development strategies drew on secular ideologies that were themselves of western origin. Socialist Muslim states thus had liberal oppositions; more notably, capitalist states had vociferous leftist oppositions. In these cases the opposition objected to close alliances between the ruling elites and the west but did not oppose the development agenda itself. Rather, they favored pursuing development based on another western ideology.

Since the late 1970s, a different form of critique of state-led development has surfaced in the Muslim world. Islamist movements now question some of the foundational principles of the postcolonial state, most notably that development is predicated on secularization and begins with accepting the qualitative superiority of western civilization values; thus, development must necessarily entail replacing some Islamic values in favor of western ones. In the Arab world Islamists have rejected the arguments of Arab nationalists regarding the "backwardness" of Islam and the superiority of socialism, just as in Iran and Turkey Islamists have refuted similar arguments presented by Kemalism and the Pahlavi state's nationalist rhetoric. Interestingly, secular Muslim states such as Malaysia and Indonesia also subscribe to a similar line of reasoning. Malaysian Prime Minister Mahathir Muhammad has been at the forefront of the movement to defend Asia's right to live by its own values, rejecting the universality of western social, legal, and human rights values.

The Islamist opposition has also challenged the wisdom of the state's industrialization policy. In Algeria, Nasser's Egypt, and Syria, inefficiencies caused by socialism and centralized economic planning produced poverty, unemployment, a breakdown in social services, urbanization, and a decline in standards of living. In Pahlavi Iran, post-Nasser Egypt, Indonesia, and Malaysia, capitalist economic development produced income disparties, corruption, urbanization, and rapid cultural change. Islamism has not specifically rejected development, but as Islamism challenged the ideological underpinnings of developmentalism and adopted the cause of the poor and the disgruntled, it became a poignant critique of development strategies. In Malaysia, Islamist forces did not initially discuss state economic strategies directly, but they criticized the state for not favoring Malays. In Iran, the Islamist revolutionaries criticized economic development for its westernization and the income disparties it generated, and they proposed greater state control of the economy. In Algeria and Turkey, conversely, the FIS and the Refah party favored open economies and less government control. The FIS actually became a force in the burgeoning private markets that provided consumer goods to the population and as such became a critique of the state's heavy industrialization strategies that had denied the population those basic goods and instead produced corruption and promoted socialism. The Refah party meanwhile was strongly tied to small merchants and the business community. In all these cases Islamism has for the most part criticized the ideological underpinnings of development. It has proposed its own development strategies as alternatives to those implemented by the state. As such, those Islamists who confront socialist and state-controlled economies favor greater market reforms, whereas those Islamists who are in opposition to capitalist development favor greater state control of the economy. Still, it is by challenging the ideological legitimacy of the development process in the secular state that Islamism poses the most fundamental challenge to state development strategies.

The Islamist opposition also challenges the validity of the state's attempts to control the role of Islam in the public arena. Since their independence, many Muslim states have sought to regulate Islam in public life. In Pakistan, Turkey, and Iran, for instance, the state took over the management of religious endowments. In Turkey the state also took over the schools that train preachers and Islamic scholars. In Malaysia and Egypt preaching in mosques now requires a license, and in Malaysia the state has gone to great lengths to establish a nationwide network of mosques that are run by state-appointed prayer leaders. From Algeria to Indonesia, Islamic law was replaced by civil codes imported from the west, and Islamic courts were disbanded. In some states, such as Morocco, Saudi Arabia, Pakistan, and Malaysia, the state has shied away from an outright secular image and has couched its policies in Islamic language and symbolism, going so far as to speak for Islam. Still, the intent of state policy clearly has been in the direction of secularizing change, and the control and marginalization of Islamic institutions, thus limiting the role of Islam in public life.

Islamism has put forward a political platform that is nothing short of a rejection of both the reality and the intent of the secular state's penetration of society—the continuation of the colonial establishment's programs of control and transformation of society to serve colonialism's aim of improving the lot of the local peoples. In this regard, Islamism has served as an important source of resistance to the expansion of state power and as the focal point for the rallying of those social forces that resist state domination. This function began in Turkey, Iran, and Egypt in the early part of the twentieth century. Since the 1950s it has gained momentum, as ulama and Islamist groups across the Muslim world have been at the forefront of opposition to land reform and nationalization of industries, and of course to state domination of education, commerce, charities, and religious endowments. The scope of Islamist resistance to state power is so broad that it undermines the entire raison d'être of the postcolonial Muslim state, as it denies the state the right to change society and to do so based on the same presuppositions that guided the colonial state.

The legacy of the colonial state has been so deeply entrenched in the postcolonial Muslim state that Islamism itself has not been able to avoid the tempta-

A few colonialists were smitten by the local culture, such as Harry St. John Philby, remembered as an early Western explorer of Arabia. In 1925 Philby gave up his post as British political officer, settled in Jidda, and converted to Islam, taking the name Abdallah. By the early 1930s he had become a confidant of the Saudi Arabian king Abd al-Aziz and was allowed to traverse and photograph previously unknown areas of the region, recording such sites as the palace of Sultan Ali.

tion of championing developmentalism. Although Islamism rejects the cultural assumptions of colonialism and the secular state's right to transform social relations, it accepts the ideal of social advancement, albeit according to Islamic norms and without westernization. In so doing, Islamism portends to float an alternative paradigm for development, what Malaysia's PAS calls "developing with the ummah." Islamism also, therefore, seeks to mold the individual and to regulate his or her music, dress, private beliefs, and cultural outlook—all as a prelude to its vision of development—and to change the distribution of resources in society. One can therefore conclude that Islamism too is concerned with development and predicates the process on top-down social engineering—the hallmark of the colonial state and its successor. Islamism's opposition to state power, therefore, emanates from the ability of the secular state to use it to further its secularist agenda. In effect, resisting state authority is tied to Islamism's rejection of state-sponsored secularization. In fact, in Iran, Pakistan, and Sudan, once Islamist forces were in a position to control policy making, they continued with the expansion of the state's power and reach and extended the control of the state over private life, religion, and education.

In essence, the public debate in the Muslim world—between secular and Islamist forces—has focused on ideology alone and has largely ignored the problem of the growing size of the state, which was a legacy of colonialism, and the reach of its public policies, which is embedded in the programs of both the state and its Islamist opposition. Muslim societies—as have many other developing societies—have become stuck with the notion of a large and intrusive state, and the ideal of defining Muslims has become central to all political discourse. The bone of contention is not the state's right to manage development but the goal and content of its policies. In short, whereas the ideological orientation—the degree to which society is secularized or Islamic identity is accepted as a part of national identity—and policy content of developmentalism have been debated and fought over in the Muslim state, the more fundamental legacies of colonialism have remained intact. All conceptions of the Muslim state—from capitalist to socialist to Islamist—view the primary function of the state to be top-down social transformation, with the aim of realizing development. The Islamist conception however, has entailed a modification of this grand vision of the state's role and function in that it no longer accepts that the West is the sole repository of the values that should guide the state in transforming society in its greater wisdom. The Malaysian Islamic youth movement, ABIM (Angkatan Belia Islam Malaysia, the Islamic Youth Force of Malaysia), for instance, directed its energies at informing the Malaysian development agenda of Islamic values, and many of its members pursued this goal by entering into government service.

The Economic Legacy of Colonialism

Muslim countries, much like other Third World countries, initially viewed development, especially in the economic sphere, to be a matter of setting in motion a set of processes that would culminate in industrialization, growth, and wealth. They were supported in this view by Western theorists who characterized economic development as a matter of reaching the "take-off" point, as Europe had following the Marshall Plan in the 1950s. Many Muslim states sought to shortcut the process by assigning to the state a greater role in managing the economy. In this they were influenced by the examples of the Soviet Union under Stalin and such Third World leaders as Jawaharlal Nehru of India.

This vision of development closely paralleled prevalent conceptions of political development that saw successful sociopolitical change to be a matter of completing a set of processes, identified to have been key in the European experience. It also sat well with the predilections of the new states, which as successors to the colonial state viewed progress as a top-down and state-managed process. Although scholars debated over the number and sequence of the stages involved, they were in agreement that the ideas drawn from the European example were readily applicable to the developing world and that development was a linear cause-effect process. Whether in the political arena or in the economic one, however, developing states, including Muslim states, defied the logic of modernization theory. States were able to bring about social change and economic growth but did not replicate western models of the state and the economy. Rather, hybrid polities and economies emerged, revealing uneven development across sectors, classes, regions, and areas of the polity.

Disappointments were often blamed on state leaders and their policy choices. The elusive nature of development eventually led many to argue that perhaps the developing state could not reproduce the European experience because the Third World society and economy was not the same as the premodern European one. Modernization theory now argued that the Third World state was hampered in its desire for development by cultural and social obstacles. Religious beliefs, social mores, customs, and the fractured society of the Third Worlders were held accountable for holding back the state—suggesting that Christianity and western values accounted for the historical achievements of the west. This "dual cultures" thesis was a reiteration of the guiding belief of the colonial state, which had also viewed the uplifting of the colonized to be a matter of the passing of their cultures and religions and their replacement with a western value system—a task that was possible only if the colonial state saw to it—which in turn, at a fundamental and "moral" level, justified colonialism.

Islam was, and continues to be, a favorite target of the advocates of this thesis. From the first versions of the "dual cultures" thesis to its recent incarnation in the "clash of civilizations" argument, this approach has pointed to various aspects of Islam—from its theology to its law, its rituals, and its views of the economy, societal relations, women, and minorities—as responsible for lackluster development in Muslim countries. Many Muslim leaders bought into this myth, which reinforced the legacy of colonialism that had already shaped state attitudes toward Muslim society and the Islamic faith. From Sukarno of Indonesia to Ayub Khan of Pakistan, the Shah of Iran, Bathist leaders in Syria and Iraq, to Suharto of Indonesia and Habib Bourgiba of Tunisia, state leaders sought to marginalize Islam and to promote secular conceptions of society and politics.

In the 1960s the anomalies in the Third World experience with development were explained in a different manner. Third World intellectuals and leftist thinkers in the West posed a "dual economies" thesis in place of the "dual cultures" one, giving shape to what came to be known as the dependency theory. It was argued that Third World societies were not the same as premodern European ones because the latter had simply been undeveloped, whereas the Third World societies had been mangled and deformed. Colonialism had damaged Third World economies by disturbing the balance between economic sectors. Colonialism had been premised on using the colonial territories as a source of cheap raw materials and a market for European products. It had therefore encouraged the development of raw materials and discouraged industrial developments. The economies of colonial territories had become unnaturally dependent on raw materials and had not developed industrial sectors. In fact, colonialism had systematically eliminated the traditional artisan classes that in Europe had evolved into the industrial sector. As Egypt grew more and more cotton, or Java and Africa agricultural commodities, for example, the export crops and raw materials dominated their economies. The dual dependency on European markets for the raw materials and the European industries for final products led to absolute dependency, which enriched the West and impoverished the developing world. Third World economies typically had overdeveloped raw materials export sectors and underdeveloped indigenous manufacturing.

Upon independence, Muslim economies displayed these characteristics of dependency. Cotton dominated in Egypt, cotton and jute in Pakistan, coffee and spices in East Africa and Java, cotton and silk in Syria, oil in the Persian Gulf, and rubber in Malaysia. Economies of the Muslim states had become tied to the fluctuations of the world economy, in which they produced the lowest value-added products and consumed finished goods. Their products were subject to greater price fluctuation and employed minimal technology; what they consumed employed far more technology and had more stable prices. The pattern of integration of these economies into the global economic order also influenced the development of infrastructure, urban development, and the like. Ports became dominant in colonial territories. In the Muslim world such cities as Karachi and Beirut emerged, sometimes in places where no major population center had existed before, and soon overshadowed the older cities of the interior. From Zanzibar in East Africa to Malacca and Penang in Malaysia, ports became the centers of wealth and power in the colonies. Lines of communications, roads, railways, and population movements followed the directions in which raw materials and finished goods flowed. In many cases the overdevelopment of the export sector led to the emergence of "enclave" economies that were largely divorced from the local economy. The oil sector in the Persian Gulf, for example, clearly had such a characteristic.

To some extent, patterns of economic change led to large-scale migration to metropolitan centers as traditional patterns of farming and the balance between urban and rural economies were altered. Colonial agricultural policy led to rural poverty, which in Java, Egypt, and Algeria broke down rural economies and led to flight to urban centers. Later economic policies of such Muslim states as Iran and Egypt would only encourage this tendency. In some instances urban development occurred in the interior. Lyallpur (later Faisalabad) in Pakistan or Kuala Lumpur were not ports, but they developed because of the new economic relations that were spawned by colonialism. For the Third World, development was therefore not a matter of simply setting in motion a set of cause-effect economic processes until "take-off" would be reached but of remedying the destructive effects of the relationship of dependency. Development would have to begin by undoing the impact of colonialism.

In many Muslim states, such as Egypt, Indonesia, Iran, and Algeria, the state saw its role in the economy in exactly such terms, as one of correcting the imbalances that were produced by colonialism. State-led industrialization thus became a means of bringing about patterns of economic change that the society and the economy were incapable of achieving on their own. In Pahlavi Iran and Pakistan the state saw its role as merely corrective; in socialist states, such as Sukarno's Indonesia, Nasser's Egypt, or the FLN's Algeria, the state saw its role as more fundamental. Development thus found an additional justification as the state became the instrument for correcting biases in the economy—expediting development but also making sure that development will happen. Remedying the ills of colonialism became a justification for states to veer society away from Islam by diverting attentions away from questions of faith and identity to ones about imperialism and its consequences.

Where state control of economy progressed unchecked, it stifled market forces to the long-run detriment of the economy. It achieved industrialization and weaned the economy away from its dependency on the export of agricultural products or raw materials, but it did not produce viable and self-sustaining

Under the impact of colonialism and with the discovery of oil, small fishing villages, such as Kuwait City, were transformed into major centers of wealth and power. Often dependent on such exports as oil, these ports exemplified the enclave economy that was largely divorced from local concerns.

industrialization. In many cases, as in Egypt under president Anwar Sadat, Iran under Ayatollah Ali Akbar Hashemi Rafsanjani, Indonesia under Suharto, or Tunisia under Ben Ali, the state now relaxed its control of the economy. Suharto and Ben Ali's reforms were more far-reaching, involving privatization and restructuring of the economy, and have thus proved more meaningful than Sadat's infitah or Rafsanjani's liberalization initiative. The belief that colonialism had thus produced fundamental imbalances in local economies added further weight to the state's view that it had the duty to oversee development. Whereas initially its function was to hasten development, now its principal role was to first correct the problems caused by colonialism—and later by imperialism—and then to see to rapid development. Where state leaders accepted the logic of dependency theory, the role of the state in the society and economy thus expanded and found further justification.

Beyond the general ways in which colonialism accounts for what Muslim states have come to view economic development to be, and the reasons development has proved to be an elusive goal, the colonial experience through its everyday policies and practices gave shape to the economies in which it operated. Land-tenure policies in Java during the Dutch period and in Syria and Algeria, the settlement of tribal lands and the conversion of forests into arable land in Punjab, patterns of capital investment, choice of crop, and the like were instrumental in shaping local economies. Whereas dependency theory underscored those legacies of colonialism that all developing and Muslim economies share, these more parochial differences in colonial policies and practices explain why Algeria was different from Morocco and why both were different from Syria. In Algeria, for instance, a large portion of the land—the best and the most productive—was owned by the European settlers. In Syria the land remained in the hands of local landowners.

In Algeria, unlike Syria, the French settlers' (*colons*) presence and appropriation of land broke down rural relations and created a strong racist-imperialist order that then decided the pattern of resistance politics. French policy also led to wide-scale pauperization of the Algerian society when it became independent. At independence, Algeria had the lowest number of professionals—administrators, doctors, engineers, and the like—of any other Arab colony or mandate. Most Algerian social and economic relations had been dismantled by the French rule in the nineteenth century. Whatever new structures replaced them were then weakened during the war of independence. The flight of the settlers during and after the war of independence went hand in hand with wanton destruction and flight of capital. Thus, French impact on the new state was profound, although not only in continuities between the colonial and postcolonial states but also in the abrupt break with the past.

The local social structure was important in these different outcomes but so was the timing of the colonial settlements. Syria was controlled by France, not as a colony but as a mandate—a temporary arrangement under the supervision of the League of Nations to see to Syria's eventual independence. This, combined with the fact that the French arrived in Syria after World War I when colonialism's heyday had passed, meant that there was very little enthusiasm in France for long-term investment in Syria. The meager capital outflow from France to Syria therefore to a good degree accounts for differences in the shape of agrarian relations and land ownership in Algeria and Syria under the same colonial power.

In some instances colonialism benefited through direct extraction of material wealth from the economy, while in other cases it helped transform the economy and earned its profits through taxation of the higher output and income. In the

A goal of colonialism was to extract material wealth from the local economy. In Java and Sumatra the agricultural system set up by the Dutch was designed to transform these areas into large-scale producers of spices and exotic agricultural goods. On this coffee estate in Sumatra around 1900, for example, female pickers labor on ladders with European overseers in the background.

first case, often witnessed in Java or Africa, colonialism could impoverish, damage, and disturb the local economy and culture, whereas in the second case colonialism could produce tangible developments. In Java the agricultural system set up by Dutch colonial administrator van den Bosch aimed to convert Java into a large-scale producer of spices and exotic agricultural export commodities. Large tracts of land and upward of 56 percent of the population were put to the service of the Dutch agricultural interest. Production of foodstuff declined, and spices and coffee replaced them. A peasantry emerged that lacked economic autonomy and the ability to sustain itself. Dependent on the Dutch for employment, this peasantry became increasingly squeezed by the local elite that controlled it and by the vagaries of the global economy. It thus became exceedingly weak and poor. In Africa, French colonialism extracted surplus, whereas in the Levant it sought to accrue wealth by enriching local agriculture. The British Empire, which was at its core mercantile, did not rely on European settlers but benefited from customs and taxes.

In many instances colonialism also invested in infrastructure that later became central to economic progress. In India, Malaya, and Egypt the British built roads, railways, and ports; in Punjab they also built canals, an infrastructure for agricultural development, and even some degree of manufacturing activity. Many roads across the Muslim world were built by the colonial powers. In some countries, such as India, the taxation system was introduced, institutionalized, and given its place in the modern economy by the colonial establishment. In those developments that infrastructure has made possible, or otherwise inhibited, colonialism has influenced economic change in Muslim states.

The Social Impact of Colonialism

Colonialism had a profound impact on both the social stratification and the cohesion of Muslim societies. The economic impact of colonialism produced new classes and altered the distribution of power among the existing ones. For instance, in North Africa French settlers emerged as a dominant social and economic class. In India the British created and maintained a feudal class through which the colonial administration could control the rural masses, and in the Dutch Indies the colonial agricultural policy reinforced the social position of the local elite. In urban areas mercantile and commercial interests tied to the colonial trade policies gained in stature, as did the emerging bureaucracy that was trained by and worked for the colonial administration. The rise of these new social groups coincided with the relative decline of artisans, small-scale agricultural producers, and in some cases the traditional elite. The political consequences of this process were momentous. In India, for instance, the decline of the old elite tied to the Mughal court was important in the Great Mutiny of 1857 and in the tensions between Muslims and the British Raj in the following century of colonial rule.

The rise of mercantile classes and an embryonic middle class in the form of educated functionaries in the colonial administration also changed the structure of local politics. Emphasis gradually shifted from the time-honored patterns of exertion of authority to the politics of nationalism and the struggles of liberation, which ultimately ended colonialism. The new nationalist elite were often tied to and emerged from the colonial order's educational, bureaucratic, and social institutions; from the metropolitan centers rather than the hinterland. Their points of reference and their ideas came from the colonial culture and did not purport to assert traditional notions of authority.

The buildings of the Hong Kong and Shanghai Banking Corporation dominated the crowded waterfront of Singapore, the most important city in the Riau Archipelago, traditional home to the Malay people. Completed in 1892, the bank offices stood until 1919, when they were demolished to make way for new premises.

Such social developments as the entrenchment of feudalism, where and when it occurred, proved to have a long-term effect on social development in Muslim societies. The political function that landowners performed in northern India allowed them to develop strong class interests and tied their economic roles to political ones. Their power and position therefore remained unaffected in the post-colonial state, in Pakistan, where feudalism remains a pillar of the political system, a legacy of colonialism's social policy. In the Persian Gulf similar trends were evident in the entrenchment of the power of tribal chieftains, who also served as means of social control for the colonial establishment and in turn used colonial patronage and policies to fully entrench their sociopolitical positions and in many cases to evolve into monarchies. Across the Persian Gulf independence has only marginally changed the political role of these traditional forms of authority.

Colonialism also affected local societies by encouraging and strengthening modernizing trends. Colonial rulers across the Muslim world encouraged education and invested heavily in educational institutions. Such institutions as the University of Punjab and the University of Malaya were established to educate those who would eventually run the machinery of colonialism. Over time these institutions produced generations of Muslim leaders and influenced intellectual developments in Muslim societies. They also helped to create the new middle classes and to provide space for this new class to develop roots. The colonial administration also encouraged the sons of the elite, and later promising middle-class youth, to study at modern educational institutions or in Europe. The Atchison College in Lahore was established for the sons of chiefs, princes, and landlords and the Kuala Kangsaw Malay College in Malaya for recruiting sons of Malay aristocrats into the bureaucracy. Over time they also became the training ground for children of the rising bureaucratic elite. Others went to school in Eton and Harrow in England and studied at Oxford and Cambridge, or in Paris and Amsterdam. The name *Pakistan* is alleged to have been coined at Cambridge; Muhammad Iqbal, the eminent Muslim poet-philosopher of South Asia, was educated at Cambridge and Heidelberg universities as well as in law at the Lincoln's Inn in England, where Muhammad Ali Jinnah, who led the Pakistan movement, also received his law degree. Many leaders in the North African liberation movements were students in the French schools in North Africa and at the university in Paris.

A similar trend was also evident in the military, whose officer corps came from the colonies but whose education occurred in Europe at such places as Sandhurst or Saint Cyr, or in officer schools modeled after European military schools and staffed by European officers, such as the Quetta Staff College in Pakistan. The colonial administration had hoped that western education for the old elite and those in positions of power would create an affinity between them and the colonial elite.

This view had gained currency after the colonial establishment encountered the first wave of resistance to its position by traditional chiefs and religious leaders. Over time, however, those educated in modern ("western") subjects proved to be equally uncompromising foes. The new leadership educated in western ways employed European ideals to question the morality of colonialism, however, whereas the old elite had relied on Islam to resist colonialism. In the end the former approach proved more potent, as it paved the way for independence.

The impact of the colonial education in the intellectual realm was equally profound. Through the educational system many indigenous thinkers became aware of western literature and philosophy. Some even wrote and thought in western languages. From Indonesia to Morocco a great deal of intellectual activity has occurred in the nineteenth and twentieth centuries in Dutch, French, and English; and an even greater amount of intellectual activity has occurred in the genre of western intellectualism, but in local languages. New forms of literature and literary activity, such as novels or free-verse poetry, began to surface in the 1920s and the 1930s. In India, so profound was the impact of western thought that the bulk of the production of its literary geniuses in the late twentieth century is in English. The political ramification of this was to shape Muslim intellectuals from North Africa to Turkey, Egypt, Iran, and Indonesia in the image of western intellectuals. First J. S. Mill or Jean-Jacques Rousseau, and in time Jean-Paul Sartre and Albert Camus, became models for dissenting intellectuals, just as Lenin, Fidel Castro, Mao, or Che Guevara captured the imagination of more militant activists such as the Marxist Fidaiyan-i Khalq (the People's Devotees) of Iran, activists in the Parcham (Flag) and Khalq (People) Parties in Afghanistan, communist activists in Yemen or Turkey, communist guerilla factions in Malaysia, Moro freedom fighters in the southern Philippines, and members of the Communist Party of Indonesia (PKI). The notion of political commitment among intellectuals and opposition to the state thus grew roots. Many such intellectuals congregated in London and Paris and interacted with European intelligentsia, which reinforced this trend. The impact of this form of intellectual activity on Algeria, the Arab world, and Iran has been profound. It undergirded Arab socialism and was an important source of power for the revolutionary movement in Iran. The leadership of the FLN and Iran's Ali Shariati were members of the same left-of-center circles in Paris and shared in the elaboration of "Third Worldism" (*tiermondisme*), which they then exported to their countries of origin.

Not all educational endeavors were motivated by the needs of the colonial administration, however. Colonial rulers as well as voluntary organizations, such as Christian missionary movements, sought to hasten the advancement of the local populations by educating them. Catholic and Protestant colleges in the Levant, such as American University in Beirut or St. Joseph's College in Lebanon, and Roberts College in Turkey and the Forman Christian College in Lahore (some of which later lost their Christian character), are examples in this regard. The impact of these undertakings on the youth culture or on the uplifting of women's status was even more pronounced. High schools, such as the American College in Tehran, and women's schools, such as the Iran Bethel school in Tehran or the Kinnard College in Lahore, introduced modern education to precollege students and to women in general. Muslims themselves would eventually adopt many of the educational principles of these institutions, thus creating a momentum for modern education and the development of the modern middle classes. In India the Jamiah-i Nizamiyah (Nizamiyah University) and the Fawqaniyah schools sought to incorporate modern education into the Islamic traditional curriculums of high school students in Hyderabad, whereas the Anglo-Oriental College at Aligarh sought to do the same at the university level, and Nadwatul-Ulama in a seminary setting. After independence, Western education would be widely adopted in India to shape the postcolonial society.

Another important legacy of colonialism involves its implications for national unity of later Muslim states. Colonial territories did little to unify the peoples that fell within those territories and thus did not result in national societies or produce national cultures. Colonial administrations were primarily concerned with protecting the boundaries of their colonies against encroachment of other colonial powers and lessening the burden of ruling over the colonies. The first concern led them to emphasize the sanctity of the borders of the colony, which accounts for the fact that the map of the Muslim world is largely the one that was originally drawn by the colonial powers. The second concern obviated the possibility of the consolidation of lasting national identities. Colonial boundaries were often drawn in competition with other colonial powers. Therefore they did not take into account the division of groups of the peoples or the inclusion of ethnically, linguistically, or religiously diverse populations within the same borders. In many ways colonial demarcations of territories helped to create nationally diverse states rather than homogeneous ones. Lebanon, Syria, Iraq, Indonesia, and Nigeria are all examples of this phenomenon.

This problem was compounded by the colonial administrations' reliance on divide-and-rule policies to reduce the burden of governance. In India the British pointed to India's diversity—which was painstakingly detailed in their census reports—to argue that only the British could bring order and cohesion to such a fundamentally divided land. Diversity was thus a necessary justification for the continuation of colonialism. The consequence was that diversity gradually developed roots and found a life of its own. It was also politicized and made center stage. In the same vein, the British also went to great lengths to show that Islam's roots were not in India and therefore India had been previously ruled by outsiders;

thus it followed that it should not be strange that India would once again be ruled by outsiders. Muslim rule in India clearly had many more indigenous sources of support than the British Raj. Still, the myth persisted and eventually shaped the Muslims' view of their own history in India as well as the Hindu views of it. The Hindu nationalist rhetoric of today echoes the British argument that Islam and Muslims are outsiders—Turkish, Persian, and Arab invaders. Similar arguments were made by the British in Egypt, again to try to give legitimacy to British rule. Here too the arguments eventually grew roots. One often hears that Gamal Abdel Nasser was the first Egyptian ruler of Egypt since the pharaohs.

Colonial administrations also encouraged rivalry among diverse ethnic, linguistic, and religious communities. Such rivalries preoccupied the various communities, diverting their attention from the question of colonialism. It also encouraged them to curry favor with the colonial establishment in their struggle with their rival communities. In India, British authorities actively sowed dissension among Muslims and Hindus. Some argue that the rumor that the Mughal emperor Babur had built a mosque on top of the birth place of the Hindu god Ram in Ayodhya were first circulated by the British to break down Muslim-Hindu comity in northern India. The British also played on tensions between Sikhs and Muslims. It was Sikh soldiers from Punjab who broke the back of the mutiny in Lucknow (in northern India) in 1858, avenging the hardships that their community had suffered under the Mughal emperor Aurangzeb. The British policy culminated in the great debate among Indian Muslims during the interwar period. Whereas some Indian Muslims advocated standing with Hindus in a common front against British imperialism, others, from the Muslim League to religious activists, questioned joining in a common cause with Hindus. The British used the Muslim ambivalence to pressure the nationalist movement. Although they did not stave off independence, the Indian subcontinent was eventually split between Muslims and Hindus.

In short, the colonial policy deliberately manipulated diversities to strengthen the rule of the state, to keep various communities busy with rivalries and confrontations, and to play the broker with the antagonists. In the process colonial society became increasingly fractured. Hence, some conceptions of the postcolonial state, such as a united India, Malaya (including Singapore), or Syria (including Lebanon), were never viable; and those states that became viable have within them, to varying degrees, disintegrative tensions. Civil wars in Sudan or Iraq and tensions between communities in Malaysia, Pakistan, Nigeria, Kenya, Tanzania, and Chad, to name only a few, are in good measure products of colonial rule.

The colonial policy toward religious minorities has been even more significant. European powers always maintained close relations with religious and ethnic minorities, especially with religious minorities. First, European powers viewed themselves as the protectors of Christian minorities. The Ottoman Empire under

There are more than 120 million Muslims in India. They constitute one of the largest Muslim populations in the world, roughly equal to that of Pakistan and Bangladesh, though the partition of British India in 1947 was meant to separate the groups along religious lines. Muslims in Delhi, the capital of India, gather here for prayer celebrating the end of Ramadan.

pressure eventually conceded such a status to them. France thus became the protector of the Catholic Maronites in the Levant, Russia of the Orthodox communities; for lack of a better candidate, Britain chose the Druze despite Druze protestations. European protection provided the religious minorities with considerable power, elevating their social standing and altering their relations with the dominant communities. The Europeans would eventually demand of the Ottoman Empire and Iran the same capitulatory privileges—exemption from prosecution by local courts—for their allies among the minorities that they themselves enjoyed.

As the local populations began to rebel against colonial rule, they came to view the minority communities as "collaborators." This label was of great importance in the future of relations between the minorities and the dominant communities in states that were born of struggles against colonialism. In some cases the differences were so irreconcilable that they led to secessionism. Singapore separated from Malaysia, and Lebanon rejected rejoining Syria. The idea of protection of minorities at times became a central aim of the colonial powers. In the case of France's rule over Syria, this idea translated into the French policy of creating a Christian Arab state in the form of Lebanon. In addition, because the minorities were often better represented in commercial affairs, it meant that they dealt with the Europeans first and then more frequently. The minorities were incorporated into the European commercial networks from which they benefited materially and developed vested interests. Christian communities in the Levant and Anatolia, Parsis in India, and Copts in Egypt are examples of this. The commercial links also helped to alter the balance of power between the dominant communities and their minorities. It also gave the two communities radically different views of colonialism.

Minority communities, which had enjoyed only limited privileges and did not view themselves as included in Muslim societies, saw only opportunities for gain in colonialism. Their reaction to colonialism was therefore very different from that of the dominant community. For example, minorities saw the opportunity for the generation of wealth in commercial alliances with the colonial powers, social uplift by relying on the colonial regime, and advancement by taking advantage of what colonial educational systems had to offer. Christians in the Arab Near East, Anatolia, and Iran embraced European values and ideals and subscribed to the ideologies of colonialism. Such ideological commitment, for instance, thoroughly transformed the Parsi religion in India and gave the Maronites of Lebanon a sense of "Europeanness." This was also because of the fact that they more readily enrolled in modern schools and therefore more easily joined the colonial administration and in greater number. In some cases, as in Africa, Indonesia, or India, Christian minorities emerged through the conversion of local populations. In these cases the minority's dependence on colonialism and the majority's disdain were all the greater.

Even in 1858, Sayyid Ahmad Khan pointed to this problem in India. There Hindus, who were not a minority in number but had been subservient to Muslims for centuries, were joining the administrative institutions of the British Raj more rapidly than Muslims, who viewed British education with disdain. One consequence of this was that minorities became better represented in the future political and intellectual leadership of their societies. In Africa, from Nigeria to Eritrea, non-Muslims have been prominent in national politics. In Senegal the most important nationalist leader, and later the president of the country, was Leopold Sedar Sengor, a Christian. Arab nationalism as an intellectual current—from the writer George Antonius to the ideologue Michel Aflaq—was dominated by Arab Christians, who also dominated in the bureaucracy and political institutions in that region. A disproportionately high number of the early leadership of the Palestinian Liberation Organization were Christians, as were some of its most radical leaders, such as George Habash and Nayif Hawatma.

Although relations between colonial powers and Christian minorities were more fecund and with greater significance for later developments, similar trends were also evident in relations with other religious and ethnic minorities. In Syria the French maintained close ties with the Alawis, and in India the British with the Ismailis. Dominant Muslim communities tended to view such relations with greater alarm than relations between colonialists and non-Muslim minorities, because they were tantamount to altering not only the balance of power between social groups but between orthodoxy and those it sought to exclude. Often the dominant communities suspected the colonial hand in all religious schisms, especially those that arose during colonial rule. Indian Muslims have viewed the Ahmediya as a creation of the British, just as Iranians have depicted Bahaism in similar terms. In recent years these sentiments have been echoed in the charge in some quarters that all schisms are the work of the U.S. Central Intelligence Agency. Such views owed to colonial administrations' recruitment among the minorities as well as to minorities' greater participation in the colonial educational system, both of which had the effect of empowering the minority, westernizing its cultural outlook, and allying it with the colonial administration. In India in 1931, 1.2 percent of the population were literate in English but only 0.9 percent of the Muslims were. In Syria this trend eventually led to the domination of the country by Alawis, which continues in President Hafiz al-Asad's rule.

A particularly important legacy of colonialism is the representation of particular communities in the police and military forces. The colonial powers often recruited among the minorities for the local army and police forces. Not only were the minorities more closely allied with the colonial order, but they were more likely to be willing to engage and to suppress members of the dominant community—with which they did not identify and against which they may have borne a grudge. Minorities were also less likely to respond to the religious call for rebellion and jihad. The legacy of the Great Mutiny of 1857 and the Muslim Sepoy army's siege of Lucknow dominated much of the colonial thinking in the twentieth century. Hence, the Syrian army was largely composed of Alawis, and the British army in India of Punjabis, Muslim as well as Sikh. Here Punjabi Muslims had a different relationship with the British than those of the Mughal territories. Consequently, the national armies that were built on the basis of the colonial army tended to be composed of a large number of minorities. This has been of importance in many Muslim states from Nigeria to Syria. In Jordan a variation of this scenario unfolded, where tribesmen—and not minorities—were recruited into the Arab Legion to control the urban and rural populations of western Jordan— the Palestinians. The only exception to this general rule were the Shiites, whom the colonial powers never incorporated into an alliance and whom in the 1920s and the 1930s served as the main source of opposition in Iraq to British rule. The Shiites were therefore not prominent in British colonial armies in the Near East.

Elsewhere the colonial powers actually created ethnic or religious diversity, which produced the same conditions as previously outlined. In Algeria, French settlers took over large tracts of land and numbered close to two million at the time of independence. They left Algeria after independence. In East Africa and South Africa, Indian and Malay labor, which was imported to work on colonial projects, remained to form important commercial communities from Kampala and Mombasa to Zanzibar, Dar es Salaam, Cape Town, and Durban. "Africanization" campaigns in East Africa eventually ended in the mass expulsion of South Asians from Uganda and their marginalization in Kenya and Tanzania. How the issue will be resolved in South Africa remains to be seen. In Palestine the British facilitated the settlement of European Jews for political and humanitarian rather than economic reasons. That policy culminated in the creation of the state of Israel in 1948. In Sind, in the late nineteenth century, Punjabi workers were brought in to work for the British. Their presence fueled resentments among Sindhis, which continue to animate ethnic politics in Pakistan.

How economic considerations led to the movements of populations, and the implications of these movements for the successor states, is best reflected in the case of Malaysia. Here the British negotiated concessions for land and mines with local chiefs but brought in Chinese and Indian migrant labor, who eventually formed large communities. These "minority" communities developed the same commercial, religio-cultural, and political alliances that colonial rulers had established with minority communities elsewhere. The Chinese and Indians as a result became financially and politically more advanced than the indigenous Malays, whose politics were controlled by chiefs and centered in rural areas. The University of Malaya, most commercial and social institutions, and the staff of the colonial establishment were dominated by Chinese and Indians. The power of the "imported" minorities led to major civil strife in Malaysia in 1969 and continues to be a major point of contention in Malaysian politics. After three decades of affirmative action policies to benefit the bumiputra ("sons of soil") 80 percent of private sector wealth is still controlled by the Chinese and Indians. The ethnic dilemmas confronting postcolonial Muslim states thus have their roots in the colonial era. Although ethnic consciousness is by no means unique to the Third World or to Muslim states, the particularities of the problem—divisive national societies, weakness of national identity, imbalances in the wealth, education, and power of minority and majority communities—are unique to the postcolonial state.

The Institutional Foundations of the Postcolonial State

An important, and yet until recently ignored, legacy of colonialism is the manner in which it has given form to the institutional foundations, and thus the parameter of politics, of the postcolonial state. Independence ended the sovereignty of European powers over their territories; it did not, however, produce states de novo.

The postcolonial state inherited the machinery of the colonial state, and to varying degrees, followed the model of the colonial state. In such cases as India, the continuity between the two was quite conspicuous. Muhammad Ali Jinnah first became the governor-general of Pakistan, and the India Act of 1935 was the law of the land until the Constitution of 1956 was promulgated some nine years after independence. Elsewhere the continuity is less apparent, as in Algeria or Libya. Still, even in these countries the manner in which the state works and relates to social forces has more in common with the colonial era than state leaders would admit. Ideological continuities generally have been easier to discern. The rhetoric of state leaders may also have had a hand in confounding the relations between the colonial and postcolonial states. It has become increasingly evident, however, that the postcolonial state, all protestations to the contrary notwithstanding, has been less a seed planted at independence and more a later growth in an old tree—new branches on the trunk that grew during the colonial era. Even when high politics of the state may have sought to chart new courses, at its foundations the state ineluctably followed in the footsteps of the colonial era. Colonialism accounts for more in postcolonial states than previously assumed. Policy choices, the way those choices have been implemented, and how the state has developed— all of this has occurred in a framework that was conceived and entrenched during colonial rule.

Although the aim and the general structure of authority of colonialism was much the same from Indonesia to Nigeria, there were important variations in how the colonial administrators actually ruled over their vassal populations. These variations account for differences among the experiences with state formation after independence. Colonial administration exerted authority directly as well as indirectly, through local elites, chiefs, and mercantile forces. In Algeria and Libya colonial rule was direct, while in Morocco, Tunisia, Malaya, Java, and India it used local elites to a good extent. In Java the numerical weakness of the Dutch led them to rely on local elites and chiefs to manage the labor supply. The consequence was to entrench the sociopolitical position of the intermediary elite, to create dependencies between the peasantry and the elite, and also to permit extensive exploitation and impoverishment of the masses in the process of generating a labor supply.

In India a third of the population were ruled, nominally at least, by some 250 maharajas (Hindu princes and kings) and nawabs (Muslim princes and kings) as well as the Nizam (hereditary rulers) of Hyderabad (a state that was larger than France) and the Aga Khan. These princes had little real autonomy and were carefully controlled by British political officers, but they wielded much authority over their populations. The relations between the subjects of the princes and those who lived under direct British rule was very different, however. Through the princes the British were able to control a large part of India with the least amount of political cost. Even in those territories in which British rule was direct, landowners, traditional elites, and local chiefs and grandees were used to bolster British rule. Beginning in 1861, landlords were inducted into the largely honorific advisory body called the Viceroy's Council and allowed to dominate local politics—this lasted until the interwar period.

A symbiotic relationship then developed between the princes and local elites and the British, whereby the British agreed to the social status of the local elites and the elites in turn provided local support and social control for the British. This pattern of politics made the local elites important power brokers, entrenched their sociopolitical positions, and encouraged them to favor the compartmentalization of the policy in place of a uniform national political arena, wherein they could wield power by controlling segments of the polity and negotiate for its support with the center. The patronage of the British often allowed the institutional power and reach of the princes and local elites to increase, which made it more difficult for the nationalist elite to penetrate their domain and later for the state to curb it. For instance, British policy in India gave the landowning class tremendous power over the peasantry, which helped to consolidate the control of the landowners over the rural population. In Pakistan this trend has been most evident. The landowning class has not only wielded tremendous power in the country, controlling politics at all levels, but it also has successfully resisted land reform. The landowning class therefore controls political support in its estates and is in a position to bargain with the center. In the Persian Gulf emi-

The British occupied Kabul in 1880 as part of the second Anglo-Afghan war. They installed Amir Abd al-Rahman Khan (r. 1880–1901) as ruler. With substantial annual subsidies and technical assistance from the British, the "Iron Amir" consolidated power over the entire country.

rates British policy helped to strengthen tribal chiefs, and in Malaysia the local kings. The power of the monarchy in the Persian Gulf emirates and in Brunei is to a large extent a result of these colonial policies. Similar trends also characterized relations between the British and tribal chiefs in East Africa and Nigeria, with a similar impact on state formation.

Although French colonial rule was generally centralized, it too at times followed policies similar to British colonialism. Where and when the French used the intermediary role of the local elites, however, it had less to do with the efficacy of this approach and more with limitations to centralized colonial rule or the perceived importance of the colony to France. Lisa Anderson has written that in Tunisia, because the protectorate was not very important to France, the French let local institutions of power persist and used the local mercantile classes as the means of pushing into the countryside. A local bourgeoisie thus emerged that helped to strengthen the colonial state and in turn benefited from the strengthening of that state. Under the Neo-Destur party in Tunisia, state consolidation followed the pattern first established under French rule and thus involved following the French pattern of extending the state's reach into untapped areas and extending Tunis' administrative reach. In Morocco, similarly, General Lyautey conceived of the French role as recognizing Moroccan political culture and accepting the social mores on which it was based. He saw France as a protector, best served if it worked through the existing political, cultural, and social institutions.

In Algeria and Libya under French and Italian rules a different pattern emerged. There the colonial state did not seek to operate through local elites as much as it sought to establish the paramount role of the colonial administration and to rule through the settlers. It can be argued that Morocco, Tunisia, and later Syria were exceptions to French rule, which typically had a penchant for centralization that may have been embedded in France's own political culture. That Morocco and Tunisia were protectorates and Syria later only a mandate may have made these territories less attractive or central to the French scheme of empire, and thus led to less investment in centralized rule and greater reliance on local

Tripoli, Libya, was occupied by the Italians in 1912, as the Ottoman Empire's hold over the region weakened. The Italians constructed Western-style buildings and insisted on segregating settlers from locals, especially in economic matters, and so no local elite developed to take over once the Italians departed after World War II.

forces. That France came to view Algeria as a part of France—a sentiment captured in a famous saying of the time: "France is cut by the Mediterranean as Paris is cut by the Seine"—encouraged ruling it directly, both because that was acceptable to the settlers and because centralized rule would guarantee greater integration into France. French rule in Algeria was not only interested in economic gain but also in the integration of Algeria into France. It is important to note that to the extent to which French colonialism in Algeria was engaged in economic gain, it was making such gains through the large numbers of French citizens who had settled the best land in Algeria, and not the local population, the mercantile classes, or the emerging bourgeoisie. Political compromises, necessary for facilitating economic gains from the local economy, were thus not necessary in Algeria. All compromises involved the economy of the settlers, whose leaders were distinctly hostile to all Algerian political expressions. It is also arguable that in Algeria, France found only a weak local power structure, one that could be easily overcome and one that would not have been a suitable basis for colonial authority. It was thus quickly replaced with direct administration.

In Libya, by contrast, the Italians had a different attitude, although they followed similar policies. Italy's main concern was not managing the economy but proving its own primacy. Hence, they too saw no need to forge political alliances with local elites that would facilitate extracting economic gain from the local economy. Italy, in fact, insisted on segregating the settlers and the locals, especially in economic matters. Therefore no local bourgeoisie emerged, and the local population was not tied to the expansion of the colonial state, whereas in Tunisia nationalist leaders had established their ties of patronage to the population as part of the expansion of the colonial state. The colonial state had thus facilitated the emergence of a Tunisian power structure centered in an urban bourgeoisie that had penetrated the rural areas at the back of the colonial state; Libya, by contrast, had no viable local state elite to take over from Italy, because no expansion of the local state involving the local bourgeoisie had happened. The urban Libyans had not developed any ties of patronage beyond their immediate locales because they had not had any reason to venture beyond them. Italian rule in Libya was absolute and led to little local institution building. At independence, Libya thus lacked a stable state machinery and was not able to continue in the footsteps of the Italians. Libya actually had to create a state. The colonial legacy gave Libya its independence and shape but not a viable state. The Libyan state was at the outset an ad hoc one, which lacked continuity and penetration of society and had little authority. It relied heavily on the writ of the monarchy, which made it vulnerable. The monarchy's collapse and the rise of the absolutist and arbitrary rule of Muammar Qaddafi occurred in this context.

Differences between how colonial powers conceived of their authority and how this authority had to be implemented had to do with two issues: how best to maximize economic gain from the colony, and whether the colonial power had a political-cultural agenda in mind. If economic gain was the primary motive, and this gain was not tied to a large settler population, it was likely that colonial administrations would appeal to local elites for political support or create conditions for the rise of a mercantile and bourgeois elite. Both of these elite groups would develop vested interests in the colonial state and would eventually become tied to the workings of the parent state centered in Europe. Both groups would therefore be important to the future workings of the successor state. Which group would eventually dominate—the landowners in Pakistan or the bourgeois elite in Tunisia—would depend on their relative power during colonial rule.

Where and when colonialism saw its economic gain in a settler community, or saw the purpose of colonialism as proving the political and cultural supremacy of the parent state, it was less likely to rule through the local elites or support the rise of a local elite. In such cases, as in Algeria and Libya, the colonial state would lack any serious local components that would have ties to the colonial administration and have vested interests in its power and reach. The postcolonial state in such cases would be weak and vulnerable, lacking in a social base and strong economic and political institutions.

Beyond the structure of colonial authority, how the colonial state exercised that authority and how it was perceived by the local population was of great importance to later state developments. The colonial state, unlike the European state, was from inception based on segregation of Europeans from locals in law, economic relations, administration, political matters, and social life. It was not based on the European conception of civil societies but on centralized and nonrepresentative bureaucracies that ruled by force and encouraged as well as managed social divisions. As a result, mass-based parties are a rarity in Muslim states. The United Malays National Organization in Malaysia or the Neo-Destur in Tunisia are examples of genuine party organizations. The National Liberation Front in Algeria or Bath parties in Syria and Iraq to a limited extent have served as genuine parties. Elsewhere, however, personalized rule has been the order of the day. Nasser's Arab Socialist Union never evolved into a genuine party, and the Shah's experiment with the Rastakhiz (Resurrection) party or the Ayatollah Khomeini's with the Islamic Republic party did not amount to much.

The essence of the colonial state became giving shape to those agencies and institutions that would assume domination. Unbound by constitutional limitations and citizenship rights, the colonial state had broad powers to act, and it did so viewing itself as bound to the "superior" European values. It acted on reasons of state (those of Europe), which in the eyes of the local population were condescending and paternal, unaccountable, and by nature avowedly transformative rather than managerial. These are exactly the attitudes that would become a part of the developmentalist ideology of the postcolonial state. The postcolonial state and its nationalist elite had rejected the colonial state's right to rule their populations and to represent their interests, but they never rejected the colonial state's views of the state's function in the colonial territories. In many regards the postcolonial state became an indigenization of the colonial state. The opposition to the state in the Muslim world today, although couched in Islamic rhetoric, in large measure reiterates these original nationalist complaints about the colonial state. Just as the nationalist elite rejected colonialism's claim to represent local aspirations in transforming society, the Islamist opposition similarly questions the ruling regime's claim to represent popular aspirations in pursuing secularization and development.

Generally speaking, the colonial state's goal was to establish domination, to ensure legitimacy as well as security (internal and external), to maintain autonomy first from the local society but eventually also from its parent state in Europe, and to extract economic surplus. These aims were achieved as the colonial state devised and refined its institutional setup. That institutional setup in turn determined the workings of the successor states, the nature of relations between the state and society within them, and the paradigm that governs their politics. The institutional setup is perhaps the most pervasive legacy of colonialism. The colonial state was by nature highly centralized and dependent on a core of institutions (such as the police, the military, and the bureaucracy) that served as the repositories of its authority. That authority guaranteed the continuation of European domination and extraction of resources to the advantage of the European power. Some institutions, such as the bureaucracy, were not designed primarily to enforce order but to efficiently manage the running of the machinery of government and the economy. Other institutions, such as the judiciary, were intended to help with the management of order within a legal framework, but their character had more to do with European traditions than with the functions they had to perform. Still, the confluence of the activities of the bureaucracy, the judiciary, and the coercive instruments of the colonial state constituted an institutional structure that allowed a small European minority to rule over vast territories with the help of local agents, and to manage the economic flow of goods and resources between colonial territories and Europe. So important were these institutions that they eventually constituted the basis of the postcolonial state and thus determined the character of that state and the nature of its relation with the society. In many ways states such as Pakistan are replicas of the colonial state, not only in the manner in which they are set up and function, but more important in how they envision their own roles. The military and the police are perhaps the most evident examples of the institutional and ideological continuity of colonialism.

Military, Police, and Civilian Bureaucratic Institutions

Throughout colonial territories, local armies and police forces were trained to support the colonial state. This was by and large a very successful undertaking, enough so that Indian soldiers fought in European battlefields during both world wars, and the elite Himalayan Gurkha soldiers continue to fight battles for the British, the last instance being during the Falkland Islands war in 1982. The Sepoy Mutiny of 1857, wherein Muslim and Hindu soldiers in northern India rose in rebellion against their English officers, was not repeated on that scale, at least not until the time of independence, when armies in Egypt and Syria took to anti-imperialism. Recruitment among minorities and deployment of soldiers in alien communities to some extent accounted for the facility with which colonial administrations created and managed their militaries. Sikh soldiers thus predominated in units that kept order in Hindu and Muslim areas, while it was Baluch troops from western Pakistan, who opened fire on Sikh worshipers in Julianwala Bagh in the Amritsar Massacre in 1919. Still, the power of colonial militaries came from the discipline and esprit de corps that intensive training had instilled in the soldiers and more important, in the officer corp. The colonial armies had internalized the military ideas and political values of the colonial administration. To the extent to which they found a role in state formation in later years, they did so with the benefit of their colonial outlooks. Even in Algeria the military has remained one of the most Francophone institutions in the country.

More important, the colonial legacy determined their attitudes toward politics. Colonial militaries were generally unnaturally large, far larger than the size of the local economies warranted. Colonial militaries were based on the economic and political interests of the European power; they were not conceived, armed, or trained based on the economic and technological abilities of the colonial territory. The size and power of the military itself was the most important legacy that post-colonial states had to deal with. Muslim states thus inherited omnipotent militaries, far too large for their relative population sizes and economic capacities. Furthermore, the militaries had fought alongside the colonial rulers right up to the time of independence. Their attitudes toward the struggles for independence and those who led those struggles were not necessarily sympathetic. Military and police forces had clashed with and arrested politicians; they had viewed the champions of the independence struggles with the same cynicism and disparaging glare that their superior European officers had. The Indonesian generals thus remained wary of Sukarno and lost no time in deposing him when the threat of communism provided them with the pretext to do so. The same may be said of those who would lead coups in Pakistan, Bangladesh, Nigeria, and Sudan. They would remain preoccupied with order and show impatience with the politics of the masses.

In the new states the officers who had served the colonial order and the politicians who had fought for independence had to share in the task of state formation. The relationship between the military and the civilian order was often determined by this reality. Even in the Arab world and Sub-Saharan Africa, where left-leaning junior officers overthrew senior officers of the old school to join the anti-imperialist struggle, they did not resolve the inherent tensions between the military and civilian orders. These tensions in Egypt, Libya, Iraq, and Syria eventually led to military takeovers. The military's disdain for politicians and their perceived right to interfere in politics to restore order were in good measure legacies of the colonial era—whose militaries, with few exceptions, were not meant for external war but for preservation of internal order. These legacies were internalized by the rank-and-file of the colonial armies and became a part of their postindependence ethos. The officers in most colonial settings, and even in the Ottoman Empire and Iran, were more educated than the average population, and at the institutional level militaries had been more exposed to Western ideas. They

Local armies and police forces were usually trained to support the colonial state. One of the few instances when they rebelled was the Sepoy Mutiny of 1857, in which Muslim and Hindu soldiers in northern India rose in rebellion against their British officers.

therefore viewed themselves as better equipped in leading the new states to development and progress. The combination of their belief in their greater capability to oversee development—a view that in the 1950s was shared by Western powers—and their disdain for politicians, whom were seen as demagogues, often set military leaders on a path of competition with the political elite. In this the military leadership filled the shoes of the former colonial rulers as they competed with the nationalist leaders for the right to represent and to deliver on the aspirations of the local population.

Much like the military, the bureaucracy also served as a pillar of the colonial order. Trained and molded in the ethos of the colonial culture, bureaucrats in the empire's service shared and followed the values and political outlook of the European rulers. Because they controlled the machinery of the colonial state, they ineluctably occupied a central role in the postcolonial order. Politicians had only limited success in controlling them, lest they disrupt the entire workings of the state. As a result, the bureaucracy had a major role in state formation in the postcolonial era and in creating continuities between the ethos and mode of operation of the state before and after independence. In Pakistan, for instance, soon after independence in 1947 the bureaucracy eclipsed the political elite in managing the country. Political leaders Muhammad Ali Jinnah (1876–1948) and Liaqat Ali Khan (1895–1951) were replaced at the helm after 1951 by senior bureaucrats Ghulam Muhammad (1895–1956) and Iskandar Mirza (1899–1969), who had risen through the ranks of the bureaucracy under the British.

The power of the bureaucracy varied across colonial territories, depending on the extent of the investment that colonial rulers had made in their administrative institutions. For example, the Indian Civil Service was exemplary in its efficient functioning and elaborate structure, but the bureaucracies in the Arab Near East and Libya were generally undeveloped. The power and efficiency of the bureaucracy was a double-edged sword. It could serve as a major source of resistance to effective exertion of authority by the political elite, and it could infuse the new states with the political values of the colonial order. Still, the same power and efficiency was often an asset in mobilizing resources for development. Over the years the standards by which colonial bureaucracies operated declined; some even lost their independence and preeminence. As a result, their political role and their contribution to socioeconomic change have been diminished.

The judiciary presents a very different case. To begin with, it is of primary importance to studying former British colonies, where the colonial state consciously promoted a system of justice modeled after Britain's and gave it autonomy to function within the structure of the colonial order. As a result, Britain's colonial subjects developed a strong respect for the judiciary, and its independence from the writ of the executive branch became embedded in the structure of the postcolonial state. In Pakistan, for example, the judiciary has defied the executive branch over the years to assert the primacy of the law and the constitution. It voted against the military government of General Ayub Khan when he banned the Islamist party (Jamaat-i Islami) in 1964; and in 1993 the judiciary ruled against President Ghulam Ishaq Khan for having dismissed the government, and they ordered the government restored—and it was. That Ayub Khan and Ghulam Ishaq Khan abided by the writ of the judiciary showed that the judiciary's institutional power, as conceived of by the colonial state, has become instituted in the postcolonial state. In 1996 Prime Minister Benazir Bhutto's attempts to rein in the judiciary and to assert the executive branch's supremacy over it was one of the principal reasons cited by President Faruq Leghari in dismissing Bhutto's government. Similarly, in Malaysia the judiciary has rendered a number of verdicts against the government. When a power struggle erupted in the ruling party, the United Malays Nationalist Organization, in 1986–88, a good deal of the wrangling occurred through the intermediary of the courts. Despite Prime Minister Mahathir Muhammad's success in curbing the powers of the judiciary in 1988–89, the courts continue to enjoy a certain degree of autonomy.

Not in every postcolonial state—even among those that had been British colonies—can this degree of judicial autonomy and power be seen. In Malaysia, for instance, since 1988 the autonomy and powers of the judiciary have been significantly reduced through legislation and strong-arm tactics by the government. Where and when the judicial branch has been weak in the new states, it was more likely that authoritarianism and arbitrary rule became the order of the day. The manner in which the colonial state established and then institutionalized the division of powers between the various branches of government thus had a great bearing on the internal politics of the successor states. British colonies generally tended to be less dependent on centralized rule and more emphatic on the autonomy of the various state agencies from the executive branch. As a result, former British colonies from Pakistan to Malaysia have been more likely to have pluralist forms of government and more benevolent and open authoritarian regimes. These colonies tend to view legal and constitutional issues more seriously as frameworks for managing both political and social relations.

The judiciary also had the effect of instituting particular patterns of political activity in the body politic of the colonial society, which continued to dominate the postcolonial scene and by the same token to allow legislations and the courts to become avenues for political activism. The judiciary's autonomy and respect for the law under British rule often led to resistance to colonial rule and the use of legal channels to assert nationalist aspirations. For instance, in 1913 Muhammad Ali Jinnah helped to push through the Mussalman Wakf (Muslim Endowments) Validating Act to protect Muslim endowments and thereby limit the penetration of Indian society by the British. Similar efforts in Southeast Asia had the same effect, delineating the boundaries of Muslim society and thereby protecting Muslim cultural life against colonial control. In Malaya the British compensated the local kings for their loss of political control by giving them the final say on all cultural and religious matters. As a result, control over Islamic law and its implementation became an important marker of monarchical authority. The local kings have guarded their prerogative with great vigilance, with the result that in Malaysia all issues pertaining to Islamic law fall under the jurisdiction of state governments. In effect, Muslims used the law and the courts of the colonial order to limit state power.

Many of these laws did not stand after independence, however. For instance, from 1959 onward the state of Pakistan has systematically reduced the scope of private religious endowments and increased the state's control of them, and since 1980 the federal center in Malaysia has stripped the sultans of some of their legal powers. Still, the legacy of Muslim legal efforts against colonial rule has continued to influence the unfolding of politics. First, the law and the courts have remained important to the resolution of political disputes. Second, the same issues that once protected Muslim society in the colonial order and were thus politicized—such as the endowments—have continued to serve as determinants in struggles between the state and the society. That the postcolonial state succeeded the colonial state made this continuity easier. Pakistan may have done away with the spirit of Jinnah's law of 1913, but the fact that endowments are still a contentious issue is proof of the continued salience of the avenues that were used by local political leaders in keeping the colonial state at bay.

On a different level, how the colonial state interacted with society has been important to the workings of the postcolonial state and how it has in turn interacted with Muslim societies. Colonial rule was often made possible by manipulating divisions within society. Colonial rule thus accentuated social divisions and helped to institute them by treating different communities differently, in the eyes of the law, at the polling booth, and in how resources were allocated. Separate electorates or patronage handed out along linguistic, ethnic, or religious lines thus encouraged politics of identity at the cost of the development of uniform civil societies. In India this encouraged the emergence of the All-India Muslim League in 1906, which lobbied with the British for separate electorates for Muslims and Hindus. In Malaysia the same trend of events led each community to form its own party. At the time of independence in 1957, Malays gathered under the United Malays National Organization, while the Indians rallied behind the Malaysian Indian Congress and the Chinese behind the Malaysian Chinese Association. In essence, elections in the colonial period provided a critical political framework that shaped the conception of communities of their relation to power at the center as well as their own identity and self-definition.

The postcolonial state leaders, many of whom came from among the colonial bureaucracy and military, often followed in the footsteps of their predecessors. State leaders in South Asia, Sub-Saharan Africa, or the Arab Near East would continue to manipulate social divisions even as they spoke of national unity. That the political leadership after independence inevitably belonged to one social group made the task of manipulating social divisions all the more difficult. There have been few cases in which the state has risen above the politics of identity or has been able to undo colonialism's divisive impact. Malaysia succeeded but did so only after the separation of Singapore and the ethnic riots of 1969. Other polities across the Muslim world continue to operate on the belief in the inherent division of society—a legacy of colonial rule. The nationalist rhetoric often belies the reality of everyday politics in which communal, tribal, or ethnic identities supersede national ones.

In the same vein, rules and procedures implemented by the colonial state to control local populations, especially during times of war, had an important effect on defining relations between the state and society in later years. For instance, restrictions placed on free expression during World War I and again during World War II in India and the Arab Near East, or during the emergency (the suspension of civil liberties) during the wars in Malaya, set the precedent for later authoritarian practices. Clauses in Pakistan's constitutions or in Malaysia's Internal Security Act of 1960 that restrict individual rights or give the state extraordinary powers often have their roots in wartime British restrictions, such as the Rowlett Act of 1919, the India Act of 1935, and emergency rules and laws in Malaya. Especially because World War II immediately preceded independence, the structure of relations between the state and society during the war had a greater impact on the politics of the independent states than the character of state-society relations during colonialism's earlier years. Across the Muslim world the World War II period was one of direct assaults by the colonial state on civil liberties. Restrictions on personal freedoms, the press, the right to due process and free association, the right to protest, and the like altered the nature of state-society relations. That independence followed shortly thereafter, and before the wartime regulations could have been rescinded and the nature of state-society relations restored to its pre–war status, profoundly affected the exercise of power and state authority in the postcolonial state. The war strengthened the colonial and postcolonial states, weakened social institutions that could have kept the state at bay, and strengthened pluralism.

Relations of patronage between state and society during the colonial era also have left an indelible mark on future states. In areas that were deemed strategically important to colonial rulers, such as northwest India, or where colonialism arrived late and thus was unable to dominate completely, control was secured through generous relations of patronage between the colonial state and the local populations. Northwest India—the territory that would later constitute Pakistan—bordered on Afghanistan and throughout the colonial era had been a source of concern to the British. Northwest India was also the area from which the Indian army drew most of its soldiers. As a result, the British asserted their control over this region through patronage, with the colonial state providing the local economy and political elite with financial support.

In Malaya a similar situation held with the rural Malay population, who did not benefit directly from the financial activities of the colonial establishment, but whose loyalty was purchased through patronage given to the rural power structure. In the Arab lands of the Ottoman Empire, colonialism arrived late after the first world war. As a result, colonialism was never able to establish the kind of state that ruled over India or Algeria. The temporary presence of European powers in the region, moreover, was often justified by strategic imperatives rather than commerce. As a result, the power relations were anchored not so much in direct exertion of power—although the French in Syria often used force—as it was in entangling the local population in the web of the colonial state's patronage. In Syria, for instance, the French were unable to attract settlers to the colony because of the temporary nature of the mandate system. The colonial economy and society therefore lacked the distinct settler domination that was the mark of French rule over North Africa. The colonial establishment therefore dealt directly with local landowners. The emerging relationship was one of state support for local agriculture, which in turn the French hoped, would establish French control over rural Syria. The absence of settlers and the patterns of colonial despotism that were associated with the French allowed them to develop a very different kind of colonial relationship in Syria. As World War II neared, the colonial establishments in the Arab Near East became more dependent on securing their hold, and minimizing the costs of control of the region, by generously supplying patronage to the population.

The consequences of state patronage, especially so close to independence, was to determine the pattern of later state–society relations. The state in such cases emerged as paternalistic, and the society came to view patronage as a function of the state. The domination of the public sector in the Arab Near East and the state's extensive patronage networks, which took shape under the ideological banner of Arab socialism, thus had its roots in the character of the colonial state. In Malaysia the relations of patronage led the Malay population to remain aloof from commercial activities and instead to rely on the state to guarantee its economic and social standing. The links of patronage between the dominant party, the United Malays National Organization, and the political structure of rural Malaysia is very much based on the colonial structure of authority. In Pakistan the relations of patronage had in part to do with the relative weakness of the Indian nationalist

Congress party in those regions—especially in Punjab—and after independence laid the foundations for the rise of a large and paternalistic state.

Although ideological factors and policies adopted by ruling governments have also been important in the eventual domination of the state over society, and growth in the size of state patronage, it is arguable that the existence of such relations during colonial rule may have greatly facilitated such outcomes. Elsewhere, where strong links of patronage did not exist, such as in Iran in the Qajar and Pahlavi eras, the state emerged as far weaker. In Iran, in fact, imperialism was very important to keeping the Iranian state weak throughout the nineteenth century. There is evidence that the British may have looked favorably on the rise of the Pahlavi state as a means of shoring up state power to prevent Iran's collapse before an expansionist Russia. Even there, though, the British support was short-lived. Soon after the rise of Reza Shah Pahlavi to power, the British fell out with him and eventually insisted that he abdicate and leave Iran on the eve of the second world war. As a consequence, the Iranian state—until the formation of the Islamic Republic in 1979—did not develop the kind of control and therefore power that characterized the states where colonialism had spawned strong relations of patronage and control.

Colonial institutions, policies, and attitudes toward governance determined the trajectory of state developments in the postindependence era, leaving a strong intellectual, legal, and institutional legacy in the Muslim world. Muslim states developed in the shadow of colonialism, and their developments, modes of operation, and politics cannot be fully understood without considering the continuities between the pre- and postcolonial eras and the manner in which colonialism determined fundamental attitudes toward politics, society, and governance.

CHAPTER FOURTEEN

The Globalization of Islam

THE RETURN OF MUSLIMS TO THE WEST

Yvonne Yazbeck Haddad

Since the early 1970s, western Europeans and North Americans have become increasingly concerned about an apparent change in the nature and patterns of human migration. For some this change threatens to alter the ethnic and religious composition of their nation-states, their democratic and capitalist traditions, and their liberal social values. The emigration and settlement of Muslims from more than seventy nations to the West has been of some concern. For those in the West who believe in the purity of race, civilization, and culture, or in a supersessionist "Judeo-Christian" worldview, this movement of Muslims is a menacing threat to what they believe to be a homogeneous Western society. For others it increasingly represents a significant demographic shift that posits a major cultural challenge, the precise consequences of which are unpredictable and unforeseen, because they require a variety of adjustments by both the host countries and the new immigrants.

Until recently many Europeans and North Americans tended to identify Islam with the Arabs. More knowledgeable scholars added parts of Asia and Africa to the abode of Islam. Other scholars were reluctant to admit that not only is Islam a universal religion with adherents throughout the globe, but that it has increasingly become part and parcel of the West. Ignoring "the facts on the ground," they persist in thinking of Muslims as displaced persons temporarily residing in the West, who will one day pack up and return to where they came from or to

(Left) Many types of mosques and community centers have been built in America to serve the large and varied Muslim community there. One of the most elegant is the Islamic Center of New York. Designed by the architectural firm Skidmore, Owings, and Merrill, and located on 96th Street on Manhattan's tony Upper East Side, it attests to the presence of an international community of Muslims in the metropolis.

"where they belong." Still others, who for religious or political reasons wish away these Muslim immigrants, have become more shrill in declaring their presence a threat.

The Encounter of Islam with the West

The Muslim encounter with "the West" dates back to the beginning of Islam's expansion. As Arab armies spread their hegemony over major parts of the Byzantine Empire in Southwest Asia and North Africa, large segments of the Eastern Christian churches (Byzantines, Jacobites, Copts, Gregorians, and Nestorians) came under their control. This close encounter generated a variety of experiences, ranging from peaceful coexistence and cooperation to mutual vilification and armed conflict. It also helped craft a corpus of polemical literature written by both Muslims and Christians, each seeking to demonstrate and proclaim the truth and superiority of their own religion. Each group faulted the other for basing their faith on falsified scriptures as well as proclaiming errant doctrines. The Muslim depiction of the Christian "other" and the Christian depiction of Islam have inevitably been forged by the historical context in which they were conceived.

Muslim expansion from North Africa into western Europe was stopped at Poitiers in 732, but the Ottomans in the East kept probing Europe's defenses for several centuries until they were halted after the failure of the siege of Vienna in 1683. European areas that came under Muslim jurisdictions in Spain, Portugal, Sicily, and southern France between the eighth and the fifteenth centuries experienced a thriving cultural revival that became a major influence in the transmission of civilization that sparked the European Renaissance. The fall of Grenada in 1492 brought Muslim rule in western Europe to an end. A significant number of the Ottomans continued to live in eastern Europe, where some of the indigenous population converted to Islam in Bulgaria, Romania, Albania, and Serbia. The recent dramatic transplantation of Muslims into western Europe and North America has thus been called "the new Islamic presence." Other scholars, noting the fact that Islam has modified the religious composition of western Europe and become its second largest religion, have begun to talk about "the new Europe."

The second major Muslim encounter with "the West" was with Catholic Christianity during the crusades and the Reconquista. Although the crusades took place at the periphery of the Islamic empire and seem to have been concerned with containing and weakening Eastern Orthodoxy as much as Islam, the bloody story of the crusaders sacking Antioch and Jerusalem and slaughtering all the inhabitants is increasingly depicted in today's Islamic literature as one of Western warriors consumed with Christian hatred, bent on eradicating Muslims and usurping their land. Similarly, the leaders of the Inquisition, armed with the assurance of Christian truth and virtue and in an effort to "de-Islamize" Spain, offered Muslims the options of conversion to Christianity, expulsion, or execution. In the process they all but eliminated the Muslim presence in western Europe, as the last Muslims were expelled in 1609. This phase provides an image of a West not so much interested in guiding Muslims away from their errant ways or debating the efficacy or truth of their beliefs as much as eradicating them. Polemics shifted from issues of errancy of doctrines and supersession to mutual declarations of kufr (unbelief) and apostasy, hence sanctioning violence as a means of restoring truth.

The third encounter is marked by Western colonial expansion into Muslim territory following the fall of Grenada in 1492. In this phase Muslims have encountered the West as a triumphant, conquering, and imperial presence. The colonial experience that initially pitted various European powers against one another in their quest to subjugate Muslims and monopolize their economic resources lasted until after the end of the second world war. By its end Europeans were able to create imaginary lines in the sand, parceling out Muslim territories in a variety of schemes, carving up the three Islamic empires (the Ottoman, Safavid, and Mughal) into what is today some fifty nation-states (members of the Organization of Islamic Conference). Meanwhile, more than one-fourth of the Muslims in the world continue to live under non-Islamic rule.

The colonial experience appears to have left a mark on the consciousness of those who were colonized. Islamist literature increasingly depicts the West as obsessed with combating Islam on all fronts. The West is often portrayed as marshaling its forces to launch a more pernicious attack under the guise of "civilizing" the Muslims and liberating them from "backwardness" and economic dependency, as seeking to subvert the influence of Islam on society by promoting the implementation of certain secular values as the foundation of political, economic, ideological, cultural, and social institutions. Dubbed as a "cultural attack" (al-ghazu al-thaqafi), it is seen as a multifaceted attack launched by colonial bureaucrats and their willing cadre of orientalists and Christian missionaries (both Catholic and Protestant). These bureaucrats and missionaries struggled to cast doubt about Islam by propagating the superiority of Western culture through such colonial institutions as schools, hospitals, and publishing firms, whose goal was to separate the Muslims from Islam.

The current encounter, still in progress, is a by-product of World War II. While this encounter has been conditioned and shaped during the third quarter of the twentieth century by the heritage of the postwar relationships between communism and capitalism, it is also marked by two distinct features. The first is the assumption of world leadership by the United States with the consequent creation and empowerment of the state of Israel and the invention of the "Judeo-Christian" worldview. The second is the emigration and settlement of Muslims and their acquisition of citizenship in the West, in western Europe, as well as in such established regions of European migration as Australia and New Zealand, Canada, Latin America, South Africa, and the United States.

Muslim Communities of the West

Although there are no reliable statistics on the number of Muslims currently living in the West, a 1986 estimate placed about twenty-three million Muslims in Europe. The majority lived in the Balkans and southeastern Europe; they were Slavic converts and remnants of the Turkish expansion into Albania, Bulgaria, Yugoslavia, and Bosnia or of the westward migration of Tatars into Finland and Poland. More recent Muslim sources speculate that the current estimate of Muslims in western Europe (Austria 100,000; Belgium 250,000; Denmark 60,000; France 3,000,000; Germany 2,500,000; Greece 150,000; Ireland 5,000; Italy 500,000; Luxembourg 1,000; the Netherlands 408,000; Norway 22,000; Portugal 15,000; Spain 450,000; Sweden 100,000; Switzerland 100,000; and the United Kingdom 2,000,000) and the Americas (Canada 250,000; Latin America 2,500,000; and the United States 5,000,000) may be as high as 17.4 million.

The composition of the Muslim communities in various nations of western Europe is in part a by-product of earlier relations established between European nations and the Muslim world as well as the European expansion into Muslim territory during the nineteenth and twentieth centuries. It is also conditioned by the predatory political, economic, and cultural relationships that were developed during the colonial period. Thus the first significant group of Muslims to settle in France in the twentieth century were North African and Senegalese mercenaries who were recruited to fight in French colonial wars, including a group that was the vanguard of the Allied troops that liberated Paris from Nazi occupation. A significant number of harkis, Algerian soldiers who fought with the French colonial government to suppress the Algerian revolution, settled in France after 1962 to avoid reprisals. In Germany early settlers were Tatars and Bosnians, many of whom enlisted in the German army. In the Netherlands the first significant Muslim migration came from its colonies of Indonesia and Surinam, and in Britain they were from South Asia and Africa. The majority of Muslims in western Europe, however, were recruited as temporary guestworkers to relieve the shortage of manual labor during the post–World War II economic reconstruction. The host European countries had the full expectation that imported foreign laborers were a transient commodity, and that once their contracts expired, they would return to their homelands. Since then a large number of asylum seekers and refugees from Albania, Algeria, Bulgaria, Afghanistan, Bosnia, Chechnya, Lebanon, Palestine, Iraq, Iran, and Kashmir have augmented the number of Muslims in the West.

The oil boycott that was declared during the Arab-Israeli war in 1973 precipitated an economic depression and widespread unemployment in Europe. Consequently, European economies underwent a dramatic restructuring that decreased the demand for unskilled labor, as more emphasis was placed on service industries while manufacturing jobs were exported to Asia. These changes exacerbated the unemployment problem in the ranks of the guestworkers. Several European nations, including Germany, France, and the Netherlands, eager to shrink the ranks of the unemployed and to expedite foreign laborers on their way home, offered financial incentives for their repatriation. A few took advantage of the offer, but the majority—faced with the prospects of unemployment in their home country and the lack of future access to the European labor market—decided to stay, preferring the unemployment and welfare benefits of living in Europe. This inadvertently led to a substantial increase in the number of Muslims in Europe, as various governments later allowed family reunification. The policy of thinning foreign labor thus backfired, swelling the ranks of Muslims with unemployed dependents, straining social services as well as the educational systems in the settlement areas. In the process the Muslims were transformed from a collectivity of migrant, predominantly male laborers to immigrant families, from sojourners to settlers, and from transients to citizens. The passage of legislation in the 1970s in most European countries that virtually halted labor migration has led to the creation of Muslim minority communities, who increasingly appear to have become a permanent fixture in western European nations.

The emigration of Muslims during the last quarter of the twentieth century to Europe and the Americas is part of the worldwide movement of people from

The largest concentrations of Muslims in western Europe live in former imperial powers. Britain, for example, is host to many Muslims from the Indian subcontinent, such as these Pakistani Muslims crossing a snowy street after prayer in the mosque in Bradford.

east to west and from south to north in search of higher education, better economic opportunities, and political and religious freedom. Other emigrants are refugees, often the by-product of Euro-American military or political activities. This movement also includes a smattering of those opposed to the authoritarian regimes that dominate the Muslim landscape. The largest Muslim concentrations in western Europe are in former imperial powers: Britain and France. As an economic powerhouse that attracts many immigrants, Germany also holds a large Muslim population. Each European nation has a particular relationship with its immigrants, which has been influenced by its colonial legacy, its historical memory, and its traditional perception of its former subject people. Each nation is in the process of developing policies and models for the treatment of its newest citizens, who put the nation's self-perception of liberal traditions and religious tolerance to the test.

The British model, formalized by the creation of the Commonwealth, permitted citizens of the member nations of the Commonwealth and the colonies to reside in the British Isles. The majority of Muslim immigrants in Britain, for example, came from the Indian subcontinent (Indians, Pakistanis, and Bangladeshis) and Africa. As members of the Commonwealth, they enjoyed the privileges of citizenship and were granted equal political and civil rights, a privilege not available to Muslims in the rest of Europe. Most of the Muslim immigrants are lower class laborers, except for a small number of professionals and a small group of wealthy Arabs from the Gulf oil-producing states who maintain luxury homes in London. More recently, conflicts in various Muslim countries have increased the ethnic mix of the Muslim community in Britain.

Muslims in France are predominantly of Maghribi (North African) origin (from Algeria, Morocco, and Tunisia), who have mostly come after World War II. They also include Muslims from such various Muslim states as Nigeria, Iran, Malaysia, Bosnia,

Most of the Muslims living in Scandinavia, as elsewhere in northern Europe, were recruited to work as laborers in the 1960s and 1970s. Sweden's liberal policies towards the settlement of refugees has meant that there is a sizable number of Muslims from various countries there, as reflected in the congregation worshiping in the mosque at Uppsala.

Turkey, Senegal, Mali, and Pakistan. More than 30 percent of Muslims in France are second generation. Because Germany has had extensive diplomatic relations with Muslim nations since Charlemagne, a small number of Muslims have lived in Berlin since 1777. A Muslim cemetery still in use by the Turks was opened at Columbia Dam in 1798 when the Ottoman envoy to Germany, Ali Aziz Effendi, died. When a Muslim society that was organized in Berlin in 1922 with members from forty-one nationalities attempted to construct a mosque, however, it failed because of a shortage of funds. The growth of the Muslim community in Germany, however, is a twentieth-century phenomenon, the result of the guestworkers' decisions not to return to their homelands.

The Muslim population in the Netherlands and Belgium is predominantly made up of Turkish and Moroccan immigrants who were recruited as laborers in the 1960s and 1970s. In the Netherlands it also includes a substantial number of immigrants from Surinam, the former Dutch colony that won its independence in 1975. The pattern for Scandinavian nations is similar except for Finland, which

Muslims, who were a significant presence in Sicily in medieval times, have immigrated to Italy in large numbers in the last two decades. Students were followed by laborers. There are now sufficient numbers to require a large congregational mosque in Rome, the heartland of Catholicism.

has a tiny minority of Tatar traders and craftspeople who have lived there since the nineteenth century, when it was part of the Russian Empire. Their number has recently increased because of the influx of Somali refugees who arrived by way of Moscow. In Sweden and Denmark, Muslim labor migration came in the late 1960s mainly from Turkey and Yugoslavia. Smaller numbers have come from Morocco, Pakistan, and Egypt. In the 1980s Sweden's liberal policies toward the settlement of refugees augmented the numbers of Muslims by a steady inflow of Iranians, Lebanese, Kurds, and Palestinians. Labor migration to Norway began a decade later than labor migration to other western European countries. The largest number of migrants in Norway are from Pakistan, with small contingents from Turkey, Morocco, Iran, Yugoslavia, Somalia, and India. The majority live around the capital, Oslo.

Muslim emigration to southern Europe came a decade after emigration to western Europe, when the southern economies began to prosper and they changed from labor-exporting to labor-importing nations. The first significant number of Muslims began emigrating to Spain in the 1970s. Muslims had a presence in Sicily as early as the seventh century, however, and dominated the island between the ninth and the eleventh centuries. Vestiges of their history can be seen all the way to northern Italy, where a small Muslim minority continued to live until the nineteenth century. Muslim emigration to Italy is a recent phenomenon that has taken place during the past two decades, spearheaded by students from Jordan, Syria, and Palestine who decided to settle. They were followed by the labor migration from other parts of the Muslim world. More recently, illegal immigrants, mostly Bosnians, Albanians, and Kurds, have been trying to settle in Italy, to the consternation of the other members of the European Union.

In Western nations with a tradition of European immigration—the United States, Canada, Latin America, and Australasia (Australia and New Zealand)—the suitability of Muslims for citizenship was questioned in a variety of ways and eventually somewhat resolved. This has not necessarily lessened the prejudice against their presence. The dominant characteristic of the Muslim population in North America is its diversity, which is apparent in national origin and class as well as in political, ideological, and theological commitment. The Muslim community in the United States and Canada is composed of several generations of Muslim people who have emigrated in a quest for a better life, beginning in the mid-1870s with groups from Syria, Lebanon, Jordan, and Palestine. A small number of displaced people came from eastern Europe after World War I. The repeal of the Asian Exclusion Act in the 1960s in the United States and the membership of Canada in the British Commonwealth brought a large number of immigrants from Bangladesh, India, and Pakistan. The majority of those immigrants initially admitted were the educated professionals (doctors, scientists, and engineers) recruited to fill the needs of the technological industry. Immigrants continue today to come from all over the world, including displaced people seeking refuge for political, ideological, or religious reasons.

Muslim immigrants found freedom in western Europe and North America not only to practice but also to propagate their faith. They have taken advantage of this opportunity and created a variety of missionary outreach activities in various coun-

African Americans make up the largest convert community to Islam; estimates show that between one and two million African Americans are Muslim.

tries. They have also created a corpus of literature geared toward proselytizing. A substantial number of Europeans and Euro-Americans have converted to Islam, including an estimated fifty thousand Germans and one hundred thousand North American "Anglos": Christians, Jews, and agnostics, the majority of whom are women. The largest convert community, however—estimated by various scholars at anywhere between one million to two million—is African American. Their conversion initially came through the teachings of the Nation of Islam, headed by Elijah Muhammad and promulgated by his disciple Malcolm X, who initially promoted a racist theology of black supremacy, a mirror image of the teachings of the Ku Klux Klan. The movement developed in the urban United States as a response to the racism encountered by African Americans who emigrated from the cotton fields of the South to the industrial North. Their relegation to particular working and living spaces in the ghettos consolidated new forms of white supremacy and oppression.

Observers estimate that more than eighty nations in Africa, Asia, and eastern Europe are represented in the mosque community of the United States and that these many groups constitute one *ummah* (Islamic nation), yet they bring with them a variety of traditions and practices as well as a kaleidoscope of doctrines and beliefs fashioned over time in alien contexts. Members of the community are initially surprised at the discrepancy between the ideals they have appropriated and the reality of their differences. Their similar experience of the West is forging some of them into a community of believers engaged in a process of creating a sense of solidarity through common traditions and seeking common ground in their quest to provide a comfort zone where they can fashion a better future for their children.

Western Immigration Policies

Han Entzinger has identified three European models for the immigration of non-Europeans. The first is the guestworker model, adopted mostly in Germanic countries (Germany, Austria, and Switzerland), in which the presence of the immigrants is considered temporary in perpetuity. The government does not expend any effort to integrate them or their families into the new environment, regardless of the fact that their children are born and raised in these countries and do not appear to have any desire to be repatriated. The second is the assimilationist model that is promoted in France. This model insists that if the immigrants seek to become French citizens, they must eschew their foreign cultural, religious, political, and ideological allegiances and accept and assimilate into the already existing consensus of reality and polity of the prevailing system, shedding all alien characteristics. The French policy of Gallicization expects that the end result of integration is that religious practice is privatized, while each

Muslim would become socially and economically assimilated. The third model is the ethnic minority model prevalent in a variety of fashions in the United Kingdom, the Netherlands, Belgium, Luxembourg, and the Scandinavian nations. This model recognizes that the immigrant has an alternative cultural identity that can be preserved and accommodated within the larger context.

In Canada the government has been promoting the idea that it is a multicultural society, providing funds for new immigrants to create ethnic organizations, maintain ethnic cultures, and teach their distinctive languages. The propagation of multiculturalism as a national model was adopted in the hope of circumventing the separatists among the French Quebecois. Questions are currently being asked about whether these efforts have gone too far in creating multiple identities, and whether the ramifications of maintaining ethnicities portend a balkanized Canada, because more than 50 percent of the populations of Toronto, Montreal, and Vancouver are foreign born.

In the United States "Anglo conformity" was perceived as the norm through the nineteenth century. Later scholars defined the United States as a melting pot until it was discovered that there were too many unmeltables. In the 1950s Will Herberg promoted the idea of an America with equal religious conglomerates: Protestant, Catholic, and Jewish. There are currently two paradigms that are competing for adoption; both are controversial, and both have their devoted advocates and detractors. The first is promoted by Christian fundamentalists, some in the Jewish community, and a large number of politicians. It identifies America as grounded in Judeo-Christian values. Its critics note that besides infringing on the idea of separation of religion and state, this model tends to maintain the current power structure, confining Buddhists, Hindus, Muslims, and a host of other faiths and values to the periphery. The second model advocates a pluralistic society that celebrates difference. This has raised the fear of the division of America according to ethnic identities, or "grievance groups," with the potential loss of a cohesive identity shared by all Americans, one that is commensurate with the demands of the only superpower in the world.

The situation of Muslims in western Europe and North America, however, is by no means static. New legislation that constrains and manipulates immigration and citizenship laws has been adopted at a fast pace since the 1970s by Western countries in an effort to stem the tide of immigration. They are driven by a variety of factors. Some countries are governed by economic necessities, given the fact that high labor costs and technological innovation in the West have reshaped European and North American economies. At the same time, most of these countries are experiencing a great deal of pressure on the resources of the welfare state because they have an aging population. They are also influenced by political considerations, given the dramatic rise in racist tendencies in a number of nations.

In Britain the government issued the first measures restricting immigration in 1962, but the restrictions did not apply to those who held British passports, which included citizens of the Commonwealth. As the flow of immigrants did not abate, the government found it necessary to institute additional measures in 1968. As a consequence, those seeking to emigrate had to prove that they had connections to a family in Britain before they were allowed into the country. In 1976 the Race Relations Act recognized ethnic communities and their right to be different, thus providing rights for Muslims by prohibiting indirect discrimination based on race. It did not provide for equal rights based on religious affiliation, however.

In the United States several measures have been taken to restrict Muslim immigration. The quota system has recently been revised to favor white European immigrants, especially from Ireland and eastern Europe. There are reports that the U.S. Department of State has given instructions to its consular offices overseas not to accept people with an Arab background.

Muslims and the Challenge of Life in the West

Muslims have emigrated to Western nation-states that have a fully developed myth of national identity, which has been inculcated in the citizens over two centuries through schools and codified through legends and a particular reading of history. This identity has shaped several generations of Europeans and Americans through the cauldron of two world wars. It has been celebrated in literature, art, music, and dance. The nation-states have fashioned distinctive identities based on collective assumptions, promoting a particular worldview that includes a core of values and attitudes that are taken for granted as unique to a superior West. At the same time, the process of nation building has delineated what is considered alien, strange, and weird.

Immigrants have also been shaped in their home countries by the particular events and perceptions of their generation. Most of the adults among them have a pre-formed distinctive identity not only of their tribe, village, town, or city but also of a national identity instilled by the schools and the institutions of the state from which they emigrated. This identity provides the immigrants with a particular understanding of who they are and what their relationship is to the state in which they live; it therefore conditions their understanding of events and reality. Immigrants also bring a pre-formed understanding of Western culture based on a particular interpretation of the shared heritage between the Muslim world and Europe, one that is particularly focused on the recent experience of colonialism and neocolonialism. These perceptions are enhanced and shaped by Western movies and television, which tend to depict Western society as imbued with drugs, violence, racism, and pornography. Muslims who come from societies that favor strong family solidarity are repelled by what they see as a degenerate Western society consumed by premarital and extramarital sex, burdened by a high rate of divorce and births to unmarried women, latchkey kids, and fragile family bonds. They condemn Western values as lacking in the responsibilities of parents and children toward one another, and they believe that Western society puts too much emphasis on individual freedom and not enough on corporate responsibility.

The formation of Muslim minority communities in the West by choice became problematic to some Muslim intellectuals, especially those from India, where "minorityness" involves the survival of Islam under non-Muslim rule. The late Mawlana Abul Ala Mawdudi, who traveled all over Europe, the United States, and Canada, admonished Muslims to avoid integration into their new environment or to leave lest they lose their souls in the West's wayward ways. Other scholars have insisted that such opinions are misguided because the proper interpretation of Islamic law allows Muslims to live outside the abode of Islam, as long as they have the freedom to practice and propagate their faith. Still other scholars are of the opinion that Muslim presence in the West provides them with an unprecedented opportunity to fulfill their Islamic duty to propagate the faith. In the process they not only obey God's commandment to call people to Islam, they also help to redeem Western society from its evil ways and to restore it to the worship of God. The empowerment of Muslims overseas and the propagation of the Islamist ideology as normative for the world should supersede personal gain.

For Zain el-Abedin, the founder of the Institute for Muslim Minority Affairs in Jidda, Saudi Arabia, the greatest challenge the Muslims face in the West is the loss of identity in an alien social and ideological context. The fear is that in its eagerness to fit in, the minority community reluctantly but steadily gives up its cherished values, while the hostile environment slowly but surely chips away at its core beliefs. To protect the community from disintegration, Abedin determined that it was necessary to promote Islam as an ethnicity and in the process erect ramparts not only to keep the aliens out but, more important, to hold the Muslims in. He was aware that this was not an easy task given the diversity of the community. He thus identified important ideological constructs as well as behavioral distinctions as indispensable markers of the cultural divide. He therefore called for the creation by consensus of a particular body of ideals, values, aspirations, goals, and doctrines. While crucial in setting the Muslim community against other worldviews, the ideals in themselves are not sufficient, nor is such a task easy, because Muslims must "squarely confront the reality of the modern secular, multinational state." While maintaining the unquestioned primacy of allegiance to Islam, Muslims in the West thus need to determine the proper attitude toward the new social reality in which they live. Also to be determined is the nature and extent of their commitment to and participation in the new environment. In the process they must clearly identify the ideological constraints that impede full participation in the economic and social spheres, fully cognizant of the consequences of adhering to a precise and ideologically exclusive stance. They also need to "see how some of the political and social effects of this stance can be softened and mitigated and learn to live with those that cannot." There must be an individual as well as a corporate willingness to pay the price for the decision to live on the social, political, and economic margins of society.

Abedin promoted the idea of fashioning Islam as an ethnicity defined by religion, admittedly a rather difficult task because most immigrants have been fashioned by the nation-state from which they came and identify with its causes and feel particular allegiances to ethnic and linguistic preferences and racial origins. The West thus becomes a laboratory in which a new modern identity is to be fused, one that fosters particular behavioral patterns and promotes a common language, distinctive customs and traditions, and recognizable styles of dress and food, among other cultural distinctions. These are easier to identify and particularize than the effort to inculcate ideas because they are more tangible. At the same time, Abedin was aware that ethnicity could be very divisive, given the diversity of migrant groups. The difficulty is in determining whose language, customs, or behavior is more Islamically legitimate. Abedin was aware of the dilemma his recommendations posed for Muslims because on a very important level, ethnicity itself is un-Islamic. Although cultural distinction promotes cohesion and functions as a barrier to being absorbed or assimilated into a multicultural society, it may also veer from the truth of Islam, which affirms that "physical traits, cultural traditions, dress, food, customs, and habits are subordinate or subsidiary to their main doctrinal identity, that God created differences in people in order to facilitate recognition, that the true identity is determined by the manner in which a person or group of any race, colour or physical type approaches the business of living, uses his faculties, selects ends and means for his worldly endeavours."

Khalid Ishaque of Britain is under no illusion that the host societies are about to accept an ideological minority that seeks to maintain its self-respect by promoting commitments and priorities that are deliberately incompatible with those of the host culture. Thus the community must realize that suffering is not only inevitable, but it is to be welcomed in some cases because it provides the opportunity to demonstrate the commitment to a higher cause and walk in the footsteps of the early Muslim community, who were persecuted for their faith, under the leadership of the Prophet Muhammad in Mecca. Ishaque notes that Muslims who choose to live in nations that are not governed by Islamic law should realize that they must assume certain obligations. While accepting adversity, they must constantly endeavor to establish a relationship with the majority that will foster an atmosphere conducive to the propagation of Islam, in which the larger society is receptive to the Muslim solutions to the problems of humanity.

By the 1990s there began to be a shift in the perspective of leaders of the Islamist movement on this issue. Azzam al-Tamimi of Britain, for example, recently identified the reality facing Muslims living in the West as a state of crisis. He feels that the options fostered for Muslims in the West in the 1970s have not succeeded. His assessment is that although not all of the obstacles in the relations of Muslims and non-Muslims in Western societies are brought about by Muslims, the more dangerous and difficult ones are the consequences of Muslim perceptions and behavior. Some Muslims erroneously seek to overcome these obstacles by melting into Western culture and abandoning some or all of their Islamic identity. Others insist on avoiding these obstacles by resorting to isolation and hiding in cocoons, which some fear could eventually form ghettos similar to those occupied by the Jewish communities in previous centuries. For al-Tamimi this discrepancy in dealing with the crisis led to the sundering of relations between the generations. On the one hand is the generation of the fathers, mothers, and grandparents, who have an emotional and cultural tie to the original homeland, who hold on to the same customs and traditions whether or not they accord with the new environment. On the other hand is the generation of the children and grandchildren, who have no emotional ties to the homeland and find little of value in those customs, which are seen as counterproductive, an impediment to progress in the society in which they have been born.

The new Muslim presence in Europe has made some Europeans more self-consciously reflective about being European. Ignoring the history of immigration into Europe over the centuries, the tendency of scholars and politicians is to depict European nations as unique, cohesive, and integrated societies with distinguishing pre-formed and established characteristics. The presence of Muslims who are able to exercise their political rights in Britain as citizens and the possibility of granting citizenship to these Muslim immigrants and their children in Germany, France, and other European countries has become a contentious matter. At the same time, the recent encounter has also made Muslim immigrants more reflective about their identity, as a growing number have become more self-consciously Muslim. Many who would not have entered a mosque in their homelands have become active in the mosque movement in the West and are increasingly defining the mosque as the center around which Muslim life should revolve. They seem to seek refuge in religion, rummaging through tradition for identifying proper belief, and eager to Islamize behavior, demeanor, and lifestyle as well as to erect cultural boundaries.

For a growing number of Muslims, strict adherence to ritual practice in the adopted country marks the boundaries of distinction. Announcing the need for a clean space for daily prayer, the act of praying, refraining from eating pork and improperly slaughtered meat, and fasting during the month of Ramadan have become important self-delineated boundaries that help the Muslim immigrant feel secure, distinct, and outside the bounds of pollution. For some, conforming to Islamic prohibitions has become a conscious act of witness of a distinctive faith despite public ridicule and a demonstration of steadfastness and perseverance in the face of social obstacles. For others the act of affirming uniqueness itself has become an important affirmation of the need to uphold their identity despite the pressure to change and to abandon the faith. It is a declaration that not only is difference normal, but in a most important way it is divinely designed, approved, and sanctioned. Some Muslims will not associate with other Muslims who do not practice these rituals. Those Muslims are deemed as being outside the pale. Inculcating this message in Muslim children is a mechanism to keep them within the fold. Thus for some, the ritual is Islam and Islam is the ritual.

Institutionalization: The Creation of the Mosque Culture

The majority of Muslim migrant laborers in the West—whose primary focus was the country they left behind, where they hoped to return with enough assets to restart their lives—demonstrated very little interest in establishing Islamic institutions. Once they decided to settle and raise families in the West, their concern centered on maintaining their children in the faith and creating space for communal activities. Their initial efforts to build mosques were generally hampered by lack of funds. In Europe the early mosques were constructed either by or for diplomats or by the Ahmadiyyah movement in Islam, which sought to convert western Christians to Islam by initiating a mosque-planting program in Europe and North America. Most of the Muslim immigrants in the West today came from Islamic states in which the government organizes, subsidizes, and administers religious institutions. In most of these states civic organizations, especially private Islamic institutions, are deemed suspect and a potential source of undermining the government's legitimacy. Furthermore, the majority of the immigrants are Sunnis, who believe that there is no clergy in Islam; thus the creation and maintenance of Islamic institutions in the West is a new experience for the majority of the Muslim diaspora community.

There is no consistent model or pattern in the West for the establishment of mosques. Each European and North American nation-state, in its efforts to provide for freedom of religious faith and practice, appears to have particular policies that govern the formation, administration, and the tax-free status of religious organizations. Every Muslim community in the West is thus predisposed to organize itself within the juridical boundaries of the place of emigra-

The founding of mosques is a key method of reinforcing Muslim identity. The mosque is often marked by a tall minaret, the signpost of Islam in the cityscape. The glass-fronted mosque at Kingsland Road, Hoxton, London, has a three-story pencil-thin minaret modeled on those found in traditional Ottoman mosques.

tion. The nature and form of its institutions are dependent on what the host country's legal system recognizes as the jurisdiction of Muslim authority. The space as well as the nature of the organizations that can be developed are constrained by the legal parameters of the relationship between the state and religious institutions in each nation-state as well as the policies that each state has toward the immigrant community. This has challenged the Muslim community to ascertain that in the process of taking advantage of or adjusting to these laws, the institutions created in the West are grounded in Islamic precedent and prescriptions. Muslims thus face a variety of legal statutes that govern the establishment of communities and regulate the construction of buildings. In the Netherlands, for example, there is a difference in the kind of jurisdiction that the government has in regulating associations and foundations. The executive of an association is elected by the membership of the group and is accountable to them for changes in policies, while the executive of a foundation can appoint himself or herself. If the leader in any way contravenes the statutes, the membership can protest only through the court system. Thus, while in the 1970s the trend for Muslims in the Netherlands was to incorporate themselves as foundations led by individual leaders, the need for more democratic forms of organization became evident in the 1980s as more groups incorporated themselves as associations.

Both western Europe and North America have the expectation that the organizational unit for religious communities would be an institution similar to the church. Thus, for example, in Germany, Sweden, and the Netherlands the host governments, as well as concerned church groups, encouraged the establishment of Muslim prayer centers and religious services. Part of the incentive was the need to develop leadership and to locate interlocutors who represent the group. Also operative was the growing apprehension of the potential for the growth of Islamic fundamentalism among the marginalized guestworkers. This eventually led to arrangements with the Turkish and Moroccan governments to supervise the community's religious affairs. Both Morocco and Turkey welcomed the opportunity in an effort to blunt the growth of fundamentalism and to curtail its dissemination in their countries by returning laborers.

Muslim immigrants in the United States began building mosques during the Great Depression, when they realized that they were not returning "home" soon. They held annual conventions to provide a venue for celebrations and an opportunity for their children to meet suitable marriage partners. Women were very active in mosque activities and in fund-raising. By 1954 there were fifty-two Islamic mosques and centers that were members of the Federation of Islamic Associations of the United States and Canada. In 1957, for example, a mosque was built in Washington, D.C., financed and furnished by various Muslim nations to serve the diplomatic community. By 1998 the Muslim population in the Washington metropolitan area had grown to about 50,000, and it is now served by more than 30 mosques and centers that cater to different ethnicities, nationalities, and ideological preferences. With the reopening of the doors of immigration and the repeal of the Asian Exclusion Act in the 1960s, the makeup of the Muslim community in both countries changed dramatically. The new immigrants were scandalized by the compromises made by those who preceded them in integrating into the society, and they set out to create their own ideological mosques with connections to the Muslim Brotherhood of Egypt and the Jamaat-i Islami of Pakistan.

The dramatic growth in the number of mosques and Islamic centers in Europe and North America since the 1970s is indicative of the rapid growth of the Muslim population that they serve in the West. This growth is also more directly affected by other factors, such as the availability of funds for such projects. Raising funds locally was an formidable task, given the fact that most of the immigrants were poor and conditioned to have governments provide for their religious needs. Both foreign donors and European governments stepped up to the task. In the 1980s there was a concerted drive to organize Muslims into congregations and to establish institutions in Europe and North America. This mosque movement was spurred by a confluence of a variety of interests, including Muslim governments flush with cash (including Saudi Arabia, Kuwait, Libya, and the United Arab Emirates) and eager to support the nascent Muslim communities in the West. Also actively supporting such efforts were various Christian denominations and Islamists. A few European governments—the Netherlands, Sweden, Norway, and France—also provided funds for the construction of Islamic centers and mosques. The estimated number of

Most people assume that mosques must have domes and minarets, but actually they can be built in any style or reuse existing structures. This Islamic center in Evansville, Indiana, was a church that has been converted to Muslim purposes.

mosques, Islamic centers, and prayer halls currently in the West include 2,000 in Germany, 1,450 in the United States, 1,000 in France, 600 in Britain, 350 in the Netherlands, 300 in Spain, 200 in Italy, 200 in Belgium, 100 in Canada, 100 in Denmark, 40 in Norway, 40 in Switzerland, 40 in Austria, and 35 in Sweden. The ideological mosques established in both Europe and North America have been able to provide a religiously based sense of solidarity in the Muslim community that is capable of transcending ethnic, linguistic, and national divisions. They have been able to integrate a diverse membership that is generally disenchanted with the leadership of the country left behind and therefore lacks the commitment to preserve its national identity. These communities generally believe that nationalism and ethnicity are "un-Islamic," and they are also opposed to the cultural reproduction of music, dance, art, celebrations, or other forms of entertainment that serve to bind people of the same ethnic or national background.

In many places, the professionals who belonged to the ideological mosques were unable to cater to the needs of the new immigrants. Policies of family reunification which brought large contingents of relatives (aunts, uncles, and grandparents from the subcontinent), as well as the growth of the refugee population from southern Lebanon, Iraq, Palestine, Somalia, Kashmir, and Afghanistan, have brought to the West a substantial number of people with little or no education. This chain migration has led to the splintering of the mosque population into distinctive groups that identify by nationality, ethnicity, or language. In the process this has also made it possible for Muslims to re-create the sectarian, ideological, and theological divisions that exist overseas; thus the development of mosques or centers persist that identify as Barelwi, Deobandi, Jamaat-i Islami, Ahli Hadith, Shiite, Ismaili, Ahmadiyya, Alawi, Tableeghi, Tahrir, or Hizbollah or affiliate with one of the various Sufi organizations.

Although some of these groups have reestablished themselves in different parts of Europe, on the whole the European patterns have been different, given the fact that the Muslim population was recruited from specific countries. Ethnic backgrounds have therefore generally determined the constitution of the mosques in Europe. In Belgium, Luxembourg, and Germany the Turkish mosques are mostly under the supervision of the Directorate of Religious Affairs in Ankara, Turkey (Diyanet Baskanligi). The second largest organization is the

The Dar al-Islam Foundation Islamic Center Village was built in Abiquiu, New Mexico, in 1980–1981. Designed by the renowned Egyptian architect Hassan Fathy, the mosque is the centerpiece of a complex that includes a school, a clinic, a shopping center, and other public buildings.

In Europe, ethnic background has generally determined who attends which particular mosque. The mosque on Shearbridge Road in Bradford, England, is a converted church, and most of the Muslims gathered for Friday prayer are originally from Pakistan, as shown by their distinctive clothes.

Sulaymanci, which runs Quran schools. Also operating among the immigrants are the politically active Milli Gorus and the apolitical Risale-i Nur movement, which is now attempting a reconciliation of religion and science.

Although mosques and Islamic centers cater to about 10 to 15 percent of the Muslim population in the West that is involved in organized religion, they meet other needs as well. The mosque functions as a social center, where the community meets for a variety of events that help to cement relationships and to provide communal celebrations. It has become the center for Islamic knowledge and education, where Islam is taught to the next generation and where people can reflect on Islam's meaning in the new environment. The mosque has also become an island of sanity where people's humanity is respected, a haven of security where their self-esteem is restored, where they can find respite from the harassment, discrimination, and humiliation of the social environment. It is a venue for the sharing of experiences, the ratification of norms, and the validating of values, a place where people's identity is affirmed in the community of friends and family and, most important, in the company of fellow believers. As such, the mosque has become a center for the confirmation as well as the dissemination of shared social and cultural values, where community is forged and formalized, where common concerns and visions are shared and reaffirmed. The mosque

Mosques function as social and community centers for the whole Islamic community. Women crowd the entrance to the mosque in Regent's Park, London, for the prayer to celebrate the end of the fast of Ramadan.

structure has become the primary symbol not only of the presence of Islam in the West but of its permanence and its future. Its cupolas and minarets are fixtures in the Western urban skyline, set in stone, tile, brick, steel, or concrete. It is the place where the demarcation line between the community and its surrounding culture are located and emphasized, or where they are carefully negotiated and formalized.

Although the message preached in the mosque may vary according to the leadership's ideological commitment, there is a consensus among some religious leaders that Islam is the antidote to what ails Europe and North America. They present Islam as the divinely sanctioned alternative to what prevails in the degenerate society in which many Muslims consider themselves living. Islam stands in condemnation of Western culture, which is depicted as hedonistic and morally depraved, with dysfunctional families, people hooked on drugs, sexual immorality, meaningless lives, and psychological disorders. Islam offers a moral order and promotes a collective responsibility that keeps the youth from being lost. Islam calls for an equitable and just society, obedience to parents and respect for elders; it restores the authority of the parents and provides a sense of purpose in life.

The Development of Umbrella Organizations

The formation of Islamic umbrella organizations that are independent of the state is a recent phenomenon in the experience of Muslim immigrants. Such organizations are the norm in the West, as governments and civic institutions expect to deal with a recognized national leadership, a religious hierarchy; simply put, it is the Western way of organizing religion, and Muslims are pressed to reformulate themselves accordingly. Another factor has been the interest of foreign-based organizations such as the Muslim Brotherhood of Egypt and the Jamaat-i Islami of Pakistan. The students who adhere to the teachings of these organizations formed the Muslim Student Association, which helped to establish several hundred mosques on U.S. and Canadian campuses. They later reformulated themselves into the Islamic Society of North America (ISNA). A more conservative group split from ISNA and formed the Islamic Circle of North America.

Also involved in the process are foreign governments who seek control of the mosques to manage their affairs and to keep their ideologies in conformity to those advocated overseas. Saudi Arabia established a European office of the Muslim World League in Belgium and two offices in North America (in New York and Toronto) in an attempt to supervise the mosque's leadership and its message by recruiting mosques to register as members of the Council of Masajid in Europe or North America. Both Morocco and Turkey have also been involved in staffing mosques that are being established for their expatriates in Europe. Muslims who have experienced minority status in other countries appear to be at the forefront initiating organizations. The Surinamese, for example, were the pioneers in forming Islamic associations in the Netherlands. They had the experience of the Dutch methods in Surinam. They knew the language and could negotiate their way in the state bureaucracy as well as in the society. They emphasized cultural identity and obtained subsidies from public funds and from the Ministry of Welfare, Health, and Culture. Other groups that were successful in creating effective organizations were the Ahmadiyya and the Ithna Ashris of Indian background, who had the earlier experience of being a minority group in East Africa.

Efforts to organize umbrella organizations that transcend ideological commitment, theological particularities, ethnic allegiances, and personal rivalries have not been too successful. This is not for lack of trying. For example, the Federation of Muslim organizations in the Netherlands functioned between 1975 and 1981. When it began to sink, its staff founded the Muslim Information Center in the Hague. In 1979 the Federation of Turkish and Cultural Associations was formed; it included eight local Turkish organizations and cooperated with the Directorate of Religious Affairs in Ankara. Another Turkish organization, the

Islamic Center Foundation (representing seventeen local groups), was inspired by the Suleymanci movement in Turkey and had no government connection. The Union of Moroccan Muslim Organizations, representing forty groups in the Netherlands, was founded in 1978. The Netherlands Islamic Society functioned between 1973 and 1982, serving the Surinamese community; it was then taken over by the Foundation for the Welfare of Muslims in the Netherlands. National Muslim umbrella organizations that were representative of more than one group included the Muslim Organizations in the Netherlands Foundation, which was established by Turks and Moroccans in 1981. A Surinamese initiative that sought the inclusion of other nationalities was the Netherlands Islamic Parliament, established in 1982. Most of these organizations failed because of lack of funds and the proper staff necessary to create coalitions.

Islamic Education

The highest priority for most Muslim parents in the West is providing Islamic instruction for their children. Where that was not available, some of the early immigrants in the United States, eager that their children acquire religious values, sent them to Christian Sunday schools. Those Muslim parents who were concerned about the values that were thought to be propagated in public schools sent their children to Catholic or Baptist schools. What parents often object to is the intrusion of school officials into what they perceive to be parental prerogatives. They are concerned about the school's inculcation of cultural patterns that are antithetical to the parents' traditions and the Islamic faith. Many object to mixing of boys and girls in class, coed gym and swimming classes, sex education, and counseling by school officials that promotes rebellion against the parents' values.

The central place for Islamic education continues to be the home, although in the United States and Canada religious instruction is increasingly being carried out in more than fifteen hundred Sunday schools, youth groups, and retreats run by

Education is an important way to create and reinforce feelings of solidarity in the Muslim community. Although the central place of Islamic education in America is still the home, many children attend primary schools run by mosques or Islamic centers. More than one hundred such primary schools are licensed in various states.

the various mosques and Islamic centers. More than one hundred Islamic religious day schools have been licensed by various states. The majority provide primary education. The most famous high school is the Saudi Academy in northern Virginia; 95 percent of its graduating class goes to college. Religious schools follow the required local curriculum and supplement it with Islamic studies and Arabic language classes. Among the converts in the African American community, Islamic education is considered crucial for the proper instruction of children. The Nation of Islam under the leadership of Elijah Muhammad established about one hundred schools that he named Universities of Islam. These

Islamic instruction is the highest priority for most Muslim parents in the West. These boys and girls, wearing traditional dress and headscarves, are attending Arabic class at the Islamic School in London. Opened in April 1998, the school was the first state-funded Islamic school in Britain.

were closed in 1976 by Warith Deen Muhammad, Elijah's son and successor. It was after a protracted process of re-educating the membership in the Sunni faith and retraining the imams and teachers that Warith Deen reconstituted some of the schools as Sister Clara Muhammad Schools.

In Britain the Queen is officially the head of the church, and there is no pretense of separation of church and state. The 1944 Education Act required that the school day should begin with a Christian-inspired assembly or collective prayer, while allowing parents with alternative religious beliefs to withdraw their children from participating in Christian activities. A 1988 law made religious instruction obligatory. Muslim requests for parity with other religious groups in Britain, such as Jews and Catholics, who receive state funding to support the operation of their religious schools, have been denied. Instead they have been offered a compromise that allows Muslim students to go to single-sex schools. In several inner-city schools in Britain 80 to 90 percent of the student body is Muslim. Several confrontations occurred in the 1970s over school uniforms that required girls to wear short skirts. Girls who did not comply with the regulations were expelled from school, and in some cases parents took their daughters out of school over the issue. A Muslim liaison committee was formed in Bradford to negotiate with the educational authorities about issues important to Muslims. Compromises were eventually worked out, allowing Muslim girls to wear trousers as long as the trousers match the colors of the school uniform. Girls are generally allowed to put on headscarves and they can wear tracksuits for physical education classes. Several schools have tried to organize separate swimming classes for boys and girls and allow Muslim students to wear swimming suits in the shower. The first state Muslim school in Britain opened in early 1998 in London. A second state Muslim school was scheduled to open in Birmingham in September 1998.

In the Netherlands about 60 percent of Moroccan and Turkish students who attend either parochial or public school receive religious education that is subsidized by the government. Because Christianity is taught in confessional schools, and rabbis and ministers teach religion in state schools, Muslims sought to have imams hired as instructors of Islamic education. Although instruction in Islamic tenets was legally guaranteed in the state schools, the law required that it must be taught in Dutch, which few of the imams mastered. In 1986 the Diocesan Catholic school board in Breda denied requests from a few Catholic schools to be allowed to give Islamic instruction. In 1988 the Council of Churches in the Netherlands wrote a letter to the Association of Dutch municipalities concerning this issue. Although Muslims were appreciative that their children, when attending Christian schools, were being educated in an atmosphere in which God is revered, they were apprehensive about efforts at conversion. In 1988 two Islamic schools were opened in Rotterdam and Eindhoven; the latter was associated with a Protestant school, and the one in Rotterdam was connected to a public school. For different reasons both Muslims and non-Muslims had reservations about the venture. Questions were raised about whether there were enough students to justify the dedication of an entire school to one group. Fear was expressed that such a school would impede integration, and serious questions were raised about the lack of qualified Muslim teachers. By 1992 there were more than twenty Islamic schools in the Netherlands, however. Efforts to make room for Islamic instruction in Christian schools appear to have foundered, as Christians began to question whether that was their responsibility. The only exception was the Juliana van Stolbergschool, where initial experiments allowing the imam to provide instruction in Dutch eventually led to the school's becoming an interreligious primary school with its own board composed of both Christians and Muslims.

The question of who decides the content of Islamic education exists in all Western nations. In Germany, for example, the government agreed that the Turkish consulate would provide religious instruction in Turkish. The curriculum, published in Turkey, strives to foster devotion to Turkey and Kemalism as well as nationalistic sentiments to a foreign nation. The curriculum continues to be structured as imported Islam taught by imported teachers who do not understand the German community and the daily issues of life that the children face. Questions are raised about whether this kind of instruction will impede the integration of the Turkish community into the German body politic that calls for tolerance and integration of all groups. Several European countries, including Belgium, Sweden, Germany, and the Netherlands, are now supporting imams imported from Turkey, Morocco, and elsewhere to provide instruction in Islam to the Muslim student population. In the Netherlands imams were recruited to serve the immigrants in their own language and inculcate them in their particular culture. By the middle of the 1980s there were an estimated 120 foreign imams (seventy Turkish, forty Moroccan, and ten Surinamese, including the Ahmadiyya).

In the United States, which constantly reaffirms the separation of religion and state, various state and federal officials have hired and credentialed imams for service as chaplains in the prison system. The chaplaincy office of the U.S. armed services has also commissioned four imams as chaplains and are introducing a novel idea in training a woman to be an assistant chaplain. In the Western context the imam's leadership, social role, and function have been enhanced and transformed to parallel that of the priest or the rabbi. He is not merely the leader of prayer as overseas; rather, he has increasingly become expected to function as a spiritual leader in a non-Muslim environment, an educator and teacher providing information on how to live an Islamic life. He presides over weddings and funerals, serves as a chaplain in hospitals, jails, and the military. He provides counseling for youth and the troubled in his congregation and has become the representative of the Muslims as well as their spokesman to the larger community, a propagator of the faith in dialogue with non-Muslims, and the ambassador to the host culture, attempting to build bridges to other faith communities.

The Muslims are hard pressed to find imams adequately equipped for such a role. Foreign-born and -trained imams have often failed to provide the community with the kind of leadership that makes Muslims comfortable in their new homes in the West. They have generally insisted on replicating foreign cultural standards and constraints as normative for all times and places. They have displayed little understanding of the pressures young people face in the Western environment and have little sympathy with those who advocate that religion should pertain only to the area of belief and not to culture. A few Muslim leaders have raised the issue of whether it is time to start training imams from among the immigrants and their children. The question is where the new breed of imams would get their education. Efforts to open schools for the training of imams in the United States and Britain have been met with skepticism from those who suspect particular theological advocacy on the part of the leadership. They also have been condemned by those who believe that any compromise or adjustment to the Western environment is tantamount to rejection of the faith.

Interfaith Relations

Efforts to create a context for interreligious dialogue and interfaith activities in the West generally have been initiated by Christians and Jews and have been a source of Muslim suspicion, focused particularly on the goals and purposes of such ventures. Several Christian umbrella organizations in the West, including the Conference of European Churches and the Council of Bishops' Conferences in Europe, sponsored a joint project focused on Islam in Europe. The World Council of Churches in Geneva opened an office that deals with interfaith issues; it has engaged overseas Muslim scholars for several decades. The National Council of Churches in the United States finds itself hamstrung by its bureaucratic structures waiting for the formation of a comprehensive Islamic umbrella organization that brings together the various groups. Only then can the organization initiate official dialogue with Muslims on the national level.

Muslims have taken note that the proclaimed underlying principles for establishing relationships with people of other faiths by these organizations and by the Vatican differ in their perception and treatment of Jews and Muslims: Judaism often receives a more amicable treatment. Because of this, Muslims have often demonstrated a great reluctance to participate. The suspicion is that dialogue and other interfaith activities are a new phase in Christian efforts to convert Muslims or that they have a hidden agenda aimed at undermining Islam. Also operative is the prevailing Muslim belief that Islam provides all pertinent information about Judaism and Christianity, thus there is no need for Muslims to learn anything more about these two religions. Some Muslims refuse to appear at a church unless it is to inform Christians about Islam's virtues and moral values. Others take interfaith activities as an opportunity to preach Islam. They disseminate a variety of publications written by overseas scholars who have no understanding of the Western context or the protocols followed in interfaith activities, or who do not package their material in the Western idiom. In fact, some of the material disseminated—such as the videotapes of dialogues by Ahmad Deedat and Jimmy Swaggart's "Is the Bible the Word of God?" Muslim literature that attempts to prove that the Bible prophesied the coming of the Prophet Muhammad, or the writing of converts from Christianity condemning their former faith—have had the opposite effect of deepening the misunderstandings between the two religious communities.

Interfaith efforts have also been hampered by Jewish suspicion of Christian-Muslim collaboration that does not include them, by the reticence by some evangelical Christian participants who see Muslims as the agents of the Antichrist, and by those Muslims who see any cooperation or collaboration between Muslims and people of other faiths as bordering on indulging in kufr, or abandoning the faith.

The Jewish community for more than half a century has been able to organize and maintain interfaith relations with various Christian groups. Generally speaking, in the United States the Jewish community has stipulated up front that such activity is conditional on the acceptance of the state of Israel as a genuine expression of Jewish expectations. Criticism of Israel and its policies toward Palestinian Christians and Muslims is characterized as being anti-Semitic. Interfaith activities are thus perceived by some Muslims as a ploy to provide a protective shield over the continuing dispossession of the Palestinian people.

In Sweden, where interfaith activities are supported by the state, a more trusting milieu has been achieved. From the beginning, a priest, a rabbi, and an imam held public dialogue sessions to which they were invited by churches, universities, and the media. Their first joint project was a study of fundamentalism. In August 1994 they went on a peace mission to Sarajevo. In 1996 they founded the Nordic Center for Interreligious Dialogue, for which they received donations from the government of Göteborg. The center has nine board members, three from each faith community. Its composition does not represent the numerical strength of the communities, because there are twelve thousand Jews, mostly around Stockholm, and two hundred and fifty thousand Muslims, while the majority of the rest of the population has Christian roots. Muslim efforts are directed toward non-Muslims. They distribute publications demonstrating Islam's virtues and moral values. In Sweden, as elsewhere, members of the Muslim Brotherhood have taken the initiative in actively promoting dialogue, while the Salafiya groups are opposed to any dialogue and vehemently oppose inviting non-Muslims, who are deemed apostate, to the mosque.

In Britain, the United States, and Canada, the initial Muslim response to interfaith overtures is being reconsidered. The theme of the 1970s and 1980s, founded on the conviction that the message of Islam is powerful and persuasive enough that all Westerners will see the light and convert to Islam, appears to be waning. What Muslims are seeing instead is actually an increased antipathy toward Islam on the part of many Westerners. This has led to a serious reassessment of the role of Muslims and Islam in the West. Such reflection is taking into account the reality that the Muslims of the West have vital interests that can best be tackled through cooperation with the larger community. Azzam al-Tamimi of Britain has identified these interests as follows: helping to address such problems as racism and the deterioration of morality in Western societies by participating in this society and trying to influence the decision makers; spreading Islamic *dawa* (the call to Islam) in a manner that is comprehensible to Western society; and trying to alleviate the conditions of Muslims overseas caused by imperialist policies of Western governments by working with those who are nonaligned in the West to help pressure their governments.

A few Muslim individuals and congregations are beginning to see the value of participating in interfaith dialogue. Meanwhile, serious questions continue to be raised about the goals and consequences of interfaith activity for believers of all faiths. There is concern that such participation involves risk, because it may weaken the religious commitment of those involved should they find virtue in the faiths of others. They question whether the openness to the other may strengthen tolerance of fanaticism, in the process sacrificing the truth, or whether the commitment to interfaith dialogue creates an alternative religious community at the expense of belonging to the participant's own. It further poses the question of whether such activity provides an atmosphere that presupposes permissiveness and relativism because the commitment is to pluralism.

The Concern for Security

The discourse surrounding the current experience of Muslims in the West has revolved around two issues deemed of paramount importance by both Muslims and the nations in which they have sought to live: security and cultural coherence. That Muslims in western Europe chose to become permanent residents rather than migrant laborers, and to become citizens where possible in some European countries and North America, has increasingly become a prominent concern of many Westerners. Muslim immigrants and their children have come to the realization that they have to cope with the prevalent pre-formed stereotypes, honed over centuries of conflict and competition. They also have to deal with the increasing rhetoric of demonization and prejudice. In the United States some conservative commentators and pundits have created such controversies. This rhetoric often holds Muslims in the West and Islam as the religion responsible for the acts of irresponsible individuals overseas.

During the revolution in Iran in 1979, an imam led a demonstration in support of Ayatollah Khomeini outside the Iranian embassy in London.

The Islamic revolution in Iran in 1978–79 was a major catalyst in refocusing Western attention on Islam's perceived potential threat. It tapped into a heritage of Western suspicion and fear of Muslims. The hostage taking, made intimate by its exposure on television, followed by the attack on Islam's holiest shrine in Mecca by what was depicted as Muslim fanatics, has resurrected the long tradition of associating Muslims with violence and jihad. In 1980 the violence came home to Europe with the bombing of a synagogue and an assassination attempt on an Iranian in Paris. This was followed by the assassination of the French ambassador in Beirut in 1981, a bomb explosion in the Paris-Toulouse train, and a shootout in Paris. Fifty-eight French soldiers were killed in Beirut on October 23, 1983. A parallel attack on the same day killed 241 American marines when trucks packed with explosives were driven into their headquarters there. A couple of years later several French citizens were taken hostage. During 1985 and 1986 several bombs exploded in Paris. The headlines in the press were no longer about events far away but about the wounded and the dead downtown. Europeans began to fear what the Muslims next door could do to them. The Muslims were depicted as the obscurantist sinister enemy, ruthless followers of a religion that promotes violence and blind adherence to tradition.

Similar attitudes have been formed in the United States as a consequence of terrorist acts that have resulted in the death and injury of American citizens. These include the bombings of Pan Am flight 103 in 1988 and the World Trade Center in New York in 1993, the murder of two Central Intelligence Agency employees in Washington, D.C., in 1993, and the discotheque bombing in Germany in 1986. Such acts have heightened fears of Islamic fundamentalism as being driven by irrational people who place no value on human life. The *fatwa* (legal opinion) by the Ayatollah Khomeini sanctioning the death of Salman Rushdi for defaming the Prophet Muhammad in his *Satanic Verses* and the debates that followed reaffirmed these perceptions. The press depicted Islam as antiliberal, antimodern, anti-intellectual—the epitome of what is not "West." The burning of Rushdi's book in Britain created fear in the British public that Muslims in their midst were intolerant and averse to freedom of thought. Some Muslims in Britain sought what they perceived to be parity of treatment. They wanted the implementation of the British blasphemy law that would at least ban the book's circulation. They found out that the law did not cover Islam but protected only the official state religion: Anglicanism. It brought home to many Muslims that their concerns are considered to be outside the pale. In the United States, Muslims noted that some books, including *Little Black Sambo*, are kept out of libraries because they offend certain segments of the society, but the same sensitivity was not shown to Muslims in the case of *Satanic Verses*.

Muslims consider some segments of the Western press to be extremely biased against them, providing unfavorable spin about issues that are of paramount importance for the welfare of Muslims in the world. The press generally condemns Islamists because they espouse an anticolonial rhetoric, that by definition is anti-West. They also condemn the West for its silence on the shedding of Muslim blood in Chechnya, Kashmir, Palestine, and Bosnia and for its unqualified support of Israel. As victims of hate speech and hate crimes, including assault, murder, and the burning of mosques in both Europe and North America, Muslims' apprehension about their security and their future has increased. They are convinced that Westerners do not value Muslim life as they do their own. How else could they have stood by in 1992 while tens of thousands of Bosnians were victims of ethnic cleansing?

In 1985 several mosques and Islamic centers were vandalized and threatened in different parts of the United States (in San Francisco and Orange County, California, in Denver, Colorado, in Quincy, Massachusetts, and in Dearborn, Michigan). Also in 1985 two pipe bombs exploded in the South West mosque in Houston, Texas, during the celebration of the eid, an Islamic holiday. No one was hurt because the Muslim community had gathered in a different place, because of the expected presence of thousands for the celebration. Various Arab organizations also received death threats at this time. These acts were brought to the attention of a few U.S. legislators, who included mosques with the other religious institutions being protected in the Hate Crime Bill that was signed into law in 1988. Although the law became effective in 1990, requiring the Justice Department to collect and publish information on hate crimes, it has not deterred the growing acts of vandalism against mosques and Islamic institutions. There appears to be a correlation between overseas events and the rise in the number of hate crimes in the United States. Mosques and Islamic centers increasingly are targeted during heightened periods of confrontation between the West and Muslim nations.

In several European countries housing discrimination as well the low income level of the Muslim laborers, many of whom are now on welfare, has confined them to particular residential areas that have become virtual ghettos of foreign residents. Some Muslims do not speak the language of the countries in which they dwell or have not had a chance to meet or interact with a single European, even after living for more than twenty years in Europe. In France the spectacular rise of the far right during the 1980s is partly a consequence of a xenophobic platform that projects all problems facing French society on the presence of immigrants. Although at first it was dismissed as being promoted by a racist fringe, its proponents gained credibility, given France's economic recession and the growth of unemployment. A consensus is slowly emerging that the immigration of North Africans presents a special set of issues that previous immigrants did not pose for French society: Their African origin and Islamic faith have become the issue.

Several European political parties have become vocally anti-Muslim. These include the Front Nationale in France, the Vlaams Blok in Belgium, and the Republikaner in Germany. The Centrumpartij of the Netherlands is less powerful than similar anti-immigrant parties of western Europe. It has only one of 150 members in the second chamber of Parliament. Although attacks on asylum centers and Islamic institutions in the Netherlands have increased, they do not match what occurs in neighboring countries. Since 1991, when Frits Bolksteini of the conservative liberal party raised some uncomfortable issues about the presence and influence of ethnic minorities on Dutch society, there has been more open public debate on immigration in the Netherlands. In 1993 there was more public expression of xenophobia and panic about the rate of immigration; the issue of whether the Netherlands can accommodate any more people was raised.

The public discussion of what do with the Muslims in Europe and the threat they pose to its security, as well as the accompanying violence against Muslim life and property, has been disconcerting. For many Muslims the massacre of 200 Algerians in Paris in 1961, in the 1993 killing of an Algerian in Paris, and the image of German hooligans burning a hostel for Turkish immigrants in Solingen in 1993—has left an indelible mark. As a consequence, Muslims in the West have generally favored keeping a low profile for security reasons. They see themselves as the latest victims of chauvinism and xenophobia. The Muslims in the West have thus become the new villains on the block, joining Jews, gypsies, Italians, and African Americans in being reviled.

The Cultural Divide

The scramble to identify the next threat to Western democracies that ensued after the fall of communism has not yet abated. Islam and Muslim culture have been depicted by certain interests in the United States as the next challenge, if not the enemy challenging the West. It is accused of being a religion that is devoid of integrity and progressive values, a religion that promotes violent passions in its adherents, a menace to civil society, and a threat to the peace-loving people of the world. Muslims are often cast as bloodthirsty terrorists, whose loyalty as citizens must be questioned because they are perceived to be obsessed with the destruction of the West.

Samuel Huntington's publication of "The Clash of Civilizations" in *Foreign Affairs*, promoting a thesis that the next conflict will not be between nation-states or ideologies but civilizations, appears to have gained support among some policy pundits. His thesis has reconfirmed to Muslims that colonialism is not over, because it has echoes of themes heard since the nineteenth century. On the surface it appears as a rehash of a century-old myth that undergirded European hegemonic policies justifying wars of colonial expansion and missionary crusades during the nineteenth century under the rubric of "civilizational mission," "white man's burden," or Manifest Destiny. It posited the superiority of European man, the acme of human civilization, who willingly assumes the burden of sharing his values and achievements with the rest of the backward world. In the process, this myth justified the ransacking of the cultures of the conquered people and confining Muslim achievements to ethnological museums or the dustbin of history.

Meanwhile, the immigrants bring with them a different understanding of their culture. Many believe that they have been victims of Western cultural hegemony. For them the preservation of distinctive culture is the last line of defense against total obliteration. Battered by Western weapons of destruction, overcome by Western scientific achievements, and reduced to vassal states, Muslims have been attempting to resist by hanging on to Islamic civilization as the last bastion of human dignity and worth, a means of galvanizing people and keeping them from total disintegration. Consequently, conformity to Islamic culture, traditions, and norms is not only a source of pride in Muslim contributions to human civilization, it has become a divine imperative, a cure for what ails Muslim society and the world. It is promoted as possessing redemptive powers. Public performance of the rituals of Islam and maintaining a distinctive culture has thus become a vehicle of healing. Deviating from the consensus of what is publicly considered normative by the majority population in which the immigrants live is not backwardness; rather, it is a willful act of coherence and an option of a more meaningful reality. In the process, for some, ritual has become an instrument of protest against a society that continues to treat Islam as an alien religion whose adherents are fixated in the seventh century.

Islamic Law

Many Muslim leaders in the West would like to see Western states recognize Islamic law as a body of public law, which would provide parallel legal status for Muslims with those of other religions. In a few instances Muslims in the West have been able to negotiate some accommodation of their particular traditional, cultural, and religious needs regarding burial practices. Among the early immigrants, the fear of being buried among the "unbelievers" led to repatriating corpses to the country of origin. The acquisition of cemeteries dedicated to Islamic burials in the West have all but put an end to this practice in the United States, Canada, and many parts of western Europe, although some families repatriate the dead for emotional reasons. Furthermore, despite laws to the contrary, in some instances Muslims have been able to prepare the corpse for burial in accord with Islamic tradition and have been allowed to use shrouds in place of coffins. A few mosques in western Europe and North America have even built rooms on the premises for the ritual washing of the dead. In other places exceptions have been made in violation of zoning laws. For example, some mosques in Britain that do not meet the specifications of religious areas, such as adequate parking space, have been legalized to accommodate the needs of the population.

Eating meat that has been slaughtered according to correct ritual practice has become increasingly important for many Muslims in the West as a means to distinguish themselves from Westerners and maintain their cultural identity. This shop in Manningham, England, advertises that it uses ritually slaughtered (halal) meat for the kebab it sells along with fish and chips.

During the 1984 general election in Britain, Muslims demanded recognition of the shariah in matters of personal status law: marriage, divorce, child custody, and inheritance. Although law in Britain covers all citizens regardless of their religious affiliation, some consideration to Muslim legal traditions appears to have been made in at least two divorce cases in which the husband had to pay the specified amount in the marriage contract rather than to follow British custom. In several cases, in both the United States and Canada, the family courts have recognized the Islamic marriage contract as a legal document, equivalent to a prenuptial agreement, whose stipulation for settlement in the case of divorce is approved by the courts.

Eating halal food (meat from animals that have been properly slaughtered and contains no pork by-products) has assumed a vital symbolic dimension. Although early immigrants followed the fatwa by the Islamic modernist Muhammad Abduh sanctioning the eating of meat killed for Christians and Jews, mosques are increasingly disseminating information and raising consciousness, declaring that eating such food is un-Islamic. The immigration of Muslims from the subcontinent since the late 1960s and the growth of the Islamist ideology among immigrants have put a great deal of emphasis on dietary laws to keep Muslims from mixing socially with non-Muslims. In the United States, African American Muslims have a tradition of using dietary laws as boundaries around the community. In Bradford, England, two Muslim butchers were fined 3,500 pounds in 1986 for operating outside the parameters governing the slaughter of animals. This brought a strong reaction from the Muslim community, but when the Bradford Council for Voluntary Services allocated special funds to take care of the dietary concerns of Muslims, other people in the community objected. The council proposed that meat sandwiches would be served on separate platters and food containing alcohol would not be served to Muslims. An ethnic menu and halal meat will, whenever possible, be provided by the catering services hired by the council. They also proposed in-service training in ethnic cooking for all council cooks.

While issues of diet and proper space for worship and burial are being negotiated and resolved by government institutions, the growing public debate concerns the consequences of the Muslim presence for liberal societies in the West. The focus is most recently on the role of women in Islam, who in Western perception are considered to be oppressed. Such views have been reinforced by televised reports about the treatment of women in revolutionary Iran and in Afghanistan under the rule of the Taliban and by the vocal rejection of the universal values for womanhood as promoted by the United Nations. The issues range from abortion, female genital mutilation, and sexual orientation to wearing the veil.

The issue of wearing the *hijab* (headscarf) took on national significance in France when several female students were banned from wearing them on the grounds that such dress is tantamount to proselytizing, a proscribed activity in the secular schools of France. The debate that followed in the French press dwelled on related issues. Is the hijab a cover for the persecution and repression of women? Is it the Muslim standard raised to challenge the French Tricolor? Is it a means of snubbing a hospitable French society by an ingrate population flaunting its reactionary customs in the midst of the center of Western civilization? For Muslims the ban was seen as an anti-Muslim act because Christians are allowed to wear crucifixes and Jews yarmulkes, both of which should similarly, under the circumstances, be interpreted as acts of propagating a faith. The issue of the hijab has surfaced under different rubrics in other Western nations. For example, in Canada feminists championed the banning of headscarfs, which they depicted as a symbol of oppression. Young Muslim women who donned the scarf insisted that it was an act of obedience to a divine injunction and was therefore protected under freedom of religion. Some Muslim women viewed wearing the hijab as an instrument of liberation from being a sex object. In the United States the Council on American-Islamic Relations reported that there was a 50 percent increase in 1996 in the number of incidents of discrimination against women who wear the hijab.

Muslims and Politics in the West

Regardless of their growing numbers in Europe and North America, and their increasing wealth in the United States and Canada, Muslims are aware that they have little political power to influence the government, the media, or the elites in the West. They have very few channels of communication to policy makers in the societies in which they live. A variety of factors hamper effective participation in the political process, including the lack of experience in participating in political activities, the fear of the consequences of political involvement, and the lack of experience in grassroots organizations or coalition building. Muslims also lack seasoned leaders and efficient organizations that are able to forge coalitions with other groups to bring about change and to influence legislation. This is generally ascribed to a lack of experience in Western-style democracy, which is based on compromise, which many Muslims believe to be tantamount to abandoning the principles of justice and truth. There are external factors as well; among them is their belief that Muslims in the West are often shunned by political candidates and parties as a perceived liability, because their participation might antagonize the Jewish lobby. Democratic presidential candidates have turned down Arab-American endorsements for fear of alienating Jewish support.

The issue of participation in the political process is now being debated within the Muslim community. Can a Muslim participate in the running of a *kuffar* (unbelievers) society? Should they vote for representatives who are accountable to various interests? Would such participation lead to defending the freedom to engage in things Islamically prohibited? Ali Kettani, a North African consultant to the Saudi government on Muslim minority affairs, has called for Islamic political representation: "Otherwise, Muslim politicians would be put in office by non-Muslim forces and would consequently be used to subjugate the Muslim community." The political interests of the immigrant generation are generally focused on the countries left behind. The second generation demonstrates more interest and savvy in local politics. Younger Muslims in Britain, for example, are increasingly involved in British politics. Their interests focus on antiracist and antideportation organizations. They have also worked on campaigns for legislation to allow family reunions and to fight police violence.

In Birmingham, Muslim political participation is mostly aimed at the local level. In 1982 the first Muslim labor representative to the ward was elected. The following year the number increased by two, and by 1987 the first Muslim woman was elected. Many Muslims in Britain vote for the Labour Party because many are laborers and would therefore benefit from the party's programs. In

1984 a Muslim charter appeared recommending that Muslims vote for those who would support their agenda concerning schools, sex education, Muslim personal laws, and provisions for Muslims in state schools. Nothing came of it; nor has the call for the establishment of a Muslim parliament. In Britain local authorities run social services, housing, leisure, and community services, public health programs, and economic, urban development, and equal opportunity programs. Most Muslim concerns are tackled on the local level. In 1993 there were twelve Muslim councilors of 117 in Britain, all members of the Labour Party.

In the Netherlands consultative ethnic minority councils were established in various areas, especially in the major cities where immigrants congregate: Amsterdam, Rotterdam, the Hague, and Utrecht. The councils are recognized by the authorities as representing the community, thus they have to be consulted on matters of interest to minorities. Under the minorities policy, immigrants were extended new rights in the 1980s that included such matters as providing for proper Islamic burial rites and halal slaughtering of animals, to the consternation of animal rights advocates. They were allowed to be employed in the civil service, except for positions in the police and the armed forces. Although they maintain their foreign citizenship, immigrants were granted the right to vote in local elections but could not participate in provincial or national elections. During the local elections of 1986 and 1990, a few foreigners were elected to municipal councils.

In the United States initial political activity came as a result of the Arab-Israeli conflict. American government support for the state of Israel, conjoined with a press that is generally considered by Muslims as acting as a gatekeeper suppressing any reports that would show Israeli policies in a negative light while promoting what is considered a defamation of Arabs, led to the development of Arab political action groups. Their activities have generally centered around three areas: providing accurate information to the American public about Arab culture, history, and religion; challenging and correcting the prevalent negative stereotypes of Arabs and Arab Americans; engaging with U.S. policy makers who seek a more equitable and balanced American policy in the Arab world, especially in regard to the Arab-Israeli conflict. The American-Arab University Graduates was founded in 1967 by professionals, university professors, lawyers, and doctors, a large number of whom had participated in the Organization of Arab Students, which flourished on U.S. campuses in the late 1950s and early 1960s. The targeting of Americans of Arab background by the Nixon administration gave the impetus to the formation of the National Association of Arab Americans, organized in 1972 and modeled after the pro-Israeli lobby, the American Israel Public Affairs Committee. Its aim was to create access to members of the U.S. Congress and to explain the issues from an Arab perspective, while educating Arab Americans about the political process.

The American-Arab Anti-Discrimination Committee, modeled after the Anti-Defamation League of the B'nai B'rith, was established in 1980 to fight racism, prejudice, and discrimination against Arabs in the United States. Founded by James Aburezk, a former U.S. senator from South Dakota, it continues to be the largest grassroots Arab organization in the United States, with chapters in various parts of the country. Its efforts focus on issues of interest to the community, from seeking to halt the production and distribution of movies that vilify Arabs and Muslims by Walt Disney Productions to helping immigrants unjustly targeted for deportation by the U.S. Immigration and Naturalization Service. It has sought apologies from television anchor Dan Rather and former secretary of state Henry Kissinger for defamation and ethnic slurs, filed legal suits to stop certain advertisements that traded on racist sentiments, and more recently advocated the lifting of the U.S. ban on travel to Lebanon and of the siege of Iraq.

The Arab American Institute (AAI) was established in 1984 by James Zoghby, who was active in Jesse Jackson's presidential campaign in 1988. Zoghby was appointed as

Muslims in the West are increasingly beginning to see the usefulness of participating in interfaith dialogue and political activities that promote common causes. In 1988, for example, the Muslim Political Action Committee hosted the Reverend Jesse Jackson when he ran for President.

national co-chair of the campaign and was able to raise $700,000 for Jackson's campaign. The AAI encourages participation in the political system and is eager to get Arab Americans to run for office. The institute establishes Democratic and Republican clubs in various parts of the country.

All Arab American organizations include both Christians and Muslims. In the 1980s several Muslim political action committees were formed, including the American Muslim Council, the Council for American-Islamic Affairs, and United Muslims of America. Their work generally parallels that of the Arab American organizations. They restrict their activities to Muslim rather than Arab concerns and cast a wider net of interest, including the fate of Muslims in Cyprus (Kibris), Kashmir, Bosnia, Kosovo, Bulgaria, and Somalia, among other locales. These political action committees have been recognized as representative institutions of the Muslim community. The leadership has been invited to the White House for Islamic celebrations; they have also cosponsored petitions and issued statements with non-Muslim political and religious organizations.

The Muslim Presence: Positing a Challenge for the West

The Muslim presence in western Europe and the Americas has posited a challenge and raised concerns that need to be addressed by both the immigrants and the host nations. These issues touch on such social and cultural matters as shifting demographics, race, class, religion, and ethnicity and challenge the very premise of democracy itself, because they impinge on areas of power sharing, law, education, and public policy. Muslim immigrants in the West are noted for their diversity. Their experiences of the West vary according to what beliefs, perceptions, and conditioning they acquired before their emigration as well as the environment into which they settled. Their experiences and their responses are conditioned by the reasons they chose to emigrate, their educational background, and their social class, as well as the historical relationship between their country of origin and the nation into which they have moved. This relationship is also influenced by the policies of the host country: whether it welcomes foreigners and grants them citizenship rights, its perceptions of Islam, and its national policies governing the relationship between religion and state.

Muslim identity in the West is influenced by the dynamic interaction between the variety of conscious and unconscious perspectives that the immigrant brings and the context in which he or she settles. It is also the by-product of the compromises with the host culture that become necessary to lead a coherent life. The immigrant's perspective is dependent on the background from which he or she comes, the class, the experience of social mobility, the level of education, whether he or she is a settler, a refugee, or a sojourner. It is also fashioned by the political identity and the religious perspective on which the immigrant was raised. These factors are constantly renegotiated and refashioned in a society that is perceived and experienced as racist and anti-Muslim, with certain sectors in it engaged or exclusively dedicated to demonize or fan distortion and fear. It also makes a difference whether the individual sees himself or herself as a born-Muslim, a born-again Muslim, or a convert; or whether he or she is defined by ethnic origin, nationality, place and language of origin, and by religious affiliation (Sunni, Shii, Ahmadi, Wahhabi, Alawi, Druze).

Although some Muslims continue to contemplate the option of returning to their homelands as a safety valve should conditions become intolerable, their children, born and reared in the schools of the West, are caught in the middle: The West is their homeland. They are bicultural, with an intimate experience and knowledge of the West, as well as an intimate experience of their parents' culture as remembered and reinvented in the West. For the immigrants the struggle to maintain their identity and to preserve it from disappearing into the Western culture appears to be an ongoing project. They are increasingly challenged and changed, as their children are becoming more indigenized into Western culture. This has brought about new interpretations by a few daring people who attempt to be relevant to the new reality in which they find themselves. The question is whether they can develop a rational means of minority jurisprudence to guide their lives in the West. If it is developed, the next question is whether the Muslims in the majority nations will recognize such jurisprudence as authentic and valid.

Meanwhile, some Western authors have continued to question whether Muslims are worthy of citizenship in a democratic nation or whether their presence will put their particular stamp on Europe and America, forever changing the West as it is known. Some European scholars fear that Muslims' presence in a multicultural environment will erode Europe's unique identity and make it similar to what exists in the United States or Canada. Still others deny that Muslims are a variable that will make a difference in reshaping Europe. They do not see any difference in the impact of their presence than what has happened in earlier migrations of poorer populations, such as the Poles and Italians. It is clear from the shrill tone of some of those engaged in the debate about whether Muslims belong in the West that they are fully aware that Muslims have become part and parcel of the West.

Still to be addressed is the Muslim demand for accountability for Western imperialism, as well as the demand that the West come to terms with Islam and recognize its equal status with Christianity and Judaism as a legitimate monotheistic religion. Will the pluralism and democratic principles espoused by both Europe and North America make room for a different culture and allow its mem-

Louis Farrakhan, the current leader of the Nation of Islam, has much of the charisma of Malcolm X (1925–1965), the enormously influential Black Muslim leader. In October 1995 Farrakhan organized the Million Man March on Washington, D.C., and hundreds of thousands of Muslims and non-Muslims raised their hands in unity on the mall, vowing to renew their commitments to family, community, and personal responsibility.

bers to operate with respect and dignity? Once again, the Muslim presence challenges Europeans not only to reflect on their self-assured perceptions of their liberalism, pluralism, democracy, and tolerance; it has also challenged Europeans to think of ways that they can guarantee the Muslims freedom of religion and the right to propagate their faith and enjoy the culture of their choice. Muslims continue to ask whether Western democracies are liberal enough to include Islamic input into the national consensus, or will there be an insistence on a Judeo-Christian culture. Will Western pluralism or multiculturalism be flexible enough to provide for Islamic input into the shaping of the future of Western society? Or will Muslims continue to be marginalized, ostracized, studied, and evaluated, always judged as lacking, always the "other"?

Finally, will the juggernaut of assimilation that has reshaped Europe and North America in a long process of secularization, modernization, and liberalization be able to reshape Muslims to the extent that they can dissolve into the Western mix, abandoning their distinctive identities, practices, and cultures? Or will they opt for integration, holding on to their distinctive identities and preferences, at the same time participating in the political and social life of their adopted countries, demanding equal rights, and proportional representation as a distinct group? The questions are not only concerned with what would happen to the Muslims when they choose between assimilation, integration, or separation, but, more important, the questions are also concerned with the manner in which Muslims' integration, assimilation, or separation would affect the fabric of Western society. What kind of a society will Europe and America become as a consequence of the introduction of the new mix of peoples and cultures who affirm a vibrant religion that they insist transcends borders and supersedes all other claims to truth?

CHAPTER FIFTEEN

Contemporary Islam

REFORMATION OR REVOLUTION?

John L. Esposito

The twentieth century has been one of the most dynamic, explosive, and innovative in Islamic history. Within a span of a few centuries Muslim societies have passed from subjugation to European imperialism to national independence, from remnants of medieval empires to modern nation-states, from a transnational but somewhat regionally fixed community to a global community not only of Muslim-majority communities in Africa, the Middle East, and Asia but also of significant Muslim-minority communities in Europe and the United States.

At every stage the predictable has proven unpredictable: mighty European colonial powers were overthrown, artificially drawn nation-states emerged and engaged in nation building, the desert Gulf sheikhdoms discovered oil and experienced rapid development, a remote and quiescent Muslim Southeast Asia has produced an Asian tiger in Malaysia, and the secular presuppositions and expectations of modernization theory were swept aside by an Islamic tide that seemed to come out of nowhere and challenged much of the Muslim world, from North Africa to Southeast Asia to the West.

The history of contemporary Islam is a story of challenge and response, tension and conflict, atavism and creativity or renaissance, retreat and advancement, religious and intellectual retrenchment, reformation and revolution. It has been dominated by two major struggles: the first, the wars of

(Left) The many faces of contemporary Islam include not only the more visible reassertion of Islam in Muslim politics but also the revitalization of Muslim piety and spirituality. These adherents of the Sufi Naqshbandi order at the Islamic Institute in Cairo represent one of the major mystical orders in Islam. Not only did they play an important role in reformist and anticolonialist movements throughout the Islamic world in the past, they also do so today.

In the twentieth century many of the old stereotypes and assumptions about Islam and the Islamic lands have been reversed. Mighty European colonial powers have been overturned. This drawing shows the pomp and circumstance surrounding the entry of the Prince of Wales at Baroda during his visit to India.

independence at the turn of the twentieth century, when much of the Muslim world struggled to free itself from dominion by European powers; and the second, in the latter half of the century, the internal battle over religio-cultural identity and integrity associated with contemporary Islamic revivalism and the reassertion of Islam into public life.

Islam, European Colonialism, and Modernity: Renewal and Reform

The nineteenth and twentieth centuries proved to be a period of major transformation in the history of Islam: a time of humiliation and subjugation, independence and revolution, revival and reform. Islamic history had witnessed the emergence of Islam, its rapid and dynamic expansion, the spawning of vast Islamic empires and sultanates, and the florescence of a rich and varied Islamic civilization, but European colonialism seemed to bring it all to a crashing halt. The age of European expansion, penetration, and dominance (euphemistically called the Age of Discovery by Europeans) began in the sixteenth century but came to fruition in the nineteenth and early twentieth centuries. By the nineteenth century the balance of power had clearly shifted toward Europe. European governments (Great Britain, France, Spain, Russia, the Netherlands, Portugal, Italy) extended their political influence or domain internationally. The emergence of the West as a dominant global power proved a military, political, economic, and ideological challenge to Hindu, Buddhist, and Muslim societies in Asia, Africa, and the Middle East.

By the nineteenth century much of the Muslim world found itself subjugated to European imperial powers, demonstrating its political, economic, and military impotence and challenging the veracity of Islam itself. Why had Europe (that is, Christendom) proved triumphant? Was it the superiority of its science and technology or of its religion and culture? Many Muslims had long believed that their historical success and florescence were due to the truth of their faith and mission, but with the political, economic, and military success of European imperial powers at hand, what were Muslims now to conclude?

Major changes to the Middle East in the twentieth century have resulted from the discovery of oil. The first well was drilled at Masjid-i Sulaiman in Iran around 1908. A gusher with wooden derrick was typical of the period when precautions taken to control the flow of oil were not always adequate.

For several centuries Muslims in diverse circumstances had recognized the decline in their communities as a result of both internal (domestic) and external (foreign) threats and had initiated various revival and reform movements. A sense of community disintegration and the corruption of "true Islam" generated revivalist movements in the seventeenth and eighteenth centuries (Wahhabi, Mahdi, Fulani, Padri, and others) that stretched across the Muslim world from Africa to Southeast Asia. Muslim responses to European colonialism and imperialism were conditioned both by the source of the threat and by Islamic tradition. They ranged from holy war to emigration and noncooperation to adaptation and cultural synthesis. Faced with Christian European dominance of the Muslim world, some Muslims concluded that the only proper responses were those of the Prophet Muhammad when he faced opposition and rejection: to fight (jihad, struggle) in defense of Islam or to emigrate (hijra) as Muhammad and his early followers had done when they went from Mecca to Medina in 622 C.E. Militant resistance in Africa, the Middle East, South Asia, and Southeast Asia, however, proved impotent in the face of the European's modern technology and army weapons. Although emigration was possible for some, it proved impractical for many. Some religious leaders counseled cultural isolation, withdrawal, and noncooperation, to resist the Western threat to their Islamic way of life. Others, ranging from secular to Islamic modernists, pursued a path of accommodation to harness the West's scientific and technological power to revitalize the community and to regain independence.

Modernist Responses: The Limits and Legacy of Islamic Modernism

For Muslim rulers in the Ottoman Empire (Morocco, Egypt, and Iran), the West's power was based upon its superior technology and weapons. These they set out to acquire. Their focus was primarily military and bureaucratic: to create a strong military and central administration. In the nineteenth and early twentieth centuries students were sent to Europe to study languages, science, and politics; European experts were brought in; translation bureaus and printing presses were introduced to make technical information more accessible. This was accompanied by modernization of education, law, and the economy. New universities and curricula were created and modern curricula were introduced to allow student to acquire the knowledge necessary to modernize. European legal codes became the basis for legal reforms, and Islamic law was restricted to personal status or family law (marriage, divorce, inheritance). Modern economic systems and institutions were established.

The state increasingly asserted its right to regulate and administer religion, creating ministries of religious affairs and endowments (waqf, sg.; awqaf, pl.) that attempted to control previously autonomous organizations and institutions, including Sufi orders, mosques, shariah courts, and religious schools and endowments. Change was mandated by the state and implemented from the top by a small political elite. Thus, the modernization process introduced by rulers was not concerned with political liberalization and greater local autonomy but rather with strengthening regime power and control through a more centralized administration and modernized military and security apparatus. Reform was imposed from above, a top-down rather than bottom-up process, with a narrow base of support. Issues of authority, legitimacy, security, and popular participation would continue to become significant issues in the contemporary Islamic revival movement.

The reformist spirit of the times was especially evident in the emergence from Egypt to Southeast Asia of

Oil is found in many regions of the Middle East. Shaykh Ahmad al-Jabir al-Sabah is about to turn a silver valve wheel inaugurating the first cargo of crude oil for export from Kuwait on June 30, 1946.

an Islamic modernist movement that called for a "reformation" or reinterpretation (*ijtihad*) of Islam. Responding to the plight of Muslim communities and the intellectual and religious challenge of the West, Islamic modernism sought to bridge the gap between conservative religious scholars (*alim*, sg.; *ulama*, pl.), characterized as clinging (*taqlid*, following or emulating) blindly to the past, and the Western-oriented secular elites, regarded as uncritical in their imitation of the West and insensitive to Islamic tradition. The ulama's static sanctification of Islam's classical or medieval formulation and their resistance to change were blamed for the backwardness and plight of the Islamic community. Islamic modernists of the nineteenth and early twentieth centuries, like secular reformers, were open to accommodation and assimilation; they wished to produce a new synthesis of Islam with modern science and learning. Thus, they distanced themselves from the rejectionist tendency of religious conservatives as well as Western-oriented secular reformers who restricted religion to the private life, and they looked to the West to rejuvenate state and society.

As Europe dubbed its age of imperialism and conquest an Age of Discovery, Islamic reformers might have called their quest or mission one of "rediscovery"—rediscovery and reappropriation of the rightful place of reason and science in the Islamic tradition. They argued that Islam and modernity, revelation and reason, were indeed compatible. In contrast to earlier seventeenth- and eighteenth-century revivalist movements, with which they shared the desire for renewal and reform, modernists did not simply wish to restore the beliefs and practices of the past. Rather, they asserted the need to reinterpret and reapply the principles and ideals of Islam to formulate new responses to the political, scientific, and cultural challenges of the West and of modern life. Most modernists combined a quest to rejuvenate the Islamic community with an anticolonialist agenda, the ultimate goal of which was national independence.

Jamal al-Din al-Afghani and Muhammad Abduh pioneered modernist visions and agendas in the Middle East, as did Sayyid Ahmad Khan and Muhammad Iqbal in South Asia. Despite some distinctive differences, each argued that Islam was a dynamic, progressive religion that was made stagnant by the forces of history and the mind-set of many ulama. They identified the sources of Muslim weakness and asserted the compatibility of religion and reason and science. They reclaimed the glories of Islamic history, reminding Muslims that although they were now weak, they had once been strong, spawning vast Islamic empires and an Islamic civilization whose wonders included major achievements in science, medicine, and philosophy. Reformers set out to initiate a reformation, to boldly redefine or reconstruct Islamic belief and thought, to reform Islamic theology and law. At the same time, they emphasized Muslim pride, unity, and solidarity to face the political and cultural threat of European colonialism.

Jamal al-Din al-Afghani (1838–97), born and educated in Iran and then British India, traveled throughout much of the Muslim world and to Europe. Al-Afghani believed that Muslims could repel European colonialism not by ignoring or rejecting the sources of its strength—science and technology—but by reclaiming and reappropriating reason, science, and technology, which, he maintained, were integral to Islam and had spawned Islamic civilization. He emphasized that Islam was both a religion and a civilization, an ideology that provided the raison d'être for Muslims both as individuals and as a sociopolitical community. Al-Afghani's critique of the status quo, call for modern reforms, and advocacy of constitutionalism and parliamentary government to limit the power of rulers made him popular with many of the younger educated generation, who had traditional upbringings but were attracted by modern reforms and calls for national independence.

Muhammad Abduh (1849–1905), a disciple of al-Afghani and a reform-minded Egyptian religious scholar, differed from the conservative outlook of many other ulama. Focusing on religious reform, he advocated significant legal, social, and educational change. Thus, Abduh argued that although the religious observances of Islam were immutable, the social aspects of Islamic law could be reformed in such areas as marriage, divorce, and inheritance. He argued that the Quranic ideal was monogamy, not polygamy; he supported women's education and modernized the curriculum at al-Azhar University, a major international center and training ground for Muslim religious scholars.

Sayyid Ahmad Khan (1817–98) surveyed the abysmal state of the Muslim community in India (defeated, powerless, and demoralized) after the Sepoy Mutiny of 1857, which resulted in formal British colonial rule and the end of Muslim dominance in the Indian subcontinent. For Ahmad Khan, Muslims needed to change the way they saw and responded to the modern world; he devoted his life to religious, educational, and social reform. Like al-Afghani and Abduh, he called for a bold "new theology" or reinterpretation of Islam and the acceptance, not rejection, of the best in Western thought. He insisted that he was reclaiming "the original religion of Islam, which God and the messenger have disclosed, not that religion which the ulama and preachers have fashioned." His interpretation of Islam was guided by his belief that Islam was compatible with reason and the laws of nature and therefore in perfect harmony with modern scientific thought. The Quran and Sunna of the Prophet (the customs and practices of the Prophet that became the example for all Muslims) were interpreted from this perspective. Ahmad Khan was quick to distinguish between literal and metaphorical or allegorical meanings of the Quran when addressing issues of evolution, angels, and miracles. He called for a critical reassessment of the *hadith* (prophetic traditions), challenging their historicity and authenticity.

Ahmad Khan combined theory with practice, seeking to implement his ideas and train a new generation of Muslim leaders. His prolific writing was accompanied by his leadership in many educational reforms: a translation society to make Western thought more accessible, the introduction of their own journals, and the formation of the Anglo-Muhammadan Oriental College (later renamed Aligarh Muslim University), which was modeled after Cambridge University.

Muhammad Iqbal (1877–1938), the poet-philosopher of the Indian subcontinent, judged the condition of the Islamic community as one of five centuries of "dogmatic slumber" as a result of the blind following of tradition, and he called for the "reconstruction" of religious thought to revitalize the Muslim community. Educated in England and Germany, where he earned a law degree and a doctorate in philosophy, Iqbal combined modern Western philosophy (that of Nietzsche, Bergson, Hegel, and Fichte) with his Islamic tradition and constructed a modern, dynamic, Islamically informed worldview.

Iqbal distinguished between eternal, immutable principles of Islam (*shariah*) and those regulations that were the product of human interpretation and thus subject to change. In contrast to the ulama, whom he charged had halted the dynamic process that originally produced Islamic law and instead were content to merely perpetuate established traditions, Iqbal believed that Muslims must once again reassert their right to reinterpret and reapply Islam to changing social conditions. He reinterpreted or redefined *ijtihad* (individual interpretation) and *ijma* (consensus), suggesting that the right to interpret Islam for the community be transferred from the ulama to a national assembly or legislature. This collective or corporate consensus would then constitute the authoritative consensus of the community.

Iqbal admired the dynamic spirit, intellectual tradition, and technology of the West but condemned its European colonialism, the economic exploitation of capitalism, the atheism of Marxism, and the moral bankruptcy of secularism. He believed that Islam provided its own religio-political alternative for Muslim societies, and thus he turned to the past to "rediscover" the principles and values necessary to reconstruct an Islamic model for modern Muslim society with Islamic versions of democracy and parliamentary government. Thus, for example, Iqbal concluded that the centrality of such beliefs as the equality and brotherhood of believers made democracy a political ideal in Islam, which, although historically unrealized, remained a duty for Muslims in the twentieth century.

The Muslim doctrine of God's oneness (*tawhid*, monotheism)—that is, Allah's role as creator, sustainer, and judge of the universe—Iqbal believed, implied that God's will or law governed every aspect of life. This, combined with Muhammad's role as Prophet and head of state, led Iqbal to maintain that the Muslim community is a religio-political state governed by Islamic law. It was this

The mosque built by late sultan Sir Omar Ali Saifuddin III (r. 1950–67) in the lagoon in Brunei is one of the largest in Asia. The substantial income from oil exports since the 1930s allowed the ruler of this tiny island on the northwest coast of Borneo to address the disaffection of his poorer subjects through an extensive social welfare system and the promotion of Islam.

belief that led Iqbal to call for an autonomous Muslim state or states in India, for which he came to be regarded as one the founders of the modern state of Pakistan.

For some time Islamic modernism remained primarily an intellectual movement among a small elite sector of society. Failure to produce an effective organization or movement with a leadership cadre, systematic program, and institutional support resulted in the diffusion of the modernist movement in many directions. Moreover, modernists were vulnerable to criticism that their reforms often resulted in a redefinition of Islam in light of Western criteria and therefore amounted to a westernization or Europeanization of Islam.

The legacy of Islamic modernists, however, was substantial, influencing the development of the Muslim community and its attitude toward the West. Their vision inspired Muslim intellectuals and activists from Algeria to Indonesia to emphasize educational reforms that incorporated a modern curriculum, legitimated legal and social change, and contributed to the formation of anticolonial independence movements. Reformers rekindled the spirit of Muslim unity, solidarity, and autonomy, restored Muslim pride in Islam's intellectual and scientific heritage, and generated modern ideological interpretations of Islam that incorporated modern concepts, disciplines, and institutions from textual criticism to nationalism, parliamentary government, and democracy. Thus, Islamic modernists introduced and reinforced a change-oriented mind-set that rejected the blind following of tradition and accepted the necessity as well as the legitimacy of reinterpretation and reform. Of equal significance, these Islamic modernists reasserted the right of laity as well as ulama to interpret Islam.

Nationalist Movements and the Emergence of Modern States

The first half of the twentieth century was dominated by two interrelated issues: nationalism and independence, and the creation of the modern state. Between World Wars I and II, Muslims increasingly pressed for an end to colonial rule. Independence movements sprang up and in some places, such as Algeria, long, bloody wars were fought before achieving autonomy. To varying degrees, depending on local populations and contexts, Islam and Muslim identity played a role in nationalist struggles. In Iran the ulama joined with secular forces and pressed for reforms to limit the shah's power. In the Tobacco Protest (1891–92) they used mosques as sanctuaries for protestors and *fatwas* (legal opinions) to oppose the selling of tobacco concessions, fearing that the shah's propensity to sell concessions for railroads, banking, and tobacco compromised Iran's independence by making it economically dependent on Europe. Similar concerns informed opposition in the 1950s to oil concessions. From 1905 to 1911 the ulama in Iran supported a constitutional revolution in an attempt to circumscribe the shah's power. In North Africa, Islamic reformers had been among the founders and leaders of early nationalist organizations and political parties emphasizing resistance to French rule and the dangers of cultural assimilation and advocating independence and national identity based on an Arab-Islamic heritage. Allal al-Fasi led Morocco's Independence party (Istiqlal), Abd al-Aziz Thalbi was a founder of Tunisia's Constitutional party (Destour), and Abd al-Hamid Ben Badis organized the Association of Algerian Ulama. In the Indian subcontinent the Muslim League used Islamic symbols and Muslim nationalism as the ideological tool in mobilizing support for its demand for a separate Muslim homeland, Pakistan.

Both the formation of modern states and independence movements in the Muslim world were the products of European colonialism whose legacy had profound long-term negative consequences. Colonial powers, controlling or influencing the selection of leaders, configured and reconfigured the borders of many countries, and created other countries such as Jordan. The breakup of the Ottoman Empire, the creation by Great Britain and France of mandate countries in the Middle East (including Lebanon, Syria, Iraq, and Kuwait), the division of South Asia into India and Pakistan, and the division of Southeast Asia into Malaysia, Singapore, Brunei, and Indonesia are examples of an often-calculated attempt to create states that would foster or at least not threaten European interests. Similarly, the first kings of Jordan, Syria, and Iraq were defeated and displaced Hashimites of the Hejaz (what is now western Saudi Arabia). The result was the image of a militant, imperialist West, whose artificially drawn states undermined Muslim unity and whose appointed or approved rulers had little legitimacy. The creation of the Jewish state of Israel was viewed as the placement of a Western colony in the Middle East, further undermining Muslim unity. This legacy would continue to have profound effects through contemporary times.

By the 1950s most Muslim communities had gained independence, although it would not be until 1962 that Algeria did so. Modern state formation varied considerably. The end result was a varied spectrum of patterns. At one end, Mustafa

Kemal (known as Ataturk, "Father of the Turks") established a thoroughly secular state, formally ending the caliphate, suppressing or marginalizing religious institutions, and replacing them with European-based laws and institutions. At the other end, Saudi Arabia was created as a self-styled Islamic state, with the Quran as its constitution and the shariah its law. The vast majority of states fell somewhere in between these two poles. They became "Muslim states" in that the majority population was Muslim, and they incorporated Islamic provisions, such as the requirement that the head of state be a Muslim and that there be some reference to the shariah as a source of law. Many Muslim states, such as Egypt, Syria, Iran, and Iraq, turned to Western models of political, legal, economic, and educational development. Implicit in their development was the prevailing paradigm that equated modernization with the progressive westernization and secularization of societies.

Although the late decades of the twentieth century were characterized by the proliferation of Islamic activist movements, their patriarchs and models were to be found in the 1930s and 1940s. Two remarkable individuals established major Islamic movements in the Middle East and South Asia during this period. Hasan al-Banna in Egypt and Mawlana Abul Ala Mawdudi in India seized the banner of Islam to create the Muslim Brotherhood and the Jamaat-i-Islami (Islamic Society) respectively. Both were critical of Western secular-oriented elites, the rigid conservatism of the ulama, and the "westernized Islam" of Islamic modernists. In contrast to earlier Islamic modernists, they championed the self-sufficiency of Islam and were far more critical of the West. Islam, they asserted, was a self-sufficient alternative to capitalism, Marxism, and socialism. Abul Ala Mawdudi in particular wrote prolifically, attempting to delineate a comprehensive Islamic system, encompassing such topics as Islam

Mustafa Kemal, commonly known as Ataturk, "Father of the Turks," established a thoroughly secular state in Turkey in 1922. He is shown here with his wife seated beside him in a Western-style portrait, taken the year after the establishment of the Turkish republic.

and government, nationalism, democracy, economics, revolution, women, and the family.

In contrast to Islamic modernists, al-Banna and Abul Ala Mawdudi emphasized organizational development to implement their visions of an Islamic state and society. Although they have been dubbed "fundamentalists" and equated with a retrogressive vision, they were in fact modern in their orientation and organization. Both men wished neither to escape nor to reimplement a seventh-century past; they did not want to reject modern science and technology. Rather, al-Banna and Abul Ala Mawdudi sought to reapply Islamic doctrine and values to the contemporary world and thus respond to the challenge of modernity. They denounced the westernization and secularization of Muslim societies. Although bitter opponents of the West—from European colonialism and secular nationalism to the cultural penetration of the West—they did not reject but rather valued modern science and education. Many members of the Muslim Brotherhood and the Jamaat-i-Islami were modern professionals (teachers and university professors, physicians, lawyers, scientists, engineers) who established modern institutions (schools, clinics, cottage industries, printing presses, publishing houses) and used modern technology.

Both the Muslim Brotherhood and the Jamaat shared a common ideological worldview: First, was the belief that Islam was a comprehensive way of life and that the union of religion and the state (*din wa dawla*) was the God-ordained Islamic ideal. Second, the separation of religion and politics, a Western secular artifact adopted by Muslim societies, was the cause of Muslim decline. Third, restoration of the unity and autonomy of Muslim societies required a return to "true Islam" and thus implementation of the shariah, the blueprint for Islamic society. Finally, this Islamic revolution was the required struggle of all true Muslims. The Muslim Brotherhood and the Jamaat differed in their organizational approaches, however. The Brotherhood was a pop-

The University of Riyadh, Saudi Arabia, was founded by Saud III ibn Abd al-Aziz (r. 1952–64). It is one of many universities and other institutions founded by Muslim rulers in the twentieth century to overcome the perceived technical and financial superiority of the West and modernize education, law, and the economy.

ulist movement that recruited from all sectors of society, while the Jamaat took a more elitist path, seeking to attract and train a new leadership cadre: modern, educated, but Islamically oriented men. While the Brotherhood espoused a bottom-up approach, the Jamaat's was top-down.

The desire to transform society invariably led to involvement in politics and confrontation with the state. Activists and authoritarian regimes accused each other of instigating violence. Activists were arrested and their organizations suppressed. Al-Banna was assassinated in 1949, and some Muslim Brotherhood leaders who in the face of state repression espoused a more militant revolutionary path were executed, imprisoned, or driven underground in Egypt under the Arab president Gamal Abdel Nasser (1918–70) in the 1960s. By the end of the 1960s most believed that the Brotherhood had been successfully suppressed. The 1970s and 1980s would witness its resurrection, however, and the extent to which violence and repression radicalized many who became the founders of radical, violent revolutionary movements. Although Abul Ala Mawdudi was condemned to death and at times the Jamaat was threatened with suppression, the Jamaat was able to participate within the political system more freely than the Brotherhood, and as a result it did not experience the same degree of alienation and radicalization.

Liberal and regional nationalism and socialism were the predominant ideologies of newly emergent Muslim states. Nationalist ideologies based on common territory, history, and language became typical means for new regimes and rulers to create a common identity and mobilize popular support. Though predominantly secular in orientation, ideologues often found it necessary to assert some link (historical, religious, or linguistic) with their Islamic past.

By the late 1960s, Arab nationalism and socialism had become the predominant ideology ushering in a number of revolutionary regimes in Egypt, Sudan, Libya, Syria, and Iraq. In time they would prove vulnerable, however. The case of Nasser, the enormously popular Egyptian leader, is particularly instructive. Nasser was part of a military coup against the government of King Farouk. Although supported by the Muslim Brotherhood, Nasser crushed its expectation that victory would usher in an Islamic government, opting instead for a more secular socialist orientation. When a frustrated Brotherhood engaged in active opposition, Nasser moved quickly to contain and repress it. Violent clashes and assassination attempts occurred in 1954 and 1965. Thousands were arrested and Brotherhood leaders—among them the militant ideologue of Islamic revolution, Sayyid Qutb (1906–66)—were executed.

By the late 1960s Islamic critics at home (chief among them the Muslim Brotherhood) and Saudi Arabian policy abroad led Nasser to seek his own brand of Islamic legitimacy. He nationalized Cairo's al-Azhar University, the venerable bastion of orthodoxy and training ground for Muslims all over the world. He created a journal, *The Pulpit of Islam*, which featured prominent religious scholars and intellectuals who legitimated Nasser's Arab social-ism in the name of Islam.

Nasser's Arab socialist-populist critique of Saudi Arabia and other Gulf monarchies as feudal was countered by Prince (later King) Faisal's develop-ment of a policy that emphasized Saudi Arabia's regional and global Islamic leadership. The Saudi government countered Nasser's appeal to Arab socialism with a pan-Islamic ideology that incorpo-rated Arab nationalism and appealed to the entire Islamic community (ummah), declaring themselves the patrons of Islam and custodians of the holy cities of Mecca and Medina. Nasser's Arab nationalism and socialism were condemned as "un-Islamic."

By the late 1960s and early 1970s events through-out much of the Muslim world reinforced a sense of the failure of many modern Muslim states and soci-eties. The Israeli rout of the combined Arab forces of Egypt, Syria, and Jordan in the 1967 Six-Day War, accompanied by the massive Arab loss of territory (Sinai, Gaza, the West Bank, and Jerusalem), was devastating. Both secularists and Islamists reeled from the shock and apparent utter impotence of the Arab-Muslim world in what came to be called "the catastrophe." Fought in the name of Arab national-ism and socialism, the disastrous defeat discredited Arab nationalism, inflamed passions against Israel and American neoimperialism (given America's prominent role in the creation of Israel and its sub-stantial support during the 1967 war), and served as a primary catalyst for an Islamic resurgence.

The loss of Jerusalem stunned the Muslim world and assured that henceforth the liberation of Palestine and Jerusalem were global Islamic issues. Similar signs of failure—the Pakistan-Bangladesh civil war of 1971 (which witnessed the secession of East Pakistan, now Bangladesh, and the failure of Muslim nationalism, Pakistan's founding ideology), the Lebanese civil war of the mid-1970s, and Malay-Chinese riots in Kuala Lumpur in 1969—signaled the military, political, economic, and cultural failures of Muslim societies and communities. Lebanon, whose capital Beirut was popularly called the "Paris of the Middle East," was torn by a civil war

Colonel Gamal Abd al-Nasser came to power in Egypt in 1952 as part of a military coup against the government of the prof-ligate King Farouk. Nasser's socialist orientation transformed his erstwhile allies, the Muslim Brotherhood, into militant opposition. Nasser and the Brotherhood became locked in a round of violent confrontations.

in the mid-1970s that shattered the mosaic of a Christian-dominated confessional state (a nation of Christian, Muslim, and Druze communities).

Disenchantment with the "failures" resulting from following the West (both its models of development and its role as an ally) produced an identity crisis, characterized by a quest for a more indigenous, authentic identity on which to base national development. From Cairo to Kuala Lumpur, Muslim societies imbued with a rich Islamically informed cultural heritage experienced a revival that saw a greater emphasis on their Islamic identity, history, culture, and values. Islam had always been present in these societies. However, the secular drift of many societies seemed reversed as Islam became more prominent and visible in personal and public life.

In many ways the Iranian revolution of 1978–79 was the defining moment that signaled and symbolized for many the contemporary resurgence of Islam. For a Western world and modernizing elites in the Muslim world, blinded to the resurgence of Islam in Muslim politics by a secular predisposition and definition of modernization, the specter of Iran's Islamic revolution was unthinkable. That a mighty shah of Iran, with oil wealth, formidable military and security forces, and Western support, could be toppled by a popular revolution led by the Ayatollah Ruhollah Khomeini (1900–89), at that time exiled in France, seemed impossible. Subsequent events reinforced fears of a militant radical Islamic resurgence, popularly referred to as "Islamic fundamentalism."

Political Islam

Islam reemerged as a potent global force throughout the 1970s and 1980s. Much of its impact in the 1970s went unnoticed, however. It was the Iranian revolution that shattered the secular bias and expectations of modernization and development theories and cast a light on the significant changes that had already been taking place in many Muslim societies throughout the 1970s. Ironically, its most potent manifestations of the Islamic resurgence, both in the 1970s and in later decades, occurred in those societies regarded as the most "modern" or modernizing, those possessing a well-trained, Western-oriented, secular elite: Iran, Egypt, Lebanon, Tunisia, Turkey, and Algeria.

From Cairo to Kuala Lumpur, the resurgence of Islam manifested itself in personal and public life, in piety and politics. Many became more religiously observant in prayer, fasting, dress, and behavior. Greater emphasis on piety and spirituality were also reflected in the revitalization of Sufism—Islamic mysticism—both within the Muslim countries and abroad. Major Sufi leaders and such orders as the Naqshbandi were to be found not only in Muslim countries from Egypt to China but also in Europe and the United States, where they continue to function as effective missionaries of Islam. At the same time, governments and opposition in countries as diverse as Egypt, Pakistan, Malaysia, and Indonesia increasingly appealed to Islam to enhance their legitimacy and mobilize popular support. Islamic ideology, rhetoric, symbols, actors, political parties, and organizations became prominent fixtures in Muslim politics and society.

Libya's Muammar Qaddafi and Sudan's Jafar Numayri seized power in the late 1960s; they did so in the name of the Arab socialism of Nasser, whom they admired. By the early 1970s, with the discrediting of Arab socialism after the 1967 war and Nasser's death in 1970, both Qaddafi and Numayri turned to Islam to buttress their Arab nationalism, legitimate their seizure of power, and broaden their base of support. Each reinforced his Islamic identity and image. Both employed a heavy does of Islamic rhetoric and posturing. Numayri published *Why the Islamic Way*, and Qaddafi issued his *Green Book*, in which he delineated his "Third Way" or Islamic alternative to Western capitalism and Soviet Marxism. Both introduced Islamic laws, regulations, and taxes. Their interpretations of Islam domestically and internationally varied significantly, however, influenced by their distinctive personalities, local experiences (domestic policies), and international ambitions. Numayri, having been betrayed by Sudan's communist party, incorporated the philosophies of Hasan Turabi (leader of Sudan's Muslim Brotherhood) into his government and assumed an anticommunist, pro-Western profile. He became an American ally and the only major Arab leader not to break relations with Egypt over than President Anwar Sadat's signing of the Camp David Accords. In contrast, Qaddafi championed a radical populist-socialist message and played an international audience more effectively. He denounced the conservative monarchies of the Arab world, used Libya's abundant oil revenues and the draw of Islam to compete with Saudi Arabia for influence and leadership in the Arab and broader Islamic world, and supported revolutionary movements internationally from Ireland's Irish Republic Army to the southern Philippines's Moro National Liberation Front.

Similarly, when Sadat (1918–81) succeeded the charismatic and enormously popular Nasser, he used Islam to enhance his legitimacy, distance himself from the left, and garner popular support. Sadat appropriated the title "the Believer president," relied on a heavy use of Quranic references and Islamic symbols in speeches and at public gatherings, and cast the 1973 Arab-Israeli war as a jihad. He attempted to co-opt Islamic organizations; for example, he permitted the outlawed and imprisoned Muslim Brotherhood, suppressed by Nasser, to function in society and fostered the growth of Islamic student organizations on university campuses to blunt the power of Nasserites and leftists.

Pakistan's Zulfikar Ali Bhutto (1928–79), a secular socialist who came to power after the 1971 civil war when Pakistan split into Pakistan and Bangladesh, turned to Islam to strengthen ties with the oil-rich states of the Arabian Gulf and to counter his Islamic critics (in particular, the Jamaat-i-Islami). Under President Bhutto,

The Afghan civil war continued after the Soviet withdrawal in February 1988. Here, a group of *mujahideen* (Muslim militias) rest during a lull in the heavy fighting with government troops over the city of Jalalabad, which was a vital link in the black-market arms trade from Peshawar, Pakistan, through the Kunar valley to Afghan guerrillas.

Pakistan became a host to numerous international Islamic conferences. Legislation was introduced to restrict alcohol use, gambling, and the frequenting of night clubs, as well as to lower bank interest and to impose Islamic taxes (*zakah* and *ushr*). Bhutto renamed or "Islamized" his secular socialism, calling it the equality of the Prophet. Reflecting the growing Islamic climate, in 1974 Pakistan hosted an international Islamic conference at the Badshahi mosque, one of the great mosques of South Asia, at which Qaddafi preached and Sadat attempted to mediate between Pakistan and Bangladesh in the name of their common Islamic brotherhood.

During the 1970s and 1980s Islam proved an effective source for opposition and popular protest in such countries as Iran, Pakistan, and Afghanistan, as well as in Egypt and Lebanon. It was used to legitimate the overthrow of the shah of Iran and of President Bhutto of Pakistan, as well as to legitimate the imposition of Islamic forms of government by the Ayatollah Khomeini and clergy of Iran, General Mohammad Zia-ul-Haq (1924–88) and the army in Pakistan, and the Taliban in Afghanistan.

Islamic symbols, slogans, ideology, religious leaders, organizations, and institutions played important roles in the organization and mass mobilization of popular support from diverse sectors of society. In Iran clerical and lay leaders such as the Ayatollah Khomeini and Ali Shariati (1933–77) became the primary ideologues of a popular revolution that brought together clergy, intellectuals, students, journalists, and men and women from diverse classes, professional backgrounds, and political positions under the banner of Islam. In Pakistan, Bhutto's appeals to Islam so incensed religious and secular leaders and parties that a broad-based opposition, the Pakistan National Alliance, representing a cross section of the political spectrum, mobilized under the banner of Islam, promising an Islamic system (*nizam-i-Islam*) of government.

The liberation of Afghanistan from Soviet occupation in 1979 did not bring peace to this war-torn country. The struggle of brave Afghan *mujahideen* (Muslim militias) against the occupation of their country by an "atheist" Soviet army had captured the support and sympathies of many in the West and the Muslim world alike. In contrast to the West's fear of the Islamic resurgence or "Islamic fundamentalism" in Iran and the Middle East, Afghanistan's Muslim militias were seen as freedom fighters whose jihad received substantial aid from the United States, Saudi Arabia, and other countries. The mujahideen victory did not bring peace, however. The common Islamic identity that had served to mobilize and inspire, to unify the militias in their jihad against the Soviet Union, was now eclipsed by Afghanistan's age-old tribal, ethnic, and religious differences and rivalries, primarily between the Sunni and Shiite branches of Islam.

Afghanistan, a predominantly Sunni country, had enjoyed a fragile unity, offset by the realities of its multiethnic tribal society (Pathans, Pashtuns, Uzbeks, Tajiks, and Persian-speaking Shiites in the west). The leadership vacuum created by the Soviet defeat now unleashed a factional power struggle. Having driven out the Soviets in 1989 and defeated the communist regime of Najibullah in Kabul in 1992, the mujahideen Islamic government then fell prey to a bloody internal power struggle as mujahideen leaders (or perhaps more accurately, warlords) vied for supremacy, resulting in more deaths and devastation than its liberation had cost. Two major groups came to the forefront: Hizb-i-Islami, led by Gulbudeen Hekmatyar, and Jamaat-i-Islami, led by Burhanuddin Rabbani. Much of Afghanistan, including Kabul, was caught in the rivalry and crossfire between these two groups.

After almost eighteen years of civil war in Afghanistan, a seemingly endless state of carnage and chaos was abruptly reversed. As if out of nowhere, a band of students (*taliban*) from the *madrasas* (colleges whose primary purpose is the teaching of Islamic law and related religions subjects) appeared in late 1994 and within two years swept across the country. Denouncing all the warlords and representing no

In Afghanistan, the Taliban government requires women to wear a full veil that allows them to see only through a screened area in front of their eyes.

outside interests, they claimed the mantle of moral leadership as representatives of the Afghan majority who were victims of the internecine warfare. Although initially portrayed as young students from the madrasas with no military background, in fact they were a force of mullahs and taliban, religious leaders and students. The mullahs were primarily veterans of the Afghan-Soviet war who had returned to the madrasas after the Soviets' departure. Their leader, Mullah Omar, reflected this older generation. Mullah Omar had been a student of Islam before joining Mohammad Nabi Mohammadi's Islamic Revolutionary Movement (Harakat-i-inqilabi-i-Islami). During the 1980s Omar fought against the Soviet occupation, losing an eye and becoming deputy commander of the movement. In 1994 he launched the Taliban campaign to restore stability and order and to establish an Islamic state. Because little was known about the Taliban and they were portrayed simply as young students from religious schools, inexperienced in warfare and poorly armed, they were initially not taken seriously. In time they proved to be a formidable force, however, feared by warlords but embraced by ordinary citizens, who captured Kabul and controlled three-fourths of the country.

Although initially hailed as liberators who secured towns, made the streets safe, and cleaned up corruption and graft, the Taliban's strict form of Islam soon became an issue for some. The Taliban subscribed to a very conservative, puritanical interpretation of Islam. Their doctrines are close to those of Saudi Arabia's Wahhabi religious establishment and Pakistan's Jamaat-i-Islami. As Sunni Muslims, they denounced their Shiite opposition as infidels. When they captured the Afghan capital Kabul after a two-year battle, the Taliban not only restored law and order but also sought to create or impose a moral shariah-governed society, mandating their brand of Islamic reform. They segregated the sexes outside the home, closed girls' schools, required that women be fully covered in public, and banned women from the workplace. They also banned television, cinema, and music, ordered men to grow beards and pray five times a day, and introduced the *hudud* punishments (punishments for certain crimes as prescribed by the Quran and hadith, such as amputation for theft, death for murder, stoning for adultery).

In Egypt, after initial periods of support, both the Muslim Brotherhood and the Islamic student organization (the Gamaa Islamiyya) became more vocal in their criticisms of the Sadat government during the late 1970s. Radical underground groups with such names as Muhammad's Youth, Takfir wal Hijra, and Islamic Jihad, committed to the overthrow of the Sadat government and the imposition of an Islamic government, sprouted and began their guerilla war against the regime, government officials, minorities, and other Muslims. In 1981 Sadat, a Nobel prizewinner for his negotiated peace (the Camp David Accords) with Israel's prime minister Menachem Begin (1913–92), was assassinated by the militant group Islamic Jihad.

In Lebanon demographic changes prompted Muslims, both Sunni and Shiite, to call for a redistribution of power in a state whose political system had been based on the proportional representation of Lebanon religious communities (Christian, Sunni Muslim, Shiite Muslim, and Druze, in that order). A prominent Shiite leader, Imam Musa Sadr, established the Movement for the Dispossessed (and subsequently its militia, AMAL, Lebanese Resistance Battalions). In the aftermath of the Iranian revolution, the Iranian-inspired, -trained, and -funded Hizbollah (Party of God) undertook its militant struggle with the Israeli occupation and the Christian (especially Maronite) dominance of Lebanon. In both cases—AMAL and Hizbollah—Shiite belief and ritual were reinterpreted, though not in precisely the same ways, to support social and political movements of protest and reform. For Hizbollah the goal was the creation of an Islamic state. For AMAL the object was a more equitable redistribution of political and economic power within Lebanon's multiconfessional state.

Anatomy of a Revolution: The Islamic Republic of Iran

Iran captured the headlines and imaginations of many throughout the Muslim world and the West, so much so that many would come to view Islam and Islamic revivalism through the lens of the Ayatollah Khomeini's Iran. A seemingly modern, enlightened, and invincible shah was overthrown by a movement led by an ayatollah in exile in France. Intellectuals, merchants (*bazaaris*), students, and journalists as well as clergy mobilized under the banner of Islam. Islam was not only a rallying cry for its supporters but also a symbol of protest for all who opposed the shah, whatever their political or religious beliefs. Islamic symbols, rhetoric, and institutions provided the infrastructure for organization, protest, and mobilization of a coalition of forces calling for reform and in the end for revolution.

Iran seemed a textbook candidate for successful modernization and development, the most unlikely prospect for revolution. Outwardly, the goal of the White Revolution, the ambitious modernization program of Shah Mohammad Reza Pahlavi (1919–80), was to bring Iran into the twentieth century within a matter of decades. Oil wealth, the best equipped military in the Middle East (with the exception of Israel), close ties with the United States, Europe, and even Israel, and a well-trained elite contributed to the image of Iran, in the words of U.S. President Jimmy Carter, as "an island of stability" in the Middle East. Beneath the surface, however, was growing discontent.

Although the shah's modernization program did improve the lot of many, the benefits of modernization tended to favor disproportionately a minority of modern elites and urban centers. Economic, educational, and military reforms were not accompanied by political liberalization. Traditional merchants (bazaaris) and religious leaders (ulama), long mutually supportive and connected through marriage and business relationships, were alienated by the shah's religious and economic reforms. State control of religious affairs (through the courts, endowments, and education) and a tilt toward Western markets and the corporate sector threatened their interests, authority, and power. Many modern, educated academics, professionals, and journalists increasingly expressed concerns over the excessive dependence of Iran on the West (economically and militarily), with its negative religio-cultural impact. Some modern, Western-educated intellectuals like Jalal al-e-Ahmad and Ali Shariati spoke of the dangers of "Westoxification," an excessive dependence on the West that threatened to rob Iranians of their independence and cultural identity. These were issues that resonated across many sectors of society.

Early in his rule, the shah worked out a tacit agreement and accommodation with many of Iran's leading clerics. However, some clerics, like Ruhollah Khomeini (later the ayatollah) from Qum, exiled first to Iraq and later France, were less compliant. In the mid-1970s, as the voices of discontent increased, gov-

By the 1970s in Iran, there was widespread discontent with the authoritarian rule of Shah Mohammad Reza Pahlavi. Shiite Islam offered the broadest basis for a mass movement, and many people united to support Ayatollah Khomeini, as in this demonstration in Tehran in February 1979.

ernment security forces moved quickly to contain and repress mounting opposition. By the late 1970s, with widespread suppression of dissident intellectuals, politicians, journalists, liberal nationalists, socialists, and Marxists, Shiite Islam (Iran's religious and cultural heritage and therefore the religion of most Iranians) offered the most indigenous broad-based basis for a mass movement.

Shiite Islam provided a common set of symbols, historic identity, and values—an indigenous, non-Western alternative. Shiite belief provided the basis for an ideological framework for opposition and protest against oppression and injustice. Clerical and lay intellectuals, such as the Ayatollah Khomeini and Ali Shariati, reappropriated Shiite history, beliefs, and rituals to support and sustain religiously legitimated opposition to the shah's regime. After an early revolutionary history, Shiite Islam had developed doctrines that enabled it to survive and coexist in a Sunni-dominated world. Now reformers turned to Shiite Islam's early revolutionary period as a base for their reformist and revolutionary ideology. Memories of a persecuted, dispossessed, and disinherited remnant's struggle and martyrdom took on modern meanings. The paradigmatic Shiite event—the martyrdom of the caliph Ali's righteous son al-Husayn (the Prophet's grandson) by the forces of the "evil" Sunni Umayyad ruler Yazid at the battle of Karbala in 680—was now likened to the oppression and injustice inflicted under the shah, the new Yazid. The mullah mosque network enabled the clergy and Iran's thousands of mosques to serve as centers for organization, propaganda (distribution of audiotapes and flyers), and mobilization.

Although the opposition united under the umbrella of Islam in a common purpose—opposition to the shah and the desire for a more independent, indigenously rooted modernity—it encompassed heterogeneous political and religious groups. They ranged from secularists to Islamic activists, from liberal democrats to Marxists. Similar differences existed among the clergy and senior ayatollahs, as would later become more evident. Nowhere was the division among Islamically oriented activists more pronounced than in the two most prominent ideologies of the revolution: the Ayatollah Khomeini, a traditionally madrasa-trained cleric, and Ali Shariati, who combined a traditional religious education with a Sorbonne doctorate. Although banners depicting each were juxtaposed in many homes and in protest marches, their interpretations of Islamic identity and ideology were in fact quite different. Khomeini, a member of Iran's Shiite religious hierarchy, privileged ulama leadership and tradition; Ali Shariati called for a bold reinterpretation of Shiite Islam to recapture its early revolutionary message. He criticized the religious establishment for its accommodation with the state (what he called Safavid Islam) and its betrayal of the true meaning and legacy of early Shiism (Alid Islam) with its radical commitment to social justice.

The revolution of 1978–79 brought together a diverse cross section of lay and clerical leadership, social and economic classes, political parties, and guerilla groups. With the passing of their common enemy, the shah, differences of vision and ideology (both religious and socioeconomic) surfaced almost immediately after the revolution. The struggle between moderates and militants became evident. Rather than returning to their mosques and madrasas, the Ayatollah Khomeini and many of his clerical disciples moved quickly to consolidate their power and control of government. The Islamic Republic's first prime minister, Mehdi Bazargan, and president, Abol Hasan Bani-Sadr, although initially approved by Ayatollah Khomeini, were driven from office. Bazargan resigned in November 1979 and Bani-Sadr fled Iran after being impeached in 1981. The ulama consolidated their power and set about fulfilling the twin goals of institutionalization and export of the revolution.

The new constitution of the Islamic Republic was a mixture of modern Western and Shiite religious institutions that incorporated modern political language and such institutions as those of a republic, parliamentary government, or the executive, legislative, and judicial branches. The overriding concept of state, however, was the notion of government by the faqih or legal expert (wilayat al-faqih, guardianship or rule by the jurist). While many, including moderate or liberal intellectuals and ulama, expected the ulama to return to their mosques and schools and at best advise the government on Islamic matters, Khomeini and the bulk of more militant and conservative ulama believed in a clerically guided state. At the apex of government it was the Ayatollah Khomeini, the supreme authority assisted by other clergy, who dominated the branches of government and its organizations in a clerical state or theocracy.

Voices of dissent, lay and clerical, were intimidated or silenced—from secularists and leftists to Islamically oriented intellectuals such as Bazargan and Bani-Sadr. Sadeq Ghotbzadeh, an early protégé of the Ayatollah Khomeini who had held a number of senior government positions including foreign minister, was executed for an alleged plot to assassinate Khomeini. Dissident clergy, in particular those who refused to accept Khomeini's interpretation of Islam, which had yielded his doctrine of "rule by the jurist," were hounded and harassed by fellow clerics. Many were silenced; the Ayatollah Muhammad Kazem Shariatmadari, a senior ayatollah revered for his knowledge and piety, was even defrocked in 1982.

Institutionalization of the revolution at home was accompanied by its export abroad. The promotion and spread of Islam and Iran's "Islamic revolution" was a foreign policy goal of the Khomeini government, explicitly stated in the exhortation of Iran's constitution: "to perpetuate the revolution both at home and abroad." Both preaching and propagation of the faith (through distribution of publications, conferences, and funding of religious institutions abroad) were combined with confrontation and armed struggle. At the same time, the Ayatollah Khomeini and other government officials, as well as Iran's radio broadcast "Voice of the Islamic Revolution," called on the Muslims of the Gulf and throughout the world to rise up and overthrow "oppressive, un-Islamic" governments. Gulf states were condemned because of the nature of their governments (monarchy was dismissed as "un-Islamic") and because of their close ties with America, which was often referred to as "American Islam," that is, offering a form of Islam acceptable to the West.

In Iran, as time passed political and ideological divisions deepened not only between those who were for and against the revolution but also among supporters of the revolution. Differences of religious interpretation and class interests divided rather than united the Islamic Republic's debate over economic and social reform. The majority of the parliament favored a social revolution that included state control of the economy and controls on the private sector and free enterprise, to improve the condition of the urban poor, farmers, and villagers. Merchants, who had been major financial supporters of the revolution, and landowners, including many clerics, strongly opposed these measures and lobbied senior clerics. The Council of Guardians, clerical experts on Islamic law who determined whether legislation was Islamically acceptable, consistently blocked such legislation. The Ayatollah Khomeini, who could have broken these deadlocks, chose not to intervene.

During the post-Khomeini period economic policy and ideological differences continued to affect Iran's development. Ineffective economic policies fed growing discontent and disillusionment, leading many to look back longingly to the relative prosperity of the shah's rule. Iran's Islamic identity seemed more wrapped up in debates over women's dress and conduct in society than in implementation of effective political and economic policies. Yet, despite what some viewed as Iran's rigid "fundamentalism," within the state's ideological limits and controls Iran did conduct parliamentary and local elections; women were able to function in society (to vote and hold elected office, to work, to publish magazines that advocated women's rights issues); and strong differences of opinion were debated in parliament and in the press. This stood in sharp contrast to the more restrictive policies of many of Iran's Gulf neighbors.

The 1980s were dominated by fears of "radical Islamic fundamentalism," the spread of Iran's Islamic revolution, or the proliferation of extremist underground militant organizations bent on destabilizing and toppling entrenched governments. Both Muslim and Western governments feared a domino effect, the spread of revolutionary Islam leading to "other Irans." The fear seemed verified by events: eruptions in Saudi Arabia's oil-rich eastern province, which was heavily populated by its Shiite minority; disturbances in Kuwait and Bahrain; Iran's significant support for militant Shiism in Lebanon, such as Hizbollah (Party of God) and Islamic Jihad; and the attempt by Khomeini to turn the Iran-Iraq war into a jihad and mobilize a revolt by Iraqi Shiites. At the same time, militant groups like

Islamic Jihad and Hizbollah were responsible for the assassination of the Egyptian president Sadat in 1981 and a rash of hijackings across the Middle East and in South Asia.

For a secular-oriented West the specter of the spread of revolutionary Islam seemed both retrogressive and a threat to Western allies and interests (oil and trade). The reality was in fact far more complex. Iran proved far more effective as a source of inspiration rather than emulation. There were no Iranian-inspired or -funded revolutions. Shiite disturbances did not lead to the fall of governments. Khomeini was not able to mobilize the Iraqi Shiites in a war in which ancient rivalries (Arab versus Persian), and modern Iraqi and Arab nationalism proved stronger than common religious affiliation. Indeed, even after the defeat of Iraq in the Gulf War in March 1991, the Iranians did nothing to encourage the emergence of a Shiite republic in the south of a devastated Iraq. Moreover, as time passed, the failures and excesses of the Iranian government became a source of disillusionment to many of its initial admirers.

As a result, few noticed or distinguished between the violent extremists who wished to seize power and populist political and social movements that quietly pursued change from below, from within their societies, like the Muslim Brotherhoods of Egypt and Jordan, the Islamic Tendency Movement (later renamed Hizb al-Nahda, the Renaissance Party or Ennahda), the Jamiyat al-Islah

In the 1980s many governments, both Muslim and Western, feared that Iran's Islamic revolution would spread. Their worst fears were realized in the outbreak of the Iran-Iraq war, and Ayatollah Khomeini's attempt to mobilize a revolt by Iraqi Shiites against Saddam Hussein.

(Reform Society) in Kuwait, the Jamaat-i-Islami in Pakistan or ABIM and PAS in Malaysia, and the Jamat al-Nasr (Society for Victory) in Nigeria.

Islam and Democracy

By the late 1980s and 1990s the two faces of Islamic activism became evident: (1) anti-Western radical revolutionary governments (in Iran, Sudan, and Afghanistan) and movements (jihad groups in the Middle East and the Gamaa Islamiyya in Cairo, for example), seeking to overthrow regimes in the Muslim world, and (2) a host of Islamic movements functioning within mainstream society to foster social and political change.

From Egypt to Indonesia, Islamic movements and organizations created alternative educational, medical, legal, and social services (schools, clinics, hospitals, youth centers, and legal aid societies, for example), publishing houses, and financial institutions. Islamists held prominent positions and participated in professional associations and unions. In countries and areas with large populations and poor economies (in which there was often poverty, high unemployment, and a lack of adequate housing and social services)—such as Egypt, Algeria, the West Bank and Gaza, and Indonesia—Islamically motivated educational, economic, and social welfare institutions (many though not all Islamist in orientation) provided an alternative to state services, which were often inadequate, too expensive, or nonexistent. Regimes regarded them as an implicit critique of the state's failure to provide for its citizens. For example, when earthquakes devastated parts of Egypt and Algeria, it was the Islamists (the Muslim Brotherhood and the Islamic Salvation Front), not the state, that were the first on the scene, providing needed relief. An embarrassed and somewhat threatened Egyptian government under President Hosni Mubarak subsequently banned nongovernmental organizations from responding to such disasters.

Social activism has always been part of the redefinition of the notion of *dawa*, the call to Islam. While the primary definition of dawa has been of preaching and spreading God's word and community (calling all to "the straight path" of Islam), it has also included the call to Muslims to *return* to Islam, to become more religiously observant. To these understandings has been added the institutionalization of Islam's teaching that Muslims are socially responsible and accountable. The Islamic requirement to promote social justice has been coupled with the view of Islam as a total way of life and provided the rationale for the growth of social welfare agencies or organizations, the creation of organizations that relate the religion of Islam to the needs of society. The social welfare organizations discussed above are known as Islamic call societies, as are the myriad of relief agencies that have been created for Palestine, Bosnia, Kashmir, and Afghanistan. The term has also been politicized by governments as well as opposition movements.

Libya's Jamiyyat al-Dawa has served as a foreign policy tool, disseminating Qaddafi's religious and political ideas and providing funds for schools, mosques, and hospitals. The Iraqi Islamic call society Hizb al-Dawa al-Islamiya was founded in opposition to military and political leader Saddam Hussein's rule.

A notable sign of the mainstreaming of Islamic revivalism or activism was the emergence of Islamists as leaders in professional associations and trade unions. Their presence underscored the extent to which the strength of Islamic revivalism was not simply due to its attractiveness to the poor and uneducated but in fact to a modern educated but Islamically oriented elite. The strength of Islamists in professional associations of physicians, lawyers, engineers, journalists, and teachers reflected the extent to which Muslim societies now had an alternative sector of society alongside the traditional Islamic and modern Western-oriented sectors, and an alternative elite to the Western secular elite.

As the Soviet Union and eastern Europe were swept along by the wave of democratization in 1989–90, the Middle East and the broader Muslim world showed signs of modest change in response to political unrest in Egypt, Sudan, Tunisia, Jordan, Algeria, Morocco, and Pakistan. Although some Muslim radicals, like secular nationalist radicals, rejected any form of parliamentary democracy as westernizing and incompatible with Islam and local Muslim traditions, many, if not most, Islamic intellectuals and activists tried to come to terms with the idea and the process. Islamic movements in Algeria, Tunisia, Egypt, Sudan, Jordan, and Pakistan chose to function within the political system and participate in electoral politics.

The majority of Muslim countries have been ruled by authoritarian governments buttressed by military and security forces. Few rulers have held elective office; most have been kings or military or ex-military officers. Where parliaments and political parties have existed, they have generally remained subordinated to the ruling government or party. While some Muslim countries, such as Pakistan and Turkey, have held elections, the military have also had significant influence on politics. In the late 1980s and early 1990s several major events led to an opening of the political system, ushering in political liberalization and democratization. Among the most important were numerous economic crises and "food riots," the fall of the Soviet Union and liberation of eastern Europe, and the Gulf War. Countries as diverse as Egypt, Tunisia, Jordan, and Algeria responded by opening their political systems, enabling Islamists to participate in electoral politics. To the surprise of many, Islamists and Islamic parties emerged as the leading opposition in Egypt, Tunisia, and Jordan. In Algeria they seemed poised to come to power.

In Pakistan opposition to Zia ul-Haq in the 1980s had been coordinated in the Movement for the Restoration of Democracy, which included secular as well as religious (Islamic) parties. In October 1990 elections Zia ul-Haq's democratically elected successor, Benazir Bhutto, was defeated by a coalition that took the name the Islamic Democratic Alliance. Throughout this period such groups as the Jamaat-i-Islami, the Jamiyyat Ulama-i Pakistan, and the Jamiyyat Ulama-i Islam called for the restoration of democracy and participated in national and provincial elections.

Egypt and Jordan, long regarded as having moderate pro-Western governments, introduced political reforms to alleviate the growing opposition due to deteriorating economic conditions and high unemployment and to defuse the threat of "fundamentalism." Both countries attempted to keep Islamic moderates separated from militants—a kind of containment policy—and to avoid radicalization. President Mubarak of Egypt distinguished more sharply than his predecessor, Anwar Sadat, between political dissent and direct challenges to the state's authority. Islamic groups such as the Muslim Brotherhood were allowed to participate in political and economic life and to express their criticism of government policies. As early as 1941, the Brotherhood had accepted participation in electoral politics. Six Brothers (including Hasan al-Banna, its founder) contested the parliamentary election of 1945, but none was successful in an election that was seen by many as corrupt. From the revolution in 1952 to the post-Sadat period in the 1980s, the Brotherhood either boycotted elections or, more often, was prohibited from operating openly as a political organization. In 1984, however, when the Brotherhood was allowed to contest parliamentary elections, although not as a political party, it formed an alliance with the New Wafd party and won twelve seats. In 1987 it created an "Islamic alliance" with the Socialist Labor Party and the Liberals and increased its parliamentary strength to thirty-two seats.

Islam has been effective in mobilizing opposition and popular protest against governments. In 1977 General Muhammad Zia ul-Haq deposed Zulfikar Ali Bhutto, a secular socialist, with the support of the Jamaat al-Islam; he then instituted an Islamic form of government.

In Jordan, King Hussein initiated a process of political reform in November 1989, following serious rioting in April of that year after government-announced increases in the price of major commodities. Parliamentary elections were held for the first time in twenty-two years. Islamic candidates, campaigning with slogans such as "the Quran is our constitution" and "Islam is the solution," scored an upset, taking thirty-two of eighty parliamentary seats. The Muslim Brotherhood won twenty seats, while twelve went to other Islamic candidates. The Brotherhood also did well in local elections. In 1990 it won nine of ten seats in a local council election in Zarqa, the second largest town in Jordan, and four of nine seats in municipal elections in Rusaifah. In January 1991, given its parliamentary strength, the Brotherhood received five cabinet positions—the Ministries of Education, Religious Affairs, Justice, Social Development, and

Most Muslim rulers in the twentieth century have been kings or military or ex-military officers, like King Hussein of Jordan, shown here just before leaving Amman in 1970. In 1989, after riots in response to reported increases in the price of major commodities, Hussein instituted political reforms, and parliamentary elections were held for the first time in twenty-two years.

Health. Moreover, a Muslim Brother was elected speaker of the parliament.

Islamic organizations in Tunisia and Algeria joined with their fellow citizens during the 1980s in pressing for a multiparty system and representative elections. Governments in both countries had a record of rigorously controlling Islamic movements. Habib Bourguiba's thirty-year reign as president in Tunisia was characterized by a Western secular orientation that excluded religion from public life. In the 1980s he imprisoned and threatened to execute leaders of the Islamic Tendency Movement. After seizing power from Bourguiba in 1987, Zein Abidine Ben Ali, the prime minister of Tunisia, promised democratization and held parliamentary elections in April 1989. However, despite the fact that the Islamic Tendency Movement renamed itself Hizb al-Nahda (the Renaissance Party) to comply with Ben Ali's insistence that no single group should monopolize the claim to be Islamic, the government did not permit it to participate as a legal political party. High inflation, growing unemployment, and increased poverty proved to be critical issues. Islamic candidates won 14.5 percent of the vote nationwide and a stunning 30 percent in such cities as Tunis, Gabes, and Sousse. In November 1989 Ben Ali reneged on his earlier promises to recognize Hizb al-Nahda as a political party, announcing that he would not allow any party to combine religion and politics. The Ministry of Education reintroduced a decree from the Bourguiba period that banned the wearing of Islamic headdress by women in schools and offices. Student demonstrations, strikes, imprisonment of Hizb al-Nahda leaders, and the closing down of its newspaper, al-Fajr, signaled the onslaught of the regime's attempt to destroy the group.

The Tunisian government's shift to a more hardline policy toward Islamic activists was influenced by events in Algeria. In what had long been regarded the most monolithic, single-party political system in the Arab world (dominated by the National Liberation Front, or FLN), President Chedli Ben Jadid introduced greater political pluralism following the bloody antigovernment riots in October 1988. This included recognition of the Islamic Salvation Front (Front Islamique du Salut, FIS), North Africa's first legal Islamic political party, led by Ali Abbasi al-Madani. The government of Ben Jadid, faced with such intractable economic difficulties as a 25 percent unemployment level, foreign debt of some $20 billion, and food shortages, felt constrained to concede these reforms.

Islamic groups flourished as Algerian state socialism failed to resolve the country's social and economic problems. The FIS, with a national organization and an effective mosque and social welfare network, emerged as the largest Islamic party and one of the strongest opposition parties. In the June 1991 municipal elections, the first multiparty election in Algeria since independence in 1962, the FIS scored a stunning victory, capturing 54 percent of the vote, while the FLN garnered 34 percent. This success was partly explained by the boycott of two main opposition parties and by a voting abstention rate of roughly 40 percent. But also contributing to the FIS victory was an electoral system that allowed husbands to vote by proxy for their wives and that awarded 51 percent of the seats on a council to whichever group secured the largest number of votes. The FIS won a majority of votes in all the major cities: 64 percent in Algiers, 71 percent in Oran, and 72 percent in Constantine.

The Algerian government moved quickly to discredit and contain the FIS victory. Funds to FIS-controlled municipalities were cut off to limit their effectiveness in office, scheduled parliamentary elections were postponed, FIS leadership (al-Madani and Ali Belhadj, a popular Algerian preacher) were imprisoned, and voting districts were redrawn to favor the FLN in future parliamentary elections. With these measures in place and with no access to an FLN-controlled media, the defeat of the FIS in parliamentary elections appeared assured.

On December 26, 1991, Algeria held the first multiparty parliamentary elections in its thirty-five-year history. With 59 percent of eligible voters casting ballots, the FIS scored another victory in the first of two rounds. It won 48 percent of the vote, 188 of 231 parliamentary seats, twenty-three votes short of a majority. The FLN finished with sixteen seats. In two government-controlled democratic elections, the FIS had won and now seemed poised to control the parliament, with an expected victory in the second round of elections scheduled for

Ali Abbasi al-Madani (b. 1931) is leader and official spokesman of the Algerian Islamic Salvation Front (Front Islamique du Salut, FIS), the first legal Islamic political party in North Africa. A professor at the University of Algiers with a doctorate from the University of London, he became active in the 1980s during the clashes between the state and Islamic students and was a founding member of the FIS. Following the FIS victory in the June 1991 municipal elections, he was arrested by the government and remains in prison.

January 16, 1992.

On January 12 the Algerian military in a de facto coup seized power to prevent the FIS from winning their democratic victory. Their rationale was that the FIS was an antidemocratic "radical" Islamic movement that would use the ballot box to "seize" power. Once in power, it was asserted, the FIS would hijack democracy, taking control of the government.

The Algerian military's message, aimed in part at the West, was unmistakable and could be encapsulated as follows: "The governments in power are worth preserving. For no matter what their shortcomings, ranging from political exclusion to severe human rights violations, they form the only barrier against fanatics who want to confront the West." According to this interpretation, local forms of authoritarianism are regrettable, but they are the only road toward Western-style political pluralism.

The military takeover was followed by a move to suppress the FIS, which precipitated a virtual civil war in which more than seventy-five thousand Algerians (in a country of twenty-nine million) lost their lives. The military and security forces moved quickly, arresting FIS leaders and imprisoning more than fifteen thousand members in detention camps, closing down their institutions, and seizing their properties and funds. As government repression and violence mounted, Islamists responded both defensively and offensively. The military's crackdown saw many in the FIS move from a nonviolent legal opposition to a combative, and in some cases revolutionary movement. The FIS split into a moderate group and a more militant wing, the Islamic Salvation Army.

The spiral of government and Islamist violence and counterviolence swept across Algeria's cities and countryside as the battle raged between government security forces and those in the FIS who formed their own militia, the Islamic Salvation Army. Moreover, both the security forces and the Islamists also spawned radical militias, the military's eradicateurs and the Armed Islamic Group (GIA). An extremist guerrilla group, the GIA, rejected any attempt at a political solution or compromise, demanded an Islamic state, waged a war (jihad) of terrorism against all opponents (pro-government, Islamist, or noncommitted). Like other radical movements in the Muslim world, the GIA divided their world into "true believers" (those who fully accepted their views and agenda) and unbelievers (kafirs), Muslim and non-Muslim alike. They condemned the FIS for its moderation and killed military and civilians (including leading secularists, journalists, and schoolchildren), combatants and noncombatants alike.

For rulers in the Gulf, response to the strength and threat of Islamic political activism was complicated by the fact that many of them were Sunni rulers with significant Shiite populations. In Kuwait, for example, although the regime had attempted to enhance its legitimacy by permitting parliamentary elections since

1963, the emir twice dissolved the National Assembly, in 1976 and 1986, in the face of open criticism of government action. When Islamists and other political groups demanded reinstitution of the National Assembly, the government responded with a crackdown on pro-democracy leaders and permanently disbanded the National Assembly. In the post–Gulf War period, Kuwait's ruling al-Sabah dynasty, overseeing the country's reconstruction, faced increasing demands for "democratization." The Gulf War strengthened sectarian relations and impelled Kuwait's Islamists, as the majority of citizens, to rally behind the government—a position that contributed to their credibility in post–Gulf War parliamentary elections in 1992. Islamists won 25 percent of the vote, holding eight to ten seats in parliament, with a total of eighteen deputies backed by Islamic groups. Although these Islamists supported in principle the application of shariah, what that meant for each in reality differed markedly.

The Saudis for many years assiduously avoided the creation of a parliamentary body. In times of crisis kings often promised one, but they did not introduce such a body. In 1962, on the heels of considerable internal unrest, Crown Prince Faisal promised the promulgation of a constitution that would allow the creation of

The conflict between government and Islamists has been particularly violent in Algeria. The imprisonment of many leaders of the Islamic opposition has spawned extreme guerrilla groups that have provoked the government to equally violent reactions.

The spiraling violence in Algeria's cities and countryside has caused many deaths on both sides. Women in Ait Said village in the Kabylie region mourn at the funeral of a young militiaman.

regional and national assemblies. Shortly after the seizure of the Grand Mosque of Mecca by a group of militants in November 1979, Crown Prince Fahd announced a "basic law of governance," which would include provision for a consultative assembly (*majlis al-shura*). To rally popular support at home in its war with Iraq in 1990–91, the House of Saud in November 1990 again promised a consultative assembly whose members would be appointed by the king; there was no intention to introduce elections or to permit political parties.

Saudi Arabia's King Fahd, forced to balance demands for political participation from both religious leaders and technocrats and the traditional concentration of power within the Saudi elite, created an appointed consultative council in March 1991, while emphasizing that Islam was incompatible with democracy. A cross section of society, from intellectuals and technocrats to women and Islamists, pressed for greater political participation and socioeconomic reforms. While the religious establishment remained supportive, younger and more militant ulama and Islamists continued to voice their opposition and press their demands. Just when the government's crackdown against religious dissidents and its policy of containment seemed to have silenced its critics, bomb attacks against U.S. military installations occurred in November 1995 and June 1996. The shock of these acts of violence, attributed to underground Islamic groups, coupled with the broader challenge from militant Islamists, led to a closing of ranks between political and religious elites.

The Compatibility of Islam and Democracy

Muslim discourse on political liberalization and democratization has embraced a broad spectrum of positions, from Muslim secularists who wish to separate religion from politics and Islamic reformers who have reinterpreted Islamic traditions in support of modern elective forms of government to those Muslims who reject democracy. Indeed, in contemporary Muslim politics Islam has often been used to legitimate democracy and dictatorship, republicanism and monarchy.

While some Islamic leaders in the past spoke out against Western-style democracy and a parliamentary system of government, this negative reaction was often part of the general rejection of European colonial influence, a defense of Islam against further dependence on the West rather than a wholesale rejection of democracy. For other Muslims, Islam is totally self-sufficient, with a divinely mandated system, based on divine sovereignty and sacred law (shariah), which is incompatible and irreconcilable with notions of popular sovereignty and civil law. Still other Muslims insist that Muslims should generate their own forms of political participation or democracy from within Islam; they have no need to look to Western forms of democracy.

The spectrum of those Muslims who believe that Islam and democracy are incompatible has been broad and diverse. In Iran during the Constitutional Movement of 1905–11, Shaykh Fadlallah Nuri, in debates over the constitution's formulation, argued that one key democratic idea—the equality of all citizens—is "impossible" in Islam. He maintained that unavoidable and insurmountable inequalities exist, such as those between believers and unbelievers, the rich and the poor, husbands and wives, the healthy and the sick, and the learned jurist and his followers. Neither is it possible for a legislative body to exist; Nuri believed that "Islam does not have any shortcomings that require completion."

Sayyid Qutb, the great theoretician of the Muslim Brotherhood who was executed by the Egyptian regime in 1966, strongly objected to any notion of popular sovereignty as incompatible with God's sovereignty. Although Qutb stressed that the Islamic state must be based on the Quranic principle of consultation, he also believed that shariah is so complete as a legal and moral system that no further legislation is possible. In addition, he believed that for one group of people to legislate for others was contrary to the equality and absolute dignity of believers.

Mawlana Abul Ala Mawdudi, founder of the Jamaat-i-Islami, combined parts of Nuri's and Qutb's perspectives and yet subtly differed from them. Abul Ala Mawdudi held that Islam constitutes its own form of democracy, but he concentrated on the relationship between divine and popular sovereignty. Arguing that

Mawlana Abul Ala Mawdudi (1903–1979), the founder of the Jaamat-i-Islami, had a far-reaching impact on Muslim thinkers and activists throughout the Islamic world.

democracy as commonly understood is based solely on the sovereignty of the people, Abul Ala Mawdudi concluded that Islam is "the very antithesis of secular Western democracy." For this reason his critics charged that he was an "absolutist" or "doctrinal purist." Yet he went on to argue that if democracy is conceived as a limited form of popular sovereignty, restricted and directed by God's law, there is no incompatibility at all. He used the term *theo-democracy* to describe this alternate view.

This argument has resonance in the current world of Muslim political activism. For example, the constitution of the Islamic Republic of Iran, which might have been expected simply to reaffirm the absolute sovereignty of God, makes reference to both divine and popular sovereignty. Principle 2 of the constitution acknowledges that God has "the faculty to rule and implement the divine law" and that there is a "necessity to obey His orders." Yet Principle 1 indicates the hold that the idea of popular sovereignty has on modern Iranian Muslim consciousness. It notes that the Republic's government was "endorsed by the Iranian nation by an affirmative vote of 98.2 percent of the majority of eligible voters." This recognition of the central importance of political participation is further delineated in other articles in the constitution that affirm that the people should participate "in determining their political, economic, and social destiny" (Principle 3). Furthermore, the Republic should provide for a popularly elected national consultative assembly (Principle 62) and for periodic referenda on issues that are submitted "directly to the people for a judgment" (Principle 59).

More conservative voices in the Muslim world could also be heard in the 1980s and 1990s, however. In 1982 Shaykh Muhammad Mutawwali al-Sharawi, a prominent Egyptian religious leader and popular preacher whose writings and television broadcasts enjoyed an audience throughout the Arab world, created controversy by saying that Islam and democracy are incompatible and that *shura* (consultation) does not mean simple domination of the majority. In Algeria in the early 1990s the popular preacher Ali Belhadj, one of the FIS leaders, accepted participation in elections but echoed the refrain that democracy is a Judeo-Christian concept and should be replaced with inherently Islamic principles of governance. He found the concept of majority rule objectionable because issues of right and justice cannot be quantified; the greater number of votes does not translate into the greater moral position.

King Fahd of Saudi Arabia, long regarded as a conservative monarch and an ally of the West, declared that democracy is a Western institution foreign to Islam, which has its own forms of participation: "[T]he democratic system prevalent in the world is not appropriate in this region. The election system has no place in the Islamic creed, which calls for a government of advice and consultation and for the shepherd's openness to his flock, and holds the ruler fully responsible before his people."

Yet, increasingly, many Muslims have accepted the notion of democracy, although they have different opinions about its precise meaning. Muslim interpretations of democracy generally build on the well-established Quranic concept of consultation, but these interpretations vary in the degree to which "the people" are able to exercise this duty. Some argue that Islam is inherently democratic, not only because of the principle of consultation but also because of the concepts of independent reasoning (ijtihad) and consensus (ijma). The attempt to generate Islamic forms of democracy is based on a reinterpretation of traditional concepts and institutions. Consultation or political deliberation and community consensus have been reinterpreted to support parliamentary democracy, representative elections, and political parties. Thus, for example, the consultative assembly or group (majlis al-shura) that selected or elected a new caliph has been transformed and equated with a parliament or national assembly. As Muhammad Asad noted in *The Principles of State and Government in Islam* (1980):

The nineteenth and twentieth centuries have been a period of transformation, as shown by this Moroccan woman, who wears traditional dress as she exercises her right to vote.

> The legislative assembly—*majlis al-shura*—must be truly representative of the entire community, both men and women. Such a representative character can be achieved only through free and general elections; therefore the members of the majlis must be elected by means of the widest possible suffrage, including both men and women.

In Tunisia the group Hizb al-Nahda accepted the democratic process and sought to become a legalized political party. This commitment to pluralist politics reflected the thinking of its leader, Rashid al-Ghannoushi. He combined the criteria of Islam with that of democracy to critique the Tunisian government and to serve as a platform in Hizb al-Nahda's appeal for popular support. For al-Ghannoushi, democracy, popular sovereignty and the role of the state ("The state is not something from God but from the people . . . the state has to serve the benefit of the Muslims"), multiparty elections, and constitutional law are all part of a "new Islamic thinking" whose roots and legitimacy are found in a reinterpretation of Islamic sources. In affirming Hizb al-Nahda's commitment to the democratic process, al-Ghannoushi chided the West for not promoting its democratic ideals: "While the West criticizes Islamic governments for not being democratic, it also supports governments who are not democratic and are keeping Islamic movements from developing their ideas."

There are differences between Western notions of democracy and Islamic traditions. Although the great majority of Muslims today would subscribe to the idea that shura (consultative government) is central to the Islamic state, the proper relationship between popular and divine sovereignty is a subject of dispute. Most Muslims would accept that the divine will is supreme, and, in theory, that God's law is immutable and cannot be altered by human desire or whim. Yet, at the same time, by the insistence on the need of rulers to consult and to rule on the basis of consensus, Muslims effectively concede that some form of popular participation is required. Questions about the specific nature and degree of participation remain unanswered. While some Muslims debate what to call such a system, Muhammad Natsir, former Indonesian prime minister and one-time leader of the Islamically oriented Masjumi party, commented, "Islam is not one hundred percent democracy, neither is it one hundred percent autocracy. Islam is . . . Islam." In many places today political participation and democratization have become a litmus test by which both the openness of governments and the relevance of Islamic groups are certified. Although democracy is not entrenched in modern Islamic political thought and practice, it is a powerful symbol of legitimacy. It is used both to legitimate and to delegitimate precisely because it is seen to be a universal good.

A major hurdle facing Islamic movements today involves their willingness to tolerate diversity when in power. Some in the Muslim world and the West believe that Islamic movement participation in electoral politics is merely tactical and that once they are successful these Islamists would impose an intolerant, monolithic order on society. This issue was raised by the electoral victory of Algeria's FIS party. Despite the fact that its leader, Ali Abbasi al-Madani, affirmed his acceptance of democracy in the face of accusations that he had opposed the democratic process in the past, some of the FIS's more impatient voices—such as that of the popular preacher Ali Belhadj—unhesitatingly questioned whether democracy can be Islamic.

The record of Islamic experiments in Pakistan, Afghanistan, Iran, and Sudan raised serious issues about religious tolerance. In both Pakistan and Iran the belief that divine sovereignty naturally sets limits on the popular will has, in practice, led to a restriction on the rights of minorities and women. This is seen in the

Jamaat-i-Islami's traditional hostility toward the Ahmadiyyah (a nineteenth-century messianic movement that has been criticized by the Jamaat and others and declared a non-Muslim minority in Pakistan) and advocacy of the separation of the sexes. In Pakistan, Zia-ul-Haq distinguished between democracy, which was presumably Western and objectionable, and "shurocracy" (consultative government), which was Islamic and desirable. He used Islam to legitimate martial law and banned political parties as un-Islamic. In Iran the government proved intolerant of the religious movement Bahai and its other political opponents.

In Sudan the military governments of both Jafar al-Numayri and Omar al-Bashir, in association with the Muslim Brotherhood, exacerbated the civil war by being unresponsive to criticism from the predominantly non-Muslim southerners (Animists and Christians) that imposition of the shariah discriminates against them. These examples raise serious questions about the willingness of Islamically oriented governments to tolerate dissent and to respect the rights of women and minorities. At the same time, the role of the military in Algeria, the Tunisian government's suppression of its Islamic opposition, and Egypt's crackdown on the Muslim Brotherhood to "restore democracy" by denying Islamists that which they earned or proved capable of winning in electoral politics have been equally problematic. The result in Algeria was a civil war that claimed the lives of more than seventy-five thousand people. Tunisia crushed its Islamic opposition (Hizb al-Nahda) and President Hosni Mubarak of Egypt no longer clearly distinguished between violent

The twentieth century has been a period of major religious, political, and social transformation as Muslim governments have responded variously to calls for democratization. Pakistan has an elected government, housed in these buildings in Islamabad.

underground movements like the Gamaa Islamiyya and Islamic Jihad and the Muslim Brotherhood, which functioned nonviolently within society. All took control of the electoral system, banned or marginalized their Islamic opposition and indeed any significant opposition, and rigged or manipulated elections. For example, in 1993 President Ben Ali of Tunisia won reelection by 99.91 percent of the vote, and President Mubarak of Egypt took 94 percent in the 1995 elections.

Issues and Prospects for the Future

Twentieth-century Muslim history reveals a period of major religious, political, and social transformation. Amid the diversity of events and issues, fundamental questions emerge regarding religious interpretations and the authority of the past. Among them are Whose Islam? and What Islam? Both questions occur at the juncture of tradition and modernity, for contemporary Muslim societies incorporate the simultaneous presence and interplay of past, present, and future.

"Whose Islam?" Historically, rulers (caliphs and sultans) were the protectors of Islam and the ulama; by self-definition, they were the guardians and interpreters of Islam. In the second half of the twentieth century, rulers as diverse as monarchs (King Fahd of Saudi Arabia and King Hassan of Morocco), military leaders (Muammar Qaddafi, Mohammad Zia-ul-Haq, Jafar al-Numayri, and Omar al-Bashir), ex-military leaders (Anwar Sadat), and religious leaders and students (the Ayatollah Khomeini and the Taliban) have overtly used Islam to enhance their legitimacy and to mobilize popular support.

The ulama have also played a significant role in the contemporary Muslim world. The Ayatollahs Khomeini, Shariatmadari, Mutahairi, and others of Iran, Abul-Qasem Khoi of Iraq, Imam Musa Sadr and Shaykh Fadlallah of Lebanon, Muhammad al-Ghazali and Yusuf Qardawi, and many popular preachers across the Muslim world have been significant clerical voices, from masters of theology and law to social and political activists. While some wish to continue that legacy in the twentieth century, however, many if not most reformers and activists have in fact been lay rather than clerical. The Islamic modernist movement and its legacy produced generations of reformers (lay and clerical) from Egypt to Indonesia: Jamal al-Din al-Afghani, Muhammad Iqbal, Sayyid Ahmad Khan, Chiragh Ali, Allal al-Fasi, Abd al-Hamid Ben Badis, Muhammad Natsir, Prof Hamka, Muhammad Asad, many of whom often found the ulama among their sharpest critics. The major founders of neorevivalist movements, from the pioneers (Hasan al-Banna, Mawlana Abul Ala Mawdudi, Sayyid Qutb) to present-day movements, are in large part non-ulama or what some might call the new ulama or intellectuals. Laity or non-ulama are the backbone of the second and third generation of Muslim intellectuals and activists across the Muslim world, among them: Sudan's Dr. Hasan Turabi and Sadiq al-Mahdi; Tunisia's Rashid al-Ghannoushi, Iran's Ali Shariati and Abdul Karim Sorush; Algeria's Dr. Ali Abbasi al-Madani; Pakistan's Professor Khurshid Ahmad; Turkey's Dr. Necmettin Erbakan; Jordan's Dr. Ishaq Farhan; Egypt's Dr. Hasan Hanafi, Kamal Aboul Magd, M. Selim al-Awa, and Fahmy Howeidy; Indonesia's Dr. Nurcholish Madjid, Abdurahman Wahid, and Dr. Deliar Noer; and Malaysia's Mohammad Kamal Hassan, Osman Bakar, and Anwar Ibrahim. They have also included women, such as Egypt's Zaynab al-Ghazali and Heba Raouf Ezzat, Pakistan's Maryam Jameelah and Riffat Hassan, Malaysia's Khalijah Mohd. Salleh, America's Amina Wadud, and others.

Both laity and the ulama write prolifically on Islamic doctrine, law, politics, science, and economics. Although there is notable cooperation among some of these activists, many continue to challenge the authority of the ulama as the sole of primary guardians of faith and belief. Emphasizing that there is no ordained clergy in Islam and that contemporary problems require a variety of experts and specialties (economics, medicine, science, and so on) that are beyond the ulama's more traditional areas of expertise, they affirm a more inclusive notion of the religious scholar or expert. As Hasan Turabi has commented: "[B]ecause all knowledge is divine and religious, a chemist, an engineer, an economist, a jurist are all ulama." Despite their common Islamic orientation, they display a diversity of intellectual positions and orientations.

The second question is *What Islam?* What interpretations of Islam? Islam, like all religious traditions, has been subject to multiple interpretations throughout history. Islamic tradition is the product of text and context, sacred scriptures (the Quran and Sunna of the Prophet) and sociohistorical contexts, divine revelation and human interpretation. The key issue is the relationship of tradition to modernity or postmodernity. Is the process of Islamization or re-Islamization to be based on a process of restoration or reformation, a reapplication of classical Islamic doctrine, or a reconstruction of Islamic thought that draws inspiration from the past but formulates new responses to the challenges and realities of a rapidly changing world? The issue is not change but rather how much change. How much change is necessary? How much is permissible? What is the Islamic rationale for change? Thus, for example, although Iran was often characterized as a fundamentalist state led by a medieval, anti-Western religious figure, its government and constitution incorporated many modern concepts and institutions—including that of a republic, elected parliament, president, and prime minister—which have no clear precedent in Islamic history.

There are four discernible orientations toward change: secular, conservative (or traditionalist), neorevivalist (or fundamentalist), and neomodernist. Secularists advocate the separation of religion and politics. While their critics sometimes characterize or dismiss them as nonbelievers who represent a small westernized elite sector of society, secularists counter that they are Muslims who believe that religion should be restricted to private or personal life (prayer, fasting, personal morality). They charge that those who mix religion and politics do so for political rather than religious ends.

The three religiously oriented positions, although differing in distinct ways, nevertheless overlap because they are orientations rather than fixed, mutually exclusive positions. While each orientation may advocate a return to Islam, they differ in their presuppositions, interpretations, and methods. The conservative or traditionalist position is that of the majority of mainstream ulama, who believe that Islam is expressed quite comprehensively and adequately in classical formulations of Islamic law and doctrine. Although change can and does occur, the orientation of conservatives to past practices severely limits substantive change. Conservatives are reluctant to distinguish between revealed, immutable principles and historically conditioned laws and institutions that were the product of human reason and experience. The hold of tradition is especially reflected in those who in principle are open to reinterpretation but reflexively cling to past practices when faced with specific changes. They see no need to go back to the Quran or Sunna to develop answers to new modern problems or questions. Nor are they interested in a broad-based reformulation or reinterpretation that alters or replaces traditional Islamic laws. Thus, conservatives emphasize the following of past traditions or practices and are wary of any innovation that they regard as "deviation" (bida), the Muslim equivalent to Christian heresy. When change does occur, it is gradual and by way of exception in areas clearly not covered by any legal precedents. Conservatives believe that it is not the law that must change but a society that has strayed from God's path. Thus, although many ulama acquiesced to state-imposed modern, Western-inspired legal systems, it was a temporary compromise rather than an internalized change.

In the 1980s and 1990s the climate and politics of Islamic revivalism led many ulama from Egypt and Iran, to Pakistan, Bangladesh, Afghanistan, Malaysia, and Indonesia, to challenge modern reforms and call for the imposition of traditional formulations of Islamic law. However, even in these cases, beneath the ostensible unity, there has been a diversity of opinion and practice reflecting different communities (Sunni and Shii), schools of Islamic law (Hanafi, Hanbali, Jafari, Maliki, and Shafii), and local customs on such issues as women's dress and education and sexual segregation. Thus, General Zia ul-Haq's call for reimplementation of Islamic law in Pakistan set off sharp differences and conflict between Sunni and Shiite and among competing schools of Sunni religious thought. Iran's mullahs, while abrogating the shah's reformist family protection act and advocating a return to Islamic law, also bitterly criticized Afghanistan's Taliban implementation of Islamic law.

Neorevivalists or Islamists, often popularly referred to as "fundamentalists," share much in common with conservatives or traditionalists. They too emphasize a return to Islam to bring about a new renaissance. Although they respect classical formulations of Islam, they are less wedded to them. Neorevivalists claim the right to go back to Islam's original sources, to reinterpret and reapply them to contemporary society. Like conservatives, they attribute the weakness of the Islamic world primarily to the westernization of Muslim societies, the penetration of its foreign, "un-Islamic" ideas, values, and practices. In contrast to conservatives, however, they are much more flexible in their ability to adapt to change. At the same time, neorevivalists have taken issue with the Islamic modernism of Muhammad Abduh and Muhammad Iqbal, which they believe succumbed to the West and produced a westernized Islam, in their insistence that Islam is fully capable in and of itself to be the sole basis for a Muslim renaissance. Neorevivalists have produced a host of Islamic political and social movements and organizations that protest and challenge the political and religious establishments in the Muslim world, and they are often sharply critical of the West. The leadership cadre is often lay rather than clerical, graduates and professionals trained in the modern sector rather than in seminaries. They are thus more likely to be educators, journalists, scientists, physicians, lawyers, or engineers than ulama.

The earlier division of elites in many Muslim societies into modern secular or traditional (the ulama)—based on the bifurcation of education in modern, Western-oriented schools and in traditional Islamic or religious schools—is complemented today by a highly educated but more Islamically oriented sector of society, an alternative elite. The contemporary revival has also produced a new generation of Islamic reformers: neomodernists, who seek to bridge the gap between the traditionally and the secularly educated. They too are activists who look to the early Islamic period as embodying the normative ideal. Although they overlap with neorevivalists or Islamists, with whom they are often grouped, neomodernists are more flexible and creative in their thought. After an early traditional education, many obtain degrees from Western-oriented national universities or at major universities in the West. They emphasize the importance of "Islamic modernization and development." This new sector has produced a diverse group of leaders and intellectuals.

Islamic neomodernists do not reject the West in its entirety; rather, they choose to be selective in approach. They wish to appropriate the best of science, technology, medicine, and intellectual thought but to resist acculturation or the assimilation of Western culture and mores, from secularism and radical individualism to the breakdown of the family and sexual permissiveness. The goal is thus to learn from the West but not to westernize Muslim society. The distinction is drawn between the rejection of change (modernization) and the uncritical, indiscriminate, blind imitation of the West.

Contemporary Islamic reformers or neomodernists also stress the need to renew Islam both at the individual and the community levels. They advocate a process of Islamization or re-Islamization that begins with the sacred sources of Islam, the Quran and Sunna of the Prophet, but that also embraces the best in other cultures. They see themselves as engaging in a dynamic process that is as old as Islam itself. Much as early Muslims interpreted and applied Islamic principles and values to their times and adopted and adapted political, legal, and economic practices from the cultures they had conquered, the neomodernist reformers wish to bring about a new Islamic renaissance (nahda) pursuing a similar selective, self-critical path. They distinguish between God's revelation and human interpretations, between that part of Islamic law which is eternal and that which is contingent and relative, between immutable principles and regulations that were human constructs conditioned by time and place. In contrast to neo-revivalists, neomodernists are more creative and wide-ranging in their reinterpretation of Islam and less tied to traditional interpretations of the ulama. For this reason, they are often accused of "deviationism" by the ulama, who charge that neomodernists lack the necessary training and credentials to interpret Islam.

Contemporary Muslim Societies: Old and New Realities

Islam in the twentieth century has been associated with reformation and revolution. Political and intellectual movements responded to the challenge of European colonialism, achieved independence, and established modern Muslim states and societies. In the last decades of the twentieth century, a second struggle emerged. This Islamic resurgence signals both the failures of Muslim societies and deep-seated, unresolved religio-cultural issues, as Muslims continue to struggle with the meaning and relevance of Islam in the world today. The issues have extended from textual criticism and interpretation of the Quran and Prophetic traditions to the role of religion in state and society. This resurgence has yielded a variety of questions, from the nature of the state and Islamic law to pluralism and the status and rights of women and minorities.

Although the Quran and Sunna of the Prophet Muhammad remain normative for most Muslims, questions of interpretation, authenticity, and application have become contentious items. Some Muslims see little need to substantially redefine past approaches and practices; others strike out into new territory. Some Muslim scholars distinguish the eternal, immutable principles and laws in the Quran from those prescriptions that are contingent responses to specific contexts. Other scholars distinguish between the Meccan and Medinan suras (chapters): the Meccan chapters are regarded as the earlier and more religiously binding texts; the Medinan are seen as primarily political, concerned with Muhammad's creation of the Medinan state and therefore not universally binding. Still other Muslim scholars have distinguished between the Quran's eternal principles and values, which are to be applied and reapplied to changing sociopolitical contexts, and past legislation that was primarily intended for specific historical periods.

Although the example of the Prophet Muhammad has always been normative in Islam, from earliest times Muslim scholars saw the need to critically examine and authenticate the enormous number of hadith (Prophetic traditions), to distinguish between authoritative texts and pious fabrications. In the twentieth century a sector of modern Western scholarship questioned the historicity and authenticity of the hadith, maintaining that the bulk of the Prophetic traditions were written much later. Most Muslim scholars and some Western (non-Muslim) scholars have taken exception with this sweeping position. Many ulama continue to unquestioningly accept the authoritative collections of the past; other Muslim scholars have in fact become more critical in their approaches and uses of hadith literature.

New approaches to the study and interpretation of Islam's sacred sources have been accompanied by similar debates over the nature of Islamic law, the shariah. As noted, many ulama continue to equate the shariah with its exposition in legal manuals developed by the early law schools. Other Muslims—from Islamic modernists such as Muhammad Abduh, Sayyid Ahmad Khan, and Muhammad Iqbal to Islamic revivalists and neomodernists—have distinguished between those laws based on clear texts of the Quran and hadith and those that are the product of human interpretation and application, the product of reason and custom. Some express this distinction as that between the eternal law of God (shariah) and its human interpretation and application (fiqh) by early jurists. The distinction is often articulated in terms of the classical division of law into a Muslim's duties or obligations to God (ibadat, worship) and his or her duties to others (muamalat, social obligations). The former (for example, the performance of the Five Pillars of Islam, the essential beliefs and practices) are seen as unchanging; the latter are contingent upon historical and social circumstances.

Contemporary Muslim discussion and debate over the role of Islam in state and society reflect a broad array of questions: Is there one classical model or many possible models for the relationship of religion to political, social, and economic development? If a new Islamic synthesis is to be achieved that provides continuity with past tradition, how will this be accomplished, imposed from above by rulers and the ulama or legislated from below through a representative electoral process?

Legal reform remains a contested issue in many Muslim communities. Many emerging Muslim states followed a pattern of implementing Western-inspired legal codes. The process of legal change did not reflect widespread social change so much as the desires of a small secular-oriented sector of the population. Governments imposed reforms from above through legislation. The process, contradictions, and tensions inherent in modernization programs in most Muslim societies were starkly reflected in family law (marriage, divorce, and inheritance) reforms. Family law, which is regarded as the heart of the shariah and the basis for a strong, Islamically oriented family structure and society, was the last area of law to be touched by reformers. Even then, unlike most areas of law that implemented Western-inspired legal systems and codes, Muslim family law was not displaced or replaced but instead subjected to selective reform. Officials often employed an Islamic modernist rationale, in an ad hoc and haphazard manner, to provide an Islamic facade and legitimacy.

Family law ordinances were drawn up and implemented by the state, not by the ulama, pitting religious leaders against both secular and Islamic modernists. The ulama tended to object to any tampering with Islamic law, maintaining that (1) they and they alone were the qualified experts in Islamic doctrine and law; (2) the law was sacred and unchangeable; and (3) modernists were unduly influenced by the West and thus family law reforms were simply an illegitimate attempt to "westernize" God's law. However, the government imposed reforms that were ultimately accepted, albeit reluctantly. Modernizing elites accommodated the force of tradition in their unwillingness to directly challenge or invalidate classical Islamic law. Thus, violation of the law did not render an act invalid, only illegal. Moreover, punishments in the form of fines and imprisonment for men who ignored reforms that limited their right to polygamous marriages or to divorce were often minimal. The contemporary resurgence of Islam triggered the ulama's reassertion of the authority of the past, as they called for a return to the shariah and sought to repeal family law reforms and reassert classical, medieval formulations of Muslim family law.

In more recent decades, the debate over whether the shariah should be part of or the basis of a country's legal system has become a sensitive, and at times contentious, issue. If it should be, to what degree? Does Islamization of law mean the wholesale reintroduction of classical law, the development of new laws derived from the Quran and Sunna of the Prophet, or simply the acceptance of any law that is not contrary to Islam? Who is to oversee this process: rulers, the ulama, parliaments? As Iran, Sudan, Afghanistan, Pakistan, and Saudi Arabia demonstrate, the implementation of shariah has not followed a fixed pattern or set interpretation even among those dubbed conservative or fundamentalist. For example, women in Saudi Arabia and Afghanistan under the Taliban cannot vote or hold public office. In Pakistan and Iran, despite other strictures and problems, women vote, hold political office in parliaments and cabinets, teach in universities, and hold responsible professional positions. However, Islamization of law has underscored several areas that have proved particularly problematic: the *hudud* (punishments as prescribed by the Quran and hadith for certain crimes, such as alcohol consumption, theft, fornication, adultery, and false witness) and the status of non-Muslims (*dhimmi*), minorities, and women. All involve the question of change in Islamic law.

Although many traditionalists and neorevivalists or fundamentalists call for the reimplementation of the hudud punishments, other Muslims argue that they are no longer appropriate. Among those who advocate imposition of the hudud (for example, amputation for theft or stoning for adultery), some call for its immediate introduction and others argue that such punishments are contingent upon the creation of a just society in which people are not driven to steal in order to survive. Some critics charge that although appropriate relative to the time period in which they were introduced, hudud punishments are unnecessarily harsh in a modern context. Although many Muslim rulers and governments try to avoid directly addressing the issue of the hudud, Prime Minister Mahathir Mohamad of Malaysia, advocate of a modernized Malaysia with a moderate, tolerant Islam, directly criticized the conservatism of his country's ulama, their legal opinions (*fatwas*), and religious courts. In addition, he refused to allow the Malaysian state of Kelantan, the only state controlled by PAS (the Islamic Party of Malaysia), an Islamic opposition political party, to implement the hudud.

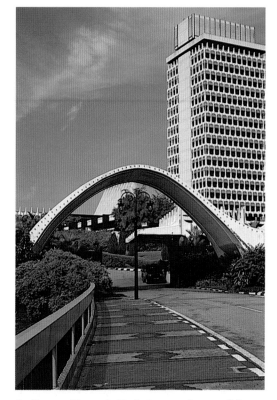

Parliament House in Kuala Lumpur is one of the government buildings in the constitutional monarchy of Malaysia. Prime Minister Dr. Mahathir Mohamad and former Deputy Prime Minister Anwar Ibrahim have advocated a modernized state with a moderate, tolerant Islam.

The reintroduction of Islamic law has often had a particularly pronounced negative impact on the status and role of women and minorities, raising serious questions about whether it constitutes a setback in the gains made in many societies. During the postindependence period, significant changes occurred in many countries, broadening the educational and employment opportunities and enhancing the legal rights of Muslim women. Women became more visible in the professions (as teachers, lawyers, engineers, physicians) and in government. Admittedly, these changes affected only a small proportion of the population and varied from one country or region to another, influenced by religious and local traditions, economic and educational development, and government leadership. The contrasts could be seen from Egypt and Malaysia to Saudi Arabia and Iran.

One result of contemporary Islamic revivalism has been a reexamination of the role of women in Islam, and at times a bitter debate over their role in society. More conservative religious voices among the ulama and Islamists have advocated a return to veiling and sexual segregation as well as restricting women's education and employment. Muslim women are regarded as culture bearers, teachers of family faith and values, whose primary roles as wives and mothers limit or exclude participation in public life. The imposition of reputed Islamic laws by some governments and the policies of some Islamist movements reinforced fears of a retreat to the past: in Afghanistan, the Taliban enforcement of veiling, closure of women's schools, restriction of women in the workplace; in Pakistan, General Zia ul-Haq's reintroduction of the hudud punishments and a law that counted women's testimony as half that of men's; greater restrictions on women in the Islamic Republics of Iran and Sudan; the murderous brutality of Algeria's Armed Islamic Group toward unveiled or more westernized professional women. In fact, the picture is far more complex and diverse, revealing both old and new patterns.

Muslim women in the twentieth century had two clear choices or models before them: the modern westernized lifestyle common among an elite minority of women or the more restrictive traditional "Islamic" lifestyle of the majority of women, who lived much the same as previous generations. The social impact of the Islamic revival, however, produced a third alternative that is both modern and firmly rooted in Islamic faith, identity, and values. Muslim women, modernists, and Islamists have argued on Islamic grounds for an expanded role for women in Muslim societies. Distinguishing between Islam and patriarchy, between revelation and its interpretation by the (male) ulama in patriarchal settings, Muslim women have reasserted their right to be primary participants in redefining their identity and role in society. In many instances, this change has been symbolized by a return to the wearing of Islamic dress. This has not simply meant a wholesale return to traditional Islamic forms of dress, however. For

Women are active participants in modern Islamic society. Many have not returned to wearing traditional dress, but have adopted new forms that are both modest and stylish, like the one displayed by these mannequins in a shop in Cairo.

some it is the donning of a head scarf (*hijab*); others from Cairo to Kuala Lumpur have adopted new forms of Islamic dress, modest but stylish, worn by students and professionals. Initially prominent primarily among urban middle-class women, this new mode of dress has become more common among a broader sector of society. For many it is an attempt to combine religious belief and values with contemporary levels of education and employment, to subordinate a much-desired process of social change to indigenous, Islamic values and ideals. The goal is a more authentic rather than simply westernized modernization.

Islamic dress has the practical advantage of enabling some women to assert their modesty and dignity while functioning in public life in societies in which Western dress often symbolizes a more permissive lifestyle. It creates a protected, private space of respectability in crowded urban environments. For some it is a sign of feminism that rejects what they regard as the tendency of women in many Muslim societies to go from being defined as sexual objects in a male-dominated tradition to being exploited as sexual objects Western-style. Western feminism is often seen as a liberation that has resulted in a new form of bondage to dress, youthfulness and physical beauty, sexual permissiveness and exploitation, a society in which women's bodies are used to sell every form of merchandise from clothing to automobiles and cellular phones. Covering the body, it is argued, defines a woman and gender relations in society in terms of personality and talents rather than physical appearance.

Contemporary Muslim societies reflect both the old and the new realities. Traditional patterns remain strong and are indeed reasserted and defended by those who call for a more widespread return to traditional forms of Islamic dress and sexual segregation or seclusion (purdah) in public life. At the same time, however, Muslim women have also become catalysts for change, empowering themselves by entering the professions, running for elective office and serving in parliament (in countries as diverse as Egypt and Iran), becoming students and scholars of Islam, conducting their own women's study groups, and establishing women's professional organizations, journals, and magazines. Women's organizations from Egypt and Iran to Pakistan and Indonesia—such as Women Living Under Muslim Laws, based in Pakistan but international in membership, and Malaysia's Sisters in Islam—are active internationally in protecting and promoting the rights of Muslim women.

The simultaneous call for greater political participation and for more Islamically oriented societies has not only had a negative impact on non-Muslim communities, but it has also sparked a lively discussion and debate among Muslim intellectuals and religious leaders over the status of non-Muslims in an Islamic state. The traditional doctrine of non-Muslims as "protected people," enabling many to practice their faith and hold positions in society, was advanced relative to its times and to the then far more exclusive approach of Western Christendom. By modern standards of pluralism and equality of citizenship, however, it amounts to second-class status. More conservative Muslim voices continue to celebrate and defend this doctrine, while other Muslims from Egypt to Indonesia have advocated a redefinition of the status of non-Muslims, in terms of their right to full and equal citizenship, which would enable an egalitarian and pluralist society of Muslims and non-Muslims. This is reflected in debates in Egypt over whether the Copts can serve in the army or should have to pay a special tax and similar discussions about issues of religious and political pluralism in countries such as Lebanon, Pakistan, Malaysia, and Indonesia.

Ironically, questions of citizenship and the exercise of political rights have become increasingly significant for Muslim minority communities in the second half of the twentieth century. At no time in history have Muslim minorities been as numerous and widespread. Both the swelling numbers of Muslim refugees and the migration of many Muslims to Europe, Canada, South America, and the United States, where Islam is now the second or third largest religion, make the issue of minority rights and duties within the majority community an ever-greater concern for Islamic jurisprudence. Can Muslim minority communities accept full citizenship and participate fully politically and socially within non-Muslim majority communities that are not governed by Islamic law? What is the relationship of Islamic law to civil law? What is the relationship of culture to religion? Are Muslims who live in the United States American Muslims or Muslims in America? How does one distinguish between culture and religion, that is, between the essentials of Islam and its cultural (Egyptian, Pakistani, Sudanese, Indonesian) expressions?

The history of Islam in the contemporary world, as throughout much of history, continues to be one of dynamic change. Muslim societies have experienced the effects of rapid change, and with it the challenges in religious, political, and economic development. Muslims continue to grapple with the relationship of the present and future to the past. Like believers in their sister traditions, Judaism and Christianity, the critical question is the relationship of faith and tradition to change in a rapidly changing and pluralistic world. As Fazlur Rahman, a distinguished Muslim scholar, observed in *Islam and Modernity* (1982), Muslims need "some first-class minds who can interpret the old in terms of the new as regards substance and turn the new into the service of the old as regards ideals."

CHRONOLOGY

ca. 570 Birth of Prophet Muhammad

610 Muhammad receives call to Prophethood

613 Muhammad begins public preaching in Mecca; first emigration of Muslims to Abyssinia, although Muhammad remained in Mecca to continue preaching against polytheists

619 Deaths of Muhammad's wife, Khadijah, and uncle, Abu Talib, leaving Muhammad without a protector; Muhammad tries to leave Mecca

621 Muhammad's first contact with Medina

622 Migration (*hijra*) of early Muslims to Medina; Islam takes form of political state; first year of Islamic calendar.

624 Battle of Badr—Muslims outnumbered, but victorious; serves as symbol for Muslims of divine intervention and guidance

625 Battle of Uhud—Muhammad and Muslims attacked and defeated by Meccans

627 Battle of the Trench—Muhammad and Muslims victorious over Meccans and bedouin mercenaries; Muhammad consolidates leadership in Medina

628 Treaty of Hudaybiyah permits Muslims to make pilgrimage to Mecca

630 Muhammad occupies Mecca

632 Death of Muhammad; Abu Bakr becomes first Caliph

632–661 Reign of the Four Rightly Guided Caliphs—normative period for Sunni Islam

634 Death of Caliph Abu Bakr; Umar ibn al-Khattab becomes second Caliph

638 Muslims occupy Jerusalem

644 Caliph Umar ibn al-Khattab stabbed. Dies one week after appointing committee to select successor, setting precedent for orderly transfer of caliphate. Uthman ibn Affan becomes third Caliph; Quran is collected and put in final format during reign of Uthman

656 Caliph Uthman ibn Affan assassinated; Ali ibn Abi Talib becomes fourth Caliph

656–661 Aisha leads Muslim opposition forces again fourth Caliph, Ali. Ali victorious. First instance of Muslim caliph involved in military action against other Muslims

661 Caliph Ali ibn Abi Talib assassinated; Muawiya ibn Abi Sufyan founds Umayyad dynasty

661–750 Umayyad caliphate—Arab military aristocracy

670 Muslim conquest of northwest Africa

680–692 Second Muslim civil war—Husayn, son of Ali, leads rebellion against Umayyad Caliph Yazid and is martyred, creating paradigm of protest and suffering for Shiites

691 Dome of the Rock completed in Jerusalem by Caliph Abd al-Malik

705–715 Great Umayyad Mosque of Damascus built

711 Berber converts to Islam cross Straits of Gibraltar and enter southern Iberia, expanding Islam into Europe

732 Charles Martel defeats Muslims at Battle of Tours, France, halting expansion of Islam into Europe

744–750 Third Muslim civil war and defeat of Umayyads by Abbasids

750–850 Consolidation of Abbasid Muslim empire in Iraq, western Iran, Khurasan, Mesopotamia, Egypt, and Syria by caliphs al-Mahdi, Harun al-Rashid, and al-Mamun

750–1258 Abbasid caliphate—height of Islamic civilization, development of Islamic law, patronage of art and culture, booming trade, commerce, agriculture, and industry

756 Emirate of Córdoba founded by Umayyad prince Abd al-Rahman

762 Baghdad founded as Abbasid capital

765 Death of sixth Shiite Imam and founder of Jafari school of Islamic law, Jafar al-Sadiq; succession disputed, creating split between Sevener and Twelver Shiites

767 Death of Abu Hanifa, founder of Hanafi school of Islamic law, dominant in Ottoman and Mughal Empires

786–809 Harun al-Rashid caliph (legendary exploits recounted in *The Thousand and One Nights*), height of Abbasid caliphate

795 Death of Malik ibn Anas, founder of Maliki school of law, dominant in Islamic Africa

9th century–1962 Zaydi imams rule Yemen

801 Death of Rabiah al-Adawiyah, female Sufi mystic credited with fusing asceticism with love of God

819–1005 Samanid dynasty rules Khurasan and Transoxiana

820 Death of Muhammad al-Shafii, founder of Shafii school of Islamic law, dominant in Arabic-speaking areas of eastern Mediterranean

830 Caliph al-Mamum establishes "House of Wisdom" (Bayt al-Hikmah) in Baghdad, responsible for translating manuscripts from other languages and cultures into Arabic

833–945 Emergence of regional states within Abbasid territories (present-day Iraq, western Iran, Khurasan, Egypt, and Syria)

836 Abbasid capital transferred from Baghdad to Samarra

855 Death of Ahmad ibn Hanbal, founder of Hanbali school of Islamic law, dominant in Saudi Arabia and prominent among fundamentalist groups

867–1480 Saffarids rule Sistan

868–905 Tulunid dynasty in Egypt and Syria

874 Twelfth Imam goes into occultation; end of direct rule of Shiite Imams

929 Andalusian caliphate founded by Abd al-Rahman III

934–1062 Buyid dynasty rules in western Iran, Iraq, and Mesopotamia

935–969 Ikhshidid dynasty rules Egypt and Syria

969–1171 Fatimid dynasty rules North Africa, Egypt, and Syria

977–1186 Ghaznavids rule Khurasan, Afghanistan, and northern India

End of 10th century–1215 Ghurid dynasty

Early 11th century–1147 Almoravid dynasty in North Africa and Spain

1009 Fatimid Caliph al-Hakim orders destruction of Church of the Holy Sepulchre in Jerusalem

1030 Death of Sultan Mahmud of Ghazni

1031 End of Andalusian caliphate

1037 Death of philosopher Ibn Sina (Avicenna)

1038–1194 Seljuk dynasty rules Iraq and Persia

1041–1186 Seljuk sultans rule Kirman

1058–1111 Abu Hamid al-Ghazali, theologian, legal scholar, and mystic who integrated Sufism into mainstream Sunni thought

1071 Battle of Mankizert—Turkish nomads defeat Byzantine emperor and enter Anatolia

1071–1178 Danishmendids rule Central and eastern Asia

1071–1243 Seljuk dynasty rules in Anatolia

1078–1117 Seljuk dynasty rules Syria

1095 Pope Urban II calls for crusade against Islam at Council of Clermont

1099 Crusaders capture Jerusalem and establish Latin Kingdom

12th century Sufi orders begin to provide organizational framework for social movements

1130–1269 Almohad dynasty in North Africa and Spain

1143 First translation of Quran into Latin commissioned to Robert of Ketton by Peter the

Venerable, Abbot of Cluny

1169–1252 Ayyubid dynasty rules Egypt

1171 Saladin conquers Egypt, restoring Sunni rule

1187 Saladin defeats Franks at Battle of Hittin and recovers Jerusalem for Islam

1191 Construction of Quwwat al-Islam Mosque in Delhi

1198 Death of philosopher Ibn Rushd (Averröes)

1206–1370 Mongols rule Central Asia

1206–1555 Delhi sultans

1220–1260 Mongol invasions of Muslim territories

1225 Almohad rulers abandon Spain

1227–1363 Chaghatayids in Transoxiana, Semirechye, and eastern Turkey

1241 Death of Sultan Iltutmish

1250–1517 Mamluk dynasty in Egypt and Syria

1256–1336 Mongol Ilkhanids rule Persia

1256–1483 Qaramanids rule central Anatolia

1258 Mongols sack Baghdad

1260 Mamluks defeat Mongols at Ayn Jalut

1261–1517 Abbasid caliphate in Cairo

ca. 1280 Ertugrul begins Ottoman expansion

1281–1924 Ottoman Empire

1292 Marco Polo visits Acheh in northern Sumatra

1295–1304 Ghazan—first Mongol Khan to convert to Islam

1297 Death of al-Malik as-Salih in Samudra

1326 Ottomans take Bursa

1334 Death of first Safavid master, Safi al-Din Ishaq

1345 Ottomans cross Straits of Gallipoli; Ibn Battutah visits Sumatra

1351 Death of Sultan Muhammad ibn Tughluq

1370–1405 Conquests of Tamerlane

1389 Ottomans defeat Serbians at Battle of Kosovo

1394 Tamerlane builds shrine of Ahmad Yasavi at Turkestan City

1400 Founding of Melaka

1407–1506 Timurids rule Herat

1444 Last anti-Ottoman European crusade defeated at Varna

1453 Ottomans capture Constantinople

1478 Islamic conquest of Majapahit kingdom in Java

1488–1528 Rule of Sultan Mahmud Shah of Melaka

1491 Granada—last Muslim stronghold in Spain—falls to Christian rulers Ferdinand and Isabella

1500–1599 Shaybanids rule Samarqand

1501–1725 Safavid dynasty in Persia

1511 Portuguese capture Melaka; Mahmud Shah sets up new capital elsewhere in archipelago and vainly tries to recapture city until he dies

1511–1659 Saadian dynasty rules Morocco

1514 Ottomans defeat Safavids at Battle of Chaldiran

1517 Ottoman conquest of Egypt, Syria, Mecca, and Medina

1520 Ottomans capture Belgrade

1520–1566 Suleyman the Magnificent ruler, high point of Ottoman Empire

1520–1857 Mughal Empire in India

1524 Death of Shah Ismail of Safavid dynasty

1526 Battle of Panipat, beginning of Mughal rule

1526–1858 Mughal emperors rule South Asia

1529 Failed siege of Vienna by Ottomans

1534 Ottoman occupation of Baghdad

1535–1536 Death of Bihzad, master of Herat school of painting

1556–1605 Akbar rules India, high point of Mughal Empire

1564–1624 Shaykh Ahmad Sirhindi, advocate of Islamic state and society in India

1571 Battle of Lepanto—Europeans block Ottoman advance into Mediterranean

1574 Sinan builds Selimiya mosque in Edirne

1583 British negotiate first trade treaty with Ottoman Empire

1588–1629 Shah Abbas ruler of Persia, high point of Safavid Empire

1599–1785 Janids in Bukhara

1603–1629 Safavids build Maydan of Isfahan

1605 Death of Emperor Akbar

1606 Treaty of Zsitva Torok—Habsburgs recognize Ottoman rule in Romania, Transylvania, and Hungary

1613–1645 Rule of Sultan Agung in second Mataram dynasty

1631 Death of Mir Damad, founder of Iranian school of illuminationist philosophy

1631–present Filali (Alawi) dynasty in Morocco

1639 Treaty of Qasr Shirin—permanent borders of Iraq and Iran established

1643 Taj Mahal nearly completed

1658–1707 Aurangzeb rules Mughal Empire, implementing religious rule of *ulama* and Islamic basis for character of state and society

1696 Russia takes Azov in Crimea

18th century Rise of neo-Sufism and renewed interest in *hadith* scholarship as means for moral reconstruction of society; Akhbari vs. Usuli debate over proper source of guidance for Islamic community

1702–1762 Shah Wali Allah of Delhi, India, leader of Islamic revival in India

1703 Edirne Incident in Ottoman Empire—Shaykh al-Islam Feyzullah dominates government and grand viziers; high point of *ulama* influence over affairs of state; ousted by Janissaries and lower-level religious leaders and students

1707 Death of Emperor Aurangzeb

1722 Afghans seize Isfahan, bringing end to Safavid rule in Iran

1736–1795 Afsharids in Persia

1737–1815 Ahmad al-Tijani, founder of Tijaniyah Sufi order, major neo-Sufi order in Morocco, which inspired West and North African jihad and resistance movements

1745 Beginning of Wahhabi movement in Arabia

1747–1842 Durranis rule Afghanistan

1750–1794 Zands rule Persia

1754–1817 Uthman dan Fodio, leader of northern Nigerian reformist opposition to Hausa states

1757–1790 Sultan Muhammad ibn Abdallah ruler of Morocco; encourages revival of Islamic scholarship and study of *hadith*

1774 Treaty of Kuchuk Kaynarja—Russians take control of Black Sea from Ottomans

1779–1924 Qajars rule Persia

1785–1868 Mangits rule Central Asia

1785–present Naqshbandiyyah movement leads anti-Russian resistance in Caucasus

1786–1831 Sayyid Ahmad Barelwi, leader of jihad movement in India against Sikhs and British

1787–1859 Muhammad Ali ibn al-Sanusi of Libya, founder of Sanusiyyah tariqah and Islamic state

1789–1807 Sultan Selim III rules Ottoman Empire and tries to implement Tanzimat reforms; resisted due to westernization inherent in reforms

1792 Treaty of Jassy—Russians consolidate control of Georgia, Black Sea, and Romania; beginning of Ottoman reforms

1794–1864 Jihad state in area of present-day Mali and Senegal

1798 French occupation of Egypt under Napoleon; Muhammad Ali comes to power, initiating period of reform of political and economic structures along Western lines

19th century European imperial expansion in the Muslim world

1803–1837 Padri movement in Sumatra

1809–1903 Sokoto caliphate

1817–1898 Sir Sayyid Ahmad Khan, leader of Islamic modernist movement in India

1818–1845 Faraidi of Bengal opposes Hindus and British

1819–1973 Barakzais in Afghanistan

1822–1895 Ahmad Cevdet Pasha Shaykh al-Islam of Ottoman Empire formulates civil code combining Islamic legal principles with new legal ideas and influences Tanzimat

1825–1830 Dipanegara leads revolt in Java

1830 French invade Algeria; Abd al-Qadir, leader of

Qadiriyyah tariqah, leads resistance until 1847 and tries to establish Islamic state

1837 Death of Ahmad ibn Idris, founder of Idrisiyyah movement

1838–1897 Jamal al-Din al-Afghani, father of Islamic modernism

1848–1885 Muhammad Ahmad, Mahdi of Sudan and founder of Islamic state

1849–1905 Muhammad Abduh, Islamic modernist and reformist and cofounder of Salafiyyah movement in Egypt

1851–1914 Ismail Gasprinski, sponsor of schools combining Russian and Muslim education to achieve modernization

1856–1873 Yunnan leads rebellion against Chinese rule and tries to establish Muslim state

1862–1867 Jihad in Senegal led by Ma Ba against French

1865–1935 Rashid Ridda, cofounder of Salafiyyah movement in Egypt and Islamic modernist movement

1873–1908 Ulama-led resistance to Dutch occupation of Acheh

1875–1938 Muhammad Iqbal, Islamic modernist who developed ideology for foundation of Pakistan

1876 Deobandi school founded to combine *hadith* studies and Sufism

1876–1909 Sultan Abdulhamid II rules Ottoman Empire and pursues pan-Islamic ideal as caliph

1879–1882 Urabi revolt against European influence in Egypt, leading to British occupation and later rise of nationalism in Egypt

1891–1892 Tobacco Protest in Iran—*ulama* and merchants opposed to Shah's government granting tobacco concessions to Europeans; sets pattern of cooperation between two social classes later used during 1979 Iranian revolution

1897–1975 Elijah Muhammad, leader of Nation of Islam movement in United States

1898 Mahdist state of Sudan defeated by British; Rashid Ridda begins publishing *al-Manar* in Egypt—journal becomes leading publication for Islamic reformist ideas

1899–1920 Muhammad Abdallah Hasan leads resistance to British in Somalia

1905–1911 Constitutional revolt in Iran places limits on Shah's power; local religious leaders play key role in opposition to Shah

1908 Young Turk revolution in Ottoman Empire

1912 Muhammadiya founded in Southeast Asia to promote educational and social reform

1919–1924 End of Ottoman Empire following World War I and creation of Turkish Republic

1919–1925 Khilafat movement in India in support of caliphate

1924 Ottoman/Turkish caliphate and *shariah* court system abolished by Mustafa Kemal Ataturk

1925–1979 Pahlavi dynasty in Iran

1926 Islamic law replaced by Swiss- and Italian-based system in Turkey

1927 Tablighi Islam founded by Mawlana Muhammad Ilyas

1928 Muslim Brotherhood founded in Egypt by Hasan al-Banna; reference to Islam as religion of state eliminated in Turkey

1932 Kingdom of Saudi Arabia founded on basis of alliance between religion and politics with *sharia* as law

1933–1977 Ali Shariati, ideologue of Iranian revolution of 1979

1941 Jamaat-i Islami founded in India/Pakistan by Mawlana Abu al-Ala Mawdudi

1943 National Pact of Lebanon agreed upon, assuring dominance of Christian Arabs in political process based on numerical superiority in 1932 census; president of country to be Maronite Christian, prime minister Sunni Muslim, and speaker of chamber of deputies Shiite Muslim; other key government positions distributed proportionally along confessional lines

1947 Pakistan founded as state for Muslims of India

1948 State of Israel declared

1949 Religious education reintroduced in Turkish schools as elective course; Hasan al-Banna assassinated by Egyptian police

1950 Religious education mandatory in Turkish schools unless parents object

1951 Idris ibn al-Mahdi, grandson of Muhammad ibn Ali al-Sanusi, becomes king of newly created Libya, highlighting leadership and nationalistic roles of Sanusiyah tariqah

1952 Gamal Abd al-Nasser seizes power in Egypt under banner of pan-Arabism and Arab socialism, supported by shaykhs of al-Azhar

1954 Muslim Brotherhood founded in Sudan, advocating Islamic political and social order via adoption of Islamic constitution based on the Quran and introduction of Islamic law

1956 Pakistan adopts constitution declaring itself an Islamic Republic with a Muslim head of state and based upon Islamic principles; Islamic research center deemed necessary for reconstruction of Muslim society on Islamic basis

1965 Crackdown on Muslim Brotherhood in Egypt after Nasser accuses them of plotting to assassinate him

1966 Execution of Sayyid Qutb, prominent writer for Muslim Brotherhood who gave movement radical, militant tone, by Nasser in Egypt

1967 Arab-Israeli war—Arab forces routed by Israel, leading to Arab disillusionment with secular policies like nationalism and socialism and sparking Islamic revival

1969 Muammar Qaddafi seizes power in Libya, later implementing own version of Islamic state as "Third Universal Alternative"; Jafar al-Numayri seizes power in the Sudan; al-Aqsa Mosque in Jerusalem burned, leading King Faisal of Saudi Arabia to call for *jihad* against Israel and to organize an Islamic summit conference combining pan-Islamism with Arabism

1970 Organization of the Islamic Conference founded—first official pan-Islamic institution for cooperation among Islamic governments

1970–1971 East-West Pakistan civil war results in declaration of independent state of Bangladesh (formerly East Pakistan)

1971 ABIM (Malaysian League of Muslim Youth) founded in Malaysia as mission movement and political party, rejecting capitalism and socialism and promoting Islam as an alternative political and economic system

1972 National Salvation Party founded in Turkey by Necmettin Erbakan; goal is Islamic state and Islamization of Turkish life

1973 "Operation Badr"—second Arab-Israeli war, with Egypt recovering some of territory lost to Israel in 1967 war; Arab oil embargo against West shows Arabs to be world economic power

1974 Musa al-Sadr founds Movement of the Disinherited, a populist movement for social and political reform in Lebanon favoring redistribution of power and resources to include Shiite majority otherwise excluded; militant wing develops into AMAL.

1975 Outbreak of civil war in Lebanon, resulting in radicalization of Shiite population; Muammar Qaddafi of Libya publishes *The Green Book*, outlining his interpretation of Islam and the world

1977 Zulfikar Ali Bhutto's government in Pakistan ousted by General Zia ul-Haq, who introduces Islamization

1978 Disappearance of Musa al-Sadr during trip to Libya, giving him popular "hidden imam" status among Shiis of Lebanon; Israel invades Lebanon; Pakistan announces creation of *shariah* courts

1979 Iranian Revolution—Islamic Republic of Iran founded; American Embassy seized by militant supporters of Khomeini protesting U.S. ties to shah; seizure of Grand Mosque of Mecca by militants led by Mahdi in Saudi Arabia; Shiite riots in Eastern Province of Saudi Arabia, calling for fairer distribution of oil wealth and services; liberation of Afghanistan from occupation by Soviet Union, largely due to efforts of *mujahidin*

1980 Hizbollah founded in Lebanon; Islamic Jihad founded in Palestine by Muslim Brotherhood

1981 Anwar al-Sadat of Egypt assassinated by militant Tanzim al-Jihad; Habib Bourguiba of Tunisia cracks down on Tunisia's Islamic Trend Movement

1982 Hafiz al-Asad of Syria levels city of Hama to put down opposition movement led by Muslim Brotherhood; Israel invades Lebanon for second time; massacre of inhabitants of Sabra and Shatilla in Lebanon

1983 September Laws implemented in Sudan, reintroducing Islamic laws and military courts; commission established by Gulf states to study and develop unified code of *shariah* law

1987 Crackdown on Tunisia's Islamic Trend movement by Habib Bourguiba government; *intifada* declared in Palestine; HAMAS founded in response to *intifada*

1988 Benazir Bhutto elected prime minister of Pakistan, first elected female head of state in Muslim world; end of Iran-Iraq War; MTI (Mouvement de la Tendance Islamique) becomes Tunisia's leading opposition group, performing impressively in national elections

1989 Death of Ayatollah Ruhollah Khomeini, first ruler of Islamic Republic of Iran and author of doctrine of *vilayat-i faqih*; Hashemi Rafsanjani elected president of Iran; Ayatollah Sayyed Ali Khamenei becomes *faqih*; Omar Hassan al-Bashir seizes power in Sudan—tied to National Islamic Front; FIS (Islamic Salvation Front) in Algeria sweeps municipal elections; Tunisia refuses to allow Renaissance party (formerly MTI, or Mouvement de la Tendance Islamique) to participate in elections in order to keep religion and politics separate

1990–1991 Persian Gulf War results from Iraq's invasion of Kuwait

1990 Islamists win 32 out of 80 seats in Jordanian Parliament and member of Muslim Brotherhood is elected speaker of national parliament; FIS (Islamic Salvation Front) wins municipal and regional elections in Algeria, coming to power through democratic process, rather than revolution

1991 FIS (Islamic Salvation Front) wins parliamentary elections in Algeria

1992 Iranian elections place conservatives in control of parliament, marginalizing hard-liners and paving way for limited liberalization of political participation and dissent; all mosques in Egypt placed under government control; military prevents FIS (Islamic Salvation Front) from coming to power in Algeria, cancelling results of democratic parliamentary elections; Algerian government crackdown on FIS, leading to civil war which has claimed over 100,000 lives

1993 Bombing of World Trade Center in New York City, tied to Shaykh Umar Abd al-Rahman

1994 Baruch Goldstein (Jewish settler) kills 29 worshipers at Mosque of the Patriarch in Hebron, provoking suicide bombings by Qassam Brigade (military wing of HAMAS); Taliban, composed of religious leaders and students, appears in Afghanistan, claiming mantle of moral leadership and ending civil war; Refah (Welfare) party wins mayoral elections in more than a dozen major cities in Turkey, including Ankara and Istanul

1995 Refah (Welfare) Party wins enough seats in National Assembly to make its leader, Necmettin Erbakan, Turkey's first Islamist prime minister

1995 Dayton Peace Agreement for resolution of the Bosnian conflict

1997 Mohammad Khatami elected president of Iran, opening door to United States for cultural, scholarly, and economic exchanges; Algeria resumed parliamentary elections, although FIS (Islamic Salvation Front) barred from participating; alternative Islamic movement MSP (Movement of Society for Peace) wins second highest number of votes

1998 Refah party declared unconstitutional and banned from political activity and assets seized by state; deputy prime minister and leader of ABIM, Anwar Ibrahim, removed from power in Malaysia

1998 Increasing violence in Kosovo leads to international sanctions against the Yugoslavian (Serbian) government

SELECT BIBLIOGRAPHY

CHAPTER ONE

For a deft survey of the Near Eastern background against which Islam emerged, consult Peter Brown's *The World of Late Antiquity* (London: Harcourt, Brace, Jovanovich, 1971). A sensible treatment of the life of the Prophet Muhammad, which manages to avoid the extremes of either undue skepticism or credulous apologetic that mar many works, is F. E. Peters' *Muhammad and the Origins of Islam* (Albany, N.Y.: SUNY Press, 1994). The best recent survey of early Islamic history in the *mashriq* is found in Hugh Kennedy's *The Prophet and the Age of the Caliphates: The Islamic Near East from the Sixth to the Eleventh Centuries* (London: Routledge, 1986). For the Islamic West, see Jamil M. Abun-Nasr's *A History of the Maghrib in the Islamic Period* (Cambridge: Cambridge University Press, 1987) on North Africa. On Spain, see tzhe many valuable essays in Salma Khadra Jayyusi, ed., *The Legacy of Muslim Spain* (Leiden, Netherlands: E. J. Brill, 1992). A concise review of developments in Iran from the eleventh to the thirteenth centuries is found in the relevant chapters of David Morgan's *Medieval Persia, 1040–1797* (London: Routledge, 1988); a much fuller treatment is provided by two rich volumes of the *Cambridge History of Iran*: volume 4, *From the Arab Invasion to the Saljuqs*, and volume 5, *The Saljuq and Mongol Periods* (Cambridge: Cambridge University Press, 1975 and 1968, respectively).

A readable overview of the early spread of Islam in Anatolia, associated with the arrival of the Turks, is Claude Cahen's *Pre-Ottoman Turkey* (New York: Taplinger, 1968). The more ambitious reader may look to Marshall G. S. Hodgson's magisterial *The Venture of Islam*, 3 vols. (Chicago: University of Chicago Press, 1973); although it is not always easy to read, this work remains the most intellectually stimulating synthesis of the entirety of Muslim history and civilization, and it is especially strong on the periods covered in this chapter. An interesting recent interpretation of the development of Islamic culture is found in Richard Bulliet's *Islam: The View from the Edge* (New York: Columbia University Press, 1994). For readers who have difficulty grasping the realities of remote periods of history, because they have little sense of what life in premodern times was actually like, Patricia Crone's *Pre-Industrial Societies* (Oxford: Basil Blackwell, 1989) is highly recommended.

CHAPTER TWO

Books have a habit of going out of print with alarming frequency in the field of Islamic studies. What follows is a short list of works that might help the reader who is interested in the issue of Islamic faith and practice and its relevance to the fields of law and ethics. Works quoted in this chapter are also listed below.

Muhammad Abul Quasem's *The Ethics of al-Ghazali: A Composite Ethics in Islam* (Delmar, New York: Caravan Books, 1978) is the best source of information on al-Ghazali's ethical theories. Although this book is out of print, it can be found in major university and public libraries. Chapter three of Vincent J. Cornell's *Realm of the Saint: Power and Authority in Moroccan Sufism* (Austin, Texas: University of Texas Press, 1998) is the sole source of information on Abu-l-Abbas al-Sabti and his teachings in the English language. Charles Le Gai Eaton's *Islam and the Destiny of Man* (Cambridge: Islamic Texts Society, 1994) is one of the best introductions to Islam for the general reader, especially with regard to the relationship between faith and practice. Although Majid Fakhry's *Ethical Theories in Islam* (Leiden and New York: E. J. Brill, 1991) focuses mostly on philosophical ethics, its chapter on scriptural morality contains useful information on ethical principles in the Quran and the hadith. Richard M. Frank's "Knowledge and *Taqlid*: The Foundations of Religious Belief in Classical Asharism," *Journal of the American Oriental Society* 109:1 (January–March 1989), 37–62, provides the classical Islamic justification for many of the theological assertions mentioned above. Although Toshihiko Izutsu's *Ethico-Religious Concepts in the Quran* (Montreal: McGill University Press, 1966) is now out of print, it should be sought in major university and public libraries as the best source of information on Quranic ethics. *God and Man in the Koran: Semantics of the Koranic Weltanschauung* (New York: Arno Press, 1980) is another classic work by Izutsu. It is especially valuable for its chapter on the ethical relationship between God and man in Islam and its discussion of the term *islam* and the concept of religion. Sayyid Qutb's *In the Shade of the Quran*, trans. M. Adil Salahi and Ashur A. Shamis (London: MWH Publishers, 1979), is the English translation of the thirtieth part of Qutb's *Fi Zilal al-Quran*, which was published after the author's death in 1966. Abu Bakr Siraj ad-Din's *Book of Certainty* (Cambridge:

Islamic Texts Society, 1992) is one of the best discussions in any language of the Quranic concepts of the "knowledge of certainty," the "eye of certainty," and the "truth of certainty." Finally, Frithjof Schuon's *Understanding Islam* (Bloomington, Indiana: World Wisdom Books, 1994), the English translation of *Comprendre L'Islam* (Paris, 1976), provides one of the best overall comparisons of the Quranic worldview with that of Catholic Christianity. This highly intellectual introduction to Islam is not suitable for every reader, however.

Copyrights in Arabic publishing are often loosely enforced. In addition, classic works of Islamic scholarship may be reprinted (often from the same original) in more than one country as a service to the Muslim community. For reasons such as these, editions of the Quran and prophetic hadith are usually cited generically in bibliographies, leaving out the mention of publisher and date. For example, the version of Muslim ibn al-Hajjaj al-Nisaburi's *Sahih Muslim* used for this chapter (the source of the Hadith of Gabriel discussed in this chapter) was copied from an unspecified original and published at an unspecified date in Beirut by Dar al-Kutub al-Arabiyya. Appended to the text is a commentary on *Sahih Muslim* by the famous Shafiite jurist Abu Zakariya al-Nawawi (1233–77). Such commentaries are often useful for determining the majority interpretation of a normative text. The other Arabic works cited in this chapter were published with full attention to copyright regulations. Abu Muhammad ibn Abi Zayd al-Qayrawani's *Matn al-Risalah* [text of the treatise] (Rabat, Morocco: Ministry of Endowed Properties and Islamic Affairs, 1984) was written by al-Qayrawani when he was only seventeen years old. Composed as a response to an earlier Shiite creed, it is the mostly widely known Sunni creed in North and West Africa. Quotations from Abu-l-Abbas al-Sabti came from Yusuf ibn al-Zayyat al-Tadili's *al-Tashawwuf ila rijal al-tasawwuf wa akhbar Abi-l-Abbas al-Sabti* [Insight into the men of Sufism and information on Abu-l-Abbas al-Sabti], ed. Ahmed Toufiq (Rabat, Morocco: College of Letters, Mohammed V University, 1984). This work, first published in the early thirteenth century, is one of the oldest sources on the founders of the Moroccan Sufi tradition.

CHAPTER THREE

A useful bibliography of English and Arabic works on Islamic law can be found in Mohammad Hashim Kamali's *Principles of Islamic Jurisprudence*, 2nd ed. (Cambridge: Islamic Texts Society, 1991). This book also provides an extensive treatment of the sources of Islamic law and legal theory. The third revised

and enhanced edition of this work is forthcoming from the Islamic Texts Society. Subhi Mahmassani's *Falsafat al-Tashri: The Philosophy of Jurisprudence in Islam*, trans. Farhat Ziadeh (Leiden, Netherlands: E. J. Brill, 1961), provides concise and reliable information on the sources, schools, and legal maxims of Islamic law and draws interesting comparisons with Roman law. This book also provides a useful bibliography of Arabic works on the subject. Noel J. Coulson's *Islamic Surveys: A History of Islamic Law* (Edinburgh, Scotland: Edinburgh University Press, 1964) and Joseph Schacht's *An Introduction to Islamic Law* (Oxford: Clarendon Press, 1964) provide useful information on the history of Islamic law and leading schools and jurists. Schacht's book also contains brief chapters on family law, inheritance, penal law, and contracts. Noel J. Coulson's *Succession in the Muslim Family* (Cambridge: Cambridge University Press, 1971) provides a detailed treatment of both the Sunni and Shiite laws of inheritance. Reliable information on the sources and various branches of Islamic law can be found in Abdur Rahim's *Principles of Muhammadan Jurisprudence* (London: Luzac & Co., 1911).

Ahmad Von Denffer's *Ulum al-Qur'an: Introduction to the Sciences of the Qur'an* (Leicester, England: Islamic Foundation, 1983) offers general but concise information on the Quran. Said Ramadan's *Islamic Law: Its Scope and Equity*, 2nd ed. (n.p., 1970) is lucid on the sources of law and *ijtihad* and has useful information on such subjects as nationality and citizenship. Another reliable work on these and such other themes as war, peace, and international law is Muhammad Hamidullah's *Muslim Conduct of State*, 2nd ed. (Lahore, Pakistan: Shah Muhammad Ashraf, 1953). Muhammad Iqbal's *Reconstruction of Religious Thought in Islam* (reprint, Lahore, Pakistan: Ashraf Printing Press, 1983) is a classic and provides concise information and thoughtful analysis on the salient aspects of Islam and the Shariah. Jamal J. Nasir's *The Islamic Law of Personal Status* (London: Graham & Trotman, 1986) is detailed and reliable on family law. There are several other good works on Islamic personal law, including Asaf A. Fyzee's *Outlines of Muhammadan Law*, 4th ed. (Delhi: Oxford University Press, 1974) and D. F. Mulla's *Principles of Mohomedan Law*, 16th ed. (Bombay, India: Tripathi Private Ltd., 1968). John L. Esposito's *Women in Muslim Family Law* (New York: Syracuse University Press, 1982) provides a lucid overview of modern reforms of Muslim family law in Egypt and Pakistan. A useful collection and extracts of the statutory laws of various Muslim countries, with special reference to modern reforms, can be found in Tahir Mahmood's *Family Law Reform in the Muslim World* (New Delhi: Indian Law Institute, 1972). Herbert J. Liebesny's *Law of the Near and Middle East*

(Albany: New York University Press, 1975) is also informative on the applied aspects of the Shariah. Norman J. Anderson's *Law Reform in the Muslim World* (London: Athlone Pess, 1976) provides background information on the modern reforms of the Shariah in various Muslim countries.

Mohammad Hahsim Kamali's *Freedom of Expression in Islam* (Kuala Lumpur, Malaysia: Berita, 1994; revised ed., Cambridge: Islamic Texts Society, 1997) is the only detailed presentation available in the English language of the freedom of expression from both the legal and moral perspectives of Islam. Kamali's article, "Siyasah Shariyyah or the Policies of Islamic Government," *American Journal of Islamic Social Sciences* 6 (1989): 39–81, is the only publication in English on the subject, although brief references to the subject can also be found in Anderson's *Law Reform*. Morteza Mulahhari's *Jurisprudence and Its Principles*, English trans., Mohammad Salman Tawheedi (Elmhurst, New York: Tahrike Tarsile Quran, Inc., 1982), provides concise information on Shii jurisprudence. Useful information on Shii legal thought and institutions can also be found in Hossein Moderressi Tabatabai's *An Introduction to Shii Law: A Bibliographical Study* (London: Ithaca Press, 1984).

Ibn Qayyim al-Jawziyya's *al-Turuq al-Hukmiyya fil-Siyasa al-Shariyya* (*Methods of Judgment in a Shariah-Oriented Policy*) (Cairo: al-Muassasa al-Arabiyya lil-Tabaa, 1961) is a work of authority on sentencing policy and methods of judgment, especially within the general framework of Siyasa shariah. Abu Ishaq Ibrahim al-Shatibi's *al-Muwafaqat fi usul al-Ahkam* (*Concordances in the Essentials of Shariah Rulings*), ed. Shaykh Abd Allah Diraz (Cairo: al-Maktaba al-Tijariyya al-Kubra, n.d.), is widely known for its pioneering contribution to the philosophy of Islamic law and marks a departure from the hallowed textualist reading of the sources of shariah that had hitherto dominated Islamic juristic thought. Muhammad Amin ibn Abidin, *Majmuah Rasail Ibn Abidin* [collection of treatises by Ibn Abidin] (Lahore, Pakistan: Suhayl Academy, 1979) is a reliable book (2 vols. in one) of Hanafi law on selected issues that stands out more for its lucidity rather than its original contribution. The contemporary Egyptian scholar Shaykh Yusuf al-Qaradawi's *Madkhal li-Darasat al-Shariah al-Islamiyya* (an entry to the study of shariah) (Cairo: Maktaba Wahba, 1990) provides a concise introduction to the shariah and contains many of the author's own responses to contemporary juristic issues. And lastly, the Ottoman Mejelle of 1876, which is a codified version, in about 1,850 articles, of the Hanafi law of civil transactions is a general work of reference that is widely accepted in the courts of shariah throughout the Muslim world. An English translation of this work is provided by C. R. Tyser, *The Mejelle: Being the English Translation of Majallah el-Ahkam el-Adliya* (Lahore, Pakistan: Law Publishing Co., 1967).

CHAPTER FOUR

The latest and most successful attempt to provide a comprehensive overview of Arabic science is Rashed Roshdi, ed., in collaboration with Régis Morelon, *Encyclopedia of the History of Arabic Science*, 3 vols. (London and New York: Routledge, 1996): *Astronomy: Theoretical and Applied*, vol. 1; *Mathematics and the Physical Sciences*, vol. 2; *Technology, Alchemy, and the Life Sciences*, vol. 3. Many of the topics discussed in this essay are treated at length in different chapters of this encyclopedia, especially in the contributions by Régis Morelon, George Saliba, and Roshdi Rashed. C.C. Gillispie, ed., *Dictionary of Scientific Biography*, 16 vols. (New York: Scribner, 1970–80), contains useful entries on several Arab scientists. For useful illustrations, see Seyyed Hossein Nasr, *Islamic Science: An Illustrated Study* (Westerham, England: World of Islam Festival Publishing Company Ltd., 1976); photographs by Roland Michaud.

On theoretical astronomy the closest work to a systematic overview of the reform tradition in Arabic astronomy is George Saliba, *A History of Arabic Astronomy: Planetary Theories during the Golden Age of Islam* (New York: New York University Press, 1994). Other collections of specialized studies with useful general overviews include E. S. Kennedy, "Colleagues and Former Students," in eds. David A. King and Mary Hellen Kennedy, *Studies in the Islamic Exact Sciences* (Beirut, Lebanon: American University of Beirut, 1983); and Julio Samso, *Islamic Astronomy and Medieval Spain* (Aldershot, England: Variorum Reprints, 1994). In addition, titles of editions, translations, and studies of important classics of Arabic astronomy can be found in the bibliography of Rashed, ed., *Encyclopedia of the History of Arabic Science* in entries under E. S. Kennedy, George Saliba, David King, Régis Morelon, and Jamil Ragep.

On practical astronomy Aydin Sayili, *The Observatory in Islam* (Ankara, Turkey: Turk Tarih Kurumu Basimevi, 1960), remains a classic. Several studies on instruments, timekeeping, and astronomical computations are conveniently collected in David King's *Astronomy in the Service of Islam* (Aldershot, England: Variorum Reprints, 1993); in King, *Islamic Mathematical Astronomy* (London: Variorum Reprints, 1986); and in King, *Islamic Mathematical Instruments* (London: Variorum Reprints, 1987).

In the past two decades the wide-ranging research of Roshdi Rashed has been instrumental in advancing scholars' understanding of the various disciplines of Arabic mathematics. Rashed has produced several critical editions, translations of, and commentaries on Arabic mathematical texts in the disciplines of algebra, geometry, arithmetic, numerical analysis, infinitesimal mathematics, and mathematical optics. An overview of some of his findings is available in Roshdi Rashed, *The Development of Arabic Mathematics: Between Arithmetic and Algebra*, trans. A.F.W. Armstrong. Boston Studies in the Philosophy of Science Series no. 156. (Dordrecht, Boston, London: Kluwer Academic Publishers, 1994).

On optics, see Ibn al-Haytham, *The Optics of Ibn al-Haytham: Books I–III on Direct Vision* 2 vols., trans. and comm. A. I. Sabra Studies of the Warburg Institute, 40/1–2 (London: Warburg Institute, University of London, 1989). See also the useful collection of articles in A. I. Sabra, *Optics, Astronomy, and Logic: Studies in Arabic Science and Philosophy* (Aldershot, England: Variorum Reprints, 1994). On technology, see Ahmad Y. al-Hasan and Donald Hill, *Islamic Technology: An Illustrated History* (Cambridge: Cambridge University Press, 1986).

On medicine and the life sciences, see M. Ullman, *Islamic Medicine*, Islamic Surveys no. 11. (Edinburgh, Scotland: Edinburgh University Press, 1978). Another useful overview is the introduction by Michael Dols to Adil S. Gamal, ed., and Michael Dols, trans., *Medieval Islamic Medicine: Ibn Ridwan's Treatise "On the Prevention of Bodily Ills in Egypt"* (Berkeley: University of California Press, 1984). A collection of several influential essays is Max Meyerhof, *Studies in Medieval Arabic Medicine: Theory and Practice* (London: Variorum Reprints, 1984). On Arabic pharmacology, see the works by Ibrahim ibn Murad, especially his *Buhuth fi Tarikh al-Tibb wal-Saydala ind al-Arab* [Studies on the history of Arabic medicine and pharmacology] (Beirut, Lebanon: Dar al-Gharb al-Islami, 1991). On hospitals in the Muslim world, the most comprehensive work to date remains Ahmad Isa, *Tarikh al-Bimaristanat fi al-Islam* (The history of hospitals in Islam), (Damascus, Syria: al-Matbaa al-Hashimiyya, 1939). For the quote from Ibn Khaldun, and also for an elaborate discussion of the classification of sciences see Ibn Khaldun, *The Muqaddimah* (Introduction [to the Science of History]), trans. F. Rosenthal, abridged N. J. Dawood, p. 371 and passim.

CHAPTER FIVE

Jonathan Bloom and Sheila Blair's *Islamic Arts* (London: Phaidon, 1997) is a readable one-volume introduction to the arts of the Islamic lands from their beginnings to the present. A more scholarly approach can be found in the two-volume set from the *Yale University Press Pelican History of Art*: Richard Ettinghausen and Oleg Grabar's *The Art and Architecture of Islam: 650–1250* and Sheila S. Blair and Jonathan M. Bloom, *The Art and Architecture of Islam:*

1250–1800 (New Haven: Yale University Press, 1994). The 34-volume *Dictionary of Art*, edited by Jane Turner (London: Macmillan, 1996) contains a long multipart article, "Islamic Art," in volume 16, as well as many entries on individual artists, dynasties, sites, techniques, styles, and so forth, all written by experts in the field and accompanied by complete bibliographies. A shorter overview, with particular emphasis on British collections, is Barbara Brend's *Islamic Art* (Cambridge, MA: Harvard University Press, 1991). Islamic architecture is treated exhaustively in Robert Hillenbrand's *Islamic Architecture: Form, Function and Meaning* (New York: Columbia University Press, 1994). Companion volumes, published as introductory works by Edinburgh University Press, are Sheila S. Blair's *Islamic Inscriptions* and Eva Baer's *Islamic Ornament* (both 1998). The classic formulation of the development of early Islamic art is Oleg Grabar's *The Formation of Islamic Art* (New Haven: Yale University Press, 1973). An ahistorical and idiosyncratic approach to Islamic art can be found in Seyyed Hossein Nasr's *Islamic Art and Spirituality* (Albany: State University of New York Press, 1987).

CHAPTER SIX

Charles Adams' *Islam and Modernism in Egypt* (London: Oxford University Press, 1933) is an authoritative account of modernism in Egypt. Henry Corbin's *History of Islamic Philosophy*, trans. Liadain Sherrard (London: Kegan Paul International, 1993) highlights the Shiite contribution to philosophy and contains a detailed bibliography. Majid Fakhry's *A History of Islamic Philosophy*, 2nd ed. (London and New York, Longmans and Columbia University Press, 1983) is the standard work on the subject in English. It has been translated into numerous languages. Also see Fakhry, trans., *The Quran* (Reading, Pa.: Garnet Publishing, 1997).

L. Gardet and M. M. Anawati's *Introduction a la theologie musulmane* (Paris: Vrin, 1948) is the major introduction to the rise and development of systematic theology in Islam. H.A.R. Gibb's *Modern Trends in Islam* (Chicago: University of Chicago Press, 1947) is a perceptive and authoritative account of Islamic theological and political developments in modern times. Ignaz Goldziher's *Introduction to Islamic Theology and Law*, trans. Andras and Ruth Hamori (Princeton, N.J.: Princeton University Press, 1981), originally written in German, continues to be one of the most perspicuous writings on Islamic theology. Malcolm H. Kerr's *Islamic Reform* (Berkeley: University of California Press, 1966) is a clear and thoughtful presentation of Islamic modernism and Muhammad Abduh's role in its development.

Arthur Jeffery's *Islam: Muhammad and His Religion* (New

York: Library of Liberal Arts, 1958) is a useful introduction by an eminent scholar. Jeffery's *A Reader on Islam* (The Hague, Netherlands: Mouton, 1962) is a representative collection of selections from important Islamic religious and theological texts. Wilfrid Cantwell Smith's *Islam in Modern History* (Princeton, N.J.: Princeton University Press, 1959) was reprinted many times and is particularly informative on Islam in India and Pakistan. A reliable English translation with introduction and notes is Simon Van den Bergh, trans., *The Incoherence of the Incoherence* (Tahafut al-Tahafut) (London: Oxford University Press, 1954). A. J. Wensinck's *The Muslim Creed* (Cambridge: Cambridge University Press, 1932) is still a valuable discussion of theological developments in Islam. A comprehensive and authoritative discussion of the development of Islamic philosophy is given in Harry Austyn Wolfson's *The Philosophy of Kalam* (Cambridge, Mass.: Harvard University Press, 1976).

Nasr, Seyyid Hossein, *Ideas and Realities of Islam* (Boston: B Beacon Press, 1964).

Rahman, Fazlur, *Islam and Modernity* (Chicago: Chicago University Press, 1982).

Watt, W. Montgomery, *The Formative Period of Islamic Thought* (Edinburgh: Edinburgh University Press).

Wolfson, Harry Austyn, *The Philosphy of the Kalam* (Cambridge, Mass.: Harvard University Press, 1976).

Hourani, Albert, *Arabic Thought in the Liberal Age* (London: Oxford University Press, 1962.)

CHAPTER SEVEN

Kenneth Cragg's *The Arab Christian: A History in the Middle East* (Louisville, Ky.: Westminster/John Knox Press, 1991) provides a study of Christianity in the Arab world from before the rise of Islam to the present. Norman Daniel's *Islam and the West: The Making of an Image* (Edinburgh, Scotland: Edinburgh University Press, 1960) is a detailed examination and analysis of medieval Christian understanding of and polemic against the religion of Islam, its Prophet, and practices. Francesco Gabrielli's *Arab Historians of the Crusades* (London: Routledge and Kegan Paul, Ltd., 1969) contains extracts from the writings of Muslim historians, chroniclers, and biographers that deal with battles between Christians and Muslims in the Crusades. Yvonne Y. Haddad and Wadi Z. Haddad, eds., *Christian-Muslim Encounters* (Gainesville: University Press of Florida, 1995) provides proceedings of a conference on relations between Muslims and Christians in historical and contemporary perspectives, including scripture, contacts, regional studies, and theological reflections. Marshall G. S. Hodgson's *The Venture of Islam*, 2 vols., *The Classical Age of Islam*, vol. 1, and *The Expansion*

of Islam in the Middle Periods (Chicago: University of Chicago Press, 1958–59) is a history of the rise, spread, and development of Islam, including its interaction with Christians and Christendom. Bernard Lewis' *Islam and the West* (New York: Oxford University Press, 1993) is a collection of essays by Lewis on the common heritage of Islam and the West and the perceptions of each party of the other. Amin Maalouf, trans., *The Crusade through Arab Eyes* (New York: Schocken Books, 1984) provides excerpts from the works of Arab chroniclers of the Crusades, including eyewitness accounts.

Jane Dammen McAuliffe's *Qur'anic Christians: An Analysis of Classical and Modern Exegesis* (Cambridge: Cambridge University Press, 1991) presents an examination of Quranic commentary concerning verses dealing with Christians and Christianity. Eugene A. Myers' *Arabic Thought and the Western World* (New York: Frederick Ungar, 1964) provides an introduction to the culture of Islam through which Greek science and philosophy reached the West. Jaroslav Pelikan's *The Spirit of Eastern Christendom* (600–1700), vol. 2 (Chicago: University of Chicago Press, 1974) presents an examination of the divisions between Eastern and Western Christendom, including the development of Greek, Syriac, and early Slavic doctrine. R. W. Southern's *Western Views of Islam in the Middle Ages* (Cambridge, Mass.: Harvard University Press, 1962) is a survey of medieval Christian responses to eight centuries of confrontation between Christian and Muslim cultures. J. Windrow Sweetman's *Islam and Christian Theology: A Study of the Interpretation of Theological Ideas in the Two Religions*, vol. 1. (London: Butterworth Press, 1955) is a study of the two religions. David J. Wasserstein's *The Caliphate in the West: An Islamic Political Institution in the Iberian Peninsula* (Oxford: Clarendon Press, 1993) is a study of the caliphate in Islamic Spain from its beginning in 929 to its demise in 1031.

CHAPTER EIGHT

Esin Atil, *Turkish Art* (Washington, D.C.: Smithsonian Institution Press, 1980) is a collective work with beautifully illustrated articles on the main forms of Ottoman art and architecture. Sheila Blair and Jonathan Bloom, *The Art and Architecture of Islam, 1250–1800* (New Haven, Conn.: Yale University Press, 1994) is the best single volume survey of Islamic arts for our period. Fernand Braudel's *The Mediterranean and the Mediterranean World*, 2 vols., tr. Sian Reynolds (New York: Harper and Row, 1972) is a classic study of the geography and culture, the societies and economies, and of the great Habsburg–Ottoman struggle for the control of the Mediterranean in the sixteenth century. Soraya

Faroqhi, *Towns and Townsmen of Ottoman Anatolia* (Cambridge: Cambridge University Press, 1984) exmines the Ottoman provinces and the changing balances of social and economic power between capital and small cities.

Neil Goffman, *Izmir and the Levantine World, 1550–1650* (Seattle, Wash.: University of Washington Press, 1990) studies the growing foreign trade of Izmir in the seventeenth century and the polyglot communities that assembled there. Godfrey Goodwin, *A History of Ottoman Architecture* (London: Thames and Hudson, 1971) is a comprehensive survey of the premier royal art. Andrew Hess, *The Forgotten Frontier: A History of the Sixteenth-Century Ibero-African Frontier* (Chicago, Ill.: University of Chicago Press, 1978) explores the culmination of the century-long struggle for the control of the Mediterranean with deep insights into the role of sea and land power in these wars.

Halil Inalcik's *The Ottoman Empire: The Classical Age, 1300–1600*, tr. N. Itzkowitz and C. Imber (London, 1973) is the classic work on Ottoman institutions. Halil Inalcik and Donald Quataert's *An Economic and Social History of the Ottoman Empire, 1300–1914* (Cambridge: Cambridge University Press, 1994) is a collective and authoritative appraisal of Ottoman economy and society. Houri Islamoglu-Inan's *State and Peasant in the Ottoman Empire* (Leiden, E. J. Brill, 1994) probes the Anatolian countryside to bring new insights into the structure and development of Ottoman rural economy and society. Cemal Kafadar's *Between Two Worlds: The Construction of the Ottoman State* (Berkeley, Cal.: University of California Press, 1995) explores the changing historiographical perspectives on the origins of the Ottoman system. Bernard Lewis's *Istanbul and the Civilization of the Ottoman Empire* (Norman, Okla.: University of Oklahoma Press, 1963) affords a convenient introduction to the largest city of the Mediterranean in the sixteenth and seventeenth centuries. Sayyid Husayn Nasr, "The School of Isfahan," *A History of Muslim Philosophy*, II, ed. M. M. Sharif (Wiesbaden, 1966, pp. 904–31) is a brief and insightful introduction to Iranian Illuminationist philosophy.

Leslie Peirce, *The Imperial Harem: Women and Sex in the Ottoman Empire* (New York, Oxford University Press, 1993), breaks new ground in her study of the role of women in the Ottoman family and political systems. Richard Repp, *Mufti of Istanbul: A Study in the Development of the Ottoman Learned Hierarchy* (London, Uthica Press, 1986), chronicles the emergence and development of the office of the Shaykh al-Islam or chief Mufti of the Ottoman Empire. Roger M. Savory, *Iran under the Safavids* (Cambridge: Cambridge University Press, 1980), is the best one-volume history of Safavid Iran. Stanford J. Shaw, *The Jews of the Ottoman Empire and the Turkish Republic* (New York: New York University Press, 1991), is a helpful single-volume history of the Jewish minority under Ottoman rule. Peter F. Sugar, *Southeastern Europe under Ottoman Rule, 1354–1804* (Seattle, Wash.: University of Washington Press, 1977), is critical to understanding the economic and social basis for the eventual emergence of nationalism and movements for independence in the Balkans.

Speros Vryonis, Jr., *The Decline of Medieval Hellenism in Asia Minor* (Berkeley, Cal.: University of California Press, 1971) is the best case study of the processes by which Christian populations were converted to Islam. Immanuel Wallerstein's *The Modern World System*, 3 vols. (San Diego, Cal.: Academic Press, 1974–89), is a grandly conceived comparative study of the development of the global economy and an important theory about historical process. Stuart Cary Welch, *A King's Book of Kings: The Shah-nameh of Shah Tahmasp* (London, 1972), is an elegant work on this most exquisite of Persian illustrated manuscripts.

CHAPTER NINE

For general texts see Joseph E. Schwartzberg's *A Historical Atlas of South Asia for South Asia* (Chicago: University of Chicago Press, 1978) and Robert L. Canfield, ed., *Turko-Persia in Historical Perspective* (Cambridge: Cambridge University Press, 1991). For texts on South Asia see Richard Eaton's "Remembering/Imagining Persia: Medieval Deccani Migrants and the Iranian Homeland," paper delivered at the Rockefeller Workshop 3 on "South Asian Islam and the Greater Muslim World" at North Carolina State University in Raleigh, N.C., from 22–25 May 1997. Simon Digby's "The Sufi Shaykh and the Sultan: A Conflict of Claims to Authority in Medieval India," *Iran* 28 (1990): 71–81, provides a major study of contested sources of authority in sultanate India. Milo C. Beach's *The Imperial Image: Paintings for the Mughal Court* (Washington, D.C.: Freer Gallery, 1981) examines the range of royal patronage for portrait art exalting the emperor during Mughal India. Milo C. Beach's *Mughal and Rajput Painting*, vol. 3. of *The New Cambridge History of India* (Cambridge: Cambridge University Press, 1992) compares the material evidence for assessing the achievements of Rajput artists and their sometime rival Mughal counterparts. Catherine B. Asher's *Architecture of Mughal India*, vol. 4 of *The New Cambridge History of India* (Cambridge: Cambridge University Press, 1992) is the first systematic overview of both the political and the cultural ideologies that inform Mughal patronage of monumental structures. John F. Richards' *The Mughal Empire*, vol. 5 of *The New Cambridge History of India* (Cambridge: Cambridge

University Press, 1993) provides a valuable synthesis of the varied, often conflicting scholarship on the major institutions of Mughal India.

For texts on Southeast Asia see Anthony H. Johns' "Islam in the Malay World," in eds. R. Israeli and A. H. Johns, *Southeast and East Asia*, vol. 2 of *Islam in Asia* (Jerusalem: The Magnes Press, 1984), 115–61. Ross E. Dunn's *The Adventures of Ibn Battuta* (Berkeley: University of California Press, 1989) is the premier translation of the most widely cited traveler in the premodern phase of Afro-Eurasian Islamicate history. M. B. Hooker, ed. *Islam in South-East Asia* (Leiden, Netherlands: E. J. Brill, 1983) includes essays by several contributors but those by Roy F. Ellen and A. Day are especially useful. Leonard Y. Andaya's *The World of Maluku: Eastern Indonesia in the Early Modern Period* (Honolulu: University of Hawaii Press, 1993) offers a comprehensive view of the formation of Indonesia on its furthest Pacific frontier. Barbara Watson Andaya and Leonard Y. Andaya's *A History of Malaysia* (London: Macmillan, 1982) is the best overview history of Indonesia's smaller but crucial northern neighbor. James Siegel's *Shadow and Sound: The Historical Thought of a Sumatran People* (Chicago: University of Chicago Press, 1979) traces both the transoceanic developments and the local patterns of influence that shaped current-day Sumatra.

CHAPTER TEN

Thomas Barfield's *The Perilous Frontier: Nomadic Empires and China* (Cambridge: Basil Blackwell, 1989) is a sweeping overview of China's four-thousand-year history of interactions between sedentary and nomadic empires, arguing that interactions were symbiotic and cyclical. Linda Benson's *The Ili Rebellion: The Moslem Challenge to Chinese Authority in Xinjiang, 1944–1949* (Armonk, N.Y.: M. E. Sharpe, 1990) is the definitive work describing the ill-fated Uighur-led rebellion that helped define the issues facing China as it sought to integrate the Xinjiang region into the People's Republic. Cyril E. Black, Louis Dupree, Elizabeth Endicott-West, Danile C. Matuszewski, Eden Naby, and Arthur N. Waldron's *The Modernization of Inner Asia* (Armonk, N.Y.: M. E. Sharpe, 1991) is a general overview of issues facing contemporary development in Central Asia, emphasizing political and cultural differences in the region and the international context. James P. Dorian, Brett H. Wigdortz, and Dru C. Gladney's, "Central Asia and Xinjiang, China: Emerging Energy, Economic, and Ethnic Relations," *Asia-Pacific Issues* 31 (May, 1–8) provides an up-to-date overview of the issues plaguing China and Central Asian relations today. James P. Dorian, Brett Wigdortz, and Dru Gladney's "Central Asian and Xinjiang, China: Emerging Energy, Economic, and Ethnic Relations," *Central Asian Survey* 16:4 (1997, 461–86), outlines recent trends in trade and political relations between China and Central Asia, with particular attention to the ways in which ethnic ties across the borders influence economic and energy trade. Robert Ekvall's *Fields on the Hoof: Nexus of Tibetan Nomadic Pastorialism* (New York: Holt, Rinehart, and Winston, 1968) is a classic text, written by a former medical missionary who lived for several years on the Gansu-Tibetan frontier, gives first-hand information on the transformation of Tibetan pastoralism in the face of expanding Chinese influence. Joseph Fletcher's *Studies on Chinese and Islamic Inner Asia*, ed. Beatrice Forbes Manz (Hampshire, England: Variorum Press, 1995) is an invaluable collection of the world's leading authority on China's historical relations and interactions with Islamic Central Asia.

Andrew D. W. Forbes' *Warlords and Muslims in Chinese Central Asia* (Cambridge: Cambridge University Press, 1986) is the definitive work on Xinjiang politics during the Republican period, 1910–40. Herbert Franke and Denis Twitchett's *Alien Regimes and Border States (907–1368)*, vol. 6 of *Cambridge History of China* (Cambridge: Cambridge University Press, 1994) is the most definitive collection of historical discussions of China's relations with its bordering peoples and states and its domination by many of them. Dru C. Gladney's *Muslim Chinese: Ethnic Nationalism in the People's Republic* (Cambridge, Mass.: Harvard University Press, 1996) is the leading work on contemporary Islam and ethnic problems facing contemporary China. Peter Hopkirk's *The Great Game: The Struggle for Empire in Central Asia* (New York and Tokyo: Kodansha International, 1994) is a popular survey of Chinese, Russian, and British rivalries as those powers attempted to divide up the region in the late nineteenth century. Jonathan N. Lipman's *Familiar Strangers: A History of Muslims in Northwest China* (Seattle: University of Washington Press, 1998) is an overview of more modern developments. Morris Rossabi's *China and Inner Asia from 1368 to the Present Day* (London: Thames and Hudson, 1981) is an invaluable overview of China's relations with Central Asia from the end of the Mongol Empire until the founding of the People's Republic. Annemarie Schimmel's *Mystical Dimensions of Islam* (Chapel Hill: University of North Carolina Press, 1975) provides a general overview of the Sufi orders that pervade not only the Muslim world but Central Asia and China as well. Denis Sinor, ed., *The Cambridge History of Early Inner Asia* (Cambridge: Cambridge University Press, 1990) is the most authoritative overview of Central Asian history available from the paleolithic era to the Mongol empire in the thirteenth century.

CHAPTER ELEVEN

A collection of documents dating from the first to the nineteenth centuries is gathered in G.S.P. Freeman-Grenville's *East African Coast: Selected Documents* (Oxford, UK: Clarendon Press, 1962). A discussion of the Oromo or Galla contribution to Islam in Ethiopia can be found in Mohammed Hassen's *The Oromo of Ethiopia: A History, 1570–1850* (Cambridge, UK: Cambridge University Press, 1990). Mervyn Hiskett's *A History of Hausa Islamic Verse* (London: School of Oriental and African Studies, 1975) traces written Hausa literature from its beginnings to the eighteenth century.

A detailed site report of the excavation of Shanga, including new evidence about the early development of Swahili civilization, can be found in Mark Horton's *The Archeology of a Muslim Trading Community on the Coast of East Africa* (Nairobi, Kenya: The British Institute in East Africa, 1996). John O. Hunwick's *Sharia in Songhai* (London: Oxford University Press for the British Academy, 1985) is the text, translation, and historical introduction to "The Replies" by al-Maghili. Nehemia Levtzion's *Ancient Ghana and Mali* (London: Metheun, 1973) is the only full book-length study of the early empires of west Sudan; the same author's *Islam in West Africa: Religion, Society, and Politics to 1800* (London: Variorum, 1994) is a collection of essays on those topics.

R. S. O'Fahey and Jay Spaulding's *Kingdoms of the Sudan* (London: Metheun, 1974) is a history of the three kingdoms of the Sudan, the Sinnar, the Wadai, and the Darfur. Randall L. Pouwells' *Horn and Crescent: Cultural Changes and Traditional Islam on the East African Coast, 800–1900* is a comprehensive analysis of the history of Islam on the east African coast. Elias N. Saad's *Social History of Timbuktu* (Cambridge, UK: Cambridge University Press, 1983) is a comprehensive history of Timbuktu up to the nineteenth century.

CHAPTER TWELVE

Rifaat Ali Abou-El-Haj's *Formation of the Modern State: The Ottoman Empire, Sixteenth to Eighteenth Centuries* (Albany: State University of New York Press, 1991) is an important reinterpretation of the evolution of the Ottoman political context. Aziz Ahmad's *Islamic Culture in the Indian Environment* (Oxford: Clarendon Press, 1964) contains helpful essays on the major movements of Islamic renewal in South Asia. Christine Dobbin's *Islamic Revivalism in a Changing Peasant Economy: Central Sumatra, 1784–1847* (London: Curzon Press, 1983) is an essential work for understanding the Padri movement and the broader context of revivalism in Southeast Asia. Richard M. Eaton's *Islamic History as Global History* (Washington, D.C.: American Historical Association, 1990) is an excellent interpretive essay that helps to place eighteenth- and nineteenth-century movements in a global perspective.

John L. Esposito, ed., *The Oxford Encyclopedia of the Modern Islamic World* (New York: Oxford University Press, 1995) is the essential general reference work for all of the specific people and groups mentioned in this chapter. Joseph F. Fletcher's *Studies on Chinese and Islamic Inner Asia*, Variorum Collected Studies series (Brookfield, Vt.: Variorum, 1995) is a very important contribution to the study of the Naqshbandiyyah order and the general development of Muslim societies in Central Asia. Marshall G. S. Hodgson's *The Gunpowder Empires and Modern Times*, vol. 3 of *The Venture of Islam: Conscience and History in a World Civilization* (Chicago: University of Chicago Press, 1974), the third volume of an extremely important interpretation of Islamic history, provides important broader perspectives for understanding the dynamics of eighteenth- and nineteenth-century Islamic history.

Ira M. Lapidus' *A History of Islamic Societies* (Cambridge: Cambridge University Press, 1988) is a useful survey of events in all parts of the Muslim world, which added breadth to the coverage in this chapter. Nehemia Levtzion and John O. Voll, eds., *Eighteenth-Century Renewal and Reform in Islam* (Syracuse, N.Y.: Syracuse University Press, 1987) is a collection of essays on specific movements of renewal in the eighteenth century. B. G. Martin's *Muslim Brotherhoods in Nineteenth-Century Africa* (Cambridge: Cambridge University Press, 1976) is a thorough study of the major movements of Islamic renewal in Africa in the nineteenth century. R. S. O'Fahey's *Enigmatic Saint: Ahmad ibn Idris and the Idrisi Tradition* (Evanston, Ill.: Northwestern University Press, 1990) is a path-breaking study of one of the major renewalist figures and his tradition. Fazlur Rahman's "Revival and Reform in Islam," in vol. 2 of *The Cambridge History of Islam*, ed. P. M. Holt and others (Cambridge University Press, 1970) pp. 632–56, is an influential definition of the broader tradition of renewal in Islamic history. John Obert Voll's "Renewal and Reform in Islamic History: Tajdid and Islah," in *Voices of Resurgent Islam*, ed. John L. Esposito (New York: Oxford University Press, 1983), pp. 32–47, is a description of the renewalist tradition by the author of this chapter.

CHAPTER THIRTEEN

Said A. Arjomand's "Constitutions and Struggles for Political Order: A Study in the Modernization of Religious Traditions," *Archives Européenes de Sociologie*, 33:1 (1992, pp. 39–82), provides an excellent comparative analysis of constitutional debates and political developments across the Muslim world.

Benedict Anderson, *Imagined Communities: Reflections on the Origin and Spread of Nationalism*, 2nd ed., (New York: Verso, 1991), presents a provocative examination of the manner in which nationalism is constructed in response to political and economic interests. Rupert Emerson's *From Empire to Nation: The Rise of Self-Assertion of Asian and African Peoples* (Cambridge, MA: Harvard, 1960) is an in-depth analysis of the evolution of anticolonial nationalism and the manner in which it unfolded at the end of the colonial era. Nikki Keddie, "The Revolt of Islam, 1700 to 1993: Comparative Considerations and Relation to Imperialism," *Comparative Studies in Society and History*, 36:3 (July 1994, pp. 463–87), provides a useful overview of the role of colonialism and imperialism in the genesis of Islamic activism. Joel S. Migdal, *Strong Societies and Weak States: State-Society Relations and State Capabilities in the Third World* (Princeton: Princeton University Press) presents an overarching conceptual treatment of the relation between the relative powers of political leaders and institutions and those of social forces in the process of state formation. On Africa, Catherine Boone, "States and Ruling Classes in Postcolonial Africa: The Enduring Contradictions of Power," in Joel S. Migdal, Atul Kohli, and Vivienne Shue, eds., *State Power and Social Forces* (New York: Cambridge University Press, 1994, pp. 108–40), discusses the importance of the colonial legacy to post-colonial state development. Frank Furedi, *Colonial Wars and the Politics of Third World Nationalism* (London: I. B. Tauris, 1994) relates resource mobilization for colonial conflicts to the development of Third World nationalist movements. Crawford Young's *The African Colonial State in Comparative Perspective* (New Haven: Yale University Press, 1994) explains state formation in Africa in the context of the colonial legacy of that continent. On the Arab world, Philip S. Khoury's *Syria and the French Mandate: The Politics of Arab Nationalism, 1920–1945* (Princeton: Princeton University Press, 1987) is a comprehensive examination of French colonial policies and administration in the Levant. William Roger Louis' *The British Empire in the Middle East, 1945–1951* (New York: Oxford University Press, 1984) provides a similar account of British colonial policies in the Middle East. Lisa Anderson's *The State and Social Transformation in Tunisia and Libya: 1830–1980* (Princeton: Princeton University Press, 1986) is an excellent comparative analysis of the differing impact of colonialism on future state formation in Libya and Tunisia. Giacomo Luciani, ed., *The Arab State* (Berkeley: University of California Press, 1990) contains a number of useful studies of the nature and functioning of the Arab state. Manfred Halpern's in *The Politics of Social Change in Middle East and North Africa* (Princeton: Princeton University Press, 1963), provides an overview of early state forma-

tion in the Arab world. Clement Henry Moore's *Politics in North Africa: Algeria, Morocco, and Tunisia* (Boston: Little, Brown, 1970) discusses the relation between nationalism and state formation in North Africa. On South Asia, Hamza Alavi's "The State in Postcolonial Societies: Pakistan and Bangladesh," in Kathleen Gough and Hari P. Sharma, eds., *Imperialism and Revolution in South Asia* (New York: Monthly Review Press, 1973, pp. 145–73) provides a compelling analysis of the importance of the colonial legacy for state formation in South Asia. Jamal Malik's *Colonizing Islam: Dissolution of Traditional Institutions in Pakistan* (New Delhi: Manohar, 1996) details the manner in which Pakistan has dealt with the role of Islam in society. C. A. Bayly, *Rulers, Townsmen and Bazaars: North Indian Society in the Age of British Expansion, 1770–1870* (New York: Cambridge University Press, 1983) is a thorough analysis of the nature of the impact of British colonialism on India. Thomas Metcalf's *Land, Landlords and the British Raj: Northern India in the Nineteenth Century* (Berkeley: University of California Press, 1979) discusses the impact of British colonialism on social structure in South Asia. His *Ideologies of the Raj* (New York: Cambridge University Press, 1994) examines the worldviews that underpinned the colonial administration of India and their implications for later state development in South Asia. Ayesha Jalal's *The State of Martial Rule: The Origins of Pakistan's Political Economy of Defence* (Cambridge: Cambridge University Press, 1990) is a detailed examination of the continuities between the British colonial state and Pakistan, and the implications of this linkage for Pakistan's politics. Seyyed Vali Reza Nasr's "Pakistan: State, Agrarian Reform, and Islamization." *International Journal of Politics, Culture and Society*, 10:2 (Winter 1996, pp. 249–72) examines the relation between state formation, feudalism, and Islamization in Pakistan. On Southeast Asia, Willard A. Hanna's *Sequel to Colonialism: The 1957–1960 Foundations for Malaysia* (New York: American Universities Field Staff, 1965) examines the continuities between the colonial and postcolonial states in Malaysia. Anthony Milner's *The Invention of Politics in Colonial Malaya* (New York: Cambridge University Press, 1994) examines the emergence of Malay nationalism and its role in formation of the Malaysian state in the context of the politics and cultural impact of colonialism. George T. Kahin, *Nationalism and Revolution in Indonesia* (Ithaca, NY: Cornell University Press, 1952) is a classic study of the independence movement and early state formation in Indonesia.

CHAPTER FOURTEEN

Barbara C. Aswad and Barbara Bilge's *Family and Gender*

Among American Muslims: Issues Facing Middle Eastern Immigrants and Their Descendants (Philadelphia: Temple University Press, 1996) covers practical issues facing families and intergenerational conflict as well as questions of identity, community involvement, gender, and the needs of youth and the elderly. Mattias Gardell's *In the Name of Elijah Muhammad: Louis Farrakhan and the Nation of Islam* (Durham, NC: Duke University Press, 1996) provides a unique and unprecedented view of the enigma of Louis Farrakhan, weaving together information from an impressive collection of documents that have not been treated by other scholars. In *The Muslims of America* (New York: Oxford University Press, 1991) Yvonne Yazbeck Haddad brings together studies in the religion of Islam as it is experienced in a variety of contexts in North America. The work addresses the history, organization, and challenges to Islam in North America, the writings of Muslim intellectuals, and the prospects of the Muslim community in the United States and Canada.

David Horrocks and Eva Kolinsky's *Turkish Culture in German Society Today* (Providence, RI: Berghahn Books, 1996) addresses the condition of Turkish guestworkers in Germany, as well as the current situation of minorities in German society. It provides a unique focus on issues of identity. In *Muslim Minorities in the World Today* (London: Mansell, 1986), M. Ali Kettani examines the position of minority communities in their struggle to maintain a Muslim way of life. The author promotes a normative path in maintaining Islamic identity in a non-Muslim environment.

In *Islamic Britain: Religion, Politics, and Identity Among British Muslims* (London: Tauris, 1994), Philip Lewis provides an overview of the status of Muslim communities in Britain, based on well-researched fieldwork from the industrial cities in the country's center, including Bradford. Kathleen M. Moore's *al-Mughtaribun: American Law and the Transformation of Muslim Life in the United States* (Albany: State University of New York Press, 1995) explores the influence of American law on Muslim life against the backdrop of liberal commitments to the ideals of pluralism and religious tolerance in America.

Jorgen Nielsen's *Muslims in Western Europe*, second edition (Edinburgh, UK: Edinburgh University Press, 1995) is an introduction to Muslim life in contemporary Western Europe. It provides an overview of the history, development, and current conditions of Muslim communities in France, West Germany, the United Kingdom, Belgium, Holland, Scandinavia, and Southern Europe. In *Muslim Communities in the New Europe* (Berkshire, Ithaca Press, 1996), the editors, Gerd Nonneman, Tim Niblock, and Bogdan Szajkowski, have gathered a collection of essays that address the effects of government

policies, citizenship rules, economics, and international linkages on immigrant and indigenous Muslims in Eastern and Western Europe. Richard Brent Turner's *Islam in the African-American Experience* (Bloomington: Indiana University Press, 1997) is a significant contribution to the understanding of the roles of individuals, religious groups, and the religion of Islam in shaping the African American Muslim identity.

CHAPTER FIFTEEN

Mohammed Arkoun's *Rethinking Islam: Common Questions, Uncommon Answers* (Boulder, Colo.: Westview Press, 1994) provides a bold and provocative critique of both Western and traditional Islamic scholarship that presents a vision of Islam that challenges that which is prevalent throughout much of the Muslim world. Muhammad Asad's *The Principles of State and Government in Islam* (1961; reprint, Gibraltar: Dar al-Andalus, 1980) provides an early and influential analysis of the basis for a modern Islamic state. John J. Donohue and John L. Esposito, eds., *Islam in Transition: Muslim Perspectives* (New York: Oxford University Press, 1982) is a collection of Muslim writings that reflects the diversity of Muslim voices in the twentieth century. Farid Esack's *Quran, Liberation, and Pluralism* (Oxford: Oneworld Publications, 1997) is a creative and challenging analysis of the role of Islam and the Muslim community in fighting apartheid. This event becomes the take-off point for the author to explore the traditional Muslim attitude toward pluralism and to advocate a rereading of Quranic texts to support a more inclusive, pluralistic vision.

John L. Esposito, ed., *Voices of Resurgent Islam* (New York: Oxford University Press, 1983) provides a collection of studies of major twentieth-century Islamic reformers and activists, with a collection of Muslim activist writings on the nature of the Islamic revival, the Islamic state, law, and social reform. John L. Esposito's *The Islamic Threat: Myth or Reality?* (New York: Oxford University Press, 1995) is a study of the history of Islam and the West that focuses on contemporary Muslim politics and the future of Muslim-Christian relations. Is this relationship one of cooperation or conflict? John L. Esposito and John O. Voll's *Islam and Democracy* (New York: Oxford University Press, 1996) gives an analysis of the nature of democracy and Muslim reactions and responses to issues of political participation and democratization, with case studies that span the Muslim world, from Algeria and Egypt to Pakistan and Malaysia.

Dale Eickelman and James P. Piscatori's *Muslim Politics* (Princeton, N.J.: Princeton University Press, 1996) presents an analysis of the diverse politics of Islam in Muslim life. The work is especially effective in its examples, which are drawn from across the Muslim world. Yvonne Y. Haddad's *Contemporary Islam and the Challenge of History* (New York: SUNY Press, 1982) provides a study of the ways in which Arab Muslims have defined and redefined the meaning of faith and history in responding to the challenges of the nineteenth and twentieth centuries. Deliar Noer's *The Modernist Muslim Movement in Indonesia* (London: Oxford University Press, 1973) provides an analysis of the origins, causes, leaders, and ideas of modernist movements in Indonesia from 1900 to 1942. Seyyed Hossein Nasr's *Traditional Islam in the Modern World* (London: KPI, 1987) is a study of the historical role and enduring significance of traditional Islam by a leading Muslim scholar. Nasr seeks to distinguish traditional Islam from modernism and fundamentalism.

Fazlur Rahman's *Islam and Modernity* (Chicago: University of Chicago Press, 1982) is a descriptive and prescriptive study of the history of Islamic intellectualism and education, which seeks to set out a methodology for reinterpretation and reform in Islam. Andrew Rippin's *Muslims: Their Beliefs and Practices*, vol. 2 of *The Contemporary Period* (London: Routledge, 1993) is a study of Muslim perceptions of and responses to the modern world, with special emphasis on the relevance of the Quran and Muhammad. John O. Voll's *Islam: Continuity and Change in the Modern World* (New York: Syracuse University Press, 1994) provides an excellent study of the role of Islam in modern Muslim history, distinctive for its comprehensive geographic coverage.

CONTRIBUTORS

The Editor

John L. Esposito is professor of religion and international affairs and founding director of the Center for Muslim-Christian Understanding at the Edmund Walsh School of Foreign Service at Georgetown University. Editor in chief of the *Oxford Encyclopedia of the Modern Islamic World*, his other books include *Islam: The Straight Path; The Islamic Threat: Myth or Reality?; Islam and Democracy* (with John Voll); *Islam and Politics; Islam in Asia; Women in Muslim Family Law; Political Islam: Radicalism, Revolution, or Reform?;* and *Muslims on the Americanization Path* (with Yvonne Haddad).

The Authors

Sheila Blair and **Jonathan Bloom** are a wife-and-husband team of scholars who have jointly and individually written many books and articles on various aspects of Islamic art and architecture. Together they have written *The Art and Architecture of Islam: 1250–1800* and *Islamic Art*; Sheila Blair has written *Islamic Inscriptions* and Jonathan Bloom is working on *Paper Before Print*. They are now both at work on a book to accompany a forthcoming PBS series on Islamic civilization.

Vincent J. Cornell is an associate professor of religion and Asian and African languages and literature at Duke University. He has written *The Way of Abu Madyan and Realm of the Saint: Power and Authority in Moroccan Sufism*. He is currently writing a biography of the North African Sufi Abu al-Hasan al-Shadhili and is collaborating with Professor John Nikdisi, dean of the law school at Loyola University in New Orleans, on a casebook of Islamic law.

Ahmad Dallal is an associate professor of Arabic and Islamic studies at Stanford University. He writes on the history of Islamic science and modern Islamic thought. He is the author of *An Islamic Response to Greek Astronomy*, and his articles have been published in *Arabic Science and Philosophy; Journal of the American Oriental Society; National Journal of Middle East Studies;* and other publications.

Fred M. Donner is professor of Near Eastern history in the Oriental Institute of the University of Chicago, where he is also professor of Near Eastern history and chair of the department of Near Eastern languages and civilizations. He is the author of *The Early Islamic Conquests* and *Narratives of Islamic Origins: The Beginnings of Islamic Historical Writing* and he has written many articles on early and medieval Islamic history.

Majid Fakhry is emeritus professor of philosophy at the American University of Beirut; he is currently a visiting research associate at Georgetown University. His English-language publications include *A History of Islamic Philosophy; Ethical Theories in Islam; A Short Introduction to Islamic Philosophy, Theology and Mysticism; Philosophy, Dogma and the Impact of Greek Though in Islam;* and *The Qu'ran: A Modern English Version*. He has also published many works in Arabic.

Dru C. Gladney is currently Dean of Academics at the Asia-Pacific Center; he is now on leave from his position as professor of Asian studies and anthropology at the University of Hawai'i at Manoa. He has written the award-winning book *Muslim Chinese: Ethnic Nationalism in the People's Republic*, and is also the author of *Ethnic Identity in China: The Making of a Muslim Minority Nationality and Dislocating China: Muslims, Minorities, and Other Sub-Altern Subjects*; he is the editor of *Making Majorities: Composing the Nation in Japan, China, Korea, Malaysia, Fiji, Turkey, and the United States*.

Yvonne Yazbeck Haddad is professor of the history of Islam and Christian-Muslim relations at Georgetown University and past president of the Middle East Studies Association. She is the author of *Contemporary Islam and the Challenge of History* and is co-author of *The Islamic Understanding of Death and Resurrection; Islamic Values in the United States: A Comparative Study;* and *Mission to America: Five Islamic Sectarian Communities in North America*. She has edited *Muslims of America* and co-edited *Islam, Gender and Social Change; Islamic Impact; Muslims on the Americanization Path?;* and *Christian-Muslim Encounters*.

Mohammad Hashim Kamali is professor of law at the International Islamic University in Malaysia. He has also studied and taught Islamic law in Afghanistan, England, Canada, and the United States. He is the author of *Principles of Islamic Jurisprudence* and *Freedom of Expression in Islam*, among other works.

Ira M. Lapidus is emeritus professor of history and former chair of the Center for Middle Eastern Studies at the University of California at Berkeley. He is the author of *A History of Islamic Societies; Muslim Cities in the Later Middle Ages;* and *Middle Eastern Cities*.

Bruce B. Lawrence is professor of history of religion and Islamic studies at Duke University, where he also serves as chair of the department of religion. He has written extensively on both the premodern and the modern phases of institutional Islam. His special interests are Indo-Persian Sufism and the comparative study of religious movements. His latest work is *Shattering the Myth: Islam Beyond Violence*.

Nehemia Levtzion is Fuld and Bamberger Professor of the History of the Muslim Peoples at Hebrew University in Jerusalem. He is former president of the Open University in Israel, and he is currently chair of the Council for Higher Education's Planning and Budgeting Committee there. Among his publications are *Muslims and Chiefs in West Africa: A Study of Islam in the Middle Volta Basin in the Pre-Colonial Period; Ancient Ghana and Mali;* and *Islam in the West: Religion, Society and Politics to 1800*.

S. V. R. Nasr is an associate professor of political science at the University of San Diego. He has written *The Vanguard of the Islamic Revolution: The Jamaat-i Islami of Pakistan* and *Mawdudi and the Making of Islamic Revivalism*. He specializes in the relations between state and society in Muslim countries and in the role of Islam in politics.

Jane I. Smith is professor of Islamic studies at Hartford Seminary and co-director of the Macdonald Center for the Study of Islam and Christian-Muslim Relations. She is active in the National and World Councils of Churches in interfaith dialogue. Her most recent book is *Islam in America;* she is editor of the journal *The Muslim World* and an associate editor of the forthcoming *Encyclopedia of Women in the Muslim World*.

John Obert Voll is professor of Islamic history at Georgetown University and associate director of Georgetown's Center for Muslim-Christian Understanding. He is past president of the Middle East Studies Association. His publications include *Islam: Continuity and Change in the Modern World* and, with John Esposito, *Islam and Democracy*.

IMAGE SOURCES

Judy Aldrick: 503; Art and History Trust Collection: 178; Bibliothèque Nationale, Paris: 84, 214; Sheila Blair and Jonathan Bloom: 2, 26, 34, 36, 45, 50, 72, 77, 101, 106, 127, 133, 178, 183, 184, 196, 197, 208, 224, 226, 229, 232, 235, 238, 244, 245, 254, 257, 258, 265, 266, 270, 285, 291, 292, 294, 295, 309, 312, 314, 319, 345, 347, 360, 365, 367, 368, 371, 377, 402, 411, 439, 476, 521, 523, 524, 526, 531; Bridgeman Art Library: 328 (British Library), 338 (Bibliothèque Nationale/Giraudon), 343 (British Library), 372 (British Library), 551; Bodleian Library, Oxford: 186, 188, 233; British Library, London: 185; British Museum, London: 210 (Goodman Bequest), 211, 223, 502; British Petroleum Company p.l.c.: 515, 556, 574, 645, 646; Camera Press: 669, 677 (Julia Guest); Cambridge University Library (Royal Commonwealth Society): 575, 577; J.-L. Charmet: 117, 167 (Bibliothèque Nationale, Paris), 199 (Nationalbibliothek, Vienna), 213; Chester Beatty Library, Dublin: 119, 241; ChinaStock/Christopher Lui: 435b, 461, 463; Carin Clinell: 606; Douglas Dickins: 141, 259, 304, 318, 406, 417, 650; Werner Forman Archive: 202, 444, 474, 485 (Mrs. Bashir Mohamed Collection); 494; Freer Gallery of Art, Smithsonian Institution, Washington, DC: 7 (30.60a), 195 (30.75R), 217 (57.24), 250 (47.8), 282, 394 (39.49), 412 (86.0402), 413 (42.15), 418 (86.0432), 438; German Archaeological Institute, Madrid: 240; Dru Gladney: 434, 435a, 436, 437, 440, 442, 443, 445, 448, 456, 458, 459; Sonia Halliday: 23, 54; Harvard University Art Museums, Cambridge, MA, Gift of John Goelet: 219; Herzfeld Archives, Smithsonian Institution: 282; Museum of the History of Science, Oxford: 180, 181; Geoff Howard: 81, 111, 616, 623, 628; Hulton Getty: 533, 608, 662, 666; Israel Antiquities Authority: 231; A.F. Kersting: 14, 35, 57, 99, 252, 310, 352, 416, 490, 505, 564; Omar Khalidi: 600, 617, 618; Khuda Bakhsh Library, Patna: 405; Bruce Lawrence: 399, 400, 401, 408, 410, 419; Los Angeles County Museum of Art: 269; Magnum: 152, 677; Magnum, Abbas: 86, 108, 432, 484, 550, 554, 582, 642, 671, 673, 674, 688; Magnum, Burt Glinn: 640; Magnum, Steve McCurry: 658; Magnum, C. Steele-Perkins: 116, 548, 659; Marlborough Photo Library: 9, 24, 40 (Edinburgh University Library), 64, 87, 114, 366, 370 (Harvard University Art Museums), 378 (Leiden University Library), 379 (Turk ve Islam Eserieri), 403, 415 (India Office Library), 511, 513, 553, 644; Mary Evans Picture Library: 560, 563, 593; Metropolitan Museum of Art, New York: 220 (gift of Horace Havemeyer, 1941. The H.O. Havemeyer Collection. (41.165.)1, 247 Purchase, Harris Brisbane Dick Fund, Joseph Pulitzer Bequest, Louis V. Bell Fund and Fletcher, Pfeiffer, and Rogers Funds, 1990. (1990.61), 383 The James F. Ballard Collection, Gift of James F. Ballard, 1922. (22.100.51)), 384 (49.97.176); Seyyed Vali Nasr: 676; Bibliothèque Nationale, Paris: 84, 167; National Library, Cairo: 234; National Library, Copenhagen: 354; Bernard O'Kane: 1, 302; Trish O'Reilly: 414; Christine Osborne: 37, 62, 69, 82, 83, 85, 112, 135, 140, 145, 209, 420, 480, 496, 498, 504, 508, 620, 679, 687; Pierpont Morgan Library, New York: 358; James Peacock: 429, 430; Pitt Rivers Museum, University of Oxford: 499; Popperfoto: 534, 587, 652, 655, 670; Josephine Powell: 20, 39, 42, 55, 79, 155, 182, 228, 239, 256, 380; Publifoto: 315; Réunion des Musées Nationaux: 242, 251, 333, 336; Royal Geographical Society, London: 3, 17, 103, 115, 518, 527, 539, 569, 588; Prince Sadruddin Aga Khan: 364; Scala: 287; Robert Selkowitz: 78, 653; Linda Shuaib: 109; Tim Smith: 113 (BHRU), 605, 619, 633; © Jolie Stahl: 622, 637; Suleymaniye Mosque Library, Istanbul: 276; Topkapi Palace Library, Istanbul: 249, 376; Staatliche Museen zu Berlin-Preussischer Kulturbesitz, Museum für Islamische Kunst: 237, 261, 262; Staatsbibliothek zu Berlin-Preussischer Kulturbesitz-Orientabteilung: 192; State Hermitage Museum, St. Petersburg: 221, 263, 264; Thyssen-Bornemisza Foundation, Lugano: 68; University Library, Istanbul: 206; Foto Vasari: 607; Courtesy of the Trustees of the Victoria and Albert Museum, London: 46, 216, 311; Estelle Whelan: 290; Caroline Williams: 479, 487.

INDEX

A

"Abbasi," as epithet for Reza, 369

al-Abbas ibn Abd al-Muttalib, Abbasid descendants of, 20, 130

Abbasids; agricultural development under, 196, 693; Alids and, 25; apologists of, 263; architecture and art of, 243, 244, 260, 693; black flag of, 259; as caliphs, 22, 24–25, 26, 28, 29, 30–31, 32, 33, 36, 37, 38, 39, 42, 48, 58, 59, 134, 159, 160, 162, 164, 181, 210, 232, 237, 277, 278, 284, 333, 354, 358, 363, 482, 492, 693; decline of, 32, 43, 44, 48, 115, 339, 351–353, 354, 355, 356, 358–359, 361; Egyptian control by, 693, 695; Ismaili challenge of, 44–49; legacy to Ottoman Empire, 371; Mongol overthrow of, 59, 60; Nestorian physicians of, 200, 271; political system of, 358; refugees from rule of, 35, 36; regional states of, 693; Sunni supporters of, 359; Umayyad conquest by, 19–20, 24, 25, 34, 692

Abbas I, as Safavid ruler, 295, 364, 370, 439, 509, 607

Abbas II, as Safavid ruler, 180

Abd al-Al, as Islamic reformer, 531

Abd al-Aziz, Shah, as Islamic reformer, 527–528

Abd al-Hamid ibn Yahya, as Islamic administrator, 29

Abd al-Hamid II, Sultan, pan-Islamic policies of, 527

Abd Alla, Khoja, as Central Asian Sufi teacher, 451

Abdallah, Shaykh, as dan Fodio's brother, 536

Abdallahi, Khalifah, as mahdist successor, 546

Abd Allah ibn al-Zubayr, as caliph, 17, 265

Abd al-Malik ibn Marwan, 142, 223–224, 322; as caliph, 17, 22, 224, 277; Dome of the Rock commissioned by, 216, 224, 265, 313, 692

Abd al-Mumin, as Ibn Tumart's successor, 51

Abd al-Rahman III, as Umayyad caliph, 54, 211, 318, 319–320, 693, 694

Abd al-Raziq, Ali, as Islamic secularist, 300–301

Abd an-Nabi, as Mughal religious officer, 409

Abduh, Muhammad, as Islamic modernist, 293, 298, 299, 565, 633, 647, 648, 683, 685, 699

Abdulhamid II, Sultan, pan-Islamism of, 699

Abdullah, Amir, King of Jordan, 556, 557

Abdul-Rahman, Tunku, as Malaysian leader, 562

el-Abedin, Zain, on preservation of Muslim identity, 612–613

ablution, prior to praying, 78, 79, 112, 147

"abode of Islam," 324

"abode of truce," 324

"abode of war," 324

abortion, Muslim views on, 634

Abu-Ala ibn Zuhr, as Arab physician, 205

Abu al-Ala Mawdudi, Mawlana Sayyid, as Islamist, 299–300, 565, 612, 652–653, 654, 676, 700

Abu Bakr al-Asamm; as first caliph, 11, 12, 15, 112, 692; Mutazilte followers of, 146

Abu Bakr ibn Muhammad, as Mogadishu ruler, 502

Abu Daud al-Sijistani, Sunan of, 75

Abu Hanifah al-Numan ibn Thabit, as early jurist, 94–95, 113, 124, 126–127, 128, 693

Abu Hashim, as Mutazilite, 280

Abu Jafar Muhammad al-Kulayni, Shiite hadith of, 75

Abu Jafar Muhammad ibn Babuyah, Shiite hadith of, 75

Abu l-Abbas al Saffah, as caliph, 25

Abul-Fazl, *Akbarnameh* of, 407, 409

Abul-Hasan-Qazwini, Sayyid, as Ishraqi philosopher, 296

Abul-Hudhayl, as Mutazilite, 279

Abul-Mawahib dynasty, of Kilwa, 504

Abu Mansur Bakhtikin, silk saddlecloth of, 225

Abu Marwan ibn Zuhr, as Arab physician, 205

Abu Musa Islands, United Arab Emirates' claim to, 559

Abu Muslim, as Abbasid agent, 25

Abu Nasr Mansur ibn Iraq, as early astronomer, 168, 191

Aburezk, James, as founder of American-Arab Anti-discrimination Committee, 637

Abu Talib, Ali Ibn, as Muhammad's uncle and guardian, 6, 8, 691

Abu Zayd, in *Maqamat*, 234

Abyssinia, early Islam in, 306, 691

Achaemenid style, of governance, 396

Acheh (Sumatra); appeals to Ottomans from, 382; Islam in, 389, 422–424,

426, 427, 428; Japanese occupation of, 430; Marco Polo in, 695; renewalist movements in, 519–520; role in Asian trade, 389, 425; ulama-led resistance to Dutch in, 699

Acre; Crusader conquest of, 56; Mongol capture of, 323

Adal sultanate, wars with Ethiopia, 501

adat (indigenous norms), 424, 425, 427

al-Adawiyah, Rabiah, as female Sufi mystic, 693

Aden, as trade center, 38

adjudication, Islamic law on, 131

Adriatic Sea, Ottoman trade routes on, 389

Adud al-Dawlah, as Buyid ruler, 42, 232

Adudi hospital (Baghdad), 208

adultery; Islamic prohibition of, 93, 687; Quranic rules on, 122

advice, sincere, as Quranic principle, 148–149

Aegean Sea, Ottoman control of, 388

Afaq, Khoja, as Naqshbandi Sufi, 451, 453, 454

Afaqiyya Sufism, in China

Afar peoples, as Muslims, 501

al-Afdal ibn Badr, as Egyptian military man, 48

al-Afghani, Jamal al-Din; as Islamic modernist, 298, 547, 550, 647, 648, 680, 699; Salafi movement of, 299

Afghanistan; Barakzais in, 698; caliph raids of, 12; civil war of, 549, 658, 659; colonialism in, 553; creation of, 557; Durrani rule of, 698; Ghaznavid regime in, 40–41, 54, 356, 694; Hanafi school in, 114; Hizb-i Islam, 562; Islamic modernism in, 682; jihad against Soviet Union, 550–551, 660; Khwarizmshah conquest of, 58; militant activists in, 579; minorities in, 679; Muslim refugees from, 605, 618; as Muslim state, 552; nomad invasion into, 351; relief agencies in, 668; revolutionary movements in, 667; Saffarid control of, 38; shariah implementation in, 151, 686–687; Soviet Union expelled from, 549, 550, 659, 660, 702; Taliban in, 91, 466, 658, 683, 687, 688, 703–704; treatment of women in, 634, 687, 688; Turkish uymaqs in, 370

Afghans, defeat of Safavids by, 370, 697

Aflaq, Michel, 583

Africa; Christian minorities in, 583; colonialism in, 564, 576; French ter-

Khitan, Chinese occupation by, 439

Khocho (Gaochang), as Uighur city, 464

Khoi, Abul-Qasem, as Iraqi ulama, 680

Khomeini, Ayatollah Ruhollah, 628, 680, 702, 703; fatwa on Salman Rushdie of, 629; government control by, 664–665; Iranian support of, 628, 662–663; as Ishraqi-Shiite, 296; as Islamist, 565, 590, 656, 658

Khosrow I, Emperor of Persia. *See* Anushirvan

Khufiyyas, as Chinese Sufi order, 449, 450, 452, 453, 454, 456, 461, 462

al-Khujandi, Abu Mahmud Hamid, as early astronomer, 168, 181, 191

Khuldabad, as Chishti tomb complex, 418, 419

khul/khula (divorce), legal rules on, 118, 127

Khurasan; Abbasid power in, 28, 29, 693; Baghdad rivalry with, 27; Ghaznavid regime in, 54, 56, 694; Islamic control of, 33, 38, 40; Khwarizmshah conquest of, 58; Mongol conquest of, 58, 400; Saffarid control of, 38, 39; Samanid dynasty of, 693; Seljuk control of, 54–55, 56, 57–58, 351; Türkmen migration into, 54, 399; Umayyad campaigns from, 21, 24–25

Khurram, Prince. *See* Shah Jehan

Khursid Bibi vs. *Muhammad Amin*, 118

Khuzestan (Iran); caliph control of, 12; Saffarid control of, 38

Khuzestan province, "Arabistan" creation from, 557

al-Khwarazmi, Abd al-Rahman. *See* Anisi

Khwarizm; astronomy in, 191; Mongol conquest of, 58; Samanid control of, 39, 54; Umayyad control of, 21

al-Khwarizmi; algebra and trigonometry development by, 157, 184–187, 188, 189; as early astronomer, 163; timekeeping text of, 180

Khwarizmshahs, Near East empire of, 58

Khyber, Christians in, 306

Kiev, Ottoman trade with, 389

Kilij Arslan II, Sultan, 55

Kilwa (Tanzania); Abul-Mawahib dynasty of, 504; early Islam in, 503

al-Kindi, Yaqub ibn Ishaq al-Sabah; as early philosopher, 273, 274, 278, 283, 287, 331, 333; optic treatises of, 191

King Abdul Aziz University (Saudi Arabia), International Center for Islamic Economic Research of, 151

King Khalid International Airport, Quranic incriptions in, 227

Kinnard College (Lahore), 580

Kirina, Battle of, 478

Kirman, Seljuk sultans of, 694

al-Kirmani, 284

Kishiev, Kunta Haji, in Qadiriyyah movement, 540

Kissinger, Henry, ethnic slurs of, 637

kiswa, as Kaaba veil, 220

Kitab al-Aghani (al-Isfahani), 354

Kitab al-Ashr Maqalat fi al-Ayn (Hunayn ibn Ishaq), 200

Kitab al-Hawi di al-Tibb al-Mansuri (al-Razi), 203

Kitab al-Hind (al-Biruni), 398

Kitab al-Istibar, 492

Kitab al-jabr wal-Muqubala (al-Khwarizmi), as first work on algebra, 157, 184–185, 186

Kitab al-Kamil fi al-Sinaa al-Tibbiya (al-Majusi), 203

Kitab al-Mabsut (al-Sarakhsi), 110

Kitab al-Malaki (al-Majusi), 203

Kitab al-Manazir (Alhazan), 190, 191, 193

Kitab al-Nabat (al-Dinawari), 211

Kitab al-Tasrif li man Ajiza an al-Talif [medical encyclopedia], 204

Kitab al-Tibb al-Mansuri (al-Razi), 202

Kitab fi al-Jadari wal-Hasba (al-Razi), 202

Kitab fi Jawami Ilm al-Nujum (al-Farghani), 164

Kitab fi Marifat al-Hiyal al-Handasiyya (al-Jazari), 196

Kitab Mizan al-Hikma (al-Khazani), 194

Kitab Suwar al-Wawakib al-Thabita (al-Sufi), 166, 167

knights; as Christian heroes, 328; role in Crusades, 338

knowledge, three types of, 64–66, 70

"knowledge by presence" (Quran), 66

"knowledge of certainty" (Quran), 64, 65, 77

kola nuts, African sources of, 486, 495, 497

Koli Beile, as Uighur leader, 464

Kong peoples, as Islamic converts, 489

Konya (Anatolia); Ince Minareli in, 53; Islamic culture of, 60; Ottoman trade route through, 389; Seljuk rule in, 55

Koprulu family, as Ottoman viziers, 511

Koran. *See* Quran

Koreans; in Central Asia, 472; in early Chang an, 442

Köösedag, Battle of, Mongol victory in, 59

Kosovo; Battle of (1389), 373, 695; Muslims in, 638; violence in (1998), 704

Kotoko, Mai Idris's conquest of, 493

Kraton, near Yogyakarta mosque, 430

Krgyzstan, Xinjiang trade with, 468, 469

Kuala Kangsar, Islam in, 420

Kuala Kangsaw Malay College (Malaya), 578

Kuala Lumpur; economic development of, 573; Malay-Chinese riots in, 655; national identity of, 558, 656

Kubrawiyyas, as Chinese Sufi order, 449, 462

Kuchuk Kaynarja, Treaty of, 698

Kufa (Iraq); Islamic conquest of, 13, 15,

16, 17, 31; Rationalists in, 112

kufic script, use for Quran, 7, 229, 242

Ku Klux Klan, 609

Kulibali, Bakary, as Islam convert, 487

Kulibali, Biton, as Ségou founder, 486–487

Kunta family, as Qadiriyyah, 519, 542

al-Kunti, Sidi al-Mukhtar; as Qadiriyyah leader, 519; revivalist movement of, 486

Kuomintang (KMT) government; Muslim oppression by, 453; Uighur recognition by, 465

al-Kurani, Ibrahim ibn Hasan, as Kurdish mystic, 451, 455

al-Kurdi, Mahmud, as Islamic revivalist, 532

Kurdish peoples; ethnic plight of, 559; as "Mountain Turks," 559; as Muslim migrants, 607; as Muslims, 55, 56, 57, 451; in Ottoman states, 378, 527

Kurdistan, 526

al-Kurdumiri, Shaykh Ismail, as Islamic reformer, 532–533

kuttab, as Abbasid clerks, 29

Kuwait; donation to Chinese mosque, 461; extremist activities in, 665; fiqh encyclopedia project of, 150; independence of, 557; Iraqi claims to, 556, 559; Islamic politics of, 673; Jamiyat al-Islah of, 667; Maliki school in, 114; as mandate country, 651; oil exports of, 556, 574; in Persian Gulf War, 703; support of mosque movement by, 617

Kuwait Parliament, 135

Kworarafa, attack on Kano by, 497

Kyrgyz; in Central Asia, 471; conquest of Karabalghasun by, 464; Russian policies affecting, 437; Turkic-Altaic language of, 443, 445; Uighars and, 466

Kyrgyzstan; Chinese military agreement with, 471; new transportation links to, 471

L

labor migrants, Muslims as, 604, 605, 608, 630

Labour Party (Great Britain), Muslim councilors in, 635–636

al-Lahiji, Fayaz, as Ishraqi philosopher, 296

Lahore, as Islamicate center, 399, 418

laity, as Islamic modernists, 681

Lake Chad, Muslim kingdoms along, 492, 493, 536

Lake Van; Byzantine defeat near, 55; Church of the Holy Cross on, 52

"la mission civilatrice," as colonial paternalism, 560, 561

Lamu Archipelago, Islam in, 504, 505

land-tenure policies, in Java, 574

Languedoc, Muslim raids of, 21

lao jiao (old teachings), of Chinese Islam, 462